MCITP Developer: Microsoft SQL Server 2005 Data Access Design and Optimization Study Guide

Exam 70-442 PRO: Designing and Optimizing Data Access by Using Microsoft SQL Server 2005

OBJECTIVE	CHAPTER
Designing Efficient Access to a SQL Server Service	
Design appropriate data access technologies.	1
Design an appropriate data access object model.	1
Design a cursor strategy for a data access component.	1
Decide when to use cursors.	1
Decide how to maximize cursor performance.	1
Detect which applications are using cursors and evaluate whether to remove them.	1
Design caching strategies.	1
Select ADO.NET caching.	1
Design custom caching functionality.	1
Design a refresh strategy for cached data.	1
Design client libraries to write applications that administer a SQL Server service.	2
Design server management objects (SMO) applications.	2
Design replication management objects (RMO) applications.	2
Design automation management objects (AMO) applications.	2
Design SQL Server Networking Interface (SNI) for asynchronous queries.	2
Design queries that use multiple active result sets (MARS).	2
Decide when MARS queries are appropriate.	2
Choose an appropriate transaction isolation level when you use MARS.	2
Choose when to use Asynchronous queries.	2
Designing a Database Query Strategy	
Write and modify queries.	3
Write queries.	3
Modify queries to improve query performance.	3
Design queries for retrieving data from XML sources.	3
Select the correct attributes.	3
Select the correct nodes.	3
Filter by values of attributes and values of elements.	3
Include relational data, such as columns and variables, in the result of an XQuery expression.	3
Include XML attribute or node values in a tabular result set.	3
Update, insert, or delete relational data based on XML parameters to stored procedures.	3
Debug and troubleshoot queries against XML data sources.	3
Design a cursor strategy.	4
Design cursor logic.	4
Design cursors that work together with dynamic SQL execution.	4
Select an appropriate cursor type.	4
Design cursors that efficiently use server memory.	4

Sybex®
An Imprint of
WILEY

NOTE

Exam objectives are subject to change at any time without prior notice and at Microsoft's sole discretion. Please visit Microsoft's website (www.microtosft.com/learning) for the most current listing of exam objectives.

Sybex®
An Imprint of
WILEY

MCITP Developer

Microsoft® SQL Server™ 2005
Data Access Design
and Optimization (70-442)

Study Guide

MCITP Developer

Microsoft® SQL Server™ 2005
Data Access Design
and Optimization (70-442)

Study Guide

Marilyn Miller-White

Cristian Andrei Lefter

BICENTENNIAL
1807
⊗WILEY
2007
BICENTENNIAL

Wiley Publishing, Inc.

Acquisitions Editors: Maureen Adams, Jeff Kellum

Development Editor: Kim Wimpsett

Technical Editor: Rick Tempestini

Production Editor: Rachel Gunn

Copy Editor: Cheryl Hauser

Production Manager: Tim Tate

Vice President and Executive Group Publisher: Richard Swadley

Vice President and Executive Publisher: Joseph B. Wikert

Vice President and Publisher: Neil Edde

Media Project Supervisor: Laura Atkinson

Media Development Specialist: Kit Malone

Media Quality Assurance: Angie Denny

Book Designer: Judy Fung

Proofreader: Jen Larsen, Word One

Indexer: Ted Laux

Anniversary Logo Design: Richard Pacifico

Cover Designer: Ryan Sneed

Compositor: Craig Woods, Happenstance Type-O-Rama

For general information on our other products and services or to obtain technical support, please contact our Customer Care Department within the U.S. at (800) 762-2974, outside the U.S. at (317) 572-3993 or fax (317) 572-4002.

Wiley also publishes its books in a variety of electronic formats. Some content that appears in print may not be available in electronic books.

Library of Congress Cataloging-in-Publication Data

Miller-White, Marilyn.

MCITP. Microsoft SQL server 2005 data access design and optimization study guide (70-442) / Marilyn Miller-White.
    p. cm.

Includes indexes.

ISBN 978-0-470-10880-2 (paper/cd-rom)

1. Electronic data processing personnel--Certification. 2. Microsoft software--Examinations--Study guides. 3. SQL server. I. Title.

QA76.3.M569 2007

005.75'85--dc22

2007002734

Sybex®
An Imprint of
⊛WILEY

To Our Valued Readers:

Thank you for looking to Sybex for your MCITP Developer: Designing and Optimizing Data Access by Using Microsoft SQL Server 2005 exam prep needs. We at Sybex are proud of our reputation for providing certification candidates with the practical knowledge and skills needed to succeed in the highly competitive IT marketplace. Certification candidates have come to rely on Sybex for accurate and accessible instruction on today's crucial technologies and business skills.

Just as Microsoft Learning is committed to establishing measurable standards for certifying SQL Server professionals by means of its certifications, Sybex is committed to providing those individuals with the knowledge needed to meet those standards.

The authors and editors have worked hard to ensure that this edition of the *MCITP Developer: Microsoft SQL Server 2005 Data Access Design and Optimization Study Guide* you hold in your hands is comprehensive, in-depth, and pedagogically sound. We're confident that this book will exceed the demanding standards of the certification marketplace and help you, the certification candidate, succeed in your endeavors.

As always, your feedback is important to us. If you believe you've identified an error in the book, please send a detailed e-mail to support@wiley.com. And if you have general comments or suggestions, feel free to drop me a line directly at nedde@wiley.com. At Sybex we're continually striving to meet the needs of individuals preparing for certification exams.

Good luck in pursuit of your MCITP Developer certification!

Neil Edde
Vice President & Publisher
Sybex, an Imprint of Wiley

I dedicate this book to Joanne and Jay for the encouragement and support they have always given me.
—Marilyn Miller-White

I dedicate this book to my grandfather Cosma Florea, who gave me my love for books.
—Cristian Andrei Lefter

Acknowledgments

I always knew I wanted to be a teacher. There was no question—it was my passion. I am so fortunate to be able to live my passion and share the results with you. I have had the privilege to be on the forefront of many new developments. I live in research, development, and education. This is what this book is all about—moving forward and surviving. When I first became involved in the SQL Server 2005 beta program, I realized that this product was a tremendous step forward in database philosophy.

This book is for you, my friend and reader—may you consume all the information that Cristian and I have put into this book to help you pass the test and help you with all the new features for accessing data in SQL Server 2005.

A very, very special set of thanks goes to all my family and friends who encouraged me to take on this project. Please start calling me again for coffee. I can now say "yes."

Joanne, Brian, Justin, Molly, and Sara—Washington is lucky to have your sunshine. (Just move it closer to New Jersey!)

Jay, Mary, Eddie, and Wickett—thanks for all your fast answers.

Dave, Millie, and my South Jersey family—I am ready to join the family again. Thanks for your patience; I'll bring the wine.

To all my friends whom I contacted, especially Steve—thanks for the lever lesson. (Forget about the book; you should see the size of the rock I moved out of my garden!)

Most important, thanks especially to that special set of people who take my words and make it into something you can touch, feel, and enjoy working with—the editors: Maureen Adams, Kim Wimpsett, and Rachel Gunn. Another editor I want to thank for telling me to add comments to the code for you, telling me to explain more in general, and really keeping me on the straight and narrow is my technical editor, Rick Tempestini. Thanks so much, Rick! All these people and the numerous staff at Wiley have worked long hours to bring you such a professional finished product.

And speaking of professional products, thanks to the Microsoft SQL Server team, Reporting Services team, and Microsoft Learning team that I have been working with over the past few years. I have enjoyed sharing with you in Redmond, Boston, and Seattle.

—Marilyn Miller-White

A book is always a team effort. I can say now when the book is finished that I was fortunate to have the best team in the world.

My first teammates were my friends and my family, and I want to say thanks for their love and support. So my first thoughts and thanks go to my mother, Ana, Narcis, Dana and Silvia.

Then I send my appreciation to Marilyn, Jeff, Kim, Maureen, Rachel, Cheryl, and Rick. You've done a very good job, guys; I really appreciate your work, and I am happy that I had the chance to meet you.

Also, I want to say thanks to you, our reader. I hope that reading this book will help you pass your exams and, more important, will help you do your job.

Finally, my thanks goes to other people who touched this book directly or indirectly, such as fellow MVPs and members of the SQL Server team.

—Cristian Andrei Lefter

About the Authors

Marilyn Miller-White

Marilyn, a SQL Server 2005 MCTS and MCITP, MCT, MCDBA, and MCSE, is the owner of White Consulting, a New Jersey–based consultancy specializing in database and systems training and solutions.

With a master's degree in education and a passion for learning, Marilyn began teaching computer science in New Jersey's schools and colleges. While teaching, she decided to branch out to both the government and private sectors, specializing in designing database, programming, and systems solutions to support the growing needs of her customers.

Currently, she spends most of her time working with or presenting at events on SQL Server 2005 throughout North America. She loves to travel, especially to Washington and Texas where she can include a visit with her children.

When home, she enjoys singing, sailing, listening to classical music, and going to orchestra concerts and plays in Philadelphia and New York City, and she enjoys the company of her cats, Holly and her new friend Sequel.

You can reach Marilyn at author@whiteconsulting.com.

Cristian Lefter

Cristian, a SQL Server MVP and also an MCT, MCSA, MCAD, MSCD .NET, MCITP: Database Developer, and MCITP: Database Administrator, is a former SQL Server developer, database administrator, and trainer, and he is currently the CEO of MicroTraining, a consulting and training company. In his spare time, he is a technical reviewer, an author, and the leader for two user groups (ITBoard and Romanian SQL Server User Group). He is based in Bucharest, Romania.

Contents at a Glance

Table of Contents

Table of Exercises

Introduction

Welcome to what is one of the most difficult exams in the current range of SQL Server 2005 exams available, the "Designing and Optimizing Data Access by Using Microsoft SQL Server 2005" 70-442 exam.

The reason why it is such a difficult exam is because it has both a breadth and a depth that does not exist in the other SQL Server 2005 exams. It is not a DBA exam that focuses on a solution to a particular event or set of circumstances. And it is not a development exam asking you what syntax to use for a particular requirement.

It is a design exam that will ask you what the best solution is, given a large set of business and technical requirements in the context of a particular environment. There will be many requirements, and they might conflict with each other at times, as in the real world. It is up to you to untangle these various requirements so as to be able to recommend the best solution.

Designing data access solutions can be a bit of an art form, requiring years of experience, a good theoretical background, and a broad knowledge of peripheral technologies and software development techniques. Consequently, we have tried to focus on best practices and database design techniques, giving alternatives and various considerations as appropriate, instead of simply giving you syntax and "a set of rules to follow."

We have had the opportunity and good fortune of several years of experience on a variety of database solutions for numerous public and private sector organizations, each with its own set of requirements, budgets, problems, and politics. We have brought those experiences and lessons learned from the field to this book.

In addition, we hope this book will go beyond helping you pass the exam and will give you some practical advice about how to develop data access solutions based on Microsoft SQL Server 2005.

Microsoft SQL Server 2005 has some amazing technology that you can leverage as a database architect or database developer, and we hope we can help you become more aware of the options you have when designing a data access solution.

The "Designing and Optimizing Data Access by Using Microsoft SQL Server 2005" exam is based purely on case studies; however, you will notice that each chapter in this book does not end in a case study. We did this deliberately by design.

This was predominantly because of the way the chapters were structured. As a result, we could not ask data access design questions at the end of each chapter that would incorporate concepts from a number of chapters. Instead, we have written questions at the end of each chapter that test and solidify what was taught in that chapter. Consequently, we have written an entire chapter at the end of the book, Chapter 12, which comprises four case studies that will test you on the concepts covered by the entire book.

Introducing the Microsoft Certified IT Professional

Since the inception of its certification program, Microsoft has certified millions of people. Over the years, Microsoft has learned what it takes to help people show their skills through certification. Based on that experience, Microsoft has introduced a new generation of certifications:

- Microsoft Certified Technology Specialist (MCTS)
- Microsoft Certified IT Professional (MCITP)
- Microsoft Certified Professional Developer (MCPD)
- Microsoft Certified Architect (MCA)

The MCITP certification program is designed to test your knowledge as an IT professional on a broader scale than that of the MCTS certification program. The MCTS certification program is an initial certification designed to test your skills and knowledge in a basic fashion on one product. To become an MCITP, one must first obtain an MCTS certification in their particular skill area.

The MCITP program has three SQL Server 2005 certifications: database developer, database administrator, and business intelligence developer. Each of these focuses on a different aspect of SQL Server 2005 in recognition that the jobs requiring SQL Server 2005 skills are diverse with varying needs that often do not overlap. For example, a database developer may never need to know how to back up a database or configure the memory used by SQL Server. Those skills are more appropriate for a database administrator and aren't tested as heavily. Instead, the focus for this certification is in using the development tools and structuring queries.

How to Become Certified as a MCITP: Database Developer

Database developers are typically employed by mid- to large-sized organizations and are in high demand. They are responsible for designing and implementing relational database models and database storage objects. They also program the database solution by using various database objects such as user-defined functions, triggers, and stored procedures. They are also responsible for retrieving and modifying data using T-SQL queries and optimizing existing queries.

Microsoft Certified IT Professional: Database Developer (MCITP: Database Developer) is the premier certification for database designers and developers. The MCITP: Database Developer credential demonstrates that you can design a secure, stable, enterprise database solution by using Microsoft SQL Server 2005.

The MCITP: Database Developer certification requires an individual to pass two examinations as well as hold an MCTS: SQL Server 2005. The two exams are 70-441 and 70-442. Both require extensive training in SQL Server 2005 to complete. In the past, the exams were structured to test knowledge of products by remembering specifications and with a minimum of extrapolation to real-world business situations. Often people memorized answers from "exam cram" books or from "brain dump" websites and were able to pass the exams.

This book focuses on the skills you should have to pass the second exam, 70-442, while another Wiley book, *MCITP Developer: Microsoft SQL Server 2005 Database Solutions Design (70-441)*, focuses on the first exam. I hope you not only use this book as a resource in exam preparation but also a reference as you seek to develop solutions for your employer.

The new Microsoft certifications have been designed to protect the integrity of the certification programs. They require extensive knowledge of the product and real-world experience to answer the questions being asked. You'll need troubleshooting skills gained from actually using the product to solve the problems on the examination.

Make sure you take a Microsoft Skills Assessments for SQL Server 2005 to help you focus your exam preparation at http://assessment.learning .microsoft.com/test/home.asp.

This book is part of a series from Wiley that is designed to help you focus your preparation for the exams, but these books do not take the place of real-world experience and hands-on use of SQL Server 2005. Be sure you have actually used most of the features described in this book prior to registering for the exam.

For information about other topics, visit the Wiley website at www.wiley.com for information about resources to use for the other exams.

Registering for the Exam

You can take the Microsoft exams at any of more than 1,000 Authorized Prometric Testing Centers (APTCs) and VUE testing centers around the world. For the location of a testing center near you, call Prometric at 800-755-EXAM (755-3926), or call VUE at 888-837-8616. Outside the United States and Canada, contact your local Prometric or VUE registration center.

Find out the number of the exam you want to take (70-442 for the "Designing and Optimizing Data Access by Using Microsoft SQL Server 2005" exam), and then register with Prometric or VUE. At this point, you will be asked for advance payment for the exam. The exams vary in price depending on the country in which you take them. You can schedule exams up to six weeks in advance or as late as one working day prior to the date of the exam. You can cancel or reschedule your exam if you contact the center at least two working days prior to the exam. Same-day registration is available in some locations, subject to space availability. Where same-day registration is available, you must register a minimum of two hours before test time.

You can also register for your exams online at www.prometric.com or www.vue.com.

When you schedule the exam, you will be provided with instructions regarding appointment and cancellation procedures, information about ID requirements, and information about the testing center location. In addition, you will receive a registration and payment confirmation letter from Prometric or VUE.

Microsoft requires certification candidates to accept the terms of a nondisclosure agreement before taking certification exams.

Taking the "Designing and Optimizing Data Access by Using Microsoft SQL Server 2005" Exam

The "Designing and Optimizing Data Access by Using Microsoft SQL Server 2005" exam covers concepts and skills related to the design and implementation of a database solution using SQL Server 2005. It emphasizes the following elements of design:

- Designing efficient access to a SQL Server Service
- Designing a database query strategy
- Designing error-handling routines
- Designing a transaction strategy
- Performance tuning a database and a database application

This exam will test your knowledge of how you can best use SQL Server 2005 to meet the business requirements of an organization in a cost-effective manner. This exam requires a decision-making ability in all of the areas listed previously and an understanding of the implication of each of those decisions. To pass the test, you need to fully understand these topics. Careful study of this book, along with hands-on experience, will help you prepare for this exam.

Microsoft provides exam objectives to give you a general overview of possible areas of coverage on the Microsoft exams. Keep in mind, however, that exam objectives are subject to change at any time without prior notice and at Microsoft's sole discretion. Please visit Microsoft's Learning website (www.microsoft.com/learning) for the most current listing of exam objectives.

Types of Exam Questions

In an effort to both refine the testing process and protect the quality of its certifications, Microsoft has focused its Windows 2000, XP, and Server 2003 exams on real experience and hands-on proficiency. The test places a greater emphasis on your past working environments and responsibilities and less emphasis on how well you can memorize. In fact, Microsoft says an MCTS candidate should have at least one year of hands-on experience.

The 70-442 exam covers a set of precise objectives. We have written this book based on these objectives and requirements for the Microsoft exam. When you take the exam, you will see approximately 52 questions, although the number of questions might be subject to change. At the end of an exam, you will get your exam score, pointing out your level of knowledge on each topic and your exam score total with a pass or a fail.

Exam questions may be in a variety of formats. Depending on which exam you take, you'll see multiple-choice questions, select-and-place questions, prioritize-a-list questions, as well as case studies:

Multiple-choice questions   Multiple-choice questions come in two main forms. One is a straightforward question followed by several possible answers, of which one or more is correct. The other type of multiple-choice question is more complex and based on a specific scenario. The scenario may focus on several areas or objectives.

Select-and-place questions   Select-and-place exam questions involve graphical elements that you must manipulate to successfully answer the question. A typical diagram will show computers and other components next to boxes that contain the text *Place here*. The labels for the boxes represent various computer roles on a network, such as a print server and a file server. Based on information given for each computer, you are asked to select each label and place it in the correct box. You need to place *all* the labels correctly. No credit is given for the question if you correctly label only some of the boxes.

Prioritize-a-list questions   In the prioritize-a-list questions, you might be asked to put a series of steps in order by dragging items from boxes on the left to boxes on the right and placing them in the correct order. One other type requires that you drag an item from the left and place it under an item in a column on the right.

Case studies   In most of its design exams, Microsoft has opted to present a series of case studies, some often quite lengthy and followed with a series of questions as to how certain design criteria will be used. Questions following the case studies may employ any of the previous formats and methodologies.

For more information about the various exam question types, refer to www.microsoft.com/learning.

Microsoft will regularly add and remove questions from the exams. This is called *item seeding*. It is part of the effort to make it more difficult for individuals to merely memorize exam questions that previous test takers gave them.

Tips for Taking the Exam

Here are some general tips for achieving success on your certification exam:

- Arrive early at the exam center so you can relax and review your study materials. During this final review, you can look over tables and lists of exam-related information.

- Read the questions carefully. Don't be tempted to jump to an early conclusion. Make sure you know *exactly* what the question is asking. This is especially true for the 70-442 exam, which is based on case studies. Remember, *all* the pieces you need to answer the question are somewhere in the "Business Requirements" section, the "Technical Requirements" section, or even the "Existing Environment" section.

- For questions you're not sure about, use a process of elimination to get rid of the obviously incorrect answers first. This improves your odds of selecting the correct answer when you need to make an educated guess.

- However, we have always given students the tip of trusting their initial "gut" instinct when they are unsure. The more you read the question that you are unsure about, the more you doubt your initial choice, although it invariably ends up being correct.

What's in the Book?

When writing this book, we took into account not only what you need to know to pass the exam but what you need to know to take what you've learned and apply it in the real world. The book contains the following:

Objective-by-objective coverage of the topics you need to know Each chapter lists the objectives covered in that chapter.

 The topics covered in this book map directly to Microsoft's official exam objectives. Each exam objective is covered completely.

Assessment test Directly following this introduction is an assessment test that you should take before starting to read the book. It is designed to help you determine how much you already know about SQL Server 2005. Each question is tied to a topic discussed in the book. Using the results of the assessment test, you can figure out the areas where you need to focus your study. Of course, we recommend you read the entire book.

Exam essentials To highlight what you learn, essential topics appear at the end of each chapter. This "Exam Essentials" section briefly highlights the topics that need your attention as you prepare for the exam.

Glossary Throughout each chapter, you will be introduced to important terms and concepts you will need to know for the exam. These terms appear in *italics* within the chapters, and at the end of the book, a detailed glossary defines these terms, as well as other general terms you should know.

Review questions, complete with detailed explanations Each chapter is followed by 20 review questions that test what you learned in the chapter. The questions are written with the exam in mind, meaning they are designed to have the same look and feel as what you'll see on the exam. Question types are just like the exam, including multiple-choice, select-and-place, and prioritize-a-list questions.

Hands-on exercises In each chapter, you'll find exercises designed to give you the important hands-on experience that is critical for your exam preparation. The exercises support the topics of the chapter, and they walk you through the steps necessary to perform a particular function.

Case studies Because reading a book isn't enough for you to learn how to apply these topics in your everyday duties, we have provided case studies in their own chapter at the end of the book and also on the CD. These case studies explain when and why a particular solution would make sense in a working environment you'd actually encounter.

We have mixed a variety of methodologies to give you the maximum opportunities to test your own knowledge of the material covered by the objective. We model the actual exam more closely in the case studies on the CD to give you a more "exam-like" environment.

Interactive CD   Every Sybex book in the Study Guide series comes with a CD complete with additional questions, flashcards for use with a PC or an interactive device, a Windows simulation program, and the book in electronic format. Details appear in the following section.

What's on the Book's CD?

This new member of the best-selling Study Guide series includes quite an array of training resources. The CD offers chapter review questions, bonus case studies, and flashcards to help you study for the exam. We have also included the complete contents of the book in electronic form. More specifically, you'll find the following resources on the book's CD:

The Sybex ebook   Many people like the convenience of being able to carry their whole study guide on a CD. They also like being able to search the text via computer to find specific information quickly and easily. For these reasons, we've included the entire contents of this book on the CD in Portable Document Format (PDF). We've also included Adobe Acrobat Reader, which provides the interface for the PDF contents as well as the search capabilities.

The Sybex test engine   This is a collection of multiple-choice questions that will help you prepare for your exam. You'll find:

- A series of case study–based exam questions designed to simulate the actual live exam.
- All the questions from the study guide, presented in a test engine for your review. You can review questions by chapter or by objective, or you can take a random test.
- The assessment test.

Sybex flashcards for PCs and handheld devices   The "flashcard" style of question offers an effective way to quickly and efficiently test your understanding of the fundamental concepts covered in the exam. The Sybex flashcards consist of over 150 questions presented in a special engine developed specifically for the Study Guide series.

Because of the high demand for a product that will run on handheld devices, we have also developed a version of the flashcards that you can take with you on your handheld device.

How Do You Use This Book?

This book provides a solid foundation for the serious effort of preparing for the exam. To best benefit from this book, you may want to use the following study method:

1. Read each chapter carefully. Do your best to fully understand the information.
2. Complete all hands-on exercises in the chapter, referring to the text as necessary so you understand each step you perform. Install the evaluation version of SQL Server, and get some experience with the product.

Use an evaluation version of SQL Server Enterprise Edition instead of Express Edition because Express Edition does not have all the features discussed in this book. You can download the evaluation version from www.microsoft.com/sql.

3. Answer the review questions at the end of each chapter. If you prefer to answer the questions in a timed and graded format, install the test engine from the CD that accompanies this book and answer the chapter questions there instead of in the book.

4. Note which questions you did not understand, and study the corresponding sections of the book again.

5. Make sure you complete the entire book.

6. Before taking the exam, go through the review questions, bonus exams, flashcards, and so on, included on the CD accompanying this book.

7. Unfortunately, there is no substitute for experience. In fact, the exam is designed for people who have had experience with SQL Server 2005 in the enterprise. So, try to get your hands dirty with the technology.

To learn all the material covered in this book, you will need to study regularly and with discipline. Try to set aside the same time every day to study, and select a comfortable and quiet place in which to do it.

If you work hard, you will be surprised at how quickly you learn this material. Again, good luck!

Hardware and Software Requirements

You should verify that your computer meets the minimum requirements for installing SQL Server 2005. We suggest your computer meet or exceed the recommended requirements for a more orgasmic experience. Table I.1 details the minimum requirements for SQL Server 2005 editions on 32-bit computers.

TABLE I.1 SQL Server 2005 Editions and Minimum Operating System Requirements

Edition	Operating System Version and Edition
Enterprise	Windows XP with Service Pack 2 or later; Windows 2000 Server with Service Pack 4 or later; Windows 2003 Server: Standard, Enterprise, or Datacenter editions with Service Pack 1 or later; Windows Small Business Server 2003 with Service Pack 1 or later; Windows 2000 Professional with Service Pack 4 or later

TABLE I.1   SQL Server 2005 Editions and Minimum Operating
System Requirements *(continued)*

Edition	Operating System Version and Edition
Standard	Windows XP with Service Pack 2 or later; Windows 2000 Server with Service Pack 4 or later; Windows 2003 Server: Standard, Enterprise, or Datacenter editions with Service Pack 1 or later; Windows Small Business Server 2003 with Service Pack 1 or later; Windows 2000 Professional with Service Pack 4 or later
Workgroup	Windows XP with Service Pack 2 or later; Windows 2000 Server with Service Pack 4 or later; Windows 2003 Server: Standard, Enterprise, or Datacenter editions with Service Pack 1 or later; Windows Small Business Server 2003 with Service Pack 1 or later; Windows 2000 Professional with Service Pack 4 or later
Developer	Windows XP with Service Pack 2 or later; Windows 2000 Server with Service Pack 4 or later; Windows 2003 Server: Standard, Enterprise, or Datacenter editions with Service Pack 1 or later; Windows Small Business Server 2003 with Service Pack 1 or later; Windows 2000 Professional with Service Pack 4 or later

Assessment Test

1. You want to display fragmentation information for all indexes in a database. What should you do?

    A. Use the sys.dm_db_index_physical_stats dynamic management function.

    B. Use the sys.dm_db_index_usage_stats dynamic management view.

    C. Use the sys.indexes catalog view.

    D. Use the sys.dm_db_index_operational_stats dynamic management function.

2. What SQL Server management object model enables you to develop database management applications in SQL Server 2005?

    A. AMO

    B. SMO

    C. RMO

    D. SNI

3. The process of adding redundancy to a normalized database for better query performance is called?

    A. Normalization

    B. Denormalization

    C. Fragmentation

    D. Partitioning

4. You are the database developer for your organization. Your company's most important SQL Server 2005 application is running very poorly. You have one extremely large table that is used for both updating and querying that is causing high contention. Which of the following solutions should you consider for this database?

    A. Add more memory to the database server.

    B. Partition the table.

    C. Split up the table among several databases and rewrite the application as needed.

    D. Move this table to its own disk from the other tables in the database.

5. What are the main components of the architecture of data access technologies? (Choose all that apply.)

    A. Databases

    B. Database applications

    C. Client components

    D. Providers

    E. Security

6. You need to determine which indexes haven't been used since the last restart of your server. What should you do?

    A. Use the Database Engine Tuning Advisor.

    B. Use the sys.dm_db_index_usage_stats dynamic management view.

    C. Use the Default trace.

    D. Use the sys.dm_db_index_physical_stats dynamic management function.

7. What SQL Server 2005 implementation permits multiple requests to execute over a single connection?

    A. AMO

    B. SMO

    C. RAMS

    D. MARS

    E. SNI

8. The architecture of accessing data in a relational database system is best utilized by which of the following data access technologies?

    A. Cursor-based data access

    B. Set-based data access

    C. Row-based data access

    D. Loop-based data access

9. Which cursor implementations are supported by SQL Server 2005?

    A. Server cursors

    B. Atomic cursors

    C. Client cursors

    D. Tridatic cursors

    E. Consolidated cursors

10. Which of the following statements can trigger a SQL Server Agent alert?

    A. RAISERROR ('The linked server is not available',10,1) WITH LOG;

    B. PRINT 'The linked server is not available';

    C. RAISERROR ('The linked server is not available',10,1) WITH NOWAIT;

    D. RAISERROR ('The linked server is not available',10,1);

11. What is XML DML?

   A. XML DML is a query language used to return single values from XML expressions.

   B. XML DML is a query language used to return the existence of a value from an XML expression.

   C. XML DML is a query language used to convert XML data to relational data.

   D. XML DML is a query language used to modify XML data stored as an XML data type within SQL Server 2005.

12. You are the database developer for your organization. You are given the task to create a scaleout solution for your SQL Server 2005 application. The solution needs to be portable, updatable, easily maintained, and loosely coupled. Your budget allocates resources for rewriting the application and implementing the necessary hardware and software. Which of the following solutions should you consider?

   A. Scalable shared databases

   B. Peer-to-peer replication

   C. Service-Oriented Data Architecture

   D. Linked servers

13. What is displayed after running the next code?

```
SET NOCOUNT ON;

BEGIN TRY

    PRINT 'Entering the Try block';

    RAISERROR ('Error Message',1,1);

    PRINT 'The end of the Try block';

END TRY

GO

BEGIN CATCH

    PRINT 'Entering the Catch Block';

    PRINT ERROR_SEVERITY();

    PRINT 'The end of the Catch Block';

END CATCH
```

A. This is displayed:

```
Entering the Try block
Error Message
The end of the Try block
```

B. A syntax error.

C. This is displayed:

```
Entering the Try block
Error Message
Entering the Catch Block
1
The end of the Catch Block
```

D. This is displayed:

```
Entering the Try block
Entering the Catch Block
1
The end of the Catch Block
```

14. Which FLWOR XQuery expressions are supported by SQL Server 2005?

   A. FOR

   B. LET

   C. WHERE

   D. ORDER BY

   E. RETURN

15. You have to design a table named Customer that will store the international customers of your company. Which data type should you use to store the customer name?

   A. VARCHAR(MAX)

   B. NVARCHAR(MAX)

   C. CHAR(256)

   D. NVARCHAR(256)

16. You have to decide what data type you should use to store the usage instructions for the products of a pharmaceutical company. The usage instructions are written in English and contain plain text. What should you do?

   A. Use a VARCHAR(MAX) data type.

   B. Use a NVARCHAR(MAX) data type.

   C. Use a VARBINARY(MAX) data type.

   D. Use a TEXT data type.

17. Which of the following isolation levels use an optimistic concurrency approach? (Choose all that apply.)

   A. Snapshot

   B. Serializable

   C. Repeatable Read

   D. Read Committed Snapshot

18. Which new feature of SQL Server 2005 allows you to have rows greater than 8,060 bytes?

   A. Row-overflow data

   B. The TEXT data type

   C. The IMAGE data type

   D. The NTEXT data type

19. You are designing a stored procedure that generates data for a report. The underlying table named Orders is used by company employees to enter sales information. You want to minimize the concurrency impact of the report query. The report data does not require high consistency. What should you do?

   A. Use the TABLOCK query hint.

   B. Use the NOEXPAND table hint.

   C. Use the ROWLOCK query hint.

   D. Use the NOLOCK query hint.

20. Which of the following are data access technologies that can be implemented in SQL Server 2005? (Choose all that apply.)

   A. ODBC

   B. OLE DB

   C. XML

   D. SQLNCLI

   E. HTTP

Answers to Assessment Test

1. **A.** The sys.dm_db_index_physical_stats dynamic management function returns size and fragmentation information for all indexes of an instance. Using arguments you can display information for a particular table, index, or database.

   The sys.dm_db_index_physical_stats and the sys.dm_db_index_operational_ stats dynamic management functions return index usage information.

   The sys.indexes catalog view contains metadata information about properties of all indexes in a database but not fragmentation information. See chapter 8 for more information.

2. **B.** SMO, or SQL Server management objects, is a .NET library that enables you to write code-based queries, procedures, reports, and any services using a .NET-supported language. Using SMO you are able to script any object in your database. See chapter 2 for more information.

3. **B.** The denormalization process adds redundant data to an already normalized database to increase the performance of read queries. See chapter 11 for more information.

4. **B.** You should partition the table horizontally over several filegroups to boost performance. This solution will alleviate the contention problems while still maintaining one table for accessing the data. Partitioning a table is a new feature in SQL Server 2005. Adding more memory or moving the table to another disk will not relieve contention in the existing table. Creating more databases and rewriting the application are not necessary when you can more easily partition a table in SQL Server 2005. See chapter 9 for more information.

5. **A, C, D.** Databases store the data and provide the server-side access components for connectivity. Client components are components that enable your client application to connect and interact with a database. Providers establish communication between the databases and the client components. Although database applications and security play an important part in data access, they are not components of the architecture of data access technologies. See chapter 1 for more information.

6. **B.** The sys.dm_db_index_usage_stats dynamic management view returns information about all the indexes used from the last restart of a server. A simple join of this view with the sys.indexes catalog view can give you unused indexes.

   The Database Engine Tuning Advisor can generate index and partitioning recommendations but in this case would not help you. The Default trace records various configuration events but not index usage. The sys.dm_db_index_physical_stats dynamic management function returns size and fragmentation information for indexes. See chapter 8 for more information.

7. **D.** MARS, or multiple active result sets, is a new technology in SQL Server 2005 that permits multiple requests to execute over a single connection. See chapter 2 for more information.

8. **B.** The architecture of relational database systems such as SQL Server 2005 is built to utilize set-based data access. Set-based data access enables usage of server resources including memory utilization and indexing. See chapter 4 for more information.

9.   A, C.   Server cursors and client cursors are supported in SQL Server 2005. Atomic, tridatic, and consolidated cursors do not exist in SQL Server 2005 cursor strategies. See chapter 4 for more information.

10.   A.   A SQL Server Agent alert is triggered when only if an error message is logged. To do that you can use the RAISERROR WITH LOG statement, the extended stored procedure xp_logevent, or create an user-defined error message and specifying 'TRUE' as the value for the @with_log parameter. See chapter 5 for more information.

11.   D.   Since the XQuery language does not provide the ability to modify XML data, Microsoft has extended the XQuery capabilities with the modify() method within SQL Server 2005. This method uses three input keywords: insert, replace value of, and delete. See chapter 3 for more information.

12.   C.   You should consider Service-Oriented Data Architecture. SQL Server 2005 offers all the features to be a full-service provider for a loosely coupled distributed application. Some of these new features include the Service Broker service, Notifications service, web service access, and SQLCLR. Including these services as a part of the architecture enables SQL Server to manage the data and to support scalability. Using a Service-Oriented Data Architecture implementation you are able to manage and integrate services within the database giving your application a greater range and flexibility. See chapter 9 for more information.

13.   B.   You will get a syntax error because the TRY block must be immediately followed by the CATCH block. You have to remove the batch separator (GO) to fix the error. See chapter 5 for more information.

14.   A, C, D, E.   LET is the only FLWOR expression not supported in SQL Server 2005. All other expressions are supported and especially useful in designing XML queries. FLWOR statements are used to iterate and filter the logic of queries that would otherwise be complex. See chapter 3 for more information.

15.   D.   The best option is to use a variable-length Unicode character data type—in this case NVARCHAR. You should choose a variable-length data type because names in general have various lengths, and use Unicode and not ANSI because you will store international customers. The MAX specifier allows you to store up to 2GB of data but it's hard to believe that you will have a customer name with more than 256 characters. See chapter 11 for more information.

16.   A.   As the usage instructions contain plain text written in English then you should use a character data type. Between TEXT and VARCHAR data types you should use the VARCHAR data type because the TEXT data type is deprecated. Using a binary or Unicode data type is not necessary for this scenario. See chapter 11 for more information.

17.   A, D.   The new isolation levels of SQL Server 2005, Read Committed Snapshot and Snapshot, use an optimistic approach based on row versioning while the Serializable and the Repeatable Read isolation levels use a pessimistic approach based on locking. See chapter 6 for more information.

18. A.   You can have rows greater than 8,060 bytes using large value data types such as TEXT, NTEXT, IMAGE, VARCHAR(MAX), VARBINARY(MAX), or XML. In addition you can use row-overflow data, a new feature of SQL Server 2005 that allows a row greater in size than 8,060 by storing columns in a separate location data types such as VARCHAR, NVARCHAR, VARBINARY, or SQL_VARIANT. When the combined widths of the columns for a table exceed the 8,060 limit, SQL Server will store one or more columns in separate data page.

The TEXT, NTEXT, and IMAGE data types do allow you to use large data but they are not new in SQL Server 2005 and, even more, they are deprecated. See chapter 11 for more information.

19. D.   The best concurrency in this case can be obtained by using the NOLOCK query hint. Read operations don't require shared locks when you use the NOLOCK query hint.

The TABLOCK and ROWLOCK query hints determine the locking behavior of SQL Server but in this case cannot help you.

The NOEXPAND table hint is related to views and not to concurrency and locking. See chapter 6 for more information.

20. A, B, D.   Although they have been around for a long time, ODBC and OLE DB are technologies that can still be used to access data in SQL Server 2005. However, if you need to be able to utilize some of the new functionalities in SQL Server 2005, you will need to use SQL Native Client (SQLNCLI) as your access technology. XML is a mark-up language and HTTP is a protocol. See chapter 1 for more information.

Chapter 1

Designing Data Access

MICROSOFT EXAM OBJECTIVES COVERED IN THIS CHAPTER:

✓ **Design appropriate data access technologies.**

✓ **Design an appropriate data access object model.**

✓ **Design a cursor strategy for a data access component.**

- Decide when to use cursors.

- Decide how to maximize cursor performance.

- Detect which applications are using cursors and evaluate whether to remove them.

✓ **Design caching strategies.**

- Select ADO.NET caching.

- Design custom caching functionality.

- Design a refresh strategy for cached data.

Database applications allow you to use the data you have stored in your database. They provide access to and manage your data. Today you have a wide variety of database access methods. Therefore, it is essential to select the technology for accessing your data that will benefit your enterprise most.

In this chapter, we cover the technologies that will better serve your access needs so that you can develop efficient and manageable database applications. We begin by focusing on the methods available. Some of these methods are new to SQL Server 2005; in fact, using the same technologies as you have in the past might not provide you with the tools you need to create a well-managed data access environment. Thus, we next explain how you can use the data access methods available to your advantage in building a data access layer.

The internal structure of the SQL Server 2005 database engine has changed. Knowledge of the changes in the data models from previous versions of SQL Server to SQL Server 2005 will assist you not only in choosing the correct access method for your data but also in administering SQL Server 2005. Therefore, we specifically target these new features.

Because SQL Server is a relational data system that works in a set-oriented manner, you will need to access data on a row-by-row process. In order to process row-oriented data using cursors, we discuss how to implement cursors for data access. (See Chapter 4 for further discussion of cursors and cursor strategy).

Finally, we conclude this chapter with a focus on ways to improve data access performance. We discuss designing and implementing caching strategies. Although SQL Server 2005 manages caching mechanisms automatically, you need to understand the processes involved so that your data access application will work optimally.

Determining the Right Access Method

We start with a look at the current technologies available to you for accessing data. Then we cover the appropriate scope in which to use these technologies. In this discussion, you will learn the two types of database applications and the components used within the data access system and the architecture of those components.

We use the term *component* to reference a part or element of an overall solution.

Designing Appropriate Data Access Technologies

As a developer you know that your application design is all about accessing data efficiently and securely. Your applications come in many shapes and sizes. However, you have two distinct types of applications: those designed for managing data and those designed for administering systems.

You can define these two types of applications as follows:

- Applications that use data access components to obtain data and store it in the database
- Administrative tools that use well-defined object models to enable you to administer your database system

You require a data access system to create the link between your data and your application. All applications, regardless of the shape or size, require the same type of data access components. Simple applications, such as a client application querying your database, might involve nothing more than a command-line utility running on the client. For example, you might use the command-line utility SQL command (SQLCMD) and connect to your database server through a network library such as *SQL Native Client (SQLNCLI)*. For more complex business applications, such as an accounting or customer management application, your need for data access components remains the same. You might build a data access interface for your client application, but you still need a data access provider such as SQLNCLI to be able to execute queries on your database.

You can classify data access components into two types (see Figure 1.1):

Server-side components These components run on a server managing requests from client computers. Server-side components can include network libraries and TSQL endpoints. TSQL endpoints have been introduced in SQL Server 2005 as a new concept for SQL Server connections. You can grant, revoke, and deny permissions for TSQL endpoints. By default, all users have permissions to access an endpoint unless the permissions are denied or revoked by a member of the sysadmin group or by the endpoint owner. SQL Server Setup creates TSQL endpoints for all supported network protocols, as well as for the dedicated administrator connection. TSQL endpoints created by SQL Server Setup include TSQL LocalMachine, TSQL Named Pipes, TSQL Default TCP, TSQL Default (Virtual Interface Adapter) VIA, and Dedicated Admin Connection (DAC).

For more information about network libraries and protocols, search "Network Protocols and Network Libraries" in SQL Server Books Online.

Client-side components These components are the initiators as well as the receivers of requests between your database application and database server. Most often you use a presentation layer user interface (UI) component on the client for this effort.

FIGURE 1.1   Data access system components

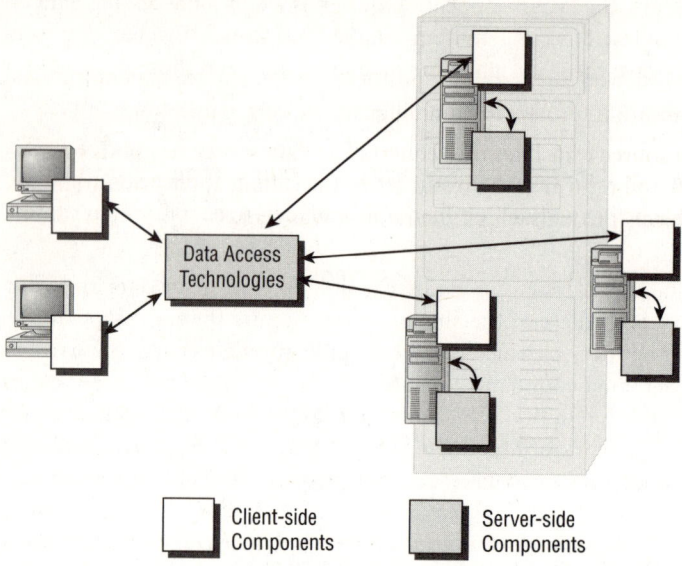

Let's take a minute to make certain you understand how database applications are built and where the data access system components fit in. A multitiered application, which is the recommended method, consists of the following:

- The presentation tier is the interface that interacts with the end user of the application.

- The business tier is the component that enforces the business rules and the workflow definitions.

- The data access tier converts the logical representation of your data into the physical schema of the database. This tier can also control the integrity of your data during the translation.

Understanding How Database Components Interact

It is important you understand how the database components interact with each other to create the connection between your application and the data source. The steps involved follow and are shown in Figure 1.2:

1. Your client application implements a data access layer. This layer will provide manageability for the connection.

2. The data access layer uses a data access application programming interface (API) to interact with the remote data. An API enables your application to exploit the power of operating system. The base services functions in the API give your application access to the resources of the computer and the features of the underlying operating system, such as memory, file systems, devices, processes, and threads. Your application uses these functions to manage and monitor the resources it needs to complete its work.

3. The API uses a specific data access provider component that will interact programmatically with the API at the remote data source.

4. The data access provider interacts with the physical network using the various systems interconnection layers to communicate with the remote data source. The data access provider will interact with the necessary network protocols, such as transactional and security, and use its data serialization formats to communicate with the data source.

5. Finally, the data source translates the request. The data source responds by executing the requested action and returning the result set to the calling application using the same channels and objects through which the request was sent.

FIGURE 1.2   Interaction of database components

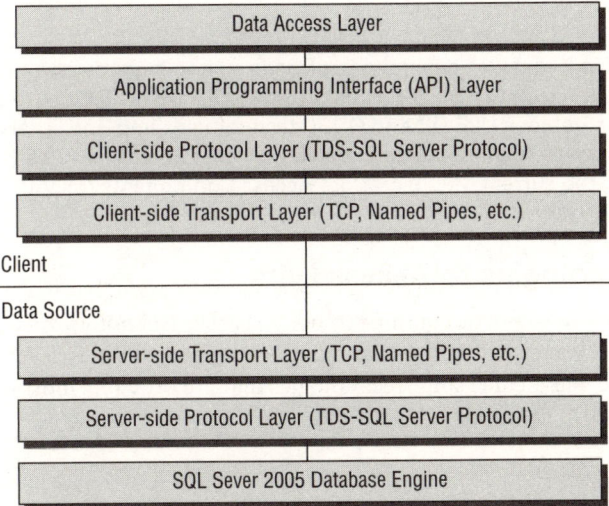

Understanding the Architecture of Data Access Technologies

Now we've covered how the components interact, we'll look at the architecture of data access technologies. Understanding the architecture will enable you to choose the appropriate technology to best meet your development needs.

You have three main players in the architecture of data access technologies:

The database   The database is your resource. Here lies your data store and the server-side components that enable your connectivity.

The provider   The provider is the communicator. Providers establish the communication connection between the client component and the data source.

The client component   Client components are both the askers and the receivers. Client components are objects that provide the capability to transform the request, reach out, and interact with a database. You can use a variety of data access technologies to create your client-side database application. Some unmanaged technologies include ODBC (Open Database Connectivity), OLE DB, ADO (Microsoft ActiveX Data Objects), and Jet. To base your database access application on managed code, you use a .NET Framework data access provider.

As we mentioned earlier, SQL Native Client (SQLNCLI) is the technology you should be using to access the new functionalities of SQL Server 2005. When you use SQL Native Client, you have no need to use an OLE DB provider, ODBC provider, or any other layer to interface with SQL Server 2005. SQL Native Client communicates directly with the SQL Server database. Since the SQLNCLI library connects to SQL Server through the server network library, which is accessed internally from a T-SQL endpoint, you are always assured of communicating with your SQL Server using data access providers. Furthermore, since this communication process is handled automatically, your database application does not need to be aware of or involved with its implementation.

SQL Native Client was designed to provide a simplified method of gaining native data access to SQL Server using either OLE DB or ODBC. It is simplified in that it combines OLE DB and ODBC technologies into one library, and it provides a way to innovate and evolve new data access features without changing the current Microsoft Data Access Components (MDAC).

Using Legacy Technologies to Access Data

It might be appropriate for you to use or continue to use an earlier technology to access your data source. We cover some legacy technologies and discuss their capabilities, level of performance, and limitations. We will include some technologies that are probably most familiar to you: DB-Library, ODBC, OLE DB, and SQLXML.

DB-Library

Consider the following when accessing data using DB-Library:

Deprecated feature   DB-Library is a client interface that originated in Sybase and is not supported by SQL Server 7.0 and later. Some legacy database applications may still be using DB-Library. However, this library, based on C code implementations, is being deprecated and will be removed from future versions of SQL Server.

No support for current versions of SQL Server   DB-Library does not support features of SQL Server 7.0 and later.

ODBC

Consider the following when accessing data using *ODBC*:

Industry standard   Open Database Connectivity is well established as an industry standard for connecting to relational database systems. Microsoft created ODBC by adapting the SQL Access Group CLI and released ODBC 1.0 in September 1992. Because ODBC dates back more than 10 years, it offers connectivity to a wider variety of data sources than other data access APIs. Many applications requiring high connectivity, including those serving SQL Server 2000, still use C language components with native ODBC.

Driver availability   You implement ODBC API functions through database management system (DBMS)–specific drivers. The core library, independent of the applications and DBMS systems, is the interpreter between the applications and the database drivers. It is the database driver that contains the DBMS-specific details. Thus you can write applications that use standard types and features without concern for the specifics of each DBMS that the applications may encounter. To implement these database drivers you need only know how to attach to the core library, thus making ODBC modular.

Data source name (DSN) connection definitions   Each ODBC data source on a client has a unique data source name (DSN). An ODBC application uses an ODBC data source to connect to an instance of Microsoft SQL Server. An ODBC data source is a stored definition that records the ODBC driver to use for connections specifying the data source—the information used by the ODBC driver to connect to a source of data and driver-specific options to be used for the connection. The connection definitions can be stored either in the registry as is the case of *System* and *User DSNs* or in the file system as is the case of the *File DSN*.

 You launch the ODBC Data Source Administrator by clicking Data Sources (ODBC) in Control Panel.

ODBC Data Source Name (DSN) Connection Definition Locations

Connection definitions are stored as follows:

System DSNs are stored in the HKEY_LOCAL_MACHINE (HKLM) portion of the registry and are available to all users of the computer.

User DSNs are stored in the HKEY_USERS (HKU) portion of the registry and are available only to the user that created them.

File DSNs are stored in the file system, which makes them available for copying to other computers or to be stored on a network drive.

OLE DB

Consider the following when accessing data using *OLE DB*:

Added functionality over ODBC   OLE DB was designed as a higher-level replacement for, and successor to, ODBC, extending its feature set to support a wider variety of nonrelational databases.

Object model data providers   OLE DB separates the data store from the accessing application through a set of abstractions, such as connections, recordsets, and attributes. OLE DB is conceptually divided into consumers and providers. The consumers are the applications that need access to the data, and the provider is the software component that implements the interface. This technology enables a variety of database sources to be queried in a uniform manner.

Flexibility of data sources   The OLE DB provider is suitable for database applications that access both relational and nonrelational data sources. Using the Microsoft OLE DB Provider for ODBC allows you to use a single OLE DB provider to connect to multiple ODBC data sources, including SQL Server. However, connecting to SQL Server clients with this provider entails more administrative overhead than using the native Microsoft OLE DB Provider for SQL Server.

Although using SQLNCLI allows you to develop an OLE DB consumer optimized for SQL Server databases, you can only use SQLNCLI with SQL Server. You can use the Microsoft OLE DB Provider for ODBC to access data from a number of OLE DB–compliant ODBC applications.

SQLXML

Consider the following when accessing data using *SQLXML*:

Updated features   SQLXML has been updated to include the new features in SQL Server 2005. For example, earlier versions of SQLXML do not have support for data types introduced in SQL Server 2005. The initial versions of SQLXML enable XML support for SQL Server 2000, bridging the gap between XML and relational data. The updated version is SQLXML 4.0. When you install SQLXML 4.0, the files installed by earlier versions of SQLXML are not removed. Therefore, you can have Dynamic-link libraries (DLLs) for several different version-distinctive installations of SQLXML on your computer. It is possible for you to run the installations side by side. SQLXML 4.0 includes both version-independent and version-dependent programmatic identifiers (PROGIDs). You should use version-dependent PROGIDs in your database applications.

Search "What's New in SQLXML 4.0" in SQL Server Books Online for more information.

Automatic installation   You automatically install SQLXML 4.0 when you install the Microsoft SQL Server 2005 server or tools with Notification Services. At installation, the components make appropriate changes to the registry.

SQLXML 4.0 is not completely backward compatible with SQLXML 3.0. Because of some bug fixes and other functional changes, particularly the removal of SQLXML ISAPI support, you cannot use Internet Information Services (IIS) virtual directories with SQLXML 4.0. Although most applications will run with minor modifications, you must test them before putting them into production with SQLXML 4.0.

Using SQL Native Client to Access Data

SQLNCLI is a data access provider specifically designed for and included with SQL Server 2005. Actually, SQL Server Management Studio and other administrative applications use SQL Native Client to communicate with SQL Server 2005.

 For another review of Microsoft's Data Access Components, check out MSDN's Data Access and Storage Developer Center's article, "Learning Microsoft Data Access Components" at http://msdn.microsoft.com/data/learning/MDAC/

You might be wondering at this point what the differences between SQLNCLI and MDAC are. Microsoft Data Access Components (MDAC) is a suite of data access APIs that ship with the Windows operating system. In many cases, an older operating system can be retrofitted with a newer version of MDAC by running the redistributable installer package. MDAC includes three major API surfaces—ODBC, OLEDB, and ADO—each of which has been optimized for a different set of applications. All three major components of MDAC employ the provider model, which allows access to a variety of data sources using a virtually identical set of programmatic calls. Although it is not a part of MDAC, SQL Native Client also exposes all three major component interfaces and is fully compatible with the latest version of MDAC. SQLNCLI and MDAC can cohabitate on the same system with no known issues.

SQL Native Client New Feature Support

SQL Native Client implements many features to take advantage of new functionalities provided by SQL Server 2005. A summary of the features follows:

- SQL Native Client supports mirrored databases, which is the ability to keep a copy, or *mirror*, of a SQL Server 2005 database on a standby server.

- SQL Native Client supports asynchronous operations, which is the ability to return immediately without blocking on the calling thread.

- SQL Native Client supports multiple active result sets (MARS), which is the ability to execute and receive multiple result sets using a single database connection.

- SQL Native Client supports the XML data type, which is a SQL Server 2005 XML-based data type that can be used as a column type, variable type, parameter type, or function return type.

- SQL Native Client supports user-defined types (UDT), which extends the SQL type system by allowing you to store objects and custom data structures in a SQL Server 2005 database.

- SQL Native Client supports large value data types, which are large object (LOB) data types that are supported in SQL Server 2005.

- SQL Native Client supports the handling of expired passwords so that passwords can now be changed on the client without administrator involvement.

- SQL Native Client supports the enhancement to row versioning that improves database performance by avoiding reader-writer blocking scenarios.

- SQL Native Client supports consumer notification on rowset modification.

- SQL Native Client supports bulk copy operations that allow the transfer of large amounts of data into or out of a SQL Server table or view.

- SQL Native Client supports the ability to encrypt data sent to the server without validating the certificate.

So, you see you have many reasons to upgrade your data access provider to SQLNCLI when using SQL Server 2005 as your data source.

You target SQLNCLI at two application types:

- Your existing applications that connect to SQL Server through OLE DB or ODBC and that you want to take advantage of any of the new SQL Server 2005 features.

- Your applications written in a development platform other than the Microsoft .NET Framework that you want to take advantage of any of the new SQL Server 2005 features.

If you do not need to use any of the new features of SQL Server 2005, you don't need to use the SQL Native Client OLE DB provider, just continue using your current data access provider. However, if you are enhancing an existing application and you need to use the new features of SQL Server 2005, you should use SQLNCLI.

SQL Native Client Connection References

When you connect to SQL Server 2005 using SQL Native Client, your applications need to reference SQLNCLI as the provider name in the *connection string* as you open the connection to the database server. Connection strings are lists of keywords and associated values that identify a particular connection attribute. Depending on your programming environment, you may also need to include a reference the SQLNCLI header files. Presuming your server is installed on the C: drive, the header files are located at C:\Program Files\Microsoft SQL Server\90\SDK\Include folder and are named SQLNCLI.h.

When you are connecting through ODBC, do the following:

- Include the SQLNCLI header file in your ODBC application by replacing the odbcss.h file with the following:

  ```
  Include "SQLNCLI.h";
  ```

- If your application is using a DSN connection, update the DSN to use the SQL Native Client driver.

- If your application uses a connection string rather than a DSN connection, update the connection string from using the SQL Server provider to using the SQL Native Client provider:

  ```
  "Driver={SQL Native Client}; Server=(local);
  Database=AdventureWorks; Trusted_Connection=yes;"
  ```

When you are connecting through OLE DB, do the following:

- Include the SQLNCLI header file in your OLE DB application by replacing the sqloledb.h file as follows:

```
Include "SQLNCLI.h";
```

- Update the connection string from using the SQLOLEDB provider to use the SQLNCLI provider:

```
"Provider=SQLNCLI;Server=(local);
➥Database=AdventureWorks;Integrated Security=SSPI;"
```

Your OLE DB applications need to reference only sqlncli.h. However, if you have an application that uses both MDAC (OLE DB) and the SQL Native Client OLE DB provider, your application can reference both sqloledb.h and sqlncli.h. However, the reference to sqloledb.h must be first.

When you are connecting through ADO, do the following:

- Update the connection string from the SQLOLEDB provider to use the SQLNCLI provider:

```
"Provider=SQLNCLI;Server=(local);
➥Database=AdventureWorks;Integrated Security=SSPI;"
```

If you are developing a new application, Microsoft recommends that you consider using ADO.NET and the .NET Framework Data Provider for SQL Server instead of SQL Native Client to access all the new features of SQL Server 2005. For more information about the .NET Framework Data Provider for SQL Server, please see Chapter 2 or the .NET Framework SDK documentation for ADO.NET.

Using ADO with SQL Native Client

If you have an existing application that uses *ActiveX Data Objects (ADO)* and you want to take advantage of the new functionality of SQL Server 2005, you should use SQL Native Client OLE DB as the data access provider. Enhancements have been made to the SQL Native Client OLE DB provider that enable ADO to use such SQL Server 2005 features as the XML data type, user-defined types, additional functionality of the VARCHAR, NVARCHAR, and VARBINARY data types and multiple active result sets (MARS),

To use the SQL Native Client OLE DB provider, define a new connection string keyword named DataTypeCompatibility. Then, set the DataTypeCompatibility keyword to 80 so that the new data types will map correctly to the ADO data types.

The changes to the connection string keyword are as follows:

- Provider=SQLNCLI
- DataTypeCompatibility=80

The following is an example of establishing an ADO connection string that is fully enabled to work with SQL Native Client, including the enabling of the MARS feature:

```
Dim con As New ADODB.Connection

con.ConnectionString = "Provider=SQLNCLI;" _
        & "Server=(local);" _
        & "Database=AdventureWorks;" _
        & "Integrated Security=SSPI;" _
        & "DataTypeCompatibility=80;" _
        & "MARS Connection=True;"
con.Open
```

Using HTTP Endpoints and SOAP to Access Data

You may want to access the data from SQL Server 2005 by using an application based on an Internet protocol. You could use many different tools, but two that have their functionality built into SQL Server 2005 are HTTP endpoints and *Simple Object Access Protocol (SOAP)*.

For previous versions of SQL Server, your clients access a SQL Server database using Tabular Data Stream (TDS). TDS is a proprietary protocol that must be supported for Windows-based desktop clients. Sometimes, SQL Server clients must use Microsoft Data Access Components (MDAC). The MDAC stack is installed on the client computer that connects to SQL Server. For SQL Server, SQLXML 3.0 is a middle-tier component that supports web-based access to SQL Server, but IIS must also be used.

In SQL Server 2005, by including the use of HTTP and SOAP, native XML web services provide an alternative for other environments to access data, as shown in Figure 1.3.

FIGURE 1.3   Web-based access to SQL Server

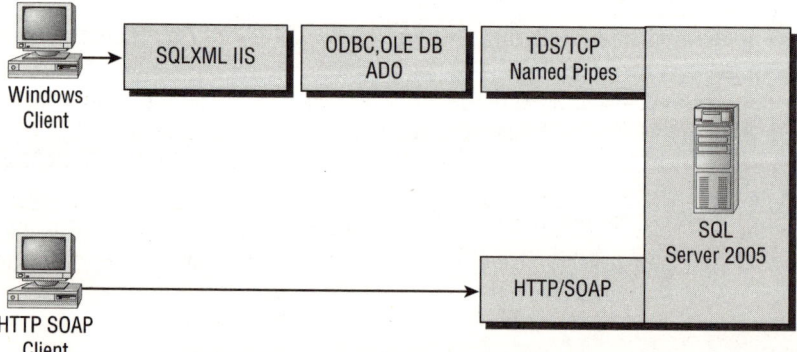

By using SOAP and HTTP, you can enable a wider range of clients to access SQL Server because you no longer need either MDAC installed at the client or SQLXML with its IIS dependency at the middle tier. These clients include web application clients that use existing client applications, such as web browsers. Furthermore, native XML web services make it easier to work with the Microsoft .NET Framework, Microsoft SOAP Toolkit, Perl, and other web development operating systems and tool sets. As you can see in our illustration, when you use HTTP or SOAP, you are making a direct call to SQL Server. Using this access method to return XML data is often more efficient than using SQLXML in the middle tier.

Exposing SQL Server as a Web Service

To expose a SQL Server as a web service, you must define an *HTTP endpoint*. An endpoint is your communication link between SQL Server and the client application. SQL Server HTTP endpoints are predefined within SQL Server to address data requests. As an object in SQL Server, the endpoint provides the necessary functions to provide SQL query responses within the security realm of SQL Server. The CREATE ENDPOINT statement is used to create both HTTP and TCP endpoints that are able to be used by Database Mirroring, Service Broker, SOAP, and T-SQL.

- The following example creates an endpoint called AWProduction, with two methods: GetProducts and UpdateProductPrice. These are the methods for which a client can send SOAP requests to the endpoint.

```
CREATE ENDPOINT AWProduction
STATE = STARTED
AS HTTP(
     SITE = 'localhost',
     PATH = '/AdventureWorks/Production',
     AUTHENTICATION = (INTEGRATED),
     PORTS = ( CLEAR ))
FOR SOAP(
     WEBMETHOD 'GetProducts' (name='AdventureWorks.Production.GetProducts',
➡FORMAT=ROWSETS_ONLY),
     WEBMETHOD 'UpdateProductPrice' (name='AdventureWorks.Production.
➡UpdateProductPrice'),
          WSDL = DEFAULT,
          DATABASE = 'AdventureWorks',
          NAMESPACE = 'http://AdventureWorks/'
     )
```

For the complete syntax of the CREATE ENDPOINT statement for Database Mirroring, Service Broker, SOAP, and T-SQL payloads, search "CREATE ENDPOINT (Transact-SQL)" in SQL Server Books Online.

Here are a few guidelines to follow when you are considering using Native XML web services for data access:

- Native XML web services are not recommended for the following:

  - Applications characterized by real-time highly concurrent access, with short duration transactions

  - Web farm-type scale-out

  - As a replacement for the middle tier, specifically where your application architecture has large-scale business logic demands that are better accommodated within middle-tier components

- You should not enable basic or digest authentications unless you must impose access limitations on a database.

- For access to sensitive data, it is preferable to adopt a Secure Sockets Layer (SSL) communication channel.

- Do not use HTTP endpoints if you are building an intensive online transaction processing (OLTP) application or must manage large data values such as binary large objects (BLOBs)

Writing Code That Uses HTTP Endpoints

The easiest way to write code that uses HTTP endpoints is by using a development environment such as Visual Studio 2005. In a development environment, all that you need to do is add a web reference to the endpoint. This creates a wrapper class, which contains one member with the function signature for each WEBMETHOD defined in the endpoint. With this class, you can access the endpoint in the same manner that you would with any other web service.

Connecting SQL Server 2005 to Other Data Stores

Let's now look at the times that you want to connect SQL Server to another data store. Your database application might use user-defined functions or store procedures to establish the connection. The queries you generate may execute wholly or partially at the remote source. For these scenarios, you must remain flexible in your approach to data access. Although OLE DB and ODBC libraries allow you to access other SQL Servers as well as other data sources, remember that you are limited by the functionality provided in the drivers themselves.

Also plan for security in your data access plan. If the remote server supports Windows Authentication, and security account delegation is available, you are able to use the same user credentials that authenticated against SQL Server to authenticate with the remote server. This delegation feature allows you to use a single credential for access to multiple data sources. Otherwise, you must create a linked server logon to map a SQL Server credential to the remote server credentials.

When your query executes against data from both remote and local sites, most often the processing for the remote data is handled at the remote server. If this process is not possible because of dialect or linked server setting difference, the remote server will return the entire data set to the local server where it will be processed with the local data. Even though local processing provides greater consistency, the cost of returning large amounts of unneeded data can be costly in terms of time and resource utilization.

Using an In-Process Data Provider to Access Data

Another consideration for connecting to an external database is to use managed code. It might be advantageous for you to create a SQL common language runtime (SQLCLR) stored procedure with the permission set to EXTERNAL_ACCESS for the following tasks:

- Process the remote information prior to combining it with your local data.

- Network with third-party data sources.

- Access data sources that are not totally compliant with the linked server implementation.

Within a SQLCLR procedure, you are able to define your connections to an external data source using ADO.NET, process and transform the data, and finally merge it with your local data. You then have full control over the behavior of the remote data source and can implement processes beyond the capabilities of the Transact-SQL technologies.

Designing an Appropriate Data Access Object Model

When creating your applications for SQL Server 2005, you are programmatically administering SQL Server itself. Therefore, you need to understand the management APIs that SQL Server 2005 uses. In the next section, we analyze the changes within the management API of SQL Server so that you will be able to choose the correct object model to use for your applications.

Managing SQL Server before SQL Server 2005

In SQL Server 2000 you used the SQL Server Enterprise Manager that used the *SQL Distributed Management Objects (SQL-DMO)* API to administer SQL Server. The SQL-DMO API is still available with SQL Server 2005, although SQL-DMO will be removed in a future version of Microsoft SQL Server. Avoid using this feature in new development work and plan to modify current applications that use this feature. In SQL Server 2000 you manage server objects using administrative tasks, evoking Data Definition Language (DDL) statements on databases and their objects and controlling services. By using SQL-DMO, your applications can administer SQL Server 2000 in the same manner that SQL Server Enterprise Manager does.

SQL-DMO objects are exposed as properties of other SQL-DMO objects. The relationship between objects is a tree-like structure that simplifies programming by using automation managers. Your objects can be referenced using the familiar dot notation used to reference properties or methods.

For example, in SQL-DMO the Database object exposes a Tables collection. Each Table object within the collection represents a single table of an instance of Microsoft SQL Server. You can obtain a SQL-DMO Table object by referencing a specific table using syntax much like the following:

```
Set oTable = oDatabase.Tables("Products")
```

Search "SQL-DMO Object Tree" in SQL Server Books Online.

Administering SQL Server 2005 Using SMO

The successor to DMO is SQL server management objects or SMO. The *SMO* object is a hierarchical structure of objects with the Server class being at the highest level in the SMO instance hierarchy. When you create a Server object variable, you are establishing a connection to SQL Server.

Search "SMO Object Model Diagram" in SQL Server Books Online.

Another important top-level class with a separate hierarchy is the ManagedComputer class. You use the ManagedComputer object to view and modify SQL Server services, network settings, and alias settings. The ManagedComputer object is made available through the Windows Management Instrumentation (WMI) Provider. In addition to the Server and ManagedComputer objects, you have several utility classes that represent tasks or operations, such as Transfer, Backup, or Restore.

The SMO object model is composed of several namespaces. Each namespace represents a different area of functionality within SMO. Table 1.1 lists the SMO namespaces.

TABLE 1.1   SMO Object Model Namespaces

Class	Function
Microsoft.SqlServer.Management.Smo	This namespace contains the instance classes, utility classes, and enumerations that you use to programmatically manage Microsoft SQL Server
Microsoft.SqlServer.Management.Common	This namespace contains the classes such as connection classes that are common to replication management objects (RMO) and SMO.
Microsoft.SqlServer.Management .Smo.Agent	This namespace contains classes corresponding to the SQL Server Agent
Microsoft.SqlServer.Management.Smo.Wmi	This namespace contains classes corresponding to the WMI Provider
Microsoft.SqlServer.Management.Smo .RegisteredServers	This namespace contains classes corresponding to Registered Server

TABLE 1.1 SMO Object Model Namespaces *(continued)*

Class	Function
Microsoft.SqlServer.Management.Smo.Mail	This namespace contains classes corresponding to Database Mail
Microsoft.SqlServer.Management.Smo.Broker	This namespace contains classes corresponding to the Service Broker
Microsoft.SqlServer.Management.Nmo	This namespace contains classes corresponding to Notification Services

The programming model of SMO has been improved over its predecessor DMO and the number of objects has grown to include all the new features in SQL Server. As you go through the following features, take a minute to reflect how each feature of SMO has brought about an increased functionality in SQL Server 2005.

You have many new features provided with SMO including the following:

- SMO gives you improved performance. Objects are loaded only when you specifically reference them. When you create an object, its properties are only partially loaded. The remaining objects are loaded when they are referenced directly.

- SMO provides capture and batched execution of Transact-SQL statements. Your network performance is improved because statements can be captured and sent as a batch.

- SMO enables you to manage your SQL Server services through the WMI Provider. SMO gives you the capability to programmatically start, pause, and stop all services on your server.

- SMO enables you to recreate any SQL Server object as well as its relationships to other objects through generated Transact-SQL scripts.

- SMO enables data transfer flexibility through its scripting functionality and use with Integration Services.

- SMO uses Uniform Resource Names (URNs).

- SMO's event handling allows you to insert code that is executed when a specific event occurs.

- SMO's exception processing allows you to identify errors specific to SMO.

- SMO gives you better control over your database objects and their security. Database objects are now managed objects and as such are controlled by their predetermined properties and methods.

Next we will look at how SMO represents some objects or properties in a number of features and components new to SQL Server 2005. These include the following:

- SMO provides support for partitioning tables and indexes on a partition scheme.

- SMO provides support for HTTP endpoints.

- SMO provides support for new concurrency controls through snapshot isolation and row level versioning.

- SMO provides support for the storage of XML data.

- SMO provides support for creating read-only copies of databases.

- SMO represents support for Service Broker communication.

- SMO supports database object Synonyms.

- SMO supports Database Mail.

- SMO supports server registration and connection.

- SMO supports SQL Server Profiler trace and replay events.

- SMO supports Notification Services.

- SMO supports security features in SQL Server 2005 through certificates and keys.

- SMO supports DDL (Data Definition Language) triggers.

 We cover how to use management object applications with the SMO object model in Chapter 2.

Administering SQL Server 2005 Replication Using RMO

You use *replication management objects (RMO)* to program SQL Server replication. SQL Server 2005 replication technologies have been enhanced in many areas. RMO supports all the new replication functionalities. The RMO object model extends and supersedes the replication-specific objects that you find in the DMO object model. You can use RMO with SQL Server version 7.0 and newer.

RMO is implemented in the Microsoft.SqlServer.Replication namespace by the Microsoft .SqlServer.Rmo.dll, a Microsoft .NET Framework assembly. Microsoft.SqlServer.Replica-tion.dll, another assembly belonging to the Microsoft.SqlServer.Replication namespace, implements a managed code interface for programming the various replication agents: Snapshot Agent, Distribution Agent, and Merge Agent. Its classes can be accessed from RMO to synchronize subscriptions.

RMO allows you programmatic control of the following types of replication tasks:

Configuring replication   You can use RMO to configure publishing and distribution, as well as to create, delete, and modify publications, articles, and subscriptions.

Synchronizing subscriptions   You can use RMO to synchronize your subscriptions.

Maintaining a replication topology   You can use RMO to perform replication maintenance tasks, such as managing partitions in a merge publication and validating subscriptions.

Monitoring a replication topology   You can use RMO to programmatically monitor your replication topology.

We cover how to use management object applications with the RMO object model in Chapter 2.

Utilizing Patterns and Practices

Microsoft has done extensive work in the development of data access technologies. The Microsoft Patterns and Practices team provides *application blocks* that they have designed and developed. Application blocks contain tested code for a variety of technologies. You can customize these reusable code templates for your own applications, thus minimizing your need to write code.

You can find the Data Access Application Block link at the Microsoft Patterns and Practices team website at http://msdn.microsoft.com/practices.

Deciding When to Implement Cursors

Your SQL Server database is a relational system and hence operates in a set-oriented manner. However, many applications work with specific objects stored within the individual rows of the tables in a database. Your application needs to access the database one row at a time, which takes place by using row-by-row processing. SQL Server supports using cursors for this row-by-row processing.

As a developer or a database administrator, you need to understand cursors and their use. We discuss their implementation in the following sections and their use in Chapter 4.

Deciding When to Use Cursors

Here are a few reasons you might use a cursor strategy in your database application:

- You decide to access data by looping through the data row by row; cursors are a natural programming technique to use.
- You do not think another type of implementation other than using cursors is optimal.
- You find it too painful programmatically to solve the data access problem without using cursors.

For when *not* to use cursors, see Chapter 4.

Designing a Cursor Strategy for a Data Access Component

Microsoft SQL Server 2005 supports three cursor implementations:

Transact-SQL cursors   These cursors are based on the DECLARE CURSOR syntax. They are used mainly in Transact-SQL scripts, stored procedures, and triggers. They are implemented on the server and are managed by Transact-SQL statements sent from the client to the server.

Application programming interface (API) server cursors   These cursors support the API cursor functions in OLE DB and ODBC. API *server cursors* are implemented on the server. Each time a client application calls an API cursor function, the SQL Native Client OLE DB provider or ODBC driver transmits the request to the server for action against the API server cursor.

Client cursors   These cursors are implemented internally by the SQL Native Client ODBC driver and by the DLL that implements the ADO API. *Client cursors* are implemented by caching all the result set rows on the client. Each time a client application calls an API cursor function, the SQL Native Client ODBC driver or the ADO DLL performs the cursor operation on the result set rows cached on the client.

Because Transact-SQL cursors and API server cursors are implemented on the server, they are referred to collectively as *server cursors*.

Deciding How to Maximize Cursor Performance

You should be careful to not mix the use of these various types of cursors. If you execute a DECLARE CURSOR and OPEN statement from an application, you must first set the API cursor attributes to their defaults. If you set API cursor attributes to something other than their defaults and then execute a DECLARE CURSOR and OPEN statement, you are asking SQL Server to map an API cursor over a Transact-SQL cursor.

Using Server Cursors

A potential drawback of server cursors is that they currently do not support all Transact-SQL statements. Server cursors do not support Transact-SQL statements that generate multiple result sets; therefore, they cannot be used when the application executes a stored procedure or a batch that contains more than one SELECT statement. Server cursors also do not support SQL statements containing the keywords COMPUTE, COMPUTE BY, FOR BROWSE, or INTO.

However, using server cursors instead of client cursors does have some advantages:

Performance   If you are going to access a portion of the data in the cursor, using server cursors provides optimal performance since only fetched data is sent over the network. In this instance, a client cursor would be inappropriate since it would cache the entire result set on the client. Therefore, if you need to access just part of the query results from the cursor, you should use a server cursor so the processing will be done on the server and the network traffic will be minimized.

Additional cursor types   If the SQL Native Client ODBC driver used only client cursors, it could support only forward-only and static cursors. By using API server cursors, the driver can also support keyset-driven and dynamic cursors. SQL Server also supports the full range of cursor concurrency attributes only through server cursors. Client cursors are limited in the functionality they support.

 For more information about cursor types, see Chapter 4. You can also search "Cursor Types" in SQL Server Books Online.

More accurate positioned updates   Server cursors directly support positioned operations, such as the ODBC SQLSetPos function or UPDATE and DELETE statements with the WHERE CURRENT OF clause. However, client cursors simulate positioned cursor updates by generating a Transact-SQL searched UPDATE statement. This action may lead to inadvertent updates if more than one row matches the WHERE clause conditions of the UPDATE statement.

Memory usage   If you use server cursors, all cursor maintenance is done at the server. The client is spared the possibility of caching large amounts of data or of maintaining information about the cursor position.

Multiple active statements   When using server cursors, no results are left outstanding on the connection between cursor operations. This allows you to have multiple cursor-based statements active at the same time.

Now that you have had an introduction to server cursors, you need to keep in mind that the operation of all server cursors, except static or insensitive cursors, depends on the schema of the underlying tables. If you change the schema of a table after a cursor has been declared on it, you will get an error on any subsequent operation on that cursor.

Implementing Client-Side Cursors

Your implementation of client-side cursors depends on the data access provider you choose. In developing data access, you usually choose providers based on factors such as database server support, transaction support, security features, performance, and technical support. You should also consider client-side features such as connection pooling and client-side cursors.

As you saw earlier in this chapter, each data access provider supports a definite feature set. Some of the data access providers, such as OLE DB and ODBC, were designed to work with multiple data sources. Other providers, such as SqlClient and the SQL Native Client, were designed to work with a single specific data source providing native support for that data source.

When OLE DB, ODBC, and ADO technologies are implemented, a cursor is implicitly opened over the result set returned by a T-SQL statement. However, you can change this behavior by modifying the properties of the object that executes the T-SQL statement.

Let's take another look at the client data access libraries, this time encapsulating the features of client-side cursors they support.

These are the features of client-side cursors that OLE DB supports:

- When you use OLE DB, the term *rowset* means a combination of the result set and its associated cursor behaviors.

- Native OLE DB does not support client-side cursors. However, you can add Microsoft Cursor Services for OLE DB to provide client-side cursors.

These are the features of client-side cursors that ODBC supports:

- When you use ODBC, the terms *result set* and *cursor* are interchangeable because a cursor is automatically mapped to a result set.

- ODBC implements client cursors through the ODBC Cursor Library.

- ODBC enables multiple active statements on a connection if used in conjunction with SQLNCLI.

- ODBC supports read-only and updatable cursor types.

- ODBC supports forward-only and scrollable cursor navigation.

- Using ODBC data access providers, you are able to configure and specify the cursor type, concurrency, and rowset size.

These are the features of client-side cursors that ADO supports:

- When you use ADO, the term *recordset* is a combination of a result set and its associated cursor behaviors.

- ADO supports only static read-only cursor types.

- ADO supports forward-only and scrollable cursor navigation.

- ADO supports asynchronous retrieval of results from the database server.

These are the features of client-side cursors that *ADO.NET*/SqlClient supports:

- ADO.NET implements classes that contain a separation between the result set (DataSet class) and the cursor (SqlDataReader and TableDataReader classes).

- ADO.NET supports only read-only, forward-only cursors.

- ADO.NET enables you to use multiple active statements on a connection.

- ADO.NET supports asynchronous retrieval of results from the database server.

Detecting Which Applications Are Using Cursors and Evaluating Whether to Remove Them

In SQL Server 2005, you have many options available to you for tracking the status and usefulness of cursors.

Using SQL Server Profiler

SQL Server Profiler enables you to analyze your application's cursor strategy. When you run a trace, you can capture the following cursor events by their start time, application name, user, client process ID, and server process ID:

CursorOpen   This event indicates when a cursor has been opened by a Transact-SQL statement.

CursorExecute   This event occurs when the Microsoft SQL Server 2005 database engine creates and populates a cursor from the execution plan created by a cursor prepare event.

CursorImplicitConversion   This event occurs when the Microsoft SQL Server 2005 database engine executes a Transact-SQL statement that is not supported by server cursors of the type requested. SQL Server database engine returns an error that indicates the cursor type has changed.

CursorClose   This event occurs when the Microsoft SQL Server 2005 database engine closes and deallocates a cursor.

CursorPrepare   This event occurs when the Microsoft SQL Server 2005 database engine compiles a SELECT statement associated with a cursor into an execution plan but does not create the cursor.

CursorUnprepare   This event occurs when the Microsoft SQL Server 2005 database engine discards an execution plan

CursorRecompile   This event occurs when the Microsoft SQL Server 2005 database engine recompiles a Transact-SQL cursor due to a schema change.

Using Performance: System Monitor

You are able to gather real-time metrics with System Monitor. You can use these metrics for a direct analysis of your cursor strategies or as a baseline to measure changes in cursor performance. Table 1.2 describes the SQL Server Cursor Manager by Type counters.

TABLE 1.2   Cursor Manager Counters in System Monitor

Cursor Manager by Type Counters	Description
Active cursors	Number of active cursors.
Cache Hit Ratio	Ratio between cache hits and lookups.
Cached Cursor Counts	Number of cursors of a given type in the cache.
Cursor Cache Use Count/sec	Times each type of cached cursor has been used.
Cursor memory usage	Amount of memory consumed by cursors in kilobytes (KB).

TABLE 1.2   Cursor Manager Counters in System Monitor *(continued)*

Cursor Manager by Type Counters	Description
Cursor Requests/sec	Number of SQL cursor requests received by server.
Cursor worktable usage	Number of worktables used by cursors.
Number of active cursor plans	Number of cursor plans.

Using Cursor Metadata

You can use either of the following ways to get metadata describing a server cursor:

- Applications using API server cursors with a database API such as ADO, OLE DB, or ODBC typically use the cursor functionality of the API to get information about the state of the cursor.

- Transact-SQL scripts, stored procedures, and triggers can use the Transact-SQL functions and system stored procedures to get information about a Transact-SQL cursor.

Using Stored Procedures

Several system stored procedures report the characteristics of a server cursor:

sp_describe_cursor   You use this system stored procedure to return a cursor describing its global attributes, such as its scope, name, type, status, and the number of rows.

sp_describe_cursor_columns   You use this system stored procedure to return a cursor describing the attributes of each column, such as the column's name, position, size, and data type.

sp_describe_cursor_tables   You use this system stored procedure to return a cursor describing the objects or base tables it references.

sp_cursor_list   You use this system stored procedure to return a listing of all the currently visible cursors for the connection.

Using System Functions

Finally, several system functions available report server cursor status information:

CURSOR_STATUS   You use this system function to indicate whether a cursor is open or closed, or whether a cursor variable is currently associated with a cursor.

@@FETCH_STATUS   You use this system function to indicate the success or failure of the last fetch operation performed for the connection.

@@CURSOR_ROWS   You use this system function to report the number of rows populated in the last cursor opened for the connection.

You should be very careful in how you use the analysis from stored procedures and functions. Their status information is often affected by other operations and other cursors. Their results may also be fleeting as in the results from the @@FETCH_STATUS function, which changes every time a FETCH statement is issued against any cursor open for the connection.

Making the Cursored Choice

When should you use cursors? Some developers would say never and manage to stay away from them whenever feasible (we believe we've heard them say, "Stay away from them like they're the plague!"). Let's take a moment to recap what we have seen thus far on the subject so you can make a well-educated decision for your strategy.

Using a cursor is less efficient than using a default result set. When you use a default result set you send only one packet from the client to the server—the packet containing the statement to execute. When you use a server cursor, each FETCH statement must be sent from the client to the server, where it must be parsed and compiled into an execution plan. It is easy to see the performance difference.

Recall that if a Transact-SQL statement will return a relatively small result set that can be cached in the memory available to the client application, and you know previous to execution that you must retrieve the entire result set, use a default result set. And finally, you should use server cursors only when cursor operations are necessary to support the functionality of the application; it is seldom "just a neat thing" to use cursors.

Planning Caching

As we complete our discussion of data access strategies, we must focus our attention on one last piece of the access structure—caching. *Caching* is the process of creating a persisted copy of data and objects local to the user.

Here are some questions to consider:

- Do you need to repeatedly access static data or data that changes rarely?
- Do you wish to minimize your expenses in data access retrieval?
- Does your data need to always be available, even when the source, such as a server, is not available?

Answering yes to each of the previous questions is a valid reason to implement a caching strategy.

Designing Caching Strategies

Although SQL Server 2005 provides many internal caching mechanisms, you can apply several available caching techniques to make your applications more robust. You can implement these caching methodologies at each of the layers of your application to improve performance and scalability as well as to optimize system resources. Furthermore, network bandwidth, physical I/O, and memory can also profit from caching strategies.

> Most often we think of caching in terms of data, but caching frequently used objects is often beneficial to performance.

You usually create database applications in layers. The layering process allows you to implement a variety of logic and scalability methodologies into your application. You can use numerous caching techniques at each layer. You can enhance each layer's functionality by applying the correct caching techniques. Next we examine the considerations you need to take into account at various layers of your application.

Caching Guidelines for Working with the Database Server Layer

Some guidelines for the database server layer follow:

Don't be greedy.   Read only the data you need when you query tables. When you read excessive amounts of data, existing data currently in the buffer cache will be forced out. The end result is that the data in cache could be useless to you and the data you need is gone.

Avoid recompiling stored procedures.   When you compile stored procedures, the query plan is put into the procedure cache. One of the main reasons for creating stored procedures is to be able to reuse the query plan for faster execution on subsequent calls of the procedure. If you recompile the stored procedure, the cache is invalidated and a new query plan must be generated. This action can be very costly in time and resources.

Monitor the buffer cache.   A variety of performance counters have been designed to assist you in monitoring the cache. One important counter is the SQL Server Buffer Manager: Page Life Expectancy counter. This counter states the number of seconds a page will stay in the buffer pool without references. In short, this is the life span of a page in the buffer cache. You want this number to be high. The higher the number, the longer data will reside in memory. This means that you will need fewer physical I/O operations to retrieve data.

Denormalization is not always a bad word.   If your queries use complex joins or aggregations, you should consider denormalizing the data. If you are creating summary reports, denormalizing the underlying data will increase the performance of the query since it will need to read fewer pages of data. The fewer the pages, the fewer I/O operations will need to be performed, the faster the query.

> You should not denormalize data that is updated often. The process of keeping the denormalized data in synchronization with the underlying normalized data might not make it worth the effort.

Caching Guidelines for Working with the Application (Middle) Layer

Some guidelines for the application layer follow:

Avoid caching data that is updatable by other processes.   The data in the cache becomes invalid when it is updated by another application or process. To overcome this problem you might need to implement logic to resolve the update issues; this logic might cause as greater drain on performance.

Use Microsoft ADO.NET connection pooling.   *Connection pooling* reduces the cost of opening and closing database connections. ADO.NET connection pooling is enabled by default, allowing you to reuse the database connection for subsequent data requests. This process can significantly improve the efficiency of your data access. Connection pooling requires that the pooled connections maintain the same parameters, including the security context.

Think of creating a cache just for your business objects.   A specialized cache will enable a more efficient reuse of these business objects.

Refrain from caching data that is sensitive in shared memory.   You tempt a security threat to this sensitive data by caching it in a shared memory location.

Caching Guidelines for Working with the Web Services Layer

Some guidelines for the web services layer follow:

Cache partial results.   When you cache intermediate results you are decreasing the calls to the application tier. This action results in a faster response time by reducing the workload of the web service.

Be aware of outdated data.   Any caching that is done at a middle-tier layer must be mindful of data changes at either the database or the application tier. You need to plan your caching strategy carefully so that you do not cause your data to be invalid.

Caching Guidelines for Working with the Front-end Application Layer

Some guidelines for the front-end application layer follow:

Cache same-session data for reuse.   When you reuse data, even if the format at the client has changed, you should cache the data. You will use fewer system and network resources. You should design your application to cache the data at the application tier.

Cache resource intensive objects with static data to disk.   For objects that are I/O and resource intensive, consider caching the objects to disk on the application's operating system. If your data is not changing often, caching provides a means to quickly retrieve the objects and their interface components.

Use time stamps to map disk-cached objects to their application retrieval time.   When you cache objects to disk, you can add a time stamp or a checksum to signify the currency of the data. Your application can use this information to retrieve data from the database based on this metric as opposed to retrieving the entire data set.

Cache dynamic user interface components in memory. Although you usually store interface components within the databases, you might consider caching them in memory. This action will save round-trips between the application and the database each time the user selects a new option.

Selecting ADO.NET Caching

ADO.NET is a cache-friendly database connection library that is designed for data reuse and database disconnection. ADO.NET uses a pooling technology to avoid repeatedly creating and disposing database connections when the database application is busy. This disconnected approach to data access provides better scalability for your application. ADO.NET leverages the ability of XML to provide disconnected access to data. ADO.NET was designed hand in hand with the XML classes in the .NET Framework. They are both components of the same architecture. Figure 1.4 shows the ADO.NET architecture.

Choosing a DataSet or a DataReader

The *DataSet* object is central to supporting disconnected, distributed data scenarios with ADO.NET. The DataSet is a memory-resident representation of data that provides a consistent relational programming model regardless of the data source. It is explicitly designed for data access independent of any data source. Therefore, you can use the DataSet with multiple data sources as well as a variety of data sources. DataSets do not require an active database connection to maintain a set of data in memory. The DataSet also represents a complete set of data. It includes the data as well as any related data, constraints, and relationships among the data. Figure 1.5 shows the DataSet object model.

FIGURE 1.4 ADO.NET architecture

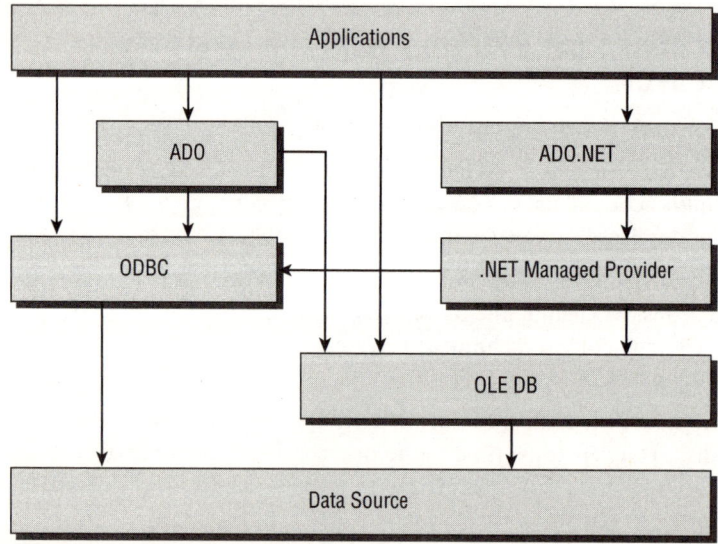

FIGURE 1.5   Relationship between a .NET Framework data provider and a DataSet

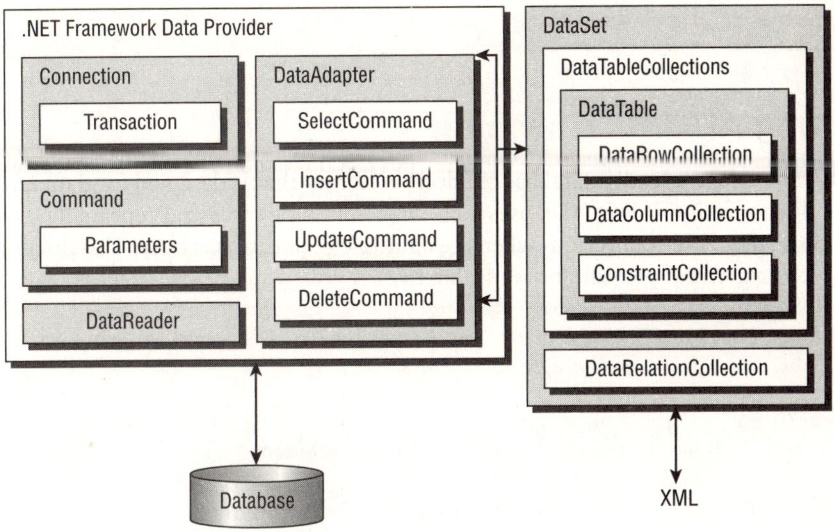

If you do not require the functionality provided by the DataSet, you can improve the performance of your application by using the *DataReader* to return your data in a forward-only, read-only fashion. By using the DataReader you can boost performance since you will be saving memory that would be consumed by the DataSet.

You need to consider the type of functionality required by your application when deciding between using a DataReader or a DataSet. You can use the DataSet to do the following:

- To cache data locally in your application so that you can manipulate it. On the other hand, if you need merely to read the results of a query, the DataReader is your better choice.

- To access remote data between tiers or from an XML web service.

- To interact with data dynamically. For example, you can use the DataSet to combine data from multiple sources or bind to a Windows Forms control.

- To execute extensive processing of data without requiring an open connection to the data source. This enables other clients and resources to use the connection.

Using Connection Settings

ADO.NET uses the ConnectionSettings class to represent the settings used by a connection to an instance of a server, such as Microsoft SQL Server. The ServerConnection class inherits the ConnectionSettings class.

Table 1.3 lists the properties exposed by the ConnectionSettings type.

TABLE 1.3   ADO.NET ConnectionSettings Members' Public Properties

Property Name	Description
ApplicationName	This property gets or sets the application's name during its connection with the server.
ConnectAsUser	This property gets or sets the Boolean value indicating whether impersonation is being used when the connection is established.
ConnectAsUserName	This property gets or sets the username when impersonation is used for the connection.
ConnectAsUserPassword	This property gets or sets the user password when impersonation is used for the connection.
ConnectionString	This property gets or sets the data source–specific connection string used to establish the connection.
ConnectTimeout	This property gets or sets the time-out period in seconds of the connection.
DatabaseName	This property gets or sets the connection database.
EncryptConnection	This property gets or sets the Boolean value indicating whether the connection is encrypted.
Login	This property gets or sets the instance logon required to establish the server connection.
LoginSecure	This property gets or sets the Boolean value indicating a trusted or SQL Server authentication connection is established with the server.
MaxPoolSize	This property gets or sets a number indicating the maximum number of connections a connection pool accepts when establishing a connection with a server.
MinPoolSize	This property gets or sets a number indicating the minimum number of connections a connection pool accepts when establishing a connection with a server.
MultipleActiveResultSets	This property gets or sets the Boolean value indicating the permission of more than one active result set.
NetworkProtocol	This property gets or sets the server network protocol used to establish the connection.

TABLE 1.3   ADO.NET ConnectionSettings Members' Public Properties *(continued)*

Property Name	Description
NonPooledConnection	This property gets or sets the Boolean value indicating the pooling state of the connection.
PacketSize	This property gets or sets the network packets in bytes of data sent between the client and the server.
Password	This property gets or sets the password used with the logon to establish a SQL Server Authenticated connection.
PooledConnectionLifetime	This property gets or sets the pooled connection lifetime.
SecurePassword	This property gets or sets the secure password used with the logon to establish a SQL Server Authenticated connection.
ServerInstance	This property gets or sets the server name.
WorkstationId	This property gets or sets the workstation's unique ID value.

As you have seen, ADO.NET provides reuse and disconnection functionality as you work with database connections. As noted above, connection pooling technology is also appropriate to avoid continually creating and disposing of database connections in highly active database application scenarios.

Using Connection Pooling

Database connection pooling allows an application to reuse an existing connection from a pool instead of repeatedly establishing a new connection with the database. This technique can significantly increase the scalability of an application, because a limited number of database connections can serve a much larger number of clients. This technique also improves performance, because the significant time required establishing a new connection can be avoided.

Data access technologies such as ODBC and OLE DB provide forms of connection pooling, which are configurable to varying degrees. Both approaches are largely transparent to the database client application. OLE DB connection pooling is often referred to as session or resource pooling.

Designing Custom Caching Functionality

As we mentioned earlier, the main cache memory pools of SQL Server 2005 are the procedure cache and the buffer cache. As a database developer, you are able to enhance your data access by controlling the contents of the caches. You want your applications to be scalable and to perform well. You want to make certain that query plan recompiles are avoided and that you do not read large amounts of data unnecessarily. You need to monitor and strive to maximize cache reuse.

Some guidelines for maximizing cache utilization follow:

Avoid reading columns you are not using.   You should always avoid returning data you don't need. The extra data will be unnecessarily forced into memory, making memory unavailable for other tasks. Especially be careful that you do not return large and variable-width columns, such as VARCHAR and TEXT columns, that are not needed. These columns may reside outside the data page. Needlessly reading these large pieces of data can create an excessive burden on your cache.

Read only rows that need to be processed.   We have mentioned this before. When you read excessive amounts of data, existing data currently in the buffer cache will be forced out. The end result is that the data in the cache is useless to you and the data you need is gone.

Avoid using nonparameterized SQL.   Nonparameterized SQL may create new rather than reusable query plans.

Monitor procedures and attempt to avoid their recompilation.   When your procedures recompile, you are not only creating extra resources to be applied but you are increasing the duration of the query process.

Use XML and relation data appropriately.   If you need to read a single scalar value, you should most likely be using relational data. If you were to read the same from an XML column, the entire column would need to be loaded into memory prior to the read.

Use multiple SQL Server instances to isolate memory.   You should use this process to adjust the memory on shared resources. Creating a new instance will isolate memory and may increase process utilization. However, other overhead also must be considered when creating a new instance, so weigh your options wisely.

Your caching scheme must include a plan to handle outdated data. If you do not update the cache when you have changes to your data, the data you retrieve might be inconsistent and yield inaccurate results. You must always give your users trustworthy data.

Designing a Refresh Strategy for Cached Data

As you have seen, caching is a broad topic. There are no concrete answers to what are the best techniques to employ for your caching implementation. However, you have tools available to assist you in monitoring your cache utilization. These tools also provide a basis for a refresh strategy that you can implement.

Using SQL Server Profiler

SQL Server Profiler provides metrics you can use to capture how the procedure cache is used in your queries. Here are a few to use in your trace:

SP:CacheHit   Indicates when a procedure is found in the cache.

SP:CacheInsert   Indicates when an item is inserted into the procedure cache.

SP:CacheMiss   Indicates when a stored procedure is not found in the procedure cache.

SP:CacheRemove   Indicates when an item is removed from the procedure cache.

SQL:StmtRecompile   Occurs when a statement in a batch (including stored procedures) recompiles. This event should be used in SQL Server 2005 instead of SP:Recompile to trace statement-level recompilations.

Using Performance Monitor

You can use *Performance Monitor* to show current buffer cache activity. Here are two BufferManager counters that you will find useful:

SQLServer:BufferManager Buffer cache hit ratio   Percentage of pages that were found in the buffer pool without having to incur a read from disk.

SQLServer:BufferManager Database pages   Number of pages in the buffer pool with database content.

Using Dynamic Management Views and Functions

You can use *dynamic management views and functions* to return server state information that can be used to monitor the health of a server instance, diagnose problems, and tune performance. There are two types of dynamic management views and functions:

- Server-scoped dynamic management views and functions. These require VIEW SERVER STATE permission on the server.
- Database-scoped dynamic management views and functions. These require VIEW DATABASE STATE permission on the database.

Some dynamic management views and functions useful in returning caching information follow:

sys.dm_exec_cached_plans   Returns information about the query execution plans that are cached by SQL Server for faster query execution.

sys.dm_exec_query_plan   Returns the Showplan in XML format for a Transact-SQL batch whose query execution plan resides in the plan cache.

sys.dm_exec_query_stats   Returns aggregate performance statistics for cached query plans. The view contains one row per query plan and the lifetime of the row is tied to the plan itself. When a plan is removed from the cache, the corresponding row is eliminated from this view.

sys.dm_exec_requests   Returns information about each request that is executing within SQL Server.

Dynamic Management Views and Functions are new to SQL Server 2005. For more information on dynamic management views and functions and their use, search "Dynamic Management Views and Functions" in SQL Server Books Online.

Using Query Notifications

You have a new functionality available that allows an application to request a notification from SQL Server when the results of a query change. This new functionality is *query notifications*. Query notifications allow you to design applications that query the database only when there is a change to information that your application has previously retrieved.

Your applications can take advantage of query notifications to reduce round-trips to the database. In lieu of writing code that periodically reexecutes a query to maintain current results, you can now design applications that are automatically notified when the results for the query may be out of date. With query notifications, your application issues a command that contains a query and a request for notification. Your application then caches the results of the dynamic content generated from the query results. When your application receives the query notification, your application clears the cached content.

The notification messages are delivered by Service Broker. Therefore, Service Broker must be active in the database where the application requests the subscription. Please note though that query notifications functionality does not require or use Notification Services. Query notifications is independent of event notifications.

For more about query notifications, search "Working with Query Notifications" in SQL Server Books Online.

Summary

In this chapter, you started your journey with data access, a topic that lays the foundation for you as you program SQL Server 2005. You were taken through the paths of some of the older technologies that are still used. We evaluated those technologies expressly built for SQL Server 2005 data access. We discussed the various technologies and when to best apply them. At this point, you should certainly be excited at what is now available to you.

Since your SQL Server database is a relational system, we then turned to the topic of row-by-row access of the data, using cursors. You learned when to use cursors and how to use cursors to maximize performance. You further learned how to use tools so you can detect which applications are using cursors. We will continue our discussion on using cursors in Chapter 4.

Finally, we focused on optimizing your system resources by caching both data and objects in the appropriate layers. You learned how to reduce your resource utilization and gain system performance in data access by implementing a caching strategy. Furthermore, you also learned you can optimize resources such as memory, physical I/O, and network bandwidth by using caching methodologies.

Exam Essentials

Before you take the exam, you need to have a good understanding of the following:

Understand how to design data access technologies. You need to be familiar with the types of data access applications, data access components and their interaction, and the architecture of data access technologies.

Be able to determine an appropriate data access method. You need to be familiar with legacy and present-day access technologies for SQL Server 2005 data access. You need to know how and why to use SQL Native Client to access data. You need to understand the data access features of HTTP endpoints and SOAP. Furthermore, you need to be familiar with the data access models of DMO, SMO, and RMO as SQL Server management APIs.

Be able to decide when to use cursors. You need to be familiar with the types of cursor implementations in SQL Server 2005. You need to know the differences in implementing server and client cursors. You need to know the data access libraries and the cursor strategies they support.

Know how to detect cursor use. You need to be familiar with the tools used to track cursors and how to evaluate their metrics.

Be able to design a caching strategy. You need to understand and be able to apply the techniques for caching at the various layers of you applications.

Understand how to evaluate caching and designing a refresh strategy. You need to be familiar with the tools used to track caching and how to use them effectively.

Review Questions

1.   Which of the following are database applications? (Choose all that apply.)

     A. Microsoft Windows Explorer

     B. Microsoft SQL Server Management Studio

     C. Microsoft Office Access

     D. Customer Relationship Management (CRM) software

2.   Which of the following is a new technology library implemented by SQL Server 2005 to provide full access to all SQL Server databases including SQL Server 2005?

     A. SQLXML

     B. SQLNCLI

     C. SQLCMD

     D. SSMS

3.   Which of the following are server-side components for data access in SQL Server 2005?

     A. Network libraries

     B. ODBC

     C. T-SQL endpoints

     D. OLE DB

     E. SQLNCLI

4.   You are the database developer for your company. You have upgraded your servers to SQL Server 2005. You have created a new version of your SalesFocus application. You need to allow the new version to run from your remote offices. All new functionalities of SQL Server 2005 must be available through this connection. What should you do?

     A. Use ODBC to connect to SQL Server.

     B. Use SQLNCLI to connect to SQL Server.

     C. Create a web service on another server. Connect this server to SQL Server using an HTTP endpoint. Have the clients at the remote offices connect to the web service.

     D. Use SQLXML 4.0 to connect to SQL Server.

     E. Use OLE DB to connect to SQL Server.

5.   You have upgraded your databases to SQL Server 2005. Now you want to update the connections in your SalesFocus application that is currently accessing SQL Server using OLE DB programmatically in the application. You need to update your code so that you can connect using SQLNCLI. What should you do? (Choose two.)

     A. Replace the OLE DB header file with the SQLNCLI header file.

     B. Add the SQLNCLI header file to the OLE DB header file.

     C. Update the DSN to use the SQL Native Client.

     D. Change the connection string to use the SQLNCLI provider.

6. Which components in the data access technology architecture act as a data transformer and local data depository?

   A. Providers

   B. Databases

   C. Client components

   D. Server endpoints

7. You are the database developer for your company. Your manager has told you to make certain that the DSN for your TaskForce ODBC application connects such that it is available to all users of each connecting computer. What should you do?

   A. You check the ODBC administrator in control panel to make certain the User DSN is being used for the TaskForce application.

   B. You check the ODBC administrator in control panel to make certain the System DSN is being used for the TaskForce application.

   C. You check the ODBC administrator in control panel to make certain the File DSN is being used for the TaskForce application.

   D. You check the HKU hive of the registry to make certain the User DSN is being used for the TaskForce application.

8. You are the database developer for your company. You need to create objects to expose SQL Server as a web service. Which of the following can you use?

   A. SSL communication channel

   B. HTTP endpoint

   C. IIS virtual directory

   D. TCP port

9. You are the database developer for your company. You have been told to develop a native XML web services strategy for data access. Which of the following guidelines are not recommended for XML web services? (Choose all that apply.)

   A. An intensive online transaction processing application.

   B. Applications that manage large values.

   C. Applications using short duration transactions with highly concurrent access.

   D. Applications that manage static data.

10. You are the database developer for your company. You want to process remote information prior to combining it with your local data sources. What type of provider should you use?

    A. An in-process data provider

    B. An ODBC data provider

    C. An OLE DB data provider

    D. An External Access data provider

11. You are the database developer for your company. You have been asked to manage your SQL Server 2005 server programmatically. What API should you use?

    A. SMO

    B. DMO

    C. RMO

    D. ADO

12. You are the database developer for your company. You have decided to use a cursor strategy in your SQL Server 2005 application. What cursor implementations are you able to use for SQL Server 2005? (Choose all that apply.)

    A. API server cursors

    B. Client cursors

    C. Transact-SQL cursors

    D. Web services cursors

13. You are the database developer for your company. You are trying to decide whether to implement server cursors or client cursors in your SQL Server 2005 application. Which of the following are advantages of using server cursors? (Choose all that apply.)

    A. Performance

    B. Memory usage

    C. Multiple active statements

    D. Choice of cursor types

14. You are the database developer for your company. You have decided to use the ODBC SQL Native Client ODBC driver with your SQL Server 2005 application. Which of the following is not a cursor type supported by the ODBC driver?

    A. Static cursors

    B. Dynamic cursors

    C. Forward-only cursors

    D. Backward compatible cursors

    E. Keyset-driven cursors

15. You are the database developer for your company. You want to gather real-time metrics on the number of active cursors in your SQL Server 2005 server. Which tool should you use?

    A. System Monitor

    B. SQL Server Profiler

    C. Dynamic Management Views

    D. System stored procedures

16. You are the database developer for your company. You need to find the number of rows populated in the last cursor opened on the connection to your SQL Server 2005 server. Which function should you use?

    A. @@CURSOR_ROWS

    B. CURSOR_STATUS

    C. @@FETCH_STATUS

    D. @@ROWCOUNT

17. You are the database developer for your company. You want to enhance your data access by controlling the contents of the caches used by SQL Server 2005. What are the two cache pools you should be controlling?

    A. Procedure cache

    B. Disk cache

    C. Buffer cache

    D. I/O cache

18. You are the database developer for your company. You want to maximize your cache utilization. Which of the following are guidelines to follow? (Choose all that apply.)

    A. Read all rows from a table, even if all are not needed.

    B. Avoid recompiling procedures.

    C. Read only rows that need to be processed.

    D. Read all columns in a table.

    E. Read only columns that need to be processed.

19. You are the database developer for your company. Which dynamic management view or function would you use to return information about the query execution plans that are cached by SQL Server?

    A. sys.dm_exec_query_stats

    B. sys.dm_exec_cached_plans

    C. sys.dm_exec_query_plan

    D. sys.dm_exec_requests

20. You are the database developer for your company. You want to use a functionality of SQL Server 2005 that will allow you to design your application so that it will inform you when there is a change to information that your application has previously retrieved. What is this functionality?

    A. Event notification

    B. Query notifications

    C. Execution plan notification

    D. Cache notification

Answers to Review Questions

1. A, B, D. A database application provides a user interface to either manage or provide access to a database system. You use Windows Explorer to manage the data in files and directories in the Windows file system. Files and directories are considered data. Thus, the Windows file system is indeed a database management system, and Windows Explorer is a database application. You use SQL Server Management Studio to manage SQL Server database objects either through a graphical or programming environment. You use CRM to enable your organization to manage its customer database through the introduction of reliable systems, processes and procedures. You use Microsoft Office Access as a client application that accesses data in a file through a Jet interface. Access is a client application but does not provide access to a database system and therefore is not a database application.

2. B. SQL Native Client (SQLNCLI) was designed to provide a simplified method of gaining native data access to SQL Server using either OLE DB or ODBC. It is simplified in that it combines OLE DB and ODBC technologies into one library, and it provides a way to innovate and evolve new data access features used in SQL Server 2005. SQLXML is being replaced by the functionality within the HTTP endpoints and new XML support in SQL Server 2005. SQLCMD is the new command-line utility in SQL Server 2005. SSMS stands for SQL Server Management Studio.

3. A, C. Server-side components run on the server managing requests from client computers. Server-side components can include network libraries and TSQL endpoints. TSQL endpoints have been introduced in SQL Server 2005 as a new concept for SQL Server connections. ODBC, OLE DB, and SQLNCLI are client-side data access technologies.

4. B. You should use SQLNCLI to connect to SQL Server 2005. SQLNCLI provides a way to innovate and evolve the new data access features used in SQL Server 2005. Although ODBC and OLE DB can be used to connect to SQL Server 2005, new functionalities will not be available. There is no mention that your application uses XML, so SQLXML 4.0 is not appropriate. Likewise creating the web service is overkill and will not provide the full functionality you are seeking.

5. A, D. You must replace the header file for OLE DB with that of SQLNCLI. You should not add the new header file. You must also change the connection string to the new provider, SQLNCLI. OLE DB does not use DSNs.

6. C. Client components enable your application to connect and interact with your data source. As a part of this process, the client components need to transform data and collect it locally in cache. Databases are your data sources. Providers supply the communication between the client and database server. Server endpoints are not a component in the data access technology architecture.

7. B. To allow all users of the computer to have access to the DSN connection, you must make certain that the DSN is a system DSN. You can check this in the ODBC administrator in the control panel of the client computer or in the HKLM portion of the registry of that computer. References to the User DSN or File DSN are incorrect.

8. B. To expose SQL Server as a web service, you need to create an HTTP endpoint. The endpoint creates your communication link between SQL Server and the client application.

9. A, B, C. Native XML web services is not recommended for applications characterized by real-time highly concurrent access, with short duration transactions. Native XML is also not recommended for web farm-type scale-out or as a replacement for the middle tier, specifically where your application architecture has large-scale business logic demands that are better accommodated within middle-tier components. Native XML does provide fast access to data in applications that manage static data.

10. A. You would use managed code to connect to an external database in this situation. It might be useful to write a SQLCLR stored procedure with permission set to EXTERNAL_ACCESS. By using the SQLCLR procedure, you are able to define your connections to the external data source using ADO.NET, then transform and process the data. Finally, you are able to merge it with your local data.

11. A. You should use SMO. SMO, the successor to DMO, is the API that is used for SQL Server 2005. SQL server management objects, or SMO, is a programming model that encompasses the new feature of all objects created with SQL Server 2005. RMO, replication management objects, allows you to programmatically control replication tasks.

12. A, B, C. API server cursors and Transact-SQL cursors are implemented on the server. They are often referenced collectively as server cursors. Client cursors are implemented internally by the SQL Native Client driver. Web services does not use cursors.

13. A, B, C, D. Server cursors provide optimal performance if you are accessing only a portion of the data in the cursor. Server cursors reduce caching at the client. Server cursors fully handle multiple active statements leaving no results outstanding. SQL Native Client supports the full range of cursor types, whereas client cursors are restricted to the functionality they support. These are "clinically" listed advantages, but you need to always know your data, its use, and its environment.

14. D. ODBC defines four cursor types supported by Microsoft SQL Server and the SQL Native Client ODBC driver: static cursors, dynamic cursors, forward-only cursors, and keyset-driven cursors. Backward compatible is not a cursor type.

15. A. You would use the Cursor Manager Active cursors object in System Monitor. System Monitor allows you to gather real-time metrics.

16. A. @@CURSOR_ROWS returns the number of qualifying rows currently in the last cursor opened on the connection. To improve performance and since Microsoft SQL Server can populate large keyset and static cursors asynchronously, @@CURSOR_ROWS can be called to determine that the number of the rows that qualify for a cursor to be retrieved.

17. A, C. SQL Server uses two main cache memory pools, the procedure cache and the buffer cache.

18. B, C, E. You should avoid reading anything you are not processing. You should also monitor your procedures and attempt to avoid their recompiling whenever possible.

19. B. The sys.dm_exec_cached_plans returns information regarding the query execution plans cached by SQL Server.

20. B. Query notifications enables your application to request a notification from SQL Server when the results of a query change. It uses the Service Broker service to allow you to design applications that are automatically notified when the results for the query may be out of date.

Chapter

2

Designing Application Access

MICROSOFT EXAM OBJECTIVES COVERED IN THIS CHAPTER:

✓ **Design client libraries to write applications that administer a SQL Server service.**

- Design server management objects (SMO) applications.

- Design replication management objects (RMO) applications.

- Design automation management objects (AMO) applications.

- Design SQL Server Networking Interface (SNI) for asynchronous queries.

✓ **Design queries that use multiple active result sets (MARS).**

- Decide when MARS queries are appropriate.

- Choose an appropriate transaction isolation level when you use MARS.

- Choose when to use asynchronous queries.

In Chapter 1 you learned the various data access technologies available for use today in SQL Server 2005. You learned that database applications can provide access to data as well as help manage it. In this chapter, we focus on the client libraries and how they are used to manage SQL Server 2005.

You will learn the roles that server management objects (SMO) and replication management objects (RMO) play in managing your SQL Server 2005 server. You will also learn how to use analysis services management objects to program administrative tasks. Yes, in SQL Server 2005, the analysis services engine has been rebuilt and is based on a defined namespace and is managed programmatically. So, just as you have SMO and RMO, you have *AMO— analysis management objects*. If you have done any studying on your own in this field, however, you will find this is indeed the new library name. But, oops—in relationship to the exam, however, the acronym AMO references the features that are used for automating the management of your server, and in the objectives, Microsoft uses AMO to refer to automation management objects. Therefore, don't get confused when you see AMO referring to automation management objects, when indeed you are studying the programmatically administrative tasks of analysis services managed objects.

In addition in this chapter, you will take a slightly different look at SQL Native Client. This time you will examine the communication process between the client and the server, examining how it has changed in SQL Server 2005. The new concept of the endpoint in the *SQL Server Network Interface (SNI)* protocol layer encapsulating the Tabular Data Stream (TDS) packet gives SQL Server the flexibility it has today.

We conclude with a focus on a technology new to SQL Server 2005, *multiple active result sets (MARS)*. MARS enables you to build applications that perform more efficiently and use fewer resources by eliminating round-trips between the client and the database. You will learn the best strategies for using MARS as well as how to design queries that use MARS. Since MARS is based on transaction isolation, you will learn how to choose an appropriate level for your MARS application.

Implementing Client Libraries

As you learned in Chapter 1, the SQL Native Client header and library files are installed with SQL Server 2005 in the *%PROGRAM FILES%\Microsoft SQL Server\90\SDK* folder. When you are developing an application, it is important that you copy and install all the required files for development to your development environment.

You should replace or add the SQL Native Client files to your client application's current header and library files using the following methods:

- For your custom C applications, the SQL Native Client header file (sqlncli.h) is all that is needed.

- For ODBC bulk copy functionality, you need to use the sqlcli.lib export library file.

- For your ODBC applications, the sqlncli.h file would be a direct replacement of your current odbcss.h file.

- For your applications using MDAC, even though SQL Native Client is backward compatible, be aware that it does not contain the class identifiers (CLSIDs) for OLE DB that the MDAC OLE DB provider includes nor the XML functionality symbols also included with the MDAC provider.

- For your OLE DB applications, if your application is continuing to use MDAC, then as mentioned in Chapter 1, you can reference both header files, sqloledb.h and sqlncli.h; however, the reference to MDAC header file must come first.

- For nonserver installs, the SQL Native Client installer only installs the client by default. If you also want the software development kit (SDK) to be installed, you need to use the ADDLOCAL option with the ALL specifier (ADDLOCAL=ALL).

When creating a connection to a data source through SQL Native Client, use "SQL Native Client" as the driver name string.

Once you have installed SQL Native client you have all the support you need for your network libraries. The network protocols are not a part of the .dll architecture. They are installed through your operating system environment. If you are upgrading from a previous version of SQL Server, most likely all protocols needed will be installed. If you are completing a pristine install, you need to concern yourself with the network environment. As a side note: SQL Server 2005 can only be enabled using with TCP/IP, Named Pipes, VIA, and Shared Memory protocols.

You also have the following configuration tools, many of which are new or refurbished for managing SQL Server 2005:

- The Surface Area Configuration (SAC) tool is the most flexible of the new tools. It has two components—one for services and connections and one for features. The features component is especially helpful in the development environment. You are able to control and view those features you need available for your applications in one easy to use interface. The view itself can be delivered by instance or component.

- The SQL Server Configuration Manager is the marrying of three tools you used previously in SQL Server 2000: the Service Manager, the SQL Server Network Utility, and the Client Network Utility. Even though the Configuration Manager is not sitting in the taskbar tray, you will find having all three management tools under one roof an enhancement to your management environment.

- The Setup command-line executable allows you to configure several parameters of your server at startup, including the network libraries. The Microsoft development team has also provided many configuration and maintenance scripts that you can run using this interface.

- You finally have available the ODBC Data Source Administrator, which is part of your Microsoft Windows operating system environment. This tool enables you to configure the data source names (DSNs), drivers, and connections for your database environment.

Thus far we have addressed client utilities and applications designed for managing data. Next we focus on those applications designed for administering systems.

Using Management Object Applications

Let's begin from the inside out! You should be more than aware of the structural differences brought forth in SQL Server 2005 than from any previous versions. SQL Server 2000 supports a COM-based object model, SQL-DMO. You no doubt have used this object model to programmatically manage your SQL servers. Enterprise Manager uses this API to manage SQL Server 2000. SQL Server 2005 has two .NET-based libraries that replace SQL-DMO: SQL server management objects (SMO) and replication management objects (RMO). Using these new libraries, you are able to write code-based queries, procedures, reports, and a variety of services using any .NET supported language.

 The SMO object model and the Microsoft Windows Management Instrumentation (WMI) APIs replace SQL-DMO. SQL-DMO has not been updated to manage features that are specific to SQL Server 2005.

The advantages of SMO are performance and scalability. SMO has a cached object model; you are able to change several properties of an object prior to effecting the changes to SQL Server. Consequently not only does SMO make fewer round-trips to the server, but it also makes its objects more flexible. You can use SMO to manage SQL Server 7, 2000, and 2005 servers programmatically.

Both SMO and RMO are implemented as classes within .NET assemblies. Microsoft .SqlServer.Smo.dll provides the main SMO classes, whereas Microsoft.SqlServer.Rmo.dll provides the main RMO classes. Actually they are two of many assemblies that you find in the %PROGRAM FILES%\Microsoft SQL Server\90\SDK\Assemblies folder, as shown in Figure 2.1.

FIGURE 2.1   The SDK\Assemblies folder for SQL Server 2005

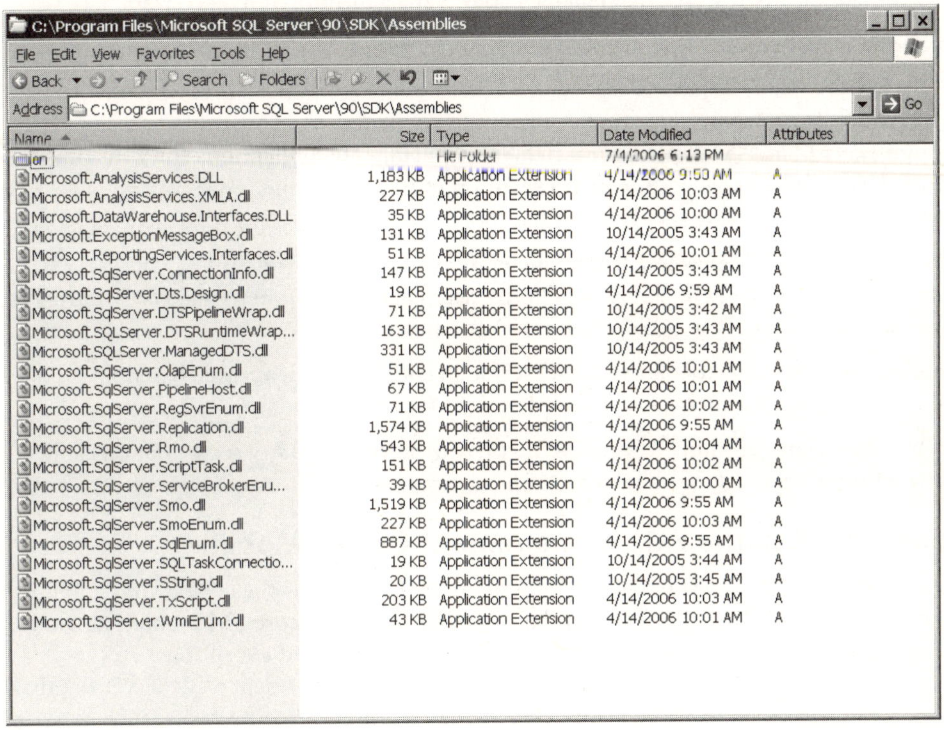

Designing Server Management Objects (SMO) Applications

Using the managed code of SMO you are able to script any database object. SMO is the primary tool you need to develop database management applications that are based on .NET Framework managed code. The classes that you require are available under the Microsoft .SqlServer namespace. As you create a new .NET project, you need to reference the following three files:

- The Microsoft.SqlServer.ConnectionInfo.dll file provides the classes for connecting to an instance of SQL Server.

- The Microsoft.SqlServer.Smo.dll file provides the main SMO classes.

- The Microsoft.SqlServer.SmoEnum.dll file contains enumerations that make working with some SMO objects easier.

Working with SMO in SQL Server 2005

SMO provides many features that enhance your management of SQL Server 2005:

Optimized instantiation   You are able to improve performance using partial instantiation where possible. You can implement full instantiation when you explicitly reference an object within your code.

Capture execution   SMO executes statements immediately by default. You can employ captured execution to defer statement execution until a later time. That way you can view the script before updating the database.

Microsoft Windows Management Instrumentation (WMI) functionality   SMO provides wrapper classes for the SQL Server WMI provider. This enables you to make WMI programming consistent with other SQL Server automation code.

Scripting   You are able to automatically script an entire dependency tree based on a single object by using the Scripter class provided with SMO.

Server option configuration   Using SMO, you can view and modify server options and configuration options in the same way as sp_configure.

Understanding the SQL Management Object Model

The Microsoft.SqlServer.Management.Smo namespace contains the classes that you use to programmatically manage your databases and servers. The core SMO objects include instances, utility classes, enumerations, event handler types, and exceptions.

The namespace contains the instance object classes that represent SQL Server database engine objects, as well as some utility classes that represent specific tasks, such as scripting. When you establish a connection to the instance of SQL Server using a Server object variable, you can access the objects on that instance using the SMO instance objects. As an example, you can use the Database object to access databases on the connected instance of SQL Server. All the instance classes are related to the Server class in the object hierarchy. Server objects are represented, such as databases, schemas, tables, and stored procedures. The hierarchy of these classes maps directly to a standard database hierarchy so that you are able to develop using a known relationship. If a parent object can have many children, then a collection class has been designed to handle the children. In the partial object model diagram shown in Figure 2.2, you can see how each class is structured in the hierarchy, giving access to that object within a server. Utility classes, on the other hand, exist outside of the Server class object hierarchy. Utility classes represent specific tasks such as backup or scripting. Note in Figure 2.2 that they are represented as a separate set from the Instance classes' hierarchy.

Referencing SQL Management Objects

You connect to a physical SQL Server installation through the Server object. The Server class is the highest level in the SMO instance object hierarchy. When a Server object variable is created, it establishes a connection to an instance of SQL Server. If you do not specify the name in the Server class constructor, the connection is always made with the local, default instance of SQL Server.

FIGURE 2.2   SQL Management object model partial diagram

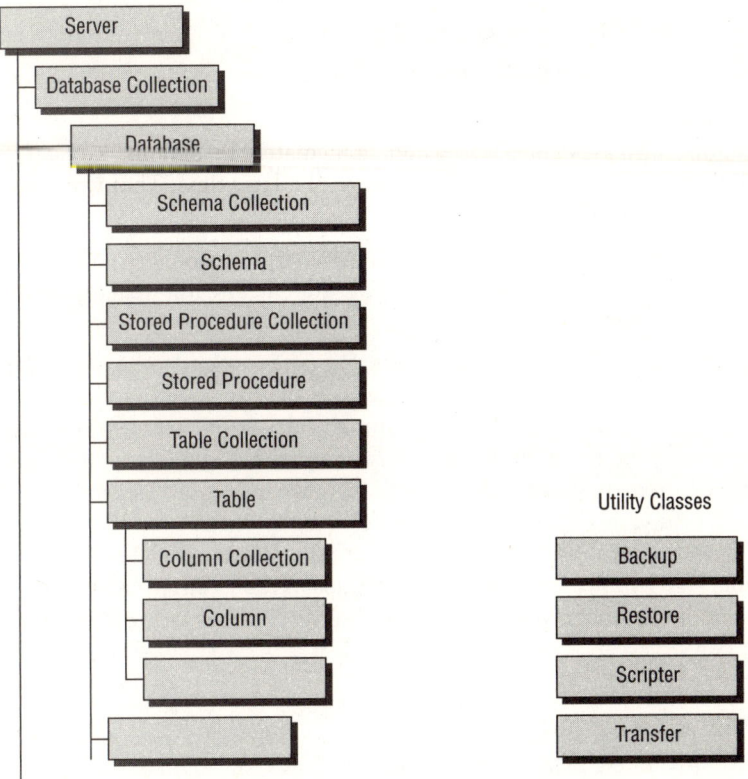

The Microsoft.SqlServer.Management.Smo namespace resides in the Microsoft.SqlServer.Smo .dll file. Additionally, some of the enumeration classes are in the Microsoft.SqlServer.SqlEnum.dll and Microsoft.SqlServer.SmoEnum.dll assembly files. You have to import all three files to access the classes in the Microsoft.SqlServer.Management.Smo namespace.

As a developer, it is important for you to learn how to use SMO to configure and maintain your SQL server. Obviously, you are using the results of SMO by using the SQL Server Management Studio application. Just take yourself out of the box and think of how you might use SMO. Here is a partial list of what the Microsoft.SqlServer.Management.Smo namespace enables you to do:

- You can connect to and manage connection settings to your SQL server using SMO.

- You can create, modify, delete, and view server objects using SMO.

- You can script dependencies using SMO.

- You can back up, restore, and attach databases using SMO.

- You can regenerate your server's master key using SMO.

- You can transfer data using SMO.
- You can create, modify, delete, and view database objects using SMO.
- You can perform a DDL (Data Definition Language) task on a server instance using SMO.
- You can execute Transact-SQL using SMO.

Automating Tasks Using SMO

You need to perform the following three steps to begin your automation tasks using SMO:

1. Create a .NET client application.
2. Reference the SQL SMO assemblies.
3. Use the Imports (using in Microsoft Visual C#) statement within your code to reference the necessary namespaces.

You can use SMO from any .NET application. The type of client you create depends on the function of your application. For instance, you are able to use console applications, Windows Forms applications, and ASP.NET Web Form applications. If you are creating an application for database management and need the flexibility to access the application from any location in your company, you may want to create an ASP.NET application. Depending on the outreach of your company, this may be an intranet or a secure Internet application.

Next, to provide your application's management tasks, you must add at least one assembly reference to your .NET project for the Microsoft.SqlServer.Smo.dll assembly. You more than likely will also need the others we mentioned above: Microsoft.SqlServer.ConnectionInfo.dll and Microsoft.SqlServer.SmoEnum.dll.

 The SMO assemblies are installed in the Global Assembly Cache (GAC) as part of the SQL Server 2005 Client Tools installation option. You need to deploy these assemblies to client computers as part of your client application installation.

Referencing an Assembly

Follow these steps to reference an assembly in a Microsoft Visual Studio .NET project:

1. On the Project menu, click Add Reference.
2. In the Add Reference dialog box, highlight each assembly you are referencing in the list and then click OK.

It is always best to keep your code as simple as possible. So import the SMO namespaces you intend to use with the Imports statement in Microsoft Visual Basic .NET or the using statement in Visual C#. These statements, a few examples of which are seen below, allow you to work with the namespace classes without having to fully qualify each class name.

```
'Visual Basic
Imports Microsoft.SqlServer.Management.Smo
Imports Microsoft.SqlServer.Management.Common
```

```
//Visual C#
using Microsoft.SqlServer.Management.Smo;
using Microsoft.SqlServer.Management.Common;
```

Now you are ready to access the server. Your next step is to determine your management tactics. Do you want to gather information? Do you want to use SMO to create server objects? Do you want to modify existing objects on your server? Remember, the world of SMO is wide open to your needs. After all, the neat SQL Server Management Studio interface is nothing more than a SMO application!

Using SMO to Retrieve Server Information

Let's start with defining the two steps you use to retrieve server and database object information. Here are the steps:

1. Instantiate a Server object, specifying the server name.
2. Your next statements are those that work with the various properties of the server or the Databases collection. Retrieve information from the server and database properties using SMO.

Step 1: Instantiate a Server Object

The following example shows how to connect to a SQL Server instance named MYSERVER:

```
'Visual Basic
Dim svr As New Server("MYSERVER")
```

```
//Visual C#
Server svr = new Server("MYSERVER");
```

By default, the Server object uses Windows authentication, as is shown in the previous code. If you need to use SQL Server authentication, or you want to control the connection explicitly, you must reference the ConnectionInfo assembly and use a ServerConnection object as shown by the following:

```
'Visual Basic
Dim conn As New ServerConnection("MYSERVER", "sa", "Pa$$w0rd")
Dim svr As New Server(conn)
```

```
//Visual C#
ServerConnection conn = new ServerConnection
("MYSERVER", "sa", "Pa$$w0rd");
Server svr = new Server(conn);
```

If you want, there is a third way to control the connection settings: instantiate a SqlConnectionInfo object as show by the following example:

```
'Visual Basic
Dim conInfo As New SqlConnectionInfo("MYSERVER")
```

```
With conInfo
  .DatabaseName = "AdventureWorks"
  .ApplicationName = "AWClient"
End With
Dim conn As New ServerConnection(conInfo)
Dim svr As New Server(conn)

//Visual C#
SqlConnectionInfo conInfo = new SqlConnectionInfo("MYSERVER");
conInfo.DatabaseName = "AdventureWorks";

conInfo.ApplicationName = "AWClient";
ServerConnection conn = new ServerConnection(conInfo);
Server svr = new Server(conn);
```

Step 2: Retrieve Information from the Server and Database Properties Using SMO

Once you have connected to the SQL Server instance, you are ready to retrieve information from the server properties. Some properties you might use are the shown in the following code. This example uses the information and configuration properties of the server to return the version of your SQL server and the value if nested triggers are enabled. The second section of code uses the server databases collection property to specify the name of each database on the instance of the server.

```
'Visual Basic
Console.WriteLine(svr.Information.VersionString)
Console.WriteLine _
(svr.Configuration.NestedTriggers.RunValue.ToString())

// Visual C#
Console.WriteLine(svr.Information.VersionString);
Console.WriteLine
(svr.Configuration.NestedTriggers.RunValue.ToString());
```

Your output to the previous statements from steps 1 and 2 will be a command window with values representing the version of your SQL Server and a 0 or 1 representing whether you are allowing triggers to call other triggers. It will appear something like this:

```
9.00.2047.00
1
```

Using the Databases property, you are able to also retrieve information at the database level. The following example shows how to display the name and size of each database for a connected instance:

```
'Visual Basic
For Each db As Database In svr.Databases
Console.WriteLine(db.Name & " " & db.Size)
Next
```

```
//Visual C#
foreach (Database db in svr.Databases)
{
Console.WriteLine(db.Name + " " + db.Size);
}
```

Your output will be a command window displaying your database names and sizes in kilobytes. It will appear something like this:

```
AdventureWorks 181.9375
AdventureWorksDW 70.5
master 5.25
model 3.1875
msdb 7.4375
Sybex 10
tempdb 8.5
```

Using SMO to Create New Objects

So let's kick it up a notch!

You can use SMO to create new database objects, yes, even the databases themselves. To do this, create a local variable to reference the object and then set the properties of the object you are creating. Finally, you call the create method on the parent object and add the new object to the server.

Here are the steps:

1. Create and instantiate a local variable for the object you are creating.
2. Set the appropriate properties of the object.
3. Add the child objects to their parent and call the Create method on the parent object to update the server.

Step 1: Create and Instantiate a Local Variable

So, the local object you create must represent a database object. As such, it has a pre-defined constructor that determines the various properties and methods that you can define on this object.

For this example, suppose you wanted to create a new table, Certification, in the AdventureWorks sample database. More than likely, you would also want to create some columns. Let's create two: CertID and CertName.

Here's how it goes. First create a local variable that references the AdventureWorks database, specifying the database name as an argument to the Databases collection property. Next create the Table object and two Column objects.

```vb
'Visual Basic
Dim AWDBase As Database = Svr.Databases("AdventureWorks")
Dim CertsTable As New Table(AWDBase, "Certifications")
Dim CertID As New Column(CertsTable, _
"CertID", DataType.Int)
Dim CertName As New Column(CertsTable, _
"CertName", DataType.NVarChar(50))
```

```csharp
//Visual C#
Database AWDBase = svr.Databases["AdventureWorks"];
Table CertsTable = new Table(AWDBase, "Certifications");
Column CertID = new Column(CertsTable,
"CertID", DataType.Int);
Column CertName = new Column(CertsTable,
"CertName", DataType.NVarChar(50));
```

Step 2: Set the Appropriate Properties of the Object

Once the object variables have been created, you can specify extra property values prior to sending the changes to the database server. In this example, we will make the first column an identity column by setting the Identity property.

```vb
'Visual Basic
CertID.Identity = True
```

```csharp
//Visual C#
CertID.Identity = true;
```

Step 3: Add the Child Objects and Call the Create Method

Now you are ready to apply the changes to the database server. You must use the Add method of a collection object to add child objects to their parent, and then call the Create method on the parent object to update the server. Let's apply this to the example:

```vb
'Visual Basic
CertsTable.Columns.Add(CertID)
CertsTable.Columns.Add(CertName)
CertsTable.Create()
```

```
//Visual C#
CertsTable.Columns.Add(CertID);
CertsTable.Columns.Add(CertName);
CertsTable.Create();
```

If your connection is operating in the default execution mode, SMO sends this change imme-diately to the database server. If your connection's SqlExecutionModes property is operating in CaptureSql mode, the underlying Transact-SQL statements are stored in the connection's Cap-turedSql property for later use.

Using SMO to Modify Existing Objects

Are you ready? There's SMO...re!

You can use SMO to modify existing objects in your server and database. Your first task is to locate the object, then, depending on your desire, either to change the property or call the appropriate methods of the object and finally alter the object.

Here are the steps to change existing objects:

1. Locate the object you want to change in the appropriate object collection.
2. Change its property values.
3. Update the database with the change.

Step 1: Locate the Object

Let's locate the CertName column of the Certifications table in the AdventureWorks database:

```
'Visual Basic
Dim AWDBase As Database = Svr.Databases("AdventureWorks")
Dim CertsTable As Table = _
AWDBase.Tables("Certifications")
Dim CertName As Column = _
CertsTable.Columns("CertName")


//Visual C#
Database AWDBase = svr.Databases["AdventureWorks"];
Table CertsTable = AWDBase.Tables["Certifications"];
Column CertName = CertsTable.Columns["CertName"];
```

Step 2: Change Its Property Values

The manner in which your change is implemented depends on the type of change you are mak-ing. If you are modifying a property value, this change will not be implemented in the database until the corresponding alter statement is employed. This example modifies the nullability of the CertName column:

```
'Visual Basic
CertName.Nullable = False
```

```
//Visual C#
CertName.Nullable = false;
```

However, if your change is through a call to a method, for instance a drop, this is handled immediately.

```
'Visual Basic
CertName.Drop( )
```

```
//Visual C#
CertName.Drop( );
```

Step 3: Update the Database with the Change

Once you have changed the database object properties, you need to update the database server. Many SMO objects have an Alter method that performs this task. This example shows the Alter method.

```
'Visual Basic
CertName.Alter( )
```

```
//Visual C#
CertName.Alter( );
```

Now you have been exposed to some aspects of SMO. In Exercises 2.1 and 2.2, you'll get a chance to use SMO for yourself. As you proceed through these exercises, be aware of the variety of properties and methods that you have available to enable you to programmatically manage your environment.

EXERCISE 2.1

Adding a Reference to SMO Assemblies

To add a reference to SMO assemblies, follow these steps:

1. Click Start ≻ All Programs ≻ Microsoft Visual Studio 2005 ≻ Microsoft Visual Studio 2005.

2. On the File menu ≻ New ≻ Project.

3. In the Project Types pane, click Visual Basic.

4. In the Templates pane, click Console Application.

5. In the Name box, type **SMOApp**. You can keep the default location if you want and leave the create directory check box checked.

6. Click OK.

7. On the Project menu, click Add Reference.

8. On the .NET tab, select Microsoft.SqlServer.ConnectionInfo, then hold down Ctrl and select the Microsoft.SqlServer.Smo and Microsoft.SqlServer.SmoEnum assemblies. Then click OK.

9. In Module1.vb, add a blank line before the Module Module1 statement at the top of the file, and insert the following Imports statements:

```
Imports Microsoft.SqlServer.Management.Smo

Imports Microsoft.SqlServer.Management.Common
```

Using SMO to Retrieve Server Properties

After completing Exercise 2.1, follow these steps to use SMO to retrieve server properties and configurations:

1. Add the following code to the Sub Main procedure:

```
Dim svr As New Server("localhost")

Console.WriteLine(svr.Information.VersionString)

Console.WriteLine _

(svr.Configuration.NestedTriggers.RunValue.ToString())

For Each db As Database In svr.Databases

Console.WriteLine(db.Name & ": " & db.Size & "K")

Next

Console.ReadLine()
```

2. On the Debug menu, click Start. The program compiles and then displays the server and database information in a command window.

3. In the Console window, press Enter to end the program.

4. Save the Solution if you want. Then close Visual Studio.

> If you want to work more with SMO, the Microsoft Development Team has put together many samples that you can download from the SQL Server Developer Center at http://msdn2.microsoft.com/en-us/sql/aa336343.aspx

Designing Replication Management Objects (RMO) Applications

Most of your replication administration tasks can be handled using the updated replication tools available in SQL Server Management Studio. You have a New Publication Wizard and a New Subscription Wizard that allow you to easily create, modify, and view replication objects.

However, if you want to manage replication programmatically, then you need to implement replication management objects that are provided with SQL Server 2005. RMO replaces the replication classes that were contained within SQL-DMO. Just as the case with SMO, RMO is compatible not only with SQL Server 2005 but also with SQL Server 7 and 2000.

The structure of RMO is much the same as SMO; RMO is implemented as classes within a .NET assembly named Microsoft.SqlServer.Rmo.dll. This assembly contains the Microsoft .SqlServer.Replication namespace, and the namespace contains the replication classes.

Connecting to a Replication Server

You use a different method to connect to a replication server than you used in SMO. You need a connection to the server namespace and to the replication namespace. The connection to an instance of your server is managed using the Microsoft.SqlServer.Management .Common namespace's ServerConnection object. Thus you need to first include a reference to the Microsoft.SqlServer.ConnectInfo assembly and import the Microsoft.SqlServer .Management.Common namespace. Once the connection to server is established, you can then use it to instantiate a connection to the replication server object. By instantiating the server connection first, you are able to use this single connection repeatedly for all your replication objects. You can supply all authentication and security information within the server connection and pass this information to the replication server object.

The next steps in the process are to include the reference to the Microsoft.SqlServer.Rmo assembly and import the Microsoft.SqlServer.Replication namespace.

To connect to a replication server, follow these steps:

1. Create a ServerConnection object.

2. Create a ReplicationServer object.

Step 1: Create a ServerConnection Object

To create a ServerConnection object, your application must include a reference to the Microsoft.SqlServer.ConnectionInfo assembly. The ServerConnection object is defined in the Microsoft.SqlServer.Management.Common namespace; so you should import this namespace by adding a using (Visual C#) or Imports (Visual Basic) statement at the beginning of your code file.

Here is the code to instantiate a ServerConnection object:

```
'Visual Basic
Dim conn As New ServerConnection("MYSERVER")
```

```
//Visual C#
ServerConnection conn = new ServerConnection("MYSERVER");
```

Step 2: Create a ReplicationServer Object

After you have created a ServerConnection, you can use it to instantiate a ReplicationServer object. The ReplicationServer object can be used to connect to any SQL Server 7.0 or later server, regardless of whether or not it has been configured for replication.

Here is the code to instantiate a ReplicationServer object:

```
'Visual Basic
Dim rs As New ReplicationServer(conn)
```

```
//Visual C#
ReplicationServer rs = new ReplicationServer(conn);
```

Using RMO for Some Common Replication Management Tasks

You can use RMO to manage all aspects of replication. Here are a few tasks you can manage with replication management objects:

Retrieve replication configuration information.   You can use the ReplicationServer class properties of IsPublisher, IsDistributor, DistributorAvailable, and HasRemotePublisher to retrieve replication configuration information.

Configure publishing and distribution.   You can use the RMO classes of DistributionDatabase and DistributionPublisher to configure publishing and distribution.

Create and manage publications and articles.   You can use classes such as TransPublication and MergePublication to create transactional, snapshot, and merge publications. You can specify the articles to be published using the TransArticle or MergeArticle class.

Create and manage subscriptions.   You can create push subscriptions with the TransSubscription and MergeSubscription classes. You can manage pull subscriptions with the TransPullSubscription and MergePullSubscription classes.

In Exercise 2.3, you will retrieve the replication information on your local server using RMO. In Exercise 2.4, you'll view it.

EXERCISE 2.3

Retrieving Replication Information Using RMO

In this exercise, you will retrieve replication information using RMO. You will connect to the replication server, and then establish a connection by adding a reference to RMO assemblies. In the next exercise, you will then use RMO to view replication settings on your local server.

To add a reference to RMO assemblies, follow these steps:

1. Click Start ➤ All Programs ➤ Microsoft Visual Studio 2005 ➤ Microsoft Visual Studio 2005.

2. On the File menu ➤ New ➤ Project.

3. In the Project Types pane, click Visual Basic.

4. In the Templates pane, click Console Application.

5. In the Name box, type **RMOApp**. You can keep the default location if you want and leave the create directory check box checked.

6. Click OK.

7. On the Project menu, click Add Reference.

8. On the .NET tab, select Microsoft.SqlServer.ConnectionInfo, then hold Ctrl and select the Microsoft.SqlServer.Replication .NET Programming Interface assembly. Then click OK.

9. In Module1.vb, add a blank line before the Module Module1 statement at the top of the file, and insert the following Imports statements:

    ```
    Imports Microsoft.SqlServer.Replication

    Imports Microsoft.SqlServer.Management.Common
    ```

EXERCISE 2.4

Viewing Replication Information Using RMO

After completing Exercise 2.3, follow these steps to use RMO to view replication settings:

1. Add the following code to the Sub Main procedure.

    ```
    Dim conn As New ServerConnection("localhost")

    Dim rs As New ReplicationServer(conn)

    Console.WriteLine("Publisher: " & rs.IsPublisher.ToString())

    Console.WriteLine("Distributor: " & rs.IsDistributor.ToString())

    Console.ReadLine()
    ```

2. On the Debug menu, click Start. The program compiles and then displays the publisher and distributor settings in a command window (both should be false unless the localhost has been defined as a publisher or a distributor previously).

3. In the Console window, press Enter to end the program.

4. You can choose to save the Solution or just close, discarding changes as you desire.

In these exercises, you viewed the status of replication objects programmatically. You could have just have easily created and modified replication objects using RMO. If you needed to automate your replication tasks, this new enhancement in SQL Server 2005 might be just the feature you need.

As mentioned earlier, if you have been using the new replication tools provided in SQL Server Management Studio, you already realize that they provide flexibility in configuration and management that was never available previously. These tools may be sufficient for your needs. However, RMO provides additional functionality in allowing you full control over any Transact-SQL scripts or stored procedures you write to customize your replication process. So not only may you want to use this new technology, you may want to use some of the newer concepts in scripting to maintain and update your server environment.

Designing Automation Management Objects (AMO) Applications

You have two tools available for working with an Analysis Services instance, analysis management objects (AMO) and Analysis Services Scripting Language (ASSL). ASSL is a command language written as an XML dialect used to execute Data Definition Language (DDL) statements on an Analysis Services instance. DDL statements include creating, modifying, and deleting objects. AMO is an application interface used to administer Analysis Services. In this section you will learn how AMO can be used to manage your Analysis Services applications. AMO is a layer between the user application and the Analysis Services instance. This layer provides access to Analysis Services administrative objects. AMO is a class library that takes commands from a client application and converts those commands into XML for Analysis (XMLA) messages for the Analysis Services instance.

Figure 2.3 shows you the relationship of AMO in the overall structure of the libraries and utilities within SQL Server 2005 Analysis Services. We have purposely simplified the illustration to the essentials to emphasize the placement of AMO. At the top section of the diagram, you will see the client or development applications. The middle section illustrates the instance of SQL Server 2005 your application will connect to, and the bottom section shows the data sources. AMO fits into that layer between your application and the SQL instance.

FIGURE 2.3 AMO in relation to SQL libraries and utilities

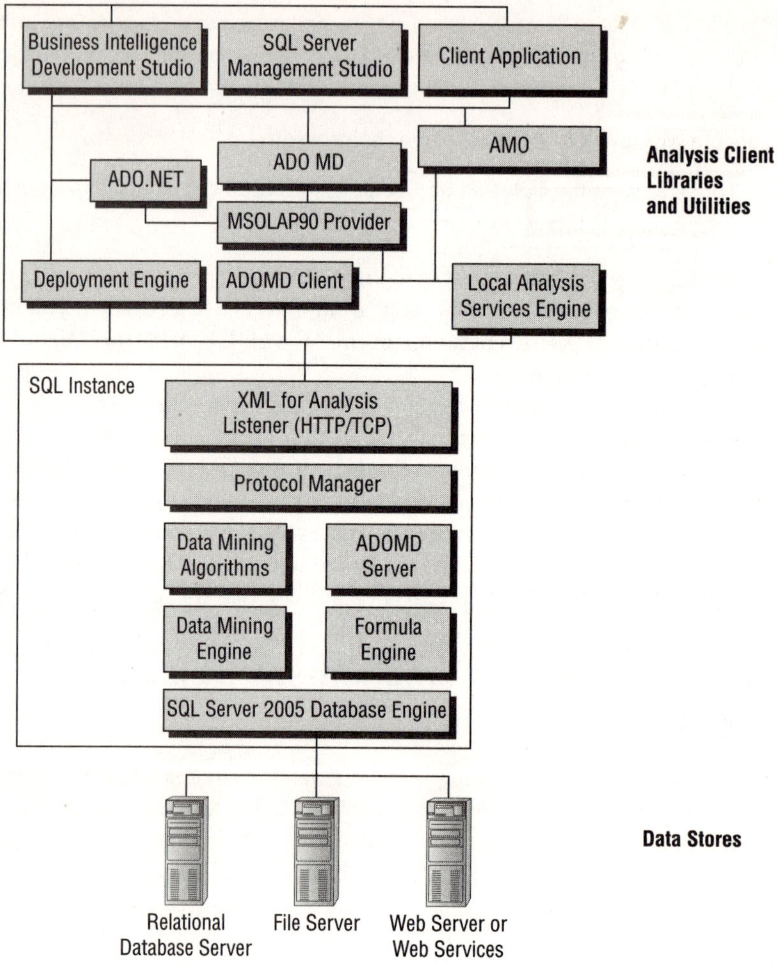

AMO presents Analysis Services instance objects as classes to your end user application, with method members that run commands and property members that hold the data for the Analysis Services objects. The AMO library of classes is designed as a hierarchy of classes, where certain classes must be instantiated before others in order to use them in your code. Also, auxiliary classes can be instantiated at any time in your code.

Figure 2.4 illustrates a high-level view of the AMO hierarchy (partial) that includes major classes, showing the placement of the classes among their containers and their peers.

To create an AMO solution in Visual Studio 2005 you must include a reference to the Microsoft.AnalysisServices namespace and perhaps also the Microsoft.DataWarehouse .Interfaces namespace. Your AMO solution can contain those tasks that you would find most useful to automate within your environment.

FIGURE 2.4   Major classes in the AMO hierarchy

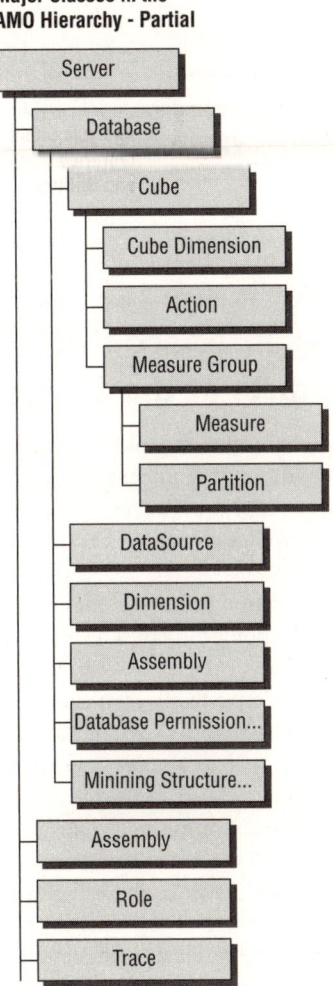

**Major Classes in the
AMO Hierarchy - Partial**

You can to create, update, or delete Analysis Services objects using AMO. You are able to control and contain versions of your objects by creating an AMO managed task. You can use AMO to create new partitions based on incoming data, and likewise to remove partitions that have outlived your project's scope. Processes that cannot be achieved using Integration Services flow tasks can be programmatically solved using AMO. You can even add a security component to your automation as well as create an entire security interface using AMO. If desired, database management such as automated backup and restore strategies can be accomplished using AMO.

We have named just a few of the many managed tasks you can develop to enhance your Analysis Services environment using AMO. This technology, along with SMO and RMO, is in its infancy for the "real-world" capabilities it is able to provide. Beneath each of these technologies lies the defined namespaces and object models built into the SQL Server 2005 environment that will provide the wide range of development features required to add definition to creating and managing applications and data.

> **TIP** AMO cannot be used to query Analysis Services data. You should be using ADOMD.NET for this purpose. For more information, see SQL Server Books Online topic "ADOMD.NET."

Now that you have learned how SMO, RMO, and AMO work with SQL Server 2005, let's investigate the client-server communication aspects, which have changed quite a bit, by the way.

Designing SQL Server Networking Interface (SNI) for Asynchronous Queries—Or, "It Starts at the Endpoint!"

SQL Server Networking Interface (SNI) is the communication protocol layer used by SQL Server 2005 to provide a robust asynchronous connection between client and server. It is important for you to understand the differences between SNI and the net libraries of SQL Server 2000 and the Microsoft Data Access Components that your applications may be currently using.

Let's take a quick refresher in the net libraries communication process so that you are able to see and appreciate the differences in the new SNI communication protocol. To keep it simple, suppose your application submits a query. The database interface at the client (API) uses the appropriate driver to encapsulate your query into packets to be transported over the network. These packets are defined by SQL Server and are called Tabular Data Stream (TDS) packets. These packets are processed from the driver, through the client net library, over the network to a receiving server net library. The appropriate server net library passes the TDS packets through its protocol stack where they are received by your server. Open Data Services is the receiving section of the server. It is here your application's query is opened and sent to the server's relational engine for processing. It is the relational engine, or sometimes referenced as the database engine itself, that compiles your query and determines the best out of several execution plans. Once the parsing, optimizing, and executing completes, the process is reversed with the result set being returned through the route to the client.

Using TDS Endpoints in SQL Server 2005

If you are envisioning the steps, or have seen the diagrams in SQL Server 2000, you see a closed communication system, a closed network. What SNI has to offer is a new playing field. SQL Server 2005 still formats its communications using a TDS packet; however, this packet is encapsulated within your network protocol. For example, if you are using TCP/IP with your SQL Native Client and your SQL Server 2005 database engine, SNI—which encapsulates your TDS packets—is an automatic piece of your communication process. The major relevance of SNI is that no longer are you bound to a synchronous client-server communication process. Your server creates server objects called endpoints for communication at installation. These are referenced as *TDS endpoints* or by the protocol or service they represent, such as TSQL endpoints. Figure 2.5 displays the default TSQL endpoints in SQL Server Management Studio.

Even though each of the default TDS endpoints, as shown in Figure 2.5, has been created, it does not mean that a protocol has been defined for the endpoint. If the underlying protocol has not been enabled, then the endpoint cannot be used. The TDS endpoint for the local Dedicated Admin Connection is also shown in the illustration. This sysadmin connection is enabled by default. If you require the DAC to be enabled remotely, you can do so using the Surface Area Configuration (SAC) Utility, Configuration for Features tool.

You must install SQL Native Client on the client and configure it to use a network protocol that is also enabled on the server. That is, you need to, if you want them to communicate!

Usually the underlying operating system network protocols (such as TCP/IP) are already installed on the client and server. If the required network protocol is not available and configured on server, the database engine will not start. If the required network protocol is not available and configured on the client, the network library will not work.

FIGURE 2.5   Default TSQL endpoints in SQL Server Management Studio

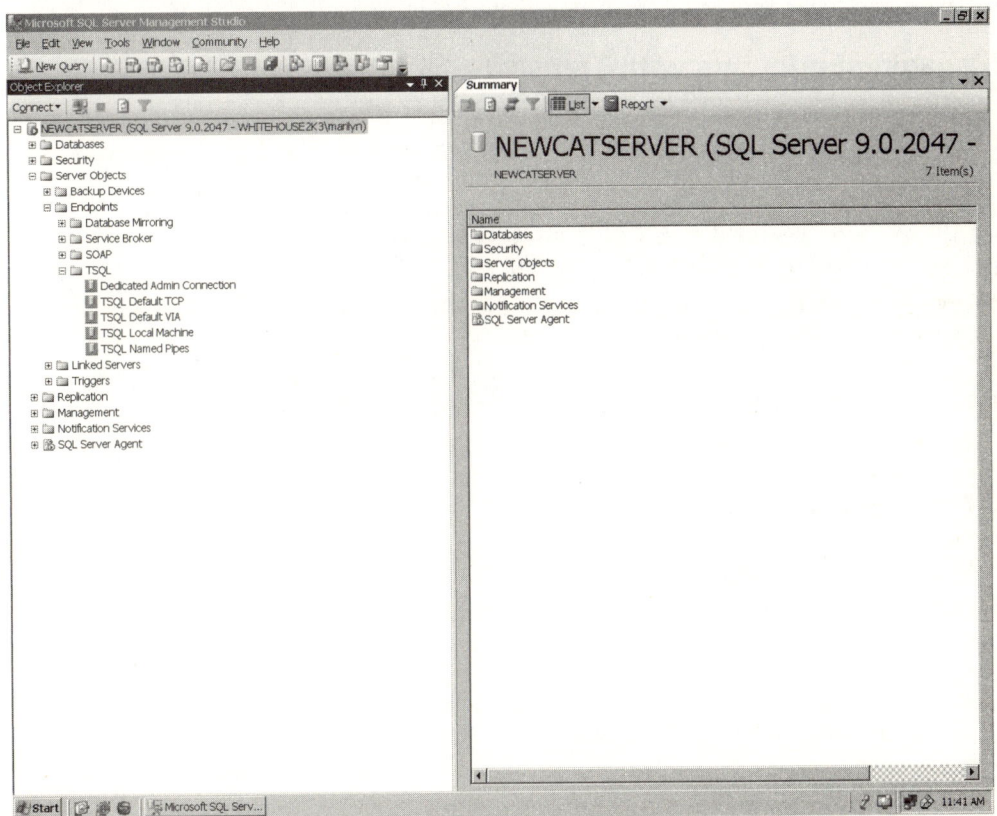

You have already learned previously how to enable the network protocols using either the SAC tool or SQL Server Configuration Manager. After the network connections are installed and configured, SQL Server can listen on any combination of the server network protocols simultaneously. Named pipes cannot have more than one endpoint per instance. However, for TCP and VIA, in addition to the default endpoints, you can create configured endpoints. All configuration settings for endpoints are stored in the registry; however, changes to endpoints and their protocol assignments must be made within SQL Server configuration tools or scripts so that they are maintained in metadata.

At times it might be helpful to verify the protocol being used for the current connection in your application. The sys.dm_exec_connections dynamic management view can be used for this purpose as shown in the following Transact-SQL statement:

```
SELECT net_transport
FROM sys.dm_exec_connections
WHERE session_id = @@SPID
```

By default, all users have access to the TDS endpoints (except the dedicated administrator connection endpoint). Because these endpoints are created internally by the server, they have no owner and you cannot associate them with a specific account.

Managing Endpoints with Transact-SQL

Endpoints are created and managed using Transact-SQL. They are created and dropped with CREATE ENDPOINT and DROP ENDPOINT statements.

The following is the CREATE ENDPOINT Transact-SQL syntax:

```
CREATE ENDPOINT endPointName [ AUTHORIZATION login ]
[ STATE = { STARTED | STOPPED | DISABLED } ]
AS { HTTP | TCP } (
    <protocol_specific_arguments>
        )
FOR { SOAP | TSQL | SERVICE_BROKER | DATABASE_MIRRORING } (
    <language_specific_arguments>
        )
<AS TCP_protocol_specific_arguments> ::=
AS TCP (
   LISTENER_PORT = listenerPort
   [ [ , ] LISTENER_IP = ALL | ( 4-part-ip ) | ( "ip_address_v6" ) ]

)
```

Here is the DROP ENDPOINT Transact-SQL syntax:

```
DROP ENDPOINT endPointName
```

If you have been following the Wiley study guides, you are well aware of the security built into SQL Server 2005. Endpoint security is no exception. When your users are granted permissions to log on to your server, they are implicitly given permission to connect to the default endpoints that have been created at the time of installation. For endpoints that you explicitly create either within the default instance of your server or to connect to a named instance of your SQL Server, you need to explicitly control the permissions. The user must have permission to log on to the server instance as well as permission on the endpoint itself through the CONNECT permission to the endpoint. You can further modify a user's permissions using the GRANT|DENY|REVOKE CONNECT ON ENDPOINT Transact-SQL statements. When you set permissions on a custom endpoint, the permissions are associated with the name of the endpoint. Therefore, if you are creating and associating permissions with endpoints beyond the default endpoints, be aware that a name change or a port number change will affect your security alignment.

 You can find information about your server's endpoints using the sys.endpoints catalog view.

Simplifying Application Design

In previous releases of SQL Server, database applications were not able to maintain multiple active statements on a connection. When you programmed in SQL Server 2000 or earlier, you were restricted by the programming model for data access APIs, such that, at any point in time, you could have at most one request pending on a given session.

What did you do to minimize the response time in your applications? How did you manage network traffic when reading related data? Obviously, you did some fancy footwork. Depending on the situation, you may have the following:

- Opened multiple connections and executed several statements in parallel.

- Implemented connection pooling at the client.

- Employed a server-side, cursor-based strategy.

These strategies can be enhanced or replaced in SQL Server 2005 by a new technology, multiple active result sets (MARS). The MARS implementation permits multiple requests to execute over a single connection. With MARS you run multiple commands on the same connection, even though all the results from running one or more of these commands might not yet be completely returned to the client.

MARS enables you to simplify your application design by giving you the following capabilities:

- Applications can have multiple *default result sets* open and can *interleave* reading from them.

- Applications can execute other statements (for example, INSERT, UPDATE, DELETE, and stored procedure calls) while default result sets are open.

You should note and remember that MARS is defined in terms of interleaving, not in terms of parallel execution. Also, MARS is not a cursor replacement.

MARS allows a batch to run and, within its execution, it allows other requests to execute. Even though the technology within MARS enables multiple batches to execute in this interleaved fashion, you should be aware that execution can be switched only at well-defined points. You should also realize that most statements require running atomically within a batch. Your statements that return rows to the client, often referenced as *yield points*, are able to interleave execution before completion. Whereas rows that are being sent to the client through SELECT, FETCH, or RECEIVE or any other statements executed as part of a stored procedure for that matter, must run to completion prior to switching to other MARS requests.

Only SELECT, READTEXT, FETCH, RECEIVE, and BULK INSERT statements will interleave.

You have a number of factors that influence the manner in which batches interleave execution. Consequently, you are often unable to predict the exact sequence in which these commands containing yield points from multiple batches will be executed. You should always test carefully to make certain that you do not realize unwanted side effects from the interleaved execution of these multiple batches. You can further avoid problems by serializing execution of such batches with consuming or canceling all results or using API calls for the connection state and transactions as opposed to using Transact-SQL statements.

To see how the execution order in interleaving works, let's have look at some examples. This is Example 1:

Time	Statement 1	Statement 2
Time1	SELECT...	
Time2	SELECT...	
Time3		UDPATE...

In example 1, the order of the statements indicates that both SELECT statements are interleaved. The UDPATE statement will execute after the last SELECT statement. This is Example 2:

Time	Statement 1	Statement 2
Time1	SELECT...	UDPATE ...
Time2	SELECT...	

In Example 2, you are dependent on which of the two statements in Time1—the SELECT or the UPDATE—is received first by your database server. If the UDPATE statement is received first, the first SELECT statement will initiate after the completion of the UDPATE statement. On the other hand, if the SELECT statement is received first in Time1, both the first SELECT and the UDPATE statements will execute; however, it is important to note that the SELECT statement will not perceive the changes since MARS uses *row versioning*. When the second SELECT statement executes, which occurs after the UDPATE statement has completed, it will perceive the changes.

Let's try one more. This is Example 3:

Time	Statement 1	Statement 2
Time1	SELECT…	
Time2	SELECT…	UDPATE …

In Example 3, we have moved the UPDATE statement into Time2. Once more, you are dependent on which of the two statements in Time2—the SELECT or the UPDATE—is received first by your database server. Obviously, the first SELECT statement in Time1 will execute first. Now if the UDPATE statement is received prior to the second SELECT statement, the SELECT statement will initiate after the UDPATE statement executes. However, if the second SELECT statement is received first, both the SELECT and the UDPATE statements will execute. In this example, neither of the SELECT statements will perceive the changes.

Two factors affect interleaving: order of execution of statements and compatibility between multiple statements.

Understanding the Features of MARS

What do you need to know about MARS?

- MARS is supported only in SQL Server 2005.

- MARS is disabled by default after opening a new connection with any data access provider. Thus connection string properties must be set accordingly.

- Even when MARS is not used, its infrastructure is created.

- When disabled, MARS indicates that an exception should be thrown to the client application when you are trying to use multiple active statements over the same connection.

"Connection is busy with results for another command" is the exception you will receive if you fail to activate MARS and are attempting to use multiple active statements over the same connection.

Understanding Row Versioning and MARS

MARS uses row versioning to control multiple active requests when you are manipulating the same data. When you issue a data modification statement during a MARS session in which there is an active result set, those rows affected by the modification are versioned.

Row versioning itself is based on the principle that multiple readers and writers should not lock each other and, furthermore, should use their own version of the data. Thus row versioning utilizes an optimistic, as opposed to pessimistic, *concurrency* control. Row versioning also lays the foundation for two new technologies in SQL Server 2005—Snapshot isolation and Read Committed Snapshot.

Row versioning works in the following manner:

1. Each time you modify a row, a version of the row imaged prior to the change is stored in tempdb.

2. The versions of the rows that you have modified are linked by a link list in tempdb.

3. The most recent version of the row is stored in your current database.

4. When you execute a read operation, you will retrieve the last version that was committed at the time that the transaction started.

Since MARS uses row versioning, you need to make certain that enough space is available in tempdb for multiple read operations to succeed. If tempdb runs out of space, update operations may continue to succeed while read operations may fail. For more information, see "Row Versioning Resource Usage" in SQL Server Books Online.

 Real World Scenario

A Case in Point: How MARS Is Being Used in Clinical Trials

Recently we have been working with pharmaceutical companies. One of the companies researches cancer drugs. During second phase clinical trials of one drug, the trial monitors wanted to compare the results of the various studies on particular populations with regard to the study drug. While it is vital that the clinics input their data into the study without delay, it is equally important that the monitors can receive the updated data quickly to evaluate the ongoing study for participant vitals and drug interaction.

In order to enable them to quickly access the drug format and choose their requirements for comparisons, we implemented a MARS solution for their SQL Server 2005 database . MARS enabled them to have quick access to their data by interleaving their requests while others are continually updating trial data. Implementing MARS also minimized connections to their database. They already had the max resources mentioned previously in this section. We also made certain we used best practices in setting up their tempdb using a RAID10 implementation.

Designing Queries That Use Multiple Active Result Sets (MARS)

As we design some queries that use MARS, keep in mind some of the factors affecting MARS that we have seen. Remember MARS is able to handle multiple requests as long as the locking, blocking, and transactional needs of each of these statements are not contradictory.

Using Client Libraries That Support MARS

To utilize the features of MARS, your clients need to have the latest versions of the *client libraries* for SQL Server 2005 installed.

The following data access libraries support MARS:

- ADO.NET 2.0 SqlClient

- SQL Native Client, including:

    - SQL Native Client for Open Database Connectivity (ODBC)

    - SQL Native Client for OLE Database (OLE DB)

    - SQL Native Client for ActiveX Data Objects (ADO)

Using Connection Strings to Configure MARS

Since MARS is disabled by default, it is important that you enable MARS when you're opening a new connection with your data access provider. The following are the connection string settings you need to provide for your client connections as specified previously:

- ADO.NET 2.0 SqlClient

    - multipleActiveResultSets = true | false (connection string setting)

- SQL Native Client ODBC

    - Set SQLSetConnectAttr with: SQL_COPT_SS_MARS_ENABLED = SQL_MARS_ENABLED_YES | SQL_MARS_ENABLED_NO

    - Mars_Connection = yes | no (connection string setting)

- SQL Native Client for OLE Database (OLE DB)

    - SSPROP_INIT_MARSCONNECTION = VARIANT_TRUE | VARIANT_FALSE (data source initialization property)

    - MarsConn = true | false (connection string setting)

- SQL Native Client for ActiveX Data Objects (ADO)

    - Mars_Connection = true | false (connection string setting)

You can improve your application's performance using MARS to read multiple related result sets on the same connection. You must decide when it is appropriate to use a MARS implementation, which is what we discuss next.

Deciding When MARS Queries Are Appropriate

You need to assess your usage scenario when seeking to provide a way for client-side logic to execute multiple read and write operations over the same connection. Using MARS could incur an unnecessary overhead. For example, if you want specific rows but not all the data to be read, you might want to use server-side cursors. Your data can also be read at a later time. Also with server-side cursors, the data is read on a row-by-row basis allowing you to apply conditional transactional updates if desired to each row. MARS on the other hand, processes results immediately and your server returns them as a complete result set to the client. But the caveat is that with SQL Server 2005 you can apply conditional transactional updating of your data over the same connection you use for reading the data. In earlier versions of SQL Server you needed to implement code for a secondary connection to update the data.

Another consideration is to determine whether MARS will improve your query response time. You want to use MARS when there is small probability that requests will block one another. An example would be a scenario where there are only requests to read information. Another scenario where MARS could have an ill effect on performance is if you are using the same connection for more than 10 commands. Presently, MARS has a hard-coded pool of 10 virtual connections to your database server. If you use more than 10 commands, the extra commands create new connections that are created on an as-needed basis and then immediately discarded, creating unnecessary overhead.

Understanding What Statements Can Be Requested Using MARS

Actually, you can send any database request over MARS. Some of the most usual ones might include those that:

- Retrieve data
- Execute stored procedures
- Execute data manipulation language statements
- Execute data definition language statements

The qualification is that you have to position your requests in an order such that your MARS execution is beneficial. You need to arrange your statements using the correct combinations and order of execution. You must program your applications to avoid blocking or piling up with other requests in the multiple buffers as well as to promote interleaving. Furthermore, you should make certain that the interleaved statements do not execute in a manner that causes conflicts.

You can interleave the following statements without being concerned with blocking or locking:

- SELECT
- FETCH
- RECEIVE
- READTEXT
- BULK INSERT

You can only run the following statements with exclusive access. MARS serializes their execution and hence they are not interleaved:

- DML statements
- DDL statements
- Calls to stored procedures
- Statements within a transaction

Mixing Reads and Writes on a Single Connection: An Example

Let's look at a sample application that will mix both a read and write over the same connection. Using the AdventureWorks database, we are going to create two procedures. The first procedure will return the top 10 bikes that have the highest sales, that is, the procedure we will call usp_GetMostPopularBikes. The second procedure will update the selling price of each particular popular bike based on its color and current price, usp_UpdateProductPrice. We have used Visual Studio 2005 to write and compile the code.

Here is the application Settings portion of the app.config file:

```
<applicationSettings>
    <Microsoft.Samples.SqlServer.Properties.Settings>
        <setting name="ConnectionString" serializeAs="String">
            <value>server=(local);database=AdventureWorks;Integrated
➡Security=true;MultipleActiveResultSets=true</value>
        </setting>
    </Microsoft.Samples.SqlServer.Properties.Settings>
</applicationSettings>
```

Notice that we have built this application to use MultipleActiveResultSets. Now let's see what happens when we execute the application and the stored procedures run. We have used just a standard template in SQL Server Profiler to show a view of the connection and order of execution of the procedures, as shown in Figure 2.6.

Notice that all the stored procedures run between the single Audit Login and Audit Logout events using the same Client process ID and SPID throughout. We have returned data to the client and updated those returned values using the same connection.

Figuring Out Whether MARS Is the Most Efficient Solution

For this application, MARS does a great job. We are reusing the same connection and pulling the results only once. But you should always consider whether is would be more efficient to use JOINs in a server-side query or update rather than implementing MARS. If you want to return various pieces of data on an item including, for example, line item totals, you might be better off to use a JOIN.

Also, since MARS resources are expensive, if you have long-running processes that require mixing read and write operations, you might find it more appropriate to use server cursors.

FIGURE 2.6   SQL Server Profiler: MARS application with reads and writes

EventClass	TextData	ApplicationName	NTUserNa..	LoginName	CPU	Reads	W..	Duration	ClientPi
ExistingCon...	-- network protocol: LPC set quoted_identifier on set arith...	Microsoft SQ...	marilyn	WHITEH...					
ExistingCon...	-- network protocol: LPC set quoted_identifier on set arith...	Report Server	SQLService	WHITEH...					
ExistingCon...	-- network protocol: LPC set quoted_identifier on set arith...	.Net SqlClie...	marilyn	WHITEH...					
ExistingCon...	-- network protocol: LPC set quoted_identifier on set arith...	Microsoft SQ...	marilyn	WHITEH...					
ExistingCon...	-- network protocol: LPC set quoted_identifier off set arit...	SQLAgent - G...	SQLService	WHITEH...					
RPC:Completed	exec sp_reset_connection	Report Server	SQLService	WHITEH...	0	0	0	0	
RPC:Completed	declare @p1 nvarchar(64) set @p1=NULL exec GetDBVersion @DB...	Report Server	SQLService	WHITEH...	0	2	0	0	
RPC:Completed	exec sp_reset_connection	Report Server	SQLService	WHITEH...	0	0	0	0	
RPC:Completed	declare @p1 nvarchar(64) set @p1=NULL exec GetDBVersion @DB...	Report Server	SQLService	WHITEH...	0	2	0	0	
RPC:Completed	exec sp_reset_connection	Report Server	SQLService	WHITEH...	0	0	0	0	
RPC:Completed	declare @p1 nvarchar(64) set @p1=NULL exec GetDBVersion @DB...	Report Server	SQLService	WHITEH...	0	2	0	0	
RPC:Completed	exec usp_GetMostPopularBikes	.Net SqlClie...	marilyn	WHITEH...	671	1853	0	1579	
RPC:Completed	exec usp_UpdateProductPrice @ProductID=782,@StandardCost=$127...	.Net SqlClie...	marilyn	WHITEH...	63	285	9	166	
RPC:Completed	exec usp_UpdateProductPrice @ProductID=783,@StandardCost=$127...	.Net SqlClie...	marilyn	WHITEH...	0	6	0	0	
RPC:Completed	exec usp_UpdateProductPrice @ProductID=779,@StandardCost=$127...	.Net SqlClie...	marilyn	WHITEH...	0	6	0	0	
RPC:Completed	exec usp_UpdateProductPrice @ProductID=770,@StandardCost=$496...	.Net SqlClie...	marilyn	WHITEH...	0	6	0	1	
RPC:Completed	exec usp_UpdateProductPrice @ProductID=762,@StandardCost=$511...	.Net SqlClie...	marilyn	WHITEH...	0	6	0	0	
RPC:Completed	exec usp_UpdateProductPrice @ProductID=780,@StandardCost=$127...	.Net SqlClie...	marilyn	WHITEH...	0	6	0	0	
RPC:Completed	exec usp_UpdateProductPrice @ProductID=760,@StandardCost=$511...	.Net SqlClie...	marilyn	WHITEH...	0	6	0	0	
RPC:Completed	exec usp_UpdateProductPrice @ProductID=781,@StandardCost=$127...	.Net SqlClie...	marilyn	WHITEH...	0	7	0	0	
RPC:Completed	exec usp_UpdateProductPrice @ProductID=784,@StandardCost=$127...	.Net SqlClie...	marilyn	WHITEH...	0	6	0	0	
RPC:Completed	exec usp_UpdateProductPrice @ProductID=761,@StandardCost=$511...	.Net SqlClie...	marilyn	WHITEH...	0	6	0	0	
RPC:Completed	exec sp_reset_connection	Report Server	SQLService	WHITEH...	0	0	0	0	
RPC:Completed	declare @p1 nvarchar(64) set @p1=NULL exec GetDBVersion @DB...	Report Server	SQLService	WHITEH...	0	2	0	0	
Audit Logout		.Net SqlClie...	marilyn	WHITEH...	0	0	0	1303016	
RPC:Completed	exec sp_reset_connection	Report Server	SQLService	WHITEH...	0	0	0	0	
RPC:Completed	declare @p1 nvarchar(64) set @p1=NULL exec GetDBVersion @DB...	Report Server	SQLService	WHITEH...	0	2	0	0	
RPC:Completed	exec sp_reset_connection	Report Server	SQLService	WHITEH...	0	0	0	0	
RPC:Completed	declare @p1 nvarchar(64) set @p1=NULL exec GetDBVersion @DB...	Report Server	SQLService	WHITEH...	0	2	0	0	
RPC:Completed	exec sp_reset_connection	Report Server	SQLService	WHITEH...	0	0	0	0	
RPC:Completed	declare @p1 nvarchar(64) set @p1=NULL exec GetDBVersion @DB...	Report Server	SQLService	WHITEH...	0	2	0	0	

```
exec usp_UpdateProductPrice @ProductID=782,@StandardCost=$1277.0209,@ListPrice=$2340.8898
```

At this point you might be wondering if there is a task that can only be implemented using MARS. Well, that answer is yes; we touched on the situation at the beginning of this section. If you need to navigate a result set at your client and also issue related statements such as an UPDATE or DELETE on a row-by-row basis over the same connection to your database server, you must implement MARS.

Using MARS and the SQL Server Lock Manager

When you make a request over MARS, as with any other database request, your connection interacts with the *SQL Server Lock Manager*. The database engine manages locks internally. As your application's Transact-SQL statements are processed within an instance of the database engine, the query processor will determine the resources that will be accessed. Furthermore, the query processor will determine the lock type required to protect your resources based on the type of access stipulated and the transaction isolation setting. The query processor requests the appropriate lock from the lock manager. The lock manager then grants the lock providing other transactions hold no conflicting locks. You should also understand that the more resources a transaction or request uses, the more Lock Manager is required to work, which might produce adverse effects in some of your applications.

Locking and isolation do not behave differently when you use a MARS-enabled connection. The difference is in how the active requests running with MARS behave with one another.

Consequently, when you are using MARS connections, the locking behavior will depend on two items:

- The type of operations you are executing
- The execution of transactional requests

Consider each of these items for a MARS connection separately:

Locking and MARS with compatible operations   When you use compatible operations over a MARS connection, they will not block one another but will be interleaved. Row-level versioning will be employed by your server.

Locking and MARS with incompatible operations   Incompatible operations will block one another, so MARS will not interleave them. Instead each incompatible operation will run to completion until the next one begins. Your server will request locks on resources from the SQL Server Lock Manager.

Locking and MARS with transactional requests   No matter the number of active requests, MARS will allow only one transaction over a physical connection. Your server will use its normal locking, blocking, and isolation paradigms at the transaction level.

Locking and MARS with nontransactional requests   MARS will execute an implicit transaction for each active request over one physical connection. Your server will use its normal locking, blocking, and isolation paradigms at the request level.

For more information about the different isolation levels and how they affect locking, check out "Managing Concurrent Data Access" in SQL Server Books Online.

Choosing How to Get the Max from MARS

You have now seen that MARS requires resources, resources, resources:

- Memory to maintain multiple sessions of requests
- Locks to control concurrency
- Disk space to support row versioning in tempdb

How can you get the max from MARS? From everything you have learned about MARS, here's the short list:

- Execute as many reads as you need over the same MARS connection. Read operations are interleaved and use row-level versioning.

- Execute writes using a different connection. Write operations do not interleave. Write operations need to run exclusively and acquire locks. Keep them separate.

- Execute transactional requests on their own connection. Recall the one transaction per physical request rule. Even over MARS, transactional requests will run to completions. So, if possible, execute them over exclusive connections.

- Execute incompatible operations as quickly as possible. Execute transactional and write requests as quickly, simply, and small as possible. The more they languish, the more contention will build.

- Monitor your resources. Check out the usage patterns to make certain the MARS is working for you, not against you.

- Maintain ample disk space, especially for tempdb. If tempdb is not able to grow, SQL Server will not be able to handle the read operations.

- Optimize tempdb access. Follow best practices especially when using MARS. Use striped disk arrays and multiple data files for tempdb.

Summary

In this chapter you learned that connections to SQL Server 2005 should always be made using SQL Native Client. Not only does the SQL Native Client .dll give you all the functionality you need to implement SQL Server 2005, it is backward compatible with previous versions of SQL Server. You then learned that you have a variety of tools available for managing your SQL Server clients: SQL Server Configuration Manager, Surface Area Configuration (SAC) tool, Setup, and ODBC Data Source Administrator.

You next learned how you are able to manage and script a variety of database objects using their object model libraries: server management objects (SMO), replication management objects (RMO), and Analysis Services automation management objects (AMO).

None of the asynchronous connectivity utilized in SQL Server 2005 would exist without SNI. You learned that SQL Server Networking Interface (SNI) is a new communication format. All communication between client and server is done through TDS endpoints.

Lastly, you have seen that support for multiple active result sets (MARS) in SQL Server 2005 gives you greater options for your application development. You now have a lightweight alternative to simplify your application design. However, you should remember that MARS is not a replacement for a cursor strategy that already scales well. To put it succinctly, MARS is a programming model enhancement allowing multiple requests to interleave in your database server that, if used correctly, may yield some performance benefits. Now the downside is that since MARS uses technologies such as row versioning, it requires the use of extra resources, including memory, disk space, and locking resources.

At this point, we hope you are feeling comfortable about the data access topics in these first two chapters. If you need to review some topics, now is the time to do so. Many of the new features of SQL Server 2005 have their foundation in the topics you learned in these two chapters. The database engine and client access pieces have been totally rebuilt, as you have discovered. In our training classes, we are always reminding the participants to upgrade their client machines to use SQL Native Client; it should be apparent now why this is so important.

Exam Essentials

Before you take the exam, you need to have a good understanding of the following:

Know how to design SMO applications.   You need to be familiar with the Microsoft .SqlServer.Management.Smo namespace and the classes contained therein. You need to understand the tasks you can perform using SMO. You need to know how to create a SMO application.

Know how to design RMO applications.   You need to be familiar with the Microsoft.SqlServer .Management.Rmo namespace and the classes contained therein. You need to understand the tasks you can perform using RMO. You need to know how to create a RMO application.

Know how to design AMO applications.   You need to be familiar with the Microsoft .SqlServer.Management.Amo namespace and the classes contained therein. You need to understand the tasks you can perform using AMO.

Know how to design SNI for asynchronous queries.   You need to be familiar with the SNI protocol layer and how it affects asynchronous queries.

Know how to design queries that use MARS.   You need to be able to understand how MARS is implemented in SQL Server 2005. You need to be able to implement MARS queries. You need to understand the transaction level MARS uses.

Review Questions

1. Which of the following SMO classes are used for automating management tasks? (Choose all that apply.)

   A. Instance classes

   B. Numerator classes

   C. Utility classes

   D. Relations classes

2. Which of the following tools are used to manage SQL Server clients? (Choose all that apply.)

   A. SQL Server Management Studio

   B. SQL Server Configuration Manager

   C. sqlcmd

   D. Surface Area Configuration (SAC) tool

3. You can use SQL server management objects (SMO) to manage SQL Server 7, 2000, as well as SQL 2005 programmatically.

   A. True

   B. False

4. What SMO object do you use to establish a connection to an instance of your SQL Server?

   A. Database

   B. Server

   C. Instance

   D. Schema

5. To automate tasks using SMO, you must import a reference to its namespace. Which of the following is the name of this namespace?

   A. Microsoft.SqlServer.SqlTask

   B. Microsoft.SqlServer.Sql

   C. Microsoft.SqlServer.Smo

   D. Microsoft.SqlServer.SqlEnum

6. Which of the following tasks can you do with SMO? (Choose all that apply.)

   A. Modify server settings.

   B. Back up a database.

   C. Attach a database.

   D. Grant permissions on a database.

   E. Create an endpoint.

7. As a database developer, you have decided to create new objects using SMO. You have established a connection to your server. What is the order of the steps you would use to create new objects? (Not all answers need to be used.)

    1. Add the child objects to their parent object.

    2. Call the Create method on the parent object to update the server.

    3. Close the connection to update the server.

    4. Set any extra properties of the object.

    5. Create and instantiate a local variable for the object you are creating.

    6. Create and instantiate a global server variable for the object you are creating.

    A. A. 6, 5, 4, 3, 2, 1

    B. B. 5, 4, 1, 2

    C. C. 1, 2, 5, 4

    D. D. 5, 6, 4, 2, 1

8. Can SMO be used to modify database object properties? If so, how would you do it?

    A. No. SMO can only be used to retrieve and create objects.

    B. Yes. Many SMO objects have an Alter method that performs this task.

    C. Yes. Many SMO objects have a Modify method that performs this task.

    D. No. SMO objects do not have a Change method that performs this task

9. Which of the following enable you to handle replication administration tasks in SQL Server 2005? (Choose all that apply.)

    A. RMO

    B. AMO

    C. New Publication Wizard

    D. New Subscription Wizard

    E. SMO

10. When you create an RMO application, what two objects must first be instantiated?

    A. ServerConnection

    B. ReplicationServer

    C. DistributionServer

    D. PublicationServer

11. You are the database developer for your organization. You want to create an interface for your Analysis Services application to restrict user access to certain objects and tasks. Which of the following should you use?

    A. RMO

    B. SMO

    C. SQL Server Management Studio

    D. AMO

12. Which of the following is not a task for AMO?

   A. Back up Analysis Services databases.

   B. Update an Analysis Services object.

   C. Query Analysis Services data.

   D. Remove temporary Analysis Server users.

13. What is the new communication protocol layer used by SQL Server 2005 for communication between client and server?

   A. SNI

   B. TCP

   C. TDS

   D. UDP

   E. SNA

14. Settings for TDS endpoints are recorded in the registry. How should you change these settings if necessary? (Choose all that apply.)

   A. You cannot change the TDS endpoint settings.

   B. You must only change the TDS endpoint settings in the registry itself.

   C. You must use a Transact-SQL statement to change the TDS endpoint settings.

15. What is the process used when MARS reads from multiple default result sets over the same connection?

   A. Parallel execution

   B. Interleaving

   C. Serializing

   D. Interlacing

16. Which two data access libraries support MARS?

   A. SQL Client

   B. SQL Native Client

   C. ADO.NET 2.0 SqlClient

   D. DAO.NET

17. Which of the following statements will not be interleaved by MARS?

   A. DDL statement

   B. SELECT statement

   C. FETCH statement

   D. BULK INSERT statement

18. What type of concurrency control does MARS use?

    A. Pessimistic concurrency

    B. Optimistic concurrency

    C. Database locking

    D. Page locking

19. Since MARS uses an optimistic concurrency control, you need to make certain that tempdb does not run out of space. What happens if tempdb run out of space in a MARS implementation?

    A. Update operations might fail but reads will be fine.

    B. Nothing, it is just a good idea to have enough space.

    C. Read operations might fail but updates will be fine.

    D. Both read and updates will most likely fail.

20. What three resources will enable you to get the max from MARS?

    A. Memory to maintain multiple sessions.

    B. Locks to control concurrency.

    C. Configuring ample disk space to support row versioning in tempdb.

    D. Configuring minimal disk space to support row versioning in tempdb

Answers to Review Questions

1. A, C. The Instance and Utility classes are the two SMO classes used for automating management tasks. The Instance class closely resembles the structure of SQL Server itself, which makes it easier to program.

2. B, D. SQL Server Configuration Manager and the Surface Area Configuration (SAC) tool are both used to manage SQL Server clients. The SQL Server Configuration Manager combines the SQL Server Network Utility, SQL Server Client Network Utility, and Service Manager of previous versions of SQL Server. The SAC tool provides a single tool to configure network features or to configure services and connections.

3. A. SMO can be used to programmatically manage SQL Server 2005 and previous versions of SQL Server starting with version 7.

4. B. You connect to a physical SQL Server installation through the Server object. The Server class is the highest level in the SMO instance object hierarchy.

5. C. You must add a reference to the Microsoft.SqlServer.Smo namespace. You will more than likely also need to add the Microsoft.SqlServer.SmoEnum and the Microsoft.SqlServer .ConnectionInfo components to your project.

6. A, B, C, D, E. You can do all of the above and more with SMO.

7. B. The steps must be in the defined order.

8. B. You need to first locate the object you want to modify. Then you need to change its property values and finally update the database. Most SMO objects have an Alter method that performs this task.

9. A, C, D. For most of your replication administration tasks, you will be able to use the New Publication Wizard and the New Subscription Wizard that are provided in SQL Server Management Studio. They enable you to create, modify, and view replication objects. However, if you want to manage replication programmatically you need to implement replication management objects (RMO).

10. A, B. The ServerConnection and the ReplicatonServer must be instantiated, and in that order.

11. D. You should use AMO. AMO provides a layer between the user application and the Analysis Services instance. As such it provides an excellent development environment for a security interface for your application.

12. C. AMO cannot be used to query Analysis Services data. You should use ADOMD.NET for this purpose.

13. A. SNI. SQL Server Network Interface protocol layer replaces the net libraries for SQL Server 2000 and Microsoft Data Access Components (MDAC). SNI is contained within SQL Native Client.

14. C. Even though the settings for the TDS endpoints are stored in the registry, since the registry is separate from the metadata, you cannot make a change within the registry and expect it to take effect in your server. You must make the change through a Transact-SQL statement and then use the Configuration Manager to enable or disable the proper protocols to start and stop the endpoints.

15. B. The process is defined in terms of interleaving. The order of execution as well as the compatibility between multiple statements affect the interleaving.

16. B, C. Both ADO.NET 2.0 SqlClient and all flavors of SQL Native Client (ODBC, OLE DB, ADO) support MARS.

17. A. The DDL statement must run with exclusive access and cannot be interleaved with other statements by MARS.

18. B. MARS uses row versioning, an optimistic concurrency control.

19. C. Since reads are moved into tempdb, they will most likely fail.

20. A, B, C. MARS uses several server resources. It uses memory to maintain multiple sessions of requests, uses locks to control concurrency, and needs an ample amount of configured disk space to support row versioning in tempdb.

Chapter

3

Designing Queries

MICROSOFT EXAM OBJECTIVES COVERED IN THIS CHAPTER:

✓ Write and modify queries.

✓ **Write queries.**

  ▪ Modify queries to improve query performance.

✓ **Design queries for retrieving data from XML sources.**

  ▪ Select the correct attributes.

  ▪ Select the correct nodes.

  ▪ Filter by values of attributes and values of elements.

  ▪ Include relational data, such as columns and variables, in the result of an XQuery expression.

  ▪ Include XML attribute or node values in a tabular result set.

  ▪ Update, insert, or delete relational data based on XML parameters to stored procedures.

  ▪ Debug and troubleshoot queries against XML data sources.

"The time has come," the Walrus said,
"To talk of many things:
"Of shoes—and ships—and sealing-wax—
"Of cabbages—and kings—
"And why the sea is boiling hot—
"And whether pigs have wings."

"But wait a bit," the Oysters cried,
"Before we have our chat;
"For some of us are out of breath,
"And all of us are fat!"
"No hurry!" said the Carpenter.
They thanked him much for that.

—From "The Walrus and the Carpenter"
(1872) by Lewis Carroll

Ah, those unsuspecting oysters! They came to a new environment, unprepared.

We are using this quote from one of our favorite mathematicians and logicians so that you realize how different your sea can be. But you need to be aware and to adjust or you will find yourselves wondering why the sea is boiling hot! Unlike the oysters, you have the chance to talk of many things. This chapter talks of many things, among them, change. The heart of the change is in the core design of the relational database engine of SQL Server 2005 itself. The relational database engine in SQL Server 2005 has been rebuilt to create a high-performance, secure environment that scales well for storing, retrieving, and modifying data in both relational and Extensible Markup Language (XML) format. In this chapter, you will learn the changes in how relational data is processed. You will write, analyze, and modify queries to improve their performance for the new database engine.

In the latter part of this chapter, you will learn how SQL Server 2005 provides extensive support for XML data processing. As you have learned in your earlier studies, XML values can now be stored natively using an XML data type column. You can index and query the XML column. Native XML can be typed—that is, delineated by using a predefined namespace or Schema collection—or untyped. You will learn how to use the components of the typed and untyped XML data type to create queries that extract data within the XML. You will also learn how to manipulate data within the XML data type using *Xquery*—the query language for XML—and XML Data Modification Language (DML). Microsoft built the XML DML to enhance the XQuery language to allow full data manipulation—insert, update, and delete—access for the XML data type.

Writing Queries

Beware, oh queries, the sea has changed! You need to understand the changes to the processing of queries and the recompilation of batches in SQL Server 2005 to be able to write queries that will perform efficiently.

In Chapter 1 you learned about the caching technologies applied to applications. In this chapter we focus on how the cache is used in queries and batches.

Understanding behind the Scenes: The Procedure Cache

Prior to a query being executed on SQL Server, it gets compiled into a plan. Most often when you execute queries, you execute them in batch. A batch can contain one or more SELECT, INSERT, UPDATE, and DELETE statements, stored procedures, DDL statements, and DML statements. A batch can also include definitions and use constructs of the Common Language Runtime (CLR). SQL Server stores the compiled plans into a part of its memory called a *plan* or *procedure cache*. In some of your readings on SQL Server you may have seen this cache referenced as the *plan cache*, but most often it is called the procedure cache. In SQL Server 2005 the procedure cache is distinct from the data cache. SQL Server's memory pool is used for both the execution plans as well as the data buffers. The percent of memory is dynamically allocated to each pool as it is needed.

 The procedure (or plan) cache can contain compiled plans, executed plans, the algebrizer tree, and extended stored procedures. You can use the SQL Server Performance Monitor SQLServer:Plan Cache Performance object to obtain information about the procedure cache. The metrics are obtained from the DBCC PROCCACHE database console command.

The algebrizer is part of the internal logic redesign process. The algebrizer, replacing the normalizer of SQL Server 2000, takes your parsed query and binds it to a best solution. The algorithms and methodologies it employs are built on the internal structure of the database engine of SQL Server 2005 and will be valid for future versions of the product. The algebrizer tree is stored in the procedure cache.

Compiled plans are stored in the procedure cache, a portion of memory in SQL Server. As your query or batch prepares for execution, the procedure cache is examined for possible plan reuse. The comparisons are done against query plans, not against query executions in the cache. If it is possible to reuse a stored plan, the compilation costs of the query or batch are avoided. In SQL Server 2000, when it is necessary for a batch to be recompiled, all the statements in the batch are compiled. SQL Server 2005 improves on this behavior by using "statement-level recompilation," which compiles only the statements that need recompiling.

> In SQL Server 2005, you do not need to break up longer stored procedures into multiple shorter ones merely to avoid the high recompiling price.

Once the batch has a query plan in the procedure cache (and there are at most two: one for all the serializable executions and one for all the parallel executions), an execution context is derived. This is a skeleton whose pieces are generated as the execution of the batch proceeds.

Understanding the Different Types of Query Plans That Promote Reuse

As you write queries and batches, you need to understand what enables them to be cached so they can be reused. If SQL Server does not place the plan for a query in its cache, it has absolutely no chance of reuse! And, consequently, a new plan must be generated. When SQL Server creates a new execution plan for a query, time and resources are spent compiling and optimizing prior to executing the query. Unnecessarily creating a new execution plan can result in your queries performing poorly.

Therefore, let's next take a look at some guidelines that will help you promote plan reuse. The best way to approach this topic is to analyze types of queries you most often write and note the factors that SQL Server 2005 utilizes when reusing the query plan.

Since this is a starting point, please be aware that the queries presented are very simplistic and may not meet sufficient conditions. With that said, we are following the more theoretical sections with practical sections on viewing your query plans. You will be studying the following types of queries for plan reuse: ad hoc queries, simple parameterization queries, the sp_executesql stored procedure, stored procedures, and batches.

Writing Ad Hoc Queries for Plan Reuse

An *ad hoc query* is one that is created from need as the situation arises. As such it may contain one of the following data manipulation language (DML) statements: SELECT, INSERT, UPDATE, or DELETE.

One of the components that makes an ad hoc query matched to an existing execution plan is that it contains fully qualified object references. For example, an ad hoc query of SELECT * FROM AdventureWorks.Production.Product will be matched with an existing plan whereas SELECT * FROM Production.Product might not. The latter query does not contain a fully qualified object reference to the AdventureWorks.Production.Product table.

A second factor affecting ad hoc query matching to promote reuse is the matching and placement of the text itself in the query. SQL Server requires ad hoc queries to match in place, space, and case sensitivity of text. The space sensitivity may be a bit difficult for you to swallow especially since this is not an aspect of Transact-SQL you normally are concerned with. The following two ad hoc queries do not share the same plan:

This is query 1:

```
SELECT EmployeeID
FROM Adventureworks.HumanResources.Employee
WHERE ManagerID = 185
```

This is query 2:

```
SELECT EmployeeID
FROM Adventureworks.HumanResources.Employee

WHERE ManagerID = 185
```

Using Simple Parameters to Increase Plan Reuse

In query 1 previously we used a simple parameter for the ManagerID value. If we were to execute query 1 using another ManagerID, SQL Server 2005 would most likely match the existing execution plan of query 1. SQL Server 2005 processes the value specified in the WHERE clause as if it had been a parameter and saves a plan internally, storing the execution plan with a simple parameter rather than a value. In SQL Server 2000 this same process is called *auto-parameterization*.

Using simple parameterization, SQL Server 2005 would use basically the same plan for the following, query 3, as it uses for query 1:

This is query 3:

```
SELECT EmployeeID
FROM Adventureworks.HumanResources.Employee
WHERE ManagerID = 3
```

The objective is to *always* have SQL Server recognize the value as a parameter and not be confused, even when the query itself becomes more complicated. You can suppose how great that works! So you might want to take matters into your own hands. Here are two suggestions to improve parameter use in complicated queries:

- Use sp_executesql to execute your query using a locally defined variable for the input parameter.
- Create a stored procedure with an input parameter.

Actually, we cover both these suggestions in the next sections.

Writing *sp_executesql* Stored Procedures for Plan Reuse

One of the best means to promote query plan reuse is to use a procedure that explicitly identifies the parameter by name and allows you to specify values into the parameter. By constructing your query in this manner, SQL Server 2005 looks at the parameter, such as the @MyManage in the example below, as part of the text that it is matching up with another query. The value replacing @MyManage is not significant in the match for query plan reuse. Using this concept, you can also list more than one parameter using a comma separator in that listing. Again, all parameters listed will be considered part of the text matching for query reuse.

For your convenience, we are restating our previous query 1. Here once again is query 1:

```
SELECT EmployeeID
FROM Adventureworks.HumanResources.Employee
WHERE ManagerID = 185
```

The following code displays how you could rewrite query 1 using sp_executesql such that the possibility of plan reuse is increased considerably. The parameters in the SELECT statement string being executed within the sp_executesql must include both the parameter definition list as well as the list of parameter values.

We have rewritten query 1 using sp_executesql and the parameter @MyManage:

```
DECLARE @MyManage INT
SET @MyManage = 185
EXEC sp_executesql
 N'SELECT EmployeeID FROM Adventureworks.HumanResources.Employee
     WHERE ManagerID = @MyManage',
 N'@MyManage INT',
 @MyManage
```

When using the sp_executesql procedure, most often you will find it more useful to use a string to define the query itself. This method makes the code more flexible and easier to reuse regarding parameters.

We have rewritten query 1 this time using sp_executesql with both the query string and the parameter defined as variables. Notice that you need to build the SQL string only once, and it can be reused with several executions and a variety of parameter values, each promoting the same plan reuse:

```
DECLARE @IntVar int;
DECLARE @SQLString nvarchar(500);
DECLARE @ParmDefinition nvarchar(500);

/* Build the SQL string once.*/
SET @SQLString =
    N'SELECT EmployeeID
      FROM AdventureWorks.HumanResources.Employee
      WHERE ManagerID = @MyManage';
SET @ParmDefinition = N'@MyManage INT';
/* Execute the string using 185. */
SET @IntVar = 185;
EXECUTE sp_executesql @SQLString, @ParmDefinition,
                    @MyManage = @IntVar;
```

```
/* Execute the same string using 3. */
SET @IntVar = 3;
EXECUTE sp_executesql @SQLString, @ParmDefinition,
                      @MyManage = @IntVar;
```

Writing Stored Procedures for Plan Reuse

A stored procedure is a collection of Transact-SQL statements that are stored within the security of the database on your server. By design, stored procedures implement execution plan reuse by providing an environment for containing repetitive tasks with multiple input and output parameters. The stored procedure defines the task and its parameters. Internally, SQL server stores the procedure using an ID that it references for plan reuse. At the initial compiling of the stored procedure, the parameters that are supplied at that time are used to optimize the query plan. Using the supplied parameter to optimize is termed *parameter sniffing*. This is a great concept and works well for your optimization as long as the "sniffed" parameter is typical. If the supplied parameter is atypical, using this parameter might cause poor performance for further executions of the procedure.

We have next created query 1 as a stored procedure with an input value of @MyManage. Also note that this is a "plain vanilla" stored procedure. We have purposely decided not to use a default value, or an implied manager, or an all managers choice; likewise, we have not defined any output values in our parameter structure. That is not our intent in this example.

```
USE AdventureWorks
GO
CREATE PROCEDURE HumanResources.uspGetEmployeesForManager
    @MyManage INT
AS
SELECT EmployeeID
FROM AdventureWorks.HumanResources.Employee
WHERE ManagerID = @MyManage
GO


/* Test the procedure using managerid 185 */
EXECUTE HumanResources.uspGetEmployeesForManager 185
/* Test the procedure using managerid 185 */
EXECUTE HumanResources.uspGetEmployeesForManager 3
```

So, now that you see how the stored procedure is implemented for plan reuse, allow us to get back to our "sniffed" saga.

SQL Server 2005 has introduced a new level of recompiling stored procedures. Stored procedures can now be recompiled at the statement level. What this means is that when a stored procedure is recompiled, the entire procedure is not necessarily recompiled, only those statements that initiated the recompiling are recompiled. Now, and here is the important part so hang on to it tightly, as the procedure is recompiled, the parameter values used at the time of recompiling are the ones implemented for the plan, not the original values. So, the "sniffed" saga continues with a new parameter being stored. Once more, for performance of your query, you can either hope or in some manner assure that this parameter is not atypical!

Writing Batches for Plan Reuse

For batches to have their query plans reused, their text must match up exactly. Once again you need to be concerned with matching place, space, and case sensitivity.

Understanding Best Practices for Reusing and Recompiling Plans

The following are the best practices for reusing and recompiling plans:

- As a general rule, if you want to reuse your query plan, establish your SET options at the initial execution of your query or batch and retain these settings for the duration of the connection.

  Changing any one of the following SET options affects plan reuse and should avoid being reset:

ANSI_NULL_DEFAULT	ANSI_NULLS
ANSI_PADDING	ANSI_WARNINGS
ARITHABORT	CONCAT_NULL_YIELDS_NULL
NUMERIC_ROUNABOURT	QUOTED_IDENTIFIER
DATEFIRST	DATEFORMAT
FORCEPLAN	LANGUAGE
NO_BROWSTABLE	

  If you are using SET options at more than one level, a hierarchy prevails. Much like rock, paper, scissors, a hint overrides an explicit SET option, a SET option overrides a database option, and a database option overrides an instance option. So, be on the safe side. Establish the SET options at connection time.

- Be aware of parameter values used in your queries. Are most values typical? If so, these queries are good candidates for plan reuse. If the values are atypical, perhaps you need to modify the recompiling process. With the new statement-level recompilation of stored procedures you may want to use the RECOMPILE query hint inside the stored procedure. You can also still force recompiling procedures by using the WITH RECOMPILE option or implementing the sp_recompile, which recompiles the procedure at its next execution.

Understanding the Cached Batch

Thus far you learned how to write queries for plan reuse. As mentioned previously, once the query is cached and compiled it is placed in the procedure cache where at most two instances of the plan are retained—one for parallel processing and one for serial processing. Within the procedure cache, an execution context is derived from the query plan. The execution context holds the results of substituting the parameter values into the executing query statements. One query plan may have multiple execution contexts. However, an execution context cannot exist without an accompanying query plan. So if a query plan is aged out of the procedure cache for any reason, all associated execution contexts are also dropped from the cache.

Understanding the Costs of the Cache

Every query plan and execution context creates a corresponding stored cost that is partially responsible for the life of these entities in the procedure cache. New algorithms are used derive the cost in SQL Server 2005. To help you with writing your queries, you should understand the old and the new:

- SQL Server 2000 query plan cost is a measure of the server resources (CPU time and I/O) it takes the query optimizer to optimize the batch. The calculation is as follows:

  - Cost c = f(cputime,ioread,iowrite)/pagecount

  The individual parts of the cost are calculated as follows:

  - cputime is the CPU time spent in generating the plan.

  - ioread is the number of pages read from disk.

  - iowrite is the number of pages written to disk.

  - pagecount is the number of memory pages occupied by the query plan of the batch.

    For the execution context, the individual costs c are calculated for every statement in the batch and are accumulated.

- SQL Server 2005 query plan cost is a measure of the amount of resources required to produce it. This cost is measured in ticks with a maximum of 31. The calculation is as follows:

  - Cost = I/O cost + context switch cost (a measure of CPU cost) + memory cost

  The individual parts of the cost are calculated as follows:

  - Two I/Os cost 1 tick, with a maximum of 19 ticks.

  - Two context switches cost 1 tick, with a maximum of 8 ticks.

  - Sixteen memory pages (128KB) cost 1 tick, with a maximum of 4 ticks.

Understanding Aging in the Procedure Cache

You have just seen how the cost factor is derived for each query plan and execution context in the procedure cache. Next you will learn how the age field that is also attached to each plan influences either the retaining or the discarding of the query plan in the procedure cache. Actually this algorithm is not quite as complicated as the previous one (even though we didn't include all the formulas!). It can be concisely stated as "Use it or lose it."

Every time the structure consisting of the query plan and its execution contexts are referenced by a connection, the age field is incremented by the above-calculated cost factor for the plan. Periodically, a lazywriter process proceeds through the cache decrementing the age field of the plans by one on each pass. A high value keeps the plan in the cache. When its age field reaches 0 or it becomes no longer referenced by a connection, the query plan is ready for deallocation from the procedure cache. The deallocation process does not take place unless memory needs to be allocated for other objects. Also recall that buffer and procedure memory are shared dynamically. Thus, if data is requesting more memory immediately from the buffer, objects in the procedure cache referenced for deallocation will immediately be dropped and the memory reallocated to the buffer. Hence, "Use it or lose it."

After the plan is in the procedure cache, you have a variety of methods available to view its processing.

Using Showplan to View Your Query Plans

Perhaps the most effective means of visualizing the query plan produced by the query optimizer is to use one of the Showplan tools. The Showplan configurations include a textual, graphical, or XML format. You use Showplan prior to your query statements by using the Transact-SQL SET statement options. Showplan provides a means of displaying the execution plan without enabling the execution itself. Your query is analyzed and the statements are displayed through a series of operators as they would be performed along with the approximated execution metrics.

If you have been using SET SHOWPLAN_TEXT, SET SHOWPLAN_ALL, or SET STATISTICS PROFILE be aware that they are scheduled for deprecation for future versions of SQL Server. You should now be using SET SHOWPLAN_XML in their place.

Understanding *SHOWPLAN_XML*

In keeping with the previous note, you must understand how SHOWPLAN_XML is used in returning the metrics of your query. First, you SET SHOWPLAN_XML ON. Then, the estimated metrics as you run your queries will be contained in a set of XML documents. The document schema that SHOWPLAN_XML uses is a component of your installation of SQL Server 2005 in the folder \Microsoft SQL Server\90\Tools\Binn\schemas\sqlserver\2004\07\showplan\ with filename showplanxml.xsd. The XSD defines the Showplan XML document in terms of the elements and attributes that appear within the document and their relationship to one another.

Did you ever wonder where you can find all SQL Server XML Schemas defined? They are all located at http://schemas.microsoft.com/sqlserver/.

Exercise 3.1 shows how to use SHOWPLAN_XML to view the query plan of query 1.

EXERCISE 3.1

Using SHOWPLAN_XML to View the Query Plan of Query 1 and Query 2

In this exercise, you'll use SHOWPLAN_XML to view the query plan of query 1. It is especially important that you execute each step as a separate batch. The following are the steps for using SSMS (SQL Server Management Studio); basically, you should highlight and run each piece of code between the comment steps and the GO. (You will notice we also commented these steps within the code.)

1. Open a new query window in the SSMS query editor. To see the most from your XML output you should set your Query Results drop-down window to Results to Grid. Set the database to AdventureWorks.

2. Use the SET statement to implement the SHOWPLAN_XML tool.

3. Execute query 1 using ManagerID = 185. Click to show the XML editor to view the XML output and notice the ParameterCompiledValue used for ManagerID is still cached at 185.

4. Execute query 2 using ManagerID = 3. Click to show the XML editor to view the XML output and notice the ParameterCompiledValue used for ManagerID is 185. The plan from query 1 has been reused.

5. Remove the SHOWPLAN_XML tool.

```
--1. Start the exercise using AdventureWorks Database

SET NOCOUNT ON

USE AdventureWorks;

GO



--2. Implement the SHOWPLAN_XML tool

SET SHOWPLAN_XML ON;

GO



-- 3. Execute query 1 and notice in the Showplan.xml

-- the ParameterCompiledValue

-- used for ManagerID is 185

SELECT EmployeeID

FROM AdventureWorks.HumanResources.Employee
```

```
WHERE ManagerID = 185;

GO



-- 4. Execute query 2 and notice in the Showplan.xml

-- the ParameterCompiledValue

-- used for ManagerID is still cached at 185

SELECT EmployeeID

FROM AdventureWorks.HumanResources.Employee

WHERE ManagerID = 3;

GO



--5. Remove the SHOWPLAN_XML tool

SET SHOWPLAN_XML OFF;

GO
```

Outputting your query plans in an XML format allows for a wide range of flexibility. One obvious caveat is that you are able to view the Showplan output on any computer, with or without SQL Server installed! If you take time to analyze the description document, you will further notice metrics that are not available in any other Showplan tools. As you become more familiar with processing XML using some of the tools in our next section, such as XPath or XQuery, you may want to revisit SHOWPLAN_XML. However, until that time, we have one last SHOWPLAN feature we want you to learn.

Saving the *SHOWPLAN_XML PLAN*

To save and view the output as XML, you need only open the XML editor and, once the editor is open, right-click and save the file as type .xml.

However, you are also able to save the output file as an XML Showplan for later viewing. To do so, follow these steps:

1. In the Results pane of the XML Showplan, right-click in the white space.

2. In the drop-down menu that appears, choose Save Results As.

3. In the Save Grid Results window, move to the appropriate folder, and in the Save As Type window change to All files (*.*), naming the file with appropriate name and ending with .sqlplan as the extension.

You are now able to capture estimated execution plans. We could continue on with so much more—the actual plans or using SSMS tools—but the waters are heating up so we must keep talking about those things you need to know to pass the SQL Server test!

Improving Query Performance

Thus far you have learned how to write queries to promote plan reuse. However, it is not surprising that some of your queries are going to consume more resources than others. Suppose you have some queries that return large result sets. Suppose also you have a set of queries that contain nonunique WHERE clauses and at the same time are very resource intensive. You need to remember that query optimization is bounded by reality. There is no query optimization wizard behind the black curtain. However, if you are able to program a less complicated set of constructs, it could eliminate the resource cost that the query optimizer is unable to eliminate.

You can use a few techniques that may improve your query performance. If your queries are complex and several of them process slowly, you might try adding more memory to the solution. If you have more than one processor available, you might try using additional processors to allow the database engine to make use of parallel query processing. Finally some considerations follow that you might use in rewriting your queries.

Modifying Queries to Improve Performance

Here are some factors you should consider to improve the performance of your queries:

- If your query uses cursors, decide whether the cursor being used is the most efficient type or whether a cursor is the most efficient means to manage the data processing. Often a query can be written using a more efficient cursor type, such as fast-forward-only cursor, or without a cursor operation, such as using a single query that usually performs better than cursor operations in general.

- If your application code itself contains a loop structure, you might build the loop structure within the query itself to enhance plan reuse, minimize round-trips between client and server, and optimize index usage—all of which will improve the performance of the query.

- Allow the query optimizer to do its job. If you are using queries with hints from previous versions of SQL Server, remove the hints and run the queries letting the optimizer choose the execution plan. View the query plan objects with and without the query hints.

- Set the *query governor* configuration option to limit the resources that your queries use. The query governor option is not set by default, so there is nothing to control long-running queries from using a large amount of system resources until they run to completion. You can set the query governor option at the server level either through the Transact-SQL statement:

```
sp_configure 'query governor cost limit', 'value'
```

where value is in seconds from 0 to 2,147,483,647 with 0 meaning no time limitation. Changing the query governor cost limit is an sp_configure advanced option.

The other way to change the query governor configuration server wide is through the SSMS interface on the Connections page under server properties. Check the use query governor check box, and fill in appropriate value. Figure 3.1 shows this change in SSMS.

You are also able to set the query governor for just a specific connection. To do so, you use the SET QUERY_GOVERNOR_COST_LIMIT Transact-SQL statement, stating a specific value in seconds you want for the particular connection. This statement, processed at the connection level, overrides the value set at the server level for the duration of the connection.

- Take heed and write your queries for plan reuse.

 You will find even more information on modifying queries to optimize performance in Chapter 7 of this book.

FIGURE 3.1   Configuring the query governor server wide in SSMS

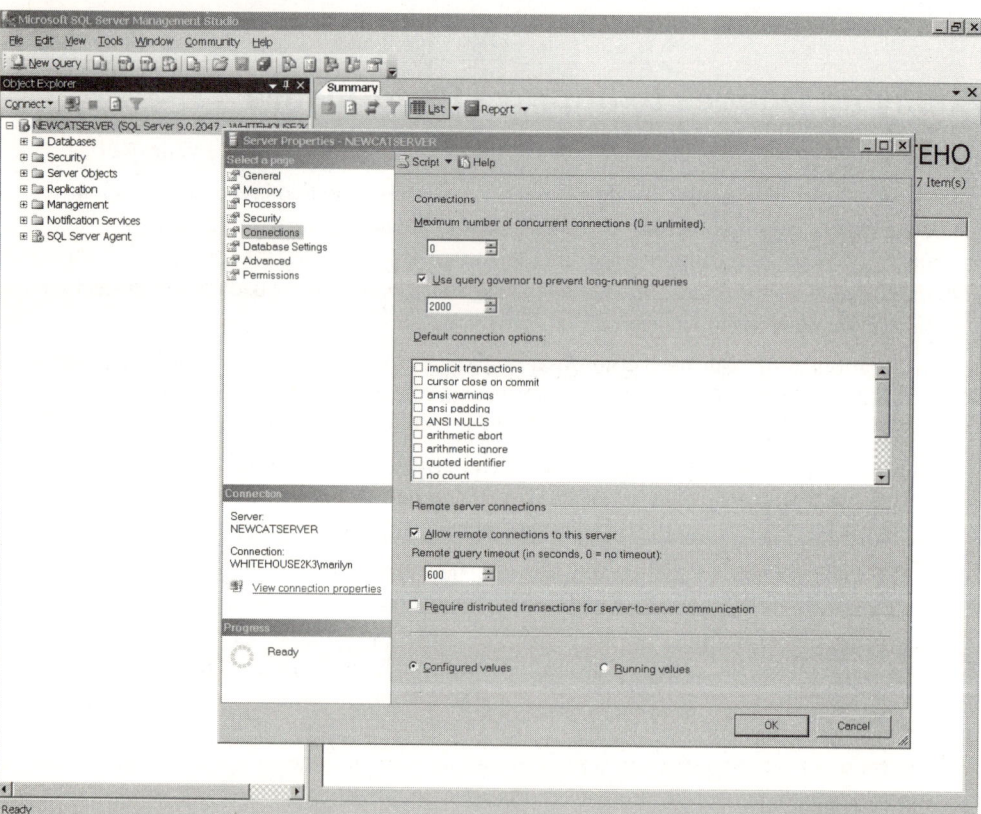

Understanding the Sea Is Full of XML

We began this chapter talking about change and quoting Lewis Carroll. You have already seen many changes within the newly designed database engine. However, change still unfolds before you. We'll start the second section of this chapter by quoting Microsoft, or at least a direct quote from Books OnLine search topic "Using XML in SQL Server" that moves you into a realm we touched on only briefly in our discussion of the Showplan tool. Here is the quote: "Support for XML is integrated into all the components in SQL Server."

You must feel comfortable with XML data. You need to understand how to retrieve XML data from the client and convert it to relational data when stored in your database. You must know how to use the Transact-SQL OPENXML function for this purpose. Likewise, you must be able to extract XML and store the XML as a data type within your database, querying the XML appropriately. You must know how to store the data as native XML and extract data from the XML using XQuery data retrieval methods. A final component of XML that you must understand is to retrieve relational data from the database and return it to the client application as XML. You use the Transact-SQL FOR XML function to return XML to the client application.

You have many choices now on how to manage XML data along with unprecedented support in SQL Server. There are merits to choosing to keep your data in relational form as well as storing it as untyped or typed XML. At the time of this writing, many articles on using XML in SQL Server 2005 are already in print from users with a variety of field experiences. It is important that you understand how to write and optimize queries containing XML. The sea has changed.

Designing Queries Using XQuery

What is XQuery? XQuery is the query language of XML. To draw a parallel, XQuery is to XML as SQL is to databases. This language is defined by the W3C and is currently supported by all major players in the database industry. At the time of SQL Server 2005 rollout, XQuery, supported and compatible with other W3C standards such as XPath, XLST, XML Schema, Namespaces, and XML, was aligned with the July 2004 working draft. More information on XQuery can be found at the W3C website: `http://www.w3.org/TR/xquery/`.

Understanding XQuery Syntax

Whenever you learn a language you must learn the syntax of that language. As in most programming languages, XQuery is built on simple expressions, operators, and constructs. Once the initial syntax is defined, you must build your queries with iterative statements, conditionals, quantifiers, sequence types, and parameters. Build all the pieces correctly and you have yourself an XML query.

Here are some basic rules of *XQuery syntax*:

- XQuery is case sensitive.
- XQuery uses only valid XML names for its elements, attributes, and variables.

- XQuery delimits comments by using a colon at either end of the comment. For example:

  `: This is an XQuery comment :`

- XQuery places strings values in either single or double quotes.

Understanding Simple XQuery Expressions

Here are some other simple expressions you will meet in XQuery along with a short definition and example for each:

Literal   A literal is a numerical or string value that must be enclosed in quotes. This is an example:

`currentmonth="February"`

Entity references can also be used to represent Unicode characters that could cause an error because of its placement. For example, since the angle bracket (<) symbol is used in XML and < is also used to mean "is less than," using < in certain situations could cause an error, therefore you need to use the entity reference < for <.

Here is a list of some entity references you will find useful:

<   represents <

>   represents >

&   represents &

"   represents "

'   represents '

Variable   A variable is a reference to a value in memory. XQuery denotes a variable by placing a dollar sign ($) prior to the identifier. This is an example:

`$MyManage`

Context item/expression   Context can be an item, node, or expression. The important concept to remember is that context is "where you are at the present time." This becomes your point of reference for parents, children, ancestors, siblings, and so on.

Path expressions   XQuery uses XPath expressions when selecting nodes within the XML document. Paths that begin with a slash (/) are absolute; that is, they describe the location of the node by stating the complete traversal of the XML tree from the root element. If the path does not begin with a slash, it is relative or described relative to a node that has been previously identified. You need to recognize the expression symbol and how it is implemented. We will list some of the path expressions you will find most valuable in your queries.

nodename	This expression selects all the children of the stated node. For example, OrderList selects all the child nodes of the OrderList element.
/OrderList	This expression selects the root element Orderlist.
/Orderlist/Order	This expression selects all the Order elements that are children of the Orderlist element
(/OrderList/Order/)[1]	This expression selects the first Order element that is the child of the OrderList element.
(/OrderList/Order/@OrderNo)[1]	This expression selects the InvoiceNo attribute of the first Order element that is the child of the OrderList element
(/OrderList/Order/)[last()]	This expression selects the last order element that is the child of the OrderList element.
/OrderList/Order/[@OrderNo=100]	This expression selects all the Order elements that are children of the Orderlist element, which have an OrderNo of 100.

Functions   You call XQuery functions to assess or manipulate data. Over 100 built-in XQuery functions are defined for string and numeric values, date and time comparisons, string and sequence manipulation, and so on. You can also create your own functions either with a query or in a separate library using a declare function statement.

You can find the latest XPath function and operator specifications from W3C at http://www.w3.org/2006/xpath-functions.

Operators   The XQuery operators fall into three categories: comparison, arithmetic, and logical. The XQuery comparison operators include the following:

=	Is equal to
!=	Is not equal to
<	Is less than
>	Is greater than
<=	Is less than or equal to
>=	Is greater than or equal to

The XQuery arithmetic operators include the following:

+   Addition

-          Subtraction

*   Multiplication

div   Division

mod   Modulus (remainder on division)

The XQuery logical operators include the following:

and   Logical conjunction, true if and only if both operands are true.

or   Logical disjunction, false if both operands are false, otherwise true.

FLWOR   You will find the FLWOR XQuery expression especially useful as you develop queries in the XML environment. You declare a FLWOR expression to iterate and filter logic that could otherwise be quite complex.

The following statements define the FLWOR clause elements:

FOR   Use one or more FOR statements in an XQuery to bind a variable to a node or nodes sequence that is iterated through to process a result set.

LET   The LET statement is the only FLWOR statement not supported in SQL Server 2005. In XQuery it is used to define a single value or match an expression in a node.

WHERE   Use the optional WHERE statement to refine or filter the sequences of your query.

ORDER BY   Use the optional ORDER BY statement to process the sorting of your result set to a defined order.

RETURN   Use the RETURN statement to process the results captured through a string value that have been extracted through the nodes iterations in the FLWOR statements. What you put in the return statement determines what you get back from the query.

Comparing FLWOR and Transact-SQL

We've talked enough. The time has come to put some of this talk into action. Exercise 3.2 shows you how to query data using FLWOR statements.

Understanding the Prolog and Body in XQuery Expressions

An XQuery expression has two parts, a prolog and a body. A prolog is a namespace declaration that provides a defined environment in an XML format. You are then able to reference the defined namespace as a prefix throughout the second part of the XQuery expression, the body. This makes for a much tighter bonding of XML namspaces or schemas and your database objects.

EXERCISE 3.2

Querying Data Using FLWOR Statements

In this exercise, you'll use SQL Server Management Studio's Query Editor to write and execute a query containing XML data.

1. Write the following query using FLWOR statements to extract data from an XML document containing data of three of our most loyal employees. Then execute the query.

```
declare @emp xml;

set @emp = '<Employees>
        <Employee id="10">
            <Name>
                <FirstName>Tweedle</FirstName>
                <LastName>Dum</LastName>
            </Name>
            <Age>52</Age>
        </Employee>
        <Employee id="20">
            <Name>
                <FirstName>Tweedle</FirstName>
                <LastName>Dee</LastName>
            </Name>
            <Age>37</Age>
        </Employee>
        <Employee id="30">
            <Name>
                <FirstName>Miss</FirstName>
                <LastName>Alice</LastName>
            </Name>
            <Age>24</Age>
        </Employee>
```

```
          </Employees>';

select @emp.query('for $e in /Employees/Employee

          where $e/Age > 35

          return $e/Name');
```

Let's first examine the FLWOR statements you have used in the query:

First, you used the **for** clause to connect the sequence you input with the $e variable.

Second, you iterated through the XPath nodes of "/Employees/Employee" using the **for** clause.

Third, you filtered the sequence against the $e variable using a value > 35 with the **where** clause.

Finally, the result is returned to the client using the **return** clause.

Now, let's compare the FLWOR clauses with Transact-SQL:

The **for** FLWOR clause compares to the FROM statement in SQL.

The **return** FLWOR clause is much like the SQL SELECT statement.

Finally, a **where** is a WHERE. What more can I say?

2. You can change the query to further filter the result by returning just the first name or even just the text of the first name. However, the change we would like you to make is one that constructs the query output to generate the FirstName attribute within the Name element. Replace the select @emp.query in the code above as follows and execute the query:

```
select @emp.query('for $e in /Employees/Employee

          where $e/Age > 35

          return

              <Employee>

                  {$e/Name/FirstName/text()}

              </Employee>');
```

Your output will look like the following:

```
<Employee>Tweedle</Employee>

<Employee>Tweedle</Employee>
```

One more time...because this is important! You can find all SQL Server XML Schemas defined at `http://schemas.microsoft.com/sqlserver/`.

As an example, let's use the StoreSurvey XML Schema or namespace. This namespace is defined as:

```
http://schemas.microsoft.com/sqlserver/2004/07/
➥adventure-works/StoreSurvey
```

In Exercise 3.3, you will write a query using the StoreSurvey XML namespace, Schema Collection, in the AdventureWorks database.

EXERCISE 3.3

Querying XML Database Data in an XML Schema

In this exercise, you will find the average quarterly sales of Exotic Bikes, one of your favorite customers. Again, this exercise shows how to do this in the Query Editor of SQL Server Management Studio. A word of caution: if you have not been trapped already, remember that XQuery is case sensitive. Be especially careful as you create your own queries to use the same case as that contained within the XML description.

1. Write the following query in the Query Editor. Be especially careful to place the entire StoreSurvery XML namespace on one line using the correct spacing and case sensitivity. Execute the query.

```
Use AdventureWorks

Go

select Demographics.query ('declare namespace

  ss="http://schemas.microsoft.com/sqlserver/2004/07/

➥adventure-works/StoreSurvey";

  for $yrsales in /ss:StoreSurvey

  return

  <StoreDetails

      AverageQuarterlySales = "{$yrsales/ss:AnnualSales div 4}">

  </StoreDetails>

') as result

FROM sales.store
```

```
WHERE customerid = 36 --Exotic Bikes
```

2. View the output. The results of the previous code returns the following:

```
<StoreDetails AverageQuarterlySales="750000" />
```

Using XQuery with the XML Data Type in SQL Server 2005

We mentioned that the XQuery specification is still evolving. However, since Microsoft has taken the stand to support XQuery directly in SQL Server, it also decided to align that support with the July 2004 version of the XQuery specification, which presents a stable platform.

So far you have seen how the XQuery language can be used to produce a result set from both an XML document and an XML column in your SQL server. Next you will look more specifically at the XML data type and how its data is manipulated by XQuery and XML Data Modification Language (DML).

XQuery Methods for Extracting Data from an XML Type Data or Column

The SQL Server 2005 XML data type provides four methods for querying XML data. You will need to understand each of these methods to be able to use them appropriately in your applications as you process data from native XML. Actually, you have been using one of them already!

The Query() method The query() method extracts the sections of an XML instance from an XML data type, column, or parameter. This is the method you have been using to extract data from the XML data type in the Exercises 3.2 and 3.3 above.

The Value() method The value() method is particularly useful when you want to extract node values of an XML instance from an XML data type, column, or parameter. Once you have extracted the values, you can execute calculations and comparisons with other data either within XML or with other non-XML data.

We'll do another exercise with the StoreSurvey defined namespace or Schema Collection to show you how this works. This time you will use the value method to extract the NumberEmployees element and the AnnualSales element. You will do a calculation as before; however, this time you will return a value.

Once again, use the Query Editor of SSMS to create and execute the query, as shown in Exercise 3.4.

The Exist() method The exist() method allows you to determine whether or not an XML fragment you are searching for exists in a particular XML instance. The method returns a 1 if the fragment is matched, a 0 otherwise. Exercise 3.5 and its steps will show you how the exist() method is used.

Using the exist() method is actually the most efficient means of writing a query of this nature. This type of query seeks a match and the desired result set is the enumeration of the matches—or nonmatches for that matter. As a developer you should recognize the most efficient query for this type of result set is a Boolean matching to True or False—you've got it—the exist()! We will illustrate this style of evaluating the Boolean method in our example in Exercise 3.5.

The Nodes() method   You use the nodes() method to return a relational view of your XML data. The nodes() method allows you to determine which nodes you will define into the new rational data set structure. You can use the nodes() method with the Transact-SQL APPLY operator to easily return your XML data into a relational table format.

EXERCISE 3.4

Querying XML Database Data Using the Value() Method

In this exercise, you'll use the value() method to find an employee's average quarterly sales at Exotic Bikes.

1. Open a new Query Editor window in SSMS. Write the following query using the Adventure-Works database. Be careful once again to place the StoreSurvey XML namespace on one line using the correct spacing and case sensitivity as noted in our code. Execute the query:

```
Use AdventureWorks

Go

SELECT Name, Demographics.value

('declare namespace ss=

"http://schemas.microsoft.com/sqlserver/2004/07/

➥adventure-works/StoreSurvey";

(/ss:StoreSurvey/ss:AnnualSales)[1] div

(4*(/ss:StoreSurvey/ss:NumberEmployees)[1])',

'numeric(11,2)') AS AverageEmployeeQuarterlySales

FROM Sales.Store

WHERE CustomerID = 36; --Exotic Bikes again!
```

2. The output is, as the name implies, a value. View your output, listed to text, as follows:

```
Name                        AvrageEmployeeQuarterlySales

------------------------    -----------------------------------

Exotic Bikes                10273.97


(1 row(s) affected)
```

Querying XML Database Data Using the Exist() Method

In this exercise, you'll use the exist() method to find all stores specializing in mountain bikes. Follow these steps:

1. Open a new Query Editor window in SSMS. Write the following query using the AdventureWorks database. Be careful once again to place the StoreSurvey XML namespace on one line using the correct spacing and case sensitivity as noted in our code. Then execute the query.

   Use AdventureWorks

   Go

   SELECT CustomerID, Name

   FROM Sales.Store

   WHERE Demographics.exist

   ('declare namespace ss=

   "http://schemas.microsoft.com/sqlserver/2004/07/

   ➥adventure-works/StoreSurvey";

   /ss:StoreSurvey/ss:Specialty[.="Mountain"]')=1

   ORDER BY CustomerID

   We'll explain some of the sections of this code:

   The exists () method is called in the WHERE clause for the Demographics XML column of the Sales.Store table.

   The existence of "Mountain" being an attribute of the Specialty element in the Schema defined column is checked for all CustomerIDs.

   The output is ordered by CustomerID.

2. View your output. Your partial output, listed as text, appears as follows:

   ```
   CustomerID  Name

   ----------- --------------------------------------------------

   2           Progressive Sports

   7           Associated Bikes

   9           Tandem Bicycle Store

   10          Rural Cycle Emporium
   ```

EXERCISE 3.5 *(continued)*

11	Sharp Bikes
14	Bicycle Warehouse Inc.
15	Budget Toy Store
17	Trusted Catalog Store
18	Catalog Store
20	Central Discount Store
21	Chic Department Stores
23	Bike World
25	Coalition Bike Company
27	Sports Sales and Rental
29	Cross-Country Riding Supplies
33	Global Sports Outlet

...

(246 row(s) affected)

Methods for Converting XML Data into Rowset Data

The nodes() method will be most useful to you as a means of converting existing XML documents into your relational data store. Previously you had only the OPENXML option available for this purpose.

Now, actually, you have three methods to convert XML into rowset data:

- Use the nodes() method.
- Use OPENXML.
- Create a user-defined function to convert the logic.

Follow these steps to use the nodes() method to convert XML data into rowset data:

- You use the nodes() method within the FROM clause of your SELECT statement. The FROM clause will include your result set. The result set will be designated with unnamed table and column names (AS nTable(nCol)).
- You use the value() method within your SELECT clause to expose the elements and attributes you want to filter into your table.
- You use the CROSS APPLY to read through all the rows of data, extracting the indicated node values and applying them into the unnamed table.

To set the stage for Exercise 3.6 and the remainder of the exercises in this chapter (Exercises 3.7–3.11), you will need to create a new table in your AdventureWorks database and fill it with some data.

We hope you are not too weary for a little more bike riding. For this set of exercises you will use an XML namespace (xmlns), StoreInvoices, directly defined within the XML itself.

EXERCISE 3.6

Querying XML Database Data Using the Nodes() Method

In this exercise, you'll use the Nodes() method to extract bike store invoicing data into relational form.

1. Create the SomeBikeStores table in AdventureWorks dbo Schema containing an XML data column StoreInvoices:

```
USE AdventureWorks

GO


-- Create table SomeBikeStores that includes an XML data column

CREATE TABLE SomeBikeStores

(StoreID integer IDENTITY PRIMARY KEY,

 BikeStoreName nvarchar(40),

 ManagerName nvarchar(40),

 StoreInvoices xml)
```

2. Insert values into the table SomeBikeStores:

```
INSERT INTO SomeBikeStores

VALUES

('Best Buys in Bikes', 'Justin Tallon',

'<InvoiceList xmlns="http://schemas.adventure-works.com/StoreInvoices">

        <Invoice InvoiceNo="500">

          <Customer>Maddox Pace</Customer>

            <Items>

                <Item ProductID="8" Price="2.99" Quantity="10"/>

            </Items>
```

```
          </Invoice>

          <Invoice InvoiceNo="501">

              <Customer>Eleanor Miller</Customer>

                  <Items>

                      <Item ProductID="2" Price="10.59" Quantity="2"/>

                      <Item ProductID="8" Price="2.99" Quantity="15"/>

                  </Items>

          </Invoice>

     </InvoiceList>')


INSERT INTO SomeBikeStores

VALUES

('Slow Sales Bikes', 'Bad Manager', NULL)


INSERT INTO SomeBikeStores

VALUES

('No Hills Mountain Biking', 'James Knarr',

 '<InvoiceList xmlns="http://

➥schemas.adventure-works.com/StoreInvoices">

          <Invoice InvoiceNo="999">

              <Customer>Mary Fehler</Customer>

                  <Items>

                      <Item ProductID="1" Price="159.99" Quantity="1"/>

                      <Item ProductID="3" Price="2.99" Quantity="10"/>

                      <Item ProductID="8" Price="2.99" Quantity="3"/>

                  </Items>

          </Invoice>
```

```
   </InvoiceList>')


INSERT INTO SomeBikeStores

VALUES

('Euro Biking', 'Cristian Lefter',

 '<InvoiceList xmlns="http://

➡schemas.adventure-works.com/StoreInvoices">

        <Invoice InvoiceNo="1001">

          <Customer>Randy Bynon</Customer>

            <Items>

                <Item ProductID="1" Price="159.99" Quantity="10"/>

                <Item ProductID="2" Price="10.59" Quantity="4"/>

                <Item ProductID="8" Price="2.99" Quantity="2"/>

            </Items>

        </Invoice>

   </InvoiceList>')
```

3. Using the nodes() method described previously with the CROSS APPLY operator, convert the filtered data into rowset data:

```
SELECT nCol.value('../../@InvoiceNo[1]', 'int') InvoiceNumber,

      nCol.value('@ProductID[1]', 'int') ProductID,

      nCol.value('@Price[1]', 'money') Price,

      nCol.value('@Quantity[1]', 'int') Quantity

FROM SomeBikeStores CROSS APPLY

   StoreInvoices.nodes('declare default element namespace "http://

➡schemas.adventure-works.com/StoreInvoices";

➡/InvoiceList/Invoice/Items/Item') AS nTable(nCol)

ORDER BY InvoiceNumber
```

4. View your output listed as text, as follows:

InvoiceNumber	ProductID	Price	Quantity
500	8	2.99	10
501	2	10.59	2
501	8	2.99	15
999	1	159.99	1
999	3	2.99	10
999	8	2.99	3
1001	1	159.99	10
1001	2	10.59	4
1001	8	2.99	2

(9 row(s) affected)

You will notice that using the nodes() method has eliminated the need to call the sp_xml_preparedocument stored procedure that is necessary with the OPENXML option. Therefore, when extracting relational data from an XML data type, the nodes() method is less memory intensive than the OPENXML. However, if this is a process you might be repeating often, you might consider creating a user-defined function.

However, it is time to change the waters. You will next look at how XML DML handles the XQuery limitation of being unable to modify XML documents.

Using XML Data Modification Language

Since so much of our time in OLTP databases is spent in modifying data, Microsoft realized a vital need for you to be able to modify XML data within your database. Therefore, they created the XML Data Modification Language (DML) to handle the tasks of inserting, updating, and deleting data within the XML data type. This language is built around and fully embraces the XQuery language. To modify or update an XML instance you use the modify() method and specify the appropriate keyword within the method statement.

We'll go through each of the three keywords and show you how you can use them to build your queries. You will use the SomeBikeStores table with the data you inserted in the previous exercise.

Be aware, the keywords insert, delete, and replace value of in XML DML are case sensitive!

The *insert* Keyword

You are able to insert one or more nodes into an existing XML document using the insert keyword. The following is the syntax for the insert keyword:

```
insert
     Expression1 (
               {as first | as last} into | after | before
                                 Expression2
               )
```

The following is the explanation of the syntax:

- Expression1 stands for the node or nodes to insert.

- The into keyword indicates that the nodes of Expression1 are inserted into Expression2 as child nodes, unless Expression2 already has child nodes, then you must also include it as first or as last to reference placement.

- The before and after keywords are used to determine where to place Expression1 with regard to Expression2; is the placement of Expression1 to come before or after any existing nodes in Expression2?

Ready for an exercise? In Exercise 3.7, you'll modify XML database data using the insert keyword in your query. Specifically, you'll insert a local contact node into the StoreInvoices XML document.

EXERCISE 3.7

Modifying XML Database Data Using the *insert* Keyword

In this exercise, Best Buys in Bikes has a local contact they want to add to their store invoices data. You'll write the query to manage the insert using the SomeBikesStores table and data created previously in Exercise 3.6.

1. Open a new Query Editor window in SSMS. Use the AdventureWorks database with the SomeBikesStores table you created in the previous exercise.

2. Use the modify method with the insert keyword to add a new LocalContact node as the first child node of the Invoice for StoreID 1.

3. Execute a SELECT statement, code is below, to view the insert.

    ```
    -- Use the modify method with the insert keyword
    ```

```
-- A new LocalContact node will be added as the first child node

-- The update will be done for StoreID 1

UPDATE SomeBikeStores

SET StoreInvoices.modify('declare default element namespace "http://

➥schemas.adventure-works.com/StoreInvoices";

  insert element LocalContact {"Molly Contact"}

  as first

  into (/InvoiceList/Invoice)[1]')

WHERE StoreID = 1


-- Run the SELECT statement to view the insert

SELECT StoreInvoices.query('declare default element namespace

 "http://schemas.adventure-works.com/StoreInvoices";

   (InvoiceList/Invoice)[1]') InsertedLocalContact

FROM SomeBikeStores

WHERE StoreID = 1
```

4. View your output as follows. For this output, we have once again used the Results to Grid. You must click to show the output in the XML editor.

```
<Invoice xmlns="http://schemas.adventure-works.com/StoreInvoices"

➥InvoiceNo="500">

  <LocalContact>Molly Contact</LocalContact>

  <Customer>Maddox Pace</Customer>

  <Items>

    <Item ProductID="8" Price="2.99" Quantity="10" />

  </Items>

</Invoice>
```

The *replace value of* Keyword

The replace value of keyword allows you to update the value of a node in place. The syntax is as follows:

```
replace value of
      Expression1
with
      Expression2
```

Expression1 and Expression2 are single nodes of a single element. In Exercise 3.8, you will replace *Molly* with *Sara*.

EXERCISE 3.8

Modifying XML Database Data Using the *replace value of* Keyword

In this exercise, you'll replace the local contact node in the StoreInvoices XML document.

1. Open a new Query Editor window in SSMS. Use the AdventureWorks database with the SomeBikesStores table you created previously.

2. Use the modify method with the replace value of keyword to update the LocalContact node text() for StoreID 1.

3. Execute a SELECT statement, code is below, to view the update.

```
-- Use the modify method with the replace value of keyword

-- The value of the local contact text()is replaced

-- The update will be done for StoreID 1

UPDATE SomeBikeStores

SET StoreInvoices.modify('declare default element namespace

  "http://schemas.adventure-works.com/StoreInvoices";

   replace value of (/InvoiceList/Invoice/LocalContact/text())[1]

   with "Sara Contact"')

WHERE StoreID = 1


-- Run the SELECT statement to view the update

SELECT StoreInvoices.query('declare default element namespace
```

```
    "http://schemas.adventure-works.com/StoreInvoices";

      (InvoiceList/Invoice)[1]') UpdatedSalesPerson

    FROM SomeBikeStores

    WHERE StoreID = 1
```

4. View your output as follows using the Results to Grid and XML editor:

```
    <Invoice xmlns="http://schemas.adventure-works.com/StoreInvoices"
    ➥InvoiceNo="500">

      <LocalContact>Sara Contact</LocalContact>

      <Customer>Maddox Pace</Customer>

      <Items>

        <Item ProductID="8" Price="2.99" Quantity="10" />

      </Items>

    </Invoice>
```

The *delete* Keyword

The delete keyword allows you to delete the nodes and all there unto appertaining from the XML instance. The syntax is as follows:

```
delete Expression
```

In Exercise 3.9, you'll will delete the local contact node.

Modifying XML Database Data Using the *delete* Keyword

In this exercise, you'll delete the local contact node in the StoreInvoices XML document.

1. Open a new Query Editor window in SSMS. Use the AdventureWorks database with the SomeBikesStores table you created previously.

2. Use the modify method with the delete keyword to delete the LocalContact node for StoreID 1.

3. Execute a SELECT statement, code is below, to view whether the LocalContact has been deleted.

```
-- Use the modify method with the delete keyword

-- The local contact is deleted

-- The update will be done for StoreID 1

UPDATE SomeBikeStores

SET StoreInvoices.modify('declare default element namespace

"http://schemas.adventure-works.com/StoreInvoices";

   delete (/InvoiceList/Invoice/LocalContact)[1]')

WHERE StoreID = 1


-- Run the SELECT statement to view the delete

SELECT StoreInvoices.query('declare default element namespace

 "http://schemas.adventure-works.com/StoreInvoices";

   (InvoiceList/Invoice)[1]') DeletedLocalContact

FROM SomeBikeStores

WHERE StoreID = 1
```

4. View your output as follows using the Results to Grid and XML editor:

```
<Invoice xmlns="http://schemas.adventure-works.com/StoreInvoices"
➥InvoiceNo="500">

  <Customer>Maddox Pace</Customer>

  <Items>

    <Item ProductID="8" Price="2.99" Quantity="10" />

  </Items>

</Invoice>
```

Binding and Parameterizing XML Queries with Relational Data

You have learned how you can use your XML queries to modify your XML data. However, sometimes you may want to just include some relational data in the XML in your query without modifying the XML content. This process is termed *binding the data*. Two functions support relational data binding: the sql:column() function and the sql:variable() function.

Using the *sql:column()* Function to Add Relational Data to Your Queries

The reference to the non-XML column specified in the argument of the sql:column() function refers to a column in the currently processed row of data. We need to put our helmets back on and pedal back to our Exotic Bikes store. So for the following two exercises we are going to return to the Sales.Store table in the AdventureWorks database we used in our earlier exercises.

In Exercise 3.10, you will add the Name and SalesPersonID row data columns to the demographics XML data column query for CustomerID 36 in the Sales.Store table.

EXERCISE 3.10

Adding Relational Data to an XML Query Using the sql:column() Function

In this exercise, you'll use the sql:column() function to insert row data into the XML query.

1. Open a new Query Editor window in SSMS.

2. Write the following query using the AdventureWorks database. Be careful once again to place the StoreSurvey XML namespace on one line using the correct spacing and case sensitivity as noted in our code. Execute the query:

```
Use AdventureWorks

Go


SELECT Name, Demographics.query

('declare namespace ss="http://schemas.microsoft.com/sqlserver/2004/07/

➥adventure-works/StoreSurvey";

<Store

  StoreName="{sql:column("Name")}"

  SalesPerson="{sql:column("SalesPersonID")}"

  BusinessType="{/ss:StoreSurvey/ss:BusinessType}"
```

```
AnnualSales="{/ss:StoreSurvey/ss:AnnualSales}">
</Store>') AS StoreSales
FROM Sales.Store
WHERE CustomerID = 36;
```

Let us take a minute to review some of the code:

StoreName and SalesPerson data are column data from the relational values of the row.

3. View your output as follows, using the Results to Grid and XML editor:

```
<Store StoreName="Exotic Bikes" SalesPerson="275" BusinessType="OS"
➥AnnualSales="3000000" />
```

We will next take the concept of adding relational data to your XML query one step further, so keep pedaling just a while longer.

Using the *sql:variable()* Function to Parameterize Your Queries

Suppose you want to define a reference variable to use as a parameter in your XML query. Since data in the variable will have a SQL data type, it can be defined outside your query as a local variable and then input into the query using a SET statement or, if the query is in the form of a stored procedure or function, an input parameter.

The sql:variable() function is used much like the sql:column() function. However, unlike the sql:column() function, the value used in the sql:variable() function will remain consistent for the entire execution of the query. In Exercise 3.11, you'll use the sql:variable() function to add a parameter to an XML query.

Adding a Parameter to an XML Query Using the *sql:variable()* Function

In this exercise, you'll use the sql:variable() function to add a parameter to the XML query.

1. Open a new Query Editor window in SSMS.

2. Write the following query using the AdventureWorks database. Be careful once again to place the StoreSurvey XML namespace on one line using the correct spacing and case sensitivity as noted in our code. Execute the query:

```
Use AdventureWorks
GO
```

```
DECLARE @salesgoal MONEY

SET @salesgoal = 500000

SELECT Name, Demographics.query

('declare namespace ss="http://schemas.microsoft.com/sqlserver/2004/07/

➥adventure-works/StoreSurvey";

<Store

   StoreName="{sql:column("Name")}"

   SalesPerson="{sql:column("SalesPersonID")}"

   AnnualSales="{/ss:StoreSurvey/ss:AnnualSales}"

   AnnualSalesGoal="{sql:variable("@salesgoal")}">

</Store>') AS StoreSales

FROM Sales.Store

WHERE CustomerID = 36;
```

Now we'll take the time again to review some of the code:

StoreName and SalesPerson data are column data from the relational values of the row.

AnnualSalesGoal is the value bound by the sql:variable() method.

3. View your output as follows, using the Results to Grid and XML editor:

```
<Store StoreName="Exotic Bikes" SalesPerson="275"

➥AnnualSales="3000000" AnnualSalesGoal="500000" />
```

Guidelines for Processing XML Queries

You have applied several strategies for querying data in both relational and XML formats. As you continue with your study of data access and query techniques in SQL Server 2005, you will continually need to analyze the requirements of your own environment with regards to the following considerations.

You need to determine whether the platform independence of XML is a necessary requirement for your situation.

If the initial format of the data is XML, you need to determine whether the data should continue to be stored in this format or whether it needs to be converted to relational data for further use in applications within the application or organization. If the data is to be converted, you further need to determine where best to handle the conversion. You must consider such factors as network load and round-trips versus converting the data to relational data at the client and sending it as a single parsed data stream.

If the data is stored as XML you need to determine whether your solution performs better with typed or untyped XML. If you want to optimize both storage and query utilization, then you should create a schema for your XML (typed) and validate the XML against the schema.

If the data is stored as XML, you need to be aware of the limitations of the XML data type that its corresponding relational SQL data types would not have.

In the processing of your XML queries, more guidelines follow, some of which we mentioned earlier in this chapter:

- When checking for existence, use the exist() method rather than the value() method. The exist() method will give you better performance and it makes use of XML indexes.

- Create typed XML to use the query optimizer.

- Eliminate the nodes() method when used with the value() method to extract single value if the node itself is a singleton. Using this reference you do not need to use CROSS APPLY, you need only to reference the context node, such as in the following partial code:

  ```
  SELECT ncol.value('@isbn',(/trainbook/@isbn)[1]',...
  ```

- Use sql:column() or sql:variable() to supply parameters to XQuery and your XML DML queries or stored procedures.

- If you use range conditions in your XML queries, their performance can benefit from typed XML with indexes on range values.

- Validate any variables you are passing into dynamic queries such as when you use sp_executesql to avoid any possibility of SQL injection attacks.

Summary

In this chapter you have learned the process that SQL Server 2005 uses to optimize and create a plan for executing your queries and batches. You have learned how to apply this knowledge to write queries so that they promote plan usage. You analyzed ad hoc queries, simple parameterization queries, the sp_executesql stored procedure, stored procedures, and batches and applied your knowledge through exercises. You learned how to analyze your queries and used SHOWPLAN_XML. You further learned how to modify them for performance.

You next moved into learning many best practices for XML queries, beginning with learning the XQuery syntax and expressions. Next you learned how to implement XQuery to build

XML queries using design and performance strategies built around SQL Server 2005 technologies. XML, its use and design, is still evolving. As you have seen, the technologies built into SQL Server 2005 embrace XML well. Enjoy the changing sea!

If you are still thirsting for more on understanding and applying XML in SQL Server 2005, see *Professional SQL Server 2005 XML* by Scott Klein (Wrox, 2006). This work is guaranteed to keep you out of the boiling waters that our dearly departed oyster friends found themselves in—we hope you did catch on that they were boiled up for lunch! But you are certain to begin a whole new adventure in grokking XML.

Exam Essentials

Know how to write queries to promote plan reuse.   You need to be familiar with the various types of queries and how to write them to promote plan reuse. You need to understand the caching process of SQL Server 2005 and what determines plan reuse and how a plan stays maintained in the procedure cache.

Know how to modify queries to improve performance.   You need to understand how to view your query plans using SHOWPLAN_XML. You need to know how to modify your queries to improve performance and configure tools involved in the process.

Know how to use XQuery syntax and expressions.   You need to know the basic XQuery syntax, expressions, and operators. You need to understand the comparisons of XQuery with SQL.

Know how to design queries to retrieve XML data.   You need to know the parts of an XQuery expression and how to create each. You need to know how to use the XQuery methods to design your queries to extract data from an XML type data or column. You need to know methods as well as best practices for converting XML data into rowset data.

Know how to design queries to update XML data.   You need to know XML DML and be conversant with the three keywords insert, replace value of, and delete.

Know how to design parameterizing XML queries.   You need to know how to use sql:column() and sql:variable() to bind and parameterize your XML queries with relational data.

Know the guidelines to process queries using XML data.   You need to know the guidelines for processing you XML queries. You need to know the methods and technologies for troubleshooting your XML queries.

Review Questions

1. Into which part of its memory does SQL Server store the compiled plans for your queries?

   A. The buffer cache

   B. The plan allocator

   C. The procedure cache

   D. The analysis processor

2. Several of your users notice that one of the SQL Server 2005 applications they use to modify client accounts has a very slow response time. This application calls a stored procedure that uses a transaction to update the client accounts.

   As the database developer for your company you need to be able to analyze the problem without impacting the resources of the environment. You also want to use a technology that will not be deprecated in future versions of SQL Server.

   Which one of the following technologies should you use?

   A. SET SHOWPLAN_TEXT ON

   B. SET SHOWPLAN_XML ON

   C. SET SHOWPLAN_ALL ON

   D. SET EXECUTION_PLAN ON

3. Which of the following ad hoc queries will match an execution plan with the given query?

   ```
   SELECT CustomerID

   FROM AdventureWorks.Sales.Individual

   WHERE ContactID = 5429
   ```

   A.
   ```
   SELECT CustomerID
   FROM Sales.Individual
   WHERE ContactID = 5429
   ```

   B.
   ```
   SELECT CustomerID
   FROM AdventureWorks.Sales.Individual
   WHERE ContactID = 5429
   ```

   C.
   ```
   SELECT CustomerID
   FROM AdventureWorks.Sales.Individual
   WHERE ContactID = 2057
   ```

   D.
   ```
   SELECT CustomerID
   FROM AdventureWorks.Sales.Individual
   WHERE contactid   > 5429
   ```

4. What is the recompile level for stored procedures in SQL Server 2005?

    A. Recompiling is done at the statement level.

    B. Recompiling is done at the procedure level.

    C. Recompiling is done at the batch level.

    D. Recompiling is done at the connection level.

5. You have several levels of SET options implemented on your SQL Server 2005 server. There are SET options specified for your database at the database level. Explicit SET options and hints are also used in various queries in the same database. How do you maintain the correct SET options?

    A. Always use the database SET options.

    B. If needed. Change the SET options at the database level.

    C. Use the options set when you wrote the query, they will never change.

    D. To be on the safe side, establish the SET options at connection time for your query.

6. You need to use a configuration tool to limit the resources used by one of the queries you are testing for a new application. You do not want to limit resources server wide, just for this particular connection. What should you do?

    A. You must set the query governor to limit the resources using the sp_configure 'query governor cost limit', 'value' Transact-SQL statement at the server.

    B. You must set the query governor to limit the resources using the SET QUERY_GOVERNOR_COST_LIMIT stating a specific value at the connection.

    C. You must set the query governor to limit the resources using the sp_configure 'query governor cost limit', 'value' Transact-SQL statement at the connection.

    D. You must set the query governor to limit the resources using the SET QUERY_GOVERNOR_COST_LIMIT stating a specific value at the server.

7. You want to put values from your rowset data into your XML query. Which of the following expression can you use? (Choose all that apply.)

    A. sql:column()

    B. modify()

    C. sql:variable()

    D. value()

8. Which of the following rules apply to XQuery syntax? (Choose all that apply.)

    A. XQuery is case sensitive.

    B. XQuery places strings in double or single quotes.

    C. XQuery delimits comments using two hyphens at the beginning.

    D. XQuery takes its naming conventions from SQL.

9. Which of the following FLWOR XQuery expressions do you use to bind a variable to a node and iterate through the node sequence to return a result set?

    A. FOR

    B. LET

    C. WHERE

    D. ORDER BY

    E. RETURN

10. What keywords are used in XML Data Modification Language (DML)? (Choose all that apply.)

    A. replace value of

    B. update

    C. insert

    D. delete

11. Given the following query:

```
declare @stu xml;

set @stu = '<Studentlist>

            <Student id="1">

                <Name>

                    <FirstName>March</FirstName>

                    <LastName>Hare</LastName>

                </Name>

                <Age>11</Age>

            </Student>

            <Student id="2">

                <Name>

                    <FirstName>Mad</FirstName>

                    <LastName>Hatter</LastName>
```

```
        </Name>

        <Age>12</Age>

    </Student>

    <Student id="3">

        <Name>

            <FirstName>Cheshire</FirstName>

            <LastName>Cat</LastName>

        </Name>

        <Age>10</Age>

    </Student>

</Studentlist>';
select @stu.query('for $s in /Studentlist/Student

    where $s/Age > 11

    return $s/Name');
```

What expression enables you to select the child elements of the Studentlist node?

A. This expression:

```
for $s in /Studentlist/Student
```

B. This expression:

```
set @stu = '<Studentlist>
  <Student id="1">
```

C. This expression:

```
where $s/Age > 11
```

D. This expression:

```
return $s/Name');
```

12. Using the query in question 11, which of the following are the results?

   A. This is the result:

   ```
   <Name>
       <FirstName>March</FirstName>
       <LastName>Hare</LastName>
   </Name>
   ```

   B. This is the result:

   ```
   <Name>
       <FirstName>March</FirstName>
       <LastName>Hare</LastName>
       <FirstName>Mad</FirstName>
       <LastName>Hatter</LastName>
   </Name>
   ```

   C. This is the result:

   ```
   <Name>
       <FirstName>March</FirstName>
       <LastName>Hare</LastName>
   </Name>
   <Name>
       <FirstName>Mad</FirstName>
       <LastName>Hatter</LastName>
   </Name>
   ```

   D. This is the result:

   ```
   <Name>
       <FirstName>Mad</FirstName>
       <LastName>Hatter</LastName>
   </Name>
   ```

13. Using the query in question 11 above, what is the $s called in XQuery?

   A. literal
   B. operator
   C. variable
   D. context

14. Use the query in question 11 above but replace the SELECT @stu.query with the following:

```
select @stu.query('for $s in /Studentlist/Student

    where $s/Age < 11

    return

        <Student>

            {$s/Name/FirstName/text()}

        </Student>');
```

What is text()?

A. The child element of FirstName

B. The value property of FirstName

C. The node of FirstName

D. The context of FirstName

15. Use the query in question 11 above but replace the SELECT @stu.query with the following:

```
select @stu.query('for $s in /Studentlist/Student

    where $s/Age < 11

    return

        <Student>

            {$s/Name/FirstName/text()}

        </Student>');
```

Which of the following is the output of the query?

A. This is the output:
```
<FirstName>Cheshire</FirstName>
```

B. This is the output:
```
<Student>Cheshire</Student>
```

C. This is the output:
```
<Student>Mad</Student>
```

D. This is the output:
```
<Student>
        <FirstName>Cheshire</FirstName>
</Student>
```

16. You need to create a query to determine whether an XML column of a table in your database contains a particular value. What is the most efficient means to create this query if the XML data type is typed XML?

    A. You should use XQuery with the query() method.

    B. You should use XQuery with the nodes() method.

    C. You should use XQuery with the value() method.

    D. You should use XQuery with the exist() method.

17. What are the two parts of an XQuery expression?

    A. Prolog

    B. Epilog

    C. Datum

    D. Body

18. Which of the following can be used to convert XML data into rowset data?

    A. OPENXML

    B. FOR XML

    C. The nodes() method

    D. Create a user-defined function.

19. If you want your XML queries to be optimized in SQL Server 2005, which of the following guidelines must be followed?

    A. Create typed XML.

    B. Create untyped XML.

    C. Use indexes only on rowset data in your database.

    D. Use indexes on XML data columns if they are beneficial to your queries.

20. When you use the nodes() method to convert XML data into rowset data, what operator must you use to format that data from your XML?

    A. PIVOT

    B. RECOMPILE

    C. APPLY

    D. JOIN

Answers to Review Questions

1. C. SQL Server stores the compiles plans in a part of its memory called the procedure cache. SQL Server memory is dynamically allocated into two parts, the buffer cache for data and the procedure cache for compiled plans. The terms *plan allocator* and *analysis processor* are not valid terms in SQL Server 2005.

2. B. Use SET SHOWPLAN_XML ON. The SET SHOWPLAN_TEXT ON and SET SHOWPLAN_ALL ON, although they provide the execution context without actually producing output, are both being deprecated in future versions of SQL Server. There is no SET statement for SET EXECUTION_PLAN ON.

3. C. For an ad hoc query to promote plan reuse, it must contain fully qualified object name references as well as match the placement, space, and case sensitivity of the text. Since the value supplied in the WHERE clause is treated as a parameter, the query in C will match with the given query.

4. A. SQL Server 2005 has introduced recompiling at the statement level for stored procedures. When a stored procedure is recompiled, the entire procedure is not necessarily recompiled, only those statements that initiated the recompiling are recompiled. The parameter values used at the time of recompiling are the ones implemented for the plan, not the original values.

5. D. To be on the safe side, establish the SET options at connection time for your query. SET options have a hierarchy and options can change. A hint overrides an explicit SET option. A SET option overrides a database option. And a database option overrides an instance option.

6. B. The query governor must be set at the connection, and the correct statement is SET QUERY_GOVERNOR_COST_LIMIT.

7. A, C. Both sql:column() and sql:variable() can be used to bind relational data to data stored within an XML document.

8. A, B. Delimiting comments using two hyphens at the beginning is incorrect because XQuery delimits comments by using the colon at each end of the comment. Taking the naming conventions from SQL is incorrect because XQuery takes its naming conventions from XML.

9. A. The FOR statement is used to bind a variable to a node and iterate through the node sequence to return a result set. The LET statement is not supported in SQL Server 2005. The WHERE statement is used to filter the sequences of your query. The ORDER BY statement is used to process the sorting of your result set. The RETURN statement is used to process the values extracted by the query.

10. A, C, D. There are three keywords used with XQuery modify() method to extend the XQuery language so that it can include modifying XML data in SQL Server 2005. These three keywords include insert, replace value of, and delete.

11. A. The XPath path expression using the slash (/) selects the elements. In this example the Student elements are the children of the Studentlist element.

12. D. Only the XML formatted name of the Mad Hatter will be chosen.

13. C. XQuery denotes a variable by placing a $ prior to the identifier.

14. B. Text() is the value of what is currently stored as the text in the FirstName element. The text() of each of the FirstName elements of the nodes in our expression above are March, Mad, and Cheshire.

15. B. The text() property will be defined by the FirstName of the student whose age is less than 11, Cheshire.

16. D. You should design an XQuery query using the exist() method. This is the most efficient way to process the query.

17. A and D. An XQuery expression includes both a prolog and a body. The prolog is a namespace declaration and the body defines the XQuery FLWOR statements.

18. A, C, D. OPENXML has been a method available to you for converting XML. However, the nodes() method and creating a user-defined function encompassing the code of the nodes() method make for a methodology that is much less memory intensive for the task.

19. A, D. Your XML should be built on a defined schema, and it should be typed XML. As typed XML, if there is a clustered index on the table, then you can create a primary index on the XML column. An index on your XML can be beneficial if you are using range conditions in your XML queries.

20. C. Since the nodes() method cannot be applied directly to the result set of a user-defined function, you must use the APPLY operator to return the data as a derived table using a table valued function.

Chapter

4

Using Cursors

✓ **Design a cursor strategy.**

- Design cursor logic.
- Design cursors that work together with dynamic SQL execution.
- Select an appropriate cursor type.
- Design cursors that efficiently use server memory.
- Design cursors that minimize blocking.
- Design a strategy that minimizes or eliminates the use of cursors.

We're introducing this chapter with a syllogism from our favorite logician, Lewis Carroll, from his *Symbolic Logic*:

a. Babies are illogical.

b. Nobody is despised who can manage a crocodile.

c. Illogical persons are despised.

The object of the puzzle is to come to the "best" conclusion using all the hypotheses. Lewis Carroll often used symbolic logic puzzles as a means to "give you clearness of thought—the ability to see your way through a puzzle—the habit of arranging your ideas in an orderly and get-at-able form—and, more valuable than all, the power to detect fallacies."

Designing a cursor strategy involves logically deciding whether to apply cursors, and in order to do that you need to understand the choices you have in SQL Server 2005, especially so to avoid using cursors only because you do not know how to handle data access in other ways. Implementing cursors because of this type of inexperience can produce poor performance and lead to many hours of modifying applications; we've seen this firsthand in the companies we have worked with throughout our consulting years.

Therefore, your cursor strategy needs to be based on understanding cursor usage in SQL Server 2005, and the appropriate use of cursors is the heart of the chapter. Also, since any implementation involves so many other factors already in place within your environment, it is important that you know how to monitor the performance of a strategy to determine whether it is the best for your situation.

So, start drawing circles to find the answer to our puzzle, clear your minds, and get ready to learn the appropriate uses for cursor implementation in SQL Server 2005. And just remember…in the Transact-SQL world, nobody is despised who can manage a cursor, but we might throw you to the crocodiles if that is all you use!

If you think your head is clear but you still want to check the answer to the syllogism, you can check out the solution in the "Summary" section of this chapter.

Understanding Data Access in Relational Data Systems

Relational database management systems are designed to use set-based data access and employ algorithms that optimize processing of multiple rows of data. This method of storing and accessing data conserves system resources and promotes quick response time. SQL Server 2005 storage architecture is designed to optimize sequential access to data. Your server's resources and memory utilization have all been optimized to use result set algorithms to provide the best performance possible. The result set algorithms are themselves a series of row-based sequential operations optimized for your server's architecture. This method of processing data is *set-based processing*, and the returned data is termed a *result set*.

Whenever possible, you should use the set-based processing of your server's architecture. This processing enables you to employ indexing. You are able to use a clustered index to efficiently return a result set from a range of data. You are able to use a nonclustered index to cover a query and return a result set quickly and efficiently.

You may find you need to process your data a single piece at a time. Unfortunately, you cannot use the architecture features of a relational database system for your data retrieval when you are accessing your data piece by piece. You need another method to process your results. This is where you might implement a cursor strategy. We'll cover both set-based and row-based processing in the following sections.

Understanding Result Set–Based Operations

Sometimes your applications will work with individual data objects. In these instances you might think it is easier for you to access this data one row at a time. This is termed *row-by-row processing*. However, you should always consider a set-based solution first. Just because it might seem easier to implement a row-by-row solution in your code, take time in the initial design of your application to clear your head and think through your logic to determine whether you are able to use a set-based operation.

Here are some of the guidelines you should follow to use *set-based operations* in your application:

Build your queries to affect grouping of rows.   As we mentioned previously, SQL Server's storage architecture and data access algorithms are optimized for this type of data handling. Searching a database for a range of data can be handled efficiently with the use of proper indexing. Query plans can be generated. Execution plans can be reused. Using set-based queries at the server is more efficient than designing algorithms to mimic that same processing at the client side.

Limit the result sets to your queries.   The performance increases and I/O lowers when you take time to filter your queries at the server. If there is no need to single out individual rows for differentiated processing, well-formed set-based queries are the answer.

Build queries and parameters such that they will have reusable execution plans.   As we mentioned in previous chapters, parameters are used as part of the stored execution plan. When using stored procedures and functions, you should make certain you are reusing plans.

Do not build too many conditional branches within your queries.   If you use too much conditional logic or too many branches or go to the extreme with filtering clauses, you are defeating the purpose of accessing the data as a set. SQL Server might serialize the execution of your query because of its complexity. Serialization of the execution inhibits the set-based algorithms from being put into place. Simplify the structure of these queries.

Take advantage of indexes as you build your queries.   Indexing is an important tool in set-based data access. Wise use of indexing strategies enables fast return of data to your users.

Understanding Row-Based Operations

Once you have determined that there is no other way to handle your data than to incur a row-by-row operation, you need to evaluate the method needed to retrieve the data. All dialects of SQL provide cursors to support *row-based operations*, but—although widely used—they are not the only methods available. Depending on your application, you might decide on a cursor strategy. If you choose to use a cursor implementation, you should understand how to choose wisely.

Cursor features have not changed from SQL Server 2000 to SQL Server 2005. You use the SQL-92 syntax standard and a set of Transact-SQL extensions.

Understanding How Cursors Work

In this section, we cover cursors to make certain you understand how they work. The analogy we present, the window washer, is a standard one used to explain cursors in programming books.

Visualize the equipment that a window washer uses, as they traverse up and down a high-rise building, stopping at each floor to wash each window. Now conceptualize your image with a data set replacing the building's floors and windows and with a cursor playing the role of the window washer. A cursor involves two procedures to complete its tasks. The first procedure is the placement that moves the cursor to the appropriate row (floor) in the data set. The second procedure is the retrieve statement that fetches the data from the designated row.

Whether the window washer can manipulate their equipment in either direction depends on the equipment type they have installed or have chosen to install; this might be a silly idea, but we hope you get the concept. Likewise, being able to go back and view already washed windows might be a different option to the window-washing equipment analogy. Keep the analogy in your mind as you learn about how to work with cursors.

Understanding Cursor Types Defined by the SQL Native Client ODBC Driver

SQL Server supports four types of ODBC cursors:

Forward-only cursor   The *forward-only cursor* moves only in one direction. It fetches the data row by row in the same direction from start to end through the data set.

Static cursor   The *static cursor* builds a temporary table in tempdb to hold the data. The data you view through the cursor is only as fresh as the time when the cursor was opened. You will not view any changes made to the data through the static cursor.

Keyset-driven cursor   The keyset-driven cursor is built on the primary key in the row. If modifications are made to nonkey members in the row, they are visible through the cursor. Membership and row order are fixed when the cursor is opened so it will not see new data rows.

Dynamic cursor   The *dynamic cursor* sees all changes made to the data set. It can see underlying changes to the data on subsequent fetches. It is the opposite of the static cursor.

Understanding the Advantages of Each Cursor Option

Initially, you need to create the cursor using the declare statement to define the appropriate cursor option. You will need to understand how each cursor option is implemented to know how to effectively determine the correct cursor to choose for a given situation. We now discuss implementation as well as when to use a particular cursor option.

Fast_Forward Cursor

This is how the *fast_forward cursor* works:

How it is implemented　The fast_forward cursor supports fetching data rows from the beginning to the end of the cursor employing the NEXT statement. This cursor moves in one direction.

> Note that there is a slight difference in syntax within the DECLARE CURSOR statement for SQL Server 2005. You are able to use both FAST_FORWARD and FORWARD_ONLY cursor options within the same declare statement without getting an error as you would have in SQL Server 2000.

When to use this cursor type　If you want to process your data rows in an order, one row at a time, without skipping rows or moving to prior rows and you are just reading data, you should use the fast_forward cursor. The fast_forward cursor defaults to read only.

Pros　The fast_forward cursor provides optimal performance under its conditions of use.

Cons　The fast_forward cursor does not allow viewing of updated data. It also does not allow bilateral movement within the data set.

Static Cursor

This is how the static cursor works:

How it is implemented　The static cursor copies all the data the cursor uses into a temporary table in tempdb. All requests to the cursor are actually responded to from this temporary table and thus are read only.

When to use this cursor type　Since the fetch statements for the static cursor are drawn on the data set in tempdb, use the static cursor when there are no real-time requirements. The static cursor will not see updates to actual data. If you need a point-in-time requirement or if you are not concerned with seeing updated data, use a static cursor. The static cursor defaults to read only.

Pros　The static cursor produces fewer concurrency problems. Each cursor gets its own copy of the data. The static cursor allows bilateral movement within the data set.

Cons　The static cursor uses more disk space than other cursors since they duplicate the data set to be used in tempdb. The static cursor does not allow viewing of updated data.

Keyset Cursor

This is how the *keyset cursor* works:

How it is implemented   The keyset cursor copies all the primary key data into a table known as the keyset in tempdb. Since the membership and order of rows is fixed when the cursor is opened, the keyset cursor will not see new rows; however, it will see modifications to existing rows.

When to use this cursor type   If you need to use a cursor solution to make modifications to your data without inserts or deletes, you should use the keyset cursor. Since the membership and order of rows is fixed when the cursor is opened, the keyset cursor maintains row order.

Pros   You are able to view modifications to existing rows. The keyset cursor allows bilateral movement within the data set.

Cons   Updates of key values from outside the cursor are not visible. The keyset cursor takes longer to open than a dynamic cursor. However, after opening, it uses fewer resources than the dynamic cursor.

Dynamic Cursor

This is how the dynamic cursor works:

How it is implemented   The dynamic cursor fetches data from the underlying base tables based on the key data that is copied in tempdb. In this manner it is much the same as the keyset cursor. However, with each modification to key data, on the base table, the key data in the cached table in tempdb is also refreshed. The dynamic cursor is a very resource intensive cursor to implement.

When to use this cursor type   The dynamic cursor should be used when you need to have all changes to the underlying data visible through the cursor. The dynamic cursor allows bilateral movement within the data set.

Pros   The dynamic cursor is the only cursor that can see data modifications as well as updates and deletes in the underlying base tables. A positioned update is an update that targets the base table for the row that you are on in the cursor.

Cons   The dynamic cursor is the most resource intensive cursor. It uses more processing power. It does not preserve order.

Guidelines for Using Row-Based Operations

Now, not all row-based operations should be handled using cursors. We discussed the concepts and use of cursors so you can make an informed decision. Some additional guidelines follow.

Do not choose a cursor strategy only because it is the most familiar programming tool. Application efficiency outweighs a small amount of time saved during development.   In our consulting experience development teams under severe time constraints to get an application deployed have chosen cursor-based strategies in lieu of a set-based process that would have been more efficient. The development time saved becomes small compared with the inefficiency of the application, the aggravation to the users, and the amount of rewrites required in the field.

Determine your method to build statements for row handling.   Determine whether you need to build rows dynamically by combining strings. In this instance you may need to use the sp_executesql stored procedure or the EXECUTE statement. If the conditions for defining each row are varied, the system will need to compile and execute each statement one at a time. This type of database application is one in which the use might generate conditions to be sent to the server as a string for processing. This procedure is a typical dynamic execution.

Determine the types and amounts of calculations you need to apply in your application. Since processing calculations involves individual columns from a table or even columns referenced from other tables, the algorithms employed can be quite complex. You need to know your data. There is no hard and fast rule as to whether cursors are better in these instances. It might even be advantageous to group the data into small sets and handle the data as small groups without using a cursor strategy.

Deciding When Cursors or Set-Oriented Operations Are Appropriate

In the following sections, we'll show how to do the same task using a cursor implementation and then using a set-oriented implementation. At the end of the example we will discuss our findings.

Here is the first task: Say you need to query the AdventureWorks database using two different queries. The first query uses the Purchasing.PurchaseOrderHeader table to select information concerning a purchase order, and the second query uses the Purchasing.PurchaseOrderDetail table to gain insight into the details of the purchase order just queried.

The header query is defined as follows:

```
SELECT PurchaseOrderID, RevisionNumber,
   Status, EmployeeID, VendorID,
   ShipMethodID, OrderDate,
   ShipDate, SubTotal, TaxAmt,
   Freight, TotalDue
   FROM Purchasing.PurchaseOrderHeader
```

The details query is defined as follows:

```
SELECT PurchaseOrderDetailID, DueDate,
   OrderQty, ProductID, UnitPrice,
   LineTotal, ReceivedQty,
   RejectedQty, StockedQty
   FROM Purchasing.PurchaseOrderDetail
```

Implementing the Purchase Order Join Task Using Client-Side Technologies

We will first show how to implement the task using cursors with client-side technology, a Windows application running on your desktop, and see how this plays out. You will be retrieving the entire list of purchase order headers. As you retrieve a purchase order header, using a loop, you need to retrieve all detail records for that purchase order. We have defined the queries as read only variables at the class level within our solution. The header and details are joined on the purchaseorderID field that they have in common after all data has been retrieved. The join is done at the client side. Let's recap what is being transferred across the network here: all the requested purchase order data, all the details for each of the purchase orders requested, and at the client a join is processed to "match up" the data.

We have created a simple timer so that you are able to see the amount of data retrieved as well as the time taken for the retrieval and processing at the client.

Figure 4.1 shows the results of running the queries and implementing the join using *client-side cursor* technologies as described previously. The elapsed time was even a little slower since we were also capturing the trace with Profiler.

FIGURE 4.1   Retrieve data timer for the client-side processing join task

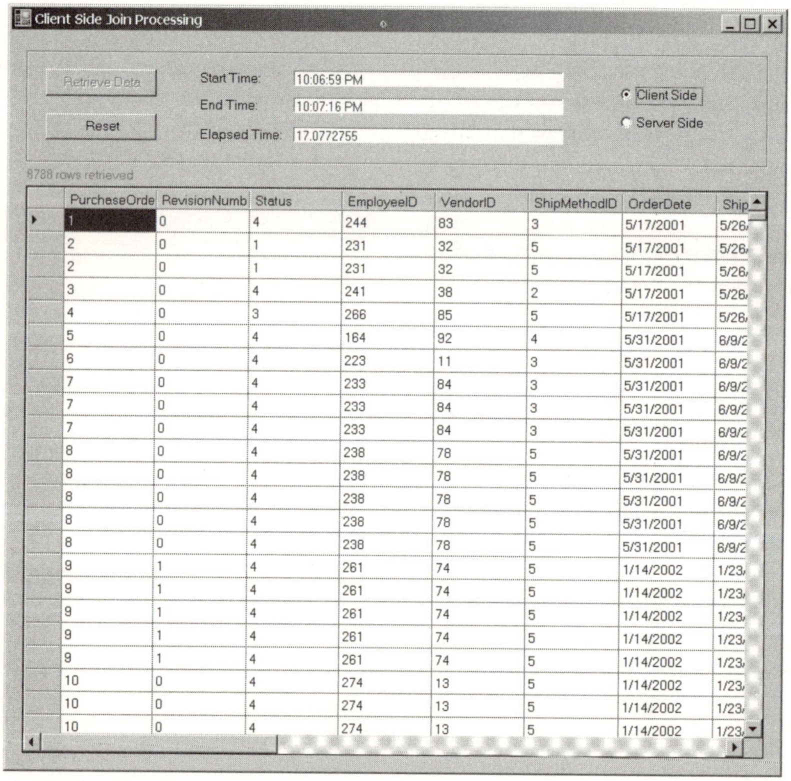

Figure 4.2 shows the Profiler trace of the client-side join processing task in Figure 4.1. Please note that each and every row connection is reset. Do you see the window washer working here? Reset, fetch, read, for each and every row of data.

FIGURE 4.2   Profiler Trace of the client-side processing join task

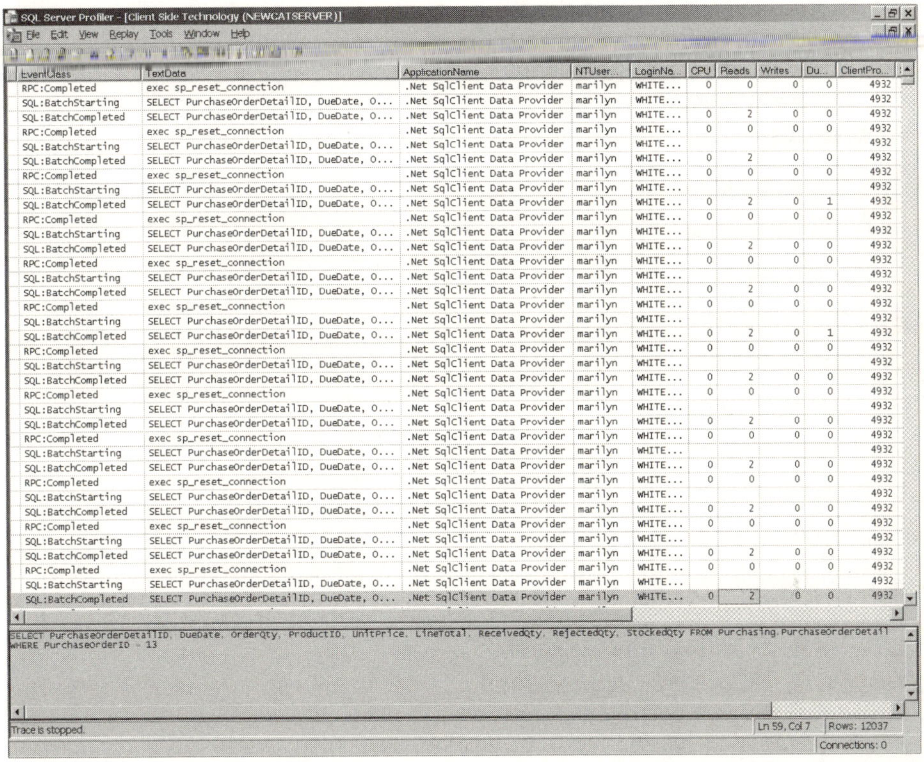

Implementing the Purchase Order Join Task Using Server-Side Set-Based Operations

Now you will implement the task again. This time you will run the queries and the join on the server using set-based operations rather than a cursor strategy. You are using the same two queries to extract the data and the same join procedure. Using the server resources also enables SQL Server to optimize the queries for performance. A Profiler trace will again be running in the background. Check out the elapsed time in the Profiler trace of the server-side join set-based task in Figure 4.3.

Figure 4.4 shows the Profiler trace of the server-side join set-based task in Figure 4.3. Notice that there is only one round-trip between the client and the server. All metrics are drastically reduced. And this is just one user accessing the data in the application!

FIGURE 4.3   Retrieve data timer for the server-side set-based join task

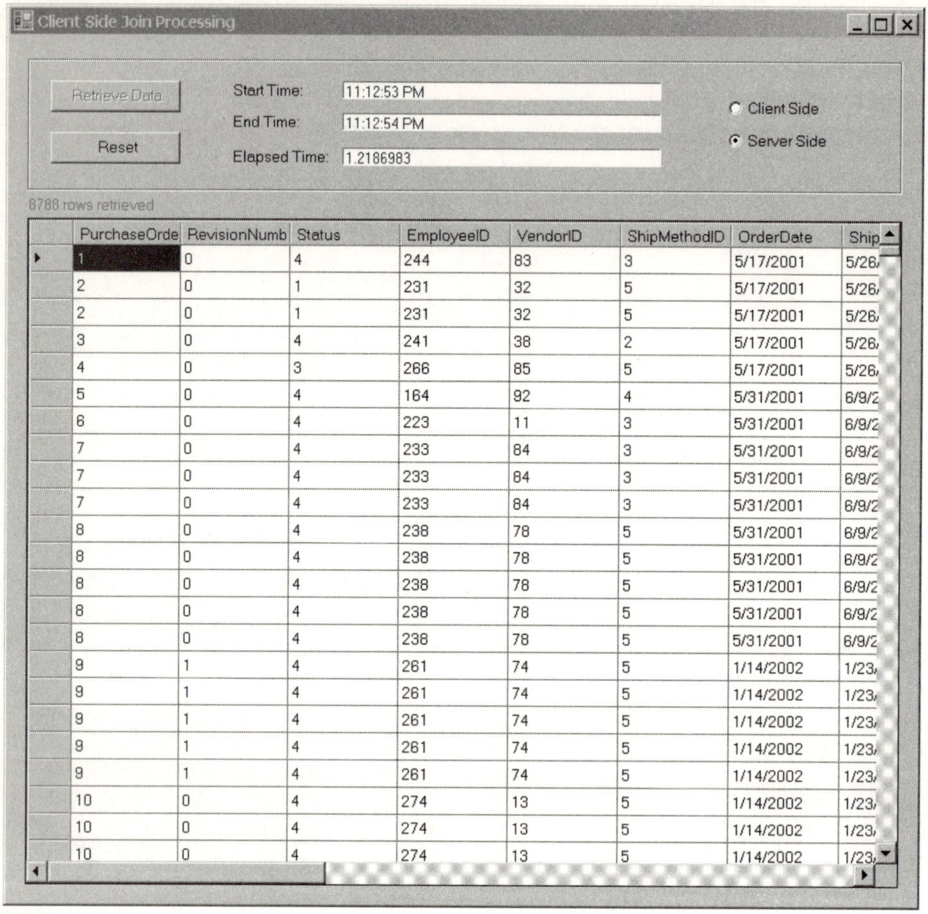

FIGURE 4.4   Profiler trace of the server-side set-based join task

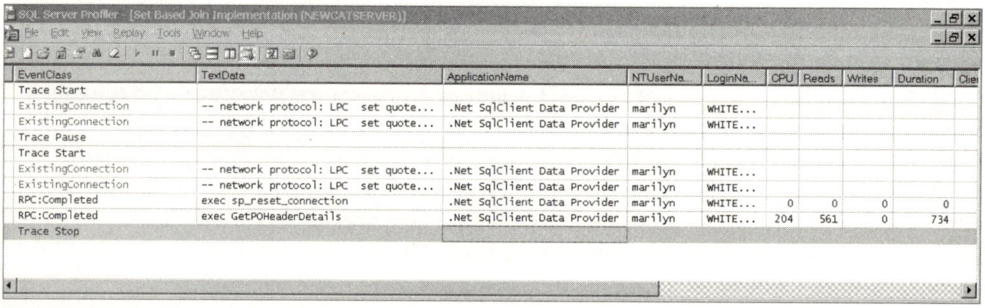

Understanding the Key Points When Differentiating between Cursors and Set-Oriented Operations

In SQL Server 2005 you have several areas to consider when using cursors and set-based operations. These considerations apply to Transact-SQL as well as the .NET CLR processing in SQL Server 2005. The following are key points when differentiating between cursors and set-oriented operations:

- Consider a set-based solution first. Your SQL Server architecture is built to optimize this technology. If you find no other choice, move to a cursor-based solution.

- Process as much of your data as possible in the database. You should avoid carrying needless amounts of data either across the network to the client or into tempdb.

- Use Transact-SQL to access data whenever possible, such as the joins in our illustration. No other language handles data at the database level more efficiently than Transact-SQL.

- Process your data where it is stored whenever possible. Thus, if your data is stored entirely within one database on your server, there is no need to carry it somewhere else, like tempdb or to a client, for processing.

A Case in Point: Views on Cursors from the Trenches

We have mentioned throughout this chapter, and rightly so, the many times we have been called into organizations to "clean up" code that was performing very poorly—mainly to find an inappropriate cursor implementation in place. The time and effort involved to get everything back on track was often very costly. The problems and additional costs could have been avoided with an appropriate data retrieval strategy from the get-go.

DBAs who are not "code savvy" often ask us what to look for in their slow-running queries. One of the culprits we often find is the sp_executesql. Programmers who use cursor strategies really love to string queries together using this means of execution. As you know from our previous chapters, this ad hoc query does not work well for plan reuse. Thus, each execution may cause a new plan to be generated. We lost count years ago on how many of these queries we changed over to other methodologies.

Cursors aren't all bad. We use them for some down-and-dirty queries ourselves in our consulting gigs. If we want to track modifications to data through metadata changes in system tables, we often use cursors. We do have DDL triggers in SQL Server 2005, but these rely on having event data retrievable for the desired data. And sometimes we decide to collect the darndest stuff, so we need the flexibility of a cursor. We have put a true example from a friend of ours (see John) in a review question at the end of the chapter to help you get the picture.

So you never know when you may need to manage a crocodile....

Selecting Cursors Appropriately

If you have decided your situation requires implementing a cursor technology, your next task is to choose the appropriate cursor strategy. We have already seen that the wrong tool can completely slow down an entire company's service.

In the following sections, you will gain insight into appropriate use of server-side and client-side cursors. We would also like you to experience performing some hands-on exercises in cursor implementation and monitoring. Thus, in the next section on server-side cursors, you will be implementing cursors in a Server Management Server solution, as well as monitoring events using Microsoft Windows Performance Monitor and SQL Server Profiler.

Selecting Appropriate Server-Side Cursors

If a cursor solution is appropriate, you need to be familiar with the placement and the type of cursor to use. A case in point is our join scenario. Obviously it was not a good choice to implement with a client-side cursor. So let's take action on that same type of join strategy. This time we will have a bit fewer deliverable records, 290 to be exact. We will use the employees and their managers to give us that same master/detail relationship that we had with the purchase orders and their details.

In the following five exercises, you will use *server-side cursors*. In Exercise 4.1, you'll set up monitoring using Microsoft Windows Performance Monitor and *SQL Server Profiler*. In Exercise 4.2, you'll use a STATIC server-side cursor implementation. In Exercise 4.3, you'll use a KEYSET server-side cursor implementation. In Exercise 4.4, you'll use a DYNAMIC server-side cursor implementation. Just to keep your minds open, in Exercise 4.5, you'll use the set-based implementation.

 Please note that Exercise 4.1 applies to Exercises 4.2 through 4.5. In other words, for the steps to work, you must do Exercise 4.1 before each of the following exercises.

EXERCISE 4.1

Exercises 4.1: Setting Up Monitoring (Preliminary Exercise for Exercises 4.2 through 4.5)

To set up the *System Monitor* console environment in Performance Monitor, perform the following steps:

1.   Click Administrative Tools ➢ Performance menu.

2.   Delete the existing three default running counters by pressing X or Delete (Delete key) three times.

EXERCISE 4.1 *(continued)*

3. Add new counters by first pressing the plus (+) sign, and choosing the following and clicking Add:

Performance Object	Counter	Instance
Processor	%Processor Time	_Total
SQLServer:Cursor Manager By Type	Active cursors	_Total
SQLServer:Cursor Manager By Type	Cursor memory usage	_Total
SQLServer:Cursor Manager By Type	Cursor Requests/sec	_Total

4. Click Close.

5. Minimize the Performance window.

6. Open Microsoft SQL Server Management Studio and connect to your server to set up the SQL Server 2005 Profiler monitoring environment.

7. Open SQL Server Profiler from the Tools menu in SSMS.

8. Create a new trace by clicking File ➢ New Trace.

9. Connect to your server.

10. The Trace Properties window will be displayed. On the General tab, if you want to save the trace, you can name it and save it to a file or table. In the Use the Template list, choose Blank.

11. On the Trace Properties window, select the Events Selection tab.

12. Select the following events. You may choose to filter or reorganize columns for the events.

    Cursors: CursorClose

    Cursors: CursorExecute

    Cursors: CursorOpen

    Cursors: CursorPrepare

    TSQL: SQL:BatchCompleted

    TSQL: SQL:BatchStarting

13. Click Run to start the trace.

EXERCISE 4.2

Server Cursor Behavior: Static Cursor

This exercise uses a FORWARD_ONLY STATIC READ_ONLY cursor to FETCH the employee/manager relationship data from the AdventureWorks database. We have assumed that the monitoring environment is now in place and active.

1. Open a new query window in SQL Server Management Studio (SSMS).

2. Set your query results to text either by pressing Ctrl+T or choosing the Results to Text icon or drop-down menu item. By setting your results to text you will not only be able to see the results but you will be able to see the statistics such as scan count and logical reads on the same screen.

3. Use the AdventureWorks database and set the Statistics IO to on.

4. Declare the FORWARD_ONLY STATIC READ_ONLY cursor and open the cursor.

5. Watch all three screens as you proceed through fetching the rows in the exercise. You can tile the three screens vertically so that you are able to monitor the performance while executing the cursor. Make certain to observe the Reads column for each row of data.

6. Fetch a row of data for each of the 290 rows, or...

7. IF you get tired of F5ing, use the WHILE loop to finish up.

8. Close the cursor.

9. Deallocate the cursor.

10. Switch to System Monitor to analyze your results.

11. Switch to SQL Server Profiler to analyze your results. You should be aware of the memory, processor, and reads values.

We have placed the steps to the exercise as comments in the code where appropriate to make it easier to follow. Here's the code:

```
-- 3.

USE AdventureWorks;

GO


SET STATISTICS IO ON;
```

```
-- 4.

-- Our first exercise uses a FORWARD_ONLY STATIC READ_ONLY cursor

-- to FETCH the data

-- This is the DECLARE CURSOR statement


DECLARE OurCrsr CURSOR   FORWARD_ONLY STATIC READ_ONLY

FOR

SELECT    Person.Contact.FirstName,

    Person.Contact.LastName,

    Person.Contact.EmailAddress,

    HumanResources.Employee.BirthDate,

    ManagerContact.FirstName AS ManagerFirstName,

    ManagerContact.LastName AS ManagerLastName,

    ManagerContact.EmailAddress AS ManagerEmail,

    HumanResources.Employee.HireDate

FROM Person.Contact INNER JOIN HumanResources.Employee ON

    Person.Contact.ContactID = HumanResources.Employee.ContactID

    LEFT OUTER JOIN

    Person.Contact AS ManagerContact ON

    HumanResources.Employee.ManagerID = ManagerContact.ContactID


OPEN OurCrsr;

GO



--6.

-- The FETCH NEXT statement retrieves one row of data
```

```
-- You need to RUN (F5) this statement for all the data

-- rows (employees in our company)

-- Until the @@FETCH_STATUS value is -1

-- If you tire of hitting F5, go on to the WHILE LOOP we

-- have provided in the next section
FETCH NEXT FROM OurCrsr

SELECT @@FETCH_STATUS




--------7.

--------NOTE:  This is an OPTIONAL STEP, IN CASE YOU TIRE OF

--------HITTING THE F5 KEY FROM THE ABOVE STEP

--------This step uses a WHILE LOOP to process the

--------remaining employees to the end of the cursor
WHILE (@@FETCH_STATUS = 0)

    FETCH NEXT FROM OurCrsr;




--8.
--Close the cursor
CLOSE OurCrsr;

GO




--9.
--Deallocate the cursor
DEALLOCATE OurCrsr;

GO
```

EXERCISE 4.2 *(continued)*

Your monitored output should look like the following:

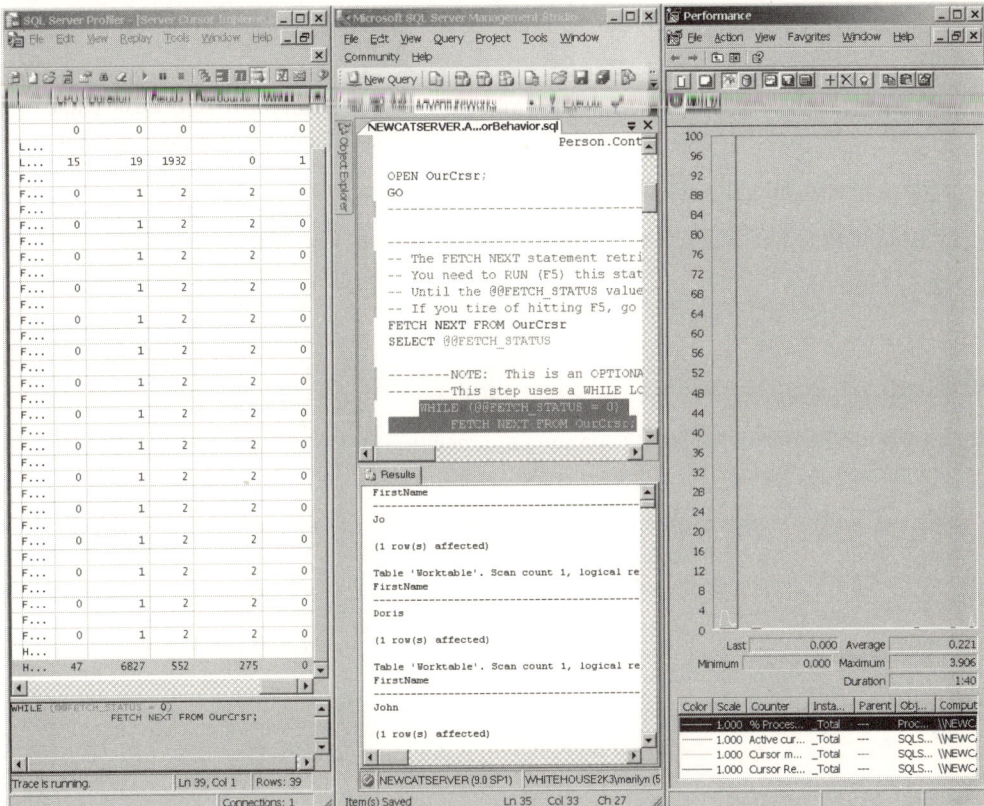

EXERCISE 4.3

Server Cursor Behavior: KEYSET Cursor

This exercise uses a FORWARD_ONLY KEYSET READ_ONLY cursor to FETCH the employee/manager relationship data from the AdventureWorks database. We have assumed that the monitoring environment is still in place and active.

1. Open a new query window in SSMS.

2. Set your query results to text either by pressing Ctrl+T or choosing the Results to Text icon or drop-down menu item. By setting your results to text you will not only be able to see the results but you will be able to see the statistics such as scan count and logical reads on the same screen.

3. Use the AdventureWorks database and set the Statistics IO to on.

4. Declare the FORWARD_ONLY KEYSET READ_ONLY cursor and open the cursor.

5. Watch all three screens as you proceed through fetching the rows in the exercise. You can tile the three screens vertically so that you are able to monitor the performance while executing the cursor. Make certain to observe the Reads column for each row of data.

6. Fetch a row of data for each of the 290 rows, or...

7. IF you get tired of F5ing, use the WHILE loop to finish up.

8. Close the cursor.

9. Deallocate the cursor.

10. Switch to System Monitor to analyze your results.

11. Switch to SQL Server Profiler to analyze your results. You should be aware of the memory, processor, and reads values.

We have placed the steps to the exercise as comments in the code where appropriate to make it easier to follow. Here's the code:

```
-- 3.

USE AdventureWorks;

GO


SET STATISTICS IO ON;



-- 4.

-- Our second exercise uses a FORWARD_ONLY KEYSET READ_ONLY cursor

-- to FETCH the data

-- This is the DECLARE CURSOR statement
```

```
DECLARE OurCrsr CURSOR  FORWARD_ONLY KEYSET READ_ONLY

FOR

SELECT Person.Contact.FirstName,

    Person.Contact.LastName, Person.Contact.EmailAddress,

    HumanResources.Employee.BirthDate,

    ManagerContact.FirstName AS ManagerFirstName,

    ManagerContact.LastName AS ManagerLastName,

    ManagerContact.EmailAddress AS ManagerEmail, HumanResources.Employee.HireDate

FROM Person.Contact INNER JOIN

    HumanResources.Employee

    ON Person.Contact.ContactID = HumanResources.Employee.ContactID

    LEFT OUTER JOIN

    Person.Contact AS ManagerContact ON

    HumanResources.Employee.ManagerID = ManagerContact.ContactID


OPEN OurCrsr;

GO



--6.

-- The FETCH NEXT statement retrieves one row of data

-- You need to RUN (F5) this statement for all the data

-- rows (employees in our company)

-- Until the @@FETCH_STATUS value is -1

-- If you tire of hitting F5, go on to the WHILE LOOP we
```

```
-- have provided in the next section

FETCH NEXT FROM OurCrsr

SELECT @@FETCH_STATUS




--------7.

--------NOTE:  This is an OPTIONAL STEP, IN CASE YOU TIRE OF

--------HITTING THE F5 KEY FROM THE ABOVE STEP

--------This step uses a WHILE LOOP to process the

--------remaining employees to the end of the cursor

    WHILE (@@FETCH_STATUS = 0)

        FETCH NEXT FROM OurCrsr;




--8.

--Close the cursor

CLOSE OurCrsr;

GO




--9.

--Deallocate the cursor

DEALLOCATE OurCrsr;

GO
```

EXERCISE 4.3 *(continued)*

Your monitored output should look like the following:

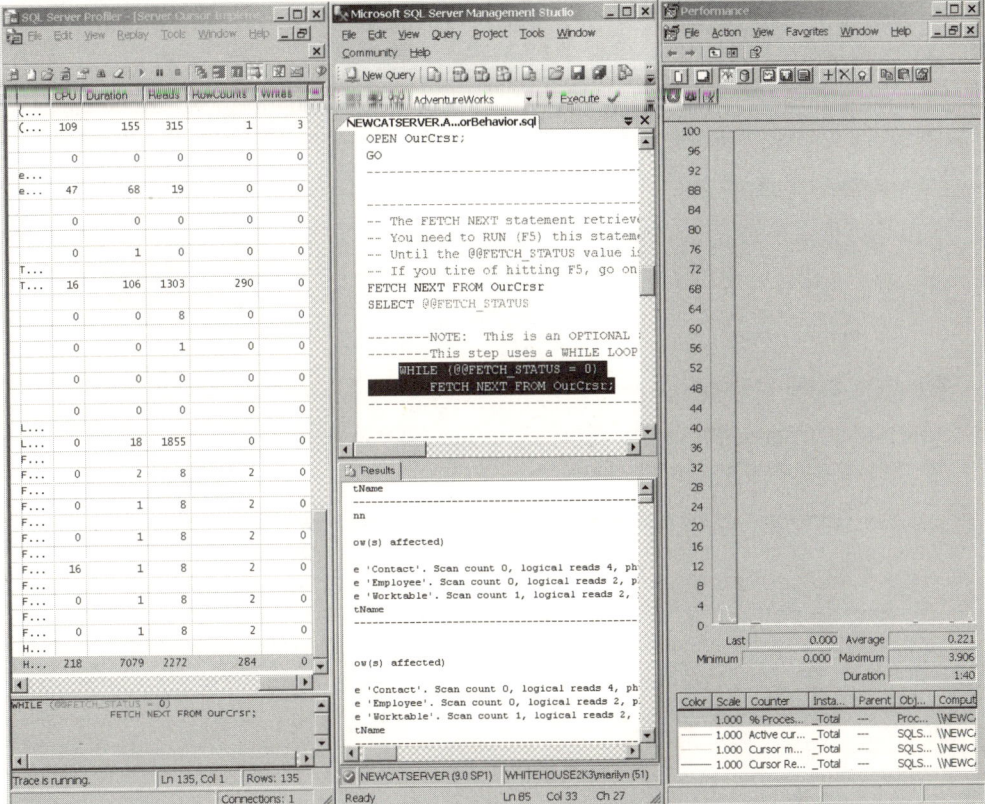

EXERCISE 4.4

Server Cursor Behavior: DYNAMIC Cursor

This exercise uses a FORWARD_ONLY DYNAMIC READ_ONLY cursor to FETCH the employee/manager relationship data from the AdventureWorks database. We have assumed that the monitoring environment is still in place and active.

1. Open a new query window in SSMS.

2. Set your query results to text either by pressing Ctrl+T or choosing the Results to Text icon or drop-down menu item. By setting your results to text you will not only be able to see the results but you will be able to see the statistics such as scan count and logical reads on the same screen.

EXERCISE 4.4 (continued)

3. Use the AdventureWorks database and set the Statistics IO to on.

4. Declare the FORWARD_ONLY DYNAMIC READ_ONLY cursor and open the cursor.

5. Watch all three screens as you proceed through fetching the rows in the exercise. You can tile the three screens vertically so that you are able to monitor the performance while executing the cursor. Make certain to observe the Reads column for each row of data.

6. Fetch a row of data for each of the 290 rows, or...

7. IF you get tired of F5ing, use the WHILE loop to finish up.

8. Close the cursor.

9. Deallocate the cursor.

10. Switch to System Monitor to analyze your results.

11. Switch to SQL Server Profiler to analyze your results. You should be aware of the memory, processor, and reads values.

We have placed the steps to the exercise as comments in the code where appropriate to make it easier to follow. Here's the code:

```
-- 3.

USE AdventureWorks;

GO



SET STATISTICS IO ON;



-- 4.

-- Our third exercise uses a FORWARD_ONLY DYNAMIC READ_ONLY cursor

-- to FETCH the data

-- This is the DECLARE CURSOR statement



DECLARE OurCrsr CURSOR  FORWARD_ONLY DYNAMIC READ_ONLY
```

```
FOR

SELECT Person.Contact.FirstName,

    Person.Contact.LastName, Person.Contact.EmailAddress,

    HumanResources.Employee.BirthDate,

    ManagerContact.FirstName AS ManagerFirstName,

    ManagerContact.LastName AS ManagerLastName,

    ManagerContact.EmailAddress AS ManagerEmail,

    HumanResources.Employee.HireDate

FROM Person.Contact

    INNER JOIN HumanResources.Employee ON

    Person.Contact.ContactID = HumanResources.Employee.ContactID

    LEFT OUTER JOIN Person.Contact AS ManagerContact ON

    HumanResources.Employee.ManagerID = ManagerContact.ContactID


OPEN OurCrsr;

GO



-- 6.

-- The FETCH NEXT statement retrieves one row of data

-- You need to RUN (F5) this statement for all the data

-- rows (employees in our company)

-- Until the @@FETCH_STATUS value is -1

-- If you tire of hitting F5, go on to the WHILE LOOP we

-- have provided in the next section
```

```
FETCH NEXT FROM OurCrsr

SELECT @@FETCH_STATUS




--------7.

--------NOTE:  This is an OPTIONAL STEP, IN CASE YOU TIRE OF

--------HITTING THE F5 KEY FROM THE ABOVE STEP

--------This step uses a WHILE LOOP to process the

--------remaining employees to the end of the cursor

    WHILE (@@FETCH_STATUS = 0)

        FETCH NEXT FROM OurCrsr;




--8.

--Close the cursor

CLOSE OurCrsr;

GO




--9.

--Deallocate the cursor

DEALLOCATE OurCrsr;

GO
```

EXERCISE 4.4 *(continued)*

Your monitored output should look like the following:

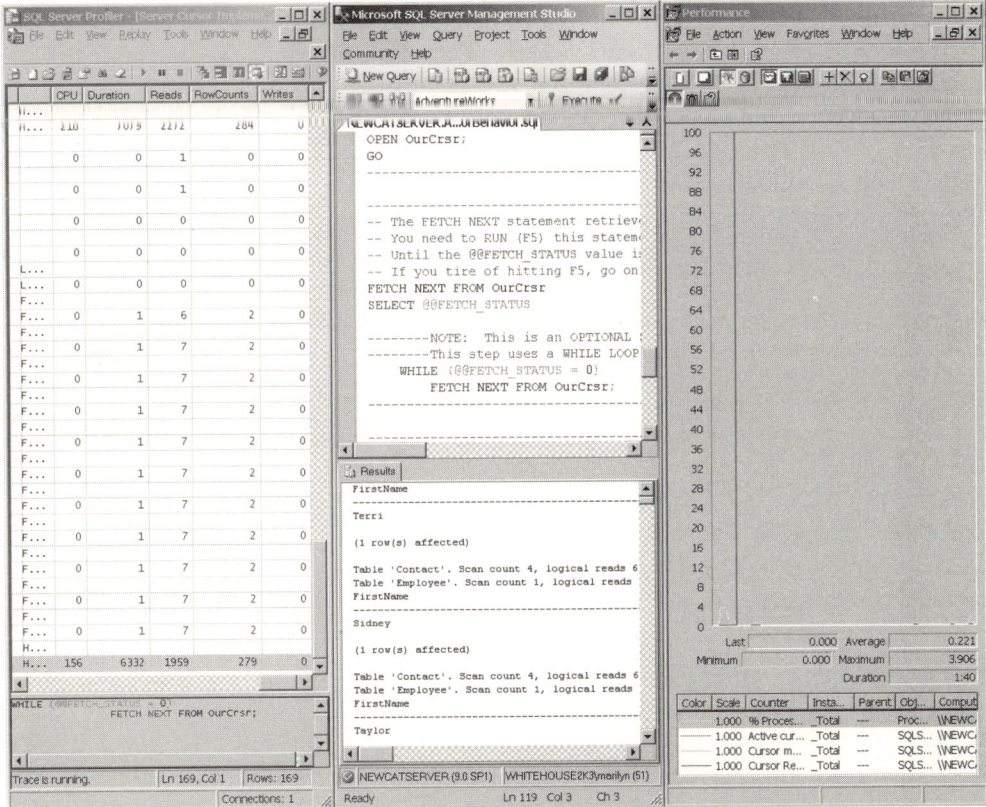

EXERCISE 4.5

Employee Join Scenario: NO Cursor

This exercise uses a set-based operation to retrieve the employee/manager relationship data from the AdventureWorks database. We have assumed that the monitoring environment is still in place and active.

1. Open a new query window in SSMS.

2. Set your query results to text either by pressing Ctrl+T or choosing the Results to Text icon or drop-down menu item. By setting your results to text you will not only be able to see the results but you will be able to see the statistics such as scan count and logical reads on the same screen.

EXERCISE 4.5 *(continued)*

3. Use the AdventureWorks database and set the Statistics IO to on.

4. Execute the select statement to retrieve the employees and their matching managers. You might further want to view the Execution Plan or the Estimated Execution Plan to view the indexes involved in generating the data retrieval.

5. Tile and view all three screens as you did in the previous exercises.

6. Switch to System Monitor to analyze your results.

7. Switch to SQL Server Profiler to analyze your results. You should be aware of the memory, processor, and reads values.

We have placed the steps to the exercise as comments in the code where appropriate to make it easier to follow. Here's the code:

```
--3.

USE AdventureWorks;

GO



SET STATISTICS IO ON;



--4.



SELECT  Person.Contact.FirstName,

    Person.Contact.LastName,

    Person.Contact.EmailAddress,

    HumanResources.Employee.BirthDate,

    ManagerContact.FirstName AS ManagerFirstName,

    ManagerContact.LastName AS ManagerLastName,

    ManagerContact.EmailAddress AS ManagerEmail,

    HumanResources.Employee.HireDate
```

EXERCISE 4.5 *(continued)*

```
FROM Person.Contact INNER JOIN

    HumanResources.Employee

    ON Person.Contact.ContactID = HumanResources.Employee.ContactID

    LEFT OUTER JOIN

    Person.Contact AS ManagerContact ON

    HumanResources.Employee.ManagerID = ManagerContact.ContactID
```

Your monitored output should look like the following:

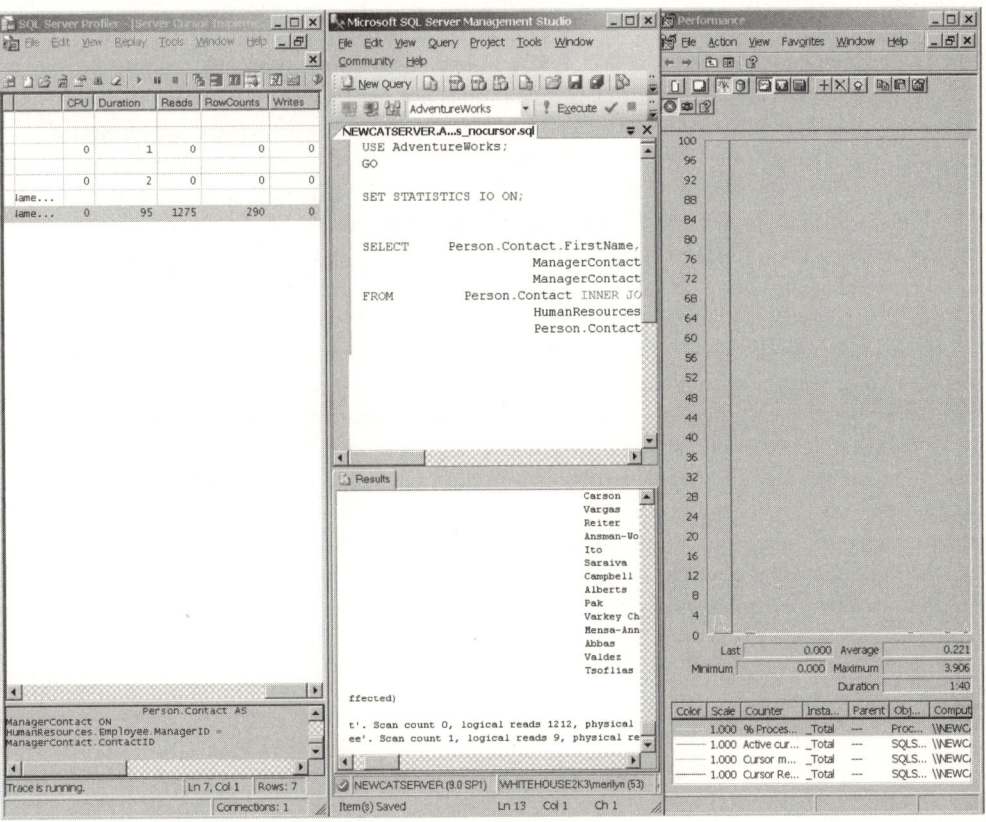

As you went through each of the previous exercises, you should have noted the cost of each of the technologies that were used to perform the join implementation task. We kept the number of rows constant and changed the cursor type. We also changed the implementation from cursor based to set based so that you could see that relationship.

We cannot stress this enough: whether the task is reading, modifying, or updating data, even though it is able to be done through a cursor strategy, try a set-based strategy first. If you decide on a cursor strategy, we have given you some performance monitoring tools to assist you in your development. These, along with our list of appropriate options, are crucial in assisting you in choosing the best strategy.

The key factors we want you to take away with you still reside in the words we bring from Lewis Carroll—keep an open mind and be aware.

Selecting Appropriate Client-Side Cursors

We had an earlier illustration of using a client-side cursor with a join that did not work out well at all. However, since we are still keeping an open mind, let's think this one out a little more. What if you needed to close the client's connection to the database once all the data was retrieved? Aha, now that client-side cursor deal does not have such a dark mark in our book!

A major benefit of client-side cursors is that the connection to the database can be closed. Once the data is held at the client, contention is reduced. The data is all yours for processing!

In Chapter 1 we defined the data access libraries of OLE DB, ODBC, ADO, and ADO.NET/SqlClient, and encapsulated the features of client-side cursors they support. As you recall, each data access library has its own feature set, making it a better choice for a given scenario. You will also recall that in both Chapters 1 and 2 we defined the SQL Native Client (SQLNCLI) data access provider and discussed in depth MARS implementations.

You should review the data access library features if you are considering a client-side cursor strategy so that you are able to choose the appropriate cursor strategy for your application. In your development and testing, make certain to set up a monitoring environment for your strategy. Recall that network performance will take a big hit in any client-side cursor implementation. The network performance involves more than you and your application; it is a very precious and watched over commodity. Another factor to consider in a client-side cursor implementation is the amount of physical memory in the client machines. The clients will need to cache large amounts of data. They must be able to handle this along with their regular workload or the application will not get off the ground.

Summary

In this chapter, we have presented all sides of the issue of determining a cursor strategy. You need to evaluate whether you are able to use a set-based implementation. SQL Server 2005 is optimized for set-based data access. Indexes, execution plan reuse, memory utilization, and locking algorithms are all based on set-based processing.

However, sometimes you may not be able to see your way through the forest because the individual trees are just too different and need to be handled so uniquely. This may be the time to call on a cursor strategy. We have given you the background of the advantages of each cursor option and how they work. We have given you some scenarios and monitoring strategies to put you on the right course. Continue to monitor and test as you develop to make certain that you have not strayed off course. A poorly chosen cursor strategy hurts more than your application; it affects your entire environment. We know. We have been there.

By the way, did you draw your circles and solve Lewis Carroll's syllogism? The answer is: *Babies cannot manage crocodiles*. However, perhaps our Australian author, Victor Isakov, can manage a crocodile! Check out Victor's book in our series *MCITP Developer: Microsoft SQL Server 2005 Database Solutions Design* (70-441) (Sybex, 2006).

Exam Essentials

Know how to design cursor logic.   You need to be able to determine when it is appropriate to implement a cursor strategy and the strategy to employ.

Know how to select an appropriate cursor type.   You need to know the cursor types and options, how each is implemented, as well as its pros and cons. You need to know how to use each type in an implementation.

Know how to design cursors that efficiently use server resources.   Once again, you need to know and understand the cursor types and their implementations at the server side. You need to understand the effects of server-side cursors on server memory, processing, and disk space. In addition you need to know the appropriate use of server-side cursors.

Know how to design cursors that minimize blocking.   Once again you need to know and understand the cursor types and their implementations at the client side. In addition to minimizing blocking, you need to know the appropriate use of client-side cursors.

Know how to design a strategy that minimizes or eliminates the use of cursors.   You need to be able to monitor server and network resources so that you do not design an inappropriate cursor strategy. You should always begin with a set-based strategy and proceed to a cursor strategy only when necessary. You need to be able to build a set-based strategy.

Review Questions

1. Which cursor option should you use if you are only interested in reading through a result set using minimal concurrency problems and not viewing modifications to underlying base tables?

   A. Dynamic cursor

   B. Static cursor

   C. Update_only cursor

   D. Keyset cursor

2. Which cursor option is the most resource intensive?

   A. Dynamic cursor

   B. Static cursor

   C. Keyset cursor

   D. Fast_forward cursor

3. Which cursor type uses the most disk space?

   A. Forward-only cursor

   B. Dynamic cursor

   C. Keyset-driven cursor

   D. Static cursor

4. Cursor strategies allow for the reuse of execution plans.

   A. True

   B. False

5. Which of the following are true about client-side cursors? (Choose all that apply.)

   A. Using client-side cursors requires several round-trips between the client and the server.

   B. Client-side cursors require more memory on the client machine for processing data.

   C. Client-side cursors are appropriate when the client is not always connected to the database.

   D. Client-side cursors are appropriate in join strategies.

6. Joe is a database developer who has implemented a keyset cursor strategy for an application that involves modifying and inserting data. While the cursor is open, he can view the modifications he makes to the underlying data but he cannot view the inserts. What has he done wrong?

   A. Joe just needs to hit F5 to refresh the data.

   B. Joe has implemented the incorrect cursor. He should use a static cursor.

   C. Joe has implemented the incorrect cursor. He should use a dynamic cursor.

   D. Joe should use a set-based solution. Cursors cannot be used for updating data.

7. John wanted to change his SQL Server's machine name. He decided to query his SQL Server metadata for the name of his machine. To do this he used a cursor solution to query all the system tables using a query string that had a format something like the following:

```
select name from sys.servers where name like '%machineName%'
```

Was John's cursor solution appropriate?

A. Yes

B. No

8. Your actuarial table uses complex accounting algorithms. Is it necessary to use a cursor to perform the row-by-row calculations if every row uses the same algorithm?

A. Yes

B. No

9. If you are using a client-side cursor strategy, which cursor implementation gives you the best performance?

A. Forward_only dynamic read_only

B. Forward_only static read_only

C. Forward_only keyset read_only

D. Forward_only non_updatable read_only

10. All the data for the Accounting application is retrieved from the Accounts database. A cursor strategy is implemented for the application. The clients are always connected to the database. Which type of strategy is more appropriate?

A. Server-side cursor

B. Client-side cursor

11. Which monitoring tools can you use to monitor cursor execution?

A. SQL Server Profiler

B. Replication Monitor

C. Activity Monitor

D. System Monitor

12. If you have the choice to implement a set-based or a cursor-based solution, which solution would be more appropriate?

A. Cursor based

B. Set based

13. Lyn has decided on a cursor strategy for an application she is designing. She needs to implement a cursor capable of modifying and viewing the modified data. No new data will be entered through this application. It is important that the modifications maintain their row order. Which cursor strategy should she use?

   A. Static cursor

   B. Keyset cursor

   C. Dynamic cursor

   D. Modifiable cursor

14. An application was written such that all the queries were executed as strings using sp_executesql. The application ran very slowly and used many resources. Which of the following might be the problem? (Choose all that apply.)

   A. The query strings were not written correctly.

   B. The query plans were not being cached.

   C. Row-based operations were being implemented.

   D. The query governor was not invoked.

15. A programmer should decide on a programming strategy based on how familiar they are with that strategy rather than how it fits the situation.

   A. True

   B. False

16. Which of the following SQL Server Profiler events are important to track for cursor execution? (Choose all that apply.)

   A. Cursors: CursorClose

   B. Cursors: CursorExecute

   C. Cursors: CursorOpen

   D. Cursors: CursorPrepare

17. What does the FETCH NEXT statement do?

   A. It retrieves the next row of data.

   B. It retrieves all remaining data to the end of the cursor definition.

   C. It moves the cursor to the beginning of the data.

   D. It moves the cursor to the end of the data.

18. What programming construct can you use if you want to process several rows of data using a cursor strategy?

   A. FOR loop

   B. WHILE loop

   C. CASE statement

   D. IF statement

19. What is a positioned update?

    A. A positioned update is a reference to a new row in the table in the same position as your cursor.

    B. A positioned update is an update that is moved to a new position.

    C. A positioned update is an update that targets the base table for the row that you are on in the cursor.

    D. A positioned update is an update that has been updated twice during the same cursor transaction.

20. Which client data access libraries that support client-side cursors enable multiple active statements on a connection? (Choose all that apply.)

    A. ADO

    B. SQL Native Client

    C. OLE DB

    D. ADO.NET 2.0/SqlClient

Answers to Review Questions

1. B. A static cursor copies all the data when opening the cursor into a temporary table in tempdb. Changes made to the underlying tables after the initial copy are not reflected in the data drawn on the fetch statements of the cursor. The dynamic and keyset cursor options both reflect modifications to the underlying base tables. Update_only is not a cursor option.

2. A. The dynamic cursor needs to run and fetch more rows on each FETCH operation making it the most resource intensive of all the cursor options. It also provides the most capabilities in that you are able to view data modified, updated, and deleted in the underlying base tables within the cursor.

3. D. The static cursor duplicates the data in a temporary table in tempdb. This procedure causes a large amount of disk space to be utilized.

4. B. Cursor strategies do not make use of SQL Server architectural resources such as caching memory.

5. A, B, C. Client-side cursors are not appropriate for join strategies. If cursors are used in joins, they should be server-side cursors

6. C. Dynamic cursors should be used when you need to have all changes to the underlying data visible through the cursor.

7. A. A cursor strategy is often very appropriate when tracking modifications. Using DDL commands within statements that are executed dynamically enable you to perform administrative tasks that would otherwise be extremely slow or cumbersome.

8. B. If every row uses the same algorithm, there is no need for a cursor implementation. This operation can be handled using a set-based implementation. Even if there were several groupings of rows, we would still choose a set-based implementation.

9. B. The forward_only static read_only gives the best performance. Forward-only cursors support fetching rows serially from the start to the end of the cursor; they do not support scrolling. The static cursor retrieves all its data when the cursor is opened and stores it in a temporary work table creating a higher performance factor than other cursor strategies.

10. A. The server-side strategy is more appropriate where all the data is in the same database. The processing can be handled at the server.

11. A, D. SQL Server Profiler and System Monitor both contain metrics that can be used to monitor cursor execution events.

12. B. If you have the choice, choose the set-based solution. The set-based solution uses the architecture and resources built into SQL Server 2005.

13. B. The keyset cursor meets Lyn's specifications. The static cursor is read only. The dynamic cursor could be implemented in this situation; however, it does not guarantee row order. There is no cursor named modifiable.

14. B, C. Possible problems might be that the query plans were not being cached so that they could be reused. Also, if a sp_executesql string was used for each row retrieval, this could cause several round-trips between the client and the server. Perhaps the queries could be rewritten using a set-based operation.

15. B. What might be comfortable in writing the code might not be applicable to the situation. The use of the application is the most important factor.

16. A, B, C, D. All are important to track cursor events.

17. A. The FETCH NEXT statement retrieves one row of data.

18. B. A WHILE loop can be used to process several row of data to the end of the cursor.

19. C. A positioned update is an update that targets the base table for the row that you are on in the cursor.

20. B, D. All flavors of SQL Native Client and ADO.NET 2.0/SqlClient enable MARS on a connection. (If you were a little rusty on this, review MARS in Chapter 2.)

Chapter 5

Planning Error Handling

MICROSOFT EXAM OBJECTIVES COVERED IN THIS CHAPTER:

- ✓ Design code that validates input data and permissions.
- ✓ Design code that detects and reacts to errors.
- ✓ Design user-defined messages to communicate application events.

Working with applications means dealing with errors from either bugs or unexpected user behavior. No matter how small an application is it will have bugs. And bugs cost the most precious resource we have: time. That includes users' time, support time, business time, and of course your time.

SQL Server 2005 comes with improved error-handling techniques that will make your applications reliable and more secure. These techniques include the new TRY...CATCH construct (available for a long time in other languages and database servers), enhanced monitoring tools (SQL Profiler, Dynamic Management Views and Functions), improved blocking and deadlocking detection.

In addition, you will see why and how to validate input data (and some reasons why you wouldn't do that), how and when to use the TRY...CATCH construct for error handling, and how to create and use user-defined messages.

Designing Code That Validates Input Data and Permissions

Every software developer should invest time making applications secure. Many developers focus on making their applications secure and reliable, but, even a SQL Server–based application running reliably and efficiently won't bring too much business value to your company if someone's code or sensitive business data is lost. Hackers using a SQL injection vulnerability can inject code into SQL Server and steal sensitive information.

To help you make your applications more secure, you should incorporate two best practices into your software development:

- Consider all user input to be malicious.
- Practice the principle of the least privilege.

Considering All User Input to Be Malicious

The first principle to help you make your applications more secure is to consider all user input to be malicious. Perhaps this seems harsh, but validating input data has an immediate result of enhanced security for your application. You can also improve reliability by preventing users from mistakenly entering a name in a field that should contain an age and generating a conversion error.

Assuming all user input is malicious means you must validate every bit of data. Failing to validate user input will make your application vulnerable to hackers or even honest users who can make an application crash by mistake. In some cases, your user may be the attacker: Don't rely on the user to be well intended.

You can take two approaches for validating user input:

- Disallowing certain characters or certain strings of characters (such as single quotes and hyphens)
- Allowing only required characters (such as digits for phone number)

The first approach is more difficult to implement and not as efficient as the second one. We strongly recommend you use the second approach whenever you have the choice because it requires testing a smaller range of characters. Think of the phone number example: it is easier to specify that allowed characters are only digits (and maybe the characters + and –) than to think of what would *not* represent a phone number.

For a practical example, suppose you want to filter the keyword SHUTDOWN. The following code sample demonstrates that you can represent the word SHUTDOWN in more ways than one. (It is more efficient to concentrate on what you should allow rather than on what you shouldn't.) The following code shows two different representations of the word SHUTDOWN, one using a hexadecimal form and one using the CHAR function (that returns the character corresponding to the specified ASCII code):

```
DECLARE @sql VARCHAR(MAX);
SET @sql = 0x53485554444F574E;
PRINT @sql;
GO


DECLARE @sql VARCHAR(MAX);
SET @sql= CHAR(83)+CHAR(72)+CHAR(85)+CHAR(84)+
    CHAR(68)+CHAR(79)+CHAR(87)+CHAR(78);
PRINT @sql;
GO
```

They both have the same output: SHUTDOWN. And these are not the only methods for representing a string.

Validating Input Data

In September 2004, CardSystems Solutions, one of several companies that process transactions for banks and merchants, had a "small" problem: hackers stole 263,000 credit card numbers and exposed another 40 million. How? The hackers used SQL injection—a technique that allows an attacker to run their own code with legitimate code.

In 2006, according to CVE (Common Vulnerabilities and Exposures), cross-site scripting (XSS) vulnerability is the favorite target of attackers followed closely by SQL injection. CVE is a list of standardized names for vulnerabilities and other information security exposures. CVE aims to standardize the names for all publicly known vulnerabilities and security exposures.

> **NOTE**   XSS is a type of computer security vulnerability typically found in web applications that an attacker can use to compromise the same origin policy of client-side scripting languages.

Last proof that SQL injection deserves your attention comes from SecureWorks in a newsletter from July 18, 2006:

> SecureWorks, a leading Managed IT Security Services Provider, announced that it has seen a dramatic increase in the number of hacker attacks attempted against its banking, credit union, and utility clients in the past three months using SQL Injection (a type of Web application attack). "From January through March, we blocked anywhere from 100 to 200 SQL Injection attacks per day," said SecureWorks CTO Jon Ramsey. "As of April, we have seen that number jump from 1,000 to 4,000 to 8,000 per day," said Ramsey.

You can prevent both cross-site scripting and SQL injection by validating input data.

We hope you are convinced that you should validate input data. In this section we tell you how. First decide what to validate and what type of validation to use. We suggest validating absolutely all input (at each layer level) and then checking the type, length, format, range, and content of user input.

We'll now show a practical example of how to validate the content of user input. One way to check the content is by using regular expressions. SQL Server 2005 doesn't support regular expressions, but you can use the power of .NET through the CLR integration. The following example illustrates a managed function written in C#:

```
using System;
using System.Data;
using System.Data.SqlClient;
using System.Data.SqlTypes;
using Microsoft.SqlServer.Server;
using System.Text.RegularExpressions;

public class ValidateFunctions
{
    [SqlFunction(IsDeterministic=true,IsPrecise=true)]
    public static bool RegExMatch(string pattern,string input)
    {
        Regex r = new Regex(pattern.TrimEnd(null));
        return r.Match(input.TrimEnd(null)).Success;
    }
}
```

You can deploy the function using Visual Studio 2005 or using the Transact-SQL statements CREATE ASSEMBLY and CREATE FUNCTION.

> For more information about deployment of CLR function, please refer to the "Deploying CLR Database Objects" topic in Books Online.

We will not go in too much detail about CLR integration since it is beyond the scope of this chapter. However, the function receives as arguments a string named input that would be validated against a regular expression pattern named, intuitively, pattern. If the input string matches the pattern, the function returns 1 and otherwise it returns 0.

The function is far from being perfect. We created it without input validation and *error handling* because we will use it again later in the chapter. Since the input is not validated, the function will crash if you use NULL arguments. The other weakness of the function is vulnerability to errors. If you pass an incorrect pattern as an argument, an exception is generated and the function will crash.

Let's see it at work:

```
SET NOCOUNT ON
-- Use a variable for the Regular Expression Pattern
DECLARE @RegExPattern varchar(MAX);
-- allow only digits and at least one digit
SET @RegExPattern = '^[0-9]+$';
-- The next statement will display 1
PRINT dbo.RegExMatch(@RegExPattern,'81818181');
-- The next statement will display 0
PRINT dbo.RegExMatch(@RegExPattern,'818181AB');
-- validate currency values
SET @RegExPattern = '^-?\d+(\.\d{2})?$';
-- The next statement will display 1
PRINT dbo.RegExMatch(@RegExPattern,'-42');
-- The next statement will display 0
-- only 2 digits are allowed after the decimal point
PRINT dbo.RegExMatch(@RegExPattern,'10.501');

-- Output
1
0
1
0
```

You've just seen a couple of simple validations, but the options are virtually unlimited. You can validate almost anything you can think of, from postal codes and e-mail addresses to filenames—anything that can be expressed as a regular expression.

Understanding SQL Injection

One of the vulnerabilities that you can prevent by properly using input validation is SQL injection. The SQL injection vulnerability can affect any database server. Basically, it consists of adding hostile code to the code submitted by an application to a database server. Most of the time the attacker does that by manipulating the input of an application. As a result, the application submits to the database server its original code plus some extra SQL statements the attacker has inserted. We will provide you with some examples later in this section. Input validation is a countermeasure for this type of threat, but we have to warn you that input validation is not enough.

Being Susceptible to an SQL Injection Attack

If you wonder what could be the impact of SQL injection or what headaches can you get from it, here's a short list:

Individual or massive identity theft   The attacker can steal identity and personal information.

Information disclosure   The attacker can access confidential information from SQL Server or from the network.

Data loss   The attacker can delete data and drop tables and databases.

Elevation of privileges   The attacker can obtain increased privileges using the account under which SQL Server instance is running.

In some extreme situations such as when a SQL Server instance runs under a domain administrator account, the attacker can gain control of your complete network. The SQL injection itself cannot do much damage without the "help" of improperly configured servers.

A classic example will give you a better image of how SQL injection can wreak havoc. Let's say a web application uses the following code written in C# to authenticate the application users:

```
01 SqlConnection myConn = new SqlConnection();
02 myConn.ConnectionString = "data source=MYSERVER;" +
03                           "initial catalog=MYDB;" +
04                           "user id=sa;password=sa;";
05 string strSql =    "SELECT COUNT(*) FROM AppUsers " +
06                    "WHERE LOGIN='" + txtLogin.Text +
07                    "'AND Password='" + txtPassword.Text + "'";
08 SqlCommand myComm = new SqlCommand(strSql, myConn);
09 myConn.Open();
10 int i = (int)myComm.ExecuteScalar();
11 if(i>0)
12 {
```

```
13  //Login successful
14 };
```

If C# or .NET languages are not familiar ground to you, we'll explain the previous code now.

You use the SqlClient provider of ADO.NET to submit a simple query to a SQL server named MYSERVER. For that you use two objects, a connection (myConn) and a command (myComm). If the execution of the query returns any rows, you can consider the user to be authenticated. Your honest user Bob may generate the following SQL query by typing his user ID and password:

```
SELECT COUNT(*) FROM AppUsers
WHERE LOGIN = 'Bob' AND PASSWORD = 'BobPwd '
```

On the other hand a malicious user can enter **Bob' OR 1=1 --** as the login, as shown in Figure 5.1, generating the following SQL query:

```
SELECT * FROM AppUsers
WHERE LOGIN = 'Bob' OR 1=1 -- ' And Password = ''
```

As you may guess, the query will count all rows from the AppUsers table, and this way our attacker will be authenticated successfully. Unfortunately, this is just the beginning. The attacker can enter **Bob' OR 1=1; SHUTDOWN; --** , as shown in Figure 5.2, generating the following query:

```
SELECT * FROM AppUsers
WHERE LOGIN = 'Bob' OR 1=1; SHUTDOWN; -- ' And Password = ''
```

FIGURE 5.1   Entering Bob' OR 1=1 --

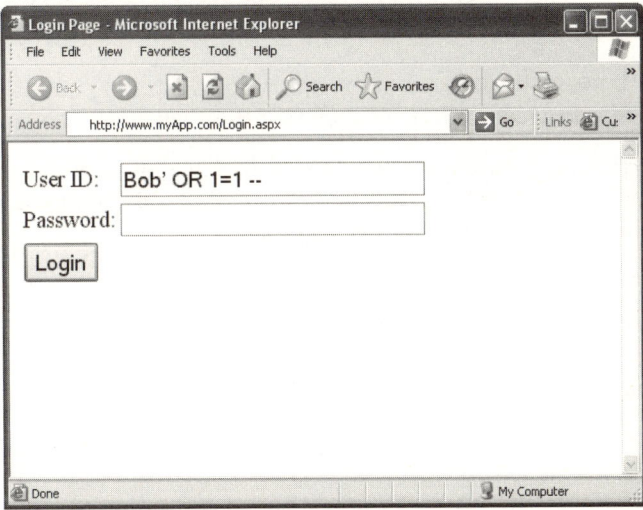

FIGURE 5.2   Entering Bob' OR 1=1; SHUTDOWN;

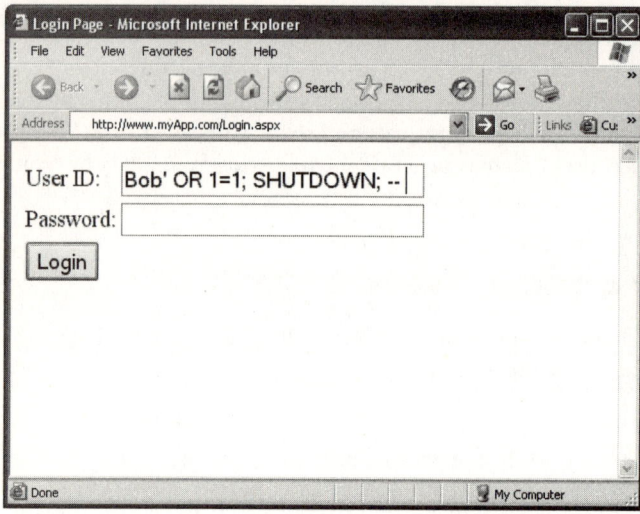

Since the application connects with sysadmin privileges, you can replace SHUTDOWN with virtually any command. One of the favorites for any attacker is the extended stored procedure xp_cmdshell that allows running operating system commands.

 In SQL Server 2005 xp_cmdshell is disabled by default, but you can enable it using either Transact-SQL or the Surface Area Configuration Utility.

Another example of vulnerable code is the following excerpt from a web application:

```
var ProductID
ProductID = Request("ProductID");
var sql = "SELECT * FROM Products WHERE ProductID=" + ProductID;
```

The previous code (written in JavaScript) retrieves information about a product using a product ID as parameter. The product ID is received from another web page by submitting a form. You can see a simplified version of the web page here:

```
<HTML>
 <HEAD><TITLE>Product Search</TITLE></HEAD>
 <BODY>
  <FORM ACTION='ProductById.asp' METHOD='GET'>
   <TABLE>
    <TR>
     <TD>Product ID:</TD>
     <TD><INPUT TYPE=Text NAME=ProductID /></TD>
```

```
    </TR>
    <TR>
     <TD><INPUT TYPE=Submit VALUE='Search'  /></TD>
     <TD><INPUT TYPE=Reset VALUE='Reset' /></TD>
    </TR>
   </TABLE>
  </FORM>
 </BODY>
</HTML>
```

You can avoid using the original form by entering the following URL in a browser:

```
http://www.myapp.com/ProductById.asp?ProductID=1000
```

Obviously, nothing will stop you to enter the following URL:

```
http://www.myapp.com/ProductById.asp?ProductID=1000;SHUTDOWN
```

By now it's clear that this application is also a perfect candidate for SQL injection. Again, lack of input validation makes your code vulnerable.

How can you prevent SQL injection? Let's identify the mistakes of the previously presented code and extract some preventive measures from them:

Mistake 1   The first mistake is using too many unnecessary privileges for an operation. A simple select from a table does not require using a login that is a member of the sysadmin fixed server role. The preventive measure in this case is to use the principle of least privilege. We will discuss this principle soon.

Mistake 2   The second mistake is that the SQL account has a weak password and the connection string is not stored secure. To correct the latter, you should encrypt your connection string and store it securely in registry or in a configuration file.

 It is preferable to store the connection string in the registry when you have the choice. If you really have to store it in a configuration file, store it encrypted.

Also there is no excuse for weak passwords. Working as consultants, we have the chance to see all kinds of weak passwords for the sa account, so here is our list of the worst passwords used in production:

- The infamous blank password—nothing can beat: " "
- Our second choice for lack of inventiveness: sa
- Reversing sa, a lame try of security by obscurity: as
- The well-known message "please enter your password": password
- And a password that will resist a brute-force attack in most cases for less than a millisecond: p

We urge you to avoid these top five production passwords. And if you don't know yet, in SQL Server 2005 you have the option to disable or to rename the sa account. The following is the code for both situations:

```
-- disable sa account
ALTER LOGIN sa DISABLE;
GO
-- rename sa account
ALTER LOGIN sa WITH NAME = [myAdminAccount];
GO
```

As an additional measure, you can use password policies to enforce the complexity of the passwords. In SQL Server 2005, password policies are available both for Windows and SQL logins. However, password policies for SQL logins require a Windows Server 2003 or newer operating system. On Windows Server 2000 and Windows XP, only a rudimentary complexity check is available (such as checking for blank passwords, and so on).

Mistake 3 The third mistake is that the user input is not validated and the remedy is to consider all user input as malicious and to treat it accordingly.

Mistake 4 The fourth mistake is using dynamic SQL instead of parameterized queries or stored procedures.

Mistake 5 The fifth mistake is that error handling is completely missing, and this can make the application vulnerable.

Preventing SQL Injection

And now let's explore the preventive measures:

Validate user input. Reject everything that doesn't represent valid input. Implement input validation in each layer of your application. For example in an ASP.NET application you can validate the user input at the client, then at the server (the web server) and finally at the database level.

Use the principle of least privilege. This recommendation is generally applicable. For example the SQL Server services should not run in the context of a domain administrator. The next topic will show you how to implement this principle at the SQL Server level.

Do not use dynamic SQL. You should avoid dynamic SQL and use parameterized queries or stored procedures instead. Besides protecting you from SQL injection, using stored procedures has several other benefits, which we will get back to soon.

Store secrets securely. Encrypt passwords or other secrets and store them securely.

Use proper exception handling. Developing exception handling is crucial. The second section of this chapter is dedicated to this best practice.

Use strong passwords. Strong passwords are a general recommendation.

Additionally, a good practice is to follow the defense-in-depth security model. Inspired from a military strategy, this model proposes seven levels of security defenses: Data, Application, Host, Internal Network, Perimeter, Physical Security, and finally Policies, Procedures, and Awareness. As a developer, you should be concerned by the data and application layers without forgetting the whole picture.

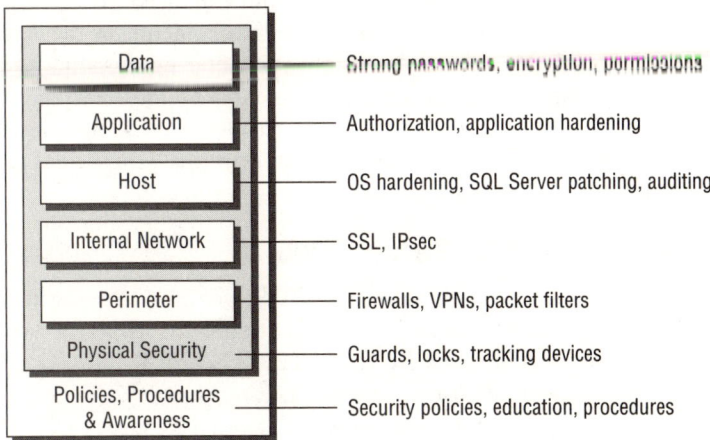

Data	Strong passwords, encryption, permissions
Application	Authorization, application hardening
Host	OS hardening, SQL Server patching, auditing
Internal Network	SSL, IPsec
Perimeter	Firewalls, VPNs, packet filters
Physical Security	Guards, locks, tracking devices
Policies, Procedures & Awareness	Security policies, education, procedures

Defense in Depth Model

 You can get more information from the Books Online topic "Security Considerations for SQL Server" and from the following site: https://www.securityguidance.com/.

Using Stored Procedures

There's an eternal debate in the programming world regarding using stored procedures versus ad hoc queries. We prefer stored procedures for the following reasons:

Greater security   Using stored procedures adds another layer of defense to your application.

Encapsulation   Somewhat similar to the object-oriented programming, you can use encapsulation at a database level by exposing your data through stored procedures and not directly.

Performance   Most of the time, stored procedures will increase the performance of your application if you replace ad hoc queries. Admittedly in some situations you can make your ad hoc queries run as fast as a stored procedure using query plan's caching. We talk more about the plan cache in Chapter 7.

Loosely coupled modules   You should be able to change your database code without affecting your application's code, and stored procedures can give you the means to do that.

Understanding the Principle of the Least Privilege

Along with considering all user input to be malicious, you can definitely improve the security of your applications by considering the "principle of the least privilege," which affirms that a user should have just the minimum possible privileges to complete a task—no more, no less.

The security model in SQL Server 2005 is way beyond enhanced, so we concentrate on several features that allow you to write code following the principle of the least privilege. The main topics of the following sections are highly granular permissions and context-switching functionality using the EXECUTE AS statement. Though we will not cover code signing and ownership chaining topics, you should consider them as options of changing the execution context. Also, when you design your applications, you should have in mind the complete security model of SQL Server 2005.

Setting Permissions in SQL Server 2005

Many SQL Server 2000 features were enhanced in SQL Server 2005. Permissions are no exception. They are more granular and can be granted at different scopes (server, database, and schema). The new ones include CONTROL, ALTER ANY, or IMPERSONATE ON.

You can grant permissions for almost any action and any object. We say *almost* because some actions still do not have a grantable permission. Yet you have more than 180 grantable permissions that allow you to give just the necessary rights for a specific action.

To get an idea of what permissions you can grant, run the following code:

```
SELECT
class_desc AS class,
permission_name AS permission,
type,
covering_permission_name AS covering_permission,
parent_class_desc AS parent_class
FROM fn_builtin_permissions(default);
GO
-- Partial Output
class      permission        type  covering_permission    parent_class
-------------------------------------------------------------------

DATABASE CREATE TABLE      CRTB  ALTER SERVER          CONTROL SERVER
DATABASE CREATE VIEW       CRVW  ALTER SERVER          CONTROL SERVER
DATABASE CREATE PROCEDURE  CRPR  ALTER SERVER          CONTROL SERVER
DATABASE CREATE FUNCTION   CRFN  ALTER SERVER          CONTROL SERVER
DATABASE CREATE RULE       CRRU  ALTER SERVER          CONTROL SERVER
DATABASE CREATE DEFAULT    CRDF  ALTER SERVER          CONTROL SERVER
   ...
```

We displayed just a partial result since the query returns 187 rows. What do you see here? The output is a list with all built-in permissions containing the securable class, the name of permission, the compact permission type code, the covering permission name, and the name of the parent class (containing the current class).

See the "sys.fn_builtin_permissions" topic from Books Online for additional details.

Using EXECUTE AS

One of the practices we recommend for developing database applications is to mediate access to base tables and objects through stored procedures and views. How to do that? The first step is to create stored procedures that implement the essential database operations for each base table: Create, Read, Update, and Delete (known as the CRUD operations). Then, grant Execute permission to your users on the stored procedures instead of the base tables. This allows you to simplify permissions management and to hide the underlying schema of your database from the end user.

To implement this practice, you have several options available:

- Ownership chaining
- Code signing (consists in signing modules within the database such as stored procedures, triggers, functions, or assemblies)
- EXECUTE AS statement

This section is dedicated to the last method—using the EXECUTE AS statement. Before using the EXECUTE AS statement or any other similar one, it is important to understand two concepts: execution context and context switching. *Execution context* establishes the identity against which the permissions are checked. In short, execution context establishes identity that will be checked for permissions to run code or execute certain actions. *Context switching* means changing the execution context of a session, a module (such as a stored procedure), or a dynamic string.

Also see Books Online to learn more about these two concepts. In particular you should look at the following topics: "Context Switching," "Understanding Context Switching," and "Understanding Execution Context."

As the proverb says, there's more than one way to skin a cat, and this is true for context switching also. However, we can promise you that the subject is not too complicated. Let's examine each case.

Changing the Execution Context of a Session

As mentioned, we will tell you how to use the EXECUTE AS statement. Here's the syntax:

```
{ EXEC | EXECUTE ] AS <context_specification>
[;]
```

```
<context_specification>::=
{ LOGIN | USER } = 'name'
    [ WITH { NO REVERT | COOKIE INTO @varbinary_variable } ]
| CALLER
```

You can change the execution context by impersonating a login or a user. If you specify the NO REVERT option, the execution cannot be reverted to the previous context. Otherwise, you can use the REVERT statement for that purpose.

If you use the option COOKIE INTO @varbinary variable, the execution context can be reverted to the previous context if you supply the exact value of @varbinary_variable in the REVERT statement. In addition, the EXECUTE AS CALLER can be used inside of a module to change the context of execution to the caller of the module.

 You must grant the caller IMPERSONATE before running the EXECUTE AS statement.

If you need to determine the login that connected to the SQL Server, you can use the ORIGINAL_LOGIN function.

The next several examples will give you a better picture. You will create two logins and two users and change the execution context several times:

```
USE tempdb;
GO
--Create temporary logins and users
CREATE LOGIN BobLogin WITH PASSWORD = 'yukon9.0';
CREATE LOGIN TedLogin WITH PASSWORD = 'shiloh8.0';
GO
CREATE USER Bob FOR LOGIN BobLogin;
CREATE USER Ted FOR LOGIN TedLogin;
GO
--Grant IMPERSONATE permissions on Ted
GRANT IMPERSONATE ON USER:: Ted TO Bob;
GO
-- Display the execution context.
--Output on my computer: MICROTRAINING\Cristi     dbo
SELECT SUSER_NAME() AS LoginName,
        USER_NAME() AS UserName;
-- Change execution context to BobLogin.
EXECUTE AS LOGIN = 'BobLogin';
-- Display the execution context.
-- Output: BobLogin     Bob
SELECT SUSER_NAME() AS LoginName,
```

```
        USER_NAME() AS UserName;
--Change the execution context.
EXECUTE AS USER = 'Ted';
-- Display the execution context.
-- Output: TedLogin    Ted
SELECT SUSER_NAME() AS LoginName,
        USER_NAME() AS UserName;
-- To check the initial login
-- Output on my computer: MICROTRAINING\Cristi
SELECT ORIGINAL_LOGIN() AS InitialLogin;
-- Change back the execution context
REVERT;
-- Display the execution context.
-- Output: BobLogin    Bob
SELECT SUSER_NAME() AS LoginName,
        USER_NAME() AS UserName;
REVERT;
-- Display the execution context.
-- Output on my computer: MICROTRAINING\Cristi dbo
SELECT SUSER_NAME() AS LoginName,
        USER_NAME() AS UserName;
GO
--clean-up.
DROP USER Bob;
DROP USER Ted;
DROP LOGIN BobLogin;
DROP LOGIN TedLogin;
GO
```

In the first part of the code sample, you create two logins and two users (each one associated to one login). Then you grant impersonate permission to the user Bob, this way allowing Bob to impersonate Ted.

In the second part, you switch the execution context several times and display the current login and the current user. The execution context changes from the original login (used to connect to SQL Server) to Bob and then to Ted and back.

The last part of the code is for cleanup, deleting the new logins and the new users.

Changing the Execution Context of a Module

Another way to change the execution context is to use the EXECUTE AS clause in modules such as functions, stored procedures and triggers. You can use the same clause for Service Broker queries.

The syntax depends on the module types:

```
Functions (except inline table-valued functions), Stored Procedures,
 and DML Triggers
{ EXEC | EXECUTE } AS { CALLER | SELF | OWNER | 'user_name' }


DDL Triggers with Database Scope
{ EXEC | EXECUTE } AS { CALLER | SELF | 'user_name' }


DDL Triggers with Server Scope
{ EXEC | EXECUTE } AS { CALLER | SELF | 'login_name' }


Queues
{ EXEC | EXECUTE } AS { SELF | OWNER | 'user_name' }
```

You have four options available for functions, stored procedures, or Data Manipulation Language (DML) triggers and only three options for Data Definition Language (DDL) triggers and queues:

CALLER   The code inside the module will be executed in the context of the caller. This is the behavior of SQL Server 2000 and the default setting.

SELF   The code will be executed in the context of the user who is creating or altering the module. EXECUTE AS SELF is the same as specifying EXECUTE AS username, where the username is the user that is creating or altering the module.

OWNER   The context of the owner of the module will be used to execute the code.

'user_name'   The identity of the specified user will be used to execute the code inside the module. You can use it to create custom permission sets.

You can change the context of execution inside of a module if you want. Here's an example:

```
USE tempdb;
     GO
     --Create temporary logins and users
     CREATE LOGIN BobLogin WITH PASSWORD = 'yukon9.0';
     CREATE LOGIN TedLogin WITH PASSWORD = 'shiloh8.0';
     GO
     CREATE USER Bob FOR LOGIN BobLogin;
     CREATE USER Ted FOR LOGIN TedLogin;
     GO
     --Grant IMPERSONATE permissions on Ted
     GRANT IMPERSONATE ON USER:: Ted TO Bob;
     GO
     -- Create a stored procedure
     CREATE PROCEDURE ups_ExecuteAS WITH EXECUTE AS 'Bob'
```

```
        AS
        BEGIN
        SELECT USER_NAME() AS UserName;
        EXECUTE AS USER='Ted';
        SELECT USER_NAME() AS UserName;
        REVERT;
        EXECUTE AS CALLER;
        SELECT USER_NAME() AS UserName;
        REVERT;
        SELECT USER_NAME() AS UserName;
END
GO
EXEC ups_ExecuteAS;
GO
-- Output: Bob Ted dbo Bob
-- The output displays dbo because my user (the caller) is a dbo
```

Similar to the earlier code sample, the previous code shows how to switch the execution context but this time in a stored procedure.

To clean up by deleting the stored procedure and the users, run the next code:

```
USE tempdb;
GO
DROP PROCEDURE ups_ExecuteAS;
DROP USER Bob;
DROP USER Ted;
DROP LOGIN BobLogin;
DROP LOGIN TedLogin;
GO
```

Creating Custom Permissions

Our favorite usage of the EXECUTE AS clause is to secure a database through encapsulation. You can prevent direct access to base objects and grant access to mediating stored procedures and views. However, you have another way to use the EXECUTE AS clause, and that is to create custom permission sets. Though SQL Server permissions cover almost every action, some do not have grantable permissions. For example, the TRUNCATE TABLE statement requires ALTER permissions on the specified table. If you want to allow a user to truncate a table and at the same time comply with the principle of least privilege, you can achieve both by using the EXECUTE AS clause in a stored procedure. For example, if the database user Bob has permissions to truncate a table named Orders and another user Ted needs to be able to truncate it, Bob can create the following stored procedure:

```
CREATE PROCEDURE TruncateOrders WITH EXECUTE AS 'Bob'
AS
```

```
BEGIN
TRUNCATE TABLE CompanyDB.Sales.Orders;
END
GO
```

When Ted executes the TruncateOrders stored procedure, it will run with Bob's permissions. This method allows you to grant just the necessary permission for a task.

Changing the Execution Context of a Dynamic String

The last method of changing the execution context we illustrate is changing the execution context of a dynamic string. We do not recommend using string concatenation or executing dynamic SQL. However, sometimes you have to use these methods, so in this section we'll provide you with a method to do it safely by customizing the execution context. You can use for that the EXECUTE statement.

The syntax is simple:

```
{ EXEC | EXECUTE }
        ( { @string_variable | [ N ]'tsql_string' } [ + ...n ] )
    [ AS { LOGIN | USER } = ' name ' ]
[;]
```

To see it at work, you can run the following example that will run a select in the context of a user named Bob. To see the effect of context switching, the query returns the username:

```
USE tempdb;
GO
CREATE LOGIN BobLogin WITH PASSWORD = 'yukon9.0';
GO
CREATE USER Bob FOR LOGIN BobLogin;
GO
-- Output: Bob
EXECUTE ('SELECT USER_NAME();') AS USER = 'Bob';
GO
DROP USER Bob;
DROP LOGIN BobLogin;
GO
```

Use context switching with care. You can lower but also elevate privileges and that combined with string concatenation can make your code vulnerable.

Designing Code That Detects and Reacts to Errors

As a software developer, you should keep in mind the following design goals for your applications:

Availability   The application should be present and ready for business.

Manageability   The administration of the application should be as easy as possible.

Performance   How the application behaves under load should be measurable.

Reliability   The application should behave in a predictable manner.

Scalability   The application should support increased demands by increasing available resources.

Securability   The application should protect its data and its resources.

Can you imagine one of the above design goals satisfied by an application built without proper error handling? Every design goal mentioned depends on error handling. That's why this topic is very important for your exam and even more important for your job as a software developer. This section will review every aspect of error handling in SQL Server 2005, especially the new TRY...CATCH construct.

What does error handling mean? Basically, error handling is the effective management of errors and may include several of the following steps:

- Preventing the error in the first place using a proactive approach to error handling
- Executing cleanup code (deallocate cursors, close open transactions, and so on)
- Logging the error information
- Recovering from the error
- Sending notifications about the error
- Propagating the error to other layers of application

 You may find the term *exception handling* used for the same purpose as *error handling*. For SQL Server, these terms can be used interchangeably but you may want to know that there is a difference between them in some languages.

Understanding the Structure of an Error

Let's take a look at an error message by running the next statement:

```
SELECT CAST('NotAnInt' AS INT)
```

Obviously, trying to convert the NotAtInt string to an integer data type will generate an error. The error message displayed will be as follows (provided you have the default language English):

```
Msg 245, Level 16, State 1, Line 1
Conversion failed when converting the varchar
value 'NotAnInt' to data type int.
```

You will notice that this particular error message has a message number, a severity level, a state, a line where it occurred, and a message text. Additionally, when the error occurs inside a stored procedure (or trigger), you will also get the procedure name. You should know the following about the error messages components:

Error number   Identifies each error message. You will find all system and *user-defined messages* in the sys.messages catalog view. The error number (or the message ID) is less than 50000 for system messages and greater than 50000 for user-defined ones. The 50000 error number is reserved for errors generated using RAISERROR when you don't specify an error number as argument. For example if you run the following statement:

```
RAISERROR ('No number specified',16,1)
```

You will get this message:

```
Msg 50000, Level 16, State 1, Line 1
No number specified
```

Severity level   Is a number between 0 and 25 that indicates how severe the error is. You will find out more about severity levels in the next section.

State   Provides additional information about an error by means of a value between 0 and 127. Some errors may occur in different situations and the state can help identify the particular case. We get back to this attribute in the RAISERROR section.

Procedure   Displayed when the error occurs in a stored procedure (or trigger) and represents the name of the stored procedure (or trigger).

Line   Identifies the line number where the error occurred.

Message text   Represents textual information about the cause of the error. It can contain parameters and supports localization.

Understanding the Levels of Severity

When SQL Server raises an error, the *severity of the error* indicates the importance of the problem and also some of the consequences. For example, an error with severity 20 or above might terminate the database connection whereas an error with severity 10 would be considered an informational message and it won't affect code execution at all.

The severity of an error can have a value between 0 and 25, and using the severity level the error messages can be grouped as shown in Table 5.1.

TABLE 5.1   Error Severity

Severity Level	Description
0–10	Informational messages or warnings
11–16	Errors that can be corrected by the user
17–19	Errors that cannot be corrected by the user and should be managed by system administrators
20–25	System problems and fatal errors

You should keep in mind that errors with the severity level between 17 and 25 are considered to be severe and can determine the following effects:

- Stop the current running batch.
- Terminate the database connection.
- Shutdown the instance of SQL Server.
- Indicate database damage and require restoring the database.
- Indicate hardware or software problems.

 If you want to get additional details about severity levels, you should read the "Database Engine Error Severities" Books Online topic.

Using @@ERROR

The @@ERROR function was the primary mechanism of handling errors in previous versions of SQL Server. It basically returns 0 if the last Transact-SQL statement executed successfully or the error number if the statement generated an error.

Something important to remember if you use this function is that each statement will reset its value. So in some cases, it would be a good idea to save its value in a variable.

The following example illustrates the use of @@ERROR function by moving an employee from an old table to a new one:

```
DECLARE @ErrorInsert INT,
        @ErrorDelete INT;
BEGIN TRANSACTION
```

```
INSERT INTO RetiredEmployees (OldEmployeeID, FirstName, LastName)
VALUES ('JSMITH','John','Smith')

SET @ErrorInsert = @@ERROR

IF @ErrorInsert <> 0 GOTO ErrorLabel

DELETE FROM Employees
WHERE EmployeeID = 'JSMITH'

SET @ErrorInsert = @@ERROR

IF @ErrorInsert <> 0 GOTO ErrorLabel

-- Success
COMMIT TRANSACTION
GOTO ExitCode

ErrorLabel:
ROLLBACK TRANSACTION

ExitCode:
-- Exit point for this code
```

As you can see, the IF...GOTO combination can easily create the so-called spaghetti code, it's not at all readable, and you will see in the next topic that the new TRY...CATCH block is by far a better way to handle errors.

Another function that you may use in your code is @@ROWCOUNT. It returns the number of rows affected by the last Transact-SQL statement. When would you use @@ROWCOUNT? In general, it is used to detect whether your UPDATE (INSERT or DELETE) statement changed anything:

```
USE AdventureWorks;
GO
UPDATE Person.Contact
SET Phone = N'398-555-0132'
WHERE ContactID = 21222
IF @@ROWCOUNT = 0
PRINT 'No rows were updated!';
GO
-- Output
No rows were updated!
```

Just like @@ERROR, the @@ROWCOUNT function is reset after each statement so if you want to use it, it may be a good idea to save its value. If you need both @@ROWCOUNT and @@ERROR, you can save them using the following code:

```
DECLARE @ErrorSave INT,
        @RowCountSave INT;


UPDATE  MyTable
SET     SomeColumn = @SomeValue
WHERE     IdColumn = @IdValue;


SELECT  @ErrorSave = @@ERROR,
        @RowCountSave = @@ROWCOUNT;
```

Using Try...Catch

Available initially in C++ and Java and later in .NET CLR, structured exception handling is a fundamental feature for all programming languages. SQL Server 2005 enhances Transact-SQL by introducing the TRY...CATCH construct for handling errors. We discuss how to use the TRY...CATCH construct as well as what errors can be caught, different usage scenarios, limitations, and best practices.

The basic syntax of the TRY...CATCH construct is as follows:

```
BEGIN TRY
    { sql_statement | statement_block }
END TRY
BEGIN CATCH
    { sql_statement | statement_block }
END CATCH
[ ; ]
```

A TRY block must be followed by a CATCH block. Inside the TRY block, you should include statements that may generate errors. Let's see a simple example:

```
SET NOCOUNT ON
BEGIN TRY
    PRINT 'Begin execution'
    SELECT CAST('NotAnInt' AS INT)
    PRINT 'Finish Execution'
END TRY
    BEGIN CATCH
    PRINT 'An error ocurred'
END CATCH
```

As you may guess, running the code will generate the following result:

```
Begin execution
An error ocurred
```

Casting the "NotAnInt" string generated an error, and that caused the execution to be transferred to the CATCH block. If we remove the SELECT statement that caused the error, the output of the construct would be as follows:

```
-- Hypothetical Output
Begin execution
Finish Execution
```

The TRY…CATCH construct has several facts and limitations you should consider:

- A CATCH block must immediately follow a TRY block. This is important.

- There is no FINALLY block. If you are not familiar with TRY…CATCH construct from other languages, the FINALLY block follows the CATCH block. It is used usually to include cleanup code as the code from a FINALLY block executes always.

- The TRY…CATCH construct block can catch errors that have a severity higher than 10. Errors with the severity level 20 or greater will be caught by the TRY…CATCH construct as long as the database connection is not closed.

- Errors with severity level 10 or lower are considered informational messages or warnings and will not be handled by the TRY…CATCH construct.

- The TRY…CATCH construct can be nested, meaning that TRY…CATCH constructs can be placed inside other TRY blocks or CATCH blocks.

- You cannot have multiple CATCH blocks for the same TRY block (as in other programming languages) and you cannot catch a specific error.

- The scope of a TRY block consists of the code between BEGIN TRY and END TRY, including new levels on the stack such as calling stored procedures, trigger execution, and so on.

- You can use GOTO statements inside of a TRY or a CATCH block and to leave a TRY or a CATCH block. However, you cannot use GOTO statements to enter a TRY or a CATCH block.

- You can rethrow errors caught with TRY…CATCH construct using the RAISERROR statement. As you will see in the RAISERROR section you cannot rethrow the exact error but, as in many other cases, you have a workaround available.

- In some situations one error will generate multiple error messages. In this case the *error functions* will be set by the last error message. Here's an example for such a case (thanks to Naveen Prakash from the SQL Programmability & API Development Team):

```
BEGIN TRY
  -- generate two errors
  -- Msg 2714, Level 16, State 6, Line 7
```

```
-- There is already an object named 'MyTable' in the database.
-- Msg 2759, Level 16, State 0, Line 7
-- CREATE SCHEMA failed due to previous errors.
        EXEC ('

                    CREATE SCHEMA MySchema

                    CREATE TABLE MyTable(id int)

                    CREATE TABLE MyTable (id int)

                ');
END TRY
BEGIN CATCH
        PRINT error_message();
END CATCH


-- Output
-- CREATE SCHEMA failed due to previous errors.
```

Catchable Errors

Using the TRY...CATCH construct allows you to catch any errors that set the @@ERROR function, which means the errors with a severity greater than 10 and less than 20 (and errors with the severity 20 and greater as long as they do not break the database connection). Considering how an error may affect code execution they can be classified as follows:

Statement abort errors Cause the current statement to be aborted and rolled back (if necessary). Execution continues with the next statement (if any). In this category of errors you may find errors such as "Violation of PRIMARY KEY constraint", "Cannot insert the value NULL", and so on. To see a short example run the following code:

```
USE tempdb;
GO
CREATE TABLE myTable (ID INT NOT NULL PRIMARY KEY)
GO
INSERT INTO myTable VALUES(1)
-- This statement will fail
-- but execution will continue
INSERT INTO myTable VALUES(1)
INSERT INTO myTable VALUES(2)
-- Check what was inserted
SELECT * FROM myTable
```

Level (scope) abort errors   Terminates the current statement's scope execution (stored procedure, user-defined function, and so on) and will have the same behavior as a statement abort error for the caller.

Batch abort errors   Causes the execution of the entire batch to be aborted. Conversion errors for example can be the cause of a batch abort error.

Transaction abort errors   Aborts the batch and rolls back the transaction.

The TRY…CATCH construct can handle successfully all of the previous errors. However, some types of error will get away from a TRY…CATCH construct and you can see which ones in the next section.

Unhandled Errors

Though the TRY…CATCH construct is more than useful and we advise you to use it whenever you can, it has its limitations. Some types of errors cannot be caught—though in some cases workarounds are available:

Compile errors   As in most programming languages, you cannot catch compile errors using a TRY…CATCH construct when the error is generated at the same level as the TRY block. However, you can catch a compile error generated at a lower level. A couple of short examples will show you the difference:

```
BEGIN TRY
     PRINT 'Entering the TRY block'
     -- generate a compile error
     SELECT *
END TRY
BEGIN CATCH
     PRINT 'Entering the CATCH block'
END CATCH


-- Output
Msg 263, Level 16, State 1, Line 4
Must specify table to select from.
```

And here is the workaround:

```
BEGIN TRY
     PRINT 'Entering the TRY block'
     -- use dynamic sql
     EXEC sp_executesql N'SELECT *'
END TRY
BEGIN CATCH
     PRINT 'Entering the CATCH block'
     PRINT ERROR_MESSAGE()
```

```
END CATCH

-- Output
Entering the TRY block
Entering the CATCH block
Must specify table to select from.
```

Using dynamic SQL generated the error at a lower level than the TRY block and this way the error became catchable. We recommend you handle all errors, and the purpose of the above technique is to show you how to do that for compile errors.

Recompile errors   Recompile errors are errors that occur when a statement is recompiled due to changes in schema, statistics, object name resolution, or errors occurring after the compilation due to deferred name resolution. Microsoft's SQL Programmability & API development team decided to use the same behavior in case of a TRY...CATCH as they did for the compile errors for consistency reasons. The bottom line is that the TRY...CATCH construct cannot catch recompile errors when they occur at the same level of execution. However, there is a workaround—to execute the offending statements in a TRY block at a lower level of execution by calling a stored procedure or using dynamic SQL. The following examples give you an idea of both workarounds:

```
BEGIN TRY
    -- the PRINT will execute
    PRINT 'Entering the TRY block'
    -- but the next statement will fail
    SELECT * FROM ThisTableDoesNotExist
END TRY
BEGIN CATCH
    PRINT 'Entering the CATCH block'
    PRINT ERROR_MESSAGE()
END CATCH

-- Output
Entering the TRY block
Msg 208, Level 16, State 1, Line 5
Invalid object name 'ThisTableDoesNotExist'.

-- first workaround
BEGIN TRY
    PRINT 'Entering the TRY block';
    -- use dynamic sql
    EXEC sp_executesql N'SELECT * FROM ThisTableDoesNotExist';
END TRY
BEGIN CATCH
```

```
        PRINT 'Entering the CATCH block';
        PRINT ERROR_MESSAGE();
END CATCH

--Output
Entering the TRY block
Entering the CATCH block
Invalid object name 'ThisTableDoesNotExist'.

-- second workaround
USE tempdb;
GO
CREATE PROCEDURE uspRecompileError
AS
BEGIN
        SELECT * FROM ThisTableDoesNotExist;
END
GO
BEGIN TRY
        PRINT 'Entering the TRY block';
        -- use a stored procedure
        EXEC uspRecompileError;
END TRY
BEGIN CATCH
        PRINT 'Entering the CATCH block';
        PRINT ERROR_MESSAGE();
END CATCH

-- Output (the same)
Entering the TRY block
Entering the CATCH block
Invalid object name 'ThisTableDoesNotExist'.
```

Errors with severity from 20 through 25   These errors terminate the database connection and cannot be caught by the TRY...CATCH block. If the error is extremely severe, the server will shutdown. No, there's no workaround for these type of errors.

KILL   The KILL statement is used to terminate a user process that cannot be caught by a TRY...CATCH construct. If you want to test this, run the following code in a SQL Server Management Studio query window:

```
SELECT @@SPID;
GO
```

```
BEGIN TRY
WAITFOR DELAY '00:05';
END TRY
BEGIN CATCH
PRINT 'Entering the CATCH block';
END CATCH
```

Note the value display, open a new query window, and run the following code:

```
-- replace 52 with the value noted before
KILL 52
```

Switch to the first query window and notice the result:

```
Msg 0, Level 11, State 0, Line 0
A severe error occurred on the current command.  The results, if any, should
be discarded.
Msg 0, Level 20, State 0, Line 0
A severe error occurred on the current command.  The results, if any, should
be discarded.
```

It's evident that the TRY...CATCH couldn't help you too much in this case (this behavior is normal) and unfortunately there is no workaround.

Attentions   Attentions such as those sent by Microsoft Distributed Transaction Coordinator (MS DTC) will determine a batch abort and cannot be handled with a TRY...CATCH construct.

Using Event Notifications to Handle Warnings

Another technique that you may find useful illustrates the use of event notifications for handling informational messages. As you may recall you cannot use the TRY...CATCH construct for handling errors with severity 10 or less but you can use event notification for this purpose.

This method can be very easily adapted to catch attentions or exceptions by modifying the event type. To make the code easier we included explanatory comments and we will give you additional details. An event notification will execute in response to SQL Trace events (like in our case) or Transact-SQL DDL (Data Definition Language) statements. Information about these events will be sent to a Service Broker service. So, in the code, you will create a Service Broker service infrastructure starting with a queue, then the service, a route, and finally the event notification:

```
USE AdventureWorks;
GO


-- Enable Service Broker for AdventureWorks database
```

```
IF EXISTS
(
    SELECT * FROM sys.databases
    WHERE database_id = DB_ID(N'AdventureWorks')
    AND is_broker_enabled = 0
)
ALTER DATABASE AdventureWorks SET ENABLE_BROKER
GO


-- Create a queue
CREATE QUEUE WarningQueue ;
GO
-- Create the service
CREATE SERVICE WarningService
ON QUEUE WarningQueue
(
[http://schemas.microsoft.com/SQL/Notifications/PostEventNotification]
);
GO
CREATE ROUTE WarningRoute
WITH SERVICE_NAME = 'WarningService',
ADDRESS = 'LOCAL';
GO


CREATE EVENT NOTIFICATION WarningNotification
ON SERVER
FOR USER_ERROR_MESSAGE
TO SERVICE 'WarningService', 'current database';
GO
```

To test it, just run the following lines of code:

```
USE AdventureWorks;
GO
RAISERROR ('Test Warning', 1, 1)
GO
SELECT CAST(message_body AS XML) EventInfo
FROM dbo.WarningQueue
GO
```

You can change the "USER_ERROR_MESSAGE" event with the "EXCEPTION" event and obtain a method to catch all exceptions that occur in your SQL Server instance. To enhance the solution you can create a stored procedure that is activated when the events are received by the WarningQueue queue and eventually logs the event's data in a table.

```
-- Create table to log information
CREATE TABLE LoggedWarningsXML(
      WarningNumber INT IDENTITY PRIMARY KEY,
      WarningData    XML
      ) ;
GO


-- Set options for the XML data type.
SET ANSI_NULLS ON
GO
SET QUOTED_IDENTIFIER ON
GO
-- Create the stored procedure
CREATE PROCEDURE uspLogEventsProc
AS
SET NOCOUNT ON;
DECLARE     @message_body XML,
            @message_type_name NVARCHAR(256),
            @dialog UNIQUEIDENTIFIER ;
--   process messages until the queue is empty.
WHILE (1 = 1)
BEGIN
    WAITFOR (
        RECEIVE TOP(1) -- receive one message
            @message_type_name=message_type_name,
            @message_body=message_body,
            @dialog = conversation_handle
            FROM WarningQueue
    ), TIMEOUT 5000 ; -- wait 5 seconds

    IF (@@ROWCOUNT = 0)
        BEGIN
            BREAK ;
        END ;
```

```
    -- Check for an end dialog message
    -- to end conversation
     IF (@message_type_name =
   'http://schemas.microsoft.com/SQL/ServiceBroker/EndDialog')
     BEGIN
          END CONVERSATION @dialog ;
     END ;
     ELSE
     BEGIN
     -- Log the information
     INSERT INTO LoggedWarningsXML (WarningData)
     VALUES(@message_body) ;
     END ;
 END ;
 GO


 -- Alter the queue
 ALTER QUEUE WarningQueue
     WITH ACTIVATION (
          STATUS = ON,
          PROCEDURE_NAME = uspLogEventsProc ,
          EXECUTE AS SELF
     ) ;
```

 If you are new to Service Broker and Event Notifications, please refer to the "Introducing Service Broker" and "Understanding Event Notification" topics of Books Online.

Error Functions

To obtain more information about the error caught, SQL Server 2005 comes with the following error functions:

- ERROR_NUMBER() returns the error number.
- ERROR_SEVERITY() returns the severity level of the error.
- ERROR_STATE() returns the error state.
- ERROR_PROCEDURE() returns the name of the stored procedure (or trigger) if it's the case.

- ERROR_LINE() returns the line number inside the routine that caused the error.
- ERROR_MESSAGE() returns the text of the error message.

You can (and should) use them anywhere within the scope of a CATCH block. If you call them outside the scope of a CATCH block, they will return NULL. The following example shows how to use the error functions:

```
01 BEGIN TRY
02        SELECT CAST('NotABit' AS bit)
03    END TRY
04    BEGIN CATCH
05        PRINT 'Error on line:' + CONVERT(varchar, ERROR_LINE())
06        -- The inner TRY...CATCH construct
07        BEGIN TRY
08            SELECT CAST('NotAnInt' AS INT)
09        END TRY
10        BEGIN CATCH
11            PRINT 'Error on line:' + CONVERT(varchar, ERROR_LINE())
12        END CATCH
13        PRINT 'Error on line:' + CONVERT(varchar, ERROR_LINE())
14    END CATCH
15 PRINT 'Error on line:' + ISNULL(CONVERT(varchar,ERROR_LINE()),'N/A')
```

Note that the line numbers are for reference only and you should remove them when you run the code. The result can surprise you:

```
Error on line:2
Error on line:8
Error on line:2
Error on line:N/A
```

An error will occur on line 2. The outer CATCH block will catch it. The execution will continue by printing the error line, which is 2. Then the execution will continue with the inner TRY block where another conversion error will occur. This error is handled by the inner CATCH block. The value of the ERROR_LINE() function will be 8. Then the execution will reenter the outer CATCH block and the value of the ERROR_LINE() function will be 2 again (as it should be). The last statement is executed outside of a CATCH block and, due to this fact, the ERROR_LINE() function, will return NULL.

RAISERROR

The RAISERROR statement can be used to generate an error message. There are multiple usage scenarios for RAISERROR:

- Send a message back to the calling batch or application.
- Rethrow an error caught using a TRY...CATCH construct.

- Test a TRY...CATCH construct.
- Log an error and cause an alert to fire.

We will discuss how to use RAISERROR after a brief description of its syntax:

```
RAISERROR ( { msg_id | msg_str | @local_variable }
    { ,severity ,state }
    [ ,argument [ ,...n ] ] )
    [ WITH option [ ,...n ] ]
```

These are the arguments:

msg_id   Represents the error message number and it should correspond to a value stored in the message_id column of the sys.messages catalog view. You should consider these some limitations regarding the message ID. All the user-defined messages have the ID greater than 50000 and our recommendation is to use RAISERROR only with user-defined messages. Undocumented you can use messages with the error message number greater than 13000. Why would you do that? To rethrow the exact exception caught with a TRY...BLOCK construct. For example:

```
BEGIN TRY
-- generate an error by omiting parameters
    EXEC msdb.dbo.sp_delete_job
END TRY
BEGIN CATCH
    DECLARE    @ErrorId INT,
            @ErrorSeverity INT,
            @ErrorState INT;
    SELECT    @ErrorId = ERROR_NUMBER(),
            @ErrorSeverity = ERROR_SEVERITY(),
            @ErrorState = CASE ERROR_STATE()
                        WHEN 0 THEN 1
                        ELSE ERROR_STATE()
                        END;
    --Check the error id and the severity
    --Errors with the severity 20 or greater require
    --RAISERROR WITH LOG
    PRINT 'An error occured';
    IF ERROR_NUMBER() >=13000 AND ERROR_SEVERITY()<20
    BEGIN
    RAISERROR(
            @ErrorId,            --msg_id
            @ErrorSeverity,       --severity
            @ErrorState           --state
```

```
            );
      END
END CATCH

-- Output
An error occured
Msg 14279, Level 16, State 1, Line 21
Supply either @job_name, @job_id or @originating_server.
```

But then again since the other errors with the error message number less than 13000 are reserved, we don't recommend you to use RAISERROR this way, the above example having more of a didactic value.

msg_str   As you can see, you can specify as the first argument a message ID, a message text, or a local variable. The error message text can have up to 2,047 characters and allows formatting similar to the printf function from the C language. We get back to this subject in the last section of this chapter.

@local_variable   Represents an alternative to specify the error message text.

severity   Allows you to specify a severity for your error. Several rules apply to this parameter:

- Any user can specify a severity level from 0 through 18.
- To specify a severity level 19 or greater you have to be a member of the sysadmin fixed server role or to run as a user that has ALTER TRACE permission.
- You have to use the WITH LOG option of RAISERROR if you specify a severity level 19 or greater.
- Errors with the severity level from 20 through 25 will be logged in the Windows application log and in the SQL Server Error log and, it is important to note, the client connection will be terminated.

state   Is an integer between 1 and 127. You can use state to identify the situation in which an error occurred for errors that can occur in multiple situations. Specifying values for the state argument such as 0 or greater than 127 will result in an "Invalid value" error.

argument   Represents the parameter (or parameters) used as substitution if the error message makes use of variables. Let's take a look at a simple example:

```
RAISERROR (N'This is a %s message with %d arguments', -- message text.
           10, -- severity,
           1, -- state,
           N'test', -- first argument
           2); -- second argument.
    GO

    -- Output
    This is a test message with 2 arguments
```

The first parameter represents a string and the second one a signed integer.

option   Represents one of the following three options:

LOG   Using this option will determine whether SQL Server logs the error in the Windows Application log and the SQL Server Error log. You should be aware that there is a limit of 440 bytes for the messages logged in the Error log. To use the WITH LOG option you have to be a member of the sysadmin fixed server role or run in the security context of a user that has ALTER TRACE permission.

Another important fact about this option is that using it allows you to define a SQL Server Agent alert that will be triggered by the specified error. You can only define SQL Server Agent alerts for errors that are logged in the Windows Application log and the WITH LOG option is one of the methods that allows you to log an error in the Windows Application log.

NOWAIT   If you specify the WITH NOWAIT option, the error message will be sent immediately to the client. One particular use of this option is reporting progress in a long-running code as follows:

```
RAISERROR ('Running first statement',10,1) WITH NOWAIT;
-- execute the first long-running statement
RAISERROR ('Running second statement',10,1) WITH NOWAIT;
-- execute the second long-running statement
-- ...
-- and so on
```

SETERROR   This option allows you to set the values for the @@ERROR and the ERROR_NUMBER functions. If a message number is specified, then the message number will be used as value for the @@ERROR and the ERROR_NUMBER functions. Otherwise the 50000 reserved value will be used:

```
EXEC sp_addmessage 80001,10,'Test SETERROR';
GO
RAISERROR (80001,10,1);
-- displays 0
PRINT '@@ERROR=' + CAST(@@ERROR AS VARCHAR);
RAISERROR (80001,10,1) WITH SETERROR;
-- displays 80001
PRINT '@@ERROR=' + CAST(@@ERROR AS VARCHAR);
RAISERROR ('Test',10,1);
-- displays 0
PRINT '@@ERROR=' + CAST(@@ERROR AS VARCHAR);
RAISERROR ('Test',10,1) WITH SETERROR;
-- displays 50000
PRINT '@@ERROR=' + CAST(@@ERROR AS VARCHAR);
GO
```

```
EXEC sp_dropmessage 80001;
GO

-- Output
Test SETERROR
@@ERROR=0
Test SETERROR
@@ERROR=80001
Test
@@ERROR=0
Test
@@ERROR=50000
```

An important use of RAISERROR is rethrowing errors. Once you've caught an error and handled it using a TRY…CATCH construct (and logged the error, eventually sending an alert to a system administrator), you also have the option to transfer the error (the same error that has occurred or a more meaningful one) to other layers such as the client application, the calling component, and so on.

As already mentioned, in most cases when a system error occurs you cannot raise the exact error but you can circumvent this limitation with the following workaround:

```
BEGIN TRY
    -- Generate an error
    SELECT CAST('NotAnInt' AS INT)
END TRY
BEGIN CATCH
    -- Declare and initialize variables
    -- to save the original error info
    DECLARE
        @ErrorMessage      NVARCHAR(4000),
        @ErrorNumber       INT,
        @ErrorSeverity     INT,
        @ErrorState        INT,
        @ErrorLine         INT,
        @ErrorProcedure    NVARCHAR(126);
    SELECT
        @ErrorNumber = ERROR_NUMBER(),
        @ErrorSeverity = ERROR_SEVERITY(),
        @ErrorState = ERROR_STATE(),
        @ErrorLine = ERROR_LINE(),
        @ErrorProcedure = ISNULL(ERROR_PROCEDURE(), 'N/A');
    --Build the error message string
    SELECT @ErrorMessage =
```

```
        N'Error %d, Level %d, State %d, Procedure %s, Line %d, ' +
          'Message: '+ ERROR_MESSAGE();

    -- Place clean-up and logging code here

    -- Rethrow the error
      RAISERROR
      (
      @ErrorMessage,
      @ErrorSeverity,
      1, -- Avoid errors in case the original state value is 0
      @ErrorNumber,     -- the original error number parameter
      @ErrorSeverity,   -- the original error severity parameter
      @ErrorState,      -- the original error state parameter
      @ErrorProcedure,  -- the original error procedure name parameter
      @ErrorLine        -- the original error line number parameter
      );
END CATCH


-- Output
Msg 50000, Level 16, State 1, Line 29
Error 245, Level 16, State 1, Procedure N/A, Line 3,
Message: Conversion failed when converting the
varchar value 'NotAnInt' to data type int.
```

Usually errors should be handled in the layer where they occurred. However, if you can't handle an error, a best practice would be to propagate the error to the caller and the best way to do that using Transact-SQL is RAISERROR.

Handling Transactions

Another scenario where you will find the TRY...CATCH construct very useful is handling errors that occur inside *transactions*.

If a transaction abort error occurs inside of a TRY block, the transaction enters in an uncommitable (or doomed) state. In an uncommitable state you can only perform read operations or issue a ROLLBACK TRANSACTION; you cannot commit the transaction or roll back to a savepoint. To give you information about the state of a transaction, a new function is available in SQL Server 2005.

The XACT_STATE function will return:

- −1 if the current request has a transaction marked as uncommitable

- 0 if there are no active transactions

- 1 if the current request has active transactions

It might be useful to combine the XACT_STATE function with the XACT_ABORT option, which when set to ON will make most of the runtime errors to become transaction abort (or batch abort) errors. And last but not least the @@TRANCOUNT function that returns the number of active transactions is another useful tool in dealing with transactions and errors.

Let's see a couple of examples to get a feel of how to use these features:

```
USE tempdb;
GO
CREATE TABLE T (I INT NOT NULL PRIMARY KEY);
GO
-- First Test
INSERT INTO T VALUES (1);
-- the next statement will fail
INSERT INTO T VALUES (1);
-- but the next one will succeed
INSERT INTO T VALUES (2);
GO
SELECT * FROM T;

-- Output : 1 2
```

What does this output mean? The first insert statement worked just fine. The second statement tried to insert the same value in a column designated as primary key. Obviously, it failed, and the following error was generated: "Msg 2627, Level 14, State 1, Line 4 Violation of PRIMARY KEY constraint." But the execution didn't stop. It continued with the third statement.

Now let's use the XACT_ABORT option to see how it modifies the behavior:

```
-- Second Test
SET XACT_ABORT ON;
GO
-- the next statement will fail
INSERT INTO T VALUES (1);
-- the next statement will fail too
INSERT INTO T VALUES (3);
GO
SELECT * FROM T;

-- Output:    1 2
```

The first insert statement failed again because of the primary key constraint violation. Though the second statement didn't generate any errors, it failed because of the XACT_ABORT setting. The whole batch failed.

The next step is to use a TRY...CATCH block:

```
-- Third Test
SET XACT_ABORT OFF;
GO
BEGIN TRANSACTION
BEGIN TRY
-- the next statement will succeed
INSERT INTO T VALUES (4);
-- but the next statement will fail
INSERT INTO T VALUES (1);
END TRY
BEGIN CATCH
    IF XACT_STATE() = -1
        BEGIN
        PRINT 'Uncomitable Transaction';
        ROLLBACK TRANSACTION;
        END;
    IF XACT_STATE() = 1
        BEGIN
        PRINT 'Comitable Transaction';
        COMMIT TRANSACTION;
        END;
END CATCH
GO
SELECT * FROM T;

-- Output: 1 2 4
```

As you can see, in some cases you can obtain unexpected results. Even though the second insert failed you still have been able to commit the transaction. That's why we recommend that you analyze whether you really want to commit the transaction when an error occurs. If you turn on the XACT_ABORT option for the previous example, the transaction will be marked as uncommitable. Let's see it:

```
-- Forth Test
SET XACT_ABORT ON;
GO
BEGIN TRANSACTION
BEGIN TRY
-- the next statement will succeed
INSERT INTO T VALUES (5);
```

```
-- but the next statement will fail
INSERT INTO T VALUES (1);
END TRY
BEGIN CATCH
    IF XACT_STATE() = -1
        BEGIN
        PRINT 'Uncomitable Transaction';
        ROLLBACK TRANSACTION;
        END;
    IF XACT_STATE() = 1
        BEGIN
        PRINT 'Comitable Transaction';
        COMMIT TRANSACTION;
        END;
END CATCH
GO
SELECT * FROM T;


-- Output: 1 2 4
```

Before moving to the next section, we will remind you: Don't leave any transaction open! Commit the transaction or rollback if you have to, but if you use them, don't forget about them! And before rolling back a transaction you should check the @@TRANCOUNT function to see whether you do have any transactions to roll back.

Handling Deadlocks

A *deadlock* occurs when two or more tasks are each waiting for another to release a resource. If you follow several simple rules, you can reduce the probability of deadlocks occurring:

- Always access objects in the same order.
- Avoid user interaction in transactions.
- Keep transactions short.
- Use snapshot isolation.
- Use lower isolation levels.
- Use a row versioning.

 To get more information about how to avoid deadlocks, please refer to the "Minimizing Deadlocks" topic in Books Online.

You will find more about isolation levels and row versioning in the next chapter, so let's concentrate now on deadlocks. In real life you cannot avoid deadlocks in all situations.

Fortunately, the TRY...CATCH construct can help you solve deadlock situations more gracefully. You can catch the 1205 deadlock victim error and you can retry the action that was aborted. Here's the code:

```
USE tempdb;
GO
-- Create a table that will be used to generate a deadlock
CREATE TABLE EmployeeVacation(
        EmployeeID INT NOT NULL PRIMARY KEY,
        DaysOff INT NOT NULL);
GO
-- Insert demo data
INSERT INTO EmployeeVacation VALUES (1,20);
INSERT INTO EmployeeVacation VALUES (2,20);
GO
```

Now run each of the following blocks of code in a separate window of SQL Server Management Studio. The purpose is to generate a deadlock. You obtain a deadlock by running two batches, each updating two rows. Each batch updates the rows in a different order. The different order is actually to blame for the deadlock.

This is the first batch:

```
USE tempdb;
GO

-- Use a variable to track
-- the number of retries
DECLARE @retry_nmb INT;
SET @retry_nmb = 10;

-- As long as the number of
-- retries is greater than 0
-- retry the update
WHILE (@retry_nmb > 0)
BEGIN
BEGIN TRANSACTION;
  BEGIN TRY
  UPDATE EmployeeVacation
  SET DaysOff = DaysOff + 1
  WHERE EmployeeID = 1;

  WAITFOR DELAY '00:00:20';
```

```
UPDATE EmployeeVacation
SET DaysOff = DaysOff + 1
WHERE EmployeeID = 2;

COMMIT TRANSACTION;
    -- If everything's fine set -- @retry_nmb to 0
    SET @retry_nmb = 0;
END TRY
BEGIN CATCH
-- Check for deadlock victim
-- error number and decrement
-- the @retry_nmb variable
-- If another error occurs
-- set the @retry_nmb to -1
-- to exit the WHILE
IF (ERROR_NUMBER() = 1205)
SET @retry_nmb = @retry_nmb - 1;
  ELSE
      SET @retry_nmb = -1;

    -- Print the error message.
    PRINT ERROR_MESSAGE();

    -- Roll back the transaction
    IF XACT_STATE() <> 0
          ROLLBACK TRANSACTION;
    END CATCH;
END;
GO
```

This is the second batch:

```
USE tempdb;
GO


-- Use a variable to track
-- the number of retries
DECLARE @retry_nmb INT;
SET @retry_nmb = 10;

-- As long as the number of
```

```
-- retries is greater than 0
-- retry the update
WHILE (@retry_nmb > 0)
BEGIN
BEGIN TRANSACTION;
  BEGIN TRY
  UPDATE EmployeeVacation
  SET DaysOff = DaysOff + 1
  WHERE EmployeeID = 2;

  WAITFOR DELAY '00:00:10';

  UPDATE EmployeeVacation
  SET DaysOff = DaysOff + 1
  WHERE EmployeeID = 1;

  COMMIT TRANSACTION;
    -- If everything's fine set -- @retry_nmb to 0
    SET @retry_nmb = 0;
  END TRY
  BEGIN CATCH
  -- Check for deadlock victim
  -- error number and decrement
  -- the @retry_nmb variable
  -- If another error occurs
  -- set the @retry_nmb to -1
  -- to exit the WHILE
  IF (ERROR_NUMBER() = 1205)
  SET @retry_nmb = @retry_nmb - 1;
    ELSE
        SET @retry_nmb = -1;

    -- Print the error message.
    PRINT ERROR_MESSAGE();

    -- Roll back the transaction
    IF XACT_STATE() <> 0
        ROLLBACK TRANSACTION;
    END CATCH;
END;
GO
```

After running both batches you can get the following output for one of them:

```
-- Output of one of the sessions:
Transaction (Process ID XX) was deadlocked on lock resources with
another process and has been chosen as the deadlock victim. Rerun the
transaction.
```

Though the TRY…CATCH can help you with deadlock situations, we recommend you to use a proactive approach and avoid deadlocks using coding best practices. How could you avoid the deadlock in the previous example? The answer is very simple—use the same access order in both batches.

Catching Errors from Managed Code

The TRY…CATCH block can be used to handle errors raised by the managed code that runs inside your database. To illustrate this we use the function RegExMatch written in C#, a function created in the "Designing Code That Validates Input Data and Permissions" section of this chapter:

```
USE AdventureWorks;
GO
SET NOCOUNT ON;
GO
DECLARE @PhoneNumber varchar(10)
DECLARE @RegExPattern varchar(MAX);
SET @PhoneNumber = '81818181'
-- Use an incorect pattern that is missing a square bracket
-- the correct one would be '^[0-9]+$'
SET @RegExPattern = '^[0-9+$'

BEGIN TRY
    SELECT dbo.RegExMatch(@RegExPattern,@PhoneNumber)
END TRY
BEGIN CATCH
    PRINT 'The following error occured:' + ERROR_MESSAGE()
END CATCH

-- Partial Output
The following error occured:A .NET Framework error occurred
during execution of user defined routine or aggregate
'RegExMatch':System.ArgumentException: parsing "^[0-9+$" - Unterminated [] set.
```

Don't worry too much if you are new to regular expressions. The regular expression used requires that in order to match, the @PhoneNumber argument should respect the following rules:

from the start to the end—indicated by the caret (^) and the dollar sign ($) characters—all characters should be digits and the plus sign (+) sign shows that the phone number should have at least one character or more. However, we intended to demonstrate that TRY...CATCH will help you even for managed code.

Using PRINT

PRINT statement allows you to return messages to the client application. In most cases you should use RAISERROR statement instead of PRINT, yet for troubleshooting Transact-SQL code PRINT statement can be very useful. It has a very simple syntax, receiving as arguments character strings, char or varchar variables (or variables that can be implicitly converted to char or varchar data types), or an expression that generates a string:

```
PRINT msg_str | @local_variable | string_expr
```

Messages produced with PRINT are considered informational messages by the client applications.

Using the sys.dm_os_ring_buffers Dynamic Management View

Imagine the following situation: you test your application and you obtain an error that you suspect to be database related. Unfortunately you can't reproduce it and none of your error logs can help you. You won't believe it, but this kind of situation does happen. We can give you another option: SQL Server 2005 maintains a ring buffer (or circular buffer), which contains 64K of exceptions. Being a ring buffer, when it fills, old exceptions will be replaced with new ones; however, interrogating this ring buffer can solve your problem. You can do that using a dynamic management view named sys.dm_os_ring_buffers. Let's see an example:

```
-- generate an error
SELECT CAST ('NotAnInt' AS INT);
-- get the error in XML format
GO
SELECT TOP 1 CAST (record AS XML) x
FROM sys.dm_os_ring_buffers
WHERE ring_buffer_type = 'RING_BUFFER_EXCEPTION'
ORDER BY [timestamp] DESC
GO
-- Output
<Record id="83" type="RING_BUFFER_EXCEPTION" time="485098">
  <Exception>
    <Task address="0x006B95B8" />
    <Error>245</Error>
```

```
    <Severity>16</Severity>
    <State>1</State>
    <UserDefined>0</UserDefined>
  </Exception>
  <Stack>
    <frame id="0">0X01463E8F</frame>
    <frame id="1">0X014645B7</frame>
    <frame id="2">0X014B1AD3</frame>
    <frame id="3">0X01059BEA</frame>
    <frame id="4">0X010251BC</frame>
    <frame id="5">0X01025741</frame>
    <frame id="6">0X01023E34</frame>
    <frame id="7">0X01041DD5</frame>
    <frame id="8">0X0103DFD4</frame>
    <frame id="9">0X01006A96</frame>
    <frame id="10">0X01006BBC</frame>
    <frame id="11">0X01006DAB</frame>
    <frame id="12">0X01447562</frame>
    <frame id="13">0X0144859B</frame>
    <frame id="14">0X0144789A</frame>
    <frame id="15">0X01447720</frame>
  </Stack>
</Record>

-- You can get the error message
-- text from sys.messages
SELECT [text] FROM sys.messages
WHERE message_id =245 AND language_id = 1033;
GO
-- Output
Conversion failed when converting the %ls value '%.*ls' to data type %ls.
```

You can use XQUERY to get better results:

```
SELECT
        c.value('(//Exception/Error)[1]','int') message_id,
        c.value('(//Exception/Severity)[1]','tinyint') severity,
        c.value('(//Exception/State)[1]','tinyint') state
    FROM(
```

```
        SELECT TOP 1 CAST (record AS XML)
        FROM sys.dm_os_ring_buffers
        WHERE ring_buffer_type = 'RING_BUFFER_EXCEPTION'
        ORDER BY [timestamp] DESC
   ) T(c)
-- Output
message_id   severity state

-----------  -------- -----

245            16       1
```

Besides the exception ring buffers, you can use the sys.dm_os_ring_buffers DMV to obtain information about other eight ring buffers dedicated to memory, schedulers, CLR Integration, and so on.

Handling Errors in Applications

A common subject to this section and the next section of this chapter is handling errors and messages in applications. Each database API (application programming interface) has a specific set of objects, structures, and functions that you can use to get information about errors and messages. We give you several facts without going into greater details (Books Online has plenty of information about this topic), but first we describe the difference between errors and messages:

- Errors have a severity 11 or greater.

- Messages can be the following:

   - Errors that have a severity of 10 or less (warnings, informational messages)

   - The output of several DBCC statements

   - The output of the PRINT statement

   And now the facts about handling errors in different APIs:

- ADO, OLE DB–based application, cannot differentiate between errors and messages

- DB-LIBRARY, ODBC, and Sql Client provider (from ADO.NET) APIs make the distinction between errors and messages

- Not all error information is returned by APIs such as ODBC, ADO, or OLE DB (usually the missing information is related to the severity and the state of the error message).

   The following is a short example of handling errors using C# and SqlClient provider:

```
try
{
    // insert database operations code
}
catch (SqlException ex)
```

```
{
    for (int i = 0; i < ex.Errors.Count; i++)
    {
        string errorMessage = "";
        errorMessage =   "Error #" + i.ToString() + "\n" +
                         " message:" + ex.Errors[i].Message + "\n" +
                " Number:" + ex.Errors[i].Number + "\n" +
                " Line:" + ex.Errors[i].LineNumber + "\n" +
                         " State:" + ex.Errors[i].State + "\n" +
                         " Procedure:" + ex.Errors[i].Procedure + "\n";
        Console.WriteLine(errorMessage);
    }
}
```

To catch an error, we use the C# TRY...CATCH construct and the SqlException class. As you can see the SqlException class exposes the error message text, the error number, the line in the Transact-SQL code where the error occurred, the state, as well as the procedure name where the error occurred, if any.

The second example shows how to process warnings and informational messages using SqlClient provider and the SqlInfoMessageEventHandler delegate. The SqlInfoMessageEventHandler delegate handles the InfoMessage event that occurs when SQL Server returns a warning or informational message. Here's the code:

```
// declaring the connection
SqlConnection myConn;
// set the connection properties
myConn = new SqlConnection();
myConn.InfoMessage += SqlInfoMessageEventHandler(myConn_InfoMessage);
// the handler
private void myConn_InfoMessage(object sender, SqlInfoMessageEventArgs e)
{
    foreach (System.Data.SqlClient.SqlError se in e.Errors)
    {
        string errorMessage = "";
        errorMessage =   " Message:" + se.Message + "\n" +
                         " Number:" + se.Number + "\n" +
                         " Line:" + se.LineNumber + "\n" +
                         " State:" + se.State + "\n" +
                         " Procedure:" + se.Procedure + "\n";

        Console.WriteLine(errorMessage);
    }
}
```

As you would expect, the same information as for exceptions is available for warnings and informational messages (the error message text, the error number, the line in the Transact-SQL code where the error occurred, the state, as well as the procedure name, if any).

Logging Errors

When your application is deployed in production and various problems start to happen (as they always do), the error logs will be one of your greatest allies. We won't spend too much time with this topic, but you should consider the following when logging error information:

- Log error information for each layer of your application.
- Consider creating several logs when you have more types of information.
- Capture all relevant information that would help solve the error.
- Do not capture warnings and informational messages if it's not required (they can generate a great volume of unnecessary information).
- Select a log format and type of storage keeping in mind how the log will be processed later.

As for the log storage types and formats, you can choose from the following:

Enterprise Instrumentation Framework (EIF)   An instrumentation API that allows handling application events including, of course, exceptions. If you develop a multitier .NET application, you should consider using EIF.

 Instrumentation means incorporating code in your application that will expose application-specific data for monitoring purposes.

Windows Event Log   Allows you to use the Windows Application log or create a separate event log for your application. Using Windows Event Log has several advantages, such as:

- Many options to view the logs (Event Viewer, SQL Management Studio, Custom application).
- WMI (Windows Management Instrumentation) can be used to manage the logs.
- RAISERROR statement and xp_logevent extended stored procedure offer support for writing to the Event logs.

The main disadvantage of using Windows Event Log is that by design it is a central repository for a single machine and it will be cumbersome to use it in a multiserver environment.

A central relational database   Will make your information accessible from any remote machine but has the main disadvantage that in the case your database is not available (due to network failure for example), you can lose information.

A custom log file   Has the main advantage of flexibility but it requires development.

In the previous section, you saw a custom logging solution based on Event Notifications. If you want to see an example of how to log errors in a relational database you can find a good one in the AdventureWorks sample database. Here is its code:

```
-- uspLogError logs error information in the ErrorLog table about the
-- error that caused execution to jump to the CATCH block of a
-- TRY...CATCH construct. This should be executed from within the scope
-- of a CATCH block otherwise it will return without inserting error
-- information.
CREATE PROCEDURE [dbo].[uspLogError]
@ErrorLogID [int] = 0 OUTPUT -- contains the ErrorLogID of the row inserted
AS                           -- by uspLogError in the ErrorLog table
BEGIN
    SET NOCOUNT ON;

    -- Output parameter value of 0 indicates that error
    -- information was not logged
    SET @ErrorLogID = 0;

    BEGIN TRY
        -- Return if there is no error information to log
        IF ERROR_NUMBER() IS NULL
            RETURN;

        -- Return if inside an uncommittable transaction.
        -- Data insertion/modification is not allowed when
        -- a transaction is in an uncommittable state.
        IF XACT_STATE() = -1
        BEGIN
            PRINT 'Cannot log error since the current transaction is in
an uncommittable state. '
                + 'Rollback the transaction before executing
uspLogError in order to successfully log error information.';
            RETURN;
        END

        INSERT [dbo].[ErrorLog]
            (
            [UserName],
            [ErrorNumber],
            [ErrorSeverity],
            [ErrorState],
```

```
            [ErrorProcedure],
            [ErrorLine],
            [ErrorMessage]
            )
        VALUES
            (
            CONVERT(sysname, CURRENT_USER),
            ERROR_NUMBER(),
            ERROR_SEVERITY(),
            ERROR_STATE(),
            ERROR_PROCEDURE(),
            ERROR_LINE(),
            ERROR_MESSAGE()
            );

        -- Pass back the ErrorLogID of the row inserted
        SET @ErrorLogID = @@IDENTITY;
    END TRY
    BEGIN CATCH
        PRINT 'An error occurred in stored procedure uspLogError: ';
        EXECUTE [dbo].[uspPrintError];
        RETURN -1;
    END CATCH
END;
GO
```

You can use the uspLogError stored procedure inside of a CATCH block. The comments make it self-explanatory so we won't spend any time analyzing its code. But we would improve this stored procedure and the logging table by adding some extra information such as the current system date and time and the original login (in case the execution context is changed, this information may be useful).

Another note, using the @@IDENTITY function to retrieve the last value inserted in a column with the IDENTITY property can be hazardous if the target table has a trigger. We would use the SCOPE_IDENTITY function to accomplish the same results but limiting it to the current scope.

Following Best Practices

The following list summarizes several methods and practices that can help you in dealing with errors:

- A very obvious practice is to use error-handling code constructs (such as TRY...CATCH) to handle errors in your applications.

- Test your CATCH blocks. Errors can occur also in the CATCH block.

- When you handle errors don't forget to clean up (deallocate cursors, close transactions, and so on).

- Don't "swallow" errors. Handling errors doesn't mean hiding errors, because you will treat the symptom but not the problem. You should at least consider logging them if not rethrowing more meaningful ones.

- When you raise or rethrow errors, do not reveal too much information. You should display just enough information to assist the user when an error occurs. If you disclose too much information, you will make your application more vulnerable. Keep the technical details of an error for a system administrator in an error log, for example.

- Fail securely. If the application fails due to an unrecoverable error make sure that it fails safely. For example, if your application cannot connect to its database, you should display an error message like "Resource unavailable," log the complete details of the error (optionally send a notification to a system administrator), and stop processing the failing request.

Designing SQL Server User-Defined Messages to Communicate Application Events

The basic use of a database is related to data retrieval and data manipulation. Beyond this simple usage, a database server offers lots of additional services, one of which is to communicate application events. SQL Server has its own mechanism for communicating application events (usually errors, warnings, and informational messages), and your application should too.

Though you can implement your own messages system or you can use alternate methods for communicating with your application (such as using return value or output parameters of stored procedures), this section focuses on how to build user-defined messages using the integrated mechanism of SQL Server 2005. As already mentioned, SQL Server 2005 has a built-in mechanism to communicate application events using messages. You can build on top this system by adding user-defined messages. Of course, you have the option to create your own mechanism, but using the existing system offers several advantages:

Zero development time   You don't have to allocate time for building a custom system.

Support for multiple languages   You can define messages for all languages installed on the server.

Simple and centralized message management   You have the RAISERROR statement for returning messages to the client applications and three stored procedures for message management (sp_addmessage, sp_altermessage, sp_dropmessage).

Support for parameterized messages   You can reuse messages by including parameters.

Support for SQL Server Agent alerts   You can define alerts and alert responses using error numbers, severities, or the message text.

The architecture of the system is pretty simple and consists of the following components:

- sys.messages catalog view that exposes all system messages and user-defined messages.
- RAISERROR statement for sending messages to the client applications.

 The RAISERROR statement is described in the previous section.

- sp_addmessage, sp_altermessage, and sp_dropmessage stored procedures to add, modify, or delete a user-defined message.
- xp_logevent stored procedure that allows you to log a message in the SQL Server log and in the Windows Application log and send an alert without sending a message to the client.
- FORMATMESSAGE statement for message formatting.

Let's take a closer look at each element that defines the integrated message mechanism of SQL Server 2005.

The sys.messages Catalog View

SQL Server 2005 stores the user-defined messages in a system table, but under normal conditions you could not directly access the system tables and there is no reason to do it. Instead you should use the sys.messages catalog view. Table 5.2 displays the column names and a short explanation for one.

TABLE 5.2   The sys.messages Catalog View

Column Name	Data Type	Description
message_id	Int	The ID of the message. It has to be unique across the server instance.
language_id	Smallint	Defines the language for the message and corresponds to the language ID column of the sys.syslanguages catalog view.
severity	Tinyint	Severity level of the message. All messages with the message_id have the same severity.
is_event_logged	Bit	1 if the message will be logged.
text	Nvarchar(2048)	Text for the message_id and language_id combination.

There's nothing too complicated about this view but we want to remind you that some columns deserve special attention. The severity and the is_event_logged columns will have the same value for all messages with the same message_id. In plain English that means that you cannot have an English message with a severity 10 and the same message in French with a severity 11.

sp_addmessage

The name of this stored procedure is self-explanatory so you can use it to add user-defined messages. Let's take a look at its syntax:

```
sp_addmessage [ @msgnum = ] msg_id , [ @severity = ] severity , [ @msgtext = ]
'msg'
    [ , [ @lang = ] 'language' ]
    [ , [ @with_log = ] { 'TRUE' | 'FALSE' } ]
    [ , [ @replace = ] 'replace' ]
```

You can specify the message ID, severity of the message, a language, and also if the message will be logged or not. If you use the replace option you can replace an existing message. Here are just a few observations related to this stored procedure:

- The message_id should be greater than 50000.
- The with_log option can be used only by the members of the sysadmin server fixed role.
- If you use multiple languages, you have to supply the English version of the message first.
- The RAISERROR statement can override the severity specified in sp_addmessage stored procedure.

The following example adds a message in two languages (English and French):

```
USE master;
GO
EXEC sp_addmessage @msgnum = 70000, @severity = 16,
    @msgtext = N'The employee %s already exists in the database.',
    @lang = 'us_english';

EXEC sp_addmessage @msgnum = 70002, @severity = 16,
    @msgtext = N'L''employé %1! existe déjà existe déjà
dans la base de données!',
    @lang = 'French';
GO
```

To test both versions of the message, use the following code:

```
SET LANGUAGE us_english;
GO
```

```
RAISERROR(  70000,    -- Message ID
            10,       -- Severity
            1,        -- State
            'John Smith' -- Parameter
        )
GO
SET LANGUAGE French;
GO
RAISERROR(   70000,   -- Message ID
            10,       -- Severity
            1,        -- State
            'John Smith' -- Parameter
        )
GO
-- Output
Changed language setting to us_english.
The employee John Smith already exists in the database.
Le paramétre de langue est passé à Français.
L'employé John Smith existe déjà existe déjà dans la base de données!
```

sp_altermessage

You may find the name of this stored procedure a little confusing and let us explain why: Once you have a message in the database, you can modify it using the sp_addmessage stored procedure with the replace option. If you want to modify the logging behavior of an existing message, you can use the sp_altermessage stored procedure.

Its syntax is simple:

```
sp_altermessage [ @message_id = ] message_number,
 [ @parameter = ] 'write_to_log',
 [ @parameter_value = ] 'value'
```

You can specify a message ID and if the message should be logged (in the Windows Application log) or not. The RAISERROR statement can override the setting specified with this stored procedure so if you specify false as value for the write_to_log parameter, you can still log a message using the WITH LOG option of the RAISERROR.

Let's see an example:

```
--Change the logging behavior of the previous created message
sp_altermessage 70000, 'WITH_LOG', 'true';
GO
```

sp_dropmessage

The sp_dropmessage stored procedure allows you to delete a user-defined message.

Its syntax allows specifying a message number and a language:

```
sp_dropmessage [ @msgnum = ] message_number
        [ , [ @lang = ] 'language' ]
```

You can specify the value "all" for the language parameter if you want to drop all language versions of the specified message. If you have multiple language versions for a message you have to drop all localized versions of the message before dropping the U.S. English version. As an observation, dropping messages requires membership of the sysadmin and serveradmin fixed server roles.

The following example illustrates how to drop the previous created messages:

```
EXEC sp_dropmessage
    @msgnum = 70000,
    @lang = 'all';
GO
```

xp_logevent

The xp_logevent stored procedure can be used to log a user-defined message in the SQL Server log file and in the Windows Application log. Unlike RAISERROR, the xp_logevent stored procedure won't send a message to the client application and you can use it to trigger a SQL Server Agent alert.

Here's the syntax:

```
xp_logevent { error_number , 'message' } [ , 'severity' ]
```

As you can see the syntax of the xp_logevent stored procedure allows you to specify a message ID and a message text and optionally you can specify a value for the severity parameter that can be one of the following character strings: INFORMATIONAL, WARNING, or ERROR (the default being INFORMATIONAL).

To use this stored procedure you have to be a member of the db_owner fixed database role in the master database or a member of the sysadmin fixed server role.

Here's a simple example for now (a more elaborate example of this stored procedure comes later):

```
USE master
EXEC xp_logevent 60000, 'The employee John Smith already exists in the
database.', INFORMATIONAL;
```

FORMATMESSAGE

The FORMATMESSAGE function allows you to format a user-defined message without sending it to the client and thus making it available for further processing.

Here's the syntax:

```
FORMATMESSAGE ( msg_number , [ param_value [ ,...n ] ] )
```

You can specify as arguments an existing user-defined message and values for its parameters (if any).

Let's see it at work:

```
USE master;
GO
EXEC sp_addmessage @msgnum = 70000, @severity = 16,
   @msgtext = N'The employee %s already exists in the database.',
   @lang = 'us_english';
GO
DECLARE @temp VARCHAR(256)
SELECT @temp = FORMATMESSAGE(70000, 'John Smith')
PRINT @temp
-- Output
The employee John Smith already exists in the database.
```

In this particular case, the function returned the message with the ID *70000* and replaced the single parameter of the message with the supplied value *'John Smith'*.

Now that you have understood all the components of the SQL Server 2005 messages system, we invite you to test them in a more complex exercise. In Exercise 5.1, you will create a user-defined message and generate a SQL Server Agent alert based on the message number.

EXERCISE 5.1

Defining a SQL Server Agent Alert

1. To create the user-defined message, open a SQL Server Management Studio query window, and run the following code:

    ```
    USE master;

    GO

    EXEC sp_addmessage @msgnum = 80000, @severity = 16,

       @msgtext = N'The specified employee already exists in the database.',

       @lang = 'us_english';

    GO
    ```

EXERCISE 5.1 *(continued)*

2. To define an operator that will receive the alert, in the Object Explorer, expand SQL Server Agent node. We make the assumption that SQL Server Agent is started.

3. Right-click Operators and select New Operator.

4. Enter 'John' in the Name textbox and your computer name in the Net send address text box and click OK. Make sure that the Messenger service is started in order to receive messages using net send command. One method to do that is by selecting Control Panel ➤ TRA Administrative Tools ➤ TRA Services. In the Services list, locate by name the Messenger service, and start it. Alternatively you can run `net start Messenger` from a command prompt window.

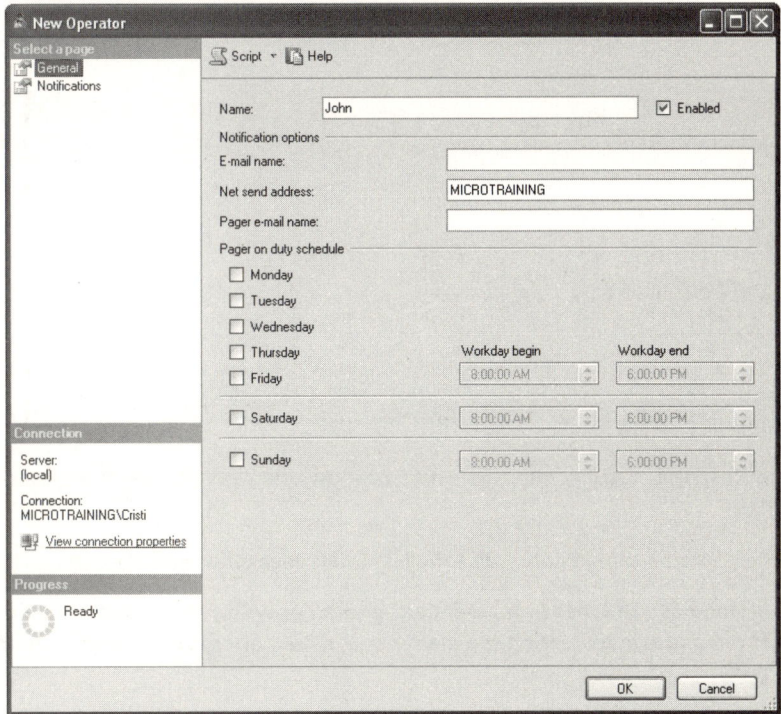

5. Define the alert. In the Object Explorer, expand SQL Server Agent node if it is not already expanded.

6. Right-click Alerts and select New Alert.

7. Enter **TestMessageAlert** as the name for this alert.

8. Select SQL Server event alert in the Type box.

9. Click the Error number radio button and enter **80000** in the Error number textbox.

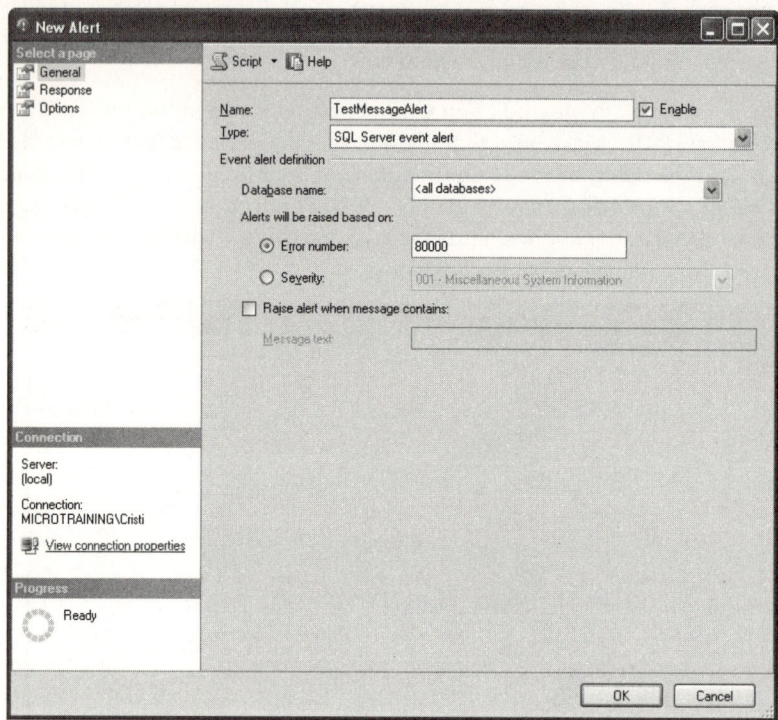

10. Click the Response page of the New Alert window and click the Notify operators check box.

11. Select the operator named John, click the Net Send check box, and click OK.

12. Now that you have the message, the alert, and an operator to receive the alert we have just one more step: testing the alert. Open a new query window and run the following code:

```
-- The message has the ID 80000, Severity 10, State 1

-- The WITH LOG option is used to trigger the alert

RAISERROR (80000, 10, 1) WITH LOG;
```

EXERCISE 5.1 *(continued)*

13. If you succeeded, you will receive a pop-up window notifying you that a SQL Server Agent Alert named 'TestMessageAlert' occurred on your computer.

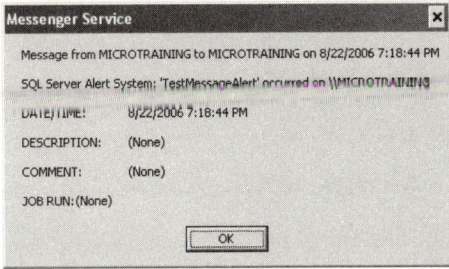

Summary

In this chapter, you learned why and how to implement error handling in SQL Server 2005 and how to create and use user-defined messages to communicate application events.

You also learned some security best practices and how to protect your applications by simply validating user input.

We hope we convinced you that you can and should invest time in writing secure code.

Exam Essentials

Know how to secure your applications.   You have to know what measures can be applied to make your applications more secure (validate user input, using permissions, and execution context).

Know how and when to change the execution context.   You need to understand and determine the necessary security context for every action performed on your database. You also have to be familiar with the options available to change execution context.

Know how to incorporate error-handling techniques.   You need to know how to use the TRY...CATCH construct to obtain more robust and reliable applications.

Know how to use and manage user-defined functions.   You need to know how to use the built in messages system of SQL Server to communicate application events effectively.

Review Questions

1. One of the junior DBAs from you company wrote the following code to test the TRY...CATCH functionality:

```
SET NOCOUNT ON;

BEGIN TRY

    PRINT 'BEGIN TRY BLOCK';

    RAISERROR ('Test Message',10,1);

    PRINT 'END TRY BLOCK';

END TRY

GO

BEGIN CATCH

    PRINT 'BEGIN CATCH BLOCK';

    PRINT ERROR_MESSAGE();

    PRINT 'END CATCH BLOCK';

END CATCH
```

However, after the running the code, he obtains different results than the expected ones. What will display the code?

A. BEGIN TRY BLOCK

BEGIN CATCH BLOCK

Test Message

B. END CATCH BLOCK

BEGIN TRY BLOCK

Test Message

C. END TRY BLOCK

BEGIN TRY BLOCK

END TRY BLOCK

D. The code will generate an incorrect syntax error.

2. You develop the code for an internal application. As a part of this application you create a stored procedure that reads content from a web service using a managed function. If the web service is not available, you want to raise an error that will trigger a SQL Server Agent alert. Which T-SQL should you use?

   A. RAISERROR ('Web Service unavailable',10,1) WITH LOG;

   B. RAISERROR ('Web Service unavailable',10,1) WITH SETERROR;

   C. RAISERROR ('Web Service unavailable',10,1) WITH NOWAIT;

   D. RAISERROR ('Web Service unavailable',10,1);

3. You write a stored procedure for an inventory application that allows modification of product codes. When the product code specified doesn't exist in the database, you want to log the incorrect product code in a table. You wrote the following code:

```
01 CREATE PROCEDURE uspChangeProductCode

02 @ProductCode VARCHAR(5)=NULL,

03 @NewProductCode VARCHAR(5)=NULL

04 AS

05 BEGIN

06 IF @ProductCode IS NULL

07 OR @NewProductCode IS NULL

08 BEGIN

09 RAISERROR('Incorrect parameters',16,1);

10 RETURN;

11 END;

12 UPDATE Products

13 SET ProductCode = @NewProductCode

14 WHERE ProductCode = @ProductCode;

15

16 INSERT INTO ErrorLog(Error)

17 VALUES ('Incorrect code:' + @ProductCode);

18 END

19 GO
```

What should you add to line 15 to complete the stored procedure?

A. IF @@ERROR <> 0

B. IF @@ROWCOUNT = 0

C. IF XACT_STATE() = 0

D. IF @@TRANCOUNT = 0

4. What type of errors can be handled by the TRY...CATCH construct running at the same execution level? (Choose all that apply.)

   A. Compile errors

   B. Statement abort errors

   C. Recompile errors

   D. Informational messages

   E. The 1205 deadlock victim error

   F. Transaction abort errors

5. As a part of your company's security policy all database access should be done using stored procedures. You want to prevent direct access to base tables by your company users. For that purpose you create a new database user named "WriteUser" and grant it permission to modify base tables. Next you have created the stored procedures that will allow data modification. What should you do next? (Choose the best option.)

   A. Create the stored procedure using the EXECUTE AS CALLER option.

   B. Create the stored procedure using the EXECUTE AS OWNER option.

   C. Create the stored procedure using the EXECUTE AS 'WriteUser' option.

   D. Use the SETUSER statement.

6. Which of the following measures can make your code more secure? (Choose all that apply.)

   A. Avoid dynamic SQL.

   B. Validate user input.

   C. Use the principle of least privilege.

   D. Use strong passwords.

7. You want to develop a system that will communicate application events. One of the requirements is that the development time allocated for this task should be minimal. What should you do?

   A. Use the SQL Server built-in error messages system.

   B. Use a Notification Services–based solution.

   C. Use Event Notifications.

   D. Use a custom solution based on CLR integration.

8. You've created a user-defined message and you want to test it. You run the following code:

```
RAISERROR(50001,20,1);
```

However you obtain an error. What can you do to solve the problem? (Choose all that apply.)

A. Change the severity of the error to 21.

B. Change the severity of the error to 10.

C. Change the severity of the error to 22.

D. Add the WITH LOG option to the RAISERROR statement.

9. You have created a user-defined message that has the severity 20. One developer from your team has to test all user-defined messages. You have to make sure that the developer has the necessary permissions to test all the user-defined messages. How can you accomplish that? (Choose all that apply.)

A. Add the developer to the sysadmin fixed server role.

B. Grant the developer the ALTER TRACE permission.

C. Add the developer to the processsadmin fixed server role.

D. Add the developer to the bulkadmin fixed server role.

10. Which of the following types of errors can be handled using a TRY...CATCH construct? (Choose all that apply.)

A. Errors with severity level 10

B. Errors with severity level 16

C. Deadlock victim errors.

D. Errors with severity level 1

11. Which of the following functions can give you the line of code at which an error occurred inside of a CATCH block?

A. ROW_NUMBER()

B. @@ERROR

C. ERROR_LINE()

D. ERROR_NUMBER()

12. You've developed an import module for an application. When an import file is missing, you want to generate a SQL Server Agent alert without sending an error to the client application. What should you do?

A. Use RAISEERROR statement.

B. Use RAISEERROR WITH LOG statement.

C. Use FORMATMESSAGE function.

D. Use xp_logevent stored procedure.

13. You have to create a stored procedure to archive data from a table. You write the following code:

```
CREATE PROCEDURE ArchiveOrder (@OrderID INT)

AS

BEGIN

BEGIN TRANSACTION

    BEGIN TRY

    INSERT INTO OldOrders (OrderID,OrderDetails)

    SELECT OrderID, OrderDetails FROM Orders

    WHERE OrderID=@OrderID


    DELETE FROM Orders

    WHERE OrderID=@OrderID


    END TRY

    BEGIN CATCH

    IF @@TRANCOUNT>0 ROLLBACK TRANSACTION

    END CATCH

END

GO
```

When you test the stored procedure, it doesn't work as expected. What should you do?

A. Add code inside the TRY block to commit the transaction.

B. Add code inside the CATCH block to commit the transaction.

C. Remove the TRY...CATCH construct.

D. Remove the BEGIN TRANSACTION statement.

14. You have to develop a module for an application that would be used to enter orders. At the database level you have an Order table and an OrderDetails table. Each order item can have one or more details. The OrderDetails table has a foreign key constraint that references the OrderID column of the Order table. The OrderID column has the IDENTITY property and is a primary key for the Order table. You need to design a strategy for inserting a new order. What should you do?

1. Start a transaction.
2. Insert data into the OrderDetails table.
3. Insert data into the Order table.
4. Check for errors.
5. If an error occurred, return a message to the application.
6. Rollback the transaction and exit.

   A. Follow these steps: 1, 2, 3, 4, 5
   B. Follow these steps: 1, 3, 2, 4, 5
   C. Follow these steps: 1, 2, 4, 5, 3, 4, 5
   D. Follow these steps: 1, 3, 4, 5, 6, 2, 4, 5, 6

15. Which of the following versions of the EXECUTE AS clause is usually used to create custom permission sets?

   A. EXECUTE AS CALLER
   B. EXECUTE AS SELF
   C. EXECUTE AS 'user_name'
   D. EXECUTE AS OWNER

16. Which of the following T-SQL elements can cause context switching? (Choose all that apply.)

   A. SETUSER statement
   B. EXECUTE AS statement
   C. EXECUTE AS clause
   D. REVERT statement

17. Inside of a stored procedure that uses a EXECUTE AS OWNER clause you want to log for auditing purposes the database user of the stored procedure caller. What should you do? (Choose the best option.)

   A. Modify the stored procedure to use the EXECUTE AS SELF clause.
   B. Remove the EXECTE AS OWNER clause.
   C. Use the ORIGINAL_LOGIN() function.
   D. Use the EXECUTE AS CALLER statement, get the username from the USER_NAME function, and then USE REVERT statement to change back the execution context.

18. You want to change the severity level of an existing user-defined message. What should you do? (Choose the best option.)

    A. Drop the message and recreate it with the new severity level.

    B. Use the sp_altermessage stored procedure.

    C. Use the sp_dropmessage stored procedure.

    D. Use the sp_addmessage stored procedure.

19. Which of the following affirmations are true about the TRY...CATCH construct? (Choose all that apply.)

    A. You can use GOTO statements inside of a TRY or a CATCH block.

    B. The TRY...CATCH construct can be nested.

    C. You cannot have multiple CATCH blocks for the same TRY block.

    D. There is no FINALLY block.

20. You review the following code written by another developer from your department:

```
BEGIN TRY

RAISERROR(80000,16,1);

END TRY

BEGIN CATCH


END CATCH

SELECT ERROR_NUMBER();
```

    The code should return the error number (80000) but instead it returns null. How can you solve this problem?

    A. Use @@ERROR instead of ERROR_NUMBER().

    B. Use the ERROR_NUMBER() function inside the TRY block.

    C. Use the ERROR_NUMBER() function inside the CATCH block.

    D. Use the ERROR_LINE() function instead of ERROR_NUMBER().

Answers to Review Questions

1. D. The TRY block must be immediately followed by the CATCH block or a syntax error will be generated. In this case the code will work by simply removing the keyword GO.

2. A. If you want an alert to fire the error message should be logged. For that purpose you have several methods available such as RAISERROR WITH LOG, using the extended stored procedure xp_logevent, or using an user-defined error message created with the sp_addmessage stored procedure and specifying 'TRUE' as the value for the @with_log parameter.

3. B. If the update statement affects no rows, the @@ROWCOUNT function will return the value 0, meaning that there is no row in the Products table having the specified product code.

4. B, E, F. Using a TRY...CATCH construct you can handle statement abort errors, deadlocks, and transaction abort errors. Warnings and informational messages that have a severity level 10 or lower are not considered errors, and the TRY...CATCH construct will not handle them. Also compile and recompile errors cannot be handled at the same execution level.

5. C. To respect the principle of least privilege, you should run the procedure in the context of the user "WriteUser". Running the stored procedures as CALLER will generate permission errors and using OWNER could mean granting unnecessary permissions. To use the SETUSER command you need to be a member of the sysadmin role, which is out of question for the proposed scenario.

6. A, B, C, D. All of the above measures make your code more secure.

7. A. Using the integrated error messages system of SQL Server is the best option in this case. The other options would require more development time.

8. B, D. You can solve the problem either using a lower severity number or the WITH LOG option of the RAISERROR. Error messages with severity 19 or greater require the WITH LOG option of the RAISERROR statement.

9. A, B. Only members of the sysadmin fixed server role or users with ALTER TRACE permission can raise errors with a severity 20.

10. B, C. Errors with severity 10 or less are considered by SQL Server warnings and informational messages and cannot be caught with the TRY...CATCH construct. However, errors with severity level 16 and deadlock victim errors can be handled using the TRY...CATCH construct.

11. C. To get the line at which an error occurred, you have to use the ERROR_LINE() function.

12. D. The xp_logevent stored procedure allows you to log a message in the SQL Server log and in the Windows Application log and send an alert without sending a message to the client.

13. A. You have to add a COMMIT TRANSACTION statement as the last action in the TRY block.

14. D. To maintain the integrity of your database you need to check for errors after each insert statement (an alternative would be to include both insert statements in a TRY block). Since the OrderID column is generated automatically, you have to insert data first into the Order table and use the new generated OrderID to insert data into the OrderDetails table.

15. C. Although in some situations you can use EXECUTE AS SELF, the preferred method to create custom permission sets is using EXECUTE AS 'user_name'.

16. A, B, C, D. All of the above options can change the execution context.

17. D. The best option would be to use the EXECUTE AS CALLER statement inside the stored procedure. The ORIGINAL_LOGIN() function returns the login that connected to SQL Server.

18. D. You can change the text and severity level of a message by using the sp_addmessage stored procedure with the replace option.

19. A, B, C, D. All the above statements are correct.

20. C. The error functions could be used only inside a CATCH block, otherwise it returns null.

Chapter

6

Planning a Transaction Strategy

MICROSOFT EXAM OBJECTIVES COVERED IN THIS CHAPTER:

- ✓ Manage concurrency by selecting the appropriate transaction isolation levels.
- ✓ Design the locking granularity level.
- ✓ Design transaction scopes.
- ✓ Design code that uses transactions.

There's an old joke that says database servers have just one problem: the users. In other words, if it weren't for the users, DBAs and database developers wouldn't have any problems at all. Leaving all the jokes behind, users do exist, and your job is to allow them to get the information needed, to protect their data, and to ensure its consistency. That translates to finding the perfect balance between the performance and concurrency requirements of your application and the need for consistent data.

In this chapter, you will learn how to maximize concurrency while maintaining data integrity. You will also learn how to use transactions and transaction scopes.

Managing Concurrency by Selecting the Appropriate Transaction Isolation Levels

What is concurrency? *Concurrency* means two or more processes using the same data simultaneously.

Concurrency and consistency are inversely proportional. If you want great concurrency, you have to reduce consistency, and vice versa. Concurrency and implicit consistency can be managed by SQL Server using transactions to block resources—thereby creating locks—or by maintaining multiple versions of data.

According to Wikipedia, consistency (or data integrity) in a relational database is concerned with three aspects of the data in a database: accuracy, correctness, and validity.

You should know by now that you have the responsibility to select an appropriate transaction isolation level. But how do you make an appropriate choice? You can determine that by considering the requirements of your application for performance, concurrency, and consistency.

The most important advice we can give you related to concurrency is as follows: don't expect that powerful hardware will replace good design. A reader blocking thousands of writers can be a serious problem no matter what hardware stands behind. Fortunately, you have lots of options to minimize concurrency problems, and you will learn about them in this chapter. We begin by reminding you of several concepts, such as the transaction, the ACID properties, concurrency side effects, methods to control concurrency, locking granularity, lock modes, and lock compatibility.

What Is a Transaction?

A database *transaction* is one set of operations performed as one unit of work having the ACID (atomicity, consistency, isolation, and durability) properties. We will discuss them later in this section.

When ATMs of a certain bank were introduced, they had the following problem: if any kind of error occurred when a customer withdrew some money, the customer could have ended up with no money either in their account or in their hands. At that time, the ATM allowed a maximum number of 25 bills at a time. Unaware of that, the customer tried to get an amount expressed as 30 bills. The machine counted them, made some strange noise, and that was all. The money magically evaporated from the account, and the customer received nothing.

If the situation were ideal, the ATMs would work in the following manner:

- They would authenticate the customer.

- When an amount of money was requested, they would block the account, subtract the specified amount specified from the account, and give the customer the money.

- They would check that the money was actually distributed and mark that success (or failure).

- If every operation completed successfully, they would unlock the account and wish the customer a good day.

- If any operation failed, the situation should be as it was when everything started, meaning that the account should have the initial amount and the customer should receive no money at all, not even a cent.

Ideally, money withdrawal from an ATM should be a transaction—one set of operations performed as one unit of work and with the following properties:

Atomicity   All or nothing. All the operations should complete successfully or all should fail.

Consistency   Data should be consistent when the transaction starts and when it ends. If any integrity rule for the data (such as a positive value for the balance of a bank account) is violated, the transaction should be aborted.

Isolation   The operations of a transaction should be isolated from operations of other transactions. Imagine this situation: the ATM checks the account to see whether there is enough money in the account. The account contains the requested amount so the ATM decides to give the customer the money. Before the actual delivery an automatic payment of a phone bill modifies the balance of the account. The ATM gives the customer the money. Because the account is not blocked (isolated) between the ATM checking for the account balance and the actual money delivery, the customer could theoretically get more money than they actually have.

Durability   Once the transaction completes successfully, the effects of the transaction are permanent even in case of system failure.

All these properties—atomicity, consistency, isolation, and durability—known as ACID properties, are implemented by SQL Server transactions. This section is focused entirely on how SQL Server implements the isolation property.

There are two different methods used to implement isolation property:

Using locking   Resources are protected by acquiring locks.

Using separate copies for any data that is modified   This method does not require locks and it was introduced in SQL Server 2005 by means of a new feature named *row versioning*. Row versioning means maintaining different versions of modified data.

Another way to classify the methods used to allow concurrent access to data is by the concurrency control mode.

Concurrency Control Modes

When several people try to modify data simultaneously, your database server can take two approaches to allow that:

Pessimistic concurrency mode   This is a preventive method and it is based on locking to avoid possible conflicts. The pessimistic concurrency mode is based on this assumption: a read operation is very likely to be affected by concurrent data modifications. Hence, the great probability of a conflict and the preventive strategy—blocking access to data used by a process. The main disadvantage of this method is reduced concurrency.

Optimistic concurrency mode   This is the preferred method for greater concurrency with a consistency drawback. The assumption used by this mode is that a read operation is very unlikely to be affected by concurrent data modifications. Conflicts can occur and have to be handled. Read data is not locked. So when an update takes place the system will verify if data has changed after it was read. If so, an error will occur.

You can control the concurrency control mode used by the database engine (pessimistic or optimistic) through transaction isolation levels, locking hints, or concurrency options for cursors.

Locking in the Database Engine

The first method used by SQL Server to prevent data modification conflicts is by using locks. Locks help maintain the integrity of data and transactions. Let's say for example that a user named Bob starts a transaction that reads a row. If another user Ted wants to modify the same row, locks will prevent Ted's modification until Bob's transaction finishes the read operation. You will learn in the following sections how to customize the locking behavior of SQL Server using *isolation levels*. Also, you will see that you can acquire locks on different types of resources, that there are several types of lock modes, and that each type of lock can be compatible or not with other types. Let's take them in turns.

Locking Granularity

SQL Server can lock different types of resources from rows to an entire database. It is obvious that locking at a row level is better from a concurrency point of view than locking at the table level. However, it will cost more in terms of overhead. Why? Because multiple row level locks cost more resources than a single table level lock. The following list enumerates some of the resource types that can be locked by SQL Server:

- RID: A physical row in a heap

 **NOTE**   A *heap* is a table that does not have a clustered index.

- KEY: A row in an index
- PAGE: A single page in a data file
- EXTENT: A contiguous group of eight data pages (or index pages)
- HOBT: A heap or B-tree
- TABLE: An entire table (meaning all data and indexes)
- OBJECT: A database object such as tables, views, stored procedures, and so on
- FILE: A database file (it can be a data file or a log file)
- APPLICATION: An application-specified resource
- METADATA: Metadata information
- ALLOCATION_UNIT: A single allocation unit
- DATABASE: An entire database

To display locking information as well as the type of resources on which the lock request is being made, you can use the sys.dm_tran_locks DMV (dynamic management view). It displays the complete list of lock requests. The columns of the view describe both the request and the resource demanded. For the current topic, we will illustrate the use of this DMV by selecting the resource_type and the request_mode columns in a simple locking situation:

```
USE tempdb;
GO
-- Create a test table.
CREATE TABLE TestLocking
    (ID INT NOT NULL PRIMARY KEY,VAL INT);
GO
-- Insert demo data
INSERT INTO TestLocking(ID,VAL) VALUES (1,10);
INSERT INTO TestLocking(ID,VAL) VALUES (2,20);
GO
```

```
BEGIN TRAN;
-- Output: VAL 10
SELECT VAL FROM TestLocking WITH(HOLDLOCK)
WHERE ID = 1;
-- Output:
-- resource_type     request_mode
-- PAGE              IS
-- KEY               S
-- OBJECT            IS
SELECT resource_type, request_mode
FROM sys.dm_tran_locks
WHERE request_session_id = @@SPID;

COMMIT TRAN;
GO
```

As you can see, the select statement generates three lock requests at a page level, at a row of an index table, and at an object level. The object is actually our table. The typical behavior of the read operation is to release the lock as soon as the operation completes. To override this behavior, we used the NOLOCK hint to maintain the locks for the duration of our transactions.

Lock Modes

If the granularity level for locks means the option to block different types of resources, the lock modes specify how a resource can be accessed by concurrent transactions or concurrent users. For example, when you modify a row, SQL Server can use an exclusive lock at the row level to prevent other processes from accessing the same row.

In SQL Server 2005 you may encounter the following types of locks:

- Shared (S) locks are typically used for read-only operations. A shared lock (S) is released as soon as the read operation completes. You can maintain the lock for the entire transaction using a locking hint or the Repeatable Read and Serializable isolation levels. Shared locks allow other transactions to acquire a shared lock on the same resource but prevent concurrent data modifications.

- Update (U) locks are used by SQL Server when it modifies data at a later point. Before data is modified, the update lock becomes an exclusive lock. Update locks are acquired during the read operation for an update. Only one transaction can obtain an update (U) lock on a resource at a time. However, an update (U) lock is compatible with shared (S) locks. In other words, shared locks and an update lock can be placed on the same resource at the same time.

- Exclusive (X) locks are used for data-modification operations to prevent access to a resource by a concurrent user or transaction. You can still read data acquired by an exclusive lock using the NOLOCK hint or using the Read Uncommitted isolation level.

 INSERT, UPDATE, and DELETE statements typically use both modification and read operations and will require exclusive locks as well as shared locks.

- Intent locks are used to minimize locking conflicts and to establish a lock hierarchy. For example, before acquiring a shared (S) lock on a row of a table, a shared intent lock is requested at the table level. The shared intent lock at the table level prevents another user or transaction from acquiring an exclusive lock on the table containing the row. At the same time, the intent lock placed at the table level will tell the database engine if a lock can be required on a table by another transaction without the examination of all the lower level locks on that table (row and page locks). There are several types of intent locks:
    - Intent shared (IS) is used with acquired or shared locks on a resource.
    - Intent exclusive (IX) is used with acquired or required exclusive locks.
    - Shared with intent exclusive (SIX) is used to protect requested or acquired shared locks on some resources and intent exclusive locks on others.
    - Intent update (IU) is used with requested or acquired update locks.
    - Shared intent update (SIU) is a combination between shared (S) and intent update (IU) locks.
    - Update intent exclusive (UIX) is a combination between update (U) and intent exclusive (IX) locks.
- Schema locks are used in two types of situations:
    - To prevent DDL statements on a table or index when a query referencing the table or the index is compiled. For this scenario a schema stability (Sch-S) lock is used.
    - To prevent access to a resource that is being modified as in the case of adding a column to a table. To achieve that, a schema modification (Sch-M) lock is used.
- Bulk update (BU) locks are used to allow multiple processes to bulk copy data in a table and prevent the other processes to access the table.
- Key-range locks are used by the Serializable isolation level to protect a range of rows.

Lock Compatibility

As you've already seen, some lock types allow some specific types of locks to acquire the same resource while disallowing others. Use these simple rules:

- Exclusive locks are not compatible with any other types of locks.
- Shared locks are compatible with all locks except exclusive locks.
- Update locks are compatible only with shared locks.
- The schema modification (Sch-M) lock is incompatible with all lock modes.
- The schema stability (Sch-S) lock is not compatible with schema modification (Sch-M) lock but it is compatible with all the others.

Table 6.1 shows the compatibility between several of the most common lock modes. For the complete lock compatibility matrix, please refer to the "Lock Compatibility" topic of Books Online.

TABLE 6.1   Lock Compatibility

				Granted Lock				
Requested Lock	IS	S	U	IX	SIX	X	Sch-M	Sch-S
Intent shared (IS)	Yes	Yes	Yes	Yes	Yes	No	No	Yes
Shared (S)	Yes	Yes	Yes	No	No	No	No	Yes
Update (U)	Yes	Yes	No	No	No	No	No	Yes
Intent exclusive (IX)	Yes	No	No	Yes	No	No	No	Yes
Shared with intent exclusive (SIX)	Yes	No	No	No	No	No	No	Yes
Exclusive (X)	No	No	No	No	No	No	No	Yes
Schema modification (Sch-M)	No	No	No	No	No	No	No	No
Schema stability (Sch-S)	Yes	Yes	Yes	Yes	Yes	Yes	No	Yes

We'll now show a short example of locking incompatibility. We will use the same table created in the previous section. You update a row and this way you place an exclusive lock. A second connection tries to access the same row and will have to wait until the first transaction finishes. To display locking information, you can use the same dynamic management function: sys.dm_tran_locks.

So, open two query windows in SQL Server Management Studio, and run the following code in the first query window:

```
-- On my computer the Session ID was 53
USE tempdb;
GO
BEGIN TRAN
-- place an exclusive lock on a row
UPDATE TestLocking
SET VAL = 30
```

```
WHERE ID = 1
-- introduce a delay
-- wait for 20 seconds to give you time to switch
 -- and run the second batch
WAITFOR DELAY '00:00:20';
-- display locks
SELECT request_session_id, resource_type, request_mode, request_status
FROM sys.dm_tran_locks
-- rollback the transaction
ROLLBACK TRAN
Run the following code in the first query window:
-- On my computer the Session ID was 54
USE tempdb;
GO
SELECT VAL FROM TestLocking
WHERE ID = 1;

-- Partial output from the first query
```

request_session_id	resource_type	request_mode	request_status
54	PAGE	IS	GRANT
53	PAGE	IX	GRANT
53	KEY	X	GRANT
54	KEY	S	WAIT
54	OBJECT	IS	GRANT
53	OBJECT	IX	GRANT

As you can see, the exclusive lock placed by the first query prevented the second query from acquiring a shared lock on the same resource, a row of a clustered index. The request status WAIT for the second query means just as the name says, that the query has to wait to acquire its shared lock.

Concurrency Side Effects

Another area of concurrency that you should be familiar with is concurrency side effects. If a database server does not use concurrency control, the side effects (or anomalies) discussed in the following sections can occur.

Lost Updates

This problem can occur when two processes update the same data. Only one of the two modifications is persisted in the database. But let us tell you more about this phenomenon by means of a short story. When ADO.NET came with .NET Framework into the programming world, it brought a new model of working with data—the disconnected model. This model was based on an object named DataSet—a "disconnected" in-memory representation of data. For short, you take your data and load a data set and then immediately disconnect from the data source. Then, you can manipulate the data as your application requires. If needed, you can connect again to the data source to update the changes made to the data. This approach can generate the "lost updates" problem.

Imagine the following situation:

- Two users of a .NET application work on the same data.

- Each of them uses the application to load the data from a database into a DataSet.

- The users modify the data and then connect again to the database to save the changes.

Chances are that only one modification (from the submitted two) is persisted, namely the last one. Of course, there are workarounds, such as verifying that the rows that are updated were not modified in the meantime. To understand the "lost update" phenomenon better, here it is in a code context:

```
---------------------------------------------------------------
-- Step 1
-- First connection
-- Read a row from the SpecialOffers table
SELECT * FROM Sales.SpecialOffer
WHERE SpecialOfferID = 10;


-- Second connection
-- No activity
---------------------------------------------------------------
-- Step 2
-- First connection
-- Modifies the row in the application interface
-- Second connection
-- Read the same row from the SpecialOffers table
SELECT * FROM Sales.SpecialOffer
WHERE SpecialOfferID = 10;


---------------------------------------------------------------
-- Step 3
-- First connection
-- Send the change to the database
UPDATE Sales.SpecialOffer
SET DiscountPct = 0.65
WHERE SpecialOfferID = 10;
-- Second connection
-- Modifies the row in the application interface
```

```
-----------------------------------------------------------------
-- Step 4
-- First connection
-- No activity
-- Second connection
-- Send the change to the database
UPDATE Sales.SpecialOffer
SET DiscountPct = 0.70
WHERE SpecialOfferID = 10;
```

When both connections finish, the DiscountPct column will have the value 0.70 and not 0.65 like the first connection specified.

Uncommitted Dependency (Dirty Read)

This type of anomaly occurs when one connection (transaction) reads data uncommitted yet by a second connection (transaction). To illustrate this behavior, we use two queries that should run separately.

This is the first batch:

```
USE tempdb;
GO
CREATE TABLE ConcurrencyEffects(
        ID INT NOT NULL PRIMARY KEY,
        VAL INT);
INSERT INTO ConcurrencyEffects (ID,VAL)
VALUES (1,10);
GO
BEGIN TRAN
UPDATE ConcurrencyEffects
SET VAL = 20
WHERE ID = 1;
-- wait for 20 seconds to give you time to switch
-- and run the second batch
WAITFOR DELAY '00:00:20';
ROLLBACK TRAN
GO
-- The original value 10 will be returned
SELECT VAL FROM ConcurrencyEffects
WHERE ID = 1;
GO
```

This is the second batch:

```
USE tempdb;
GO
-- The uncommitted value 20 will be returned
SELECT VAL FROM ConcurrencyEffects WITH (NOLOCK)
WHERE ID = 1;
GO
```

To avoid blocking, we used the NOLOCK query hint for the second query. We will get back to query hints in the next section of this chapter. For now you should know that the NOLOCK hint modifies the behavior of the read operation. When you use the NOLOCK hint, shared locks are no longer required for read operations.

Inconsistent Analysis (Nonrepeatable Read)

The nonrepeatable read anomaly occurs when the data read multiple times by a transaction is modified by another transaction, and the first transaction obtains different values for each read.

This is the first batch:

```
USE tempdb;
GO
BEGIN TRAN
-- The original value 10 will be displayed
SELECT VAL FROM ConcurrencyEffects
WHERE ID = 1;
GO
-- wait for 20 seconds to give you time to switch
-- and run the second batch
WAITFOR DELAY '00:00:20';
-- The updated value(20) will be displayed
SELECT VAL FROM ConcurrencyEffects
WHERE ID = 1;
ROLLBACK TRAN;
GO
```

This is the second batch:

```
USE tempdb;
GO
UPDATE ConcurrencyEffects
SET VAL = 20
WHERE ID = 1;
GO
```

Phantom Reads

A phantom read occurs when after a first read operation of a transaction, a row (or multiple rows) is inserted or deleted and that specific row (or rows) belongs to the range of rows retrieved by the read operation. This type of concurrency effect can be avoided if the entire range of rows generated by the read operation will be blocked for the duration of the transaction. This way inserting new rows or deleting rows in the specified range will be prevented. This is exactly what the Serializable transaction isolation level does. You'll now see an example.

This is the first batch:

```
USE tempdb;
GO
BEGIN TRAN
-- One row will be returned
-- Output: 20
SELECT VAL FROM ConcurrencyEffects
WHERE ID > 0 AND ID < 30;
GO
-- wait for 20 seconds to give you time to switch
-- and run the second batch
WAITFOR DELAY '00:00:20';
-- Two new rows will be returned
-- and the one row displayed initially will be missing
-- Output: 30 40
SELECT VAL FROM ConcurrencyEffects
WHERE ID > 0 AND ID < 30;
GO
ROLLBACK TRAN;
GO
```

This is the second batch:

```
USE tempdb;
GO
BEGIN TRAN
INSERT INTO ConcurrencyEffects (ID,VAL)
VALUES (3,30);
INSERT INTO ConcurrencyEffects (ID,VAL)
VALUES (4,40);
DELETE FROM ConcurrencyEffects WHERE ID = 1;
COMMIT TRAN;
GO
```

You will see later in this section how you can use isolation levels to protect your application from these anomalies.

Row Versioning Framework

SQL Server 2005 introduces the row versioning framework based on maintaining multiple versions of modified rows. This framework is designed to support several new features of SQL Server 2005, such as the following:

Triggers   The inserted and deleted tables accessible in triggers are built using row versioning instead of reading the transaction log.

Multiple Active Result Sets (MARS)   Row versions are used to protect an active result set from a concurrent batch of the same MARS connection that will modify the same data.

Online index operations   Using row versioning allows building indexes or rebuilding indexes without taking the index (or the underlying table) offline.

Two new transaction isolation levels   Use Read Committed Snapshot isolation level and Snapshot isolation level.

Row versioning works relatively simply:

- When a row is to be modified, before the row can be modified, a copy of the row is copied in tempdb Version Store.

Version Store is a collection of data pages that contain row versions generated by data modification transactions that use Snapshot or Read Committed Snapshot or by features such as online index operations, Multiple Active Result Sets (MARS), and triggers.

- If the row is modified by multiple transactions, the versions of the row are linked by a link list in tempdb.
- All read operations will use the last version of the row that was committed when the transaction started.
- A background thread will remove row versions as they are no longer needed.

The 70-442 exam does not require an in-depth knowledge of row versioning framework but chances are that your job will. So we invite you to use Books Online to learn more about this new framework, about its performance impact, and about the tools that support monitoring and troubleshooting row versioning (dynamic management views and performance counters).

Database Engine Isolation Levels

SQL Server 2000 implemented the following isolation levels defined by the SQL-99 standard:

Read Uncommitted   The lowest level of data consistency and highest for concurrency.

Read Committed   The default level for the database engine, a bit more consistent than the Read Uncommitted isolation level, protecting a transaction from dirty reads.

Repeatable Read   Gives higher consistency than the Read Committed isolation level, protecting a transaction not just from dirty reads but also from inconsistent analysis phenomenon.

Serializable   Offers complete isolation for a transaction with the downside of having the lowest concurrency.

With the exception of the Read Uncommitted isolation level that will not use locks to read data, all the others use the pessimistic concurrency model.

In addition to the isolation levels supported by SQL Server 2000, SQL Server 2005 introduces another two that follow the optimistic concurrency model by using multiple versions of data:

Read Committed Snapshot   It's a new flavor of Read Committed isolation level based on row versioning instead of locking. It provides statement-level read consistency.

Snapshot   It offers transaction-level read consistency using the same row versioning framework.

You can specify a transaction isolation level using SET TRANSACTION ISOLATION LEVEL and indicating one of the following values: READ UNCOMMITTED, READ COMMITTED, REPEATABLE READ, SNAPSHOT, SERIALIZABLE. For row versioning based isolation levels—Snapshot and Read Committed Snapshot, you have to follow one more step by setting to ON a database option: ALLOW_SNAPSHOT_ISOLATION and READ_COMMITTED_SNAPSHOT.

We will discuss each isolation level in greater detail, focusing on implementation and appropriate use.

Read Uncommitted

Reading data without acquiring shared locks characterizes this isolation level. It allows reading the data that another transaction has locked exclusively. In short, readers won't block writers and writers won't block readers. As a result this is the less restrictive isolation level, and offers the best concurrency and the lowest consistency.

Facts about the Read Uncommitted Isolation Level

You should also know about this isolation level:

- It operates the same way as the NOLOCK hint.
- Transactions running in this isolation mode are exposed to anomalies such as dirty reads, inconsistent analysis, and phantoms.
- For reading operations, Sch-S (schema stability) locks are used and as an immediate result, the read operations will be blocked by concurrent DDL operations.
- Exclusive locks are used for data modification.
- Use SET TRANSACTION ISOLATION LEVEL READ UNCOMMITTED to set this isolation level.

When Should You Use the Read Uncommitted Isolation Level?

You should utilize this isolation level if your application does not require high consistency of data and when transactional performance is the most important requirement. It is supposed that your application will accept *concurrency effects* that can occur, such as dirty reads, inconsistent analysis, and phantom reads. As an example, in reporting applications, most of the time report data is not required to be real time and consistent.

Examples

To illustrate the behavior of this isolation level as well as for the others, you will create first a new database and two tables with demo data:

```
-- Create a demo database
USE master;
GO
CREATE DATABASE IsolationLevelsDB;
GO
USE IsolationLevelsDB;
GO
CREATE TABLE T1 (ID INT NOT NULL PRIMARY KEY,VAL VARCHAR(16));
GO
CREATE TABLE T2 (ID INT NOT NULL PRIMARY KEY,VAL VARCHAR(16));
GO
-- Insert demo data
DECLARE @I INT;
SET @I = 1;
WHILE @I < 21
BEGIN
INSERT INTO T1 (ID,VAL) VALUES (@I,'VALUE ' + CAST(@I AS VARCHAR(2)));
INSERT INTO T1 (ID,VAL) VALUES (100+@I,'VALUE ' + CAST(100+@I AS VARCHAR(2)));
INSERT INTO T2 (ID,VAL) VALUES (@I,'VALUE ' + CAST(@I AS VARCHAR(2)));
INSERT INTO T2 (ID,VAL) VALUES (100+@I,'VALUE ' + CAST(100+@I AS VARCHAR(2)));
SET @I = @I + 1;
END
GO
```

Now open two query windows and run the first example. You should run the first batch in a window and then the second in the other window before the first batch completes. You will see how the second batch will read uncommitted data.

This is the first batch:

```
USE IsolationLevelsDB;
GO
BEGIN TRAN;
```

```
-- place an exclusive lock on an index key of T1 table
UPDATE T1
SET VAL = 'temporary value'
WHERE ID = 1;
-- wait for 20 seconds to give you time to switch
-- and run the second batch
WAITFOR DELAY '00:00:20';
ROLLBACK TRAN;
GO
```

This is the second batch:

```
USE IsolationLevelsDB;
GO
SET TRANSACTION ISOLATION LEVEL READ UNCOMMITTED;
GO
BEGIN TRAN;
-- this will work returning : VAL 'temporary value'
-- the value will change, the returned value is an uncommited one
-- this phenomenon is known as dirty reads
SELECT VAL FROM T1 WHERE ID = 1;
GO
ROLLBACK TRAN;
GO
-- switch back to the default isolation level
SET TRANSACTION ISOLATION LEVEL READ COMMITTED;
GO
BEGIN TRAN;
-- this will block and will return
-- after the first batch completes : VAL 'VALUE 1'
SELECT VAL FROM T1 WHERE ID = 1;
GO
ROLLBACK TRAN;
GO
```

The second example illustrates that the Read Uncommitted isolation level still needs exclusive locks for data modifications. It is true that for a read operation a transaction running under the Read Uncommitted isolation level does not require shared locks, but for data modification exclusive locks are a must.

This is the first batch:

```
USE IsolationLevelsDB;
GO
```

```
BEGIN TRAN;
-- place an exclusive lock on an index key of T1 table
UPDATE T1
SET VAL = 'temporary value'
WHERE ID = 1;
-- wait for 20 seconds to give you time to switch
-- and run the second batch
WAITFOR DELAY '00:00:20';
ROLLBACK TRAN;
GO
```

This is the second batch:

```
USE IsolationLevelsDB;
GO
SET TRANSACTION ISOLATION LEVEL READ UNCOMMITTED;
GO
BEGIN TRAN;
-- the update will be blocked and will wait to aquire an exclusive lock
UPDATE T1
SET VAL = 'another value'
WHERE ID = 1;
GO
ROLLBACK TRAN;
GO
```

Read Committed

This is the default isolation level for database engines. It is more restrictive than Read Uncommitted because shared locks are used to protect read operations. The shared locks are released as soon as the read operations complete. Because shared locks are used to protect data, a reader using the Read Committed isolation level will be blocked by a writer and vice versa. This behavior changes if the READ_COMMITTED_SNAPSHOT database option is set to ON, row versioning being used instead of locking. We will discuss this particular situation in the Read Committed Snapshot isolation level topic.

Facts about the Read Committed Isolation Level

Here are some additional facts to consider, if you plan to use the Read Committed isolation level:

- Under this isolation level, writers will block readers and readers will block writers.
- The shared locks used by a read operation will be released as soon as the read operation completes. We remind you this detail because we consider it significant. You will see later in the chapter that you can change this behavior by using the HOLDLOCK hint.

- Possible anomalies for this isolation level are inconsistent analysis and phantoms.
- Use SET TRANSACTION ISOLATION LEVEL READ UNCOMMITTED to set this isolation level.
- If the READ_COMMITTED_SNAPSHOT database option is ON, you can use the READCOMMITTEDLOCK hint in case you want to use shared locks instead of row versioning.

When Should You Use the Read Committed Isolation Level?

You should consider using this default isolation level for your application when you need transaction consistent data and you want to avoid the performance impact of repeatable reads or row versioning.

It is supposed that inconsistent analysis or phantoms anomalies would not be a problem for your application.

Examples

When you use the Read Committed transaction isolation level, you can encounter the inconsistent analysis phenomenon. The first example demonstrates this anomaly. The first query will obtain two different values for the same repeated read.

This is the first batch:

```
USE IsolationLevelsDB;
GO
-- the next stament is redundant and I use it for readability
-- Read Commited being the default isolation level
SET TRANSACTION ISOLATION LEVEL READ COMMITTED;
BEGIN TRAN;
-- Output: VAL 'VALUE 1'
SELECT VAL FROM T1 WHERE ID = 1;
GO
-- wait for 20 seconds to give you time to switch
-- and run the second batch
WAITFOR DELAY '00:00:20';
GO
-- Output: VAL 'NEW VALUE 01'
SELECT VAL FROM T1 WHERE ID = 1;
GO
ROLLBACK TRAN;
GO
```

This is the second batch:

```
USE IsolationLevelsDB;
GO
```

```
-- Update the first row
UPDATE T1
SET VAL = 'NEW VALUE 01'
WHERE ID = 1;
GO
```

The second example demonstrates how readers blocking writers and vice versa can generate a bigger problem, a deadlock.

This is the first batch:

```
USE IsolationLevelsDB;
GO
SET TRANSACTION ISOLATION LEVEL READ COMMITTED;
BEGIN TRAN
-- Update first table
UPDATE T1
SET VAL = 'SOME VALUE'
WHERE ID = 1;
GO
-- Wait for 20 seconds to give you time to switch
-- and run the second batch
WAITFOR DELAY '00:00:20';
GO
-- Select from second table
SELECT VAL FROM T2 WHERE ID = 1;
GO
COMMIT TRAN;
GO
```

This is the second batch:

```
USE IsolationLevelsDB;
GO
SET TRANSACTION ISOLATION LEVEL READ COMMITTED;
BEGIN TRAN
-- Update first table
UPDATE T2
SET VAL = 'OTHER VALUE'
WHERE ID = 1;
GO
-- Select from second table
```

```
SELECT VAL FROM T1 WHERE ID = 1;
GO
COMMIT TRAN;
GO
```

One of the batches generates the following error message:

```
"Msg 1205, Level 13, State 51, Line 2
Transaction (Process ID XX) was deadlocked on lock resources
with another process and has been chosen as the deadlock victim.
Rerun the transaction"
```

An extra error is generated because once the deadlock occurs, the deadlock victim batch cannot commit the transaction and thus the following error:

```
"Msg 3903, Level 16, State 1, Line 1
The ROLLBACK TRANSACTION request has no corresponding
BEGIN TRANSACTION".
```

Repeatable Read

The Repeatable Read transaction isolation level is even more restrictive to concurrency than Read Committed. Yet, restrictive means a benefit added to the consistency by preventing the "inconsistent analysis" (nonrepeatable read) phenomenon. Unlike the Read Committed isolation level, shared locks placed on read data are not released when the read operations finishes but when the transaction ends.

Facts about the Repeatable Read Isolation Level

Additional information that you should know about this isolation level includes:

- Readers will block writers (who try to modify the read data) until the transaction ends.
- The only concurrency effect that is not prevented by this isolation level is the phantom reads phenomenon. Rows that match the result sets returned by read operations can be inserted by other transactions.
- Use SET TRANSACTION ISOLATION LEVEL REPEATABLE READ to set this isolation level.

When Should You Use the Repeatable Read Isolation Level?

You should consider this isolation level when your application needs consistent data and when read data should not change until the transaction ends. One of the cases when you may find this isolation level a perfect fit is when your application reads data and modifies the same data later (in the same transaction). If you plan to use the Repeatable Read, you have to accept the concurrency penalty imposed by this isolation level.

Example

Here is a single example for the Repeatable Read isolation level, to illustrate the locking behavior on the read data:

```
USE IsolationLevelsDB
GO
SET TRANSACTION ISOLATION LEVEL REPEATABLE READ;
GO
BEGIN TRAN;
-- place shared locks on the T1 table
SELECT AVG(ID) FROM T1 WHERE ID < 21;
GO
-- display locking info
-- Output Partial
-- resource_type request_mode
-- KEY          S
-- . . .
-- KEY          S
SELECT  resource_type, request_mode
FROM sys.dm_tran_locks
WHERE request_session_id = @@SPID;
GO
ROLLBACK TRAN;
GO
```

You may notice that a shared lock protects all 20 rows affected by the read operation.

Serializable

The Serializable transaction isolation level provides the most restrictions and the best consistency for your transactions. No anomalies can happen under this isolation level, because the following situations are forbidden:

- Reading uncommitted data of other transactions

- Allowing other transactions to modify rows that have been read by the current transaction before the current transaction ends

- Allowing other transactions to insert rows that can appear in a result set read by any statements of the current transaction until the current transaction ends

Obviously, this degree of isolation comes with a concurrency cost—range locks are used to protect data.

Facts about the Serializable Isolation Level

In addition to what we already mentioned, you should know the following facts about the Serializable isolation level:

- Use it only when really necessary. It adds a great concurrency and performance penalty to your application.

- You can achieve the same behavior if you specify the HOLDLOCK hint for all SELECT statements in a transaction.

- Use SET TRANSACTION ISOLATION LEVEL SERIALIZABLE to set this isolation level.

When Should You Use the Serializable Isolation Level?

If you require absolute accuracy, no phantom reads, same output for the same read operations, and modifying the read data later in the same transactions, then use of the Serializable isolation level.

Example

The next example demonstrates the locking behavior of the Serializable isolation level:

```
USE IsolationLevelsDB
GO
SET TRANSACTION ISOLATION LEVEL SERIALIZABLE;
GO
BEGIN TRAN;
-- place shared locks on the T1 table
SELECT SUM(ID) FROM T1 WHERE ID BETWEEN 1 AND 100;
GO
-- display locking info
-- Output Partial
-- resource_type request_mode
-- KEY       RangeS-S
-- . . .
-- KEY       RangeS-S
SELECT  resource_type, request_mode
FROM sys.dm_tran_locks
WHERE request_session_id = @@SPID;
GO
ROLLBACK TRAN;
GO
```

Unlike for the Repeatable Read isolation level, the Serializable isolation level will require range locks (like RangeS-S) and stops other transactions to insert new rows that fall in the specified range. If a concurrent connection tries to insert a row with an ID between 1 and 100, it will block it and have to wait until the current transaction ends.

Read Committed Snapshot

The Read Committed Snapshot isolation level comes with statement-level consistency for your transaction and great concurrency, both in the same package. In plain English, that means that a statement of your transaction no longer acquires shared locks for read operations, using just Sch-S locks. This way the modification of read data by other transaction is allowed (readers will not block writers and writers will not block readers). Statement-level consistency implies that a statement obtains the latest consistent version of data that was available when the statement started.

Let us show you a short example. We start by enabling the Read Committed Snapshot isolation level:

```
USE IsolationLevelsDB;
GO
-- Enable READ_COMMITTED_SNAPSHOT on the database.
-- make sure that this is the only connection to the IsolationLevelsDB
ALTER DATABASE IsolationLevelsDB
    SET READ_COMMITTED_SNAPSHOT ON WITH ROLLBACK IMMEDIATE;;
GO
```

The next step is to open two query windows and run the two concurrent batches.
This is the first batch:

```
USE IsolationLevelsDB;
GO
-- Start a read committed transaction
-- this statement is redundant the default mode
-- being Read Committed
SET TRANSACTION ISOLATION LEVEL READ COMMITTED;
GO
BEGIN TRAN;
-- Output: VAL 'VALUE 1'
SELECT VAL FROM T2 WHERE ID = 1;
GO
-- Wait for 10 seconds to give you time to switch
WAITFOR DELAY '00:00:10';
GO
-- The second transaction is not commited yet
--so the same value will be displayed
-- Output: VAL 'VALUE 1'
SELECT VAL FROM T2 WHERE ID = 1;
GO
-- Give time to the second batch to finish
WAITFOR DELAY '00:00:30';
```

```
GO
-- The second transaction should be commited by now
-- Output: VAL 'BATCH02 VALUE'
SELECT VAL FROM T2 WHERE ID = 1;
GO
ROLLBACK TRAN;
GO
```

This is the second batch:

```
USE IsolationLevelsDB;
GO
BEGIN TRAN;
-- Update the first row of table T2
UPDATE T2
SET VAL = 'BATCH02 VALUE'
WHERE ID = 1;
GO
-- Verify the update
-- Output: VAL 'BATCH02 VALUE'
SELECT VAL FROM T2 WHERE ID = 1;
GO
-- wait for 20 seconds before committing
-- to allow the first batch to read again
-- and to diplay the same version of the row
WAITFOR DELAY '00:00:20';
GO
COMMIT TRAN;
GO
```

If you managed to run the first batch and then the second one within a 10-second time frame, you should obtain the following behavior:

- The first batch reads the row with the ID=1 of table T2.

- The second batch updates the same row but does not commit yet. That causes the previous version of the row to be copied in Version Store.

- The first batch reads the same row again but this time it reads "the latest consistent version of the data that was available when the statement started," ergo the original version of the row from the Version Store. If the first batch uses the locking version of Read Committed isolation level, it will be blocked by the UPDATE statement.

- The second batch ends its transaction by committing.

- The first batch reads the same row again and since the second transaction has committed, the first batch reads the committed version of the row.

Facts about the Read Committed Snapshot Isolation Level

You should know of the following facts about this isolation level if you intend to use it and, of course, to pass the exam:

- Readers will not block writers and writers will not block readers.

- Writers will block writers, data modification following the same approach as for the locking version of the Read Committed isolation level:

  - Rows that will be updated are locked using an update (U) lock as the selected rows are read.

  - Exclusive locks will be used to protect the data that will be modified.

- Given that Sch-S locks are used to read data, concurrent DDL statements will block.

- Anomalies such as inconsistent analysis and phantom reads can occur at the transaction level.

- When you set the READ_COMMITTED_SNAPSHOT option to ON all connections will use by default the Read Committed Snapshot isolation level.

- In order to set the READ_COMMITTED_SNAPSHOT database option, your connection must be the single active connection to the database.

- You cannot use the Read Committed Snapshot isolation level for master, tempdb, and msdb system databases.

- To find out the current setting for the READ_COMMITTED_SNAPSHOT database option, you can use the is_read_committed_snapshot_on column of the sys.databases catalog view.

- When you use the ALTER DATABASE statement to change the setting of the READ_COMMITTED_SNAPSHOT database option you can customize the behavior of the ALTER DATABASE statement in case any locks are preventing the change. By default the ALTER DATABASE can wait indefinitely but you can choose to roll back incomplete transactions immediately or after a specified number of seconds using the ALTER DATABASE statement and the WITH termination clause:

```
-- roll back incomplete transactions after 5 seconds
ALTER DATABASE MyDB
SET READ_COMMITTED_SNAPSHOT ON
WITH ROLLBACK AFTER 5;

-- roll back incomplete transactions immediately
-- after 5 seconds
ALTER DATABASE MyDB
SET READ_COMMITTED_SNAPSHOT ON
WITH ROLLBACK IMMEDIATE;
```

If you want to abort immediately the request when locks are preventing changing the specified setting, you can use the NO_WAIT option of the WITH clause:

```
ALTER DATABASE MyDB
SET READ_COMMITTED_SNAPSHOT ON
WITH NO_WAIT;
```

- You can use the Read Committed Snapshot isolation level in *distributed transactions.*
- If you decide to use this isolation level with existing applications, you will not have to modify anything but set the READ_COMMITTED_SNAPSHOT database option to ON.
- If the READ_COMMITTED_SNAPSHOT database option is set to ON and you need to use the locking version of the Read Committed isolation level, you can use the READ-COMMITTEDLOCK hint.
- When using row versioning–based isolation levels you should be aware of the following costs:
  - Read performance may be reduced—the older the snapshot used the longer the version link list that must be traversed.
  - Transactions that update or delete rows generate row versions even when there are no concurrent transactions that use Snapshot or Read Committed Snapshot isolation levels. That means a performance overhead for CPU, memory, disk, and of course tempdb.
  - Version Store is located in tempdb so row versioning will increase the tempdb usage and it will consume tempdb space.
  - Updates to data will be slower due to generation of row versions.
- To support row versioning each row will be added a 14-byte versioning tag that contains the transaction sequence number of the transaction that committed the version and a pointer to the versioned row.

When any of the two row versioning database options is enabled, a transaction sequence number (XSN) is assigned to each transaction that uses row versioning. The transaction sequence number will start with the first read or write operation (on data) of the transaction and will be incremented by one each time it is assigned.

- Row versions required by a transaction that uses the Read Committed Snapshot isolation level will be maintained for the entire duration of the transaction and not for the duration of the statement as you would expect.

When Should You Use the Read Committed Snapshot Isolation Level?

Several scenarios will make using row versioning–based isolation levels a perfect candidate:

- Reporting or ad hoc queries on concurrently updated data.
- Requirements for consistent aggregate values without the locking cost of Repeatable Read or Serializable isolation levels.

- Migration to Microsoft SQL Server 2005 from other database systems that support similar isolation levels.
- High contention between readers and writers.

Besides that some arguments may require the use of the Read Committed Snapshot isolation level instead of the Snapshot one:

- Less tempdb space used. The Read Committed Snapshot Isolation level requires only statement-level consistency as opposed to transaction level. Therefore, row versions would be kept for a shorter period.
- No conflicts in update operations. The Snapshot isolation level does not acquire locks on data until the data is to be modified. That can generate a conflict in case another transaction modifies the data read by the transaction running under the Snapshot isolation level when the later tries to update the same data.
- You can use the Read Committed Snapshot isolation with distributed transactions.
- It works with existing applications (that used previous versions of SQL Server) without requiring any modification.

Snapshot

Similar to the Read Committed Snapshot isolation level, the Snapshot isolation level is based on the row versioning framework. One of the major differences between them is that the Snapshot isolation level provides transaction-level consistency (instead of statement level). A snapshot transaction uses for read operations the last version of each row that had been committed at the time the transaction started. This behavior has the same advantage as the Read Committed Snapshot isolation level—readers will not block writers and writers will not block readers.

Another major difference between the two and also a drawback (for the Snapshot transactions) is the data update approach:

- Rows that will be updated are selected using row versions.
- Exclusive locks will be acquired on the actual data unless the data has been modified and committed by another transaction after the snapshot transaction began. If this situation happens, an update conflict occurs, the snapshot transaction is terminated, and an error is generated.

The vulnerability to update conflicts is one of the most important disadvantages of the Snapshot isolation level.

Facts about the Snapshot Isolation Level

Some of the facts that apply to the Read Committed Snapshot isolation level will apply also to the Snapshot isolation level:

- Readers will not block writers and writers will not block readers.
- An integrated update conflict detection mechanism will notify you when update conflicts occur. You can minimize the chances of an update conflict if you use the UPDLOCK hint for your SELECT statements.

- The Snapshot isolation level offers the same protection as the Serializable isolation level for read operations. None of the concurrency effects can occur under this isolation level.

- Existing applications will have to be modified to use the Snapshot isolation to solve potential update conflicts. You can use for that a retry approach. If you intend to use a T-SQL-based retry method, we recommend you use the TRY...CATCH construct. A retry approach consists of trying the update operation and if it fails to resubmit the update statement.

- To use this isolation level, you have to set to ON the ALLOW_SNAPSHOT_ISOLA-TION database option and to set the isolation level using SET TRANSACTION ISO-LATION LEVEL SNAPSHOT.

- When you use the ALTER DATABASE statement to change the setting of the ALLOW_SNAPSHOT_ISOLATION database option, the ALTER DATABASE will wait until all existing transactions in the database are committed.

- You can query the sys.databases catalog view to get information about the state of the ALLOW_SNAPSHOT_ISOLATION database option. The following example shows you how:

```
-- Possible results:
-- state description
-- 0      OFF
-- 1      ON
-- 2      IN_TRANSITION_TO_ON
-- 3      IN_TRANSITION_TO_OFF
SELECT  snapshot_isolation_state AS state,
        snapshot_isolation_state_desc AS description
FROM    sys.databases
WHERE database_id = DB_ID(N'IsolationLevelsDB')
GO
```

- You can use the ALLOW_SNAPSHOT_ISOLATION settings also for the master, model, msdb, and tempdb system databases. By default it is OFF for model and tempdb and ON for master and msdb databases.

- To support row versioning, each row will be added a 14-byte versioning tag.

- Several DDL statements are disallowed inside Snapshot transactions since the database engine would not maintain multiple versions for the system metadata:

  - CREATE INDEX
  - CREATE XML INDEX
  - ALTER INDEX
  - ALTER TABLE
  - DBCC DBREINDEX
  - ALTER PARTITION FUNCTION

- ALTER PARTITION SCHEME
- DROP INDEX
- CLR (Common Language Runtime) DDL, such as CREATE, ALTER, DROP ASSEMBLY, and so on

All the previous statements work under the Read Committed Snapshot isolation level.

Some DDL are statements allowed under Snapshot isolation level such as:

- CREATE TABLE
- CREATE PROCEDURE
- CREATE TYPE
- CREATE STATISTICS
- Distributed transactions are not supported under the Snapshot isolation level.

When Should You Use the Snapshot Isolation Level?

The same scenarios enumerated for the Read Committed Snapshot isolation level are also suited for the Snapshot isolation level. When you decide which row versioning–based isolation level to use, the following requirements of your application can indicate when the Snapshot isolation level is the best suited:

- Your application requires transaction-level consistency.
- The probability to have update conflicts is low.
- You need the benefit of repeatable reads without the concurrency penalty of using shared locks.
- You have to generate reports that need consistent data and that are based on long-running, multi-statement queries.

Example

Here is just one example to demonstrate the update conflict problem. First we have to allow the Snapshot isolation level to run the following statement:

```
ALTER DATABASE IsolationLevelsDB
SET ALLOW_SNAPSHOT_ISOLATION ON;
GO
```

The next step is to open two query windows and run the following two batches concurrently. This is the first batch:

```
USE IsolationLevelsDB;
GO
SET TRANSACTION ISOLATION LEVEL SNAPSHOT;
BEGIN TRAN
-- begin the actual transaction by using a read operation
```

```
-- Output: VAL 'VALUE 10'
SELECT VAL FROM T2 WHERE ID=10;
GO
-- wait for 20 seconds to give you time to switch
-- and run the second batch
WAITFOR DELAY '00:00:20';
GO
     try an update and generate an update conflict and the error message:
-- Msg 3960, Level 16, State 2, Line 2
-- Snapshot isolation transaction aborted due to update conflict.
-- You cannot use snapshot isolation to access table 'dbo.T2' directly
-- or indirectly in database 'IsolationLevelsDB' to update, delete,
-- or insert the row that has been modified or deleted by another
-- transaction. Retry the transaction or change the isolation level for
-- the update/delete statement.
UPDATE T2
SET VAL = 'BATCH01 VALUE'
WHERE ID=10;
GO
-- the COMMIT will also fail since the transaction is aborted
COMMIT TRAN
GO
```

This is the second batch:

```
USE IsolationLevelsDB;
GO
-- Update a row in table T2
UPDATE T2
SET VAL = 'BATCH02 VALUE'
WHERE ID=10;
GO
```

A quick solution to the update conflict can be the replacement of the SELECT statement with this one:

```
SELECT VAL FROM T2 WITH (UPDLOCK) WHERE ID=10;
```

In this case, the second batch will have to wait until the first batch completes.

At this point we will renew the recommendation to use Books Online to expand your knowledge on row versioning–based isolation, as the subject can make several chapters of a book if not a complete one.

Summary of Concurrency Effects for the Existing Transaction Isolation Levels

Before ending this section we included just one more topic, a review of the possible concurrency side effects for each isolation level, as shown in Table 6.2.

TABLE 6.2   Concurrency Effects and Isolation Levels

Isolation Level	Dirty Read?	Inconsistent Analysis?	Phantoms?
Read Uncommitted	Yes	Yes	Yes
Read Committed	No	Yes	Yes
Read Committed Snapshot (for a single statement)	No	Yes	Yes
Repeatable Read	No	No	Yes
Snapshot	No	No	No
Serializable	No	No	No

Designing the Locking Granularity Level

You have several options in SQL Server to customize the locking granularity level. You have already seen how to use transaction isolation levels for that purpose, and in this section you will see how to use locking hints and index locking behavior customization.

Using Locking Hints

You should not take the word "hint" literally. You can use hints to "force" the behavior of query optimizer and not to offer a kind suggestion. Since the query optimizer does a pretty good job in most cases, you should be very careful when you decide you could do better. Test whether hints really improve the performance of your queries. In some situations hints can be very useful:

- To improve performance.
- To obtain a better customizable lock granularity than through the use of isolation levels.
- To lower the isolation level for specific queries to avoid locking problems.

From a syntactic point of view, there are join hints, query hints, and table hints, or if we consider their functionality, hints can be classified as locking hints, join hints, index hints, compilation hints, parallelism hints, and so on. We will concentrate only the locking hints in this section but you will meet all types of hints in the next chapter.

Locking hints, just as the name says, control the locking behavior of Query Optimizer, giving you a more granular control than the isolation levels. We will continue to remind you that you should interfere with the normal behavior of the Query Optimizer only if you have to do so.

Let's have a look at the types of locking hints that can be specified at the table (or view) level:

- HOLDLOCK
- SERIALIZABLE
- NOLOCK
- READUNCOMMITTED
- NOWAIT
- PAGLOCK
- READCOMMITTED
- READCOMMITTEDLOCK
- READPAST
- REPEATABLEREAD
- ROWLOCK
- TABLOCK
- TABLOCKX
- UPDLOCK
- XLOCK

Here they are in more detail:

HOLDLOCK, SERIALIZABLE   These two hints are equivalent and have the same behavior as a transaction running on the Serializable isolation level. We already explained the Serializable isolation level earlier in the chapter, but just to remind you, we'll elaborate. When you use the Serializable isolation level, a shared lock is not released when it's no longer needed and instead it is maintained until the transaction completes. The following example illustrates this behavior:

```
USE tempdb;
GO
CREATE TABLE TestHints (ID INT NOT NULL PRIMARY KEY);
GO
INSERT INTO TestHints (ID) VALUES (1);
GO
BEGIN TRAN;
-- Ilustrate normal behavior
```

```
SELECT ID FROM TestHints
WHERE ID = 1;
-- Display locks for current session
-- No lock will be maintained
-- Output: none
SELECT  resource_type, request_mode
FROM sys.dm_tran_locks
WHERE request_session_id = @@SPID;
GO
SELECT ID FROM TestHints WITH (HOLDLOCK)
WHERE ID = 1;
GO
-- Display locks for current session
-- Output:
-- resource_type request_mode
-- PAGE          IS
-- KEY           S
-- OBJECT        IS
SELECT  resource_type, request_mode
FROM sys.dm_tran_locks
WHERE request_session_id = @@SPID;
ROLLBACK TRAN;
GO
```

As you can see, the first SELECT query released the locks at completion but the second one maintained them.

NOLOCK, READUNCOMMITTED   Both hints force the Query Optimizer to read data without requesting shared locks. This way dirty reads are allowed but the advantage of this read method is high concurrency. Don't be fooled by the name NOLOCK. All queries acquire Sch-S (schema stability) locks and queries that use NOLOCK (or READUNCOMMITTED) hints—make no exception. Let's prove that.

We will use three batches for this example so open three query windows in SQL Server Management Studio. You should use the Session IDs from your own machine in the third batch:

This is the first batch:

```
-- Session ID 53 on my machine
USE tempdb;
GO
BEGIN TRAN;
-- Place a Sch-M (schema modification) lock on the table
ALTER TABLE TestHints ADD VAL INT NULL;
```

```
GO
-- wait for 20 seconds to give you time to switch
-- and run the second batch and then the third batch
WAITFOR DELAY '00:00:20';
ROLLBACK TRAN;
GO
```

This is the second batch:

```
-- Session ID 54 on my machine
USE tempdb;
GO
BEGIN TRAN;
-- query will be blocked
SELECT ID FROM TestHints WITH (NOLOCK)
WHERE ID = 1;
ROLLBACK TRAN;
GO
```

This is the third batch:

```
USE tempdb;
GO
-- Output partial:
-- 53    OBJECT    Sch-M    GRANT
-- 54    OBJECT    Sch-S    WAIT
SELECT   request_session_id,
         resource_type,
         request_mode,
         request_status
FROM sys.dm_tran_locks
WHERE request_session_id IN (53,54);
GO
```

As you can see, the second batch is blocked and will wait to acquire a Sch-S (schema stability) lock.

NOWAIT   This hint causes an immediate abort for a query if a lock is forcing the query to wait. It is equivalent with the SET LOCK_TIMEOUT 0 statement that has the same effect.

The SET LOCK_TIMEOUT statement allows you to set the time (in milliseconds) that a query will wait for a lock to be released.

Let's see an example. You need two query windows for this one.

This is the first batch:

```
USE tempdb;
GO
BEGIN TRAN;
-- Place an exclusive lock on the table
DELETE FROM TestHints
WHERE ID = 1;
GO
-- wait for 20 seconds to give you time to switch
-- and run the second batch
WAITFOR DELAY '00:00:20';
ROLLBACK TRAN;
GO
```

This is the second batch:

```
USE tempdb;
GO
-- the query will return the following message:
-- Msg 1222, Level 16, State 51, Line 4
-- Lock request time out period exceeded.
SELECT ID FROM TestHints WITH (NOWAIT)
WHERE ID = 1;
GO
```

PAGLOCK   This locking hint determines page locks in operations that would normally acquire row level, key level, or table level locks.

READCOMMITTED   The behavior of this hint depends on the READ_COMMITTED_ SNAPSHOT database option. If set to ON, this hint has the same effect as setting the Read Committed Snapshot isolation level, the database engine using row versioning. If the READ_ COMMITTED_SNAPSHOT database option is set to OFF, the database engine uses locks just like it would do when Read Committed isolation level is used.

READCOMMITTEDLOCK   If you need to use locks (instead of row versioning) regardless of the READ_COMMITTED_SNAPSHOT database option setting, you can use the READ-COMMITTEDLOCK hint. It causes the database engine to acquire shared locks for read operations. After the read operation is completed, the shared locks are released just like for the Read Committed transaction isolation level.

READPAST   This hint was enhanced in SQL Server 2005 and allows you not only to skip locked rows (like in SQL Server 2000) but also locked pages. The READPAST hint can be specified in transactions using the Read Committed or Repeatable Read isolation level. If you need it in transactions using the SNAPSHOT isolation level, the READPAST lock hint has to be combined with other locking hints such as UPDLOCK and HOLDLOCK

You'll now see an example that needs two query windows.

This is the first batch:

```
USE tempdb;
GO
-- Add three more rows to our table
INSERT INTO TestHints (ID) VALUES (2);
INSERT INTO TestHints (ID) VALUES (3);
INSERT INTO TestHints (ID) VALUES (4);
GO
BEGIN TRAN;
-- put an exclusive lock on the row having the ID=1
UPDATE TestHints
SET ID = 10
WHERE ID = 1;
-- wait for 20 seconds to give you time to switch
-- and run the second batch
WAITFOR DELAY '00:00:20';
ROLLBACK TRAN;
GO
```

This is the second batch:

```
USE tempdb;
GO
-- Output: 3
-- 2 + 3 + 4 / 3 = 3 instead of
-- 1 + 2 + 3 + 4 / 4 = 2.5 which would be truncated to 2
SELECT AVG(ID) FROM TestHints WITH (READPAST);
GO
```

In the example above, one row is locked by the update. If the row wouldn't be locked, the query will return the value 2. Because the row is locked and the READPAST hint is specified, the locked row is skipped and the average value is calculated from the remaining rows.

REPEATABLEREAD   Has the same behavior as the Repeatable Read isolation level.

ROWLOCK   Row locks are acquired instead of page level or table level locks.

TABLOCK   A shared lock is maintained on the specified table until the end of the statement. If the HOLDLOCK hint is also specified, the lock is maintained until the end of the transaction. It can be used with the OPENROWSET bulk rowset provider to improve the parallel import of data (only when your table doesn't have indexes).

TABLOCKX   Is characterized by maintaining an exclusive lock on the specified table until the end of the statement or transaction (if the HOLDLOCK is also specified).

UPDLOCK   This hint allows you to block the data you read, data that will be modified later. You can use this hint for SELECT statements under the Snapshot isolation level to minimize update conflicts.

XLOCK   This hint was also improved in SQL Server 2005, allowing exclusive locks to be held at page level, table level, and row level. To set the locking granularity level you have to use the XLOCK hint in combination with granularity hints such as ROWLOCK, PAGLOCK, and TABLOCK.

Customizing Index Locking Behavior

Another option you have to override the default locking actions is to customize locking behavior at the index level using either CREATE INDEX and ALTER INDEX statements or the sp_indexoption stored procedure. The CREATE INDEX or ALTER INDEX statements are preferred over the sp_indexoption stored procedure since the later will be replaced in future versions of SQL Server.

The partial syntax of ALTER INDEX statement that allows you to customize locking behavior follows:

```
ALTER INDEX { index_name | ALL }
    ON <object>
...
<set_index_option>::=
{
    ALLOW_ROW_LOCKS= { ON | OFF }
  | ALLOW_PAGE_LOCKS = { ON | OFF }
  ...
}
```

Basically you can specify whether or not row locks and page locks are allowed when accessing the index. The database engine will determine when to use row locks or page locks if these options are enabled. It is obvious that if you disallow row level locks, only page level and table level locks will be available. And if you go further and disable the page level locks, the database engine will remain with a single option—table level locks. You will see how this option works in the following example. We build first a table with more pages, 20 to be more precise, to see how the locking is escalated from a row level to the table level when you disallow both page level and row level locks:

```
USE tempdb;
GO
-- Create a test table with 10 pages and 20 records
CREATE TABLE TestIndexLocking
```

```sql
(ID INT NOT NULL PRIMARY KEY,VAL CHAR(4000) NOT NULL);
GO
DECLARE @I INT;
SET @I = 1;
WHILE @I < 21
BEGIN
INSERT INTO TestIndexLocking (ID,VAL)
VALUES (@I, 'VALUE ' + CAST (@I AS VARCHAR(2)));
-- Increment @I
SET @I = @I + 1;
END
GO
-- Check the number of pages
SELECT page_count,record_count
FROM sys.dm_db_index_physical_stats(DB_ID('tempdb'),
 OBJECT_ID('dbo.TestIndexLocking'),NULL,NULL,'DETAILED')
WHERE index_level = 0;
-- Test locking
BEGIN TRAN;
UPDATE TestIndexLocking
SET VAL = 'Test Value'
WHERE ID = 10;
-- Output Partial
-- resource_type request_mode
-- KEY          X
SELECT  resource_type, request_mode
FROM sys.dm_tran_locks
WHERE request_session_id = @@SPID;

ROLLBACK TRAN;

-- Disable rowlocking and pagelocking
ALTER INDEX ALL ON dbo.TestIndexLocking
SET (
    ALLOW_ROW_LOCKS = OFF,
    ALLOW_PAGE_LOCKS = OFF
    ) ;
GO

-- Test locking again
```

```
BEGIN TRAN;
UPDATE TestIndexLocking
SET VAL = 'Test Value'
WHERE ID = 10;
-- Output
-- resource_type request_mode
-- OBJECT          X
SELECT  resource_type, request_mode
FROM sys.dm_tran_locks
WHERE request_session_id = @@SPID;


ROLLBACK TRAN;
```

Before you move to the next section, we remind you to test all queries that use hints or modify the default locking behavior. You have to be completely confident that your way is the best way.

Designing Transaction Scopes

You have learned what a transaction is and how to use the isolation levels and locking hints. In this section, you will discover the transaction modes supported by SQL Server 2005.

 **NOTE** The responsibility for maintaining logical consistency of data by using transactions belongs to the SQL developer. You are responsible for starting and ending transactions while the database engine is responsible for atomicity, consistency, isolation, and durability in your transactions.

Since you are responsible (as a developer) for managing transactions, you should be aware of the following transaction modes:

Explicit transactions   The start and the end of the transaction are explicitly defined using Transact-SQL statements (BEGIN TRANSACTION, COMMIT TRANSACTION, ROLLBACK TRANSACTION) or through API functions.

Autocommit transactions   Each T-SQL statement is committed or rolled back automatically. This is the default transaction mode for the SQL Server database engine.

Implicit transactions   When the implicit transaction mode is on, the database engine will start a transaction automatically for the first statement from the following set: SELECT, INSERT, DELETE, UPDATE, CREATE, OPEN, and so on. You have to end the transaction manually by specifying a COMMIT or a ROLLBACK. After ending a transaction, the database engine starts a new one automatically.

Batch-scoped transactions   When an explicit or implicit transaction is used under a MARS (multiple active result sets) session, the transaction becomes a batch-scoped transaction and is managed at the batch level unlike regular connections where transactions are managed at the connection level.

Let's examine each transaction mode in more detail.

Explicit Transactions

Known also as user-defined transactions, *explicit transactions* allow you to define both the start and the end of a transaction. Usually, you start a transaction using the Transact-SQL statement BEGIN TRANSACTION. However, you can start in several other ways using different API functions:

- In DB-Library applications, you should use the same statement (BEGIN TRANSACTION).
- In OLE DB, you can call the ITransactionLocal::StartTransaction method to start a transaction.
- In ADO, the Connection object provides the BeginTrans method that allows you to start an explicit transaction.
- In ADO.NET, the SqlClient managed provider allows you to start an explicit transaction using the BeginTransaction method of the SqlConnection object.
- In ODBC API, explicit transactions are not supported.

To end a transaction, you have several methods as well:

- In Transact-Sql and DB-Library, you can use COMMIT TRANSACTION or COMMIT WORK to commit a transaction and ROLLBACK TRANSACTION or ROLLBACK WORK to roll it back.
- In OLE DB, you can call the ITransaction::Commit method to commit the transaction or the ITransaction::Abort method to roll it back.

> The fRetaining argument of the ITransaction::Commit and the ITransaction::Abort methods should be TRUE for explicit transactions.

- In ADO, the Connection object has two methods for ending a transaction: CommitTrans for committing the transaction and RollbackTrans for rolling back an explicit transaction.
- In ADO.NET, the SqlConnection object of the SqlClient provider provides the Commit() and the Rollback() methods for ending the transaction.

The following is a simple example:

```
USE tempdb;
GO
CREATE TABLE TestTransactions (ID INT NOT NULL PRIMARY KEY);
```

```
GO
BEGIN TRANSACTION
BEGIN TRY
INSERT INTO TestTransactions (ID) Values (1);
INSERT INTO TestTransactions (ID) Values (1);
COMMIT TRANSACTION
END TRY
 BEGIN CATCH
ROLLBACK TRANSACTION
END CATCH
GO
-- No rows will be returned
SELECT * FROM TestTransactions;
```

The code inserts two rows into a test table. Since the second insert violates the primary key constraint, the execution will jump to the CATCH block and the transaction will be rolled back. We strongly suggest you to use error handling in your code and if you want a reminder of how to use the TRY...CATCH construct with transactions, you should review Chapter 5.

Autocommit Transactions

When we were introduced to SQL Server at the beginning of our professional careers we had lots and lots of questions, some of them quite silly. One that troubled us for days was what if we run an INSERT...SELECT query that inserts a million rows in a table and someone unplugs the power cable before SQL Server finishes? What if it had just one more row to insert? You probably know that when SQL Server starts again, the entire insert operation will be rolled back. Why? Well, the autocommit transaction mode is the default transaction mode in the database engine. This means every statement runs in its own transaction that is committed or rolled back automatically. It's obvious that if the statement encounters any error, its transaction will be rolled back or otherwise committed.

So returning to the beginner questions, if 999,999 rows are inserted and an error is generated for the last one, and you're talking here about any kind of error from power failures to constraint violations, the complete set of 999,999 rows will be lost or, more accurately said, the transaction will be rolled back. As mentioned, the autocommit mode is the default mode for a connection and can be overridden by explicit or implicit transactions. It is also the default mode for ADO, OLE DB, ODBC, and DB-Library. You may also want to consider the fact that the database engine will return to the autocommit mode when an explicit transaction ends or when the implicit transaction mode is turned off.

Implicit Transactions

When you use the explicit transaction mode, you have to specify both when the transaction starts and when it ends. In the autocommit mode, the database engine takes care of everything.

Well, the implicit mode is somewhere in the middle. The database engine starts the transaction but you have to take care of ending it. After ending a transaction, a new one will be generated and you have to end it, and so on.

The following T-SQL statements generate a new transaction when the database engine first encounters them and when the implicit mode is on.

ALTER TABLE	INSERT	DROP	SELECT
CREATE	OPEN	FETCH	TRUNCATE TABLE
DELETE	REVOKE	GRANT	UPDATE

To use the implicit transaction mode in DB-Library applications as well as for SQL Scripts, you should use the SET IMPLICIT_TRANSACTIONS ON statement. The same SET statement can be used to turn off the implicit transaction mode (SET IMPLICIT_TRANSACTION OFF). If you use ADO as the API for your application, you can use only explicit transactions or the autocommit mode. As for the implicit transaction mode, ADO doesn't support it. But you can use it with OLE DB and ODBC APIs:

- For OLE DB, you cannot use directly implicit transactions in OLE DB.

  - However, there is an indirect method to set the implicit transaction mode and that is to start an explicit transaction by calling the ITransactionLocal::StartTransaction method and then calling either the ITransaction::Commit or ITransaction::Abort method with the *fRetaining* parameter set to TRUE.

  - To stop the implicit transaction mode, call any of the two methods and specify FALSE for the *fRetaining* parameter.

- For ODBC, you can use implicit transactions following the next steps:

  - To start the implicit transaction mode call the SQLSetConnectAttr function. The *Attribute* parameter should be set to SQL_ATTR_AUTOCOMMIT and *ValuePtr* set to SQL_AUTOCOMMIT_ON. Behind the scenes, the ODBC driver will issue a SET IMPLICIT_TRANSACTIONS ON statement.

  - To commit or roll back a transaction, call the SQLEndTran function and specify the value for the *CompletionType* as SQL_COMMIT or SQL_ROLLBACK.

  - To turn off the implicit transaction mode, call again the SQLSetConnectAttr this time with *ValuePtr* set to SQL_AUTOCOMMIT_ON and the same value for *Attribute* (SQL_ATTR_AUTOCOMMIT).

As usual, an example makes this transaction mode easier to understand. You use the same table defined in the "Explicit Transactions" section:

```
USE tempdb;
GO
--set the implicit transaction mode on
SET IMPLICIT_TRANSACTIONS ON;
```

```
GO
--start the implicit transaction using
--a SELECT statement that will return no rows (the table is empty)
SELECT * FROM TestTransactions;
GO
--insert a row
INSERT INTO TestTransactions (ID) VALUES (1);
GO
--run the query again
--Output (1 row): ID 1
SELECT * FROM TestTransactions;
GO
-- On a second connection you can run
-- USE tempdb; SELECT * FROM TestTransactions;
-- to see that the table is locked

--insert another row
INSERT INTO TestTransactions (ID) VALUES (2);
--Commit the transaction
COMMIT TRANSACTION;
GO
--start a new transaction
--Output (2 rows): ID 1 2
SELECT * FROM TestTransactions;
GO
--Commit the new transaction
COMMIT TRANSACTION;
--switch back to the autocommit mode
SET IMPLICIT_TRANSACTIONS OFF;
```

When we first met implicit transactions they seemed to be somehow awkward to us. We prefer the explicit transactions where the transaction boundaries are better defined. Yet if you need to use implicit transactions, don't forget that you are responsible for ending them.

Batch-Scoped Transactions

MARS introduced a special type of transaction. Before MARS you could have at most one request per transaction. This behavior changed with MARS because you can have multiple requests for the same transaction. When MARS is enabled for a connection and an implicit or an explicit transaction is started by a batch or a stored procedure, the transaction should complete before the batch ends or it will be rolled back automatically by SQL Server. This new type of transaction mode is managed at the batch level, hence the name batch-scoped transaction.

We have to warn you that under MARS, in some cases, it would be hard to determine the exact order in which commands from multiple batches are executed. That combined with Transact-SQL statements that deal with transactions (BEGIN TRANSACTION, COMMIT TRANSACTION, ROLLBACK TRANSACTION) or that change connection state (SET, USE) can determine random results.

Let us give you just a short example:

```
-- Batch 1
USE AdventureWorks;
-- do some work


-- Batch 2
USE tempdb;
-- do some other work


-- Batch 3
SELECT * FROM MyTable;
```

If we tell you that first and second batches are submitted concurrently, what would you say that the database context for the third batch would be, if the third batch runs after the first two batches finish? The answer is that it depends on which batch finishes last. If the first batch finishes last, the database context will be AdventureWorks and tempdb otherwise.

Similar problems can be encountered for transactions and can be avoided if you use API calls to manage connections state and transactions instead of Transact-SQL statements.

We included two code examples written in C# to illustrate the problems you may encounter when dealing with transactions and MARS. The first example creates two requests, starts an explicit transaction using Transact-SQL, and "forgets" to end it. The second example uses the proper way—API calls instead of Transact-SQL.

But first you have to create a simple table that has two columns and then you will have to insert three rows:

```
USE tempdb;
GO
CREATE TABLE TestMARS (ID INT NOT NULL PRIMARY KEY,VAL INT);
GO
INSERT INTO TestMARS (ID, VAL) VALUES (1,10);
INSERT INTO TestMARS (ID, VAL) VALUES (2,20);
INSERT INTO TestMARS (ID, VAL) VALUES (3,30);
GO
```

The next step is to run the following code from Visual Studio .NET (personally we run it in a Windows application as the response for a button click event). You have to make just one

modification to the default code of form, and that is to include the statements using
System.Data; and using System.Data.SqlClient;. The rest of the code follows:

```
SqlConnection conn = new SqlConnection();
conn.ConnectionString = "data source=(local);initial catalog=tempdb;" +
"Integrated Security=SSPI;" + "MultipleActiveResultSets=True;";
string sql1 =    "BEGIN TRANSACTION; " +
"SELECT * FROM TestMARS;" +
"INSERT INTO TestMARS (ID,VAL) VALUES(4,40);";
string sql2 = "UPDATE TestMARS SET VAL=@v WHERE ID=@id;";

        SqlCommand comm1 = new SqlCommand(sql1, conn);
        SqlCommand comm2 = new SqlCommand(sql2, conn);

        // add parameters for the second command
        comm2.Parameters.Add("@v", SqlDbType.Int);
        comm2.Parameters.Add("@id", SqlDbType.Int);

        conn.Open();
        SqlDataReader dr1 = comm1.ExecuteReader();

        // update each row by increasing the value of VAL column by 10
        while (dr1.Read())
        {
            comm2.Parameters["@v"].Value = (int)dr1["VAL"] + 10;
    comm2.Parameters["@id"].Value = (int)dr1["ID"];
    comm2.ExecuteNonQuery();
}

        // clean-up
        dr1.Close();
        conn.Close();
        conn.Dispose();
        comm1.Dispose();
        comm2.Dispose();
```

After the code runs, if you open a query window in SQL Server Management Studio and
run the following script, you will notice that the first batch was rolled back (because a COM-
MIT TRANSACTION is missing), whereas the second completed successfully:

```
USE tempdb;
GO
SELECT * FROM TestMARS;
```

```
-- Output
-- ID     VAL
-- 1      20
-- 2      30
-- 3      40
```

The second example displays the proper way to run the two batches under the same transaction. This time we use the SqlClient API functions and methods instead of Transact-SQL:

```
SqlConnection conn = new SqlConnection();

conn.ConnectionString = "data source=(local);initial catalog=tempdb;" +
                        "Integrated Security=SSPI;" +
                        "MultipleActiveResultSets=True;";

string sql1 = "SELECT * FROM TestMARS;" +
  "INSERT INTO TestMARS (ID,VAL) VALUES(4,40);";
string sql2 = "UPDATE TestMARS SET VAL=@v WHERE ID=@id;";
conn.Open();
SqlTransaction tr1 = conn.BeginTransaction();

SqlCommand comm1 = new SqlCommand(sql1, conn, tr1);
SqlCommand comm2 = new SqlCommand(sql2, conn, tr1);
comm2.Parameters.Add("@v", SqlDbType.Int);
comm2.Parameters.Add("@id", SqlDbType.Int);

SqlDataReader dr1 = comm1.ExecuteReader();

// update each row by increasing the value of VAL column by 10
while (dr1.Read())
{
    comm2.Parameters["@v"].Value = (int)dr1["VAL"] + 10;
    comm2.Parameters["@id"].Value = (int)dr1["ID"];
    comm2.ExecuteNonQuery();
}

tr1.Commit();
conn.Close();
conn.Dispose();
comm1.Dispose();
comm2.Dispose();
dr1.Close();
```

This time both batches use the same transaction and after running the above code our demo table will reflect all modifications—a new row inserted and the VAL column is updated:

```
USE tempdb;
GO
SELECT * FROM TestMARS;
-- Output
-- ID    VAL
-- 1     30
-- 2     40
-- 3     50
-- 4     40
```

The next section reminds you to end your transactions in batches that run under MARS or when you use implicit transactions.

Bound Sessions

If you have two or more sessions that need to share the same transaction and operate on the same data without getting lock conflicts, SQL Server allows you to use bound sessions.

Before SQL Server 2005, extended stored procedures used bound sessions to join the transaction space of the calling process. Now you can replace extended stored procedures with CLR managed code so bound sessions can work in multi-layer applications in the same transaction.

When you use bound sessions, you should be aware that at any point in time a single session executes code. There is no parallel execution since bound sessions share the same data and the same locks. We will not spend more time on bound sessions since they are not subject for your exam and because bound sessions can be replaced by MARS or distributed transactions.

Distributed Transactions

A distributed transaction is a transaction that spans two or more databases that can be located on the same server or on separate servers. Although to a database user or an application a distributed transaction looks just like a local one, it is managed somewhat differently. Multiple data sources involved in a distributed transaction are managed by multiple resource managers. To guarantee the atomic property (all or nothing) of a distributed transaction, a transaction manager will coordinate the resource managers. In case of SQL Server, a transaction manager can be MSDTC (Microsoft Distributed Transaction Coordinator).

MSDTC uses the two-phase commit technique for managing the commit process of a distributed transaction. A two-phase commit consists of two parts:

Prepare phase   When MSDTC (or other type of transaction manager) receives a commit request, a prepare command is sent to all resource managers involved. As a result, all operations for a standard commit are performed (flushing out buffers, writing transaction logs) but unlike a standard commit the transaction is not marked as committed and locks are not released. If the prepare phase was successful, a resource manager returns a success signal to the transaction manager (or otherwise a failure signal).

Commit phase   In the second part, the commit actually takes place if all resource managers signal success of the prepare phase. This time a commit command is sent to all resource managers and if all resource managers successfully commit, the application is notified that the transaction succeeded. Otherwise a rollback command is sent to all resource managers and the application is notified that the transaction failed.

You will see how to use distributed transactions in the next section.

Designing Code That Uses Transactions

The last section of this chapter is dedicated to practical usage of transactions.

Using Explicit Transactions

As we already mentioned, an explicit transaction starts with an API function call or with the BEGIN TRANSACTION statement.

The complete syntax of BEGIN TRANSACTION statement is the following:

```
BEGIN { TRAN | TRANSACTION }
    [ { transaction_name | @tran_name_variable }
      [ WITH MARK [ 'description' ] ]
    ]
[ ; ]
```

At minimum you need to specify BEGIN TRANSACTION or the shorter version BEGIN TRAN.

You can use a name for your transaction, and you can specify the name directly or through a variable.

When you specify the WITH MARK clause, your transaction becomes a marked transaction. A marked transaction allows you to restore your database to the specified mark.

How Would You Typically Use Marked Transactions?

Before using marked transactions you have to know that this feature is available only for databases that have the recovery model full or bulk logged. You can follow the next steps to use a marked transaction for a single database:

- Create a full or differential database backup for your database.
- Start a transaction using the WITH MARK option.
- Back up the transaction log for your database.
- Restore the database backup (or backups) using the WITH NORECOVERY option.
- Restore the transaction log using the WITH STOPATMARK option.

The following example illustrates how to apply the steps mentioned above and also how to use transaction names:

```
-- switch the recovery model of AdventureWorks database to full
-- in order to use WITH MARK option
USE master;
GO
ALTER DATABASE AdventureWorks SET RECOVERY FULL;
GO
-- Obtain a full backup of AdventureWorks database
BACKUP DATABASE AdventureWorks
TO DISK='C:\AdventureWorksFullBackup.bak';
GO


USE AdventureWorks;
GO
-- Check the VacationHours value for EmployeeID 1
-- Output: 21
SELECT VacationHours FROM HumanResources.Employee
WHERE EmployeeID = 1;
-- Update all employees vacation hours
DECLARE @TransactionName VARCHAR(32);
SET @TransactionName = 'UpdateVacation';
BEGIN TRANSACTION @TransactionName
    WITH MARK 'Update vacation hours for all Employees'

UPDATE HumanResources.Employee
SET VacationHours = VacationHours - 1
WHERE VacationHours > 1;

COMMIT TRANSACTION @TransactionName;
GO
-- Check the VacationHours value for EmployeeID 1
-- Output: 20
SELECT VacationHours FROM HumanResources.Employee
WHERE EmployeeID = 1;

-- Backup the transaction log
USE master;
GO
BACKUP LOG AdventureWorks
```

```
TO DISK='C:\AdventureWorksLogBackup.bak'
WITH NORECOVERY;
GO
-- Restore the database before the update
RESTORE DATABASE AdventureWorks
FROM DISK='C:\AdventureWorksFullBackup.bak'
WITH NORECOVERY;
GO
RESTORE LOG AdventureWorks
    FROM DISK='C:\AdventureWorksLogBackup.bak'
    WITH RECOVERY,
    STOPATMARK = 'UpdateVacation';
GO
-- Switch back to simple recovery model
ALTER DATABASE AdventureWorks SET RECOVERY SIMPLE;
GO
USE AdventureWorks;
GO
-- Check the again the VacationHours value for EmployeeID 1
-- Output: 21
SELECT VacationHours FROM HumanResources.Employee
WHERE EmployeeID = 1;
```

Using Savepoints

Savepoints allow partial rollback for a transaction. You can undo portions of a transaction without losing all the work as with a rollback operation. You can define a savepoint using the SAVE TRANSACTION statement. The syntax follows:

```
SAVE { TRAN | TRANSACTION } { savepoint_name | @savepoint_variable }
[ ; ]
```

The name of the savepoint can be specified directly or by using a variable and can have a maximum of 32 characters.

Savepoints are not supported in distributed transactions or when MARS is enabled.

You'll now see a short example adapted from the uspLogError sample stored procedure from the AdventureWorks database:

```
USE [tempdb]
GO
```

```
CREATE TABLE MyLog(
    LogID INT IDENTITY(1,1) NOT NULL,
    UserName VARCHAR(128) NOT NULL,
    ErrorNumber INT NOT NULL
);
GO
CREATE PROCEDURE [dbo].[LogError]
    @LogID [int] = 0 OUTPUT
AS
BEGIN
   SET NOCOUNT ON;
   -- Set the output parameter value to 0 to indicate
   -- that information was not logged
   SET @LogID = 0;
   -- Return if the procedure is not called from a CATCH block
   IF ERROR_NUMBER() IS NULL
       RETURN;

   BEGIN TRAN;
   SAVE TRANSACTION BeforeInsert;
   BEGIN TRY
     INSERT MyLog(UserName,ErrorNumber)
     VALUES ( CONVERT(sysname, CURRENT_USER),ERROR_NUMBER());

     -- Return the LogID of the row inserted
     SET @LogID = SCOPE_IDENTITY();
   END TRY
   BEGIN CATCH
    ROLLBACK TRANSACTION BeforeInsert;
    END CATCH
    COMMIT TRANSACTION
END;
GO
-- To test the stored procedure run the following code
BEGIN TRY
    RAISERROR ('Test',16,1);
END TRY
BEGIN CATCH
BEGIN TRANSACTION
    DECLARE @LogID INT
```

```
    EXECUTE LogError @LogID OUTPUT;
    -- Output at first run: 1
    SELECT @LogID;
    COMMIT TRANSACTION;
END CATCH
```

The stored procedure logs errors in a table. It makes use of savepoints to protect external transactions if any. If the procedure is invoked as part of a transaction and the logging operation generates an error, only the work done by the stored procedure will be rolled back, without affecting the external transaction.

Nesting Transactions

The name of the topic can be somewhat misleading. SQL Server allows nesting explicit transactions though they are not exactly nested. Let us show you what we mean by "not exactly nested."

You may know by now that the @@TRANCOUNT function returns the number of active transactions for current connection. Each BEGIN TRANSACTION statement increments the value of the @@TRANCOUNT function by one. Each COMMIT WORK or COMMIT TRANSACTION statement decrements the value of the @@TRANCOUNT function by one.

A possible surprise for your logic would be the behavior of ROLLBACK WORK or ROLL-BACK TRANSACTION statement. A ROLLBACK transaction statement rolls back all nested transactions and sets the @@TRANCOUNT to 0.

The following code, conceptually possible, would fail in SQL Server:

```
-- both versions will fail
-- version 1
BEGIN TRANSACTION T1
 BEGIN TRANSACTION T2
 ROLLBACK TRANSACTION T2
ROLLBACK TRANSACTION T1


-- version 2
BEGIN TRANSACTION
 BEGIN TRANSACTION
 ROLLBACK TRANSACTION
ROLLBACK TRANSACTION
```

The next example shows how @@TRANCOUNT is affected by nesting transactions, savepoints, and rollbacks:

```
BEGIN TRANSACTION
 -- Output: 1
 SELECT @@TRANCOUNT;
 BEGIN TRANSACTION
```

```
-- Output: 2
SELECT @@TRANCOUNT;
SAVE TRANSACTION SAVEPOINT1;
  -- @@TRANCOUNT is not affected
  -- Output: 2
  SELECT @@TRANCOUNT;
 ROLLBACK TRANSACTION SAVEPOINT1;
  -- @@TRANCOUNT is not affected
  -- Output: 2
  SELECT @@TRANCOUNT;
 ROLLBACK TRANSACTION;
 -- Output: 0
 SELECT @@TRANCOUNT;
-- The next ROLLBACK TRANSACTION will generate the error:
-- The ROLLBACK TRANSACTION request has no corresponding BEGIN
-- TRANSACTION.
ROLLBACK TRANSACTION;
```

If you use transaction names, a ROLLBACK TRANSACTION *transaction_name* statement should specify the name of the outermost BEGIN TRANSACTION statement. The next code illustrates this requirement:

```
-- incorrect version
BEGIN TRAN T1
 BEGIN TRAN T2
-- Rollback will fail
ROLLBACK TRAN T2


-- correct version
BEGIN TRAN T1
 BEGIN TRAN T2
ROLLBACK TRAN T1
```

Another fact to consider is that the database engine ignores names specified in a COMMIT TRANSACTION statement. You can use the names just to increase the readability of your code. The following three versions of code are equivalent:

```
-- version 1
BEGIN TRAN T1
 BEGIN TRAN T2
 COMMIT TRAN T2
COMMIT TRAN T1
```

```
-- version 2
BEGIN TRAN T1
 BEGIN TRAN T2
 COMMIT TRAN T1
COMMIT TRAN T2
-- version 3
BEGIN TRAN T1
 BEGIN TRAN T2
 COMMIT TRAN
COMMIT TRAN
```

So you should remember that in nested transactions only the outermost COMMIT TRAN will actually commit the transaction. The other inner COMMIT TRANSACTION statements will just decrement @@TRANCOUNT by one.

If you use savepoints, a ROLLBACK TRANSACTION *savepoint_name* will not affect @@TRANCOUNT.

Another case when @@TRANCOUNT value will be incremented by one is when a trigger is executed. Entering a trigger means an indirect nested transaction for the database engine.

Statements Not Allowed in Transactions

In an explicit transaction you can use almost any Transact-SQL statement with the following exceptions:

- Full-text system stored procedures such as sp_fulltext_catalog, sp_help_fulltext_ catalogs_cursor, or sp_fulltext_column. You can find the complete list in Books Online.
- The next Transact-SQL statements
  - ALTER DATABASE
  - DROP DATABASE
  - ALTER FULLTEXT CATALOG
  - DROP FULLTEXT CATALOG
  - ALTER FULLTEXT INDEX
  - DROP FULLTEXT INDEX
  - BACKUP
  - RECONFIGURE
  - CREATE DATABASE
  - RESTORE
  - CREATE FULLTEXT CATALOG
  - UPDATE STATISTICS
  - CREATE FULLTEXT INDEX
- Any system procedures that modify the master database.
- The sp_dboption stored procedure.

Errors and Transactions

When an error occurs inside of transaction don't expect that to have the transaction automatically rolled back. We recommend you use the new TRY...CATCH construct for handling errors in your code and in particular to handle errors in transactions. See Chapter 5 for more information on handling errors.

For this section we remind you of the XACT_ABORT setting and the XACT_STATE function. The XACT_STATE setting controls if a runtime error is in addition a transaction abort error. If you set the XACT_STATE to ON, most runtime errors become also transaction abort errors and that means that the transaction is aborted and rolled back automatically.

Another situation where you may find the XACT_STATE setting useful is within distributed transactions. If the transactions modify data and if the providers involved in the distributed transaction do not support nested transactions, you have to set the XACT_ABORT option to ON. Otherwise you will receive errors.

Finally, SQL Server 2005 introduces a new function, a function that can help you in dealing with errors and transactions: the XACT_STATE function. This function tells you if you have active transactions for the current connection and if the existing transactions are committable or not. It does that by returning three values: 1 if there are active transactions, 0 if there are no transactions, and −1 if there are active transactions but they are in an uncommittable state.

Using Distributed Transactions

From Transact-SQL the most obvious way to start a distributed transaction is by using the BEGIN DISTRIBUTED TRANSACTION statement. The syntax follows:

```
BEGIN DISTRIBUTED { TRAN | TRANSACTION }
    [ transaction_name | @tran_name_variable ]
[ ; ]
```

You can specify a transaction name that can be used to track the distributed transaction. Once a distributed transaction was started a remote server is enlisted in the transaction if it is the target of a distributed query or of a remote stored procedure call. There are some situations that are not so obvious when a local transaction is promoted to a distributed one:

- When a distributed query is executed in a local transaction.

- When the REMOTE_PROC_TRANSACTION connection option is set to ON and your local transaction executes a remote stored procedure (from another database engine instance).

You'll now see an example of using two instances of SQL Server 2005 (a Developer and an Express instance) to run the example. Since the machine we're using is a Windows XP SP2, the security settings of SP2 require enabling MSDTC following the next steps:

1. Go to Control Panel, open Administrative Tools, and double-click Component Services.

2. Use the left pane of the Console Root, expand the Component Services node, and then expand Computers.

3. Right-click My Computer, and select Properties.

4. Click the MSDTC tab, and then click Security Configuration button.

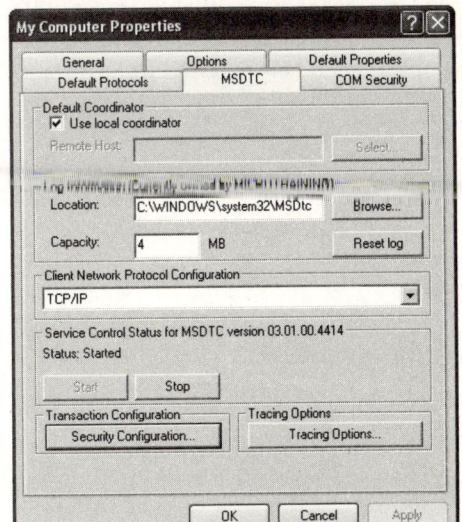

5. Under Security Settings, select Network DTC access check box (we will not use remote servers and because of that this setting alone is enough).

6. Verify that the DTC Logon Account is NT AUTHORITY\NetworkService.

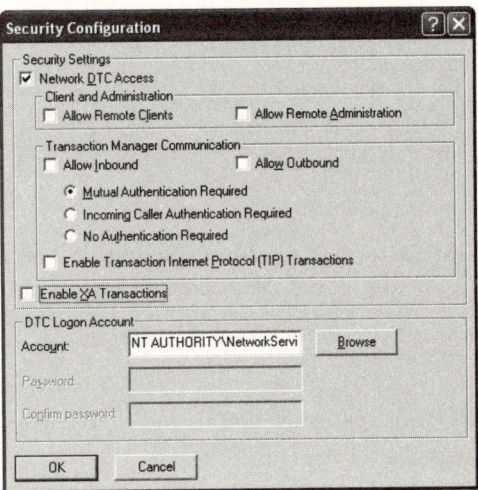

7. Click OK in the Security Configuration window, and click Yes on the pop-up window that will notify you of MSDTC service restart.

8. Click OK in My Computer Properties window, and close Component Services.

Our server's name is MICROTRAINING. We have two instances of SQL Server 2005, a default instance that runs the Developer edition of SQL Server 2005, and a named instance (named by default SQLEXPRESS) for the Express edition.

The next step for our example is to add my SQLEXPRESS instance as a linked server in the default instance:

```
USE master;
GO
EXEC sp_addlinkedserver
    @server='EXPRESS_Instance',
    @srvproduct='',
    @provider='SQLNCLI',
    @datasrc='MICROTRAINING\SQLEXPRESS';
GO
```

Now that everything is set, you can run the following code:

```
SET XACT_ABORT ON
GO
BEGIN DISTRIBUTED TRAN T1
UPDATE EXPRESS_Instance.AdventureWorks.HumanResources.Employee
SET vacationhours = vacationhours + 1;
;
UPDATE AdventureWorks.HumanResources.Employee
SET vacationhours = vacationhours + 1;
;
GO
COMMIT TRAN;
GO
```

The transaction simply updates two tables from two separate instances of SQL Server 2005. You used the XACT_ABORT option set to ON to allow the update on the linked server.

Best Practices

Whenever you use transactions in your code, you should consider the following guidelines:

- Keep your transactions short.
- Do not wait for user input during a transaction.
- Reduce blocking using row versioning–based isolation levels, proper indexing, or data access methods.
- Use the lowest transaction isolation level possible.
- Use locking hints to obtain custom and more granular locking.

- Limit the accessed data in your transaction to just the required data.
- Minimize the errors and prevalidate data to reduce the number of transaction rollbacks.
- Monitor for transaction rollbacks and take action: retry, inform users, or log the rollback cause.
- For large transactions consider splitting them into smaller ones.
- Also for large transactions consider using savepoints for allowing partial rollbacks.

Summary

In this chapter you've seen how to plan a transaction strategy by using transaction scopes, transaction isolation levels, and locking hints. We showed you local and distributed transactions, transactions under MARS, and how to deal with errors in transactions. You've learned how to customize the locking behavior of database engine either by isolation levels or by hints.

Also, you have learned the various flavors of transactions and how to balance the consistency with the concurrency needs of your application.

Exam Essentials

Know how to set isolation levels.   You have to know what isolation level you should use considering the consistency and concurrency requirements of your application.

Understand how to modify the locking granularity.   When the transaction isolation level is not a perfect fit for your application needs, you have to know how to modify the locking behavior of database engines using locking hints. You have to be familiar with each locking hint as well as when a specific locking hint will be useful.

Know how to use the proper transaction scopes.   You should know when your business requirements translate into local transaction or distributed ones.

Know how to use transactions.   You need to know how to use each transaction type and how to make your transactional code efficient.

Review Questions

1. Which of the following properties are required by a logical unit of work to qualify as a transaction? (Choose all that apply.)

    A. Atomicity

    B. Durability

    C. Consistency

    D. Isolation

2. You write a stored procedure that will return data for a report. The accuracy of the data is not so important; however, you want to avoid dirty reads. Which isolation level should you avoid?

    A. Read Committed

    B. Read Uncommitted

    C. Repeatable Read

    D. Serializable

3. Which isolation level can you specify if you want to avoid all concurrency side effects such as dirty reads, inconsistent analysis, and phantom reads?

    A. Read Committed

    B. Read Uncommitted

    C. Repeatable Read

    D. Serializable

4. You are designing a query that will return data for a report from a table that contains millions of rows of data. The report data is dynamic as a result of a preliminary search and will be used by 200 users. You want to minimize the concurrency impact of the report query by considering the following facts: the data of the table is rarely modified and the number of users that will request the report will increase. Which of the following query hints should you use?

    A. TABLOCK

    B. HOLDLOCK

    C. ROWLOCK

    D. NOLOCK

5. You design an application that will be used to sell car parts. The architecture of your application specifies one central database at the company headquarters and several other databases located at the company dealers. When a dealer sells a car part, the inventory of the local and central database should be updated. How can you accomplish that?

    A. Use implicit transactions.

    B. Use savepoints.

    C. Use the Snapshot isolation level.

    D. Use a distributed transaction.

6. Which of the following isolation levels use a pessimistic concurrency approach? (Choose all that apply.)

   A. Snapshot

   B. Serializable

   C. Repeatable Read

   D. Read Committed Snapshot

7. Which of the following isolation levels prevents readers from blocking writers and updates conflict detection?

   A. Serializable

   B. Repeatable, Repeatable Read

   C. Snapshot

   D. Read Committed Snapshot

8. Which actions are required to use Snapshot isolation level? (Choose all that apply.)

   A. Set the READ_COMMITTED_SNAPSHOT database option to ON.

   B. Set the ALLOW_SNAPSHOT_ISOLATION option to ON.

   C. Use the READCOMMITTEDLOCK hint.

   D. Set the isolation level for your session to Snapshot using SET TRANSACTION ISOLATION LEVEL SNAPSHOT.

9. You want to display locking information on a specific database. What should you do?

   A. Use the sys.dm_version_store dynamic management function.

   B. Use the sys.dm_tran_current_transaction() dynamic management function.

   C. Use the sys.dm_tran_current_snapshot() dynamic management function.

   D. Use the sys.dm_tran_locks dynamic management view.

10. You design a stored procedure for a CRM application. The stored procedure will update several tables in a single transaction. You have to decide what transaction isolation level to use for your stored procedure considering the following requirements:

    ▪ Readers should not be blocked.

    ▪ Concurrency side effects such as dirty reads, inconsistent analysis, and phantoms should be prevented.

    What should you do?

    A. Use the Serializable isolation level.

    B. Use the Read Committed isolation level.

    C. Use the Repeatable Read isolation level.

    D. Use the Snapshot isolation level.

11. You are tuning a stored procedure that returns data for a report. The consistency requirements for data specify that dirty reads should be avoided. The stored procedure was created using the following code:

```
CREATE PROCEDURE GetOrders

@BeginDate DATETIME,

@EndDate DATETIME

AS

BEGIN

SET TRANSACTION ISOLATION LEVEL SERIALIZABLE;

SELECT OrderID, OrderDate, TotalAmount

FROM Orders

WHERE OrderDate BETWEEN @BeginDate AND @EndDate;

END

GO
```

You want to minimize locking generated by the stored procedure and satisfy the data consistency requirements.

What should you do?

A. Use the NOLOCK hint.

B. Use the Read Uncommitted isolation level instead of Serializable.

C. Use the Read Committed isolation level.

D. Use the Repeatable Read isolation level.

12. You have to upgrade an application from SQL Server 2000 to SQL Server 2005. As part of the migration, you have to tune several stored procedures used for data analysis. To get consistent data, the stored procedures makes use of the Repeatable Read or the Serializable isolation levels. You want to reduce the locking while maintaining data consistency for your stored procedures. What should you do?

A. Use the Read Committed isolation level.

B. Use the Read Uncommitted isolation level.

C. Use the Read Committed Snapshot isolation level.

D. Use the NOLOCK hint.

13. You want to run a query using the Read Committed isolation level. The READ_COMMITTED_ SNAPSHOT database option is set to ON. What should you do? (Choose the best option.)

   A. Nothing, the default isolation level is Read Committed.

   B. Set the READ_COMMITTED_SNAPSHOT database option to OFF.

   C. Use SET TRANSACTION ISOLATION LEVEL READ COMMITTED.

   D. Use the READCOMMITTEDLOCK hint.

14. You are troubleshooting a stored procedure that should archive data. The stored procedure contains the following code:

```
CREATE PROCEDURE usp_ArchiveUser

@UserID INT

AS

BEGIN

SET IMPLICIT_TRANSACTIONS ON;

INSERT INTO tblArchivedUsers (UserID, UserName)

SELECT UserID, UserName

FROM tblUsers

Where UserID=@UserID;


IF @@ERROR<>0 RETURN -1;


UPDATE tblUsers

SET Archived=1

WHERE UserID=@UserID


IF @@ERROR<>0 RETURN -1;


END

GO
```

For some reasons the stored procedure doesn't seem to work.

What should you do?

A. Add code to commit transaction at the end of the stored procedure.

B. Remove the error checking.

C. Use savepoints.

D. Use a distributed transaction.

15. You want to use the implicit transaction mode to run several queries. What should you do? (Choose all that apply.)

A. Set the IMPLICIT_TRANSACTIONS option to ON.

B. Set the IMPLICIT_TRANSACTIONS option to OFF.

C. Explicitly end transactions using COMMIT TRANSACTION or ROLLBACK TRANSACTION statement.

D. Explicitly start transactions using the BEGIN TRANSACTION statement.

16. What is the default transaction mode for a regular connection (where regular means that you don't use MARS)?

A. Explicit transaction mode

B. Implicit transaction mode

C. Batch-scoped transaction mode

D. Autocommit transaction mode

17. You write a stored procedure that will implement a complex task for an application. The task consists of several logical steps. Each logical step contains multiple read/write operations. If one of the operations of a step fails, you need to roll back all the other operations of the same step.

How can you implement the stored procedure?

A. Use implicit transactions.

B. Use nested transactions.

C. Use autocommit transactions.

D. Use savepoints.

18. You want to set the READ_COMMITTED_SNAPSHOT database option to ON for a database named TestInventory. You want to roll back any incomplete transactions that will prevent the change taking place immediately.

    Which Transact-SQL code should you use?

    A. Use this:

    ```
    ALTER DATABASE TestInventory
    SET READ_COMMITTED_SNAPSHOT ON;
    ```

    B. Use this:

    ```
    ALTER DATABASE TestInventory
    SET READ_COMMITTED_SNAPSHOT ON
    WITH NO_WAIT;
    ```

    C. Use this:

    ```
    ALTER DATABASE TestInventory
    SET READ_COMMITTED_SNAPSHOT ON
    WITH ROLLBACK AFTER 5;
    ```

    D. Use this:

    ```
    ALTER DATABASE TestInventory
    SET READ_COMMITTED_SNAPSHOT ON
    WITH ROLLBACK IMMEDIATE;
    ```

19. You have to decide the isolation level that will be used by a stored procedure for a transaction with multiple operations. The requirements on which you should base your decision are:

    ▪ The transaction should be completely isolated from other concurrent transactions.

    ▪ Update conflicts must be avoided at all costs.

    Which transaction isolation level should you use?

    A. Use the Read Uncommitted isolation level.

    B. Use the Snapshot isolation level.

    C. Use the Serializable isolation level.

    D. Use the Read Committed isolation level.

20. You write code for a transaction that modifies data from a local server as well as from a remote server. On the local server you add the remote server as a linked server. The next step you should take is to decide the scope of transaction.

    What should you do?

    A. Use a Multiple Active Result Sets (MARS) connection.

    B. Use a local transaction.

    C. Use an implicit transaction.

    D. Use a distributed transaction.

Answers to Review Questions

1.   A, B, C, D. All of the above properties are required.

2.   B. If you want to avoid dirty reads, then you definitely should not use the Read Uncommitted isolation level since it is the only isolation level that can have this side effect.

3.   D. In this case you should use the Serializable isolation level.

4.   D. There is no reason to hold locks in this situation so you should use the NOLOCK query hint.

5.   D. To update the inventory of the two databases, you need to use a distributed transaction.

6.   B, C. The Serializable and the Repeatable Read isolation levels use a pessimistic approach based on locking. The new isolation levels of SQL Server 2005, Read Committed Snapshot and Snapshot use an optimistic approach based on row versioning.

7.   C. The Snapshot isolation level prevents readers from blocking writers (and vice versa) and offers updates of conflict detection.

8.   B, D. You need to allow Snapshot isolation level at database level first and then request it explicitly.

9.   D. To display locking information, you should use the sys.dm_tran_locks dynamic management view.

10.   D. To satisfy all requirements, you have to use Snapshot isolation level.

11.   C. You should use the Read Committed isolation level to satisfy the requirements.

12.   C. You should use Read Committed Snapshot isolation level to obtain consistent data and to reduce locking.

13.   D. To use the locking version of the Read Committed isolation level, when the READ_COMMITTED_SNAPSHOT database option is ON, you have to use the READ COMMITTEDLOCK hint.

14.   A. Implicit transactions should be explicitly committed or rolled back by the user.

15.   A, C. To use the implicit transaction mode you have to set the IMPLICIT_TRANSACTION option to ON and explicitly end transactions. The database engine will start new transactions automatically.

16.   D. The default transaction mode for a regular connection is the Autocommit mode.

17.   D. The simplest way to implement the complex task of your application is using savepoints.

18.   D. You have to use the ROLLBACK IMMEDIATE option of the WITH clause to roll back incomplete transaction immediately.

19.   C. The only isolation level that satisfies the requirements is the Serializable isolation level.

20.   D. Since you modify data that spans multiple servers, you should use a distributed transaction.

Chapter 7

Optimizing and Tuning Queries for Performance

MICROSOFT EXAM OBJECTIVES COVERED IN THIS CHAPTER

✓ Optimize and tune queries for performance.

✓ Evaluate query performance.

- Analyze query plans.
- Modify queries to improve performance.
- Test queries for improved performance.

✓ Detect locking problems.

✓ Modify queries to optimize client and server performance.

✓ Rewrite subqueries to joins.

✓ Design queries that have search arguments (SARGs).

✓ Convert single-row statements into set-based queries.

Some people say that performance tuning is a science. Others say that it's an art. Probably, both affirmations are true. In this chapter we will help you get started with the science of performance tuning, leaving you the responsibility of the creative part. Maybe you've noticed by now that the entire book is dedicated to database performance tuning and optimization, because the exam 70-442 requires you to have this type of knowledge. We focus now on improving query performance, continuing the introduction provided in Chapter 3. Later in the book, Chapter 10 continues the work of this chapter, focusing on performance tuning at the server level.

Evaluating Query Performance

Why do your queries slow down? There are a lot of reasons. Here are just a few:

- Inefficient query plans
- Blocking issues
- Indexes (unused or missing)
- Missing or out-of-date statistics
- Compilations and recompilations
- Resource (CPU, I/O, tempdb, memory) bottlenecks
- Slow network connections
- Improper database design
- Improper server configuration

Efficient performance tuning means considering all items on the list. We will address just the first five of the items here and the rest in the remaining chapters.

Understanding the Query Life Cycle: High-Level View

Did you ever wonder what happens with a query when it gets to SQL Server? The query is compiled into a plan. Then, the compiled plan is used to generate an execution context. The execution context gets "executed" and you receive the results.

Both the query plan and the execution context are cached for potential reuse.

Compiled plans and execution contexts are stored into a memory region named *plan cache*. You may find the term *procedure cache* used to refer to the same notion. However, we prefer using the term *plan cache* as the plan cache stores plans for various types of batches (such as ad hoc queries) and not just for stored procedures.

There are some significant differences between query plans and execution contexts

Query plan   The query plan is a read-only re-entrant structure multiple users share. The query plan is agnostic to user context. SQL Server 2005 retains maximum two copies of a query plan in the plan cache—one for all the serial executions and one for all the parallel executions.

Execution context   The execution context contains data specific to each user that executes a query such as parameter values. Execution contexts can be reused but they are single threaded. At any point in time an execution context can be used by one and only one batch.

You may find the term *execution context* used as an identity against which the permissions are checked. However, in this chapter we refer to a different kind of context.

For example, let's say that a user named John runs the following query:

SELECT * FROM AdventureWorks.Person.Contact WHERE ContactID=11.

If another user, Mary runs the query:

SELECT * FROM AdventureWorks.Person.Contact WHERE ContactID=32

both queries will use the same query plan, but different execution contexts.

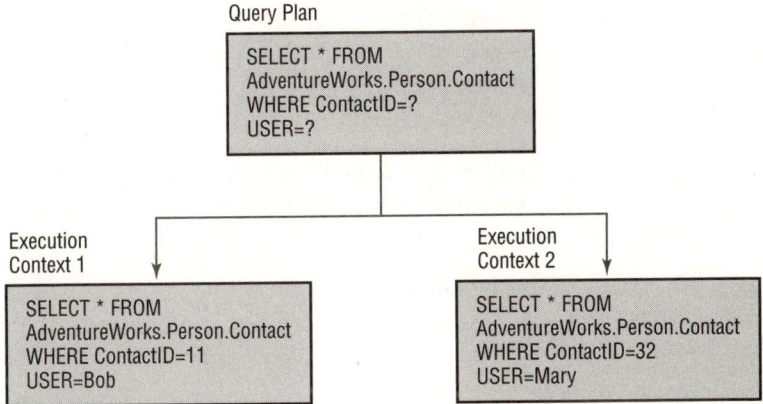

Understanding the Query Life Cycle: A Closer Look

That was the short version. The complete story of the query life cycle is somewhat longer. But understanding how the Query Processor works is important for query tuning, so we decided to give you more details. You can view the query life cycle from two perspectives: logical and physical.

Logical Query Processing

To show how the Query Processor works from a logical point of view, we'll use a query that includes almost all constructs of a typical SELECT query. The query is based on two simple tables: Books and Authors.

```
USE tempdb;
GO
CREATE TABLE Authors (AuthorID INT, AuthorName VARCHAR(128));
GO
CREATE TABLE Books (
 AuthorID INT,
 BookName VARCHAR(128),
 IsPublished BIT);
GO
INSERT INTO Authors VALUES(1,'Danndy Weyn');
INSERT INTO Authors VALUES(2,'Joseph L. Jorden');
INSERT INTO Authors VALUES(3,'Victor Isakov');
INSERT INTO Authors VALUES(4,'Marilyn White');
INSERT INTO Authors VALUES(5,'Cristian Lefter');

INSERT INTO Books VALUES(1,'70-431',1);
INSERT INTO Books VALUES(2,'70-431',1);
INSERT INTO Books VALUES(3,'70-441',1);
INSERT INTO Books VALUES(4,'70-442',0);
INSERT INTO Books VALUES(5,'70-442',0);
INSERT INTO Books VALUES(6,'70-445',0);
GO
```

The tables represent books and authors writing the books. Our sample query has the job of returning all books that haven't been published yet and have no author or a single author assigned. To see a better representation of steps, we included the step numbers as comments in the code:

```
SELECT                      -- Step 7
 TOP 3                      -- Step 9
 B.BookName,
 COUNT(A.AuthorID) AS NmbOfAuthors
FROM Books B                   -- Step 1
```

```
LEFT OUTER JOIN Authors A          -- Step 3
     ON B.AuthorID = A.AuthorID    -- Step 2
WHERE B.IsPublished = 0            -- Step 4
GROUP BY B.BookName                -- Step 5
HAVING COUNT(A.AuthorID) < 2       -- Step 6
ORDER BY NmbOfAuthors              -- Step 8
GO
```

The query returns just one row:

```
-- Output
BookName NmbOfAuthors
70-445    0
```

Here's how the query is processed:

1. The Query Processor identifies the data sources using the FROM and the JOIN clauses. It builds a virtual table similar to a Cartesian product of all participating tables. The virtual table is made from all the columns and rows of all tables just like a cross join. To get an idea of it, just run the following code:

```
SELECT
*
FROM Books B
CROSS JOIN Authors A
```

The output has a number of rows equal to the number of rows in the Books table multiplied by the number of rows in the Authors table ($6 \times 5 = 30$):

B.AuthorID	B.BookName	B.IsPublished	A.AuthorID	A.AuthorName
1	70-431	1	1	Danndy Weyn
2	70-431	1	1	Danndy Weyn
3	70-441	1	1	Danndy Weyn
4	70-442	0	1	Danndy Weyn
5	70-442	0	1	Danndy Weyn
6	70-445	0	1	Danndy Weyn
1	70-431	1	2	Joseph L. Jorden
2	70-431	1	2	Joseph L. Jorden
3	70-441	1	2	Joseph L. Jorden
4	70-442	0	2	Joseph L. Jorden
5	70-442	0	2	Joseph L. Jorden
6	70-445	0	2	Joseph L. Jorden
1	70-431	1	3	Victor Isakov
2	70-431	1	3	Victor Isakov
3	70-441	1	3	Victor Isakov

4	70-442	0	3	Victor Isakov
5	70-442	0	3	Victor Isakov
6	70-445	0	3	Victor Isakov
1	70-431	1	4	Marilyn White
2	70-431	1	4	Marilyn White
3	70-441	1	4	Marilyn White
4	70-442	0	4	Marilyn White
5	70-442	0	4	Marilyn White
6	70-445	0	4	Marilyn White
1	70-431	1	5	Cristian Lefter
2	70-431	1	5	Cristian Lefter
3	70-441	1	5	Cristian Lefter
4	70-442	0	5	Cristian Lefter
5	70-442	0	5	Cristian Lefter
6	70-445	0	5	Cristian Lefter

2. Apply the join condition to the virtual table that resulted from step 1. The new virtual table, in our particular case, has just five rows:

B.AuthorID	B.BookName	B.IsPublished	A.AuthorID	A.AuthorName
1	70-431	1	1	Danndy Weyn
2	70-431	1	2	Joseph L. Jorden
3	70-441	1	3	Victor Isakov
4	70-442	0	4	Marilyn White
5	70-442	0	5	Cristian Lefter

3. Add the outer rows when the join is an outer join (LEFT, RIGHT, or FULL OUTER JOIN). For the virtual table, just one row is added:

B.AuthorID	B.BookName	B.IsPublished	A.AuthorID	A.AuthorName
1	70-431	1	1	Danndy Weyn
2	70-431	1	2	Joseph L. Jorden
3	70-441	1	3	Victor Isakov
4	70-442	0	4	Marilyn White
5	70-442	0	5	Cristian Lefter
6	70-445	0	NULL	NULL

4. The Query Processor applies the WHERE conditions to the rows of the virtual table. Thus, your table remains only with three rows—the rows that have the value 0 for the IsPublished column:

B.AuthorID	B.BookName	B.IsPublished	A.AuthorID	A.AuthorName
4	70-442	0	4	Marilyn White

| 5 | 70-442 | 0 | 5 | Cristian Lefter |
| 6 | 70-445 | 0 | NULL | NULL |

5. Existing rows from virtual tables are arranged in groups using the expression specified in the GROUP BY clause:

```
Group   Rows
------------      ---------      -------------------------------------------
B.AuthorID B.BookName B.IsPublished A.AuthorID A.AuthorName
------------------------------------------------------------
70-442
4          70-442     0             4          Marilyn White
5          70-442     0             5          Cristian Lefter
------------------------------------------------------------
70-445
6          70-445     0             NULL       NULL
```

6. Apply the HAVING filter. For your query, the HAVING filter leaves just one group:

```
Group   Rows
------------------------------------------------------------
B.AuthorID B.BookName B.IsPublished A.AuthorID A.AuthorName
------------------------------------------------------------
70-445
6          70-445     0             NULL       NULL
```

7. Use the list of columns specified to reduce the list of columns included in the result set. The output is:

```
B.BookName NmbOfAuthors
------------------------------------------------------------
70-445     0
```

8. Apply the ORDER BY clause. It cannot change anything since you have just one row left.

9. Finally, before you see the results, apply the TOP operator. To your only row again, the top operator can't change too much and ta-dah, here's the result:

```
B.BookName NmbOfAuthors
------------------------------------------------------------
70-445     0
```

That was the logical side. The other perspective of the story is done by the physical query processing.

Physical Query Processing

To make our job easier we use the following image:

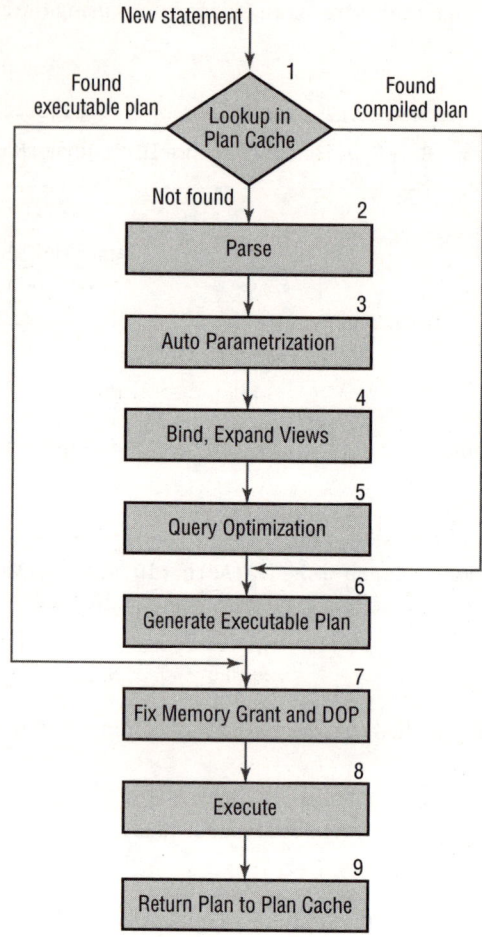

1. Search a reusable query plan. If a plan is found, the next step is obtaining an execution context. How? By reusing an existing one from the plan cache or by generating a fresh execution context. If there is no plan found, a new query plan is generated.

2. The first phase of the compilation process is the parsing phase. In this phase, the syntax of your query is verified and the query is transformed into a parse tree. The existence of the object specified by your query is not checked at this stage. So, if you submit the following query SELECT MyColumn FROM MyTable and the column MyColumn does not exist, the query is still parsed successfully.

3. In some cases the query plan for the submitted batch does not depend on the particular values of the constant literals. Such an example is the next query:

```
SELECT * FROM Person.Contact WHERE ContactID=1
```

The plan for this query is the same no matter what value is specified for the constant literal. In such cases the query is auto-parameterized—the constant literals are replaced by parameters. The query in the previous example becomes:

```
SELECT * FROM Person.Contact WHERE ContactID=@1.
```

4. Next is the binding phase. In the binding process, the objects specified in your sql statements are bound to real objects. This is the job of a new component in SQL Server 2005 named the algebrizer. The algebrizer takes as input the parse tree—the output of the parse phase. Among its responsibilities, the algebrizer is responsible for name resolution. It also verifies that what you ask for is possible. For example, if you try to select from a stored procedure your query will fail in this stage. The output of the algebrizer is the relational operator tree—a tree of logical operators.

5. The relational operator tree is the input for the query optimizer. The goal of the optimization phase is to find a good enough plan in a reasonable amount of time. Why not a perfect plan? Because the query optimizer has to maintain a balance between the optimization time and the estimated execution time. Imagine the following hypothetical situations:

   - The optimization time for a query takes 3 milliseconds to generate a "good" plan. The query runs in 10 milliseconds.

   - The optimization time takes 5 minutes to generate the "best" plan and the query runs in 8 milliseconds.

   In most of the cases the first approach is the right one. If you need a "perfect" plan, unfortunately you have to find it yourself because query optimizer is a cost-based optimizer. It tries to find an execution plan with a low cost (as close as possible to the estimated best cost) that is fast enough. The cost of a plan reflects the computing resources used. The query optimizer uses the cost of a plan to choose from the various alternatives of executing the query. What is very important to mention here is that the cost of a plan relies on statistics. The more accurate statistics you have the better execution plan you get for a query.

   Without diving into greater details, you should know that the query optimization process consists of two steps:

   - First, the query optimizer tries to find an obvious and inexpensive plan—the so-called trivial plan. For example, the SELECT * FROM MyTable query (where MyTable is a heap with no indexes) has only one way to execute and that is a table scan. In this case, the trivial plan is used to run the query.

   - Second, if the query is more complex, the query optimizer begins the cost-based optimization, which consists of three search phases. Each search phase consists of trying different transformations rules (such as reordering joins) to produce an execution plan. You can take a look at what the query optimizer is doing by using the sys.dm_exec_query_optimizer_info dynamic management view (explained pretty well in Books Online).

6. To execute the plan found in the optimization phase, an execution plan is needed. If there is already an execution plan in the plan cache, it is reused. If not, a new one is created.

7. Before query execution, memory is allocated for the query execution and the degree of parallelism is established.

8. The query executes.

9. The plans are returned to cache and that's all.

Unfortunately some of the query execution internals (such as the work of the algebrizer) is not publicly available. But to give you a clearer picture, we use the following example to illustrate partially a query's life cycle. The query selected for that consists of a join between two tables T1 and T2:

```
SELECT *
FROM T1
JOIN T2 ON T1.ID = T2.ID
WHERE T1.ID > 10
```

A possible parse tree resulting from parsing this query is shown below:

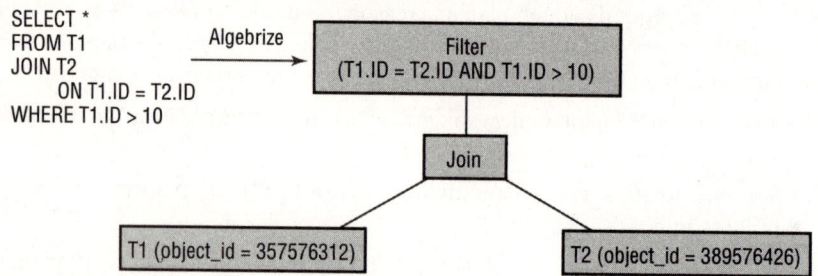

1. And here are two possible transformations (simplification and implementation):

Simplification

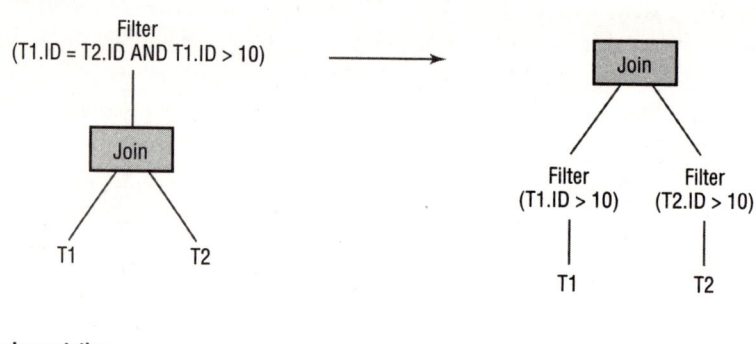

Implementation

Next, we move onto query plans.

To enhance your knowledge about query processing, we recommend Craig Freedman's WebLog at `http://blogs.msdn.com/craigfr`.

Obtaining Query Plans

If you want a better understanding of a query, you have to look at its plan. In SQL Server 2005, you have several options to obtain the query plan information:

- Use the Transact-SQL SET statement options.
- Use SQL Server Management Studio.
- Use SQL Profiler.
- Use the sys.dm_exec_query_plan dynamic management function.

All methods offer you logically equivalent outputs. The objective of the following sections is to teach you each method's strengths and weaknesses. First, let's establish a common language.

Understanding Short Query Plans Terminology

The terms used to refer to the different formats of the query plan are showplan and execution plan. The showplan can have three forms: text, graphical, and XML. If the query plan is generated without executing the query, we refer to the query plan as the *estimated execution plan*. Finally, if the query plan is generated after the execution of the query, we refer to it as the *actual execution plan*.

Using Showplan SET Statement Options

Using various SET statement options, you can obtain the text and the XML format of a query execution plan. In addition, you can get statistical information for query execution such as disk activity, number of rows returned, and so on.

The complete list of options follows:

SET SHOWPLAN_TEXT   When set to ON, the queries that follow are not executed and their execution plan is returned as text.

SET SHOWPLAN_ALL   Similar to SET SHOWPLAN_TEXT, it includes additional information.

SET SHOWPLAN_XML   When set to ON, the query plan is returned as a well-formed XML document and the query is not executed.

SET STATISTICS XML   Similar to the SET SHOWPLAN_XML, the XML form of the query plan is returned only after the queries that follow are executed. Also the query plan contains execution information.

SET STATISTICS PROFILE   The execution counterpart for the SET SHOWPLAN_ALL option. The queries are executed and then the query plans are returned, including execution information.

SET STATISTICS IO   When set to ON, queries that follow are executed and information is displayed about the disk activity generated.

SET STATISTICS TIME   When set to ON, the queries that follow are executed and additional information is returned. The information includes the number of milliseconds required for parsing, compiling, and executing each statement for every query executed.

To illustrate each option, we use several examples based on the following query:

```
SELECT C.FirstName, C.LastName
FROM Person.Contact C
JOIN Sales.SalesOrderHeader O
    ON C.ContactID = O.ContactID
WHERE OrderDate = '2001-08-14'
```

The query returns a list of four rows with customer names for all the customers that have an order on the specified date.

SET SHOWPLAN_TEXT

The simplest method to obtain the query plan in text format is using the SET SHOWPLAN_ TEXT option. Let's see the example first:

```
SET SHOWPLAN_TEXT ON
GO
SELECT C.FirstName, C.LastName
FROM Person.Contact C
JOIN Sales.SalesOrderHeader O
    ON C.ContactID = O.ContactID
WHERE OrderDate = '2001-08-14'
GO
SET SHOWPLAN_TEXT OFF
GO
```

You have to turn the option ON to get the query plan, and after that we recommend you turn it OFF. The output of the query follows:

```
StmtText
-------------------------------------------------------------------
SELECT C.FirstName, C.LastName FROM Person.Contact C
JOIN Sales.SalesOrderHeader O ON C.ContactID = O.ContactID
WHERE OrderDate = '2001-08-14'
```

```
StmtText
------------------------------------------------------------------------
  |--Nested Loops(Inner Join, OUTER REFERENCES:([O].[ContactID]))
       |--Clustered Index Scan
(OBJECT:([AdventureWorks].[Sales].[SalesOrderHeader].
[PK_SalesOrderHeader_SalesOrderID] AS [O]),
WHERE:([AdventureWorks].[Sales].[SalesOrderHeader].[OrderDate]
as [O].[OrderDate]='2001-08-14 00:00:00.000'))
       |--Clustered Index Seek (OBJECT:([AdventureWorks].[Person].[Contact].
[PK_Contact_ContactID] AS [C]),
SEEK:([C].[ContactID]=[AdventureWorks].[Sales].[SalesOrderHeader].
[ContactID] as [O].[ContactID]) ORDERED FORWARD)
```

The query is not executed and instead its execution plan is returned in text format. The first row returned displays the query text for our SELECT statement and the following three rows display the operators that make our query plan.

If you remember, the query plan is a hierarchical tree of operators (or iterators). In the text format of the showplan, each operator is displayed on a separate line. The tree is represented by using vertical bars "|" and indentation. In our example, we have three iterators: Nested Loops, Clustered Index Scan, and Clustered Index Seek.

Nested Loops is a physical operator that implements the Inner Join logical operator. The Nested Loops Join operator (named also Nested Iteration) used two inputs—an outer table (displayed at the top of an execution plan) and an inner table (displayed at the bottom). In our case, the outer table is the Sales.SalesOrderHeader table and the inner table is the Person.Contact table.

The algorithm of the Nested Loops Join in pseudo-code is the following:

```
for each row R1 in the outer table do:
   for each row R2 in the inner table do:
      if R1 joins R2 then
          accept the row and return (R1,R2)
      end if
   end for
end for
```

Each row of the outer table is compared to each row of the inner table. In our case, the outer table is scanned using a Clustered Index Scan operation. Since there is a clustered index on the ContactID column of the inner table (the Person.Contact table), the operator used to match the row from the outer table with rows from the inner table is a Clustered Index Seek operator. A seek operation is usually better than a scan operation from a performance point of view.

The index seek depends on the O.ContactID column and is referred to as a "correlated parameter." You can see it in the OUTER REFERENCES section of the plan.

We continue exploring our query in the next sections.

SET SHOWPLAN_ALL

The SET SHOWPLAN_ALL option builds on the output of the SET SHOWPLAN_TEXT option by adding several columns.

```
SET SHOWPLAN_ALL ON
GO
SELECT C.FirstName, C.LastName
FROM Person.Contact C
JOIN Sales.SalesOrderHeader O
    ON C.ContactID = O.ContactID
WHERE OrderDate = '2001-08-14'
GO
SET SHOWPLAN_ALL OFF
GO
```

We cannot display all output because you cannot scroll to the left in a book. Instead we display several of the new columns included in the result:

```
StmtText                EstimateRows Type      EstimateExecutions
----------------------------------------------------------------
SELECT C.FirstName,Last... 5.206897      SELECT     NULL
  |--Nested Loops(Inner... 5.206897      PLAN_ROW 1
    |--Clustered Index... 5.206897       PLAN_ROW 1
    |--Clustered Index... 5.206897       PLAN_ROW 5.206897
```

Again, we have the text of the plan and the operators in the StmtText column, as well as some new columns:

- StmtId represents the number of the statement in the batch. Since we have just one statement, the value of StmtId is 1 for our example.

- NodeId is the ID of the node in the query. The SELECT statement has the NodeId 1, the Nested Loops 2, and so on.

- Parent represents the NodeId of the parent step. In our example the Nested Loops has the value for NodeId 2. The Nested Loops operator is the parent for both the Clustered Index Scan and the Clustered Index Seek operators. Consequently, the Parent value for the Clustered Index Scan and the Clustered Index Seek operators is 2.

- PhysicalOp is the physical operator used. For example, the Nested Loops is a physical operator.

- LogicalOp is the logical operator represented by the node. For example, the second row has the Inner Join logical operator (that is implemented by the physical operator Nested Loops).

- Argument adds information about the operation performed. In the previous example, the value of the Argument column for the second row is OUTER REFERENCES:([O] .[ContactID]), the correlated parameter.

- DefinedValues contains a list with expressions or values for the current operator. In our example, the Clustered Index Seek operation on the Person.Contact table returns the "DefinedValues": [C].[FirstName], [C].[LastName] (the columns needed from the Person .Contact by the SELECT statement).

- EstimateRows represents the estimated number of rows of output produced by the current operator. In our case the SQL Server estimates that approximately five rows will be returned if you run the query.

- EstimateIO represents an estimation of the I/O cost for this operator.

- EstimateCPU represents an estimation of the CPU cost for this operator.

- AvgRowSize represents an estimation of the average size in bytes of the row that goes through this operator.

- TotalSubtreeCost is the estimated sum of costs this operation and all child operations costs.

- OutputList represents the list of columns generated by this operator.

- Warnings contains warning messages in case statistics are missing or a join operation is missing a join predicate. For example, run the following query:

```
SET SHOWPLAN_ALL ON
GO
SELECT C.FirstName, C.LastName
FROM Person.Contact C, Sales.SalesOrderHeader O
GO
SET SHOWPLAN_ALL OFF
GO
```

  To implement the join operation, the same Nested Loops operator is used. On the Warnings column for the Nested Loops operator, you will find the value "NO JOIN PREDICATE" that notifies you that your query is missing the join predicate.

- Type represents the type of the node. The parent node for each query is the query statement and has the value SELECT, INSERT, DELETE, UPDATE, EXECUTE, and so on. The subnodes represent the execution plan and the value for the type column is "PLAN_ROW."

- Parallel tells you whether the operator is running in parallel (value 1) or not (value 0). On our machine (a single processor laptop), the only value that can be returned is 0.

- EstimateExecutions represents the estimated number of times that this operator will be executed. For our example, if you run the query, there will be approximately five index seeks and one index scan.

SET SHOWPLAN_XML

The XML showplan is new in SQL Server 2005 and is the most comprehensive type of query plan.

You can find the schema for the XML showplan at http://schemas .microsoft.com/sqlserver/2004/07/showplan/ or in your install directory at Microsoft SQL Server\90\Tools\Binn\schemas\sqlserver\2004\07\ showplan\showplanxml.xsd.

It contains information that is not available in the textual or graphical query plan. Here's an example:

```
SET SHOWPLAN_XML ON
GO
SELECT C.FirstName, C.LastName
FROM Person.Contact C
JOIN Sales.SalesOrderHeader O
    ON C.ContactID = O.ContactID
WHERE OrderDate = '2001-08-14'
GO
SET SHOWPLAN_XML OFF
GO
```

The output is large so we will display just a small fragment:

```
<StmtSimple StatementText="SELECT C.FirstName,
C.LastName&#xD;&#xA;FROM Person.Contact C&#xD;&#xA;JOIN Sales.SalesOrderHeader
O &#xD;&#xA;&#x9;
ON C.ContactID = O.ContactID&#xD;&#xA;
WHERE OrderDate = '2001-08-14'&#xD;&#xA;"
StatementId="1" StatementCompId="1"
StatementType="SELECT" StatementSubTreeCost="0.583988"
➥StatementEstRows="5.2069" StatementOptmLevel="FULL"
➥StatementOptmEarlyAbortReason="GoodEnoughPlanFound">
<QueryPlan CachedPlanSize="10">
    <MissingIndexes>
     <MissingIndexGroup Impact="96.9486">
      <MissingIndex Database="[AdventureWorks]"
Schema="[Sales]" Table="[SalesOrderHeader]">
       <ColumnGroup Usage="EQUALITY">
        <Column Name="[OrderDate]" ColumnId="3" />
       </ColumnGroup>
      </MissingIndex>
     </MissingIndexGroup>
    </MissingIndexes>
```

You can see the statement of the query, the estimated number of rows, and so on. So what's new in this representation? Among other things, you can see that the optimization of the statement is FULL (StatementOptmLevel="FULL"), and that the query optimizer terminated the optimization because it found a good enough plan (StatementOptmEarly-AbortReason="GoodEnoughPlanFound"). You can also see the size of the plan in the plan cache (CachedPlanSize="10"). To finish the analysis of this fragment, take a look at the

MissingIndexes section. As the name says, in this section you can find indexes that could help your query. When the query optimizer tries to find a good enough execution plan, it analyzes what could be the best indexes for a filter condition. If the best theoretical indexes are missing, you can see that either in the XML showplan or using several dynamic management views.

For more details about the missing indexes feature, please refer to the Books Online topic "About the Missing Indexes Feature" http://msdn2.microsoft.com/en-us/library/ms345524.aspx.

One great feature of the XML format of showplan is that you can view it in a graphical form following these steps:

- In the Results tab, click XML showplan.

- An XML editor displays the XML showplan. Select File ➢ Save Microsoft SQL Server 2005 XML *Showplan1.xml* AS. In the Save as Type drop-down list change the type to All Files (*.*).

- Replace the file extension with .sqlplan, select a location, and click Save.

- Now using Windows Explorer, go to the saved location and double-click the saved file.

- If you've done everything properly, you should see the following representation of the plan:

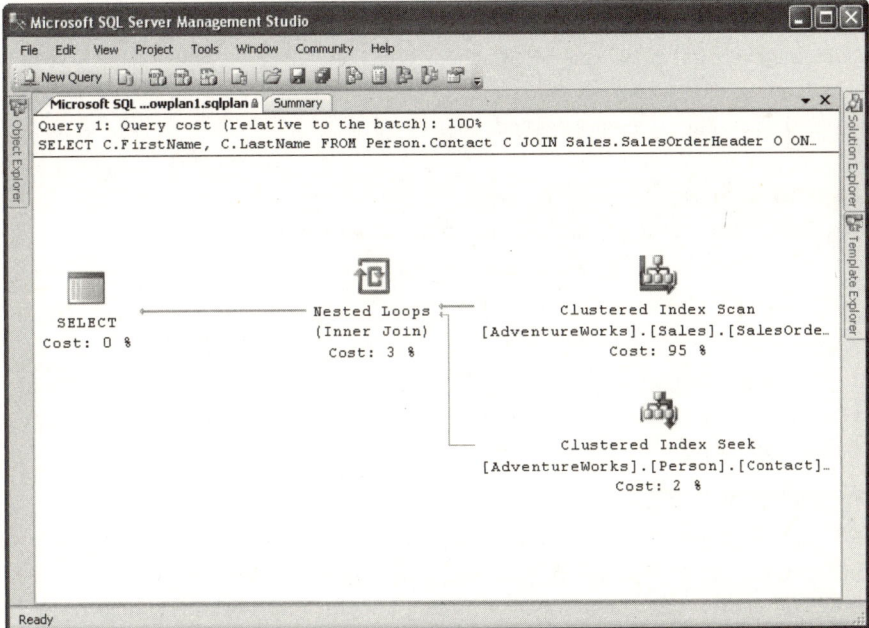

We'll give you one more reason to use the XML showplan instead of the text version: the SET SHOWPLAN_TEXT and the SET SHOWPLAN_ALL options will be replaced by the SET SHOWPLAN_XML in future releases of SQL Server.

SET STATISTICS XML

If you need execution information in your XML showplan, you can use the SET STATISTICS XML option. It has very similar output to the SET SHOWPLAN_XML option.

```
SET STATISTICS XML ON
GO
SELECT C.FirstName, C.LastName
FROM Person.Contact C
JOIN Sales.SalesOrderHeader O
    ON C.ContactID = O.ContactID
WHERE OrderDate = '2001-08-14'
GO
SET STATISTICS XML OFF
GO
```

Again, we can display just some small (but relevant to illustrate the information included) portions of the XML showplan:

```
...
<QueryPlan DegreeOfParallelism="0" CachedPlanSize="11">
...
<RelOp NodeId="0" PhysicalOp="Nested Loops" ...>
...
 <RunTimeInformation>
  <RunTimeCountersPerThread Thread="0" ActualRows="4"
     ActualEndOfScans="1" ActualExecutions="1" />
 </RunTimeInformation>
...
```

You can see the degree of parallelism at the runtime—DegreeOfParallelism="0"—that means a serial execution. The second fragment shows the actual number of rows and executions for the Nested Loops operator.

SET STATISTICS PROFILE

The SET STATISTICS_PROFILE option adds to the output of the SET SHOWPLAN_ALL option just two columns—Rows and Executes, representing the actual number of rows returned by an operator and the number of times an operator has been executed respectively.

```
SET STATISTICS PROFILE ON
GO
SELECT C.FirstName, C.LastName
```

```
FROM Person.Contact C
JOIN Sales.SalesOrderHeader O
    ON C.ContactID = O.ContactID
WHERE OrderDate = '2001-08-14'
GO
SET STATISTICS PROFILE OFF
GO
```

You can see from the output (we included just the partial output) that the estimated row count is actually different from the actual row count. A significant difference between estimated and the actual row count may indicate missing or outdated statistics.

Rows	Executes	StmtText	EstimateRows	EstimateExecutions
4	1	SELECT C.FirstName...	5.206897	NULL
4	1	|--Nested Loops(I...	5.206897	1
4	1	|--Clustered I...	5.206897	1
4	4	|--Clustered I...	5.206897	5.206897

The SET STATISTICS XML option will replace the SET STATISTICS PROFILE option in next releases of SQL Server.

SET STATISTICS IO

The SET STATISTICS option of the SET statement displays information about the disk activity of a query:

```
SET STATISTICS IO ON
GO
SELECT C.FirstName, C.LastName
FROM Person.Contact C
JOIN Sales.SalesOrderHeader O
    ON C.ContactID = O.ContactID
WHERE OrderDate = '2001-08-14'
GO
SET STATISTICS IO OFF
GO
```

The output of the query is the following:

```
Table 'Contact'. Scan count 0, logical reads 8, physical reads 5,
read-ahead reads 0, lob logical reads 0, lob physical reads 0,
lob read-ahead reads 0.
Table 'SalesOrderHeader'. Scan count 1, logical reads 703,
physical reads 620, read-ahead reads 699, lob logical reads 0,
lob physical reads 0, lob read-ahead reads 0.
```

And here's the explanation:

- Table represents the name of the table (Contacts and SalesOrderHeader in our example).

- Scan count represents the number of scans performed. You can see that is 0 for the Contact table (because the method of access is seeking an index) and 1 for the table SalesOrderHeader. A clustered index scan means actually scanning the table and, if you remember, the access method for the SalesOrderHeader is a Clustered Index Scan operation.

- Logical reads represent the number of pages read from the cache.

- Physical reads represent the number of pages read from disk.

- Read-ahead reads give you the number of pages placed into the cache.

- Lob logical reads represent the number of pages read from the data cache that contain text, ntext, image, or large value type (varchar(max), nvarchar(max), varbinary(max)).

- Lob physical reads represent the number of pages read from disk that contain text, ntext, image, or large value type (varchar(max), nvarchar(max), varbinary(max)).

- Lob read-ahead reads represent the number of pages placed into the cache containing text, ntext, image, or large value type data.

SET STATISTICS TIME

The SET STATISTICS TIME options returns the time spent parsing, compiling, and executing a query. To illustrate the behavior of this option, see the next example. First, run the following statement to turn ON the SET STATISTICS TIME option:

```
SET STATISTICS TIME ON
GO
```

Then, run our query:

```
SELECT C.FirstName, C.LastName
FROM Person.Contact C
JOIN Sales.SalesOrderHeader O
    ON C.ContactID = O.ContactID
WHERE OrderDate = '2001-08-14'
GO
```

The previous example has the following output on our laptop (on your machine results may vary):

```
SQL Server parse and compile time:
   CPU time = 15 ms, elapsed time = 48 ms.


(4 row(s) affected)


SQL Server Execution Times:
   CPU time = 0 ms,   elapsed time = 128 ms.
```

Now run the query again. The results on our machine are the following:

```
SQL Server parse and compile time:
    CPU time = 0 ms, elapsed time = 1 ms.


(4 row(s) affected)


SQL Server Execution Times:
    CPU time = 0 ms,   elapsed time = 7 ms.
```

Why are the results different? The first time, it took 15 milliseconds of CPU time to parse and compile the query, and 128 milliseconds to run it. The second time, obviously, the values are considerably smaller. The answer is simple. When you run the query the second time, the query plan is already in the cache and the query benefits from cached data.

So if you intend to test your query and want accurate results each time you run queries, it may be a good idea to clear the plan cache and the data cache, using the CHECKPOINT, DBCC FREEPROCCACHE and the DBCC DROPCLEANBUFFERS commands. These commands will be covered later in the chapter.

WARNING   Do not clear the cache on a production system because you can adversely affect its performance.

Displaying Graphical Execution Plans Using SQL Server Management Studio

Why would you use the graphical version of the execution plan? One of the reasons is that you can spot potential problems very easily. For example, if a table is missing, the table name will be displayed in red. In addition, some people may find the graphical format of the query plan easier to read. To get the graphical execution plan, you have several methods:

▪   Save an XML showplan in a text file having the extension .sqlplan.

▪   In SQL Server Management Studio, from the Query menu select either Display Estimated Execution Plan (to get the estimated execution plan) or Include Actual Execution Plan (to obtain the actual execution plan after you run the query).

Using the same query, let's see the graphical execution plan. First, open a Query window and type our query:

```
SELECT C.FirstName, C.LastName
FROM Person.Contact C
JOIN Sales.SalesOrderHeader O
    ON C.ContactID = O.ContactID
WHERE OrderDate = '2001-08-14'
GO
```

Then, in the Query menu of SQL Server Management Studio select Include Actual Execution Plan and run the query. A new tab is displayed named Execution Plan. Click on it to see the showplan. The information displayed is similar to the information returned by the other types of showplan. The tree structure of the query plan is represented as graphical icons connected by arrows.

To get information about each node, you can point at it with the cursor (the information is displayed as a tooltip) or click on it and press F4 to display the Properties window. The Properties window includes more details than the tooltips:

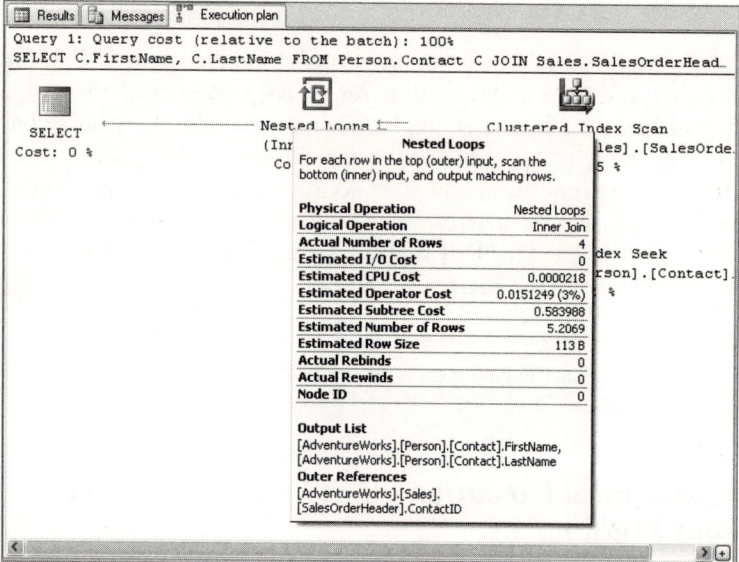

In the next topic, we show you how to obtain the graphical execution plan using SQL Profiler.

Obtaining the Execution Plan for a Query Using SQL Profiler

Another method to obtain the execution plan for a query is using the following Event Classes of SQL Server Profiler:

- Showplan XML occurs when a query executes. It captures the estimated execution plan of a query in XML format.

- Showplan XML For Query Compile occurs when a query is compiled or recompiled. It is similar to the Showplan All event class.

- Showplan Text occurs when a query executes. The text format of the estimated execution plan is captured.

- Showplan Text (Unencoded) is similar to the Showplan Text event class except for the formatting of the event information. You will get the information as a string instead of binary data.

- Showplan All occurs when a query executes. It captures the text format of the estimated execution plan.

- Showplan XML Statistics Profile occurs at runtime. The XML format of the execution plan is captured.

- Showplan Statistics Profile occurs at runtime. The text format of the execution plan is captured.

- Performance statistics occurs when a query plan is cached for the first time, compiled, or recompiled, and when the plan is flushed from the cache. Using this event you can monitor the performance of the executed queries.

In Exercise 7.1, we show you how to obtain the graphical version of a query showplan using the SQL Profiler, using the XML Statistics Profile Class Events.

EXERCISE 7.1

Use SQL Server Profiler to Obtain the Query Showplan

1. Open a new Query window in SQL Server Management Studio.

2. Type the following query:

```
SELECT C.FirstName, C.LastName

FROM Person.Contact C

JOIN Sales.SalesOrderHeader O

    ON C.ContactID = O.ContactID

WHERE OrderDate = '2001-08-14'

GO

SELECT C.FirstName, C.LastName

FROM Person.Contact C

JOIN Sales.SalesOrderHeader O

    ON C.ContactID = O.ContactID

WHERE OrderDate = '2001-07-15'

GO
```

EXERCISE 7.1 *(continued)*

3. On the Tools menu, click on SQL Server Profiler.

4. On the File menu of SQL Server Profiler, click New Trace, and then connect to the same instance of SQL Server (as for SQL Server Management Studio).

5. In the Trace Properties dialog box, type Getting XML Showplans as the Trace Name.

6. From the Use the template list, select Blank.

7. Click Save to File to capture the trace to a file and select the C:\ as the location (you can specify an alternate location if you want).

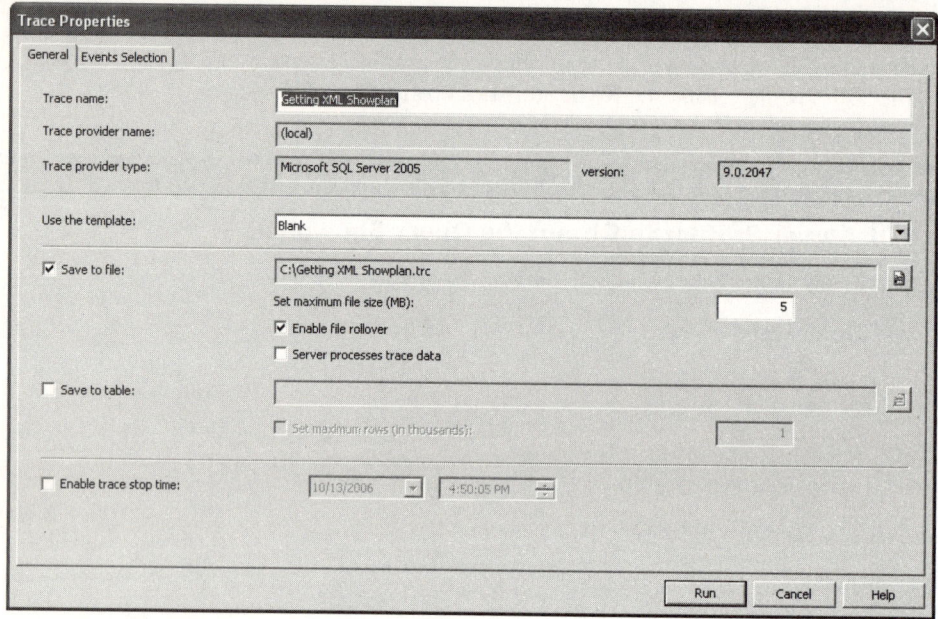

8. Click the Events Selections tab of the Trace Properties.

9. In the Events data column, expand the Performance event node, and select the Showplan XML Statistics Profile check box. A new tab named Events Extraction Settings is displayed.

EXERCISE 7.1 *(continued)*

10. Click the Events Extraction Settings tab and click Save XML Showplan Events Separately.

11. In the Save As dialog box, enter PlanDemo as the filename and save it to C:\. You can choose any alternate location.

12. Click on All Batches In A Single File.

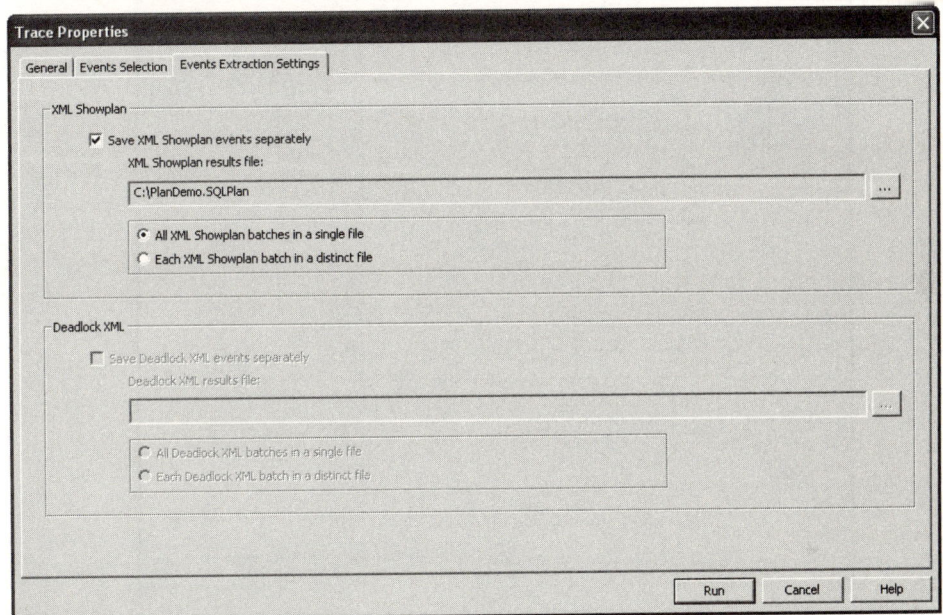

13. Click Run.

14. Switch back to SQL Server Management Studio and run the query.

15. Switch back to the SQL Server Profiler. The query produced two rows having the event class Showplan XML Statistics Profile. Click on each row to see the plan displayed in SQL Server Profiler.

16. Stop the trace and close the SQL Server Profiler.

17. Using Windows Explorer, navigate to C:\ (or to the folder you specified in step 11). Click on the file PlanDemo.SQLPlan. SQL Server Management Studio displays the graphical form of the query plan for the two statements.

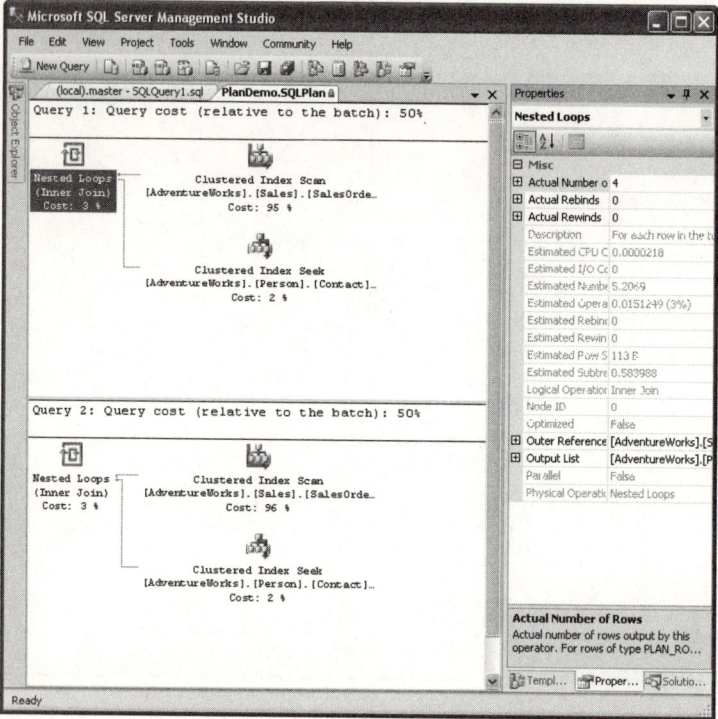

Using the sys.dm_exec_query_plan Dynamic Management Function

The last (but not least) method to obtain a query plan is using the sys.dm_exec_query_plan dynamic management function and a few other dynamic management views and functions such as:

- sys.dm_exec_query_stats, which returns aggregate information for cached query plans (recompilations, number of executions, physical reads, logical reads, and so on).

- sys.dm_exec_sql_text, which returns the text of a SQL statement identified by a sql handle.

- sys.dm_exec_cached_plans, which returns information about cached objects.

- sys.dm_exec_plan_attributes, which returns a row for each attribute associated with a plan identified by a plan handle.

For details about "Execution Related Dynamic Management Views and Functions" please refer to the topic with the same name from Books Online.

We have selected just a single example here, though the topic is really huge. The purpose of the example is to show you a simple method to obtain the XML showplan for a query:

```
SELECT
qp.query_plan
FROM sys.dm_exec_requests r
CROSS APPLY sys.dm_exec_query_plan(r.plan_handle) qp
WHERE r.session_id = @@SPID;
```

The sys.dm_exec_requests dynamic management view returns the current executing requests. In our example, we filter for our query by specifying the query's session ID in the WHERE clause. And to obtain the query plan we apply the dynamic management function sys.dm_exec_query_plan to each row returned by the query (in this case just one row).

```
-- Partial Output
<ShowPlanXML xmlns="http://schemas.microsoft.com/sqlserver ...
```

If you want the plan for all cached queries, you can run the following code:

```
SELECT
qp.query_plan
FROM sys.dm_exec_cached_plans cp
CROSS APPLY sys.dm_exec_query_plan(cp.plan_handle) qp;
GO
```

Analyzing Query Plans

Now that you have the query plan, the next step is to look for potential problems. A large list of possible problems can be detected using a query plan. The following sections highlight several important things you should look for.

Check Out Table Scans

A table scans means reading all rows of a table. Most of the time a seek operation is more efficient than a scan. So, if you see a table scan or a clustered index scan (which is the same thing if the table is clustered) in a query plan, you should investigate the cause for the scan. The following reasons help determine when query optimizer will use table scans:

- Missing indexes support. You don't have useful indexes for your query. To fix that you can use the Database Engine Tuning Advisor or alternatively look at the XML showplan (the MissingIndexes feature).

- Not using filters in your query. If you can limit the results of your query, using a WHERE clause for example, we urge you to do it.

  Using our sample query, if you limit the search for a specific customer by specifying the customer ID, the query is greatly improved because the table scan operator is replaced by a join between two seek operators. To prove that, run the following queries together:

```
-- Clear the cache
CHECKPOINT;
DBCC FREEPROCCACHE WITH NO_INFOMSGS;
DBCC DROPCLEANBUFFERS WITH NO_INFOMSGS;
GO

SET STATISTICS IO ON
GO
-- New Query
SELECT C.FirstName, C.LastName
FROM Person.Contact C
JOIN Sales.SalesOrderHeader O
    ON C.ContactID = O.ContactID
WHERE O.OrderDate = '2001-08-14'
AND O.CustomerID = 28017;
GO

-- Clear the cache
CHECKPOINT;
DBCC FREEPROCCACHE WITH NO_INFOMSGS;
DBCC DROPCLEANBUFFERS WITH NO_INFOMSGS;
GO

-- Old Query
SELECT C.ContactID,C.FirstName, C.LastName
FROM Person.Contact C
JOIN Sales.SalesOrderHeader O
    ON C.ContactID = O.ContactID
WHERE O.OrderDate = '2001-08-14'
GO
SET STATISTICS IO OFF
GO
```

  In the Messages tab of the results, you can find the proof that the new query is better than the original one:

```
-- Partial Output
```

```
Table 'SalesOrderHeader'. Scan count 1, logical reads 5,
physical reads 4, read-ahead reads 0, lob logical reads 0,
lob physical reads 0, lob read-ahead reads 0.

Table 'SalesOrderHeader'. Scan count 1, logical reads 703,
physical reads 1, read-ahead reads 699, lob logical reads 0,
lob physical reads 0, lob read-ahead reads 0.
```

What does the output tell you? The new query needed five pages from the buffer cache compared to 703 pages needed by the old query. That's enough to prove the efficiency of the new query.

- Table scan operations can be a good choice in some situations. For example, when you need most of the data (more than 70 percent of the table data) or when the table is not large, it is usually better to perform a scan operation rather than a seek.

Look for Index Scans

An index scan, as the name says, means reading all rows of an index. Index scans occur on non-clustered indexes and are usually better than table scans from a performance point of view since they are smaller. However, index seeks are preferable so if you have the option, rewrite the queries to use index seeks instead of index scans. Instead of scanning each leaf-level page of an index, a seek operation uses the index keys to get to the data. For example, if you look in the index of this book for the page number where this chapter starts and then go to that page you are doing an index seek.

A simple example illustrates how can you rewrite a query to use index seeks instead of index scans. Suppose you need all email addresses that start with "g" from the Contacts table. One way to obtain them is by comparing the first character of the email address with the letter "g":

```
USE AdventureWorks
GO
SELECT EmailAddress
FROM Person.Contact
WHERE LEFT(EmailAddress, 1) = 'g';
GO
```

The problem with this method is that it would force an index scan. The same results with an index seek can be obtained running the next query:

```
USE AdventureWorks;
GO
SELECT EmailAddress
FROM Person.Contact
WHERE EmailAddress >= 'g' AND EmailAddress < 'h'
GO
```

The solution consists of removing the function from the WHERE filter. You will find more about these types of queries in the section, "Designing Queries That Have Search Arguments (SARGs)."

Watch Out for Red

In the graphical execution plan, a table name is displayed in red if the statistics are missing or out of date. If you encounter this situation, make sure that the AUTO_CREATE_STATISTICS and AUTO_UPDATE_STATISTICS database options are turned ON. When set to ON, these options allow Database Engine to create and update statistics automatically. You can run the sp_updatestats stored procedure to update statistics for all user tables from a database.

Look for Thick Arrows

Arrow width in the graphical execution plan is proportional with the number of rows produced by an operator. The thicker the arrows are the bigger the number of rows. They do not necessarily indicate problems, but they can give you an idea of where to start looking. Investigate whether you can make your WHERE clauses more restrictive to reduce the number of rows.

Watch for Parallel Execution Plans

The job of the query optimizer is to provide a plan with a fast and reasonable response time. In case that the cost of a query is greater than the value specified for the cost threshold for parallelism option (the default value is 5), the optimizer can select a parallel execution plan. There's nothing wrong with parallel execution plans except for the fact that they reduce the throughput of OLTP systems and are more appropriate for OLAP (Online Analytical Processing) installations.

What can you do to prevent parallel execution plans for a specific query? The best solution is to reduce its cost by rewriting it, adding necessary indexes, and even modifying the database schema. Pay attention to the use of XML documents in your query. The performance of your query can be dramatically improved if you add indexes on your XML columns—that is, of course, if you use XML data type methods in your query, such as exist().

Look for Inefficient Query Plans

A query plan is efficient if the query optimizer receives accurate input. As you know, the query plan is generated based on (among other things) the cardinality estimates for each operator (part of the query plan). Cardinality estimates are based on statistics. If the cardinality estimates are wrong, chances are that your query plan will be inefficient.

Where should you look to determine whether the cardinality estimates are wrong? You should look at the EstimateRows and EsitmateExecution values of the query plan as well as the actual execution values. If the values differ too much, that indicates wrong cardinality estimates.

What can you do? Check the statistics-related database options. Tune the query using the Database Engine Tuning Advisor.

A great resource about the how the query optimizer uses statistics can be found here: "Statistics Used by the Query Optimizer in Microsoft SQL Server 2005" http://www.microsoft.com/technet/prodtechnol/sql/2005/qrystats.mspx.

In some cases your query is to blame for inaccurate cardinality estimates:

- Your query has predicates that use comparison operators between multiple columns of the same table.

- The predicates of your query are not equal to (!=) comparison operator or NOT logical operator.

- Your query uses joins with criteria based on arithmetic operators.

A short example illustrates how to obtain better cardinality estimates using a computed column instead of comparing two columns of the same table:

```
SET NOCOUNT ON
GO
USE tempdb
GO
CREATE TABLE T1(
    ID INT IDENTITY(1,1) PRIMARY KEY,
    col1 INT,
    col2 INT)
GO
DECLARE @I INT
SET @I = 1
WHILE @I < 100
BEGIN
INSERT INTO T1(col1,col2) VALUES (@I*2, @I);
SET @I = @I + 1;
END
GO

SET STATISTICS XML ON
GO
SELECT *
FROM T1
WHERE col1>col2
GO
SET STATISTICS XML OFF
GO
```

The query returns 99 rows and is executed using a clustered index scan. If you look at the EstimateRows attribute of the clustered index scan operator, you will see the 29.7 value, approximately a 70 percent error.

The solution that generates better estimates (but in this case not better performance) is to add a computed column to the table:

```
ALTER TABLE T1 ADD col3 AS (col1-col2)
GO
```

```
SET STATISTICS XML ON
GO
SELECT *
FROM T1
WHERE col3>0
GO
SET STATISTICS XML OFF
GO
```

This time the EstimateRows attribute value is very accurate: 99.

Identify Sorts, Filters, and Hash Operators

Sorts, Filters, and Hash operators scan their input and can be CPU consuming. Try to add indexes to support them and remove unnecessary operations from your query, such as SELECT DISTICT, ORDER BY, or UNION.

Verify Hints

If your query is making use of hints, test whether they really improve performance and remove them if not.

Testing Queries for Improved Performance

You've detected the problems of a query, you've modified it, and now the next step is to test it to see whether the performance is really improved. How? You run the queries again and compare the new plans or performance statistics (duration, number of pages read from disk, CPU time) with the old plans (and old statistics). Before you do that, we recommend you run the following commands: CHECKPOINT, DBCC FREEPROCCACHE, and the DBCC DROPCLEANBUFFERS. In a test environment (we do not recommend using them on a production server because they clear the cache), running these commands gives you a clean environment so you can get accurate results from your tests.

The CHECKPOINT statement generates a cold buffer cache by writing all dirty pages for the current database to disk. Dirty pages are data pages (in the buffer cache) that have been modified but are not written to disk yet. Then, the DBCC DROPCLEANBUFFERS command removes all buffers from the buffer pool. Finally, the DBCC FREEPROCCACHE cleans the plan cache.

The next example shows you a possible approach to query testing. You start by creating some demo tables based on two existing tables from AdventureWorks database. We don't want you to modify your sample database so you will modify instead two new tables:

```
USE tempdb;
GO
DROP TABLE Orders, Contact;
GO
CREATE TABLE Contact (
    ContactID INT NOT NULL PRIMARY KEY,
    FirstName NVARCHAR(128),
    LastName NVARCHAR(50));


GO
CREATE TABLE Orders (
    OrderID INT NOT NULL PRIMARY KEY,
    ContactID INT REFERENCES Contact(ContactID),
    OrderDate DATETIME,
    Amount DEC(38,2))
GO


-- Insert Demo Data
INSERT INTO Contact (ContactID, FirstName, LastName)
SELECT ContactID, FirstName, LastName
FROM AdventureWorks.Person.Contact
GO
INSERT INTO Orders (OrderID,ContactID,OrderDate,Amount)
SELECT SalesOrderID,ContactID,OrderDate,TotalDue
FROM AdventureWorks.Sales.SalesOrderHeader
WHERE SalesOrderID < 70000;
GO
```

The next step is to examine the current performance for a query. To start fresh, clean the data cache and the plan cache:

```
USE tempdb;
GO
CHECKPOINT;
DBCC FREEPROCCACHE WITH NO_INFOMSGS;
DBCC DROPCLEANBUFFERS WITH NO_INFOMSGS;
GO
SET STATISTICS IO ON;
```

```
GO
SET STATISTICS TIME ON;
GO
SET STATISTICS XML ON;
GO

-- Tested Query
SELECT C.FirstName, C.LastName
FROM Contact C
JOIN Orders O
    ON C.ContactID = O.ContactID
WHERE OrderDate = '2001-08-14'
GO

SET STATISTICS XML OFF;
GO
SET STATISTICS TIME OFF;
GO
SET STATISTICS IO OFF;
GO
```

The query should be familiar to you by now. We selected the XML showplan, but you can use any other version of the plan. What's the problem with this query? Looking at its execution plan, you can see the following important elements:

```
-- Partial Output of the XML showplan
<StmtSimple StatementText="SELECT ...
 StatementSubTreeCost="0.159515"
...
<MissingIndexes>
<MissingIndexGroup Impact="89.3439">
<MissingIndex Database="[tempdb]" Schema="[dbo]" Table="[Orders]">
<ColumnGroup Usage="EQUALITY">
<Column Name="[OrderDate]" ColumnId="3" />
</ColumnGroup>
</MissingIndex>
</MissingIndexGroup>
</MissingIndexes>
...
<RelOp NodeId="1" PhysicalOp="Clustered Index Scan"...
EstimateIO="0.104606" EstimateCPU="0.0291321" AvgRowSize="19"
EstimatedTotalSubtreeCost="0.133739"
...
```

```
-- Partial Output of IO Statistics
Table 'Orders'. Scan count 1, logical reads 140, physical reads 0,
 read-ahead reads 0, lob logical reads 0, lob physical reads 0,
lob read-ahead reads 0.
-- Partial Output of the Time Statistics
SQL Server Execution Times:
   CPU time = 16 ms,  elapsed time = 13 ms.
```

What do you get from this information? First, there is a missing index on the OrderDate column of the Orders table. The missing index is causing a Clustered Index Scan operation, in fact a table scan. The I/O statistics shows that the Orders table is scanned once. The time statistics may differ on your machine.

If you run the query again, including the graphical execution plan (that prevents the XML showplan from being displayed), you will see that the Clustered Index Scan operation has an estimated cost of about 84 percent.

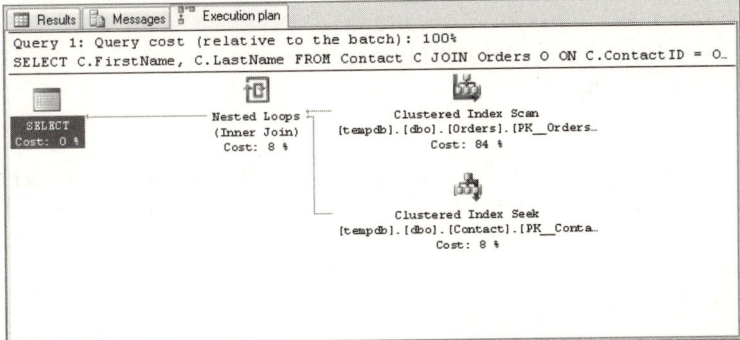

You can get the same information from the XML showplan: the estimated cost (Statement-SubTreeCost) of the query is 0.159515 and the cost of the Clustered Index Scan operator (EstimatedTotalSubtreeCost) is 0.133739. The formula is EstimatedTotalSubtreeCost * 100 / StatementSubTreeCost equivalent to 0.133739 * 100 / 0.159515. The result is 83.8410180860734, which is rounded to 84.

The first assumption you can make analyzing the information is that creating an index on the OrderDate column can improve the query. And you would be right. To make the index more useful, you should create a composite index on the OrderDate and ContactID columns of the Orders table. Why? This way you limit the search to the composite index.

```
USE tempdb;
GO
CREATE NONCLUSTERED INDEX idx_Orders_OrderDate_ContactID
 ON Orders(OrderDate,ContactID)
GO
```

After creating the index, you have to test whether the performance is improved, by running the code again.

The output that matters follows:

```
-- Partial Output of the XML showplan
<StmtSimple StatementText="SELECT ...
 StatementSubTreeCost="0.0164198"
...
<RelOp NodeId="1" PhysicalOp="Index Seek"...
EstimateIO="0.003125" EstimateCPU="0.0001625"
AvgRowSize="11" EstimatedTotalSubtreeCost="0.0032875"
...
-- Partial Output of IO Statistics
Table 'Orders'. Scan count 1, logical reads 2, physical reads 0,
read-ahead reads 0, lob logical reads 0, lob physical reads 0,
lob read-ahead reads 0.
-- Partial Output of the Time Statistics
SQL Server Execution Times:
   CPU time = 0 ms,  elapsed time = 4 ms.
```

The results may vary on your machine but they would illustrate the improvement of performance: lower cost for the query, better algorithm (index seek versus table scan), and lower I/O.

Unfortunately, in real life, you cannot stop here. You should analyze the impact of creating a new index on the other queries that use the Orders table.

 **WARNING** When physical database schema is modified to improve performance, other queries can be affected.

Each new index on a table affects the performance of data modification, and you should consider this fact. We will stop here with this topic, continuing with another area of problems that can make your queries slow down: locking.

Detecting Locking Problems

Can you imagine the speed and the grace of a Formula One race car in a traffic jam? We assure you that even this car would be as blocked as any other one. It will have to wait. And that holds true for your queries and the traffic jam caused by locking issues. It won't matter how tuned and fast your query is, if it waits for temporararily unavailable resources.

This section shows you the methods available in SQL Server 2005 to detect what "blocks" prevent your queries from running at full speed through your server. These are the available tools, which are described in detail in the following sections:

- SQL Profiler
- System Monitor

- Summary Reports from SQL Server Management Studio
- Dynamic management views and functions
- SQL Management Objects (SMO) API
- Backward-compatibility features such as SQL Distributed Management Objects (DMO) API, system stored procedures, and compatibility views

SQL Profiler

SQL Profiler exposes several event classes that allow you to detect blocking problems and deadlocks:

- Deadlock Graph provides a very nice XML description of a deadlock.
- Use Lock:Acquired Event Class to notice when a lock is acquired on a resource.
- Lock:Cancel deals with canceled requests for lock.
- Use Lock:Deadlock Chain if you need information about all participants in a deadlock situation.
- Lock:Deadlock is similar to the previous event but information is displayed only for the victim of a deadlock.
- Lock:Escalation indicates lock escalation.
- Lock:Released allows you to track lock releases.
- Lock:Timeout (timeout > 0), when lock timeout is greater than 0, indicates that a request cannot be completed because of a blocked resource.
- Lock:Timeout is similar to Lock:Timeout (timeout > 0) except it displays the events where timeout value is 0.

In SQL Server 2005, SQL Profiler allows you to correlate a System Monitor trace with a SQL Trace. We recommend you to consider this feature when you investigate locking.

System Monitor

To obtain locking information using System Monitor you can use the SQLServer:Locks object. It provides information about locks on various resource types such as rows, files, and so on. You can monitor multiple instances of the SQLServer:Locks object at the same time to obtain information for multiple resource types.

The following list represents the information available:

- Average Wait Time (ms) represents the average wait time (in milliseconds) for each lock request that had to wait.
- Lock Requests/sec represents the number of lock requests per second.
- Lock Timeouts (timeout > 0)/sec represents the number of lock requests that timed out excluding requests with timeout value 0.
- Lock Timeouts/sec represents the number of lock requests that timed out.
- Lock Wait Time (ms) represents the total wait time for locks in the last second.

- Lock Waits/sec represents the number of lock requests where the caller had to wait.
- Number of Deadlocks/sec represents the number of lock requests that ended in a deadlock.

You can display information about all locks or you can see the lock information for each of the following resource types:

- AllocUnit: A single allocation unit
- Application: An application-specified resource
- Database: An entire database
- Extent: A contiguous group of eight data pages (or index pages)
- File: A database file (it can be a data file or a log file)
- Heap/BTree Heap or BTree (HOBT): A heap or B-tree
- Key: A row of an index
- Metadata: Metadata information
- Object: A database object such as tables, views, stored procedures, and so on
- Page: A single page in a data file
- RID (Row ID): A physical row in a heap

SQL Server Management Studio

SQL Server Management Studio can help you in diagnosing blocking problems. You can use the Activity Monitor or the Summary Reports.

You can use the Activity Monitor by following these simple steps:

1. Connect to the server with Object Explorer.
2. Expand Management node.
3. Double-click Activity Monitor.

   The Activity Monitor has three pages. The Process Info page displays information about the current processes. The Locks by Process page displays locks sorted by their process. The Locks by Object page displays locking information sorted by the object name.

Another great feature of SQL Server Management Studio is the Summary Reports. Based on catalog views, the default trace and dynamic management views and functions, the Summary Reports offer you complete information about your server. To make things even better, the complete source of the report is publicly available so you can create your own custom reports.

> To find out more about Summary Reports and download their source code, visit the SQL Server Relational Engine Manageability Team Blog site at http://blogs.msdn.com/sqlrem/default.aspx.

To use Summary Reports, you have to display the Summary window by pressing F7 or from the View menu by clicking Summary. Then, click the Report drop-down to select a report. The reports available depend on the object selected in Object Explorer. Thus, if you have your server selected, you obtain information about the server instance. If you want information related to a specific database, you have to select the database in Object Explorer.

To get a better feel of Summary Reports, we'll use a simple example. You will run two queries, the first one blocking the other, and then you will display locking information using the Summary Reports. First, open two query windows and run the following code.

This is the first query:

```
USE AdventureWorks
GO
BEGIN TRAN;
UPDATE HumanResources.Department
SET [Name]='Information Technology'
WHERE DepartmentID = 10;
-- wait to give you time to switch
WAITFOR DELAY '00:10';
ROLLBACK TRAN;
GO
```

This is the second query:

```
USE AdventureWorks
GO
BEGIN TRAN;
SELECT * FROM HumanResources.Department
WHERE DepartmentID = 10;
ROLLBACK TRAN;
GO
```

Then, click the AdventureWorks database in Object Explorer.

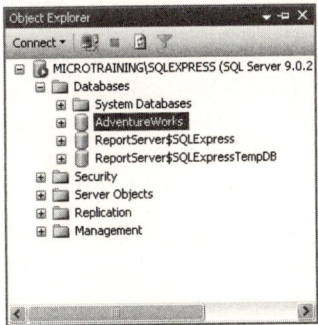

Display the Summary window, and from the Reports drop-down list, select the All Blocking Transactions report. The result is the following:

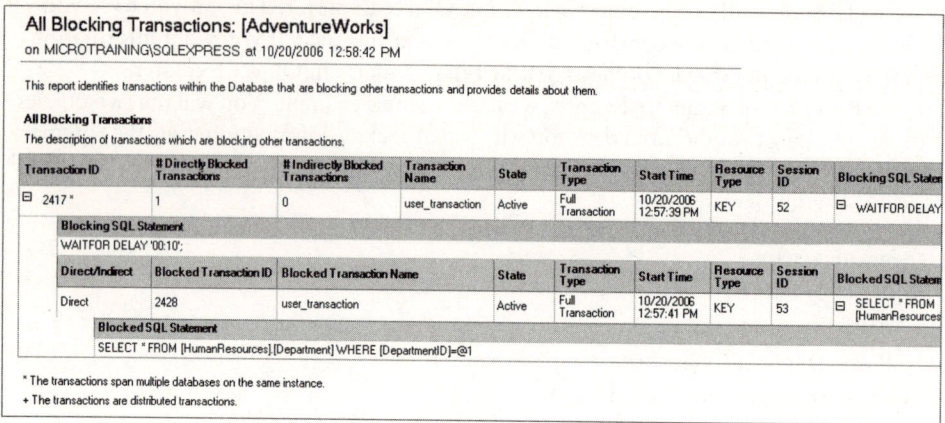

You can see in the report both blocking and blocked connections and their SQL statements. The Summary Reports are a great tool but not perfect. The report used (All Blocking Transactions) has a minor bug. It displays only explicit transactions blocked. That's why we used the BEGIN TRAN statement for the second query.

Besides the All Blocking Transactions report, you can use the following reports to display locking information:

- Activity–All Blocking Transactions is similar to the All Blocking Transactions at the database level. This report provides information about all blocked transactions on specific database engine instance.

- All Transactions retrieves information about all open user transactions within a Database.

- Resource Locking Statistics by Logins retrieves locking information sorted by individual logins.

- Resource Locking Statistics By Objects retrieves information about locks acquired and the objects involved.

- Top Transactions by Blocked Transactions Count displays the top transactions that block the highest number of other transactions. This report is available both at an instance and a database level.

- Top Transactions by Locks Count will identify which transactions obtained the highest number of locks. This report is available both at an instance and a database level.

Dynamic Management Views and Functions

Dynamic management views and functions provide another way to obtain locking information. These DMVs are covered in Chapters 8 and 10:

- sys.dm_tran_locks displays active lock requests.

- sys.dm_os_wait_stats displays information about waits for threads currently executing.

- sys.dm_os_waiting_tasks returns information about tasks waiting for a resource.
- sys.dm_db_index_operational_stats returns information about locking and access information (among others) for tables and indexes.

SQL Management Objects (SMO) API

An alternative method for displaying locking information is to use SQL Managements Object API. You can program against SMO from C#, Visual Basic .NET, and even from VBScript. You can get the list of active locks at the instance or database level by using the EnumLocks methods of Server and Database objects. The following sample written in C# illustrates a possible use of the Server.EnumLocks() method:

```csharp
using System;
using System.Collections.Generic;
using System.Text;
using System.Data;
using Microsoft.SqlServer.Management.Smo;

namespace DemoSMO
{
class Program
{
static void Main(string[] args)
{
Server srv = new Server();
DataTable d = srv.EnumLocks();
foreach(DataRow r in d.Rows)
{
Console.WriteLine("SPID:" + r["RequestorSpid"].ToString());
Console.WriteLine("Lock Type:" + r["LockType"].ToString());
Console.WriteLine("Database:" + r["Database"].ToString());
Console.WriteLine("Schema:" + r["Schema"].ToString());
Console.WriteLine("Table:" + r["Table"].ToString());
Console.WriteLine("Index:" + r["Index"].ToString());
Console.WriteLine("Status:" + r["Status"].ToString());
Console.WriteLine("----------------------------------");

}}}}
```

To see some results, you can run a previous code sample to create locks and then the previous code:

```sql
USE AdventureWorks
GO
```

```
BEGIN TRAN;
UPDATE HumanResources.Department
SET [Name]='Information Technology'
WHERE DepartmentID = 10;
-- wait to give you time to switch
WAITFOR DELAY '00:10';
ROLLBACK TRAN;
GO
```

We recommend you use Visual Studio 2005 to run the code. The partial output should look like this:

```
SPID:52
Lock Type:Sch-M
Database:AdventureWorks
Schema:
Table:
Index:
Status:1
----------------------------------------
SPID:52
Lock Type:IU
Database:AdventureWorks
Schema:HumanResources
Table:Department
...
```

Backward Compatibility Features

The SMO API replaces the SQL Distributed Management Objects (SQL DMO) in SQL Server 2005. But you can still use DMO for compatibility reasons. If you want to display locking information using SQL DMO, you can use the SQLServer class. The method has the same name, EnumLocks, and only the class is different (SQLServer instead of Server).

Besides SQL DMO, you can use two stored procedures for the same purpose, displaying locking info:

- The sp_lock stored procedure returns information about active locks in an instance of the Database Engine. For SQL Server 2005, you can use the sys.dm_tran_locks dynamic management view.

- The sys.syslockinfo compatibility view returns information about the active locks in an instance of the Database Engine. It is replaced in SQL Server 2005 by the sys.dm_tran_locks dynamic management view.

Modifying Queries to Optimize Performance

In the previous section, you saw how to detect performance problems for a query by analyzing its query plan. For each performance problem identified, you have one or more solutions, such as adding indexes, maintaining statistics, and even rewriting the query. In the following sections, you will see how to modify a query in order to obtain better performance.

Modifying Queries to Optimize Client and Server Performance

In Chapters 1 and 2, you saw how to design an effective data access strategy that responds to your application requirements. This topic serves as a reminder for you. We will go quickly through several recommendations that you should consider in selecting the data access strategy:

- Reduce round-trips to the server by caching both server side and client side.

- Minimize the resources used where resource can be memory, connections, and so on.

- Release resources; when a resource completes its job, don't forget to release it.

- Limit the returned data; do not use SELECT * and SELECT queries without a WHERE clause unless you really need all columns or all rows.

   When you select the data access technologies, remember that each one has advantages and drawbacks. Here are several examples:

ADO .NET DataSet   This is good for caching data or passing data between layers. Caching means minimizing round-trips to the database server by storing data either on the application server or at the client. On the other hand, you should be careful when you decide to cache data using DataSets on an application server where memory consumption is critical, for example, on a web server. When you need extensive data processing you can use DataSets. You can also replace cursors with DataSets or use them to access multiple data sources at the same time. The drawbacks of DataSets are memory consumption and the overhead associated with creation of DataSet objects (due to creation of other subobjects, such as DataTables, DataRows, and DataColumns).

ADO .NET DataReader   If you need fast data retrieval and low memory consumption, you can choose a DataReader object. A DataReader doesn't have the flexibility of a DataSet nor the instantiation overhead. Also it is more cumbersome to cache data using a DataReader.

MARS (Multiple Active Result Sets)   MARS is a good candidate if you want an alternative to server-side cursors or to reduce the number of connections for your application. And in some cases MARS can bring performance improvements over server-side cursors. However, don't forget that MARS is about interleaving multiple requests and not parallel execution.

ADO .NET XmlReader   Do you have data returned by a SELECT FOR XML query? Or do you need to consume streams of well-formed XML documents? Then an XmlReader object can be a very good choice.

These are just a few; we recommend you review the previous chapters for more recommendations.

Rewriting Subqueries to Joins

We begin this short section with an important statement: there is no subquery operator in SQL Server 2005. SQL Server transforms every subquery that you write in joins, most of the time. So why would you want to rewrite subqueries as joins? Because in some rare cases, the query optimizer can find a better plan if you do.

Another important statement that we want you to consider: test, test, and retest your queries. Make sure that rewriting the query results in performance gains.

The following example shows you a case where rewriting a subquery to a join would not result in better performance. Before running the code sample, don't forget to include the actual execution plan:

```
-- First Variant
SELECT ContactID
FROM Person.Contact
WHERE ContactID NOT IN
(SELECT ContactID FROM Sales.SalesOrderHeader)

-- Second Variant
SELECT
ContactID
FROM Person.Contact P
WHERE NOT EXISTS
  (SELECT * FROM Sales.SalesOrderHeader S
    WHERE P.ContactID = S.ContactID)

-- Third Variant
SELECT
ContactID
FROM Person.Contact
EXCEPT
SELECT
ContactID
FROM Sales.SalesOrderHeader

-- Fourth
```

```
SELECT
P.ContactID
FROM Person.Contact P
LEFT JOIN Sales.SalesOrderHeader S ON P.ContactID = S.ContactID
WHERE S.ContactID IS NULL
GO
```

All four variants of the query are logically equivalent. All use a Hash Match, an Index Scan, and a Clustered Index Scan operator. If you would expect that the last query (based on a join rather than on a subquery) to have better performance, you are wrong. Actually, from the last query you will get slightly less performance because of an additional Filter operator (that removes the rows with S.ContactID NULL), missing from the execution plans of the other three queries.

The next example shows you one of the rare situations where a subquery is actually better than a join:

```
SELECT
SalesOrderID,
TotalDue,
(SELECT MIN(TotalDue) FROM Sales.SalesOrderHeader) AS Min_TotalDue,
(SELECT MAX(TotalDue) FROM Sales.SalesOrderHeader) AS Max_TotalDue,
(SELECT AVG(TotalDue) FROM Sales.SalesOrderHeader) AS Avg_TotalDue,
TotalDue-(SELECT MIN(TotalDue) FROM Sales.SalesOrderHeader)
AS Diff_Total_Min
FROM Sales.SalesOrderHeader
GO


SELECT
SalesOrderID,
TotalDue,
Min_TotalDue,
Max_TotalDue,
Avg_TotalDue,
TotalDue - Min_TotalDue AS Diff_Total_Min
FROM Sales.SalesOrderHeader
CROSS JOIN
(SELECT
    MIN(TotalDue) AS Min_TotalDue,
    MAX(TotalDue) AS Max_TotalDue,
    AVG(TotalDue) AS Avg_TotalDue
FROM Sales.SalesOrderHeader) SQ
GO
```

Both queries perform the same task; they return the information about each sales order header. However, if you run the queries and look at their execution plans, you will notice that the second one performs more than twice as well as the first one.

Designing Queries That Have Search Arguments (SARGs)

Indexes can speed up your queries tremendously, especially when you let them do their job. Indexes can really help search queries when you filter the query's results using a search argument (SARG). A SARG is useful and can have an index seek operation instead of a scan as a result. A search argument can have the following forms:

- column_name operator constant(or variable)
- constant(or variable) operator column_name

It can specify the following:

- An exact match: ContactID = 1000
- A range of values: ContactID > 10 AND ContactID < 1000
- A combination of two or more items joined by AND: ContactID < 10 AND DepartmentID=10

Search arguments allow the following operators: =, >, <, >=, <=, BETWEEN, and LIKE. The operator LIKE is somewhat special. Prior to SQL Server 2005, LIKE was allowed in a SARG only for prefix matches such as FirstName LIKE 'Kim%'.

SQL Server 2005 introduces string summary statistics that extend the use of LIKE for SARGs to the following constructs:

- column_name LIKE 'string%'
- column_name LIKE '%string'
- column_name LIKE '%string%'
- column_name LIKE 'string'
- column_name LIKE 'str_ing'
- column_name LIKE 'str[abc]ing'
- column_name LIKE '%abc%xy'

What is not allowed as a SARG? Operators such as NOT, < >, NOT EXISTS, NOT IN, NOT LIKE, and functions are not allowed.

If you want to improve performance for a query, a simple method is to convert non-SARGs into SARGs. Here are some simple examples. We start by looking at a simple query demand: count the orders on a certain date from the Sales.SalesOrderHeader table from the Adventure-Works database. Use 14 August 2001 as the date. To make sure that your query can be supported by an index, you will create one:

```
USE AdventureWorks;
GO
```

```
CREATE INDEX idx_SalesOrderHeader_OrderDate
    ON Sales.SalesOrderHeader (OrderDate);
GO
```

Here are several non-SARG approaches:

```
SELECT COUNT(*)
FROM Sales.SalesOrderHeader
WHERE DATEDIFF(day,OrderDate,'2001-08-14')=0
```

If you look at the execution plan, a table scan operator is used. And an index scan operator is used for the following query:

```
 SELECT COUNT(*)
FROM Sales.SalesOrderHeader
WHERE YEAR(OrderDate)=2001
    AND MONTH(OrderDate)=8
    AND DAY(OrderDate)=14
```

The solution is simple and consists of using only operators allowed in SARGs:

```
SELECT COUNT(*)
FROM Sales.SalesOrderHeader
WHERE OrderDate >= '2001-08-14'
    AND OrderDate < '2001-08-15'
```

This time, an index seek operation is used and the query's performance is dramatically improved. To convince yourself of that, run all three queries together. On our machine, the last query had 1 percent cost of the total cost of running all three queries.

A function on a table column creates a non-SARG. Usually, you can convert the non-SARG to a SARG by removing the function. Here are several examples:

- LEFT(FirstName)='K' (non-SARG) is equivalent to FirstName LIKE 'K%' (SARG) and FirstName < 'L' AND FirstName >='K' (SARG).

- ABS(Temperature) < 10 (non-SARG) is equivalent to Temparature > –10 AND Temperature < 10 (SARG).

To conclude, though an expression may seem to be a SARG, don't base your tuning efforts on intuition only. Use tests!

Converting Single-Row Statements into Set-Based Queries

Some people say that cursors are evil. We do not necessarily agree with this statement. We would say that cursors can be improperly used by programmers who are not familiar with the set-based model of SQL queries and prefer the iterative model. Yet, SQL Server offers the best performance for the set-based model, as it should do.

Cursors can dramatically reduce concurrency so if you have a set-based alternative to cursors, use it. We already discussed cursors in previous chapters, but we will summarize the alternatives to cursors and WHILE loops:

- You can refactor cursors as set-based queries, as user-defined functions, or as complex queries using case expressions.
- You can use the disconnected model of ADO.NET (using DataSets).
- You can replace cursors with Common Table Expressions.
- You can perform operations in multiple sets.

As an example, we use a question that was posted on a community forum dedicated to SQL Server: How can I use a set-based query instead of the following cursor-based query?

```
USE tempdb
GO


CREATE TABLE MyTable (
    ID INT PRIMARY KEY IDENTITY(1,1),
    FirstName VARCHAR(64))
GO
INSERT INTO MyTable (FirstName) VALUES ('Kim');
INSERT INTO MyTable (FirstName) VALUES ('Marilyn');
INSERT INTO MyTable (FirstName) VALUES ('Cristian');
GO


DECLARE @NameList VARCHAR(MAX);
DECLARE @Name VARCHAR(64);
SET @NameList = '';
DECLARE NameList_Cursor CURSOR
        FOR SELECT FirstName FROM MyTable;
OPEN NameList_Cursor;
FETCH NEXT FROM NameList_Cursor INTO @Name;
WHILE @@FETCH_STATUS = 0
  BEGIN
   SET @NameList =
     CASE
         WHEN @NameList='' THEN @Name
         ELSE  @NameList + ','+ @Name
     END;
   FETCH NEXT FROM NameList_Cursor INTO @Name;
  END
CLOSE NameList_Cursor;
```

```
DEALLOCATE NameList_Cursor;

SELECT @NameList;
GO
```

The query returned all names separated by commas in a variable. The alternative to this query (and the answer to the question) is simple:

```
DECLARE @NameList VARCHAR(MAX);
SET @NameList = '';
SELECT @NameList =
 CASE
    WHEN @NameList='' THEN FirstName
    ELSE  @NameList + ','+ FirstName
 END
FROM MyTable;

SELECT @NameList;
GO
```

Summary

In this chapter, you learned how to troubleshoot and improve the performance of a query.

We started with how a query is executed. Then we showed you several ways to obtain a query plan as well as what potential problem can be detected by looking at a plan.

Next, we covered testing queries and the methods available to help you detect blocking problems. We continued by reminding you of several techniques to maximize client and server performance.

Finally, you saw different methods of rewriting queries for performance gains.

Exam Essentials

Before you take the exam make sure that you are familiar with the following topics:

Understand how to evaluate query performance.   You should know the methods that allow you to obtain an execution plan and the advantages and drawbacks of each method.

Be able to improve the performance of a query.   Using the query plan or the query's text you should be able to improve performance by rewriting the query, by adding support indexes, by using a different algorithm, and so on.

Know how to test queries.   You should know how to clear the buffer and the plan cache to obtain accurate results when testing your queries.

Be able to detect locking.   Several methods allow you to diagnose locking problems on your database server. You should be familiar with the practical usage of each one of them.

Review Questions

1. Which of the following are reasons for slow queries? (Choose all that apply.)

    A. Inefficient query plans

    B. Blocking issues

    C. Missing indexes

    D. Missing statistics

2. You have to investigate unusually high disk activity on your server. You want to obtain I/O information for several of the most-used stored procedures. Which statement should you use?

    A. SET STATISTICS IO OFF

    B. SET STATISTICS IO ON

    C. SET SHOWPLAN_TEXT ON

    D. SET SHOWPLAN_TEXT OFF

3. You are tuning a query and you want to obtain information about the query's parse, compile, and execution time. What should you do?

    A. Run SET STATISTICS TIME ON before you run the query.

    B. Run SET STATISTICS TIME OFF before you run the query.

    C. Run SET STATISTICS IO ON before you run the query.

    D. Run SET STATISTICS IO OFF before you run the query.

4. Which of the following methods allow you to obtain the XML showplan for queries? (Choose all that apply.)

    A. Use SET STATISTICS XML ON.

    B. Use SQL Server Profiler.

    C. Use sys.dm_exec_query_plan dynamic management function.

    D. Use SET SHOWPLAN_XML ON.

5. You are tuning a query by using the graphical query plan. Which of the following operators can indicate performance problems.? (Choose all that apply.)

    A. Index scan

    B. Table scan

    C. Clustered index scan

    D. Clustered index seek

6. You have completely redesigned several queries that had performance problems. You want to test their performance and compare it with previous performance. You want to clear the data cache and the plan cache to obtain accurate results. What should you do? (Choose the best method.)

    A. Restart the server.

    B. Use the DBCC DROPCLEANBUFFERS command.

    C. Use the DBCC FREEPROCCACHE command.

    D. Use CHECKPOINT, DBCC DROPCLEANBUFFERS, and DBCC FREEPROCCACHE.

7. You are tuning a query by using the query's graphical plan. The code of the query is the following:

```
SELECT *

FROM MyTable

WHERE ID = 12000;
```

You've notice a table scan operator. Your table has one million rows and the query returns a single row. How can you improve the query?

    A. Add an index on the ID column.

    B. Check whether the statistics are updated.

    C. Check for missing statistics.

    D. Clear the buffer cache.

8. The graphical plan for several queries displays some table names in red. What should you do? (Choose all that apply.)

    A. Set to ON the AUTO_CREATE_STATISTICS database option.

    B. Set to ON the AUTO_UPDATE_STATISTICS database option.

    C. Use the DROP STATISTICS statement.

    D. Use the sp_updatestats stored procedure.

9. You have to write a query that counts all orders from the Orders table for a specific date. One requirement for your query is good response time. Knowing that there is an index on the OrderDate column of the Orders table, which of the following code should you use to count all orders from 28 August 2001?

    A. Use the following:

```
SELECT COUNT(*) FROM Orders
WHERE OrderDate='2001-08-28';
```

    B. Use the following:

```
SELECT COUNT(*) FROM Orders
WHERE OrderDate>='2001-08-28'
AND OrderDate<'2001-08-29';
```

C. Use the following:

```
SELECT COUNT(*) FROM Orders
WHERE DATEDIFF(day,OrderDate,'2001-08-28')=0;
```

D. Use the following:

```
SELECT COUNT(*) FROM Orders
WHERE YEAR(OrderDate)=2001
AND MONTH(OrderDate)=08
AND DAY(OrderDate)=28;
```

10. You want to optimize a query that is used to search all names starting with the letter "H." Which WHERE clause should you use?

A. `WHERE LastName='H';`

B. `WHERE LEFT(LastName,1)='H';`

C. `WHERE LastName>='H' AND LastName<'I';`

D. `WHERE SUBSTRING(LastName,1,1)='H';`

11. You have to improve the performance of the following query:

```
SELECT ProductName

FROM Products

WHERE SUBSTRING(ProductName,1,3)='NET';
```

Which of the following options is better?

A. Use the following:

```
SELECT ProductName FROM Products
WHERE ProductName='NET';
```

B. Use the following:

```
SELECT ProductName FROM Products
WHERE LEFT(ProductName,3)='NET';
```

C. Use the following:

```
SELECT ProductName FROM Products
WHERE ProductName LIKE '%NET';
```

D. Use the following:

```
SELECT ProductName FROM Products
WHERE ProductName LIKE 'NET%';
```

12. A developer from your department wrote the following query:

```
INSERT INTO OrdersReport(
    OrderID,
    TotalAmount,
    OrderDate,
    CustomerID)
SELECT DISTINCT
    O.OrderID,
    O.TotalAmount,
    O.OrderDate,
    C.CustomerName
FROM Orders O, Customers C
ORDER BY O.OrderID
```

The code that creates the Customers and the Orders table is displayed below:

```
CREATE TABLE Customers (
    CustomerID INT NOT NULL PRIMARY KEY,
    CustomerName VARCHAR(128));
GO
CREATE TABLE Orders(
    OrderID INT NOT NULL PRIMARY KEY,
    TotalAmount DEC(19,2),
    OrderDate DATETIME,
    CustomerID INT REFERENCES Customers(CustomerID));
GO
```

The query should copy all orders from the Orders table to the OrderReport table. It should also include the customer name for each order. The table OrdersReport is used by a stored procedure to generate a report. The order of rows in the OrdersReport table is not important. You have to tune the data transfer query. What should you do? (Choose all that apply.)

A. Remove the ORDER BY clause.

B. Remove the DISTINCT clause.

C. Include the following WHERE clause:

```
WHERE O.CustomerID = C.CustomerID.
```

D. Use GROUP By instead of DISTINCT.

13. You have to improve the performance of the following query:

```
DECLARE @NameList VARCHAR(MAX);

DECLARE @Name VARCHAR(64);

SET @NameList = '';

DECLARE NameList_Cursor CURSOR STATIC
        FOR SELECT FirstName FROM Contacts;

OPEN NameList_Cursor;

FETCH NEXT FROM NameList_Cursor INTO @Name;

WHILE @@FETCH_STATUS = 0
  BEGIN
   SET @NameList =
      CASE
      WHEN @NameList='' THEN @Name
      ELSE  @NameList + ','+ @Name
      END;
    FETCH NEXT FROM NameList_Cursor INTO @Name;
  END
CLOSE NameList_Cursor;

DEALLOCATE NameList_Cursor;


SELECT @NameList;

GO
```

What should you do?

A. Replace the cursor with a SELECT statement.

B. Change the cursor type to DYNAMIC.

C. Replace the cursor with a WHILE loop.

D. Change the cursor type to KEYSET.

14. You have to write a query that modifies the discount for all products that have a specific category. You wrote the following query:

```
UPDATE Product

SET DISCOUNT=CASE WHEN CategoryID=10

        THEN 5

        ELSE DISCOUNT

        END

GO
```

You add an index on the CategoryID column to improve the performance of your query. However, the query performance is the same. What should you do?

A. Replace the query with a cursor.

B. Use a WHILE loop instead of the existing query.

C. Use the following query instead of the existing one:

```
UPDATE Product
SET DISCOUNT=5
WHERE CategoryID=10
GO
```

D. Add an index to the Price column.

15. You need to obtain statistics about the number of lock requests per second on your SQL Server 2005 server instance. What should you do?

A. Use the SQLServer:Locks object and the Lock Requests/sec counter.

B. Use the SQLServer:Locks object and the Lock Timeouts/sec counter.

C. Use the SQLServer:Locks object and the Lock Waits/sec counter.

D. Use the sys.dm_tran_locks dynamic management view.

16. Which of the following statements is true?

A. The use of subqueries is always better for performance than joins.

B. The use of joins is always better for performance than subqueries.

C. The use of joins is better for performance than subqueries in some particular situations.

D. Subqueries have always the same performance as joins.

17. You have to improve the performance of your application using client caching of static data. What technology should you use?

A. ADO .NET DataSet

B. ADO .NET DataReader

C. ADO .NET XMLReader

D. MARS (multiple active result sets)

18. You have to design the data access strategy for a Windows-based application. One of the requirements is to reduce the number of connections used. What technology should you select?

  A. ADO .NET DataSet

  B. ADO .NET DataReader

  C. ADO .NET XMLReader

  D. MARS (multiple active result sets)

19. Which of the following technologies should you use to fill controls for pages of a web application if the memory consumption is critical?

  A. ADO .NET DataSet

  B. ADO .NET DataReader

  C. ADO .NET XMLReader

  D. MARS (multiple active result sets)

20. You design an application that has multiple tiers. You have to select a technology that can be easily passed between various tiers of your application. What should you do?

  A. Use the ADO .NET DataSet

  B. Use the ADO .NET DataReader

  C. Use the ADO .NET XMLReader

  D. Use MARS (multiple active result sets)

Answers to Review Questions

1. A, B, C, D. All are reasons for slow queries.

2. B. If you want to obtain I/O statistics, prior to running a query you should set the SET STATISTICS IO option to ON.

3. A. To get time statistics for a query, you can use the SET STATISTICS TIME ON statement.

4. A, B, C, D. All of the methods can help you obtain the XML showplan for queries.

5. A, B, C. Seek operators are usually better from a performance point of view than scan operators.

6. D. Although you can clean the buffer cache and the plan cache by restarting your server, it is not recommended. A simple method that cleans the data cache and the plan cache is running the CHECKPOINT, DBCC DROPCLEANBUFFERS, and DBCC FREEPROCCACHE commands.

7. A. You can definitely improve the query by adding an index on the ID column.

8. Answers: A, B, D. When the table names are displayed in red, statistics are missing or out of date. You should verify that the AUTO_CREATE_STATISTICS and AUTO_UPDATE_STATISTICS database options are turned ON and you can use the sp_updatestats stored procedure to update the statistics.

9. B. To obtain better performance, you should use a search argument in the WHERE clause. The option A has the filter OrderDate='2001-08-28' that qualifies as a search argument, but it would not count all orders for the specified date. For example an order having the value for the Order-Date column '2001-08-10:30' is not counted. The options C and D don't use search arguments.

10. C. The best option (that also satisfies the requirements) is option C because a search argument is used to limit the results.

11. D. The best option has the WHERE clause WHERE ProductName LIKE 'NET%'. The other options are not equivalent with the original query (options A and C) or do not improve performance (option B).

12. A, B, C. There would be no need for a DISTINCT clause if you specify the join condition between the Orders and Customers table. In addition, there are no requirements to sort the results so you can remove the ORDER BY.

13. A. The best option is to replace the cursor with a SELECT statement.

14. C. The best option is to the filter rows to be updated by using a WHERE clause.

15. A. To obtain statistics about the number of lock requests per second, you have to use the SQLServer:Locks object and the Lock Requests/sec counter.

16. C. Joins can offer better performance than queries in particular cases.

17. A. The best answer in this case is the ADO .NET DataSet.

18. D. MARS allows interleaved execution and it can minimize the number of connection used.

19. B. The ADO .NET DataReader gives you fast access and low memory consumption.

20. A. The best option in this case is a DataSet.

Chapter 8

Optimizing Indexing Strategies

MICROSOFT EXAM OBJECTIVES COVERED IN THIS CHAPTER:

✓ **Optimize indexing strategies.**

- Design an index strategy.
- Analyze index use across an application.
- Add, remove, or redesign indexes.
- Optimize index-to-table-size ratio.

When it comes to performance, indexes can boost performance by a 1,000 factor or more without requiring any change in your application. Imagine searching for a needle in a small box versus the proverbial haystack. Imagine the difference between searching for a teaspoon in a kitchen drawer (in an organized house) versus searching the entire place for it. Indexing information does make a difference whether it is used in books, search engines, or databases.

Though indexes are not necessarily a cure-all, we discuss in this chapter the types of indexes SQL Server 2005 supports, when you should use each type, new features related to indexes, the maintenance tasks indexes require, and more.

Designing an Index Strategy

In the following sections, we cover the whole range of indexes that you can use in SQL Server 2005 and how and when to use them. Chapter 10 continues this topic by explaining when you have too many or too few indexes.

What Are Indexes?

Before we define indexes, we will define a few database concepts:

Database   A collection of tables.

Table   A collection of rows or records.

Page   The fundamental unit of storage for SQL Server with a size of 8KB. Records are stored in pages. Your disk data files are divided logically into pages. All I/O operations are performed at the page level. Consequently, if you need to read or modify a row, the page that contains it is read and loaded completely in memory even though the same page may contain another 99 rows.

Extent   A collection of eight physically contiguous pages. Extents are used for page management. An extent is uniform if all 8 pages of the extent are used by the same object. Otherwise the extent is called mixed.

What Are Pages?

Pages come in a variety of types:

Data pages   Contains data rows.

Index pages   Contains index records, which are defined later.

Text/image pages   Contains LOBs (large object data types): TEXT, NTEXT, IMAGE, NVARCHAR(MAX), VARCHAR(MAX), VARBINARY(MAX), and XML. Also they contain the following data type columns (when the row size exceeds 8K): VARCHAR, NVARCHAR, VARBINARY, and XML.

 The row-overflow feature of SQL Server 2005 allows you rows bigger than 8,060 bytes by storing one or more columns off row.

Global Allocation Map (GAM) pages   Records the allocated extents.

Shared Global Allocation Map (SGAM) pages   Records the mixed extents that have at least a page free.

Page Free Space (PFS) pages   Records information about free space available on pages.

Index Allocation Map (IAM) pages   Holds information about extents allocated to tables or indexes.

To recap, data lives in pages, pages are grouped in extents, and SQL Server uses GAM, SAGM, IAM, and FPS pages to track pages and extents allocation. Pages are used to help you get to your data.

Types of Indexes

The following types of indexes are available in SQL Server 2005:

Clustered   A *clustered index* is a B-tree structure that stores the data rows of a table or view in an order dictated by the clustered index key. The index key consists of one or more columns of the base table. For the clustered index, the leaf pages contain the base table's rows.

Nonclustered   A *nonclustered index* is similar to a clustered one, the difference being the leaf-level pages. In the leaf-level page of a nonclustered index, each row of data contains a subset of the base table's columns (the columns that make the index key and included columns) and a pointer to the actual data row.

Unique   A *unique index* is characterized by an index key with no duplicate values. Clustered and nonclustered indexes can also be unique.

Index with included columns   A nonclustered index can be extended by including nonkey columns in the leaf-level pages of the index; this is called an *index with included columns*.

Indexed views   A view can be materialized by creation of a unique clustered index. Once you've defined the unique clustered index you can also add nonclustered indexes to the view.

Full-text   A *full-text index* is a special type of index used by the Microsoft Full-Text Engine service. It allows complex string searches on character data types.

XML   To improve the performance of interrogations that use the XML data type, SQL Server 2005 comes with two flavors of XML indexes: primary and secondary.

Throughout this chapter you will meet each one of these types.

Heaps, Clustered, and Nonclustered Indexes

To explain the differences among heaps and clustered and nonclustered indexes, we'll use the analogy of a bookstore. Imagine that a new bookstore is about to open in a few months. The bookstore has nothing but empty shelves. You are the one and only salesperson in this shop.

The first book shipment arrives. If you take the books and put them on shelves without being concerned of their title, subject, or category, you will create a *heap*—a table where data is stored in no particular order.

Is this way of storage efficient? On the one hand, yes! You don't have to think where to put each book, and you have a tremendous speed in putting the books wherever there is free space. In a fictional world where a bookstore contains just a single shelf that is also very small, you can put the order of the books from the shelf in your "cache," (that is, your memory). Or, if the bookstore carries just two or three titles, it would be no problem for you to find a book requested by a customer.

On the other hand, most bookstores have many shelves and each title may have multiple copies available, making the "heap" method inefficient for finding a specific book. So unless you have an extraordinary recollection, the cache (your memory) cannot help you too much in finding a book, due to the very large volume of information.

To find efficiently a book, you could organize books by category. For example, shelves 1, 2, and 3 are for art books, shelves 4, 5, 6, and 7 for computer books, and so on, organized like this:

Art books: shelf 1

Art books: shelf 2

Art books: shelf 3

Computer books: shelf 4

Computer books: shelf 5

Computer books: shelf 6

Computer books: shelf 7

If you think of the bookstore as a table, then organizing it using each book's category is like building a *clustered index* for a table. Organizing the books this way makes it very easy to find a book from a specific category.

But what if a customer asks for all books from a certain publisher? You can go from shelf to shelf to find them (and do *table scan* or *clustered index scan*), or you can make your job easier following this method. Each time a new book arrives, after placing it on a shelf, you note in a notebook its location and its publisher. For each publisher, you use a different notebook. The entries in the Wiley's notebook look like this:

Wiley: shelf 4, 5th book

Wiley: shelf 3, 21st book

This method simulates a *nonclustered index*. While you organize books by category, you can also order them in shelves by the book title. What happens if shelves 4 to 7 are filled with computer books and a new book shipment arrives containing more computer books? You have to make room for the new books. Since the shelves are full you have no choice but redistribute a part of the books on new shelves. The computer books would now be stored on shelves 4, 5, 6, 7, and 23 for example.

When you have to locate a computer book you can easily scan the 4, 5, 6, and 7 shelves and then you have to walk to shelf 23. In database terms, this is called *fragmentation*. Leaving the bookstore behind, let's see the actual definitions for heaps and indexes.

Heaps

A heap is a table without a clustered index defined. There is absolutely no order for the stored rows (remember the unorganized shelves). This is what a heap looks like:

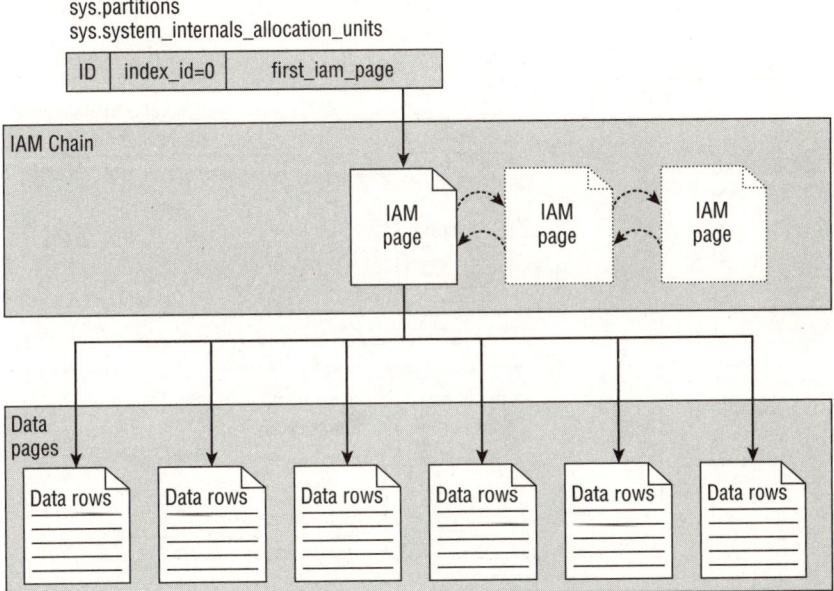

One or more IAM pages track the allocation of data pages. An IAM page covers the allocation of 4GB disk space from a database file. If the table needs more space or uses more files, then it uses more IAM pages. You can find the first IAM page for a table using the sys.system_internals_ allocation_units system view.

If someone submits the following query SELECT * FROM MyTable WHERE MyColumn=MyValue and MyTable is a heap with no indexes defined, the only way to answer to the query is to scan all data pages (a table scan). SQL Server goes to the first IAM pages to find out in which extents the table is stored. If the table has multiple IAM pages, SQL Server goes to the next IAM page in the chain and so on. Add to this hypothetical table a few million rows. It is obvious that this search method is inefficient (that's why we have indexes).

How about the next query SELECT * FROM MyTable ORDER BY MyColumn? The execution plan of the query consisting in a table scan is inefficient especially if the table is large.

Are heaps always poor design choices? No! In several cases heaps can be beneficial. For starters, heaps make very good staging tables. If you import large volumes of data, heaps with no indexes and all constraints disabled are the best choice. Why? Each modification of the base table data generates modifications for all indexes defined on a table. Hence, non-indexed heaps work better than indexed tables for the load operations. Also, you may find heaps useful for small tables or tables that have many duplicate rows.

Clustered Indexes

An index is a B-tree structure. In plain English that means a tree with a root node, optionally intermediate nodes, and leaf nodes. Also *balanced* means that if you start from the root, you will always need the same number of steps (levels) to get to a leaf node. Since an image is worth a thousand words (in this case, approximately three printed pages) take a look at the next illustration:

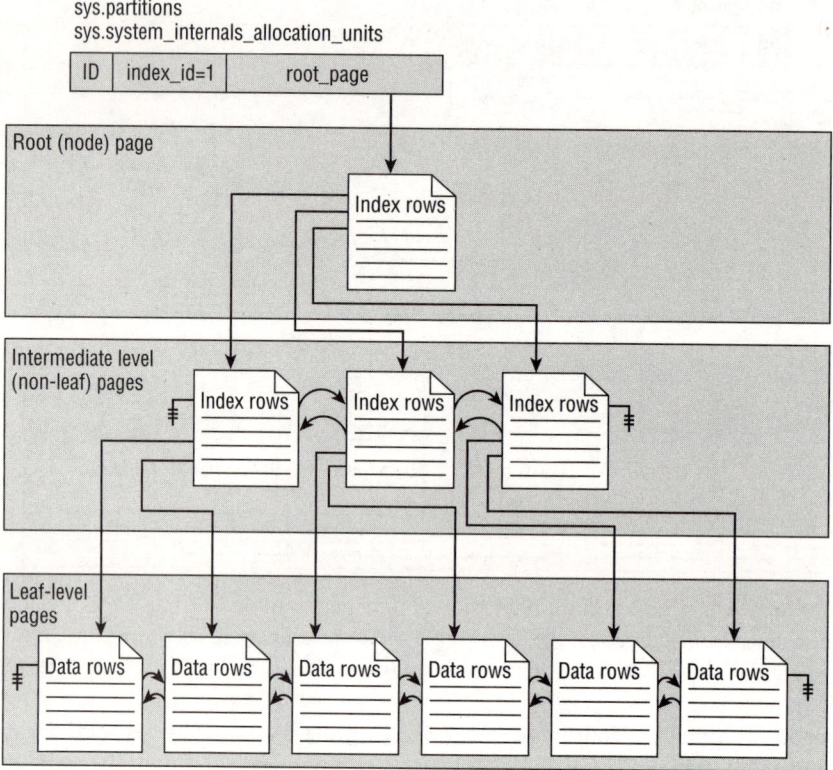

This time instead of a first IAM page, you could find in the sys.system_internals_allocation_ units system view the root page of the index. The root page of the index and the intermediary-level pages contain the index key (made of one or more columns of the base table) and a pointer to a page in the level below. The leaf pages contain the actual data. All pages on the same level except the root page are linked in a doubly linked list (each page containing a reference to the previous and the next page if any).

How can you tell that the index in the picture is a clustered one? The only thing that indicates that is the index_id=1 (clustered indexes always have the ID 1). Otherwise the picture could represent a nonclustered index. The difference between clustered and nonclustered indexes is that at the leaf level the clustered index contains the table's rows whereas the nonclustered index contains rows that have only a subset of the table's columns.

Let's get a closer look by examining the HumanResources.EmployeeAddress table from the AdventureWorks database. The table has four columns, 290 rows, and maps the employees from the HumanResources.Employee table to their address from the Person.Address table. The table columns are:

- EmployeeID int
- AddressID int
- rowguid uniqueidentifier ROWGUIDCOL
- ModifiedDate datetime

The primary key of the table is composed from the columns EmployeeID and AddressID. The same columns are the key columns of the clustered index for the HumanResources.Employee-Address table. SQL Server 2005 creates automatically a unique clustered index for the primary key constraints. Making the columns EmployeeID and AddressID the index keys means that the data is sorted using the values of these columns. The next illustration shows the actual content of the table.

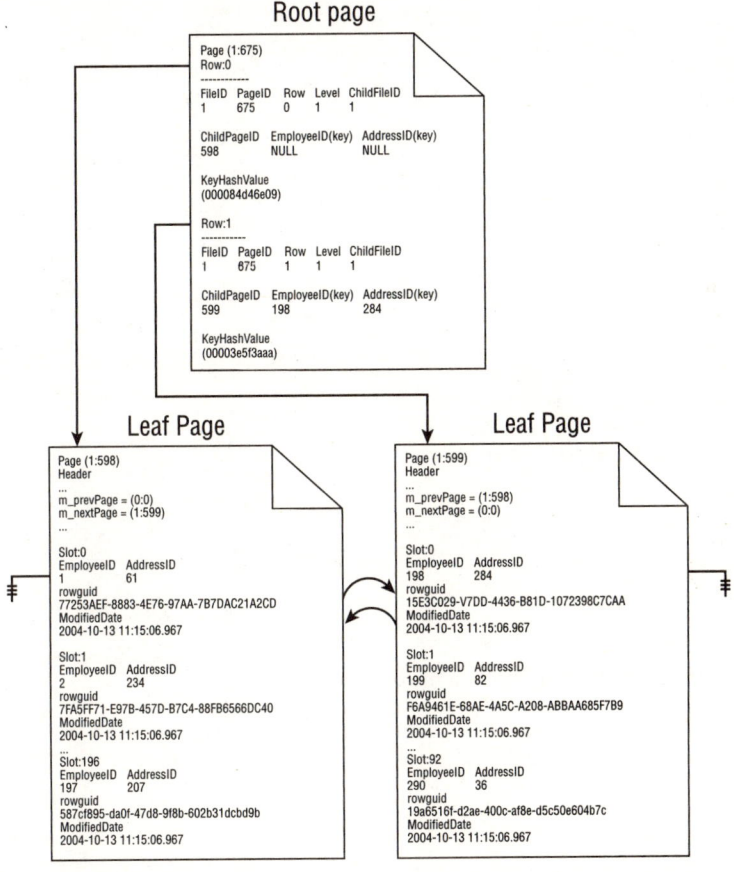

You can see that the index has a root page and two data pages. An index is built starting with the leaf-level pages. Then, the nonleaf pages are built, and the nonleaf pages contain the index key and a pointer to a page in the level below. In this case, we have just two leaf-level pages and a root page containing two rows.

Why is this structure better than a heap? If you search for a row having the EmployeeID 199, the SQL Server goes to the root page of the index and finds out that all employees with an ID greater than 198 are stored in page 599. It then reads page 599 and finds the requested row. Only two pages were necessary to find the row. You may say, "all right but the whole table has two pages" and you would be right. But, imagine that you have 4 million rows instead of 290. For 4 million rows SQL Server will read three pages maximum to find the record (the index can have a root page and an intermediary level). Comparing 3 pages with the number of pages necessary to hold 4 million rows (roughly 4,000,000 x 8,096 / row_size_in_bytes) you can easily see that there is indeed a difference. If you want to test it, try the next code. You will create a simple table having a PRIMARY KEY constraint. SQL Server automatically creates a unique clustered index to enforce the constraint:

```
USE tempdb;
GO
CREATE TABLE T(
ID INT NOT NULL PRIMARY KEY,
COL CHAR(7) NOT NULL);
GO
SET NOCOUNT ON;
GO
DECLARE @I INT;
SET @I=1;
WHILE @I<=4000000
BEGIN
  INSERT INTO T(ID,COL)
  VALUES(@I,CAST(@I AS CHAR(7)));
  SET @I=@I+1;
END
GO
SET NOCOUNT OFF;
GO
```

Then to get index information run the next code:

```
SELECT
index_level,
page_count,
record_count
FROM sys.dm_db_index_physical_stats(
DB_ID(N'tempdb'),OBJECT_ID('T'),1,
DEFAULT,'DETAILED');
```

The output is self-explanatory; the index has three levels (the leaf level, an intermediary level, and a root page):

```
--Output:
index_level page_count record_count
----------- ---------- ------------
0               9901      4000000
1                 36         9901
2                  1           36
```

Now to prove that a query seeking a specific value uses a very small number of pages, run the following:

```
SET STATISTICS IO ON;
GO
SELECT * FROM T WHERE ID=2345678;
GO
SET STATISTICS IO OFF;
GO
```

The output in the messages window shows that SQL Server needed only three pages:

```
-- Output
Table 'T'. Scan count 0, logical reads 3, physical reads 0,
read-ahead reads 0, lob logical reads 0, lob physical reads 0,
lob read-ahead reads 0.
```

SQL Server used an *index seek* instead of a *table scan*.

Now what would you use a clustered index for? Well, among other things, all nonclustered indexes use the clustered index key. We'll get back soon to the clustered index key, but for now you should know that the clustered index is appropriate for the queries that use the base table the most, such as:

- Queries that return a range of values using BETWEEN, >, >=, <, and <= operators. The data in the clustered index is already sorted by the clustered key so SQL Server has to find the page for first value indicated by the range and then read all pages in sequence until the end of the range value is reached. Remember that the pages of an index are linked—each page having a reference to the previous and the next page.

- Queries that return large result sets. Having a clustered index on table can help you reduce external fragmentation. More about this later.

- Queries that use JOIN clauses. The clustered index is typically defined on the columns that make the primary key of a table.

- Queries that use ORDER BY or GROUP BY clauses. A clustered index on the columns specified by the ORDER BY or GROUP BY columns removes the need to sort the returned data since the rows of the clustered index are already sorted.

Choosing a clustered index key is a very important decision so we dedicated the next topic to discussion the factors involved.

What Makes a Good Clustered Index?

When you design a clustered index, you should keep several aspects in mind. The clustered index should occupy the minimum amount of disk space possible. After all, it is the largest index for a table (since it includes all the table's columns) and the less space it consumes the better I/O performance you'll get. Also less space means easier maintenance. At some point all the read-write data needs maintenance (backup, defragmentation or restore).

The second aspect you should consider is that the clustered index key is used by all the non-clustered indexes of your table. So ideally this key should not be large or modified often.

Third, the clustered index is the most expensive from a maintenance point of view as it is the largest index so you should minimize the necessity of maintenance by reducing for example page splits (that cause fragmentation).

Finally, decide whether you need online operations for your clustered index or for your table. If the application is a 24/7 one, then you may not have time allocated for maintenance. In this, case you need online index operations such as online index rebuild. If your clustered index contains LOB data type columns, your clustered index cannot be rebuilt online.

Using these factors, you can extract the following characteristics for a good clustered index key:

Narrow   A narrow key minimizes the space occupied and the memory usage for the clustered index as well as for all nonclustered indexes of the table.

Unique   If the clustered index key contains duplicate values, SQL Server adds a 4-byte integer (a uniquifier) to make the duplicate values distinct. That means that duplicate values waste space.

Static   Ideally the clustered index key is not modified. Each modification of the clustered index key is reflected by all nonclustered indexes. And worse than that it may cause the move of the underlying record. Take for example using a LastName column as a clustered index key. If the name changes from Jones to Duncan (for example, in the case of marriage or divorce), then the row should be moved to maintain the index order.

Ever-increasing pattern   A clustered index key with a value that follows an ever-increasing pattern would not cause page splits for INSERT operations because new rows will be added at the end of the table.

Now you have some rules for deciding whether or not clustering your index key is good. These are some of the most encountered cases:

IDENTITY column   A column having the IDENTITY property is one of the best options you can have. It is narrow, static, unique, and ever increasing. If the column is also the PRIMARY KEY of the table (we recommend that), you have the perfect combination. Also you can use the IDENTITY and DATETIME combination.

GUID (globally unique identifier) column   We recommend you avoid selecting a GUID (globally unique identifier) column as the key of your clustered index. Though it is unique, it is not as narrow as an INT data type column but, even worse, this data type generates fragmentation. If you really need a unique identifier use it, but use another choice for the clustered index key.

If you really need to build a clustered index on this type of column, use the NEWSEQUEN-TIALID() function to generate the unique identifier's values. Unlike the values generated by the NEWID() function that are completely random, the values generated by the NEWS-EQUENTIALID function are just like the name says—sequential.

LastName column A clustered index on a LastName or FirstName column is a poor choice for many reasons. It fails all of the four rules that characterize a good clustered index key. It is not unique, it is wide, it is not static, and obviously it is not ever increasing and can generate fragmentation.

For now let's move on to nonclustered indexes.

Nonclustered Indexes

The nonclustered index has a similar structure as the clustered index, as you can see here:

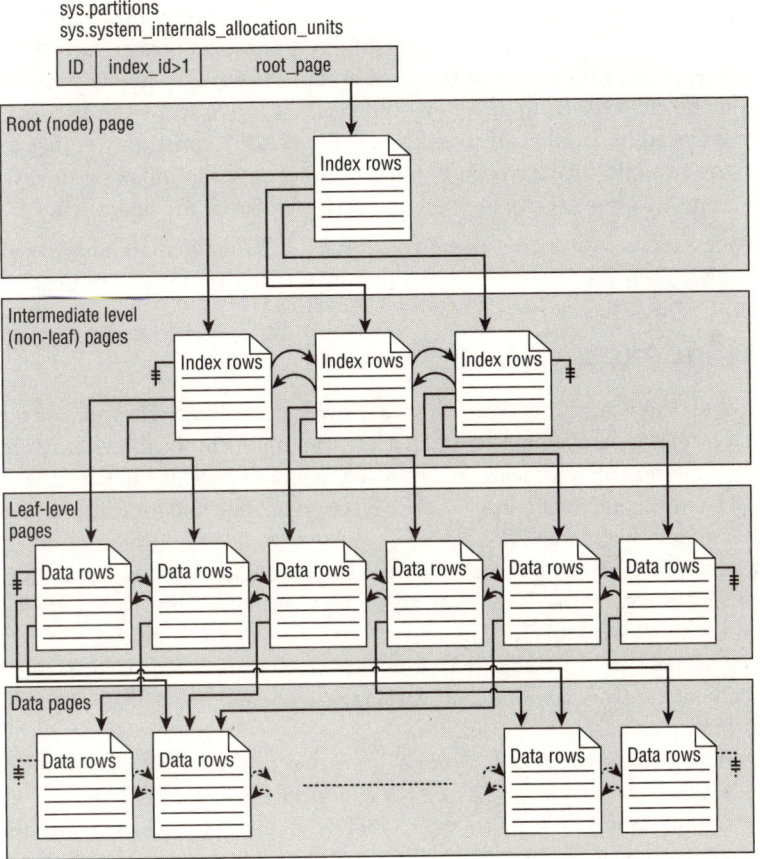

If your database contains a table having the columns COL1, COL2, COL3, and a clustered index on COL1 and you define a nonclustered index on COL2, the resulting index is similar to a clustered index on column COL2 for a table that has only two columns (COL2 and COL1).

One major difference between clustered and nonclustered indexes is at the leaf-level pages. For nonclustered indexes at the leaf level you will find the index key columns, a pointer to the actual rows (to a heap or if the table has a clustered index to the clustered index data rows), and optionally nonkey columns. Another difference between the two types is that the nonclustered index is a smaller copy of data and not the actual data as it is for the clustered index.

Why would you use nonclustered indexes? First, they are smaller than the base table or the clustered index of the table. Second, you might use nonclustered indexes for the following reasons:

- To cover queries. An index covers a query when all the columns requested by the query can be found in the index. As the nonclustered index is smaller than its underlying table, a covering index will use less I/O this way, improving performance.

- To improve JOIN queries by manually indexing columns participating in the JOIN. There is a misconception that states that SQL Server creates indexes on foreign keys automatically. It doesn't and it never did. You should put indexes on foreign keys for multiple reasons, such as to improve performance of join queries and to improve performance of queries that delete rows from the referenced table. When SQL Server deletes a row from a table referenced by another (through a FOREIGN KEY constraint), it has to check whether any rows (in the referencing) reference that row. An index on the FOREIGN KEY column (or columns) can increase the performance of the operation.

- To improve queries with search arguments (SARGs). We talked about SARGs in the previous chapter. They represent filters used by the queries to limit the returned result sets.

Full-Text Indexes

When you have to search large text data columns for specific words or phrases, you may find the full-text search feature to be the right solution. The main argument for this choice is the performance benefit of full-text search versus regular string functions such as LIKE, CHARINDEX, or PATINDEX. The string functions perform very well on small data and for character patterns, but for very large data full-text search is better.

The full-text search is based on the Microsoft Full-Text Engine for SQL Server (MSFTESQL) service that can index not just the documents stored in your database but also external documents from Word to Exchange mailboxes.

Full-text queries use a full-text index that stores information about words for a specific column. The column can be char, varchar, nvarchar, varbinary(max), and image. Full-text indexes are grouped in full-text catalogs.

The last things you need to know for your exam is that full-text queries use four predicates: *CONTAINS, CONTAINSTABLE, FREETEXT,* and *FREETEXTTABLE.*

The next example shows how to use the CONTAINS predicate starting with the assumption that a full-text index on the Production.ProductDescription table of the AdventureWorks database is already defined. You can use the CONTAINS predicate to search all rows of this table that contain the word "competition":

```
USE AdventureWorks;
GO
SELECT
[Description]
FROM Production.ProductDescription
WHERE CONTAINS(Description, N'competition');
```

The query returns just two rows:

```
-- Output (partial)
Description
----------------------------------------------------------------
Serious back-country riding. Perfect for all levels of competition...
Top-of-the-line competition mountain bike. Performance-enhancing ...
```

The full-text index on the table can be created by right-clicking the name of the table in SQL Server Management Studio—Object Explorer and using the full-text index wizard (accessible from the context menu).

 For more information about full-text searches, please refer to the "Full-Text Search Concepts" topic from Books Online.

XML Indexes

The XML type columns are stored on your disk in a binary format and can have up to 2GB size. If you interrogate an XML column, the binary objects (that make the values for the column) are shredded (or parsed) at run time. To avoid the performance penalty imposed by the shredding operation, you can use XML indexes. There are two categories of XML indexes:

- Primary XML index
- Secondary XML index

Primary XML Indexes

A *primary XML index* is a persisted B-tree representation of an XML data type column. The index associates the primary key of the base table with the nodes of the XML instances. The rows of the index store the node tag name, node value, node type, the path from the node to the root of the XML instance, and the primary key of the base table.

Most queries that interrogate the underlying XML column use the primary XML index, unless the query requires explicitly the full XML instance.

The next example shows the syntax for creating a primary XML index:

```
USE tempdb;
GO
-- Create a table
CREATE TABLE MyTable(
MyID INT IDENTITY(1,1) NOT NULL PRIMARY KEY,
XmlCol XML);
GO
-- Insert demo data
INSERT INTO MyTable(XmlCol) VALUES(
'<booklist>
  <book name="70-442 Study Guide" bookid="1"/>
  <book name="70-431 Study Guide" bookid="2"/>
</booklist>');
INSERT INTO MyTable(XmlCol) VALUES(
'<booklist>
  <book name="70-441 Study Guide" bookid="3"/>
  <book name="70-443 Study Guide" bookid="4"/>
</booklist>');
GO
-- Create a primary XML index
CREATE PRIMARY XML INDEX PXML_MyTable_XmlCol
ON MyTable(XmlCol);
```

Secondary XML Indexes

To improve the performance of queries targeting the XML columns, once you have defined a primary XML index, you can create *secondary XML indexes*. There are three types of secondary XML indexes:

- PATH secondary XML index
- VALUE secondary XML index
- PROPERTY secondary XML index

PATH secondary XML indexes improve the performance of queries that use XQUERY path expressions. The following example gives you an idea of such a query:

```
SELECT
MyID
FROM MyTable
WHERE XmlCol.exist('/booklist/book[@bookid="1"]')=1;
```

The query returns the row IDs for the rows that contain books with the bookid value 1, in this case a single row:

```
-- Output:
MyID
------
1
```

To make the query more efficient, you can create a secondary XML index using this code:

```
CREATE XML INDEX IXML_MyTable_XmlCol_Path
ON MyTable(XmlCol)
USING XML INDEX PXML_MyTable_XmlCol FOR PATH;
```

Likewise, you can define VALUE secondary indexes for value-based queries such as the next one:

```
SELECT
MyID
FROM MyTable
WHERE XmlCol.exist('//book[@*="4"]')=1;
-- Output
MyID
------
2
```

The query returns the row IDs for all rows that have any of the attributes of a book element equal to 4. Only the second row qualifies because it has a book element with the bookid equal to 4.

The above query may benefit from the following secondary XML index:

```
CREATE XML INDEX IXML_MyTable_XmlCol_Value
ON MyTable(XmlCol)
USING XML INDEX PXML_MyTable_XmlCol FOR VALUE;
```

Finally, queries that retrieve values from XML instances can be improved using PROPERTY secondary XML indexes such as the next one:

```
CREATE XML INDEX IXML_MyTable_XmlCol_Property
ON MyTable(XmlCol)
USING XML INDEX PXML_MyTable_XmlCol FOR PROPERTY;
```

A query that can use the IXML_MyTable_XmlCol_Property index is:

```
SELECT
XmlCol.value('(/booklist/book/@name)[2]','VARCHAR(50)')
AS BookName
```

```
FROM MyTable
WHERE MyID=1;
-- Output
BookName
-------------------
70-431 Study Guide
```

As you may guess, the query returns the value of the name attribute for the second book element of the XML instance that is stored in the XmlCol column for the row with the ID 1.

Chances are that the Query Processor would choose VALUE secondary indexes more often than PROPERTY or PATH indexes. However, you can force the use of a specific index using query hints.

We recommend you use XML indexes when you use XML data type methods such as value(), exist(), query(), and modify(). Just by creating a primary XML index, you can boost the performance of your XML based queries by 80 percent. Secondary indexes can improve the performance up to 1,000 percent. So if you query very large tables containing XML columns and your queries target them, you should consider XML indexes.

Indexes on Computed Columns

A *computed column* is a virtual column detained as an expression that can include noncomputed column names, constant values, functions, variables, or any combination of these connected by operators.

An example of a computed column is the TotalDue column of the Sales.SalesOrderHeader table from the Adventure Works sample database. The partial definition of the Sales.SalesOrderHeader table follows:

```
CREATE TABLE Sales.SalesOrderHeader(
...
SubTotal MONEY NOT NULL,
TaxAmt MONEY NOT NULL,
Freight MONEY NOT NULL,
TotalDue AS SubTotal + TaxAmt + Freight
...
);
```

In SQL Server 2005 you can physically store computed columns on a disk by marking them as PERSISTED. From an indexing perspective you can index computed columns to obtain better performance for special types of queries (queries that use the computed column).

In the previous chapter you saw that the query optimizer selects a query plan considering, among other things, the cardinality (the number of rows processed) of your queries constructs. Cardinality is primarily determined using statistics. In some cases, cardinalities cannot be calculated accurately, hence poor query plans are selected.

Two particular types of queries may generate poor cardinality estimates:

- Queries that use operators connecting two or more columns of the same table:

```
SELECT COUNT(*) FROM HumanResources.Employee
WHERE VacationHours<SickLeaveHours;
GO
```

- Queries that use functions with any arguments other than constant values:

```
SELECT COUNT(*) FROM HumanResources.Employee
WHERE MONTH(HireDate)=12;
```

A simple redesign of the table and of the query can solve the performance problem. For example, the first query can be improved with the following code:

```
ALTER TABLE HumanResources.Employee
ADD SVDifference AS SickLeaveHours-VacationHours;
GO
CREATE INDEX IX_Employee_SVDifference
ON HumanResources.Employee(SVDifference);
GO
-- The modified query
SELECT COUNT(*) FROM HumanResources.Employee
WHERE SVDifference>0;
GO
```

The second one can use a similar approach:

```
ALTER TABLE HumanResources.Employee
ADD MonthHireDate AS MONTH(HireDate);
GO
CREATE INDEX IX_Employee_MonthHireDate
ON HumanResources.Employee(MonthHireDate);
GO
SELECT COUNT(*) FROM HumanResources.Employee
WHERE MonthHireDate=12;
```

To test them, you can run both versions at the same time, including the actual execution plan:

```
SET STATISTICS IO ON
GO
SELECT COUNT(*) FROM HumanResources.Employee
WHERE VacationHours<SickLeaveHours;
GO
SELECT COUNT(*) FROM HumanResources.Employee
```

```
WHERE SVDifference>0;
GO
SET STATISTICS IO OFF
GO
```

In the Messages tab, the output should be similar to the next one:

```
(1 row(s) affected)
Table 'Employee'. Scan count 1, logical reads 9, physical reads 1,
 read-ahead reads 7, lob logical reads 0, lob physical reads 0,
lob read-ahead reads 0.


(1 row(s) affected)
Table 'Employee'. Scan count 1, logical reads 2, physical reads 1,
 read-ahead reads 0, lob logical reads 0, lob physical reads 0,
lob read-ahead reads 0.
```

In the actual execution plan you should see the improvement:

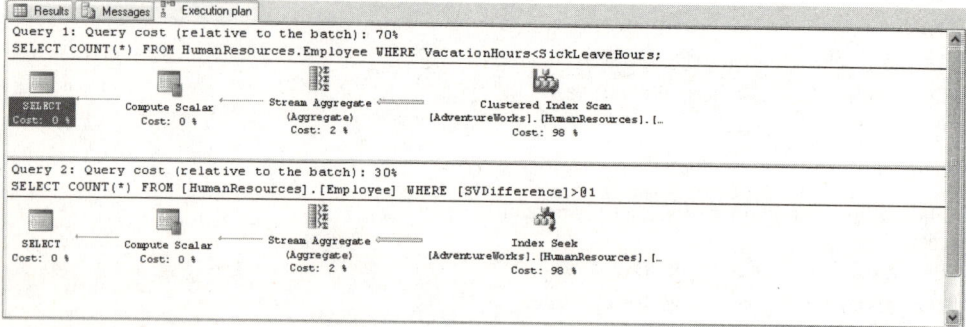

The new version is twice as good as the old one judging by its cost alone. For the second query, the test follows the same method:

```
SET STATISTICS IO ON
GO
SELECT COUNT(*) FROM HumanResources.Employee
WHERE MONTH(HireDate)=12;


SELECT COUNT(*) FROM HumanResources.Employee
WHERE MonthHireDate=12;
GO
SET STATISTICS IO OFF
GO
```

The output in the Messages tab should surprise you:

```
(1 row(s) affected)
Table 'Employee'. Scan count 1, logical reads 2, physical reads 1,
read-ahead reads 0, lob logical reads 0, lob physical reads 0,
lob read-ahead reads 0.


(1 row(s) affected)
Table 'Employee'. Scan count 1, logical reads 2, physical reads 0,
read-ahead reads 0, lob logical reads 0, lob physical reads 0,
lob read-ahead reads 0.
```

The queries are identical from a performance point of view. If you look at the query plan, you will see that this time the query optimizer managed to use the same index for both queries—namely the INDEX IX_Employee_MonthHireDate index that you've just created.

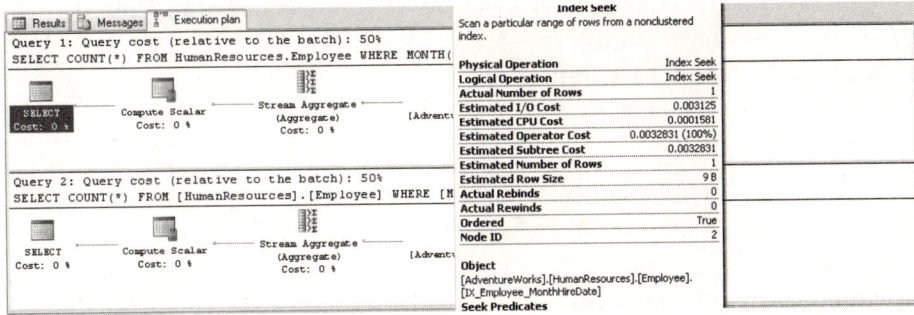

The explanation comes from Books Online:

> SQL Server 2005 sometimes evaluates expressions in queries sooner than when they are evaluated in SQL Server 2000. This behavior provides the following important benefits: The ability to match indexes on computed columns to expressions in a query that are the same as the computed column expression.

You just saw that in our case, which is just another argument for creating indexes on computed columns. However, you should consider the overhead added to data modifications by any type of index.

Indexes with Included Columns

One of the new features of SQL Server 2005, an index with included columns, is a nonclustered index that has nonkey columns in the leaf level. The main advantage of this type of index is improved query coverage.

An index covers a query when it contains all the columns referenced by the query.

Reading a nonclustered index is better from a performance perspective than reading the underlying table because the nonclustered index is usually smaller. Indexes with included columns override some limitations of nonclustered indexes:

- The maximum index key size is 900 bytes - the size of included columns is not counted.

  For example, if you need an index on the columns LastName, FirstName, and Resume of a table Persons, such as the following:

```
CREATE TABLE Person(
PersonID INT NOT NULL,
DepartmentID INT,
LastName NVARCHAR(30),
FirstName NVARCHAR(30),
Resume NVARCHAR(512));
```

  you simply can't do it in SQL Server 2000. The maximum size of the three columns is (30 + 30 + 512)*2=1,144, which is greater than 900. However, you can define the index in SQL Server 2005 as:

```
CREATE INDEX IX_Person_Name_Resume
ON Person(LastName,FirstName)
INCLUDE(Resume);
```

- Only 16 columns can be included in a composite index key—using indexes with included columns you can use up to 1,023 nonkey columns in a nonclustered index.
- Large object (LOB) data types are not allowed as key columns for an index—indexes with included columns can include LOB columns with the exception of TEXT, NTEXT, and IMAGE columns.

There is one more fact we want you to consider: indexes with included columns allow you to redesign existing nonclustered indexes and make them more efficient by limiting the index key to the columns used for lookups or searching. For example, consider an index that can cover this query adapted from Books Online:

```
SELECT
AddressLine1,AddressLine2,PostalCode
FROM Person.Address
WHERE PostalCode BETWEEN '95000' AND '99860'
```

You can use this index:

```
CREATE INDEX IX_Address_PostalCode
ON Person.Address(PostalCode,AddressLine1,AddressLine2);
```

but the next one is better:

```
CREATE INDEX IX_Address_PostalCode
ON Person.Address(PostalCode)
INCLUDE(AddressLine1,AddressLine2);
```

Indexed Views

A *view* is simply a stored SELECT statement's definition. Just like stored procedures, views add a layer of encapsulation to your application. You can expose your data through views and stored procedures, improving security and maintainability for applications.

In terms of performance, interrogating a view does not give better performance than running the underlying SELECT statement. Enter the indexed views. An indexed view is a materialized view through a unique clustered index.

The primary reason for creating an indexed view is to increase query performance. You would be surprised to notice that the query optimizer can use indexed views even when they are not referenced directly in the FROM clause of your queries.

Now, why a unique clustered index and not just a regular clustered index? As you may guess, when the rows of the view's underlying tables are modified, the modifications are reflected in the indexed view. Since the clustered index of the indexed view is unique, the rows that have to be modified (to reflect the changes of the base tables) are more efficiently found.

Why would you consider indexed views over regular indexes? One reason could be that indexed views offer more freedom in expression. For example, you can create an indexed view on the following query:

```
SELECT
ProductID,
SUM(OrderQty) As TotalQty
FROM Sales.SalesOrderDetail
GROUP BY ProductID;
```

The query returns all products from the Sales.SalesOrderDetail table and the sum of the ordered quantity for each product. You can create an index to support this query but an indexed view would give you better performance due to the aggregate function presence.

The downside of an indexed view, just like for any other index, is the overhead generated for data modifications.

Consider using indexed views in the following situations:

- Queries that include joins and aggregations, and process many rows.

- Queries that include joins and aggregations frequently used by other queries.

- Decision support queries, queries that need summarized and aggregated data, and when the underlying data is infrequently updated.

There are cases when the cost of an indexed view is higher than the benefit or when indexed views don't bring any performance value:

- OLTP systems with high volumes of new records and modifications.

- Queries without joins and aggregations.

- Aggregations of data where the cardinality of the GROUP BY key is very high—that means many different values for the column (or columns) used in the GROUP BY clause.

An indexed view improves performance when the volume of data read is far less than reading directly the base tables.

- Expanding joins. Views with result sets larger than the data of the underlying tables usually don't benefit from indexing.

If you decide that an indexed view can help you, before you create the indexed view, you have several requirements to consider:

- The view should reference only base tables and not other views.

- All referenced base tables need to have the same owner as the view and they must be in the same database as the view.

- Specify the SCHEMABINDING option in the view definition, to prevent the modification of schema for the referenced base tables.

- If you use aggregate functions inside your view definition, include the COUNT_BIG(*) expression in the SELECT list.

- All tables and functions from your view definition must be referenced using a two-part naming scheme. One-part, three-part, and four-part names are not permitted.

NOTE   To see the complete list of requirements, please refer to the "Creating Indexed Views" topic in Books Online.

Before you create a view make sure that you follow these steps:

1. Ensure that the tables referred by the view have the value ON for these SET options:
   - ANSI_NULLS
   - ANSI_PADDING
   - ANSI_WARNINGS
   - ARITHABORT
   - CONCAT_NULL_YIELDS_NULL
   - QUOTED_IDENTIFIER

   And the NUMERIC_ROUND_ABORT option set to OFF.

2. Verify the same SET option values specified in the step 1 for the session that creates the view.

3. Verify that the definition of your view is deterministic.

4. Include the WITH SCHEMABINDING option in your view's definition to make sure that the underlying objects will not change.

Here's a practical example. Let's suppose that you want to improve the performance of the following query:

```
USE AdventureWorks;
GO
SELECT
```

```
ProductID,
SUM(OrderQty) As TotalQty
FROM Sales.SalesOrderDetail
GROUP BY ProductID;
```

One way to do that is by creating an indexed view:

```
USE AdventureWorks;
GO
--Set the options to support indexed views.
SET NUMERIC_ROUNDABORT OFF;
SET ANSI_PADDING, ANSI_WARNINGS,
 CONCAT_NULL_YIELDS_NULL, ARITHABORT,
 QUOTED_IDENTIFIER, ANSI_NULLS ON;
GO
CREATE VIEW Sales.vTotalQtyPerProduct
WITH SCHEMABINDING
AS
SELECT
 ProductID,
 SUM(OrderQty) As TotalQty,
 COUNT_BIG(*) AS NmbOfRecords
 FROM Sales.SalesOrderDetail
 GROUP BY ProductID
GO
--Create an index on the view.
CREATE UNIQUE CLUSTERED INDEX IDX_vTotalQtyPerProduct
    ON Sales.vTotalQtyPerProduct (ProductID);
GO
```

What have you done? You have set the options required to create an indexed view, and created the view and then a unique clustered index. The COUNT_BIG(*) is required (if you want to index the view) because we used aggregate functions.

The next step is to test the performance improvement, if any. For that you will clear the cache and run the original query two times. The first time use hints that disallow the use of indexed views and the second time let the query optimizer make its own choice. You can use the EXPAND VIEWS query hint to prevent query optimizer from using indexed views. Conversely, you can use the NOEXPAND query hint to allow the query optimizer to consider any index defined on the view.

For more information about query hints related to index views refer to the "Resolving Indexes on Views" topic from Books Online.

To see the difference between the two include the actual execution plan:

```
CHECKPOINT;
DBCC FREEPROCCACHE WITH NO_INFOMSGS;
DBCC DROPCLEANBUFFERS WITH NO_INFOMSGS;
GO
SET STATISTICS IO ON
GO
USE AdventureWorks;
GO
-- Disallow use of views
SELECT
ProductID,
SUM(OrderQty) As TotalQty
FROM Sales.SalesOrderDetail
GROUP BY ProductID OPTION(EXPAND VIEWS);
-- No restriction
SELECT
ProductID,
SUM(OrderQty) As TotalQty
FROM Sales.SalesOrderDetail
GROUP BY ProductID;
GO
SET STATISTICS IO OFF
GO
```

The previous code works on Enterprise or Developer editions of SQL Server 2005. If you use another edition, replace the last query with this one:

```
SELECT
ProductID,
TotalQty
FROM Sales.vTotalQtyPerProduct WITH(NOEXPAND);
GO
```

On the Messages tab you should have the following output:

```
(266 row(s) affected)
Table 'Worktable'. Scan count 0, logical reads 0,
physical reads 0, read-ahead reads 0, lob logical reads 0,
lob physical reads 0, lob read-ahead reads 0.
Table 'SalesOrderDetail'. Scan count 1, logical reads 1241,
```

```
physical reads 3, read-ahead reads 1251, lob logical reads 0,
lob physical reads 0, lob read-ahead reads 0.

(266 row(s) affected)
Table 'vTotalQtyPerProduct'. Scan count 1, logical reads 2,
physical reads 1, read-ahead reads 0, lob logical reads 0,
lob physical reads 0, lob read-ahead reads 0.
```

The number of logical reads (and read-ahead reads) shows the clear difference between ignoring the indexed view and using it. Also the execution plan should tell you that the cost of the first query is 100 percent and for the second one 0.

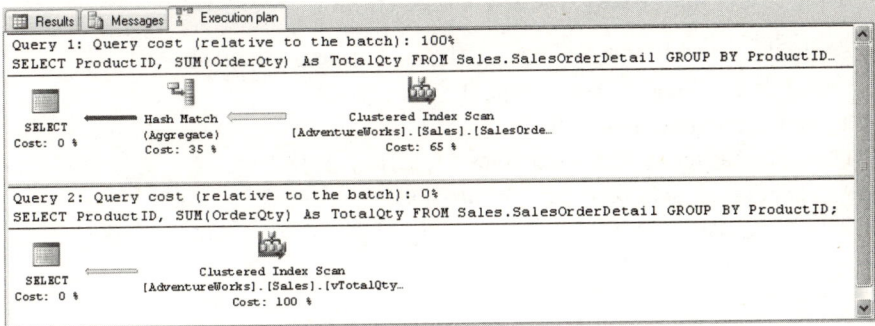

Index Limits

If you ever had to answer the question "How many indexes do I need for my tables," what would you say? The correct answer is it depends. For online transaction processing (OLTP) applications, very rarely you would add more than four or five indexes on single table. Remember that each index must be updated every time your data is modified. At the opposite pole, the Decision Support System databases (where data is seldom updated) are usually heavily indexed.

The more indexes you have, the more queries you can cover and some would say that for the number of indexes, the sky is the limit. Is this true? Well, not quite. You should add only the indexes you really need, and you should be aware that SQL Server has its own limits such as:

- One clustered index per table.

- A maximum of 249 nonclustered indexes for each table.

- The same number, 249, is the maximum number of XML indexes per table.

- Maximum 16 columns make the index key of a composite index. If you have a primary XML index on your table, the clustered index for that table is limited to 15 columns.

- Maximum 900 bytes for the size of an index key except XML indexes.

Are these enough? We would say yes, or it should be.

Creating and Maintaining Indexes

This section deals with index creation, modification, and maintenance as well as with obtaining information about existing indexes.

Creating Indexes

You can create an index using the Object Explorer of SQL Server Management Studio and programmatically through the CREATE INDEX statement. Both methods offer the same functionality and flexibility.

The partial syntax for the CREATE INDEX statement is as follows:

```
CREATE [ UNIQUE ] [ CLUSTERED | NONCLUSTERED ] INDEX index_name
    ON <object> ( column [ ASC | DESC ] [ ,...n ] )
    [ INCLUDE ( column_name [ ,...n ] ) ]
    [ WITH ( <relational_index_option> [ ,...n ] ) ]
    [ ON { partition_scheme_name ( column_name )
        | filegroup_name
        | default
        }
    ]
[ ; ]


<object> ::=
{
    [ database_name. [ schema_name ] . | schema_name. ]
        table_or_view_name
}


<relational_index_option> ::=
{
    PAD_INDEX  = { ON | OFF }
  | FILLFACTOR = fillfactor
  | SORT_IN_TEMPDB = { ON | OFF }
  | IGNORE_DUP_KEY = { ON | OFF }
  | STATISTICS_NORECOMPUTE = { ON | OFF }
  | DROP_EXISTING = { ON | OFF }
  | ONLINE = { ON | OFF }
  | ALLOW_ROW_LOCKS = { ON | OFF }
  | ALLOW_PAGE_LOCKS = { ON | OFF }
  | MAXDOP = max_degree_of_parallelism
}
```

You have to specify first the index type: CLUSTERED, NONCLUSTERED, and optionally UNIQUE. The default index type is NONCLUSTERED. Then you need to supply an index name and the base table (or view) name. Next, you have to indicate the index key columns and their sort order.

For a nonclustered index, you can specify a list with columns that will be added to the leaf level of the index. You can also specify a partitioning scheme for the index as well as the filegroup where the index will be created.

You can use several relational options when you create the index (the default values are underlined):

- PAD_INDEX = {ON|OFF} allows you to leave free space in the intermediary-level pages of an index. When set to ON, the intermediary-level pages of the index are filled using the percentage value specified by the FILLFACTOR argument.

- FILLFACTOR specifies how full the leaf-level pages of the index should be. If the PAD_INDEX is ON, the same value is used for intermediary-level pages of the index.

- SORT_IN_TEMPDB={ON|OFF} allows you to use tempdb for building the index.

- IGNORE_DUP_KEY={ON|OFF} is used for unique indexes; the setting determines the behavior of SQL Server when you try to insert rows with duplicate keys. When ON, only the inserted rows within an INSERT operation that violates the unique index fail. When OFF, the entire INSERT operation fails. The setting applies to INSERT operations occurring after the index is created or rebuilt.

- STATISTICS_NORECOMPUTE= {ON|OFF} specifies whether the statistics for the index are automatically updated (OFF) or not (ON).

- DROP_EXISTING= {ON|OFF} determines whether the index should be dropped and rebuilt if the specified index already exists.

- ONLINE= {ON|OFF} determines if the index operation is ONLINE or OFFLINE. ONLINE means that the underlying tables and associated indexes are still available for querying during the index operation.

- ALLOW_ROW_LOCKS= {ON|OFF} determines whether row locks are allowed (ON) or not (OFF) when accessing the index.

- ALLOW_PAGE_LOCKS= {ON|OFF} specifies whether page level locks are allowed when accessing the index.

- MAXDOP specifies the number of processors that can be used by the index operation.

Besides the CREATE INDEX statement and New index window of SQL Server Management Studio there is another method, somewhat indirect, to create indexes. The method consists of defining a PRIMARY KEY or UNIQUE constraint. By default SQL Server creates automatically a unique clustered index to enforce the PRIMARY KEY constraint and a unique nonclustered index for a unique constraint.

For example, the following statement creates a unique clustered index on MyID column:

```
CREATE TABLE MyTable(
MyID INT NOT NULL PRIMARY KEY,
Val VARCHAR(50));
```

Modifying Indexes

To modify the properties of an index, you can use the Index Properties window of SQL Server Management Studio (right-click an index and choose Properties) or the ALTER INDEX statement.

Here is the syntax:

```
ALTER INDEX { index_name | ALL }
    ON <object>
    { REBUILD
        [ [ WITH ( <rebuild_index_option> [ ,...n ] ) ]
          | ...
            ]
        ]
    | DISABLE
    | REORGANIZE ...
    | SET ( <set_index_option> [ ,...n ] )
    }
[ ; ]


<rebuild_index_option > ::=
{
    PAD_INDEX  = { ON | OFF }
  | FILLFACTOR = fillfactor
  | SORT_IN_TEMPDB = { ON | OFF }
  | IGNORE_DUP_KEY = { ON | OFF }
  | STATISTICS_NORECOMPUTE = { ON | OFF }
  | ONLINE = { ON | OFF }
  | ALLOW_ROW_LOCKS = { ON | OFF }
  | ALLOW_PAGE_LOCKS = { ON | OFF }
  | MAXDOP = max_degree_of_parallelism
}


<set_index_option>::=
{
    ALLOW_ROW_LOCKS= { ON | OFF }
  | ALLOW_PAGE_LOCKS = { ON | OFF }
  | IGNORE_DUP_KEY = { ON | OFF }
  | STATISTICS_NORECOMPUTE = { ON | OFF }
}
```

You can modify all indexes of a table with a single operation. Also you can *rebuild indexes* and *reorganize indexes* (via the REBUILD and REORGANIZE options) to reduce fragmentation of your indexes. In addition, an index can be disabled using the DISABLE option. When the index is disabled, only its definition is stored without index data. If you disable a clustered index, the data of the underlying table becomes unavailable.

To enable the index again, you can use the ALTER INDEX REBUILT statement or CREATE INDEX WITH DROP EXISTING.

Performing Online Index Operations

To help you achieve a database application that is available 24 hours a day, 7 days a week, SQL Server 2005 allows you (in the Enterprise Edition) to perform *online index operations*. Thus, your indexes can be created and rebuilt (or dropped) online, where online means that the index is available for querying.

Behind the scenes, SQL Server 2005 makes use of the row versioning framework. Practically, instead of one index, two indexes are used, one available for querying the "source" index and the other one modified internally—the "target" index.

The hidden costs of online index operations are as follows:

- Additional space required (for the temporary index)

- Reduced performance if the update activity on the base table is high. The performance hit is due to changing two indexes instead of one for each data modification.

- Additional overhead for tempdb. Row versions allow concurrent user updates and deletes while the index is rebuilt online. This can add overhead to tempdb. The overhead can increase if you use the SORT_IN_TEMPDB option.

When you plan for using online index operations consider these facts:

- Online index operations are not available for clustered indexes when the base tables contains large object data types, such as IMAGE, NTEXT, TEXT, VARCHAR(MAX), NVARCHAR(MAX), VARBINARY(MAX), and XML.

- Nonclustered indexes that have LOB data types in their definition cannot be created or rebuilt online.

- Indexes on local temporary tables cannot use online index operations.

Finding the Missing Index

The answer for this task is usually the Database Engine Tuning Advisor, the replacement of the Index Tuning Wizard. SQL Server 2005 offers another answer, the missing indexes feature.

The *Database Engine Tuning Advisor* (DTA) is not the Index Tuning Wizard with a new name. It is far better than its predecessor at providing what-if analysis, partitioning recommendations, time-bound tuning, and reports that give detailed information for each tuning recommendation. To use it, you need a trace, a script file, or you can launch it directly from the SQL Server Enterprise Manager to analyze an existing query.

Also considering your workload, DTA may suggest dropping existing indexes. Before implementing the recommendations of DTA you should analyze their impact on the other queries that use your database. If the workload used by DTA is a trace file, you would obtain the best suggestions when the trace contains representative activity for your application. You'll see Database Engine Tuning Advisor at work soon, in an exercise.

The other way you can identify indexes to support your queries is by using the missing indexes feature. For short, when the query optimizer generates an execution plan for a query, it considers optimal indexes for the query "indifferent" of whether or not they exist. If the optimal indexes exist, they are used in the generated execution plan. Otherwise, the query optimizer uses a less optimal execution plan.

Fortunately for you, the information about the missing indexes is exposed by the XML Showplan of the query and through a set of dynamic management views and functions. There are actually four of them:

- The sys.dm_db_missing_index_group_stats dynamic management view displays information about groups of missing indexes. Each query can benefit from one or more indexes. The hypothetical index or indexes that can improve your query make a missing indexes group.

- The sys.dm_db_missing_index_groups dynamic management view displays the indexes included in a specific missing indexes group.

- The sys.dm_db_missing_index_details DMV returns details for each missing index, such as the base table for the index the columns that should make the index key as well as index nonkey columns.

- The sys.dm_db_missing_index_columns dynamic management function returns all columns for an individual index.

Exercise 8.1 shows how they work.

EXERCISE 8.1

Finding a Missing Index for a Query

In this exercise you have to tune the following query by adding support indexes:

```
SELECT

COUNT(*)

FROM Sales.SalesOrderHeader

WHERE ShipDate='2001-10-11';
```

The query counts the number of orders shipped at the specified date. There are two orders shipped on 11 October 2001.

1. Run the query.

2. Run the following code to check what indexes are suggested for the query by the missing index feature:

```
SELECT

s.avg_user_impact,

d.equality_columns,

d.[statement]

FROM sys.dm_db_missing_index_group_stats s

JOIN sys.dm_db_missing_index_groups g

 ON s.group_handle=g.index_group_handle

JOIN sys.dm_db_missing_index_details d

 ON g.index_handle=d.index_handle

WHERE d.database_id=DB_ID(N'AdventureWorks')

AND d.object_id=OBJECT_ID(N'Sales.SalesOrderHeader');
```

3. Look at the resulting output. The missing indexes feature suggests an index on the ShipDate column for the AdventureWorks.Sales.SalesOrderHeader table. The index can generate an estimated improvement of 99.32 percent:

```
-- Output

avg_user_impact equality_columns statement

99.32           ShipDate         AdventureWorks.Sales.SalesOrderHeader
```

4. Next use the XML Showplan of the query to obtain the same recommendation. Turn ON the XML STATISTICS SET option and run the query again:

```
SET STATISTICS XML ON;

GO

SELECT

COUNT(*)

FROM Sales.SalesOrderHeader
```

EXERCISE 8.1 *(continued)*

```
WHERE ShipDate='2001-10-11';

GO

SET STATISTICS XML OFF;

GO
```

5. In the resulting XML Showplan, locate the <MissingIndexes> section. It should look similar to the next output:

```
-- Output

<MissingIndexes>

 <MissingIndexGroup Impact="99.3212">

  <MissingIndex Database="[AdventureWorks]" Schema="[Sales]"

Table="[SalesOrderHeader]">

    <ColumnGroup Usage="EQUALITY">

     <Column Name="[ShipDate]" ColumnId="5" />

    </ColumnGroup>

   </MissingIndex>

  </MissingIndexGroup>

</MissingIndexes>
```

The same information returned by the missing indexes dynamic management objects is present in the query's XML Showplan.

In the second part of the exercise you will use the Database Engine Tuning Advisor to obtain index recommendations

6. In the Query Window, highlight the query you are tuning (using SHIFT and arrow keys or SHIFT and the mouse cursor).

7. Right-click the selected query and, from the Context menu, select Analyze Query in the Database Engine Tuning Advisor.

8. Enter **Query Tuning** as the name of the session and leave the default values for the other options.

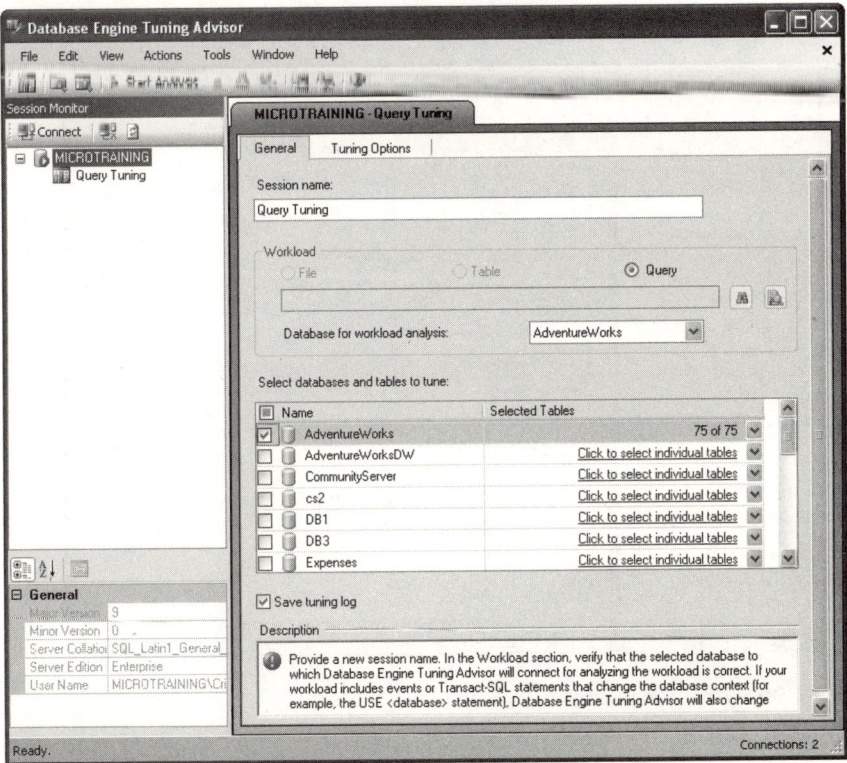

9. In the Select Databases and Tables to Tune section, select just the SalesOrderHeader table of the AdventureWorks database.

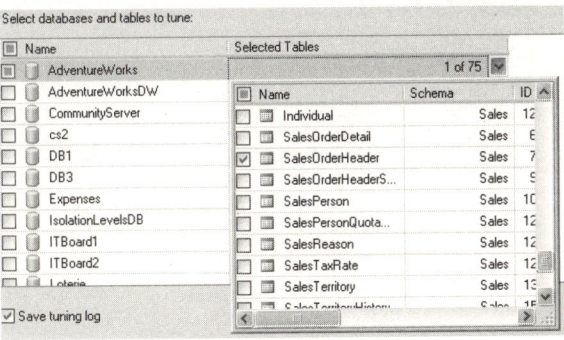

EXERCISE 8.1 *(continued)*

10. On the Tuning Options tab, uncheck the Limit Tuning Time and click on the Keep All Existing PDS option in the Physical Design Structures (PDS) to keep in the database section. This option forces Database Engine Tuning Advisor to suggest new indexes and keep the existing ones.

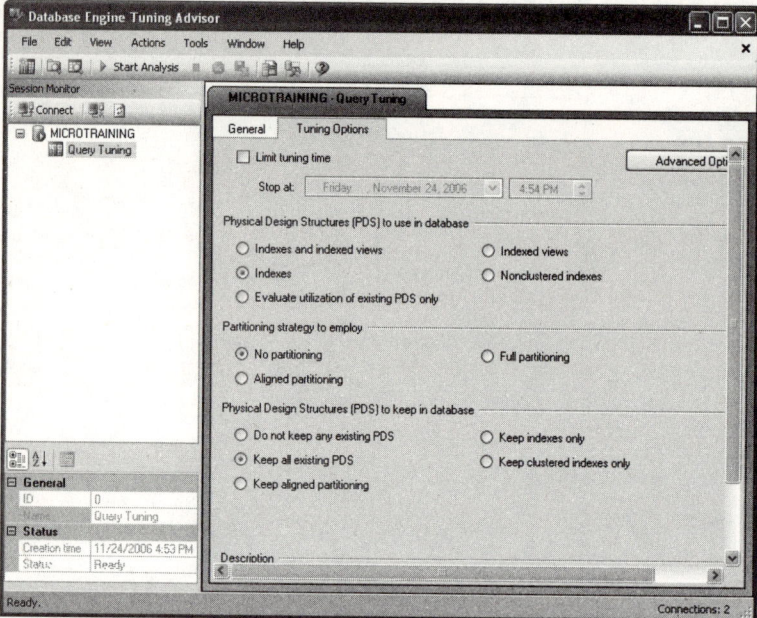

11. Click the Start Analysis button.

   The result consists of two recommendations: one new index and statistics for the new index.

   There is no surprise that the Database Engine Tuning Advisor suggests the same index as the missing indexes feature.

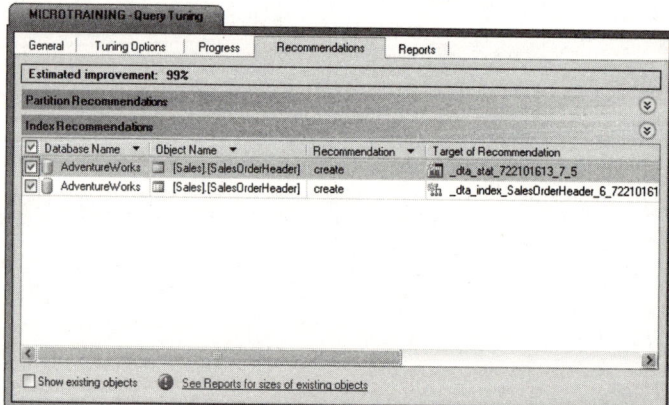

12. In the reports page you can see, among other things, the details about the estimated performance improvements in case you decide to implement the recommendations.

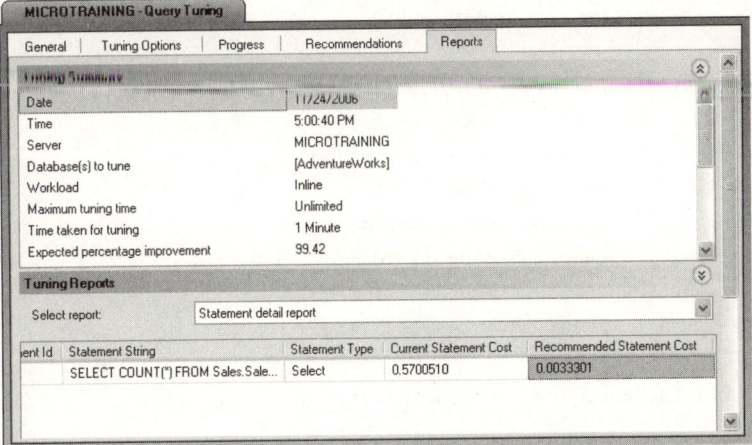

13. Choose from implementing the recommendations, saving them, or just exiting.

14. Since you don't want to create a new index, close the Database Engine Tuning Advisor window.

Fragmentation

One of the factors that can greatly impact your database performance is fragmentation. Fragmentation means inefficient space usage for an index. It can be internal when the pages of the index are not full (or almost full) and external when the logical order of the index pages differ from the physical order.

Internal fragmentation is bad for performance due to the wasted disk space and more importantly because of the inefficient use of cache. A page used by a query is loaded completely in memory no matter whether the page is 80 or 10 percent full. If the wasted disk space is not a problem for most database servers (disk storage becomes cheaper and cheaper), the inefficient use of cache is still a great problem for most applications. Also internal fragmentation generates more I/O because the data is stored in more pages than necessary.

External fragmentation can generate I/O overhead, disk head seeking being one of the most expensive operations in terms of I/O activity.

How does fragmentation occur? Fragmentation is primarily caused by data modifications. As SQL Server tries to accommodate new rows or update rows with a greater size, it may use page splits. It moves half of the existing data to a new page to make room for the new or updated rows. Delete operations can also cause internal fragmentation as the space occupied by the deleted rows remains free. Furthermore, the fragmentation is not index specific; heaps can suffer from fragmentation too.

To understand the phenomenon better, take a look at the following example:

```
CREATE TABLE Events
(
    EventDate DATETIME NOT NULL PRIMARY KEY,
    EventDescription CHAR(2000) NOT NULL);
GO
INSERT INTO Events(EventDate, EventDescription)
VALUES('2006-11-10', 'Event on 2006-11-10');
INSERT INTO Events(EventDate, EventDescription)
VALUES('2006-11-15', 'Event on 2006-11-15');
INSERT INTO Events(EventDate, EventDescription)
VALUES('2006-11-20', 'Event on 2006-11-20');
INSERT INTO Events(EventDate, EventDescription)
VALUES('2006-11-25', 'Event on 2006-11-25');


INSERT INTO Events(EventDate, EventDescription)
VALUES('2006-12-05', 'Event on 2006-12-05');
INSERT INTO Events(EventDate, EventDescription)
VALUES('2006-12-10', 'Event on 2006-12-10');
INSERT INTO Events(EventDate, EventDescription)
VALUES('2006-12-15', 'Event on 2006-12-15');
INSERT INTO Events(EventDate, EventDescription)
VALUES('2006-12-20', 'Event on 2006-12-20');
```

The size of one row for this table is approximately 2,011 bytes (2,000 bytes for the Event-Description column + 4 bytes for the EventDate + 7 bytes internal information) so the 8 rows are stored using 2 pages. Remember that a page can store almost 8K (8,192 – page header – additional overhead = 8,060 bytes) of data.

For convenience, let say that the page numbers are 1050 and 1051. If you insert a new row into the table using INSERT INTO Events VALUES('2006-11-11', 'Event on 2006-11-11'); SQL Server has to put the new row in page 1050 but the page is full. So, SQL Server splits page 1050 and moves half of the rows (the rows with EventDate values '2006-11-20' and '2006-11-25') to a free page having the number, let's say, 2015. Then the new row is inserted into page 1050.

The single INSERT statement caused both types of fragmentation. Page 1050 is 75 percent full and page 2015 only 50 percent.

The logical order of pages is 1050, 2015, and 1051, which is obviously different from the physical one (1050, 1051, 1052,..., 2014, 2015, 2016,...).

Is fragmentation always bad? No! For insert operations, pages that have free space limit the number of page splits.

Detecting Fragmentation

You have two options for obtaining the fragmentation percentage for an index. The first option is to use the Object Explorer from SQL Server Management Studio. The information is displayed in the Properties window, which you can get with a simple click for each index of a table. The Properties page displays average page fullness and the total fragmentation of the index.

The second option to get fragmentation information is by using the sys.dm_db_index_physical_stats dynamic management function. The DMF replaces the DBCC SHOWCONTIG command used in SQL Server 2000 for the same purpose. You can specify as arguments for the function a database ID, the ID of a table or a view, a specific index ID, a partition number (if the table or the index is partitioned), and a scan mode. The syntax follows:

```
sys.dm_db_index_physical_stats (
    { database_id | NULL | 0 | DEFAULT }
  , { object_id | NULL | 0 | DEFAULT }
  , { index_id | NULL | 0 | -1 | DEFAULT }
  , { partition_number | NULL | 0 | DEFAULT }
  , { mode | NULL | DEFAULT }
)
```

If you leave NULL (the default) for one of the arguments (except the scan mode), the function returns information about all objects in the class specified by that argument. For example, the next query returns size and fragmentation information about all indexes from the AdventureWorks database:

```
SELECT *
FROM sys.dm_db_index_physical_stats(
DB_ID('AdventureWorks'),NULL,NULL,NULL,DEFAULT);
```

The scan mode argument specifies the method of scanning for generated results.

There are three methods, LIMITED, SAMPLED, or DETAILED, with LIMITED being the default. LIMITED mode is the fastest due to the limited number of scanned pages (only the non-leaf-level pages for an index and all pages for a heap). The second scan mode, SAMPLE, uses 1 percent of the pages of an index or heap—when the scanned index or heap has at least 10,000 pages. For less than 10,000 pages, the DETAILED scan mode is used. The DETAILED mode scans all the pages of the target index or heap. Also this scan mode returns complete statistical information about the scanned index or heap.

To check fragmentation, you should look at the avg_fragmentation_in_percent column of the result set returned by the sys.dm_db_index_physical_stats.

Other columns that can help you are as follows:

- fragment_count displays the number physically consecutive leaf pages for an index. Ideally this column would have the value 1. The worst possible situation is when the fragment count is equal to the number of leaf-level pages.

- avg_page_space_used_in_percent indicates the average page fullness. It should be close to 100.

- page_count displays the number of data pages.

Fixing Fragmentation

To solve fragmentation problems for an index, you have three options: drop and recreate the index, reorganize the index (using the ALTER INDEX REORGANIZE), or rebuild the index (using the ALTER INDEX REBUILD).

If the fragmentation of index is less than 30 percent you should reorganize it. The operation is online and consists of reordering physically the leaf-level pages of indexes to match the physical order.

More than 30 percent of fragmentation indicates as a solution an index rebuild operation that can be done online in SQL Server 2005. It basically recreates the index.

You can manually drop and recreate the index but this method can only be performed offline. However, you should be aware that if you drop and recreate a clustered index, all non-clustered indexes of the base table are rebuilt.

To reduce the fragmentation for heaps, you can create a clustered index and then drop it. Dropping the clustered index does not impact the distribution of data.

Preventing Fragmentation

For a clustered index, you can prevent fragmentation by starting with a good index key. When the key is static and ever increasing, only DELETE and UDPATE operations can determine fragmentation (but not INSERT operations).

For all indexes, you can delay the appearance of page splits by leaving free space in the index pages. You can do that when the index is created or rebuilt using the FILLFACTOR and PAD_INDEX settings. The FILLFACTOR specifies how full each index page is going to be. It is expressed as a percentage.

The default value is 0 and has the same significance as the value 100—meaning that SQL Server will try to make the pages 100 percent full. But it won't always succeed. For example, if the table's row has a size of 5,000 bytes, SQL Server has no choice but to store a single row on a page (as the page size is 8K).

The PAD_INDEX setting allows you to leave free space at the nonleaf-level index pages. When PAD_INDEX is ON the value specified for FILLFACTOR is used for nonleaf-level index pages as well as for leaf-level ones. By default it is turned OFF and in this case SQL Server leaves room only for one more entry in the intermediary-level pages of the index.

How should you set FILLFACTOR? For OLAP systems, it should be 100 (or the default 0). For OLTP, you can specify any value between 1 and 99, considering very carefully the fact that the lower the value, the more space you waste and the more you affect your cache.

The next example shows you how to rebuild all indexes of the Production.Product table from the AdventureWorks database, leaving 20 percent free space for both intermediary-level and leaf-level pages:

```
ALTER INDEX ALL ON Production.Product
REBUILD WITH (FILLFACTOR=80, PAD_INDEX=ON);
GO
```

To illustrate how fragmentation occurs and the preventive measures to use against fragmentation, we use the following example. Create a demo table using data from the Person.Contacts table of the AdventureWorks database. We use a new table and tempdb to protect your sample database:

```
USE tempdb;
GO
CREATE TABLE Contacts
(
    ContactID INT NOT NULL,
    Title NVARCHAR(8) NULL,
    FirstName NVARCHAR(50) NOT NULL,
    MiddleName NVARCHAR(50) NULL,
    LastName NVARCHAR(50) NOT NULL,
    Phone NVARCHAR(25) NULL
);
GO
INSERT INTO Contacts(
ContactID,
Title,
FirstName,
MiddleName,
LastName,
Phone)
SELECT
ContactID, Title, FirstName, MiddleName, LastName, Phone
FROM AdventureWorks.Person.Contact
WHERE ContactID < 1000;
GO
```

At this point you have 995 rows in your table. You don't have to trust our word for it—you can check by issuing a SELECT COUNT(*) FROM Contacts query.

In the next step, create a clustered index on the LastName column of the table. We did mention that the LastName column is a bad choice, didn't we? You will see in a few seconds how quickly a table that has such a column as a clustering key gets fragmented:

```
CREATE CLUSTERED INDEX CL_IDX_Contacts_LastName
ON Contacts(LastName);
```

At this point the fragmentation of your index should be minimal but let's check that using the sys.dm_db_index_physical_stats dynamic management function:

```
SELECT
index_level AS [idx_level],
```

```
avg_fragmentation_in_percent AS [avg_fragmentation],
avg_page_space_used_in_percent AS [avg_page_space_used],
fragment_count AS [fragments]
FROM sys.dm_db_index_physical_stats(
DB_ID(N'tempdb'),
OBJECT_ID('Contacts'),
1,
DEFAULT,
'DETAILED');
```

The fragmentation on all levels of the index is 0 as it should be since you've just created the index:

```
-- Output
idx_level  avg_fragmentation  avg_page_space_used   fragments
---------  -----------------  --------------------  ---------
0          0                  95.8072275759822      1
1          0                   3.49641709908574     1
```

Let's see what happens if we add 100 new rows:

```
INSERT INTO Contacts(
ContactID,Title,FirstName,MiddleName,LastName,Phone)
SELECT
ContactID, Title, FirstName, MiddleName, LastName, Phone
FROM AdventureWorks.Person.Contact
WHERE ContactID BETWEEN 1000 AND 1100;
GO
```

If you run again the query that displays the fragmentation, you will get the following results:

```
-- Output
idx_level  avg_fragmentation  avg_page_space_used   fragments
---------  -----------------  --------------------  ---------
0          95.2380952380952   54.9278230788238      21
1          0                   6.83222139856684     1
```

By inserting 100 rows in a table that had 995 rows (10 percent) you have generated 95 percent fragmentation. Instead of one contiguous fragment as before, you have 21 fragments. And to make things worse, only 54 percent of the page space is used. This means that almost half of the disk space and cache memory used by the table is wasted.

How can you limit the disaster? Leave space in the leaf-level pages for the new rows (using the FILLFACTOR option).

To see whether FILLFACTOR can help you, in this case you need a fresh start so drop the table Contacts (by running DROP TABLE Contacts), create it again, and run the first insert statement (the one that inserts 995 records).

Then recreate the clustered index, only this time leave 20 percent of free space:

```
CREATE CLUSTERED INDEX CL_IDX_Contacts_LastName
ON Contacts(LastName)
WITH (FILLFACTOR=80);
```

If you run the query that checks fragmentation again, it will display:

```
-- Output
idx_level avg_fragmentation avg_page_space_used  fragments
--------- ----------------- -------------------- ---------
0         0                 75.271806276254      1
1         0                 4.57128737336298     1
```

As you can see, the fragmentation is 0 and the leaf-level pages of the index that are filled in average almost 75 percent. Now, insert the 100 rows again using the same statement as before:

```
INSERT INTO Contacts(
ContactID,Title,FirstName,MiddleName,LastName,Phone)
SELECT
ContactID, Title, FirstName, MiddleName, LastName, Phone
FROM AdventureWorks.Person.Contact
WHERE ContactID BETWEEN 1000 AND 1100;
GO
```

After the insert, check the fragmentation. The results of the query that checks the fragmentation shows absolutely no external fragmentation:

```
-- Output
idx_level avg_fragmentation avg_page_space_used  fragments
--------- ----------------- -------------------- ---------
0         0                 82.4040770941438     1
1         0                 4.57128737336298     1
```

And the data pages are filled 82 percent.

How could you estimate the value for FILLFACTOR to prevent fragmentation? There is no precise method for that. To estimate a value for the FILLFACTOR setting, you have to consider the following:

- The volume of data inserted between the indexes' rebuilds.
- Low values for the FILLFACTOR settings may adversely impact the performance of your SELECT queries.

Using Index Metadata

You can get information about your indexes (their configuration and state) graphically by using SQL Server Management Studio or programmatically by making use of catalog views, dynamic management objects, functions, and system stored procedures.

Some of the methods to obtain index information are described in detail in this chapter but to offer you a complete image we put them together here.

Getting Metadata from SQL Server Management Studio

The SQL Server Management Studio displays index information by two primary methods: Object Explorer and Summary Reports. The Object Explorer displays the indexes for each table or view and allows you to obtain detailed information about each index using the Index Property window. The Index Usage Statistics and Index Physical Statistics are two Summary Reports that exhibit index usage and index configuration information.

Using Stored Procedures to Obtain Index Metadata

Two of the system stored procedures that you may want to use to get information about your indexes are sp_help and sp_helpindex. The first one, sp_help, returns details about an object and in particular about the indexes of a table. A simple example shows the usage of this stored procedure (the output is not displayed as it is very large):

```
USE AdventureWorks;
GO
EXEC sp_help N'HumanResources.Employee';
GO
```

The second stored procedure, sp_helpindex, is dedicated as the name suggests to indexes. Here's an example:

```
EXEC sp_helpindex[HumanResources.Employee];
GO
-- Output
index_name                  index_description           index_keys
----------------------      ----------------------      -----------------

AK_Employee_LoginID         nonclustered, unique...     LoginID
AK_Employee_NationalID...   nonclustered, unique ...    NationalIDNumber
AK_Employee_rowguid         nonclustered, unique...     rowguid
IX_Employee_ManagerID       nonclustered located ...    ManagerID
PK_Employee_EmployeeID      clustered, unique, ...      EmployeeID
```

Using Index Catalog Views

The index catalog views are sys.indexes, sys.indexes_columns, sys.stats, sys.stats_columns, and sys.xml_indexes. The first two, sys.indexes and sys.indexes_columns, return the indexes of a database and their columns. Next, the sys.stats and sys.stats_columns display the information about indexes, associated statistics, and the related columns. Finally, the last one, sys.xml_indexes, gives you metadata for XML indexes.

To give you an idea of the output for these catalog views, here are a couple of examples:

```
USE AdventureWorks;
GO
SELECT
index_id,
[name],
type_desc
FROM sys.indexes
WHERE [object_id]=OBJECT_ID(N'HumanResources.Employee');
GO
-- Output
index_id name                            type_desc
-------- ------------------------------- ---------
1        PK_Employee_EmployeeID          CLUSTERED
2        AK_Employee_LoginID             NONCLUSTERED
3        AK_Employee_NationalIDNumber    NONCLUSTERED
4        AK_Employee_rowguid             NONCLUSTERED
5        IX_Employee_ManagerID           NONCLUSTERED

-- Second Example
USE AdventureWorks;
GO
SELECT
[name],
type_desc
FROM sys.xml_indexes
WHERE [object_id]=OBJECT_ID('Person.Contact');
GO

-- Output
name                         type_desc
---------------------------- ---------
PXML_Contact_AddContact      XML
```

Using Index Metadata: System Functions

We mention here INDEXPROPERTY, INDEX_COL, and INDEXKEY_PROPERTY functions. The INDEXPROPERTY function helps you find out the number of index levels, the type of index, the fill factor used when the index was created or last rebuilt, and the type of locking allowed for a specific index. The function INDEX_COL displays the name of the key column for a specific index. The INDEXKEY_PROPERTY returns the position of a column within an index as well as the column sort order (ascending or descending).

The next example uses the INDEXPROPERTY function to display the index depth and fill factor of the pk_Employee_EmployeeIDindex of the Employee table:

```
USE AdventureWorks;
GO
DECLARE @TblID INT;
SET @TblID=OBJECT_ID(N'HumanResources.Employee');
SELECT
INDEXPROPERTY(@TblID,'PK_Employee_EmployeeID','IndexDepth') AS IndexDepth,
INDEXPROPERTY(@TblID,'PK_Employee_EmployeeID','IndexFillFactor') AS
IndexFillFactor;
GO
-- Output
IndexDepth    FillFactor
----------    ----------
2             0
```

Getting Index Metadata from Dynamic Management Objects

Last but not least, you should remember a few dynamic management views and functions that return index fragmentation, usage, and I/O statistics, as well as missing indexes.

They are as follows:

- The *sys.dm_db_index_physical_stats* dynamic management function returns fragmentation statistics and the size of specified indexes.

- The *sys.dm_db_index_operational_stats* dynamic management function displays index and base usage and I/O statistics.

- The *sys.dm_db_index_usage_stats* dynamic management view displays how your indexes are used.

- The sys.dm_db_missing_index_details, sys.dm_db_missing_index_groups, sys.dm_db_missing_index_group_stats and sys.dm_db_missing_index_columns display information about indexes that may improve the performance of your queries.

Summary

In this chapter, you learned what indexes are and how they can help you tune your database. You also learned about some of the new features of SQL Server 2005 related to indexes, such as online operations and indexes with included columns.

In addition, we touched on some types of indexes only briefly where the exam did not require extensive knowledge, such as full-text or XML indexes. You can use Books Online to expand your knowledge if your job requires.

Because indexes are one of the critical factors for your database performance, we talked about them not only in this chapter but also in Chapters 7 and 10 of this book.

Exam Essentials

Know the types of indexes available in SQL Server 2005.   You have to know what indexes you can use to improve the performance of your queries and more importantly when you should use them. You have to be familiar with concepts such as covering indexes and how to achieve covering using, for example, a nonclustered index with included columns.

Also you have to know what type of index each situation requires. For example, querying large text data for complex phrases or words may require a full-text index.

Understand the index design considerations that affect database performance.   You should know the index design factors that can affect your database performance, such as choosing a clustered index key, how full the pages of an index should be, the locking behavior of database engine related to indexes, how to use online operations, physically placing indexes for performance, and so on.

Know how to obtain index information.   SQL Server Management Studio, dynamic management objects, and system functions are just a few of the options you have for getting index metadata. You have to know all the options not just for the exam but also for your daily work. In addition, knowing how to use Database Engine Tuning Advisor or the missing indexes feature can definitely support your index strategy.

Understand index maintenance.   One of the enemies of your indexes is fragmentation. You should know how to detect it, how to prevent it, and how to fix it.

Review Questions

1. What types of indexes are supported by SQL Server 2005? (Choose all that apply.)
    A. Clustered
    B. Nonclustered
    C. Unique
    D. XML indexes

2. You have to determine the fragmentation of all indexes on a specific database. What should you do?
    A. Use the sys.dm_db_index_usage_stats dynamic management function.
    B. Use the sys.dm_db_index_operational_stats dynamic management function.
    C. Use the sys.indexes catalog view.
    D. Use the sys.dm_db_index_index_physical_stats dynamic management function.

3. You have created a table named Person with the following definition:

    ```
    CREATE TABLE Person(

    PersonID INT NOT NULL PRIMARY KEY,

    FirstName VARCHAR(64),

    LastName VARCHAR(64),

    Resume VARCHAR(MAX),

    Picture IMAGE,

    EmploymentHistory XML);
    ```

    Which of the columns of the Person table disallow online index operations on the clustered index created automatically for the primary key of the table? (Choose all that apply.)
    A. Resume
    B. PersonID
    C. EmploymentHistory
    D. LastName

4. Your department uses several internal applications. One of them records the temperature in the server room once every hour. The information is recorded in the following table:

```
CREATE TABLE SrvRoomTemperature(

MeasureDate DATETIME,

Temperature DEC(5,2));
```

Only one query uses the table having the code:

```
SELECT

MIN(Temperature) AS MinTemperature,

MAX(Temperature) AS MaxTemperature,

AVG(Temperature) AS AvgTemperature

FROM SrvRoomTemperature

WHERE MeasureDate BETWEEN @Date1 AND @Date2
```

You want to optimize the performance of the query. What should you do? (Choose the best option.)

 A. Create a nonclustered index on the Temperature column.

 B. Create a clustered index on the MeasureDate column.

 C. Create a nonclustered index on the MeasureDate column.

 D. Create a nonclustered index on the MeasureDate column with the Temperature column included.

5. Which of the following measures improves the performance of your queries? (Choose all that apply.)

 A. Place the largest table of your database on a separate filegroup on a different disk.

 B. Place the nonclustered indexes on a filegroup separate from the other objects of your database.

 C. Place the frequently joined tables on separate filegroups on different disk drives.

 D. Place all objects of your database on the same filegroup.

6. In which situations can you use the CONTAINS predicate?

 A. To search a specific value in a clustered index.

 B. To seek a specific value in a nonclustered index.

 C. To search a specific value in an XML index.

 D. To search a specific value in a full-text index.

7. Which of the following are good choices for a clustered index?

   A. An INT column having the IDENTITY property

   B. A VARCHAR(MAX) column

   C. An XML column

   D. A TEXT column

8. Which are the characteristics of a good clustering key? (Choose all that apply.)

   A. Unique

   B. Narrow

   C. Static

   D. Ever-increasing value

9. You want to improve the performance of several queries that interrogate one of your database tables named Address. The Address table has a column named PersonID that references a column with the same name from a table named Person. You decide to improve the performance of queries that join the Address and Person tables by creating an index on the PersonID column of the Address table. You also want to maximize the INSERT operations' performance by limiting the number of page splits. For that purpose, you want to leave a 10 percent free space on both nonleaf- and leaf-level progress of the new index. Which statement should you use?

   A. Use this:

   ```
   CREATE INDEX IX_Address_PersonID
   ON Address(PersonID)
   WITH(FILLFACTOR=90);
   ```

   B. Use this:

   ```
   CREATE NONCLUSTERED INDEX IX_Address_PersonID
   ON Address(PersonID)
   WITH(FILLFACTOR=90);
   ```

   C. Use this:

   ```
   CREATE INDEX IX_Address_PersonID
   ON Address(PersonID)
   WITH(FILLFACTOR=90,
   PAD_INDEX=ON);
   ```

   D. Use this:

   ```
   CREATE INDEX IX_Address_PersonID
   ON Address(PersonID)
   WITH(FILLFACTOR=10,
   PAD_INDEX=ON);
   ```

10. You have to design an index strategy for your database applications. Which of the following recommendations should you consider first? (Choose all that apply.)

    A. Use heaps instead of clustered indexes.

    B. Use narrow, static, and unique columns (or combination of columns) as clustered index keys.

    C. Manually create indexes on foreign keys.

    D. Use clustered indexes instead of heaps.

11. How can you determine whether indexes will improve the performance of a database application? (Choose all that apply.)

    A. Use the Database Engine Tuning Advisor.

    B. Use the sys.dm_db_index_usage_stats dynamic management function.

    C. Use the sys.dm_db_index_operational_stats dynamic management function.

    D. Use the missing indexes feature.

12. You have to improve the performance of an application used by a network radio. The application records votes of the radio listeners for the most popular songs of all time. The votes are recorded over a three-month period and are stored in a table created using this code:

```
CREATE TABLE SongVote(

SongID INT NOT NULL PRIMARY KEY,

SongName VARCHAR(128),

VotesByInternet INT,

VotesBySMS INT,

VotesByMail INT,

VotesByPhone INT);
```

A web page displays the most popular songs using the following query:

```
SELECT TOP 10

SongName

FROM SongVote

WHERE VotesByInternet + VotesBySMS +

 VotesByMail + VotesByPhone > 100

ORDER BY

 VotesByInternet +

 VotesBySMS +
```

```
VotesByMail +

VotesByPhone DESC
```

The SongVote table is static and has 20,000 records. The web page that displays the top songs of all time is accessed daily by 2,000 unique visitors. How can you improve the performance of the query?

A. Create a nonclustered index on each of the following columns: VotesByInternet, VotesBy-SMS, VotesByMail, and VotesByPhone.

B. Create a nonclustered index on the most updated column from the columns: VotesByInternet, VotesBySMS, VotesByMail, and VotesByPhone.

C. Run the following script:

```
ALTER TABLE SongVote ADD TotalVotes
 AS VotesByInternet + VotesBySMS +
 VotesByMail + VotesByPhone;
GO
CREATE INDEX IX_SongVote_TotalVotes
 ON SongVotes(TotalVotes DESC);
Replace the original query with this one:
SELECT TOP 10
SongName
FROM SongVote
WHERE TotalVotes > 100
ORDER BY TotalVotes DESC;
```

D. Create a table value function that returns all songs that have over 100 votes and modify the query to use the function.

13. You design a database dictionary consisting of several tables that store the dictionary's data in VARCHAR(MAX) columns. To help search various words, expressions, and phrases you add full-text indexes on each table. Which of the following predicates and string functions use full-text indexes to search data? (Choose all that apply.)

A. FREETEXT

B. CONTAINS

C. CHARINDEX

D. PATINDEX

14. As a part of maintenance tasks for a database application you have to solve index fragmentation problems for several of the most used tables. You use the sys.dm_db_index_physical_stats dynamic management function to check the fragmentation of the largest index in your database. The value returned for the avg_fragmentation_in_percent column of the result set returned by the DMF is 15. What should you do?

A. Do nothing. The value is acceptable.

B. Rebuild the index.

C. Reorganize the index.

D. Disable the index.

15. One table of a database application is named Products and contains the products of a multi-national company. The structure of the table is very simple; the script that was used to create the table follows:

CREATE TABLE Products(

ProductID INT NOT NULL PRIMARY KEY,

ProductName NVARCHAR(50)

 COLLATE SQL_Latin1_General_CP1_CS_AS);

Most of the queries join the Products table to a table named Orders while a few others search for a product using a string expression. Some of the queries that search for a product name require a comparison with a string expression that has the collation French_CI_AS. You want to optimize those queries. What should you do?

A. Use an indexed view.

B. Create a nonclustered index on the ProductName column.

C. Run the following script:

ALTER TABLE Products

ADD ProductNameFr AS ProductName

 COLLATE French_CI_AS;

GO

CREATE INDEX IX_Products_ProductNameFr

ON Products(ProductNameFr);

Modify the queries to use the ProductNameFr column.

D. Rewrite the queries as stored procedures.

16. You've designed a help-desk application that is used to manage support cases for a software product. One table of the application, SupportIncidents, was created using this code:

```
CREATE TABLE SupportIncidents(

IncidentID INT IDENTITY(1,1) NOT NULL PRIMARY KEY,

Description VARCHAR(512),

OpenDate DATETIME,

Status TINYINT,

ClosedDate DATETIME);
```

You have to optimize the response time for the following query:

```
SELECT COUNT(*) AS NmbOfCases

FROM SupportIncidents

WHERE MONTH(OpenDate)=@MonthValue;
```

What should you do?

A. Create a nonclustered index on the OpenDate column.

B. Create a composite nonclustered index on the OpenDate and IncidentID columns.

C. Create a unique index on the OpenDate column.

D. Run the following code:
```
ALTER TABLE SupportIncidents
ADD MonthOpenDate AS MONTH(OpenDate);
GO
CREATE INDEX IX_SupportIncidents_MonthOpenDate
ON SupportIncidents(MonthOpenDate);
```
And modify the original query:
```
SELECT COUNT(*) AS NmbOfCases
FROM SupportIncidents
WHERE MonthOpenDate=@MonthValue;
```

17. Which of the following facts are true about indexes? (Choose all that apply.)

A. You can have up to 254 nonclustered indexes on a table.

B. The maximum key size for an index is 960 bytes.

C. You can have a maximum of 3 clustered indexes per table.

D. The maximum number of XML indexes per table is 249.

18. Which of the following statements are valid? (Choose all that apply.)

    A. Use this:

    ```
    CREATE PRIMARY XML INDEX PXML_Products_Catalog
    ON Sales.Products(Catalog);
    ```

    B. Use this:

    ```
    CREATE XML INDEX IXML_Products_Catalog_Path
    ON Sales.Products(Catalog)
    USING XML INDEX PXML_Products_Catalog
    FOR PATH;
    ```

    C. Use this:

    ```
    CREATE XML INDEX IXML_Products_Catalog_Property
    ON Sales.Products(Catalog)
    USING XML INDEX PXML_Products_Catalog
    FOR PROPERTY;
    ```

    D. Use this:

    ```
    CREATE XML INDEX IXML_Products_Catalog_Value
    ON Sales.Products(Catalog)
    USING XML INDEX PXML_Products_Catalog
    FOR VALUE;
    ```

19. Among the new indexing features of SQL Server 2005, there is one that allows your indexes to cover more queries. Which one is it?

    A. Indexes with included columns

    B. XML primary indexes

    C. Online index operations

    D. XML secondary indexes

20. You want to create an indexed view to speed up the execution of a query. What steps should you perform? (Choose all that apply.)

    A. Verify that the NUMERIC_ROUNDABORT option value is OFF and that the following SET options have the value ON for all the tables referenced by the view:

    ```
    ANSI_NULLS
    ANSI_PADDING
    ANSI_WARNINGS
    ARITHABORT
    CONCAT_NULL_YIELDS_NULL
    QUOTED_IDENTIFIER
    ```

    B. Verify the same SET option values (specified previously) for the session that creates the view.

    C. Verify that the view definition is deterministic.

    D. Include the WITH SCHEMABINDING option in your view's definition.

Answers to Review Questions

1. A, B, C, D. SQL Server 2005 supports the following types of indexes: clustered, nonclustered, XML, unique, and full-text. It also supports indexed views.

2. D. The sys.dm_db_index_index_physical_stats dynamic management function returns information about the size and fragmentation of indexes.

   The sys.dm_db_index_operational_stats dynamic management function and also the sys.dm_db_index_usage_stats dynamic management function return index usage statistics but no information about the fragmentation of indexes.

   The sys.indexes catalog view returns metadata information about indexes such as index type, index options, file group, and partition scheme ID.

3. A, C. Online index operations on a clustered index are disallowed if the underlying table contains LOB data types such as IMAGE, TEXT, NTEXT, VARCHAR(MAX), NVARCHAR(MAX), VARBINARY(MAX), and XML.

   The PersonID column has the type INT and the LastName column is VARCHAR(64). Both data types permit online index operations on clustered indexes as well as on nonclustered indexes.

4. B. A clustered index on the MeasureDate column is the best option because the query returns range-based data. Also this choice is optimal for insert operations because the MeasureDate value is ever increasing and this way an insert operation does not generate page splits (and fragmentation).

   A nonclustered index on the Temperature or on the MeasureDate columns won't have any performance benefits.

   A nonclustered index on the MeasureDate column with the Temperature column included covers the query but it duplicates information unnecessarily.

5. A, B, C. The rule of thumb for obtaining performance by physical placement of your database objects is that the more disk drives you use, the better performance you get. Thus, whenever possible you should place the largest and the most queried tables on different disk drives. Also you can use the same technique for nonclustered indexes and frequently joined tables.

   Placing all objects of your database on the same disk drive does not improve the performance but, on the contrary, it may adversely affect it.

6. D. The CONTAINS predicate can be used only with full-text indexes.

7. A. The characteristics that define an optimal clustered index require an index key that is narrow, unique, and static. A column with the identity property is the only choice in this case. LOB columns—XML, TEXT, NTEXT, IMAGE, and VARCHAR(MAX)—cannot be used as index keys.

8. A, B, C, D. All of the above are characteristics for a good clustering key.

    If the key of a clustered index is not unique, SQL Server will add a uniquifier (a 4-byte integer) to make duplicate index keys unique. Since the clustered index keys are used by all nonclustered indexes of a table, duplicate values of the clustering index key waste disk space and add overhead to INSERT or UPDATE operations.

    A large clustered index key determines larger nonclustered indexes and implicitly wastes space and is a bigger performance overhead. Obviously, a narrow clustered index key is a better choice than a large one.

    The clustered index key should be static because each modification of its value can determine the move of the record (potentially creating fragmentation) and also would cause the update of all nonclustered indexes of the table.

    Finally, if the values for the clustered index keys are ever increasing such as for columns with the property, new records are added at the end of the clustered index (at the end of the table) to avoid fragmentation.

9. C. To indicate the percentage of how full the database engine should make the leaf-and non-leaf-level pages, you should specify ON for the PAD_INDEX setting and give a value for the FILLFACTOR argument. The specified value is used for both leaf- and nonleaf-level pages. The correct value in this case is 90 because you want 10 percent free space pages and not 10 percent full pages.

    The first two code samples are equivalent but they do not set the PAD_INDEX argument to ON.

10. B, C. A good clustered index key is static, unique, narrow, and optionally its value is ever increasing.

    Manually indexing foreign keys adds performance benefits to join operations and to divide operations (on the referenced table).

    Choosing heaps over clustered indexes or vice versa should be made on a case-by-case basis. Heaps are very good as staging tables and for small amounts of data, while clustered indexes have their own benefits such as support for seek operations, increased performance for joins, or queries that return a range of values (based on the clustering key).

11. A, D. The Database Engine Tuning Advisor can indicate support indexes for database activity recorded in a trace or in script file.

    The missing indexes feature indicates indexes that can improve query performance. It is exposed through XML Showplans and a set of dynamic management views and functions.

    The sys.dm_db_index_operational_stats and sys.dm_db_index_usage_stats dynamic management functions return information about existing indexes.

12. C. An indexed computed column is the best option in this case. All of the other options would not improve the performance of the query.

13. A, B. The FREETEXT and CONTAINS predicates make use of full-text indexes, searching indexed VARBINARY(MAX), VARCHAR(MAX), IMAGE, and XML columns. The CHARINDEX and the PATINDEX string functions do not use full-text indexes.

14. C. A fragmentation percent of 0 through 10 may be acceptable. An index that has less than 30 percent fragmentation can benefit from reorganization. Over 30 percent fragmentation requires an index rebuild. Disabling the index is not a solution.

15. C. The best option is to use an indexed computed column.

An indexed view or stored procedures may improve performance but they are not as straightforward as our solution (an indexed computed column).

An index on the ProductName column would have no effect for the queries that use a French collation for the search argument.

16. D. You've learned about SARGs (search arguments) in the previous chapter. So you should know that, if you apply a function to a column in the filter of a query or use an expression that involves multiple columns of the same table, most of the time the query optimizer is forced to do a scan instead of a seek operation. A solution for these situations is to create a computed column and index it. For example, instead of a filter WHERE Col1>Col2 or WHERE Col1-Col2>0 you can add a computed column Col3 having the definition Col3 AS Col1-Col2 and modify your queries to use as filter WHERE Col3>0.

To return to our question, an index on the OpenDate column does not help you because you apply the MONTH function to the value of OpenDate.

A composite index on the OpenDate and IncidentID columns is not only impractical but also useless theoretically. The IncidentID column is added anyway at the leaf level of any nonclustered index as it is the clustered index key for the SupportIncidents table.

A unique index on the OpenDate column is not recommended as you can have multiple support cases opened at the same time. One may argue that two dates may differ at the time part level (one case opened two seconds after another, for example) but in any case a unique index does not improve the query.

17. D. The number of nonclustered indexes you can have on a table is 249. The same number is the maximum for XML indexes. The maximum key size for an index is actually 900 bytes. And of course, you can have just a single clustered index per table.

18. A, B, C, D. All code samples are valid and illustrate how to create primary and secondary XML indexes.

19. A. The indexes with included columns allow you to cover more queries by including additional columns (not just the columns that make the index key) in the leaf level of the nonclustered indexes. This way you can work around the maximum value for the index key size, 900 bytes, including the columns you need in the leaf-level pages of your index, without affecting the size of the index key. Also you can add VARCHAR(MAX), VARBINARY(MAX), or XML columns to the leaf level of your indexes. As you may know, you cannot use these columns in an index key definition.

Online operations and XML indexes are indeed new features of SQL Server 2005 but they are not the answer we expected.

20. A, B, C, D. All the options (and in the order of A, B, C, D) represent steps you should perform before creating an indexed view.

Chapter

9

Scaling Out Applications

MICROSOFT EXAM OBJECTIVES COVERED IN THIS CHAPTER:

✓ **Scale database applications.**

- Specify a data-partitioning model.
- Design queries that target multiple servers.
- Implement scaleout techniques like federated database, server broker distributed partitioned views.
- Design applications to distribute data and workload transparently.
- Identify code or processes that can be moved to a different tier to improve performance.
- Rewrite algorithms to improve efficiency.

Give me a place to stand, and I will move the earth.

—Archimedes

Now that is really scaling out! Archimedes had the picture all right. Let's let him leverage our applications.

Archimedes understood the principle involved to leverage the earth. He knew the tools he needed. He knew the design to use. He understood the principle involved for his design to move a large object: where to place the fulcrum, how much force, and how much distance. But more than 2,200 years later we still cannot give him a place to stand. In SQL Server 2005 Microsoft has implemented many new features. Some important design features have an impact on leveraging your applications: data partitioning, peer-to-peer replication, and service-oriented data architecture.

Previously we noted how the architectural design of SQL Server 2005 has changed from previous versions. This redesign of the server infrastructure enables you to scale out your applications with very little effort. However, a combination of many factors will enable you to take your application that is performing in a medium environment to one that is scaled out into an enterprise situation.

In this chapter, we will target two key areas in creating enterprise-level applications: the new performance features of SQL Server 2005 and designing your applications for scaling out.

Preparing to Leverage Your Database Applications

As a fully featured application server, SQL Server 2005 creates the foundation for your applications. However, to create a well-performing enterprise-level application, you need do more than just write the application or run the upgrade wizard. You must take advantage of these features as you leverage your application.

A technique that has served us well in our years of consulting and training is to build a firm and broad foundation first. Then lay the layers, one by one, creating a pyramid effect. The base must be secure and well defined to hold the layers or the pyramid will crumble.

Building the Foundation

SQL Server 2005 and its new features supply the foundation. The next layer in a well-performing enterprise application is to create a well-formed database schema to resourcefully contain the data.

On that layer users must efficiently query the data and retrieve the result sets they need. You have seen that the data query layer has indexing built as another layer on it to enhance query handling. To make certain all users are able to secure the data they need, you must make certain concurrency is performing optimally for your application. As you have probably already noticed, the four layers shown in Figure 9.1 have been the focus of the previous chapters in this book.

FIGURE 9.1   Leveraging a well-performing database application

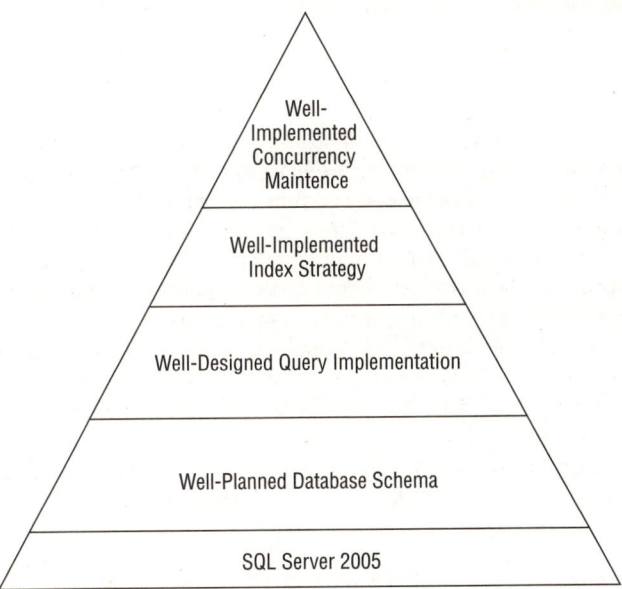

Stepping Up to Create a Well-Performing Database Application

As you review these steps once more, you should be confident you understand how to implement each layer in building a database application.

SQL Server 2005   SQL Server 2005 is your foundation. It not only provides the database engine to implement the storage and retrieval of your data but it also provides the features of your application server. Service-oriented architecture (SOA), a relatively new term in the software development arena, provides a secure basis for your database applications. The built-in application architecture provided with SQL Server 2005, such as the Service Broker messaging platform and notification services event processing, allows you to develop robust enterprise applications. You need to further ensure your physical server is sufficient and properly tuned to your requirements.

A well-planned database schema   A well-planned database schema enables you to access and manage your data efficiently. A well-built database design allows for easy access to your data. You have many new schema security features in SQL Server 2005 to assist you in your planning. However, foremost in your plan should be the amount of normalization you want to build into your model.

Normalizing a database is the process of using well-known technologies to separate your data into a related multi-table structured set to reduce redundancy. In relational database theory, third normal form is defined as the relation where "the relation is based on the key, the whole key and nothing but the key," to which some add, so help me Codd.

 Edgar F. Codd, a British computer scientist (1923–2003), is the person who originally defined the first three normal forms. The first normal form requires that tables in a database consist of a primary key and a number of atomic fields with no repeating groups. The second normal form (2NF) requires that the database meets the requirements of the first normal form and furthermore all non-key fields be dependent on the key. The third normal form (3NF) requires that the database meets the requirements of the second normal form and furthermore all non-key fields be dependent only on the key, the whole key, and nothing but the key. In other words, the non-key fields can be transitively dependent in 2NF, but must be directly dependent in 3NF.

Normalization spirals upward. Performance is increased at the query level just due to the nature of the data storage algorithms used. Indexes can be created more quickly and efficiently because the planning has been thought out.

Consider also the data manageability aspect of a well-developed database schema. It allows you to access and secure objects within the database, as well as to define a data abstraction layer through stored procedures to access your data securely and efficiently.

A well-designed query implementation   A well-designed query implementation provides for reuse of query plans and fast retrieval of data with minimal resource usage. Queries written using set-based algorithms are optimized for SQL Server by using indexes, promoting plan reuse, and utilizing server memory and disk space efficiently.

A well-implemented index strategy   A well-implemented index strategy enables fast look up and processing of data within the database. If your query implementation does not use your indexing strategy, your application will not process optimally. The two go hand in hand. For this reason it is important that set-based queries are an important part of your design.

A well-implemented concurrency maintenance solution   A well-implemented concurrency maintenance solution is necessary to make certain that your application is performing optimally. In your design, you should keep your transactions as short as possible. You also should avoid implementing cursors and implement set-based code in your queries. Once your application is deployed, concurrency maintenance may mean capturing baseline performance levels and monitoring the levels periodically or regularly. You will need to continually visit your locking procedures and locking isolation levels. You should always use the minimum transaction isolation level required.

It is easy to see the bottom-up spiraling effect. One layer strengthens the next. It is important to understand the features in SQL Server 2005 and then be able to apply them as you design your database application.

If you have done well, you are ready for scalability.

Leveraging Your Database Applications

Your application is a living document. For it to continue to function optimally, it must reflect change. Here are some examples of change:

- Your application may have an increasing workload. Sustaining that workload is essential and begins at the database architecture layer. Your architecture must have the flexibility to endure various means of improvising scalability.

- Load management may change. A middle tier may be added. Maintaining 24/7 availability may take priority over every other issue. Your application, initially built to service a particular geographic area on a local server, may now need to be implemented on a web interface so that it can be accessed internationally.

Deciding to Scale Up or Scale Out

Scaling up is the process of increasing a server's resources such as memory, CPU speed, and disk subsystems. *Scaleup* could involve nothing further than adding another processor to an existing server, or it could be an extreme overhaul to a much-improved multiprocessor system. In either case, you are still using a single server solution. No matter what your solution encompasses, you are putting more punch behind your application by providing a bigger and better box to boost it out into the world. Essentially you will not need to make any major changes to your application or the underlying database if you decide to scale up.

Scaleout involves expanding the data to multiple servers. The "how" of this is not a simple task. This procedure involves understanding your data and its use in your application.

What Type of Data Do You Have?

Ask yourself the following questions to figure out what type of data you have:

Do you use reference data?   *Reference data* is relatively stable data like airline schedules or parts catalog references. Since this type of data seldom changes, reference data scaleout is easily implemented.

Do you use activity data?   *Activity data* is generally relevant for a particular business activity and as such can be replicated or partitioned effectively.

Do you use resource data?   This data is the heart of the matter: your account data, your inventory, your customer list, your invoices, and your high availability data. This data has high concurrency requirements. As *resource data* gets "worn out"—or would you rather we said stale or old?—it becomes your reference data.

Do you use service interaction data? This data is used to communicate between services. All parties must understand the format and the rules of communication for the exchange to be complete. Embracing *service interaction data* is a basis for service-oriented data architecture in SQL Server 2005.

For more information about "Scaling Out SQL Server 2005" see the Microsoft white paper by that name at http://msdn2.microsoft.com/en-us/library/aa479364.aspx.

Factors That Affect Scaleout

After determining the types of data you are using in your database solution, let's go one step further and examine how the usage of this data affects the manner in which you develop your scaleout implementation.

Data update frequency If your update frequency is low, replication might be a good option for scaleout. On the other hand, stay away from replication if updatability is high.

Availability of a key column on which to partition data If your data contains a column on which you can partition a table horizontally, you are able to effectively scale out your application.

Data isolation If your data can be isolated such that it can be moved from resource data to reference data, you can implement a sliding window scaleout strategy. For example, the Orders table can be kept current with only 12 months of orders. At the beginning of each new month a trigger slides the noncurrent (13-month-old) data into the archived data table for the previous year. This scaleout is accomplished by a partitioning strategy similar to our previous strategy using dates for our partitioning values and implementing partition switching.

For more about switching partitions, search "Transferring Data Efficiently by Using Partition Switching" in SQL Server Books Online.

Application design flexibility Although changing your application design is not always necessary, you should be ready to accept that your application may require certain revisions so that it will work optimally in a new environment. Remember, it is a living document.

Scaling Out Data through Partitioning

In SQL Server 2005 you have a scaleout advantage over previous versions in that you can *partition* the actual base table to improve your application's performance or make it more manageable. This is accomplished by choosing a key on which to partition your table horizontally such that the rows of data are spread across filegroups. It is your call as to how you want to physically manage the filegroups to contain the data. That is to say, you can create the partitioning scheme and merely map all partitions to one filegroup or do just the opposite, map each partition to its own filegroup. You can even create more filegroups than you need at first so you are prepared for switching and archiving data at a later time.

Understanding How Partitioning Works

To partition your data, you need to determine the filegroup structure of the database and alter the database accordingly. You must create filegroups and files within the filegroups. When you create or rebuild the table to be partitioned, it will use these filegroups.

Next, the partitioning structure needs to be specified. First, you must determine the column on which you are partitioning. Only one column can be used in a table for this purpose. Then, the number of partitions and the range of values for each partition need to be specified by creating a partition function and a partition scheme.

As data is entered in the table, it will automatically be stored in its proper partition in the table. This gives you physical control over that data. You can use the $partition function to retrieve information regarding in which partition a particular row is stored.

A Case in Point: Organized Information

One of the reasons we are very excited to be writing this book for you is that we can share our own experiences with SQL Server 2005. Not long after SQL Server 2005 launched, we became involved in a project for an organization that collects extremely large amounts of data for medical studies. The group stores every piece of data it receives. The database is extremely large, several tens of gigabytes, and most of it is contained in one data table.

Personnel are continually updating this table as new data becomes available. Since so many medical institutions provide data, contention is a concern.

The purpose of the database is to enable medical personnel globally to search the stored data. Medical personnel must be able to quickly search on keywords to get up-to-the-minute results from the database on a given drug or a disease scenario. They are able to use the results from the database in their overall medical solution.

We used a partitioned table for this extremely large data table with great success. By partitioning the table across a set of filegroups, we were able to relieve contention, index the data, and back up the data.

In the next section, we use a scenario with the AdventureWorks database much like our medical database project to show you how you can leverage your application in the same manner.

Partitioning a Table to Improve Performance

Partitioning a table enables you to make an extremely large table more manageable. As you proceed through Exercise 9.1, note that although a table is spread across several filegroups for data storage it is thought of as a single logical unit for data querying and updating. In a like manner, using the same partition function, you are able to build an index on the table. You now have a manageability and performance enhancement feature never before offered in SQL Server.

Exercise 9.1 shows you how it works.

EXERCISE 9.1

Scaling Out AdventureWorks Using Partitioning

In this exercise you will create a table called NewProdReview in the Sales Schema of the AdventureWorks database. You alter the database to create three filegroups. You will create a partition function to define the horizontal partitioning values of the data on the new product name column, NewProdName, in the table. You will next create a partition scheme that maps the partitions to the appropriate filegroups. Finally, you create or rebuild the table on the partition scheme.

Use the following the steps for SQL Server Management Studio (SSMS). We also commented these steps within the code:

1. Open a new query window in the SSMS query editor.

2. Copy and execute the code to set the database to AdventureWorks and alter the database to contain three filegroups.

3. Copy and execute the code to alter the database to contain a file in each filegroup.

4. Copy and execute the code to create the partition function using range right. All values through H are included in the first partition. Values H through N are included in the second partition. All values from N on are included in the third partition.

5. Copy and execute the code to create partition scheme.

6. Copy and execute the code to create a partitioned table on the partition scheme, noting the column used for partitioning.

7. Copy and execute the code to retrieve the partition information, noting the $partition function output.

8. Copy and execute the code to clean up the objects created.

    ```
    -- Set the database to AdventureWorks

    USE AdventureWorks

    GO



    -- Alter the AdventureWorks database to contain three filegroups

    ALTER DATABASE AdventureWorks ADD FILEGROUP flg1
    ```

```
ALTER DATABASE AdventureWorks ADD FILEGROUP flg2

ALTER DATABASE AdventureWorks ADD FILEGROUP flg3

GO


--Alter the database to contain a file in each filegroup

ALTER DATABASE AdventureWorks

ADD FILE

( NAME = data1,

  FILENAME = 'c:\Program Files\Microsoft SQL

➥Server\MSSQL.1\MSSQL\Data\AWdata1.ndf',

  SIZE = 1MB,

  MAXSIZE = 100MB,

  FILEGROWTH = 1MB)

TO FILEGROUP flg1


ALTER DATABASE AdventureWorks

ADD FILE

( NAME = data2,

  FILENAME = 'c:\Program Files\Microsoft SQL

➥Server\MSSQL.1\MSSQL\Data\AWdata2.ndf',

  SIZE = 1MB,

  MAXSIZE = 100MB,

  FILEGROWTH = 1MB)

TO FILEGROUP flg2


ALTER DATABASE AdventureWorks
```

```
ADD FILE

( NAME = data3,

  FILENAME = 'c:\Program Files\Microsoft SQL

➡Server\MSSQL.1\MSSQL\Data\AWdata3.ndf',

  SIZE = 1MB,

  MAXSIZE = 100MB,

  FILEGROWTH = 1MB)

TO FILEGROUP flg3

GO


-- Create partition function using range right

-- All values through H are included in the first partition.

-- H through values up to N are included in the second partition.

-- All values N on are included in the third partition.

CREATE PARTITION FUNCTION CollectorPF (nvarchar(30))

AS RANGE RIGHT FOR VALUES ('H', 'N')

GO


-- Create partition scheme

CREATE PARTITION SCHEME CollectorPS

AS PARTITION CollectorPF TO (flg1, flg2, flg3)

GO


-- Create partitioned table

CREATE TABLE Sales.NewProdReview

(RevID int, CustName char (15), NewProdName nvarchar(30), NewProdReview
nvarchar (50))
```

```
ON CollectorPS (NewProdName)

GO


-- Insert data

INSERT Sales.NewProdReview

VALUES

(1, 'Lefter','Self-Pedaling Bike', 'Easy to use')


INSERT Sales.NewProdReview

VALUES

(2, 'Miller-White','Uphill Motor bike','Works great')


INSERT Sales.NewProdReview

VALUES

(3, 'Knarr','Level Riding Bike','Great in Texas')


INSERT Sales.NewProdReview

VALUES

(4, 'Tallon','Basic Mountain Bike','Worked well on Rainier')



-- Retrieve partition information

SELECT NewProdName, CustName, NewProdReview,

  $partition.CollectorPF(NewProdName) Partition

FROM Sales.NewProdReview
```

EXERCISE 9.1 *(continued)*

Your retrieved data should look like the following:

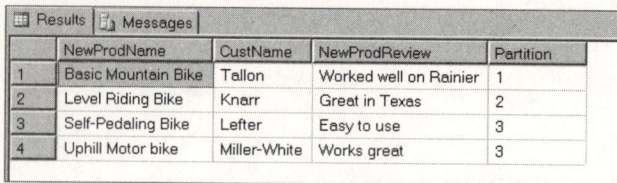

	NewProdName	CustName	NewProdReview	Partition
1	Basic Mountain Bike	Tallon	Worked well on Rainier	1
2	Level Riding Bike	Knarr	Great in Texas	2
3	Self-Pedaling Bike	Lefter	Easy to use	3
4	Uphill Motor bike	Miller-White	Works great	3

Prior to executing the following code to clean up your database, revisit Object Explorer in SSMS, noting dependencies and scripting of the objects you recently created in the exercise:

- The files and filegroups are found on the AdventureWorks property sheet.

- The CollectorPS partition scheme can be found under the Partition Scheme folder under Storage.

- The CollectorPF partition function can be found under the Partition Function folder under Storage.

- The Sales.NewProdReview table can be found under AdventureWorks.

- The disk usage report can be found under the Summary reports. Pay special note to the disk space partitions report uses.

Here is the code to clean up the objects created in AdventureWorks by Exercise 9.1:

```
-- Clean up objects created in AdventureWorks

DROP TABLE Sales.NewProdReview

GO

DROP PARTITION SCHEME CollectorPS

DROP PARTITION FUNCTION CollectorPF

GO

ALTER DATABASE AdventureWorks REMOVE FILE data1

ALTER DATABASE AdventureWorks REMOVE FILE data2

ALTER DATABASE AdventureWorks REMOVE FILE data3

ALTER DATABASE AdventureWorks REMOVE FILEGROUP flg1

ALTER DATABASE AdventureWorks REMOVE FILEGROUP flg2

ALTER DATABASE AdventureWorks REMOVE FILEGROUP flg3
```

Partitioning a Table to Make Your Data More Manageable

An example of this type of partitioning has been built into the AdventureWorks database samples. The default location for this sample script, PartitionsAW.sql is C:\Program Files\Microsoft SQL Server\90\Samples\Engine\Administration\Partitioning\Scripts.

The Production.TransactionHistory table records every piece of transaction information for the company, current for the past 12 months. Every transaction prior to that date is kept in the Production.TransactionHistoryArchive table. The partition functions, schema, and appropriate switching algorithm to move the oldest month's records for the current year into the archive table for that year are all included as a part of the queries contained within PartitionsAW.sql in the Samples folder.

The following explanation is from the readme of the PartitionsAW.sql sample. To create the partitions for these tables, the sample performs these operations:

- Creates partition function TransactionRangePF1 on the TransactionDate column of the TransactionHistory table, so that each partition contains one month of data.

- Creates partition scheme TransactionsPS1 to map the partitions to filegroups. In this sample, all partitions reside on the same filegroup.

- Drops and re-creates the TransactionHistory table specifying the partition scheme TransactionsPS1 as the location for the table.

- Creates partition function TransactionRangePF2 on the TransactionDate column of the TransactionHistoryArchive table.

- Creates partition scheme TransactionsPS2 to map the partitions to filegroups. In this sample, all partitions reside on the same filegroup.

- Drops and re-creates the TransactionHistoryArchive table specifying the partition scheme TransactionsPS2 as the location for the table.

- Bulk inserts data into the two tables.

The transfer of monthly "chunks" of data between the tables is performed by switching partitions between the two tables. This typically takes just seconds, instead of minutes or hours in earlier releases, because it is a metadata operation only instead of a physical relocation of the data. Partition switching is demonstrated in the sliding window sample.

 If you do not have an updated version of SQL Server 2005 samples, you can download them from http://www.microsoft.com/sql/downloads/2005/default.mspx.

This scenario leads you through a very nice example of the archiving sliding window to keep the current TransactionHistory table small while maintaining an active archive table for analysis and reporting.

Understanding Scaleout Solutions

Your database system is designed to handle real-time business operations. A generalized scaleout solution of multiple databases servicing customers such as that used in a web farm approach does not work for updatable database technologies. An example is the database application you might use to book an airline ticket online. When you buy your ticket for a flight and pick your seat number, that seat on that particular flight is assigned to you only. If multiple copies of the database were available for customers to book tickets on the same flight, it is possible that more than one customer could book the same seat. So you can see that making copies of the same database just won't work if data is frequently updated. However, this solution could perform fine if all users need to do is read the data, such as in viewing flight schedules, flight history, or reward miles.

It is not just a matter of deciding to scale out. You need to be able to know the data type usage in your application as well as the scaleout solutions that are available for SQL Server 2005. It is not easy to put the two together to create an optimal scaleout solution. Quite often, your application will contain multiple data usage types, for example, both reference and resource data. Resource data is volatile and requires necessary mechanisms be in place for transactions and concurrency to occur, such as in the flight-booking example. If database contains multiple data usage types but the application you want to scale out uses only one type, you may need to make minimal modifications to the application.

How do you handle an application that consists of multiple usage data types? Is there a best solution for scaleout? The best solution in this instance is to refocus. Determine the section of the application you want to scale out. Work only with that portion of the data and the application to build the best scaleout solution for your scenario. This may mean rewriting the application or restructuring of the underlying data, such as using data partitioning. Regardless of what method you employ, you must remain focused on just those sections defined in the project for the scaleout while ascertaining those sections still "fit" the overall application.

> If you use our A Case in Point: Organized Information study as an example for a scaleout solution, you notice it is the medical study retrieval section of the database or application that needs a scaleout solution. A large number of users need to retrieve information concerning patient drug response at the same time drug data is being entered into the database.

In a very broad sense, scaleout solutions in SQL Server 2005 can be categorized into three areas: transparent scaleout, nontransparent scaleout, and scaleout through *service-oriented data architecture* (SODA).

- *Transparent scaleout* is ideally loosely coupling many networked database computers, each with the same database, such that the user sees one virtual server—the database farm, so to speak. This effort has been trying to be born for nearly 20 years now without success.

  Even though no full implementation of transparent scaleout has made it out the door, it can be implemented in two special-case environments. The first is the read-only scenario that we depicted previously. The database can be copied and queried with no contention or update issues. The second, for minimal updating, is a replication scenario. You have a variety of replication technologies available in SQL Server 2005, including a new paradigm, peer-to-peer replication. You will learn more about peer-to-peer replication in the following section.

- *Nontransparent scaleout* is generally defined by the use of multiple servers running their own databases. It becomes the job of the application to pull together the resources to appear as one central repository. For example, each database, on a separate server, may hold a different activity of the company. For example, Production, Accounts, Sales, HumanResources are all separate databases. Take note how this differs from the AdventureWorks model of these concepts being schemas within one database. Partitioning technologies might be employed successfully in this scaleout strategy also. You might also find one of the replication strategies could be used in the right scenario.

- SODA is new to the scaleout scene. We have been waiting for over a decade for SODA to become a part of our database architecture and here it is. Our database system now supports our business logic natively through a set of services. You can move and change services without making any changes to your database or to your application.

Now that you have had a short introduction, let's learn more about each of the scaleout solutions.

Scaleout Using Scalable Shared Databases

You can implement a *scalable shared databases* scaleout solution with minimum effort. Its disadvantage is that you are using a single image of your database, the "shared disk," for each scaleout presence.

Here is how it works. You create a database on a storage area network (SAN). You attach up to eight instances of SQL Server. Eight is a tested workable maximum recommended by Microsoft. Each instance, on its own SQL server and set up using the same drive letter specifications, must actively attach to the database. The only way this concept can work is if no locking mechanism is allowed within each individual database. If locking were allowed, you would have the situation of the scenario you saw previously where more than one person could buy a ticket for the same seat on a plane.

The databases are read only, making scalable shared databases good scaleout solutions for reporting services marts or data marts. Other applications use read-only data, which might make this a worthwhile scaleout solution for you. For querying purposes, your clients see identical views of the data on all servers. This solution also eliminates the impact of a query that could hog the system resources, holding up all other queries. Each server uses its own CPU, memory, and tempdb database. Figure 9.2 shows a scalable shared database scaleout solution.

Consider one other piece of information before you decide that this solution is calling your name. Just how *do* you update the data on the SAN? Well, as we said, this is an easy implementation. You start all over again somewhat. That is, you need to detach all the SQL Server instances from the database. Attach one of the instances in read-write mode and refresh your database with the most current data available. Once the refresh has completed, reattach all the SQL Server instances to the database.

FIGURE 9.2 Scalable shared database scaleout solution

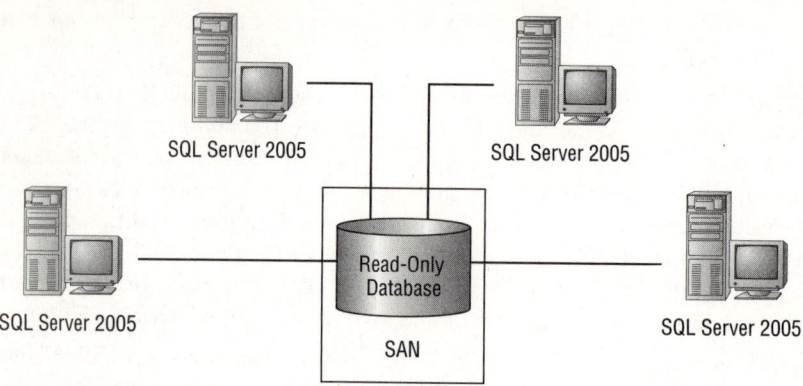

If you have the disk resources available, it might make more sense for you to update your database using a second database. The second database is read-write and in synchronization with your production server. You have a choice of two technologies you can implement, synchronized or rolling update. If you require your clients to have identical versions of the data at all times, you will need to use a synchronized update.

For a synchronized update you must first detach the older read version of the database from every server instance. Once every server instance is detached, as quickly as possible, each server instance must be attached to the second database. You will have a small amount of time where the database will be unavailable for use, so you need to plan this turnover operation. The second technology, the rolling update, requires your clients to have different views of the data during the time of the rolling update window. Each server instance is detached and attached in a round-robin fashion from the stale database to the fresh database. This round-robin operation should be done at a planned time and as quickly as possible because the client data views will be different during this window.

To find more information on implementing refresh strategies for a scalable shared databases solution search Books Online topic "Maximizing Availability of a Scalable Shared Database."

Scaleout Using Peer-to-Peer Replication

Replication is often a good scaleout solution if you have a moderate number of updates in your environment. With an installation of SQL Server 2005, you have a new choice for replication, peer-to-peer replication.

Peer-to-peer replication gives you independence without isolation. Each node in a peer-to-peer replication propagates its changes to all other nodes in the replication topology. Every node is both a publisher and a subscriber of every other node using the same schema and data.

The transactional replication relationship is a peer relationship in contrast to the hierarchical relationship found in other forms of standard transactional replication. Figure 9.3 shows a peer-to-peer replication scaleout solution.

FIGURE 9.3   Peer-to-peer replication scaleout solution

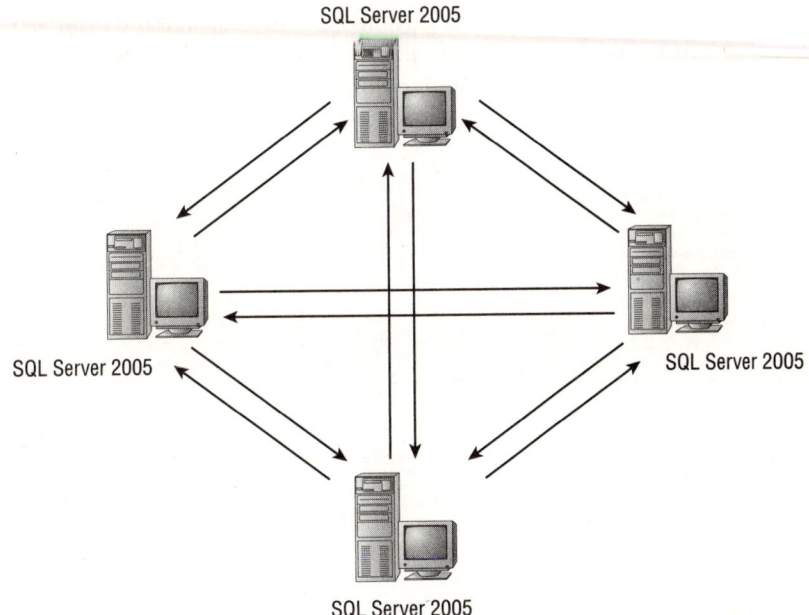

In this solution you have multiple copies of the database with each database engine maintaining its own copy. This implementation allows for updatability. The replication technology recognizes the hosting node change and propagates the change appropriately to the peer members.

In those database applications employing a peer-to-peer scaleout solution, you need to ensure that data modifications processed at one node are synchronized with all peers prior to being processed at another node. You can use a few techniques to accomplish this. One is termed data stewardship. Data stewardship means that you can only update the data you own. Let's use a retail store chain as our example. If you allow each store to have full access to its own data and read access to all other stores' data you have made them stewards of their data. This concept avoids update conflicts, eliminates the overhead of merge replication, and prevents potential server bottlenecks. Peer-to-peer replication provides high availability of your data while allowing local maintenance of the participating databases. If another store is opened or closed, you are adding or subtracting a node to the replication topology. If you have a situation where data stewardship is not a practical solution, you can still use merge replication to handle the conflicts.

With its capability to handle updates and ease of use, peer-to-peer replication can be used to scaleout solutions over all the data usage types. Replication can be used for the entire database or just a table or even parts of a table. Replication can be used just for the data in a particular application. Since it is flexible and can be used along with other scaleout solutions, peer-to-peer replication is one of the most widely applicable scaleout solutions of SQL Server 2005.

Scaleout Using Linked Servers and Distributed Queries

You can implement a *linked server* scaleout solution to give your users access to remote server objects as if they were on their local server. Synonyms in SQL Server 2005 can be used to address the four part naming convention needed to address the linked object name. Using a synonym enables you to change the data source without changing the query. Figure 9.4 shows a linked server scaleout solution.

FIGURE 9.4   Linked server scaleout solution

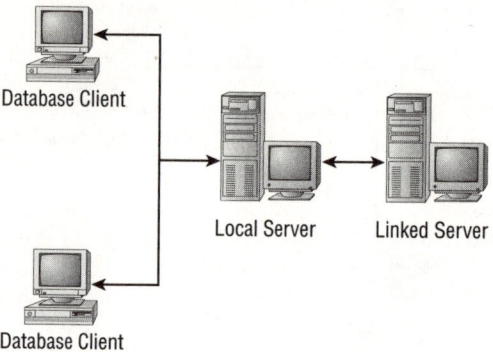

Usually you use linked servers when you need to access data that is loosely coupled to your local database. This data may be in the form of reference data. For example, if your archived data is transferred to another database on a different server, using linked servers enables you to access this data as if it were local. And just the opposite is also true. If you have an application that references your historical data and seldom accesses current data, you can use linked servers to access the current data as if it were local.

To make an effective linked server scaleout solution, you need to be certain your data coupling remains loose between the databases. If data coupling is high, the overhead of the joins of your distributed queries will be very expensive. This expense will cancel any gain you expect from your scaleout.

Scaleout Using Distributed Partitioned Views

Distributed partitioned views is a scaleout solution that supports the transparent partition of data horizontally across a group of servers. Although these servers cooperate in managing the partitioned data, they operate autonomously. Each server is managed independently, has separate operational rules, and can support independent processes and data. A group of autonomous servers that cooperate to process a workload is known as a federation.

You build federated database servers by creating databases on each server. You then partition tables across the databases. Each original table has a member table on each server, which has been split from the original table. Each member table is a subset of the original table. Your application uses a set of routing rules to access the data it needs from the proper server quickly. For instance, if more than one member server holds the needed data, the routing rules will identify the best retrieval method to get the data most efficiently.

For example, suppose you have a customer table that you partition into member tables on different servers as follows. 1–1,000 in a table on one database on one server, 1,001–2,000 in a table on a second database on another server, 2,001–3,000 in a table on a third database on a third server, and so on. You have implemented check constraints so that SQL Server knows which customer is associated with which database. If you execute a query that references a particular customer number, your routing rule will direct the query to the correct database for data retrieval. If multiple customer numbers are requested by your query such that the customer numbers span more than one database or if the requested data is not identified by the customer number, perhaps the name instead, then all databases might need to be queried.

Distributed partitioned views yield good performance in update-intensive applications since most updates concentrate on a confined set of rows within a single database Therefore, this solution is a good choice for high update frequencies.

However, this solution has not been widely embraced because it takes a great deal of management to set up and get running efficiently. The partitions need to be synchronized at all times. A disaster recovery scenario depends on the synchronization of the federation.

Scaleout Using Data-Dependent Routing

Data-dependent routing (DDR) can allow your application to do what SQL Server cannot yet do. Many extremely large, or some may call humongous, databases with a large amount of transactions need a method to handle distributed queries. Generally these databases are partitioned using distributed processing with tables built on separate databases such as in our example for distributed partition views. In keeping with our example, since such a vast amount of data is stored for each customer, it makes sense to store all related data for that customer in one place. These self-contained groups of data are called entities. So if you are looking to query customer 1,024, for example, you would be directed through data-dependent routing to server B where the entity for customer 1,024 lies. Reading as well as updating data runs faster since it is stored in and retrieved from one location. Figure 9.5 shows a data-dependent routing scaleout solution.

The design for the data retrieval is in the DDR application. You need to implement the logic in the DDR that will map the customer's ID along with where their entity data is located. When data and retrieval needs get this voluminous, you need to make certain you know your data as well as your application. Many applications fail because programmers have not taken the time to know and understand the data; they only knew the application.

Data-dependent routing is a scaleout solution designed for large volumes of data with high levels of transactions. You need to plan well prior to building the databases and the application. DDR should be used in a new application, not a retrofit. Remember to take the time to understand both your data and your application.

FIGURE 9.5 Data-dependent routing scaleout solution

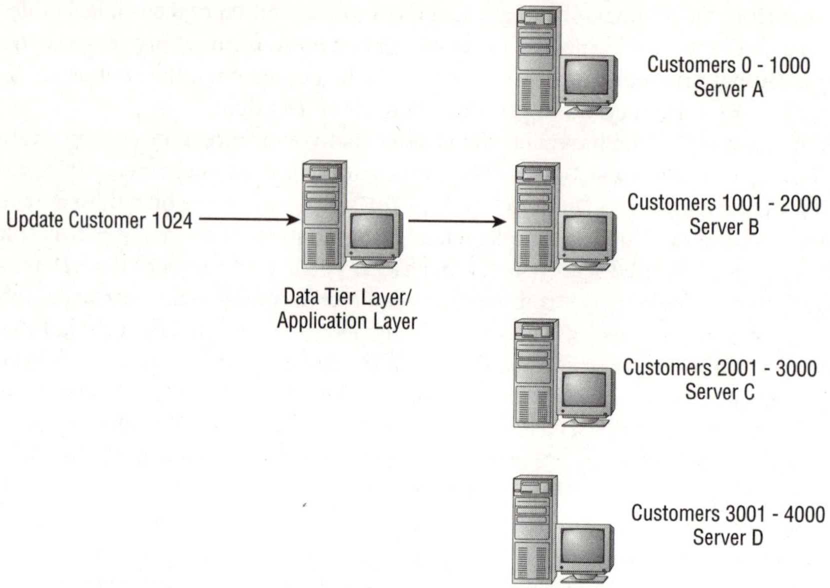

Customers 0 - 1000
Server A

Update Customer 1024 →

Data Tier Layer/
Application Layer

Customers 1001 - 2000
Server B

Customers 2001 - 3000
Server C

Customers 3001 - 4000
Server D

Scaleout Using Service-Oriented Data Architecture (SODA)

Over the past several years we have seen a change in the way database systems are used. Internet e-commerce has moved usage from the traditional realm of client-server well-connected systems to loosely coupled systems in a multitiered global environment. Microsoft SQL Server architects not only took note of this shift but felt that this shift would create the next trend in database service needs. They tasked themselves with redesigning the Microsoft SQL Server DBMS to accommodate these changes. Their vision has created the architecture features that provide the services, normally supplied through applications or middleware products, right in your database. This implementation of service-oriented architecture within the database is called service-oriented data architecture (SODA).

SQL Server 2005 is now a one-stop service shop. It provides all the features to be a full-service provider for a loosely coupled distributed application. Some of these new features include the Service Broker service, notifications service, web service access, and SQLCLR. Including these services as a part of the architecture enables SQL Server to manage the data and to support scalability.

For an inside view on the background of SQL Server service-oriented database architecture, see David Campbell's Technical Report "Service Oriented Database Architecture: App Server-Lite?" at http://research.microsoft.com/research/pubs/view.aspx?tr_id=983.

There are several reasons why it is beneficial to put service architecture in the structural design of the database engine. The most important to you at this point is that incorporating services in the database architecture enables you to scaleup or scaleout your applications by using services. This means that a scaleout decision can be made at the deployment timeframe rather than at development.

Features of a Service-Oriented Data Access Provider

Let's take a look at what you further need to consider to create a scaleout solution using SQL Server 2005 as a service provider:

- A service provider must present endpoint support for the message communication in the form of endpoints. Typical endpoints include TCP, HTTP, and SOAP.

- A service provider must process and, if needed, transform service requests. It must also be able to participate in a dialogue and conversation structure as messages are sent and received through the service queues.

- A service provider must be a logic host. It must be able to perform the logic to process the message and furthermore hand off instructions to other services involved.

SQL Server 2005 Service-Oriented Data Access Features

Let's next take a look at some of the new features of SQL Server 2005 in regards to how they are applied in scaleout solutions.

Native Web Service Access: Provides Endpoint Support

A *web service* is a message-based communication based on SOAP and other protocols that are built on the Windows Server 2003 HTTP kernel-mode driver, http.sys.

The server takes the web service request from the client in the form of an HTTP listener. The server then routes the request to the designated endpoint. The request is passed through the SOAP processing layer in SQL Server. There can be several endpoints within each SQL Server instance with each of these endpoints having multiple web methods.

You are able to bind stored procedures or scalar-valued, user-defined functions to a single web method. You can also configure an endpoint to automatically generate and provide Web Service Definition Language (WSDL) data.

For scaleout, services can provide a lot of flexibility in your solution. You are able to move services to different locations easily. Moving services in this manner does not just include web services but also applies to the remaining services that we mention in this section.

Service Broker: Provides Reliable Messaging

Service Broker provides a reliable, secure, asynchronous, and scalable messaging infrastructure for your applications. Service Broker provides the messaging host for your service provider. Service Broker contains a variety of features and objects that provide guaranteed delivery of ordered messages for your applications. It provides a total framework to support your application's messaging requirements by containing the infrastructure of the message-conversation contract and the queue delivery process. Service Broker handles all service bindings. A single Service Broker queue is able to handle multiple service programs.

Since Service Broker is built into the SQL Server 2005 database engine, you use stored procedures, user-defined functions, and .NET Framework code in Transact-SQL using Service Broker extensions to build your applications.

Once again the flexibility provided with this messaging service is easy to scale out to different servers or locations at deployment.

Query Notifications: Provides Caching Support

Query Notifications provide you with the ability to design your applications to query a database when the underlying data to which that application has previously retrieved is changed. The notification is generated on an original cache being populated from the query.

Your application relies on cached data until a notification message arrives. If SQL Server is no longer able to guarantee that the cached data is reliable, SQL Server sends a notification message. SQL Server sends a query notification for event subscriptions such as changing the results of a query, restarting your server, dropping or modifying subscription objects, and overloading of server processing.

Using Query Notifications enables you to improve the performance of loosely coupled applications that are widely distributed by caching data and reducing round-trips to the database. Query Notifications works by caching data that rarely changes at a service provider that can be located remotely from the source database. Using Query Notifications allows your messages to be smaller and use fewer network resources.

SQLCLR: Provides Logical Host

SQLCLR provides the logic host. A service provider must run high-level code capable of performing very complex business logic. Transact-SQL, although excellent at delivering data, just does not handle complex business logic. Bringing .NET Framework code that runs within the SQL Server process has provided us the last piece in our SODA infrastructure.

You can use SQLCLR to write functions that you would have previously written as extended stored procedures. You also have a variety of user-defined functions that can now be written using the CLR. SQL Server creates the hosting environment for your code; it is integrated within the security of your database. Code assemblies are loaded and kept within the confines of the database, not the file system.

For your applications that are written based on SODA, employing the CLR execution environment enables multiple programming languages, system resource management, and the security of your code access. You can develop custom objects: types, aggregates, triggers, and stored procedures built on logic-based code. Once you have developed and installed a CLR function, it is available to be used within any implemented query.

Using a service-oriented application you can now place all the logic within the database. This gives you the option of developing a single code base as opposed to having separate tiers to host or process your business logic.

SODA Implementation of Service-Centric Applications

A main advantage of a service-oriented data architecture implementation is the capability to manage and integrate services within the database. Services can be deployed anywhere, moved anywhere. With SODA you have a new alternative to the traditional approach to your application development, service-centric applications.

 For further reading on SQL Server 2005 service-oriented architecture, see Microsoft's white paper "Why Consider a Service-Oriented Database Architecture for Scalability and Availability," downloadable at http:// www.microsoft.com/sql/techinfo/whitepapers/why-soda.mspx. See also the TechNet article "Boost Performance with New Features in SQL Server 2005" by Paul Nielson at http://www.microsoft.com/tech-net/technetmag/issues/2006/01/BoostPerformance/default.aspx.

Summary

You have seen how the architectural design of SQL Server 2005 provides a foundation for new methodologies in scaling up and scaling out your database applications. You have seen how important it is to understand your data and build its structure well. A well-planned database schema is important in boosting the performance of the applications you create. You looked at the factors of data type and usage as to how they affect your scaleout solution.

You learned how to design transparent, nontransparent, and SODA scaleout solutions. You applied the scaleout solutions using scalable shared databases, peer-to-peer replication, linked servers, distributed partitioned views, data-dependent routing, and service-oriented data architecture.

Exam Essentials

Know how to specify a data-partitioning model.   You need to be able to specify the various means of data partitioning. You should to know when to apply a particular partitioning model in a scaleout solution.

Know how to design solutions that target multiple servers.   You need to understand scaleout solutions that retrieve data from multiple databases and how that affects the query process.

Know how to implement scaleout technologies.   You need to be able to identify the various scaleout solutions and how each would be applied.

Know how to design transparent, nontransparent, and SODA scaleout solutions.   You need understand the concepts and features of service-oriented data architecture (SODA). You need to know how to design service-centric applications.

Know how to write and identify code to improve performance.   You need to be able to adapt your code to boost performance for your scaled out applications.

Review Questions

1. You want to create a related multi-table structured database consisting of a primary key and a number of atomic fields. What process should you be using?

   A. Database rationalization

   B. Database normalization

   C. Relational organization

   D. Schema relationalization

2. Which type of data having a high concurrency requirement do you use for your current business data?

   A. Reference data

   B. Activity data

   C. Resource data

   D. Service interaction data

3. Which process describes increasing your server's resources such as memory, disk subsystem, and CPU speed?

   A. Scaleup

   B. Scaleout

4. Which of the following is not a factor that affects scaleout?

   A. Data isolation

   B. Data update frequency

   C. Data longevity

   D. Available key column on which to partition data

5. Which of the following objects need to be created in partitioning a table in a database? (Choose all that apply.)

   A. Create a partition scheme.

   B. Create a partition function.

   C. Create a partitioned table.

   D. Create the filegroups and files.

6. State the order of creation for the following objects used in partitioning a table in a database.

    1. Create a partition scheme.

    2. Create a partition function.

    3. Create a partitioned table.

    4. Create the filegroups and files.

    A. 1, 2, 3, 4

    B. 4, 2, 1, 3

    C. 3, 1, 4, 2

    D. 4, 3, 2, 1

7. You have a SQL Server 2005 database consisting basically of an extremely large table filled with gigabytes of data that is used for both data entry and data retrieval. Contention is high and queries run slow in this table. Which of the following provide a solution for this database?

    A. Partition the table.

    B. Add memory to the database server.

    C. Move this table on a new disk from the other tables in the database.

    D. Add another processor to the database server.

8. In your company's SQL Server 2005 database, you have a table called Transactions containing transaction data. This table is extremely large. You wish to remove older transactions from this table and place them into another table called TransactionHistory. Which of the following would be an appropriate solution for your database?

    A. Create a new database for the TransactionHistory table and implement bulk load to move the data.

    B. Create the tables using partitioned tables and use partition switching to move the data to the history table.

    C. Move the data from the Transactions table to the TransactionHistory table by moving the older data to an Excel spreadsheet and loading it into the TransactionHistory table.

    D. Create a new database for the TransactionHistory table and implement SSIS to move the data.

9. You are looking for a scaleout solution for users who are creating reports. You have created a reporting services database but want to scale out the solution. Which of the following is an appropriate scaleout solution?

    A. Distributed partitioned views

    B. Data-dependent routing

    C. Peer-to-peer replication

    D. Scalable shared databases

10. Which of the following describes a scaleout technology new to SQL Server 2005 in which each server replicates its changes to every other server in the scaleout solution?

    A. Distributed partitioned views

    B. Snapshot replication

    C. Peer-to-peer replication

    D. Scalable shared databases

11. Which of the following scaleout strategies is the easiest to implement?

    A. Replication

    B. Service-oriented data architecture

    C. Data-dependent routing

    D. Distributed partitioned views

12. Which of the following describes the technology used in peer-to-peer replication that only allows the owner of a data item to update the data?

    A. Data isolation

    B. Data stewardship

    C. Data replication

    D. Data lineage

13. Which of the following scaleout solutions allows you to query remote database objects as if they were local?

    A. Replication

    B. Service-oriented data architecture

    C. Linked servers

    D. Distributed partitioned views

14. Which of the following scaleout solutions provides good performance in update-intensive applications?

    A. Replication

    B. Service-oriented data architecture

    C. Linked servers

    D. Distributed partitioned views

15. Which of the following scaleout solutions works well with large volumes of data with high levels of transactions?

    A. Replication

    B. Service-oriented data architecture

    C. Linked servers

    D. Data-dependent routing

16. What term is used to describe a group of autonomous servers that cooperate to process a workload?

   A. Delegation

   B. Federation

   C. Cluster

   D. Farm

17. Which of the following scaleout solutions is built on being a service provider?

   A. Replication

   B. Service-oriented data architecture

   C. Linked servers

   D. Data-dependent routing

18. Which feature of SQL Server 2005 provides endpoint support for a service-oriented data architecture scaleout solution?

   A. Service Broker

   B. SQLCLR

   C. Distributed queries

   D. Native web services access

19. Which feature of SQL Server 2005 provides messaging infrastructure for a service-oriented data architecture scaleout solution?

   A. Service Broker

   B. SQLCLR

   C. Distributed queries

   D. Native web services access

20. Which feature of SQL Server 2005 provides the logic host for a service-oriented data architecture scaleout solution?

   A. Service Broker

   B. SQLCLR

   C. Distributed queries

   D. Native web services access

Answers to Review Questions

1. B. Database normalization is the process of using well-known technologies to separate your data into a related multi-table structured set to reduce redundancy. In relational database theory, third normal form is defined as the relation where "the relation is based on the key, the whole key, and nothing but the key." None of the other options are appropriate answers.

2. C. Resource data is the data you use for your current business data. Reference data is relatively stable data. Activity data pertains to a particular business activity. Service interaction data is used to communicate between services.

3. A. Scaleup is the process of boosting your single server system to improve your application performance. Scaleout involves expanding your data to multiple servers.

4. C. Data longevity does not affect scaleout. However, it might affect the type of scaleout solution that you decide to use. The other mentioned options are all factors that affect scaleout.

5. A, B, C, D. All options are needed in the implementation of partitioning a table.

6. B. You must alter the database to create the appropriate filegroups and files. You need to create a partition function before you create a partition scheme. It is possible to create the filegroups after the function and scheme are created. Finally, the partitioned table is created and, data is added to the partitioned table.

7. A. You should partition the table horizontally over several filegroups to boost performance. This solution will alleviate the contention problems. Adding memory and adding a processor will not relieve contention. Moving the entire table will not relieve the contention of the queries within the table.

8. B. The transfer of scheduled amounts of data between the tables can be performed by switching partitions between the two tables. The data is still available within the same database but is contained on different disks, which allows you to maintain an active archive table. None of the other solutions are viable solutions.

9. D. In a scalable shared databases solution, you are using a single image of your database, the "shared disk," for each scaleout presence. This is an excellent solution for reporting scaleout. This solution is only viable if there is no locking, so it is good for data that is read only. Shared databases take less effort to implement and is a more effect solution for report scaleout than the others mentioned.

10. C. Peer-to-peer replication propagates changes made to any copy of the data to all other copies. This is a new replication technology to SQL Server 2005. Snapshot replication does not propagate change in both directions in its publication-subscription paradigm. Distributed partitioned views and scalable shared databases are not replication technologies.

11. A. In general, replication is the easiest to implement and most widely applicable scaleout strategy for SQL Server 2005.

12. B. The rules that permit only the data owner to update data items belonging to them is termed data stewardship.

13. C. Linked servers give you the ability to query objects in remote databases as if they were local objects.

14. D. Since most update transactions affect a small number of rows, distributed partitioned views provide good performance in update-intensive applications.

15. D. Data-dependent routing is designed for large volumes of data that have high level of transactional processing. However, you should plan well when using this scaleout solution.

16. B. A group of autonomous servers that cooperate to process a workload is a federation. You build federated database servers by creating databases on each server. You then partition tables across the databases.

17. B. Service-oriented data architecture (SODA) enables you to build service-centric applications. This gives you all the features of being a full-service provider for your loosely coupled distributed applications.

18. D. Native web services access provides the endpoint support for SODA from the client in the form of an HTTP listener.

19. A. Service Broker provides a reliable, secure, asynchronous, and scalable messaging infrastructure for your applications. Service Broker provides the messaging host for your service provider.

20. B. Using a service-oriented application you are able to place all the logic within the database. The host for this logic is SQLCLR.

Chapter

10

Resolving Performance Problems

In this book, we've taken you through various methods that can improve an application's performance. You have seen how to work with indexes, how to improve a query's performance, and how to customize SQL Server's locking behavior. In this chapter, you will attack performance problems at a different level. You'll learn how to tune performance at the server level.

Getting Started

As you know from Chapter 7, your application can slow down because of the following reasons:

- Inefficient query plans
- Blocking issues
- Indexes (unused or missing)
- Missing or out-of-date statistics
- Compilations and recompilations
- Resource (CPU, I/O, tempdb, memory) bottlenecks
- Slow network connections
- Improper database design
- Improper server configuration

You've already learned about the first five of these issues, so in this chapter we concentrate on the others. We discuss how to detect the problems and possible resolutions. The solutions proposed in this chapter concentrate on improving performance with the existing hardware configuration and application design. Though it's easier to replace a CPU with a faster one than to troubleshoot CPU-intensive queries, we will concentrate on the troubleshooting path rather than the scaleup or scaleout resolutions. For scaleup or scaleout methods, refer to Chapter 9.

We'll start by reminding you of the tools that can help you in your performance quest.

Using Performance-Related Tools

Most of the tools you can use to improve performance should be already familiar to you from the previous chapters. However, we list them here to give you an overall picture of the performance toolbox available in SQL Server 2005. You will see different usage scenarios for them throughout this chapter.

System Monitor (PerfMon)   Allows you to track resource usage on local and remote machines.

Task Manager   Displays information about programs and processes running on a computer.

Performance Logs and Alerts   Allows you to collect the same performance data as the System Monitor but automatically.

Network Monitor Agent   Allows you to monitor network traffic and detect network problems.

SQL Server Profiler   Is the graphical tool for capturing events such as the start of a Transact-SQL statement, a deadlock event, and many others.

SQL Trace   Offers the trace events capability similar to SQL Server Profile but without a graphic interface. A trace can be defined and managed using the following system stored procedures:

>   **sp_trace_create**   Defines a trace.
>
>   **sp_trace_setevent**   Adds or removes events or event columns.
>
>   **sp_trace_setfilter**   Filters the trace.
>
>   **sp_trace_setstatus**   Starts, stops, or closes a trace.
>
>   **sp_trace_generateevent**   Generates a user-defined event.

Dynamic Management Views and Functions   Expose server state information such as memory allocation, lock requests, current connections, and so on.

SQL Server Management Studio   Offers insight about your server activity through:

>   **Summary Reports**   A set of reports based on dynamic management views, default trace, and catalog views. Starting with Service Pack 2 you can use your own reports.
>
>   **Activity Monitor**   Returns information about current connections and lock requests.
>
>   **Error logs**   The Log File Viewer of SQL Server Management Studio integrates SQL Server, SQL Server Agent, and the Windows logs into a single list.

Database Console Commands   Although partially replaced by dynamic management views and functions, you may find some situations when Database Console commands can help you.

System Functions   @@CONNECTIONS (the number of attempted connections), @@TOTAL_READ (represents the number of the disk reads), and @@TOTAL_WRITES (represents the number of the disk writes) are a few of SQL Server's built-in functions for troubleshooting performance issues.

Trace Flags   If you need to go really deep with your troubleshooting, you can use the trace flags to get additional information for specific situations. For example, the trace flag 1204 can be used to enhance the information obtained for a deadlock situation.

Database Engine Tuning Advisor   Replaces Index Tuning Wizard (ITW) and can be used to optimize the physical design structure of your database through adding, removing, or modifying indexes, indexed views, and partitions.

System Stored Procedures   Some of the system stored procedure such as sp_monitor (that is used to display statistical information for CPU and I/O usage) can be added to your performance toolbox.

Dedicated Administrator Connection   When blocking or any other reason makes your server unresponsive and your server does not respond to new connection requests, you can try DAC. The DAC is the backdoor to your server in emergency situations.

The list is not complete but includes the tools you will use in this chapter. One of the tools that could be new to you is the default trace.

Using the Default Trace

One of the new tools introduced by SQL Server 2005 is the *default trace*—a lightweight trace that records mainly configuration changes on your server. You may have used the default trace without even knowing it when you opened a summary report. The default trace along with dynamic management functions, dynamic management views, and catalog views are the data source for summary reports of SQL Server Management Studio.

Why should you use the default trace? With it, you can identify server configuration changes that had an impact on your server's performance, such as dropping an index or flushing the cache. To make things even better, the default trace runs implicitly on your server and needs absolutely no configuration.

To explain more about the default trace, we will show several queries starting with locating the default trace:

```
SELECT *
FROM fn_trace_getinfo(1)
GO
-- Output on my machine
traceid property value
1        1        2
1        2        C:\Program Files\Microsoft SQL
 Server\MSSQL.1\MSSQL\LOG\log_1908.trc
1        3        20
1        4        NULL
1        5        1
```

The function fn_trace_getinfo returns information about the specified trace ID. You probably guessed that the default trace has the trace ID 1.

If you want to know what events the default trace records, you can use the next query:

```
SELECT DISTINCT
    T.eventid, E.[name]
FROM fn_trace_geteventinfo(1) T
JOIN sys.trace_events E
  ON T.eventid = E.trace_event_id
```

```
GO
-- Output
eventid name
18       Audit Server Starts And Stops
20       Audit Login Failed
??       ErrorLog
46       Object:Created
47       Object:Deleted
55       Hash Warning
69       Sort Warnings
79       Missing Column Statistics
80       Missing Join Predicate
81       Server Memory Change
92       Data File Auto Grow
93       Log File Auto Grow
94       Data File Auto Shrink
95       Log File Auto Shrink
102      Audit Database Scope GDR Event
103      Audit Schema Object GDR Event
104      Audit Addlogin Event
105      Audit Login GDR Event
106      Audit Login Change Property Event
108      Audit Add Login to Server Role Event
109      Audit Add DB User Event
110      Audit Add Member to DB Role Event
111      Audit Add Role Event
115      Audit Backup/Restore Event
116      Audit DBCC Event
152      Audit Change Database Owner
153      Audit Schema Object Take Ownership Event
155      FT:Crawl Started
156      FT:Crawl Stopped
157      FT:Crawl Aborted
164      Object:Altered
167      Database Mirroring State Change
```

As you can see, you can find out about some events in the default trace, but the trace will not fill up your disk. The default trace is a rollover trace kept in five files of 20MB each. So it records a maximum of 100MB worth of events. The default trace can support many scenarios, such as auditing schema modifications, backup or restore events, and so on. To get an idea of some of them, look at the results of the previous query.

To get the complete list of the events that can be monitored using a trace as well as the list of the columns that can be added for an event, refer to the "sp_trace_setevent" topic from Books Online.

To show the default trace at work, we use a simple example that allows you to identify the login of the user who used the DBCC FREEPROCCACHE command to clear the cache. As you know, don't run this command on a production server:

```
-- free plan cache
DBCC FREEPROCCACHE WITH NO_INFOMSGS;
GO
-- Get the file name
DECLARE @FileName NVARCHAR(245);
SELECT @FileName = CAST([value] AS NVARCHAR(245))
FROM fn_trace_getinfo(1)
WHERE [property] = 2;
-- select DBCC audit events
SELECT TextData,
       StartTime,
       LoginName,
       *
FROM fn_trace_gettable
(@FileName, default)
WHERE EventClass = 116
GO
```

First use the DBCC FREEPROCCACHE to free the procedure cache and to give the default trace something to record. Then, the default trace provides all events that have the EventClass 116 (which means Audit DBCC Event) using the fn_trace_gettable function. The first argument is the trace location and the second the file to read from. In our case, the value default specified for the second argument has the role of forcing the reading of all five files that make the default trace.

Performance Monitoring Recommendations

As mentioned, many tools are available for performance troubleshooting and performance improvement. Which one should you use? Well, it depends. We offer several scenarios. Whatever your situation, you will need some best practices related to performance monitoring:

Don't rely on a single tool   Using multiple tools gives a better picture than limiting yourself to just one tool. A classic example is correlating a SQL Profiler trace with a System Monitor log.

Remember that monitoring tools come with overhead   Performance tools can adversely affect the performance of a system. For example, using System Monitor can add up to 20 percent overhead to a low-end server. Limit overhead by selecting the *performance counters* you really need.

In another example, in SQL Server Profiler the overhead can reach 30 percent. You can reduce it using SQL Server Profiler just to define the trace and run it without the graphical interface through SQL Trace stored procedures. Also you can limit the events selected. For example, use only the completed classes for an event and remove the starting ones as the latter usually don't contain useful information (SQL:BatchCompleted is more useful than SQL.BatchStarting).

The dynamic management views and functions have a great advantage over the other tools when it comes to the added overhead. They are based on internal structures that are maintained by the database engine. Their overhead is usually 1 or 2 percent for most of the DMVs and DMFs. However several DMVs can be quite expensive, such as the sys.dm_os_buffer_descriptors dynamic management view that returns information about all the pages from the buffer pool.

Create baselines   Baselines for performance are invaluable for monitoring performance. You can say that a server performs better or worse only by comparison.

Finding Out the Cause of Performance Problems

Before we get to work, we'll introduce the Microsoft SQL Server Development Customer Advisory Team. This team works directly with the Microsoft customers. The best description of the team comes from its blog (`http://blogs.msdn.com/sqlcat/archive/2006/06/23/ Tom-Davidson-SQLCAT-Best-Practices.aspx`):

> This team spends 75% of their time away from the halls of Redmond, Washington working directly with the largest and most challenging SQL Server implementations across the world. We have implemented several systems 10TB+ in size, high volume banking systems as well as trading systems. Many of the deployments we've worked on were on hardware with 32–64 processors, large amounts of memory and on the most sophisticated SAN solutions. When SQL Server or any database management system is stressed at these levels you learn a lot about the internals of the product and what it can and cannot do.

Why should you care about this team? Well, this team really knows how to troubleshoot performance. After all, who could know SQL Server better than the team that built it? They actually released a best practices document named "OLTP Blueprint: A Performance Profile of OLTP Applications." This chapter is based on that document.

You can read "OLTP Blueprint: A Performance Profile of OLTP Applications" at `http://blogs.msdn.com/sqlcat/archive/2006/06/23/Tom-Davidson-SQLCAT-Best-Practices.aspx`.

The blueprint is a best practices document that describes the performance for an OLTP application through a set of rules. The set of rules applies to several areas of your application, such as database design, CPU, memory, I/O, and blocking.

Troubleshooting Database Design

No existing hardware can make up for bad design. So the following sections present a few rules that can help you optimize your database applications.

Rule 1: Pay Attention to a High Frequency of Queries Having More Than Four Join Operations

Frequent queries that have more than four join operations can be bad for OLTP performance.

Value

The number is debatable, and in some cases you can have up to seven joins without performance penalties.

Description

Though normalization is usually good for OLTP applications, sometimes you can improve performance by reducing the number of joins through denormalized tables.

Resolution

Another technique you can use is maintaining one (or more) denormalized tables through triggers. For example, if you have the following hypothetical query:

```
SELECT
  T1.COL1,
  T2.COL2,
  T3.COL3,
  T4.COL4,
  T5.COL5
FROM T1
JOIN T2 ON T1.T1_ID=T2.T1_ID
JOIN T3 ON T2.T2_ID=T3.T2_ID
JOIN T4 ON T3.T3_ID=T4.T3_ID
JOIN T5 ON T4.T4_ID=T5.T4_ID
```

You can reduce the number of joins by creating the table T123 that contains the columns of tables T1, T2, and T3.

Then each time a row is inserted in T1, T2, or T3, you should insert data into T123 using a trigger similar to the next one:

```
CREATE TRIGGER T1_INSERT_T123 ON T1
 FOR INSERT
AS
INSERT INTO T123
 (T1_ID, T2_ID, T3_ID, COL1, COL2, COL3)
SELECT
 I.T1_ID, I.COL1,
 T2.T2_ID, T2.COL2,
 T3.T3_ID, T3.COL3
FROM INSERTED I
JOIN T2 ON I.T1_ID=T2.T1_ID
JOIN T3 ON T2.T2_ID=T3.T2_ID;
GO
```

In this case, we started with the assumption that data is inserted into table T1, and we obtained the inserted rows from the INSERTED temporary table.

The original SELECT query becomes the following:

```
SELECT
 T123.COL1,
 T123.COL2,
 T123.COL3,
 T4.COL4,
 T5.COL5
FROM T123
JOIN T4 ON T123.T3_ID=T4.T3_ID
JOIN T5 ON T4.T4_ID=T5.T5_ID
```

Source

You can use various methods to identify queries with multiple joins, such as looking at the text of the queries from the plan cache, using OBJECT_DEFINITION to see the text of your code modules (stored procedures, views, triggers), and so on.

Rule 2: Avoid Using More Than Three Indexes for Frequently Updated Tables

Each data modification on an indexed table generates the update of the table's indexes. For tables that are frequently updated, the index maintenance overhead can be more important than the query performance benefit from the indexes.

Value

The value specified, three, can go up to seven in some cases. For example, Microsoft recommends a maximum of seven indexes per table for SAP OLTP databases.

Description

Indexes are your greatest friends for data retrieval, and in some cases they may be useful for finding data you want to modify. However, every modification of a row in a table means index maintenance. So, if your table is heavily updated, too many indexes can become a big problem. Why? Because data modifications have to wait for indexes to update.

Source

You can identify tables having these problems by using the sys.dm_db_index_operational_stats and the sys.dm_db_index_usage_stats dynamic management functions. The first one gives you details about each operation on an index such as inserts, deletes, updates, scans, seeks, and so on. Here's an example:

```
USE AdventureWorks;
GO
DECLARE @dbid INT;
SET @dbid=DB_ID();
SELECT
OBJECT_NAME (S.[object_id]) AS ObjName,
I.[name] AS IndexName,
I.index_id,
range_scan_count + singleton_lookup_count AS Reads,
leaf_insert_count + leaf_update_count + leaf_delete_count AS LeafWrites,
nonleaf_insert_count + nonleaf_update_count +
 nonleaf_delete_count AS NonLeafWrites
FROM sys.dm_db_index_operational_stats (@dbid, NULL, NULL, NULL) S
JOIN sys.indexes I
 ON S.[object_id]=I.[object_id]
 AND S.index_id=I.index_id
WHERE OBJECTPROPERTY(S.[object_id],'IsUserTable')=1
ORDER BY Reads DESC, LeafWrites, NonLeafWrites;
```

The query lists the reads and the update operations for all tables and indexes in the Adventure-Works database. If you did not run any queries on the AdventureWorks database, chances are that the previous query will not return any rows. Having the number of reads and the number of writes for an index, you can decide whether the index costs too much in terms of performance. Similarly, the sys.dm_db_index_usage_stats can return index usage information in a simpler format:

```
USE AdventureWorks;
GO
```

```
DECLARE @dbid INT;
SET @dbid=DB_ID();
SELECT
 OBJECT_NAME (S.object_id) AS ObjName,
 I.[name] AS IndexName,
 I.index_id,
 user_seeks + user_scans + user_lookups AS Reads,
 user_updates AS Writes
FROM sys.dm_db_index_usage_stats S
JOIN sys.indexes I
 ON  S.[object_id]=I.[object_id]
 AND S.index_id=I.index_id
WHERE OBJECTPROPERTY (S.[object_id],'IsUserTable')=1
ORDER BY Reads DESC
```

The difference between the two objects is the level of detail and the method to count object access. The sys.dm_db_index_usage_stats counts each access as 1, while the sys.dm_db_index_operational_stats columns' values are incremented depending on the operation level (leaf or nonleaf and row or data page).

For more information about each dynamic management view or dynamic management functions, please refer to Books Online.

Rule 3: Look for Large I/O Activity Due to Table Scans or Range Scans (scans >2)

Missing indexes or poorly designed queries may cause large I/O activity using scan operations. You should avoid scan operations especially for large tables.

Value

The OLTP blueprint document mentions two as the value that should trigger an investigation for this type of problem. But, we recommend that you react table scans only if your I/O activity is high. There is no need to worry about scan operations on small tables because they can perform better than seek operations.

Source

Use System Monitor to determine a problem due to a large number of table scans or range scans by monitoring the SQL Server: Access Methods performance object.

Resolution

To find a solution for this problem, you have to drill down to find the cause:

Identify the missing indexes   One of the potential causes for scan operation is the lack of index support. You can identify the missing indexes by using the Database Engine Tuning Advisor, by examining the query's plan and looking for the <Missing Indexes> section (you saw that in Chapter 7), or by using dynamic management views.

We show you an example that uses dynamic management views and functions. The example uses the missing indexes feature.

When the query optimizer generates an execution plan for a query, it determines what would be the best index for a filter condition. If the hypothetical best index is missing, you can see that in the XML Showplan of the query or you can use a set of dynamic management functions:

```
SELECT TOP 10
s.*,
d.*
FROM sys.dm_db_missing_index_group_stats s
JOIN sys.dm_db_missing_index_groups g
 ON s.group_handle=g.index_group_handle
JOIN sys.dm_db_missing_index_details d
 ON g.index_handle=d.index_handle
ORDER BY avg_total_user_cost * avg_user_impact
   * (user_seeks + user_scans)DESC;
```

The query returns the top 10 missing indexes groups that can have the highest improvement for your queries. If you don't get any results, it may be because you have not run any queries on the AdventureWorks database since the server started. To get results back, you can run the next query (that counts the number of Orders on a specific date) and then rerun the previous code:

```
SELECT
COUNT(*)
FROM Sales.SalesOrderHeader
WHERE OrderDate='2001-09-17'
```

Find out more about the missing indexes feature by reading the "About the Missing Indexes Feature Components" topic in Books Online.

Identify the problematic queries   Another reason for scan operations can be queries with poor or missing filter conditions. How do you identify these queries?

First, from a trace, obtain the trace file using the tuning template of SQL Server Profiler in which you've added the Reads column. Then, you can query the trace file:

```
SELECT TOP 10
*
FROM fn_trace_gettable ('E:\MyPerfTrace.trc', DEFAULT)
ORDER BY Reads DESC;
```

Second, use the *sys.dm_exec_query_stats* dynamic management view. This view should be your first choice for spotting resource intensive queries. In this particular case use the total_physical_reads and total_logical_reads columns:

```
SELECT TOP 10
  SUBSTRING(qt.text,qs.statement_start_offset/2,
  (CASE WHEN qs.statement_end_offset = -1
  THEN LEN(CONVERT(NVARCHAR(MAX), qt.text)) * 2
  ELSE qs.statement_end_offset
  END - qs.statement_start_offset)/2) AS SqlText,
  qs.total_logical_reads,
  qs.total_physical_reads
FROM sys.dm_exec_query_stats QS
CROSS APPLY sys.dm_exec_sql_text(qs.sql_handle) AS qt
ORDER BY
  (total_logical_reads + total_physical_reads) DESC
```

The query returns the top 10 queries still in cache that have the highest read operations. The sys.dm_exec_sql_text dynamic management functions returns the query's text.

Rule 4: Remove Unused Indexes

Unused indexes cause maintenance overhead without any benefit. You should consider removing them.

Description

Indexes that are not used can add on unnecessary performance overhead to your application.

Detection

You can detect unused indexes with the help of sys.dm_db_index_usage_stats DMV. All indexes that are not present in the returned result of this DMV haven't been used since the last restart of your server. The next query uses the sys.indexes catalog view to find out the unused indexes:

```
USE AdventureWorks;
GO
```

```
DECLARE @dbid INT;
SET @dbid=DB_ID ();
SELECT
OBJECT_NAME (I.[object_id]) AS ObjName,
I.[name] AS [IndexName],
I.index_id
FROM sys.indexes I
JOIN sys.objects O
 ON I.[object_id]=O.[object_id]
WHERE OBJECTPROPERTY (O.[object_id],'IsUserTable')=1
AND I.index_id NOT IN
(SELECT index_id
 FROM sys.dm_db_index_usage_stats S
 WHERE S.database_id=@dbid
  AND S.[object_id]=I.[object_id]
  AND S.index_id=I.index_id);
```

You can use this query to identify the indexes that are not used and that can be removed.

Troubleshooting CPU Problems

You can investigate CPU problems following three rules described by the OLTP performance blueprint document. We add a few other rules required by the exam objectives. But before we proceed to the actual rules, we'll explain some of the SQL Server internals.

Scheduling in SQL Server 2005

SQL Server 2005 has a component named SQL Server Operating System (SQL OS) that is responsible for managing SQL Server resources. SQL OS is a user-mode operating system that handles memory management, scheduling, resource monitoring, hosting, exception handling, and so on. Inside SQL OS, SQL OS schedulers do the scheduling work. A *scheduler* is a logical CPU used by workers. A *worker thread* represents a logical thread mapped to a Windows thread or to a fiber (when the lightweight pooling is enabled).

For each CPU the operating system reports, a scheduler is created. SQL Server does not check whether the CPUs reported are physical or just logical. For example, if you work on a machine with one hyper-threaded CPU, the operating system reports two CPUs to SQL Server and consequently two logical schedulers are created.

When you send a batch to the database engine, the batch is broken down in one or more tasks. The task or the request is the unit of work for a worker thread. The single task or multiple tasks that represent your batch are assigned to a scheduler with the fewest tasks. Then a task is associated with a worker thread. The worker thread will process the entire task before processing another one or entering into an idle state. Only one worker thread can own a scheduler at a point in time; thereby you increase the scalability by limiting the number of active workers. Consequently only one task is active at a time.

Each scheduler manages several constructs such as a runnable queue, a work queue, and a waiter list. The runnable queue contains the workers that are available to execute. The workers that are waiting for a resource are placed into a waiter list for the specified resource. When the worker thread that owns the resource is ready to release it, it scans the waiter list for workers waiting for the resource and places them into their running queue. If a task does not have an available worker thread, the task is put into the work queue until a worker becomes available.

For example, let's say you submit three batches simultaneously to the SQL Server having sessions ID 51, 52, and 53. The runnable queue contains SPIDS 51, 52, and 53. The SPID 51 begins to run and needs a page that is not currently in cache. Then the SPID 51 is moved to the waiter list until the data page is read from disk. The SPID 52 begins to run. The runnable queue contains, at this point, the SPID 53. When the I/O operation that reads the data page for SPID 51 is complete, the SPID 51 is moved to the runnable queue that exists in SPID 53, 51.

The time spent in the runnable queue measures the CPU's pressure. You can see the CPU's pressure by using the following query:

```
SELECT
SUM(signal_wait_time_ms)
 AS [signal_wait_time_ms],
CAST(100.0 * SUM(signal_wait_time_ms)
 / SUM(wait_time_ms) AS numeric (20,2))
 AS [%CPU waits],
SUM(wait_time_ms-signal_wait_time_ms)
 AS [resource_wait_time_ms],
CAST(100.0 * SUM(wait_time_ms - signal_wait_time_ms)
 / SUM(wait_time_ms) AS NUMERIC (20,2))
 AS [%resource waits]
FROM sys.dm_os_wait_stats;
```

The query returns the time spent by the worker thread waiting for CPU or for other resources. The signal_wait_time_ms column of the sys.dm_as_wait_stats dynamic management view represents the time in the runnable queue and is the difference between the time the waiting request was signaled and the time it started running. In the technical reference for SQL Server you will encounter the term *signal waits* and you should know that it represents the time waiting in the runnable queue for a worker.

The wait_time_ms represents the time expressed in milliseconds (ms) for each type of wait present in the *sys.dm_os_wait_stats* dynamic management view.

And now you are ready for the rules for troubleshooting CPU problems.

Rule 1: Watch Out for Signal Waits Greater Than 25 Percent

When the time percent waiting for the CPU is greater than 25 percent, you should investigate whether you have a CPU problem.

Detection

To detect a problem, use the previous query to interrogate the sys.dm_os_waiting_stats DMV.

To make the returned value relevant, clear out the existing data and monitor the total signal wait time for a specific period (for example 1, 2, or 5 minutes).

To clear out the existing data, use the following statement:

```
DBCC SQLPERF('sys.dm_os_wait_stats',CLEAR)
WITH NO_INFOMSGS ;
```

How should you interpret the results?

Let's say you use a 5-minute period that means 300 seconds. If the total signals wait time is 100 percent (the sum of signal_wait_time_ms is 300000 milliseconds), then you need at least another CPU to handle the workload.

If the value is below 25 percent, you could say that there are no CPU problems. Keep in mind the time of day you measure the CPU waits. It may be normal to have a higher value for signal waits during the busiest period of the day for your application.

Resolution

Before going out and buying new hardware, try reducing the load on your CPU. Eliminate high recompilation and unnecessary sorts, use indexes if you really need sorts, and so on. You can start by finding the most expensive queries for your CPU.

Here's how:

```
SELECT TOP 10
qs.total_worker_time/qs.execution_count AS [Avg CPU Time],
SUBSTRING(qt.text,qs.statement_start_offset/2,
(CASE WHEN qs.statement_end_offset = -1
THEN LEN(CONVERT(NVARCHAR(MAX), qt.text)) * 2
ELSE qs.statement_end_offset
END - qs.statement_start_offset)/2) AS SqlText,
db_name(qt.dbid) AS DbName
FROM sys.dm_exec_query_stats qs
CROSS APPLY sys.dm_exec_sql_text(qs.sql_handle) qt
ORDER BY
        [Avg CPU Time] DESC
```

The query is using the sys.dm_exec_query_stats dynamic management view to return the top 10 CPU intensive queries. Again the sys.dm_exec_sql_text dynamic management function is used to retrieve the text of the query.

Rule 2: Strive for More Than 90 Percent Plan Reuse

An ideal OLTP application is characterized by small identical transactions. As a result, the *plan reuse* should be over 90 percent.

Detection

You can use the SQL Server: Plan Cache\Cache Hit Ratio performance counter to monitor the plan reuse on your server.

An alternative to the SQL Server: Plan Cache\Cache Hit Ratio performance counter is the sys.dm_exec_cached_plans dynamic management view that returns information about the cached execution plans:

```
DECLARE
 @single INT,
 @reused INT,
 @total INT

SELECT @single=
    SUM(CASE(usecounts)
        WHEN 1 THEN 1
        ELSE 0
    END),
    @REUSED=
    SUM(CASE(usecounts)
        WHEN 1 THEN 0
        ELSE 1
    END),
    @total=COUNT(usecounts)
FROM sys.dm_exec_cached_plans

SELECT
'Single use plans (usecounts=1)'= @single,
'Re-used plans (usecounts>1)'= @reused,
're-use %'=CAST(100.0*@reused / @total AS DEC(5,2)),
'total usecounts'=@total
```

The query returns the percent of plans that have been reused as well as the total number of plans existing in cache and the plans that have been used only once.

Additionally, using the same DMV, you can retrieve the statements with the lowest plan reuse number:

```
SELECT TOP 10
cp.cacheobjtype,
```

```
cp.usecounts,
SUBSTRING(qt.text,qs.statement_start_offset/2,
(CASE WHEN qs.statement_end_offset = -1
     THEN LEN(CONVERT(NVARCHAR(MAX), qt.text)) * 2
     ELSE qs.statement_end_offset
 END - qs.statement_start_offset)/2) AS SqlText
FROM sys.dm_exec_query_stats qs
CROSS APPLY sys.dm_exec_sql_text(qs.sql_handle) qt
JOIN sys.dm_exec_cached_plans cp
ON qs.plan_handle=cp.plan_handle
WHERE cp.plan_handle=qs.plan_handle
    AND qt.dbid IS NULL
ORDER BY usecounts,SqlText ASC
```

The result represents the ad hoc SQL statements with the lowest plan reuse. If you remove the condition qt.dbid IS NULL, you will see the results for all types of statements.

Resolution

We handled this subject in Chapter 3, but as a reminder, you can take the following measures to ensure a better plan reuse:

- Make sure that ad hoc queries have the exact same text for plan reuse. The plan of an ad hoc query is searched in the cache using a hash value obtained from the text of the query. Even a space character can differentiate two queries.

- Don't change the values of SET options between different executions of the same query.

- Keep the same connection-level settings.

- Qualify your object names. SELECT * FROM Table1 is arguably equivalent with SELECT * FROM dbo.Table1 (when the schema of the first query is dbo) but the latter has better chance of plan reuse.

- If you have a stored procedure created using a statement similar to the next one CREATE PROCEDURE myProc WITH RECOMPILE, or executed like EXECUTE myProc WITH RECOMPILE, investigate whether you can use *statement-level recompilation* to recompile just a part of the stored procedure.

Rule 3: Decide Whether Parallelism Is the Best Choice for Your Environment

Parallel execution of a query improves the performance for OLAP systems but reduces the throughput for OLTP. The CXPACKET *wait type* occurs when trying to synchronize the parallelism operator. The parallelism operator, known also as the exchange operator, handles the partitioning and the movement of data between the multiple threads of a parallel execution.

Detection

When more than 5 percent of the waits on your system returned by the sys.dm_os_wait_stats dynamic management view are due to the CXPACKET wait type, then you should investigate whether parallel queries are a performance problem for your server.

 You can find a script that lists the top wait types on your server at http://www.microsoft.com/technet/scriptcenter/scripts/sql/sql2005/perf/sql05vb021.mspx?mfr=true.

A simple query to calculate the percent for the CXPACKET wait type is the following:

```
DECLARE
    @CXPACKET_Wait NUMERIC(20,2),
    @TotalResource_Wait NUMERIC(20,2);
SELECT @CXPACKET_Wait=wait_time_ms-signal_wait_time_ms
FROM sys.dm_os_wait_stats
WHERE wait_type='CXPACKET';

SELECT @TotalResource_Wait=
    SUM(wait_time_ms - signal_wait_time_ms)
FROM sys.dm_os_wait_stats
WHERE wait_type NOT IN
('CLR_SEMAPHORE','LAZYWRITER_SLEEP','RESOURCE_QUEUE',
'SLEEP_TASK','SLEEP_SYSTEMTASK','Total','WAITFOR');

SELECT
CAST(100.0 * @CXPACKET_Wait /
@TotalResource_Wait AS NUMERIC(20,2))
 AS '% CXPACKET Wait',
@CXPACKET_Wait AS 'CXPACKET Wait (ms)',
@TotalResource_Wait AS 'TotalResourceWait (ms)';
```

We ignore several wait types as they are caused either by system processes (such as LAZYWRITER_SLEEP wait type) or they should not be counted (WAITFOR).

Resolution

You can establish the degree of parallelism at the server level using the max degree of parallelism option or per query using the OPTION (MAXDOP) hint. You can identify the queries with parallel plans by considering several characteristics.

The first characteristic is represented by multiple execution contexts for the same Session ID:

```
SELECT
r.session_id,
```

```
r.request_id,
MAX(ISNULL(exec_context_id, 0)) AS nmb_of_workers,
r.sql_handle,
r.statement_start_offset,
r.statement_end_offset,
r.plan_handle
FROM sys.dm_exec_requests r
JOIN sys.dm_os_tasks t
 ON r.session_id = t.session_id
JOIN sys.dm_exec_sessions s
 ON r.session_id = s.session_id
WHERE s.is_user_process = 1
GROUP BY r.session_id, r.request_id,
    r.sql_handle, r.plan_handle,
    r.statement_start_offset, r.statement_end_offset
HAVING MAX(ISNULL(exec_context_id, 0)) > 0
```

The query returns the current executing statements that have multiple workers for the same Session ID and therefore a parallel execution plan. You obtain the sql_handle and the plan_handle for the statements that allow you to obtain the statements' text and plan using the sys.dm_exec_sql_text and sys.dm_exec_query_plan dynamic management functions.

The next characteristic of query that runs in parallel is that their total worker time is greater than their total execution time since they use multiple workers. To identify them you can use the following query, which displays the top 10 statements that may use a parallel plan:

```
SELECT TOP 10
qs.total_worker_time,
qs.total_elapsed_time,
SUBSTRING(qt.text,qs.statement_start_offset/2,
(CASE WHEN qs.statement_end_offset = -1
    THEN LEN(CONVERT(NVARCHAR(MAX), qt.text)) * 2
    ELSE qs.statement_end_offset
 END - qs.statement_start_offset)/2) AS SqlText,
DB_NAME(qt.dbid) AS DbName,
qt.objectid,
qs.sql_handle,
qs.plan_handle
FROM sys.dm_exec_query_stats qs
CROSS APPLY sys.dm_exec_sql_text(qs.sql_handle) AS qt
WHERE qs.total_worker_time > qs.total_elapsed_time
ORDER BY qs.total_worker_time DESC
```

We want to mention that the technique is not always reliable because this method does not return all parallel queries.

Once you've identified the query that uses parallel execution, you have several options to improve their performance:

- Use the Database Engine Tuning Advisor to add support indexes for the query and reduce this way the query cost.
- Check cardinality estimates in the query's plan.
- Check for missing statistics.
- Consider rewriting the query.
- Force the serial execution of the query using the OPTION (MAXDOP 1) query hint.

Additional Rules

Besides the three rules for detecting CPU performance problems, two additional performance indicators can signal a CPU problem:

Processor: % Processor Time >80%   When this counter (that represents the amount of time a CPU spends executing a non-idle thread) is consistently over 80 percent, you may have a CPU bottleneck.

System: Processor Queue Length >2   This counter represents the number of threads waiting for processor time. If the value is greater than two, then you may have a CPU-related problem. As a word of caution: don't rely solely on this indicator. On a machine dedicated to SQL Server, this indicator can have low values (because the scheduling is done by SQL OS and not by Windows) but still you may have CPU problems indicated by high signal waits.

Additional Causes for CPU Problems

You may run into these three additional causes of CPU problems:

- Excessive compilations and recompilations
- Inefficient query plans
- Poor cursor usage

All these problems have solutions that we mentioned in previous chapters. However, we'll mention a few other measures that can reduce the number of recompilations on your server and can improve the execution plans.

Reducing the Number of Recompilations

To reduce the number of recompilation, we suggest you this simple strategy: identify queries with the highest number of recompilations and fix them.

To identify the queries with most recompilations, you can use the plan_generation_num column of the sys.dm_exec_query_stats dynamic management view:

```
SELECT TOP 10
plan_generation_num,
execution_count,
qt.[Text],
SUBSTRING(qt.text,qs.statement_start_offset/2,
(CASE WHEN qs.statement_end_offset = -1
      THEN LEN(CONVERT(NVARCHAR(MAX), qt.text)) * 2
      ELSE qs.statement_end_offset
 END - qs.statement_start_offset)/2) AS SqlText,
DB_NAME(qt.dbid) AS DbName
FROM sys.dm_exec_query_stats AS qs
CROSS APPLY sys.dm_exec_sql_text(sql_handle) qt
WHERE plan_generation_num >1
ORDER BY plan_generation_num DESC
```

The plan_generation_num column is self-explanatory, representing the number of times the plan has been recompiled. To test the previous query, you can run the following script:

```
USE tempdb;
GO
DBCC FREEPROCCACHE;
GO
CREATE PROCEDURE uspRecompilation AS
BEGIN
CREATE TABLE #t (i INT);
SELECT * FROM #t;
END
GO
EXEC uspRecompilation;
GO
```

The script creates a stored procedure that queries a temporary table (and due to that the temporary table is recompiled). If you run the previous query again, you can obtain the following values:

```
-- Output
plan_generation_num: 2
```

```
execution_count: 1
Text: CREATE PROCEDURE uspRecompilation AS BEGIN CREATE TABLE #t ...
SqlText: SELECT * FROM #t;
DbName: tempdb
```

We displayed the results not as you see them on screen but pivoted to have enough space. As you can see from results, the stored procedure was recompiled and the statement to blame for recompilation is SELECT " FROM #t;.

If you worked with SQL Server 2000, you are probably familiar with using SQL Server Profiler to identify recompilations. We elected to showcase this method as complementary method to the sys.dm_exec_query_stats DMV. Exercise 10.1 shows you how.

EXERCISE 10.1

Monitoring Recompilations Using SQL Server Profiler

1. In SQL Server Management Studio, open a new query window.

2. In the query window, type the following query:

   ```
   USE tempdb;

   GO

   IF  EXISTS

   (SELECT * FROM sys.objects

    WHERE object_id = OBJECT_ID(N'uspRecompilation')

    AND type in (N'P', N'PC'))

   DROP PROCEDURE uspRecompilation;

   GO

   CREATE PROCEDURE uspRecompilation AS

   BEGIN

   CREATE TABLE #t (i INT);

   SELECT * FROM #t;

   END

   GO
   ```

```
EXEC uspRecompilation;

GO
```

3. From the SQL Server Management Studio Tools menu, click SQL Server Profiler.

4. On the File menu of SQL Server Profiler, select New Trace.

5. Use the same connection as for the SQL Server Management Studio.

6. Specify TraceRecompiles as the name of the trace, and select the TSQL_SPs template.

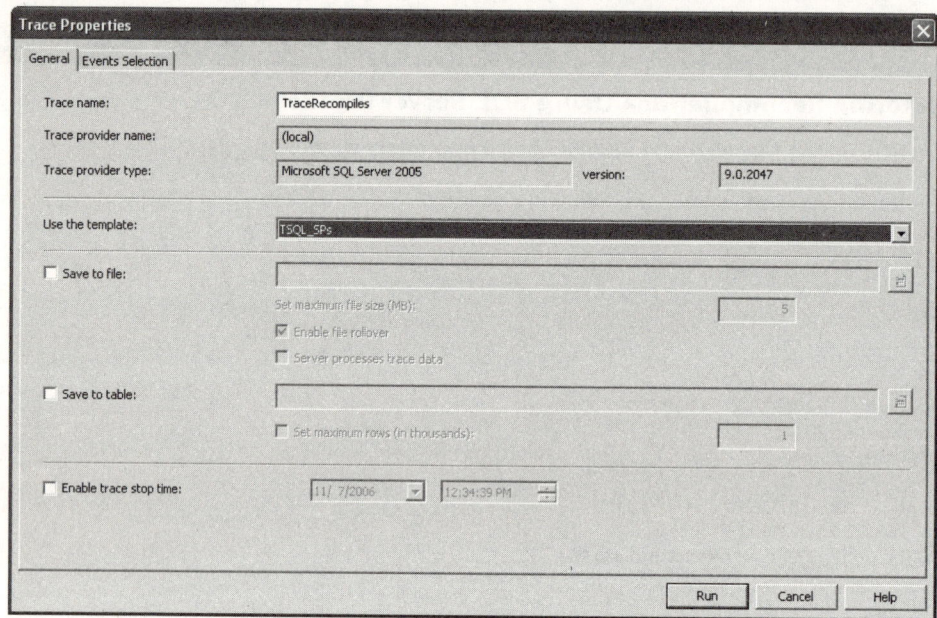

7. On the Events Selection tab, make sure only these events are selected:

SP:Starting

SP:StmtStarting

SP:Recompile

SP:Completed

EXERCISE 10.1 *(continued)*

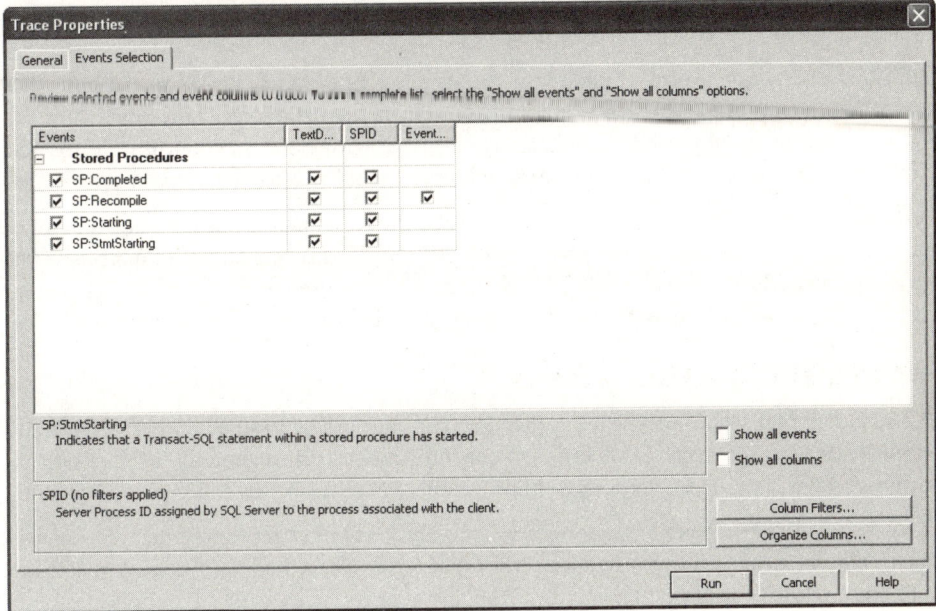

8. Select only the TextData, SPID, and EventSubClass columns.

9. Press the Run button.

10. Switch back to the SQL Server Management Studio, and run the query.

11. If you've done everything right, you should see the following results (in SQL Server Profiler):

Here are the trace results:

EventClass	TextData	SPID	EventSubClass
SP:Starting	EXEC uspRecompilation;	54	
SP:StmtStarting	CREATE TABLE #t (i INT);	54	
SP:StmtStarting	SELECT * FROM #t;	54	
SP:Recompile	SELECT * FROM #t;	54	3 - Deferred compile
SP:StmtStarting	SELECT * FROM #t;	54	
SP:Completed	EXEC uspRecompilation;	54	

Once you've identified the problematic queries, you can limit the number of recompilations for each of them by using one of the subsequent query hints.

KEEP PLAN query hint The KEEP PLAN query hint modifies the recompilation thresholds for temporary tables making them equal to those for permanent tables. So, if the temporary tables are the cause of recompilation, you can use this hint to limit them.

KEEPFIXED PLAN query hint When you specify the KEEPFIXED PLAN query hint, the query optimizer won't recompile the query in case of updated statistics. This query hint can help you reduce the number of recompilations but use it with care. As you know, statistics have their role and ignoring them may cause incorrect query plans.

RECOMPILE query hint The most useful usage for the RECOMPILE query hint is to avoid the recompilation of an entire stored procedure by recompiling only a subset of queries. If you have a stored procedure that uses the WITH RECOMPILE clause, investigate whether you can remove the clause and use the RECOMPILE query hint inside your stored procedure.

Improve Inefficient Query Plans

Inefficient query plans can become a big problem for your application as they might not just add unnecessary load to your CPUs but also consume memory and generate I/O activity.

Fortunately, you have many options to improve query plans using the following query hints.

FAST <number_rows> When your application requires a very fast response time, you can use this query hint to optimize a query for fast retrieval of the first specified number of rows. This method can give the perception of a very fast response time to the users of your application.

MAXDOP <number> The *max degree of parallelism* configuration option determines the number of processors considered by the query optimizer for execution of a query plan. You can override this setting per query basis by using the MAXDOP query hint.

OPTIMIZE FOR Sometimes the parameter detection behavior of the query optimizer may not be so beneficial for performance. The following example illustrates that and shows you how to use the OPTIMIZE FOR query to fix the problem. You will start by creating a sales table for a company that sells two major products and very rarely sells custom-made products. Run the following statements in the same query window:

```
USE tempdb;
GO
CREATE TABLE SalesOrders
(SalesOrderID INT PRIMARY KEY NOT NULL,
ProductID INT NOT NULL,
Quantity INT NOT NULL
);
DECLARE @I INT;
SET @I=1;
WHILE @I<20000
BEGIN
INSERT INTO SalesOrders(
```

```
SalesOrderID,ProductID,Quantity)
VALUES(@I,@I % 2 + 1,@I % 10 + 1);
SET @I=@I+1;
END
GO
INSERT INTO SalesOrders(
SalesOrderID,ProductID,Quantity)
VALUES (30000,3,5);
GO
CREATE INDEX idx_SalesOrders_ProductID
ON SalesOrders(ProductID);
GO
```

You also create an index on the ProductID column of the table and INSERT 20000 rows with demo data. After running the script the SalesOrder table contains 9,999 rows having the product ID 1, 10,000 having the product ID 2 and a single row having the product ID 3. One of the procedures named uspGetAverageQuantity has the following code:

```
CREATE PROCEDURE uspGetAverageQuantity
@ProductID INT
AS
BEGIN
SELECT
ProductID, AVG(Quantity) AS AvgQuantiy
FROM SalesOrders
WHERE ProductID = @ProductID
GROUP BY ProductID;
END;
GO
```

It returns the average quantity sold for the specified product. Since the product has the product ID 1, most of the executions for the uspGetAverageQuantity stored procedure specify the value 2 for the ProductID parameter.

Now let's see the problem happening:

```
DBCC FREEPROCCACHE;
GO
SET STATISTICS IO ON;
EXEC uspGetAverageQuantity 3;
GO
EXEC uspGetAverageQuantity 2;
GO
SET STATISTICS IO OFF;
GO
```

If you look at the execution plan, both queries will be executed using an index seek operation. You don't have to be a performance expert to realize that for the second query, a table scan operation would be a better choice. Why? Let's see the output:

```
-- Output
ProductID AvgQuantity
--------- -----------
3         5
1 row(s) affected)
Table 'SalesOrders'. Scan count 1, logical reads 4,
physical reads 0, read-ahead reads 0, lob logical reads 0,
lob physical reads 0, lob read-ahead reads 0.


ProductID AvgQuantity
--------- -----------
2         6
(1 row(s) affected)
Table 'SalesOrders'. Scan count 1, logical reads 20017,
physical reads 0, read-ahead reads 0, lob logical reads 0,
lob physical reads 0, lob read-ahead reads 0.
```

The second query has 20,017 logical reads due to the inefficient query plan. The same query plan is selected for subsequent executions of the stored procedure as for the first execution of the stored procedure. Why 20,017 is a bad number? Because running the next query to find out the number of pages for your table returns 52:

```
SELECT
page_count
FROM
sys.dm_db_index_physical_stats(DB_ID(),
   OBJECT_ID(N'SalesOrders'),
   1,DEFAULT,DEFAULT);
```

The sys.dm_db_index_physical_stats returns information about indexes and in this case about the index with the ID 1 that is your table.

So your table is stored on 52 pages but the execution of your stored procedure uses 20,017 pages. If no plan for the stored procedure is in cache and you run the stored procedure specifying the value 2 for the ProductID parameter, you would get better results:

```
DBCC FREEPROCCACHE;
GO
SET STATISTICS IO ON;
GO
```

```
EXEC uspGetAverageQuantity 2;
GO
SET STATISTICS IO OFF;
GO


-- Output
ProductID AvgQuantity
--------- -----------
2         6


(1 row(s) affected)
Table 'SalesOrders'. Scan count 1, logical reads 54,
physical reads 0, read-ahead reads 0, lob logical reads 0,
lob physical reads 0, lob read-ahead reads 0.
```

So we have 54 instead of 20,017, definitely a better result. How to solve it?

You can use the RECOMPILE option or since the most executions specify the value 2 for the input parameter you can use the OPTMIZE FOR query hint to instruct the query optimizer to use this value for the compilation and optimization of the query:

```
ALTER PROCEDURE uspGetAverageQuantity
@ProductID INT
AS
BEGIN
SELECT
ProductID,AVG(Quantity) AS AvgQuantiy
FROM SalesOrders
WHERE ProductID = @ProductID
GROUP BY ProductID
OPTION (OPTIMIZE FOR (@ProductID=2));
END;
GO
```

WARNING   Using query hints can adversely affect your server's performance, so use them with care.

No matter what parameter is specified for the stored procedure, the compilation and optimization (but not the execution) of the query uses the value 2. You can check that by running again the next query:

```
DBCC FREEPROCCACHE;
GO
```

```
SET STATISTICS IO ON;
EXEC uspGetAverageQuantity 3;
GO
EXEC uspGetAverageQuantity 2;
GO
SET STATISTICS IO OFF;
GO


-- Output
ProductID AvgQuantity
--------- -----------
3         5


 (1 row(s) affected)
Table 'SalesOrders'. Scan count 1, logical reads 54,
physical reads 0, read-ahead reads 0, lob logical reads 0,
lob physical reads 0, lob read-ahead reads 0.


ProductID AvgQuantity
--------- -----------
2         6


(1 row(s) affected)
Table 'SalesOrders'. Scan count 1, logical reads 54,
physical reads 0, read-ahead reads 0, lob logical reads 0,
lob physical reads 0, lob read-ahead reads 0.
```

This time the first query has 54 reads instead of 4 but it doesn't matter since most executions of the stored procedure use the value 2 for the ProductID parameter, so we want the execution of the second query to be optimal.

USE PLAN N'xml_plan' The USE PLAN query hint allows you to specify the execution plan that will be used for a query by the query optimizer. This is an example of how you can use this query hint:

```
SELECT ProductID, AVG(Quantity) AS AvgQuantiy
FROM SalesOrders
WHERE ProductID = 2
GROUP BY ProductID
OPTION (USE PLAN N'
<ShowPlanXML
 xmlns="http://schemas.microsoft.com/sqlserver/2004/07/showplan"
```

```
   Version="1.0" Build="9.00.3027.00">
    <BatchSequence>
      <Batch>
        <Statements>
          <StmtSimple StatementText="SELECT ProductID, AVG(Quan...

            ...
        </Statements>
      </Batch>
    </BatchSequence>
  </ShowPlanXML>
  ');
  GO
```

To save space we include just a part of the query's execution plan that we've obtained by running:

```
SET STATISTICS XML ON
GO
SELECT ProductID, AVG(Quantity) AS AvgQuantiy
FROM SalesOrders
WHERE ProductID = 2
GROUP BY ProductID
```

We won't go into greater detail here since is a very broad topic, but we invite you to refer to Books Online for the USE PLAN query hint topic.

Plan guides   Let's use the same example from the OPTIMIZE FOR topic. What if you are not allowed the code of the uspGetAverageQuantity stored procedure to optimize its performance?

Since you cannot modify the stored procedure, you cannot use query hints directly to be sure that each ad hoc query is using an optimal plan. But you can indirectly force the query optimizer to use a specific plan for a query using a *plan guide*. A stored procedure named sp_create_plan_guide can be used for this purpose.

Find out more about plan guides from the white paper "Forcing Query Plans with SQL Server 2005" at http://www.microsoft.com/technet/prodtechnol/sql/2005/frcqupln.mspx.

To see how this works, let's create the stored procedure again:

```
CREATE PROCEDURE uspGetAvgQtyNonModifiable
@ProductID INT
AS
BEGIN
```

```
SELECT
ProductID,AVG(Quantity) AS AvgQuantiy
FROM SalesOrders
WHERE ProductID = @ProductID
GROUP BY ProductID;
END;
GO
```

Then you will create a plan guide:

```
EXEC sp_create_plan_guide
@name = N'PlanGuide_AvgQuantity',
@stmt = N'SELECT ProductID, AVG(Quantity) AS AvgQuantiy
FROM SalesOrders
WHERE ProductID = @ProductID
GROUP BY ProductID',
@type = N'OBJECT',
@module_or_batch = N'dbo.uspGetAvgQtyNonModifiable',
@params = NULL,
@hints = N'OPTION(OPTIMIZE FOR (@ProductID=2))';
GO
```

You've created a plan guide named PlanGuide_AvgQuantity for the query 'SELECT ProductID…' of the uspGetAvgQtyNonModifiable stored procedure. The actual work is done by the hints parameter that, in this case, forces each execution of the uspGetAvgQtyNonModifiable stored procedure to be optimized for the value 2 of the ProductID parameter.

Verify that by running EXEC uspGetAvgQtyNonModifiable 3 and include the actual execution plan. Note that a table scan is used as it should be if the query is optimized for the value 2 of the ProductID parameter.

You can disable the plan guide using the sp_control_plan_guide stored procedure:

```
USE tempdb;
GO
EXEC sp_control_plan_guide
N'DISABLE',
N'PlanGuide_AvgQuantity';
GO
```

Run the query EXEC uspGetAvgQtyNonModifiable 3 again and include the actual execution plan. This time an index seek is used instead of a table scan.

We could go on, but Books Online explores usage scenarios for plan guides in depth.

Troubleshooting Memory Problems

A high number of requests characterize a typical OLTP application compared to an OLAP application. Ideally, those requests should get their data from cache. Otherwise you may have a memory bottleneck and, indirectly, an I/O problem. Here are the rules from the OLTP performance blueprint that you should verify.

Rule 1: The Average Page Life Expectancy Should Be Greater Than 300 Seconds

You can identify this situation by using the SQL Server: Buffers Manager: Page life expectancy performance counter of the System Monitor.

Resolution

To determine a resolution for memory problems you have to identify the cause. As a general recommendation you may follow these steps:

- Determine whether you have external memory pressure. External memory pressure is caused by other memory consumers on your system and can be physical or virtual. Investigate whether you can remove the other processes that run on your server or consider adding more memory. Also check the swap file and increase its size if you are low on virtual memory.

- Determine the cause for internal memory pressure. You can identify the memory consumers and ensure SQL Server is using several DMVs such as sys.dm_os_memory_clerks and sys.dm_os_memory_objects.

- Check and modify if necessary the server's configuration options related to memory, such as min memory per query, min server memory, max server memory, and awe enabled. You can track a possible modification of these options using the default trace.

- Verify whether the workload on the server has increased significantly. If you have a large number of sessions or queries, the memory consumption might be normal.

- Check whether you have missing indexes. Missing indexes on very large tables may determine cache-related problems.

For more information on troubleshooting memory problems as well as for other types of performance issues, you can read a great white paper, "Troubleshooting Performance Problems in SQL Server 2005" that is located at http://www .microsoft.com/technet/prodtechnol/sql/2005/tsprfprb.mspx.

Rule 2: Watch Out for Sudden Drops (of More Than 50 Percent) for the Average Page Life Expectancy Value

If the *average page life expectancy* suddenly drops by 50 percent or more, you may have a memory problem.

Resolution

The same recommendations for Rule 1 apply here. Additionally you may check whether the cause of the sudden drop is a configuration change by looking in the default trace. You should investigate the execution of DBCC FREEPROCCACHE command, DROP INDEX statements, or any other reason for cache flush. In SQL Server 2005 Service Pack 2, the usage of DBCC FREEPROCCACHE or DBCC FREESYSTEMCACHE is recorded in the SQL Server error log.

Rule 3: Make Sure You Have Less Than One Memory Grant Pending

In case of memory problems, one phenomenon that can occur is a high number of processors waiting for a work space memory grant.

Detection

You can detect this situation using the SQL Server: Memory Manager*Memory Grants Pending* performance counter.

Optionally you can use the sys.dm_exec_query_resource_semaphores and sys.dm_exec_query_memory_grants dynamic management views introduced by Service Pack 1 for SQL Server 2005.

The first one, the sys.dm_exec_query_resource_semaphores, returns the number of queries waiting for memory grants (through the waiter_count column). The sys.dm_exec_query_memory_grants DMV lists queries that have acquired a memory grant or require a memory grant to run.

Resolution

The same measures specified for Rule 1 applies also in this case.

Additional Signs of Memory Problems

Besides the three rules just mentioned, several other indicators of memory problems exist:

- Explicit memory errors. If your server lacks memory, it can generate errors such as these:

    - Error 701: There is insufficient system memory to run this query.

    - Error 802: There is insufficient memory available in the buffer pool.

    - Error 8628: A timeout occurred while waiting to optimize the query. Rerun the query.

    - Error 8645: A timeout occurred while waiting for memory resources to execute the query. Rerun the query.

    - Error 8651: Could not perform the requested operation because the minimum query memory is not available. Decrease the configured value for the 'min memory per query' server configuration option.

- The memory: Available Mbytes performance counter shows the amount of memory available on your system. When the value drops to the 50–100MB range, you should check for memory problems. A value under 10MB represents a real problem. A similar counter is the Memory: Available Bytes that displays the available memory in bytes rather than in megabytes.

- Memory: Page/sec represents the rate at which pages are read from or written to disk as the result of hard page faults. Over 20 Pages/sec for a longer period of time should cause additional investigations.

Detecting I/O Performance Problems

Next under your microscope is the I/O subsystem. Sometimes the I/O problems are actually memory problems but you already have the recipes for dealing with lack of memory. The following rules show what characterizes an I/O bound system.

Rule 1: Look Out for Values Greater Than 20 Milliseconds for the Average Disk Second/Read Performance Counter

When the value of the Avg. Disk sec/Read counter (of the Physical Disk object) is greater than 20 milliseconds you have a slow I/O subsystem.

Value

Any value less than 10 milliseconds is considered very good. Values between 10 and 20 ms are acceptable. In the 20 and 50 milliseconds range the value indicates slow I/O subsystem that may generate performance problems. Over 50 ms the value indicates a really serious I/O problem.

Detection

To track the values of the specified counter, you can use the System Monitor. The counter returns the average time, in seconds, for a read from disk operation.

Resolution

Here are the possible resolutions:

- Identify possible memory problems (see the previous topic).
- Add more physical drives and distribute the current load.
- Replace current disks with faster ones.
- Add faster I/O controllers or replace the existing ones.
- Identify queries that generate the most I/O activity and tune them. You can use the sys.dm_exec_query_stats for that purpose.

To detect the top 10 queries that generate a large amount of I/O activity just run the next interrogation:

```
SELECT TOP 10
(qs.total_logical_reads + qs.total_logical_writes)
```

```
/qs.execution_count as [Avg IO],
SUBSTRING(qt.text,qs.statement_start_offset/2,
 (CASE WHEN qs.statement_end_offset = -1
 THEN LEN(CONVERT(NVARCHAR(MAX), qt.text)) * 2
 ELSE qs.statement_end_offset
 END - qs.statement_start_offset)/2) AS SqlText,
db_name(qt.dbid) AS DbName
FROM sys.dm_exec_query_stats qs
CROSS APPLY
 sys.dm_exec_sql_text(qs.sql_handle) qt
ORDER BY [Avg IO] DESC
```

Rule 2: Average Disk Writes (Indicated by the Average Disk Sec/Write Counter) Should Be Less Than 20 Milliseconds

Similar to the previous rule but for write operations, a value greater than 20 milliseconds for a write to disk operation indicates a slow I/O subsystem.

The detection and resolutions are the same as for Rule 1.

Rule 3: A Number of Scan Operations (Full Scans, Range Scans) Greater Than One Requires Further Investigation

Table scans and range scans can determine huge I/O activity on very large tables. You've already met this rule in the first troubleshooting. You can apply the same indications for detection and resolutions described in the Rule 3 from the "Troubleshooting Database Design" section.

Rule 4: The Top Two Wait Type Values Should Not Include I/O Waits

There are 76 wait types in SQL Server 2000. SQL Server 2005 adds more than 100 other wait types that allow you to determine what you're waiting for.

 **NOTE** The complete list of wait types can be found in Books Online under the sys.dm_os_wait_stats topic. At the time we wrote this book there were exactly 229 wait types described.

Obviously you can use the sys.dm_os_wait_stats and wait types to determine whether you have an I/O bound system.

Detection

To detect whether you have this problem, you could use the following query:

```
SELECT TOP 2
wait_type,
wait_time_ms
FROM sys.dm_os_wait_stats
WHERE wait_type NOT IN
('CLR_SEMAPHORE','LAZYWRITER_SLEEP','RESOURCE_QUEUE',
'SLEEP_TASK','SLEEP_SYSTEMTASK','Total','WAITFOR')
ORDER BY wait_time_ms DESC;
```

You should be concerned by your I/O activity if you see one of these wait types in the result of the query:

- ASYNCH_IO_COMPLETION

- IO_COMPLETION

- LOGMGR

- WRITELOG

- PAGEIOLATCH_* (PAGEIOLATCH_DT, PAGEIOLATCH_EX, PAGEIOLATCH_KP, PAGEIOLATCH_NL, PAGEIOLATCH_SH, PAGEIOLATCH_UP)

Resolution

For resolution, follow the steps described for Rule 1.

Additional I/O Rules

In addition to the four rules specified by the OLTP blueprint, you should be aware of the following indicators of I/O problems:

- The PhysicalDisk Object: % Disk Time performance counter represents the percentage of time the disk is busy servicing read or write requests. If the value of this counter is over 90 percent, then take a look at the PhysicalDisk: Avg. Disk Queue Length counter. For RAID devices, the counter can indicate values over 100 percent. That's why you need to correlate it with the disk queue counters to see if there's a real I/O issue.

- The PhysicalDisk: Avg. Disk Queue Length performance counter shows you the number of waiting I/O requests. A value greater than 2 for over a longer period of time indicates an I/O problem. When your disk has more than one spindle (like for example RAIDs), you should multiply the margin value (2) by the number of spindles.

Troubleshooting Blocking Problems

We talked about blocking in Chapters 6 and 7, and here we jump directly to the rules you should check.

Rule 1: Block Percentage Value Should Be Less Than 2

The sys.dm_db_index_operational_stats dynamic management function displays detailed index usage statistics including blocking information.

Value

When the blocking percent for an index has a greater value than 2 then you should investigate if you have a blocking issue.

Detection

For detection of this potential problem, you can use a query similar to this one:

```
USE AdventureWorks;
GO
DECLARE @dbid INT;
SET @dbid=DB_ID();
SELECT
 DB_NAME(database_id) AS DbName
,OBJECT_NAME(s.[object_id]) AS ObjName
,i.name AS IndexName
,i.index_id
,partition_number
,row_lock_count
,row_lock_wait_count
,CAST (100.0 * row_lock_wait_count /
(1 + row_lock_count) AS NUMERIC(15,2))
 AS [block %]
,row_lock_wait_in_ms
,CAST (1.0 * row_lock_wait_in_ms /
(1 + row_lock_wait_count) AS NUMERIC(15,2))
 AS [Avg Row Lock Waits (ms)]
FROM sys.dm_db_index_operational_stats
    (@dbid, NULL, NULL, NULL) s
JOIN sys.indexes i
 ON i.[object_id] = s.[object_id]
    AND i.index_id = s.index_id
```

```
WHERE OBJECTPROPERTY(s.OBJECT_ID,'IsUserTable') = 1
ORDER BY row_lock_wait_count DESC
```

The query returns the blocking information for all indexes in the AdventureWorks database. To test the query, run the following two scripts in separate query windows. Here's the first one:

```
BEGIN TRAN
UPDATE Person.Contact
SET Title='Dr.'
WHERE ContactID = 1;
-- introduce a wait
WAITFOR DELAY '00:01';
ROLLBACK TRAN;
GO
```

And here's the second:

```
SELECT * FROM
AdventureWorks.Person.Contact
WHERE ContactID=1;
```

When both queries finish (after about a minute), run the blocking detection script. Make sure that you run the scripts in order. The partial output you may get should look like:

```
-- Output
... ObjName IndexName           ... block %  Avg Row Lock Waits (ms)
--- ------- ------------------- --- -------  -----------------------
... Contact PK_Contact_ContactID ... 12.50    28156.50
```

The value of the block % column indicates in this case a possible locking problem as it should since you've blocked a row of the Person.Contact table for almost a minute.

Resolution

For resolution you should look for missing indexes, alternate methods of access, inefficient query plans, or inappropriate isolation level for your queries.

Rule 2: Investigate Locking Problems If the Block Process Report Displays Blocks Longer Than 30 Seconds

You can identify long running blocks using the Blocked Process Report event class. The event is triggered when the wait for a lock exceeds a threshold. You can customize the value for the threshold by configuring the blocked process threshold option.

Value

The Customer Advisory Team from Microsoft recommends a 30-second value. You can set your own value based on the average (or maximum) duration values for locks in your database. If you specify a value lower than 5 seconds, you could cause the Blocked Process Report event to be triggered irregularly (so refrain from doing that).

Detection

Once you've configured the threshold, you can use either SQL Server Profiler or the Event Notifications to capture the Blocked Process Report event. The following example demonstrates how. First, let's configure the value for the blocked process threshold option. Open the SQL Server Management Studio and run the next script:

```
EXEC sp_configure 'show advanced options', 1 ;
GO
RECONFIGURE ;
GO
EXEC sp_configure 'blocked process threshold', 30 ;
GO
RECONFIGURE ;
GO
```

Next, you should start SQL Server Profiler to capture the event. So open SQL Server Profiler and from Microsoft SQL Server 2005—Performance Tools program group and create a new trace. Use the Blank template to customize easier the trace events and select from the Errors and Warnings group the Blocked Process Report event as shown here:

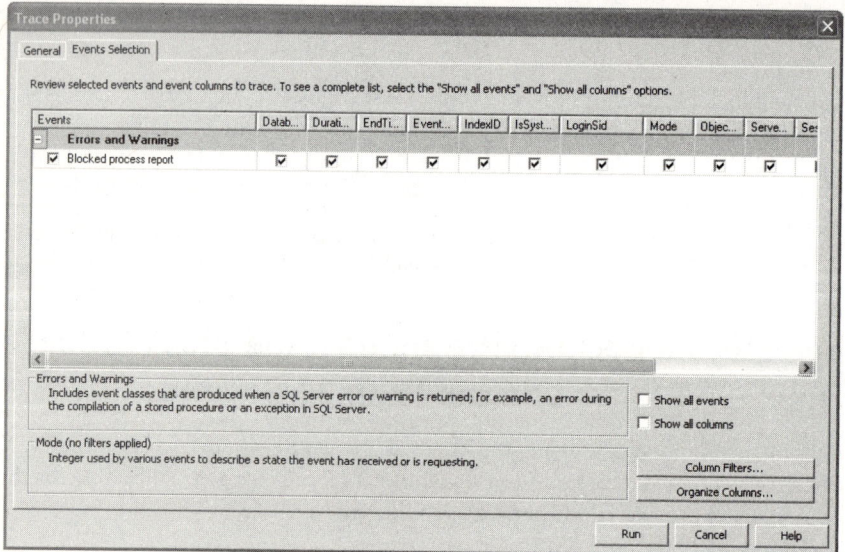

Click Run and switch back to SQL Server Management Studio. Run the same queries from the previous topic to generate blocks longer than 30 seconds. Again, make sure you run the scripts in two separate query windows using the specified order:

```
BEGIN TRAN
UPDATE Person.Contact
SET Title='Dr.'
WHERE ContactID = 1;
-- introduce a wait
WAITFOR DELAY '00:01';
ROLLBACK TRAN;
GO


-- the second batch
SELECT * FROM
AdventureWorks.Person.Contact
WHERE ContactID=1;
```

Switch back to the SQL Server Profiler to see the event captured:

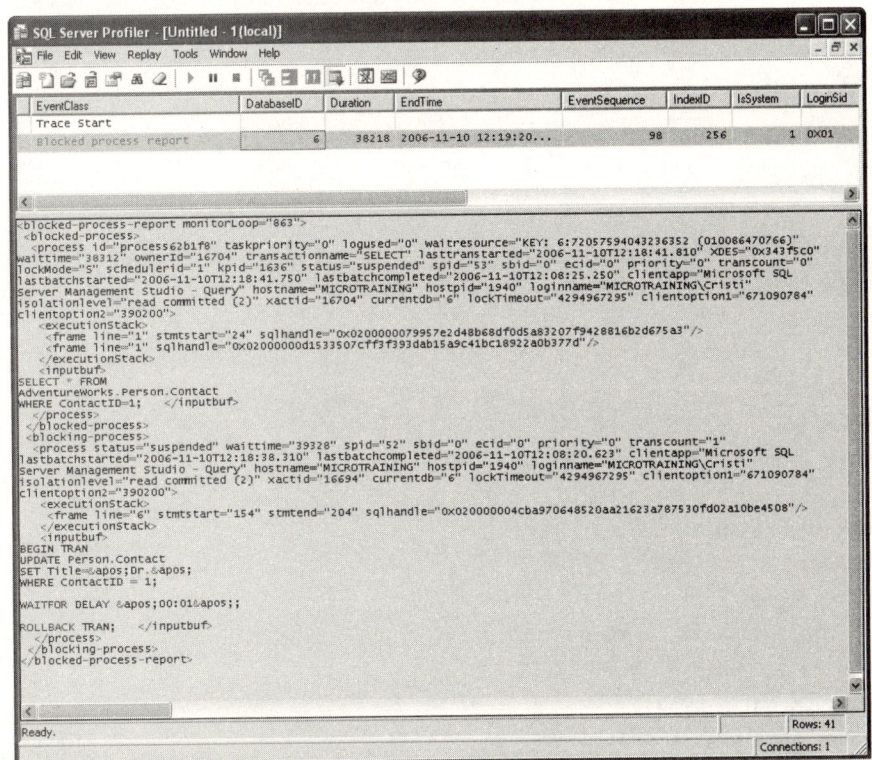

You can see the blocked process as well as the blocking one and their sql text.

Resolution

Using the Blocked Process Report event you can pinpoint the troublesome queries and concentrate your troubleshooting efforts on them. Refer to Chapter 6 for measures that allow you to avoid locking problems (such as lowering the transaction level or using locking hints). Also you could refer to Chapter 7 for specific measures that can result in improving the identified queries.

Rule 3: The Average Row Lock Waits Value Should Be Less Than 100 Milliseconds

The same dynamic management function, sys.dm_db_index_operational_stats, can tell you the average time you wait due to row-level locking for each index in your database.

Value

The OLTP Performance blueprint indicates values greater than 100 milliseconds could be a sign of a blocking problem.

Detection

For detection of this potential problem, you can use the same query as for Rule 1 but add an extra condition to the WHERE clause:

```
USE AdventureWorks;
GO
DECLARE @dbid INT;
SET @dbid=DB_ID();
SELECT
 DB_NAME(database_id) AS DbName
,OBJECT_NAME(s.[object_id]) AS ObjName
,i.name AS IndexName
,i.index_id
,partition_number
,row_lock_count
,row_lock_wait_count
,CAST (100.0 * row_lock_wait_count /
(1 + row_lock_count) AS NUMERIC(15,2))
 AS [block %]
,row_lock_wait_in_ms
,CAST (1.0 * row_lock_wait_in_ms /
(1 + row_lock_wait_count) AS NUMERIC(15,2))
 AS [Avg Row Lock Waits (ms)]
FROM sys.dm_db_index_operational_stats
    (@dbid, NULL, NULL, NULL) s
```

```
JOIN sys.indexes i
 ON i.[object_id] = s.[object_id]
    AND i.index_id = s.index_id
WHERE OBJECTPROPERTY(s.OBJECT_ID,'IsUserTable') = 1
AND
CAST (1.0 * row_lock_wait_in_ms /
(1 + row_lock_wait_count) AS NUMERIC(15,2)) > 100
ORDER BY row_lock_wait_count DESC
```

Resolution

Just like for Rule 1 you should try to identify possible missing indexes, alternate methods of access (seek operations instead of scans, views instead of a table, row versioning), inefficient query plans, or inappropriate isolation levels for your queries.

Rule 4: The Top Two Wait Type Values Should Not Include Locking-Related Waits

The sys.dm_os_wait_stats dynamic management view is the source for wait information. If the top two waits as duration are lock related, then you have a locking problem.

Detection

For detection of this problem, you can use the next query:

```
SELECT TOP 2
wait_type,
wait_time_ms
FROM sys.dm_os_wait_stats
WHERE wait_type NOT IN
('CLR_SEMAPHORE','LAZYWRITER_SLEEP','RESOURCE_QUEUE',
'SLEEP_TASK','SLEEP_SYSTEMTASK','Total','WAITFOR')
ORDER BY wait_time_ms DESC;
```

The query returns the top two wait types, ignoring system or irrelevant wait types.

If the result contains a wait type having the name LCK_*, you have a blocking problem. The LCK_* belongs to this list: LCK_M_IS, LCK_M_IU, LCK_M_IX, LCK_M_RIn_NL, LCK_M_RIn_S, LCK_M_RIn_U, LCK_M_RIn_X, LCK_M_RS_S, LCK_M_RS_U, LCK_M_RX_S, LCK_M_RX_U, LCK_M_RX_X, LCK_M_S, LCK_M_SCH_M, LCK_M_SCH_S, LCK_M_SIU, LCK_M_SIX, LCK_M_U, and LCK_M_UIX.

Resolution

The same resolution techniques for the blocking rules 1 and 3 apply also to Rule 4.

If you need to identify the queries with performance problems due to blocking, one approach is to use a SQL Trace that includes the Duration, Reads, and Writes columns. Usually queries with high values for the Duration column and low values for the Reads and Writes data columns may have problems due to blocking. If you saved the trace in a file, you could use this query to retrieve the first 10 queries that may experience blocking issues. The next query works provided you have a trace file saved at the specified location:

```
SELECT TOP 10
Duration,
Reads,
Writes,
TextData
FROM fn_trace_gettable('E:\MyBlockingTrace.trc', DEFAULT)
ORDER BY
 Duration DESC,
 Reads + Writes ASC ;
```

In the next topic we mention an extra technique for handling extreme locking situations. "Extreme situation" means a completely hung server due to blocking.

Using the Dedicated Administrator Connection to Solve Blocking Problems

One of over a thousand new features of SQL Server 2005 is the Dedicated Administrator Connection (DAC). It has its own separate memory area, its own scheduler, and even its own port that remains available even when your server becomes unresponsive.

You can initiate a DAC from either SQL Server Management Studio or sqlcmd command-line utility, by prefixing the instance name you will connect to with ADMIN: prefix. For sqlcmd you have a second option, the –A switch.

The Dedicated Administrator Connection should be used only for emergencies so, to practice, you are going to create an emergency situation. In the next exercise you will create a blocking chain by locking a row and then trying to select that row from other connections.

If you paid attention to the scheduling topic, you know that each task is bound to a worker thread until the task finishes. So if the task waits, the worker thread waits. If all workers wait, then you cannot connect to the SQL Server—not by a regular connection. In Exercise 10.2, you'll create a number of connections equal to the number of worker threads. You will need a tool named OSTRESS that you can download from the Web.

You can download the OSTRESS tool from http://www.microsoft.com/downloads/details.aspx?familyid=5691AB53-893A-4AAF-B4A6-9A8BB9669A8B.

EXERCISE 10.2

Using the Dedicated Administrator Connection

1. In SQL Server Management Studio, open a query window, and run the following code and write down the results:

    ```
    -- determine the number of worker threads

    SELECT max_workers_count FROM sys.dm_os_sys_info

    -- Output on my machine: 256
    ```

2. In the same query window, run the next query to lock a row in the AdventureWorks database:

    ```
    USE AdventureWorks;

    GO

    BEGIN TRAN;

    UPDATE Person.Contact

    SET Title='Dr.'

    WHERE ContactID = 1;
    ```

3. Open a command prompt window by clicking Start ➢ Run, typing **cmd**, and pressing the OK button. As an alternative, you can open the command prompt window from the Accessories program group.

4. Navigate to the folder where you have the OSTRESS tool.

5. Type the following command:

    ```
    ostress.exe -1600 -E -S1pc:%COMPUTERNAME% -n255 -Q"SELECT * FROM

     AdventureWorks.Person.Contact WHERE ContactID = 1;" -q
    ```

    The command launched the OSTRESS utility with a timeout of 600 seconds; it connects to the default instance of SQL Server (from your local computer) and spans 255 threads that execute the specified query. Why 255? On our machine the number of worker threads is 256. One is already busy so another 255 are necessary. Adjust this value for your configuration.

6. Wait for about 2 or 3 minutes to let the OSTRESS utility span all the specified threads.

7. Open the SQL Server Error Log file, located on C:\Program Files\Microsoft SQL Server\MSSQL.1\MSSQL\LOG\ERRORLOG. On your machine the location may vary.

8. You may notice the following message: "All schedulers on Node 0 appear deadlocked due to a large number of worker threads waiting on LCK_M_S. Process Utilization 0%." The message already tells you that you have a locking situation. All the threads try to acquire a shared lock.

9. To verify that you're in trouble, open a new query window in SQL Server Management Studio. You should get the error "Timeout expired. The timeout period elapsed prior to completion of the operation or the server is not responding." That confirms that there is indeed a problem.

10. Open a new query window but this time instead of the server name, type **ADMIN:ServerName** (to use DAC instead of a regular connection).

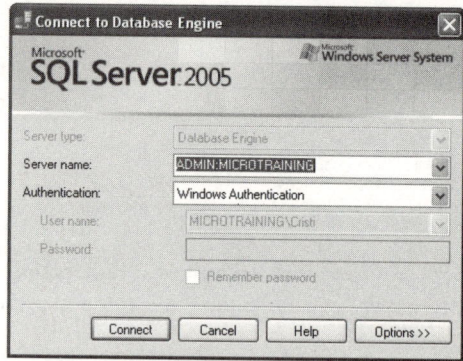

For a remote server scenario, make sure that the specified server allows remote connections (for DAC) by enabling the remote admin connection option using the Surface Area Configuration tool.

11. Once connected with DAC, start the troubleshooting using the premise that everyone's waiting due to a lock. To confirm this run the next query:

```
SELECT

    t1.resource_type,

    t1.request_mode,

    t1.request_session_id,

    t2.blocking_session_id

FROM sys.dm_tran_locks as t1

JOIN sys.dm_os_waiting_tasks as t2
```

```
    ON t1.lock_owner_address = t2.resource_address;
```

The output may be different on your machine but it should be similar to this one:

```
-- Output
resource_type request_mode request_session_id blocking_session_id

KEY           S            55                 54

KEY           S            56                 54

KEY           S            57                 54

KEY           S            65                 54

KEY           S            78                 54

...
```

Apparently everyone is waiting for session 54 (your machine may have a different value).

12. Let's see now what the session 54 is doing:

```
SELECT

  request_session_id AS spid,

  resource_type AS rt,

  request_mode AS rm,

  request_status AS rs,

  resource_database_id dbid,

  resource_associated_entity_id eid

FROM sys.dm_tran_locks

WHERE request_session_id = 54;
```

The output should be similar to the following (just the values may differ):

```
-- Output
spid rt         rm    rs     dbid eid

54   DATABASE   S     GRANT  6    0

54   OBJECT     IS    GRANT  6    309576141
```

EXERCISE 10.2 *(continued)*

```
54   METADATA  Sch-S  GRANT  6    0

54   KEY       S      WAIT   6    72057594043236352

54   PAGE      IS     GRANT  6    72057594043236352
```

Looking at the output you can realize that the session 54 tries to acquire a shared lock on an index key but it waits so someone blocks it.

13. The next step is to find out who is blocking the resource requested by the Session ID 54:

    ```
    SELECT

      request_session_id AS spid,

      resource_type AS rt,

      request_mode AS rm,

      request_status AS rs,

      resource_database_id dbid,

      resource_associated_entity_id eid

    FROM sys.dm_tran_locks

    WHERE resource_database_id=6

    AND resource_type='KEY'

    AND resource_associated_entity_id=72057594043236352

    AND request_status='GRANT';
    ```

    The output of the query is as follows:

    ```
    -- Output

    spid rt  rm rs    dbid eid

    52   KEY X  GRANT 6    72057594043236352
    ```

    Now that you've identified the session that blocks all the others, you can solve the problem by ending session 52.

14. Run KILL 52.

15. At this point you should be able to connect again to your server.

Additional Performance Factors

The OLTP blueprint document concludes with blocking issues, but you should not stop your performance investigation here. You should consider several other resources:

The tempdb database   The tempdb database is one of the shared resources that can dramatically affect your performance. We say shared because the tempdb database is the temporary storage common for all databases of a SQL Server instance. You probably know (or you should) that in SQL Server 2005 the tempdb database is used for a lot more features than in SQL Server 2000. To name only some of the features supported by the version store framework, we have online index operations, multiple active result sets (MARS), AFTER triggers, and transactions running under the snapshot or read committed snapshot isolation levels. In addition to the row versioning–based features, the tempdb also contains user objects and internal objects. We won't discuss this subject in depth but you should consider it in your performance strategy.

Read more about tempdb and SQL Server 2005 in the white paper "Working with tempdb in SQL Server 2005" at http://www.microsoft.com/technet/prodtechnol/sql/2005/workingwithtempdb.mspx.

Network adapters   Last but not least it may be worth it to take a look at the network activity for your servers. You can easily monitor your network adapters using performance counters and System Monitor or for a longer period without the graphical interface Performance Logs and Alerts. Some of the counters you should look at are:

- Network Interface:Bytes Total/sec returns the rate at which bytes are sent and received for network adapters. An average value over 50 percent of a NIC capacity can indicate network congestion.

- Network Interface:Current Bandwidth returns the current bandwidth of your network adapters in bits per second.

- As a practical example some values for the specified counters on our laptop are as follows: Network Interface:Bytes Total/sec: Minimum:200 Average: 14157 Maximum:254785 or Network Interface:Current Bandwidth: Minimum: 100000000 Average: 100000000 Maximum: 100000000.

The average value 14,157 bytes is far from being a problem for a 100 Mbits network adapter.

Summary

In this chapter, you learned how to troubleshoot and improve the performance of a database application. For a performance troubleshooting template, we used the OLTP performance blueprint, which is a document Microsoft created that describes the performance characteristics of a transactional application. In addition, you saw how to detect performance issues from CPU high utilization to high I/O activity and then how to drill down to find out the root cause. Also, you learned possible resolutions for each type of problem. Finally, you learned about other resources (besides this book) that you can use to enhance your knowledge such as Books Online and various white papers.

Exam Essentials

Before you take the exam ensure that you know the following topics:

Know various utilities of the SQL Server 2005 performance toolbox.   As you've seen in this chapter there are quite a few tools that you can use to monitor, troubleshoot, and improve performance. Each one of them could easily have a dedicated book so you have to use supplementary work to learn about them from the best SQL Server book available—Books Online.

Be able to evaluate the performance of a database application.   You should know how to identify the performance of a database application by considering the various resources that can affect it. You have to evaluate performance from various angles—response time, performance from a user perspective, resource utilization, or effective database design.

Understand how to find resolutions.   You have to provide resolutions to performance issues, resolutions that range from adding a query hint to replacing the disk subsystem with a faster one or even replacing the entire box.

Review Questions

1. You want to identify the top 10 queries that have been recompiled the most times on your server. What can you do?

    A. Use the sys.dm_exec_requests dynamic management view.

    B. Use the sys.dm_exec_sessions dynamic management view.

    C. Use the sys.dm_exec_query_stats dynamic management view.

    D. Use the sys.dm_exec_query_optimizer_info dynamic management view.

2. You want to identify the queries that use the most CPU time on your server. What should you do?

    A. Use System Monitor and the SQL Compilations/sec counter of the SQL Statistics objects.

    B. Use the sys.dm_exec_query_stats dynamic management view.

    C. Use the sys.dm_exec_requests dynamic management view.

    D. Use the sys.dm_exec_sessions dynamic management view.

3. You have to improve the performance of a stored procedure named usp_ContactSearch. The stored procedure consists of several operations such as finding all contact IDs that correspond to a search criteria, updating a table that contains the most recent search interrogations, and retrieving properties for the contact persons found. Occasionally the stored procedure has very slow response time. You analyze time execution plan of the stored procedure and find out that the SELECT statement used to search the contact persons is using an inefficient plan in some cases. For example, the SELECT statement is using an index seek where a table scan would be a better option. What should you do to improve the performance of the query?

    A. Use a query hint to force a table scan for the SELECT statement.

    B. Add the RECOMPILE option to the stored procedure.

    C. Add the RECOMPILE option to the SELECT statement.

    D. Rewrite the SELECT statement as a function.

4. You have to improve the performance of a stored procedure used by a web application to display products that have the price in a specific range. You want to optimize the query for a specific range, which is indicated by collected statistics to be the most commonly used. What should you do?

    A. Use the WITH RECOMPILE option for the stored procedure.

    B. Create separate stored procedures for each search interval.

    C. Modify the stored procedure to include the NOLOCK query hint.

    D. Create a plan guide and modify the stored procedure to include the OPTIMIZE FOR query hint.

5. After investigating some performance problems, you discovered the top 10 most frequently run queries. You want to optimize their performance and start with the first one. The code of the query is quite simple:

    ```
    SELECT FirstName, LastName

    FROM Contact

    WITH(INDEX=idx_Contact_LastName_FirstName)

    WHERE ContactID=?
    ```

    The Contact table has a clustered index on the ContactID column named idx_Contact_ContactID. For some reason the execution plan of the query is not using the idx_Contact_ContactID index. What should you do?

    A. Drop the idx_Contact_LastName_FirstName index.

    B. Rebuild the idx_Contact_ContactID index.

    C. Remove the WITH (INDEX=idx_Contact_LastName_FirstName) table hint.

    D. Update statistics.

6. You want to identify the slow running queries that are slowed down by blocking issues. You collect performance data using a SQL trace. Which of the following data columns can help you? (Choose all that apply.)

    A. Duration

    B. Reads

    C. TextData

    D. Writes

7. Which of the following allows you to determine recent configuration changes on your server?

    A. The sys.dm_exec_query_stats dynamic management view

    B. The default trace

    C. The sys.configurations catalog view

    D. The sys.system_components_surface_area_configuration catalog view

8. You have to troubleshoot the performance of an application that uses SQL Server as a back end. After reviewing several trace files with inconclusive results, you want to monitor the CPU utilization. Which of the following tools should you use?

    A. Database Engine Tuning Advisor

    B. SQL Server Profiler

    C. SQL Trace

    D. System Monitor

9. You need to find queries with the longest-running duration. You have already a trace file captured during the work hours. What should you do?

   A. Use SQL Server Profiler and group the trace information by Duration data column.

   B. Use the SQL Server Profiler and group the trace information by the End Time data column.

   C. Use the SQL Server Profiler and group the trace information by the CPU data column.

   D. Use the SQL Server Profiler and group the trace information by the Reads data column.

10. You have to troubleshoot the query performance of a database application. Which of the following tools is the best option?

    A. SQL Server Profiler

    B. Database Engine Tuning Advisor

    C. Network Monitor

    D. Task Manager

11. You have to determine whether a test server can handle the workload of a production server. For that purpose you run a stress test and collect performance statistics for the server using System Monitor. The results are the following:

    - Physical Disk: Avg. Disk Queue Length - Min:0 Max:1 Avg:0.1

    - Processor: % Processor Time - Min:60 Max:100 Avg:85

    - Memory: Pages/sec - Min: 0 Max:160 Avg:5

    - Memory: Available Mbytes - Min:200 Max:500 Avg:300

    Which of the following resource has problems?

    A. Memory

    B. CPU

    C. I/O subsystem

    D. Network

12. For which of the following values of the Physical Disk: Avg. Disk sec/Read performance counter should you investigate if your I/O subsystem has serious problems? (Choose all that apply.)

    A. 8 ms

    B. 11 ms

    C. 51 ms

    D. 55 ms

13. You have to troubleshoot a database application that had a very slow response time for the last 2 hours. One of the steps you take to detect the possible performance problem is verifying the network adapter of the database server. The Network Interface:Current Bandwidth performance counter has the following values—Min: 100000000 Max: 100000000 Avg: 100000000. What values of the Network Interface:Bytes Total/sec performance counter indicates a network problem?

   A. Min: 800 Max: 5560850 Avg: 984545

   B. Min: 1500 Max: 3265877 Avg: 1200545

   C. Both A and B

   D. None of the specified values

14. Which of the following hints allows you to optimize the execution plan of a query for a specific parameter value?

   A. NOLOCK

   B. TABLOCK

   C. OPTIMIZE FOR

   D. RECOMPILE

15. You troubleshoot the performance of an internal inventory application. The application is used by 10 of your company's employees and is hosted by a test server. The server has 2GB of RAM, 1 Pentium 4 CPU at 3GHz, and a single disk drive of 80GB size. You suspect that the disk drive is the cause for the recent performance problems experienced by the users of the inventory application. Knowing that the server's disk has a single spindle, which of the following indicates a disk problem?

   A. Physical Disk: Avg. Disk Queue Length: Min:0 Max:1 Avg:0.1

   B. Physical Disk: Avg. Disk Queue Length: Min:0 Max:1.2 Avg:0.5

   C. Physical Disk: Avg. Disk Queue Length: Min:0 Max:6 Avg:2.5

   D. Processor: % Processor Time: Min: 20 Max: 70 Avg: 50

16. What does a value of 50 seconds for the SQL Server:Buffer Manager:Page life expectancy performance counter on a database server indicate?

   A. A CPU problem

   B. A memory problem

   C. An I/O problem

   D. A network problem

17. A CXPACKET wait type indicates which of the following:

   A. A lock wait

   B. A CPU wait

   C. A synchronization wait for a parallel operation

   D. A network-related wait

18. What you can measure using signal waits?

    A. How long a query waits for CPU time

    B. The degree of contention due to locking

    C. The usefulness of your indexes

    D. The fragmentation of indexes

19. What events are recorded by the default trace? (Choose all that apply.)

    A. Audit DBCC

    B. Server Memory Change

    C. Audit Addlogin

    D. Object:Deleted

20. Which of the following affirmations are true about the default trace? (Choose all that apply.)

    A. You have to configure and start the default trace in order to run on your server.

    B. The default trace may eventually fill up your disk.

    C. The default trace contains maximum 100MB of data.

    D. The default trace is a rollover trace.

Answers to Review Questions

1. **C.** All the options represent execution-related dynamic management view. However, you can find the queries that have been recompiled the most by querying the sys.dm_exec_query_stats dynamic management view. The plan_generation_num column of this DMV returns the information you need.

2. **B.** If you need statistical data about query execution, a good place to start is the sys.dm_exec_query_stats DMV. You can use it to identify queries with most CPU consumption, most recompilations, most I/O activity, and so on.

3. **C.** The best option for this particular case is to recompile the problematic statement. Nothing in the problem statement indicates that you should recompile the entire stored procedure every time it is executed. Rewriting the SELECT statement as a function does not necessarily guarantee obtaining better performance (quite the contrary in most cases). If you modify the SELECT statement by including a hint to force a table scan operation, you would get an inefficient execution plan for cases where index seek operations are appropriate. To give you an example, searching for all customers that have a name starting with "Mary" can benefit from an index seek operation. On the other hand, retrieving all customers that have the letter "a" in their name is done better through a table scan.

4. **D.** The best option is to create a plan guide for the most common parameters of the stored procedure and force the use of the plan using the OPTIMIZE FOR query hint. Recompiling the stored procedure each time it's executed can improve its response time but has as a drawback the compilation overhead. Creating separate stored procedures for each parameter can be a solution when there are just a few parameter values (1 to 10) but when the range of values is larger, the method is totally impractical. The NOLOCK query hint can reduce the locking issues for an application but in this case it would not solve the problem.

5. **C.** The table hint specified on the query is causing the use of the specified index. By simply removing the hint you can allow the query optimizer to do its job. Dropping the used index is unnecessary and not recommended since it can be used by some other queries. Updating statistics and rebuilding the clustered index will have no effect whatsoever.

6. **A, B, C, D.** To answer the request, you have to identify the queries with high values for the Duration column and low values for the Reads and Writes data columns. The TextData column is also necessary to identify the queries.

7. **B.** The default trace is a lightweight trace that logs changes in your server configuration as well as other events like Data Definition Language or Security events. The sys.dm_exec_query_stats dynamic management view can give you a very good idea of how your queries perform but it has nothing to do with the server's configuration. The sys.system_components_surface_area_configuration and the sys.configurations catalog views return information about the current configuration of your server but not historical data.

8. **D.** The best tool for the job is the System Monitor. It can help you identify CPU, memory, or I/O bottlenecks. In this particular scenario, SQL Server Profiler and SQL Trace won't help. The Database Engine Tuning Advisor is a tool used to generate indexes and partitioning recommendations and cannot be used for monitoring purposes.

9. A. In this case the data column that can help you is the Duration column. You don't need the CPU time, the time when an event ended, or the number of read operations.

10. A. The best tool in this case (considering the available options) is the SQL Server Profiler. The other tools specified cannot help you in a direct manner for this particular case.

11. B. The single counter that shows problems is the Processor: % Processor Time performance counter. A value over 80 percent for this counter indicates a CPU bottleneck. All the other counters have values in the normal range.

12. C, D. Values less than 10 milliseconds indicate a very good I/O subsystem. Values in the 10 to 20 milliseconds range are acceptable. Values over 20 milliseconds but less than 50 milliseconds indicate a slow I/O subsystem that may generate performance problems. Values over 50 milliseconds indicate a really serious I/O problem.

13. D. Network congestion is characterized by an average value of more than a half of the network capacity value. The Network Interface:Current Bandwidth counter value indicates that you have an 100Mbs NIC so none of the specified values represent a problem.

14. C. The OPTIMIZE FOR query hint is the correct answer. The TABLOCK and NOLOCK hints are locking hints that modify the locking behavior of database engine. The RECOMPILE hint allows statement-level recompilation.

15. C. The value you should look for is a value greater than 2 for the Physical Disk: Avg. Disk Queue Length performance counter. The Processor: % Processor Time performance counter cannot help you for this situation.

16. B. A value under 300 seconds for the SQL Server: Buffer Manager: Page life expectancy performance counter may indicate a memory problem.

17. C. The CXPACKET wait type is related to parallel execution of a query.

18. A. The signal waits allow you to measure the time your queries wait for CPU.

19. A, B, C, D. The default trace records all the events specified as well as many others.

20. C, D. The default trace is a rollover trace that runs by default on your server. It is not necessary to configure it or start it since and it won't fill your disk since it can have maximum 100MB of data.

Chapter

11

Optimizing Data Storage

MICROSOFT EXAM OBJECTIVES COVERED IN THIS CHAPTER:

✓ **Optimize data storage.**

- Choose column data types to reduce storage requirements across the enterprise.
- Design appropriate use of varchar across the enterprise.
- Denormalize entities to minimize page reads per query.
- Optimize table width.

You've learned in the previous chapters about cursors, caching, queries, indexes, and other performance topics. In this chapter, we return to the basics, to the foundation of your database—the table. Everything you've learned so far depends on this structure and the effectiveness of your database application on this fundamental component.

Specifically, the goal of this chapter is to teach you how to optimize data storage using proper design and optimal data type selection. Why you should care about saving a few bytes of storage since you can buy huge disks with a few hundred bucks?

A few bytes here multiplied with a few million rows can become a few megabytes. A few megabytes can increase the size of your indexes (if any) to another few megabytes. Then, if you have queries that sort or join those *just a little-bit larger* columns, you can add another few megabytes. Add to this scenario a few thousand concurrent users who run those queries, and those few megabytes can become very important. Finally, imagine wasted cache, not just wasted disk space, and you can have suddenly a different perspective of what a few bytes mean.

If you are not convinced yet of the importance of a few bytes, we'll tell you a real story. One of our consulting customers had a large table with about 7 million records. SQL Server can handle successfully tables having billions of rows so a few million records should not have been a problem at all. In this case, the table was the most queried one. Long story short, the rows of the table had roughly one kilobyte plus a few bytes in size. After saving a few bytes here and there, we managed to squeeze an extra row per data page, each page having 8 rows instead of 7. Before we did that, almost 1KB was free in every page. We managed to save 1GB disk space, the table having initially 8GB. We also put some indexes on a diet and reduced the backup and restore time.

Thus, in this chapter, you will learn how to achieve an optimal logical design from a performance point of view. We teach you how to choose the right data type for your table's columns, how to eliminate redundant data through normalization, and, when necessary, how to use denormalization for better read performance.

Picking the Right Data Type

We start with data types. If you compare a database with a house, the data types would be the bricks. Choosing the right data type for your table's columns is essential not only for performance but also for database management operations. You will see why pretty soon, but first let's see what a table is.

A *relational* database is a set of related tables. A *table* is a collection of rows (or records) that have the same attributes. The attributes are the columns of the tables and have values in the same domain, which means in the same data type.

Data types represent the domain for the attributes (columns) of a record. They specify what type of data tables columns can hold and the views, variables, and parameters. Also, data types specify the type of data returned by functions.

Understanding Your Data Type Options

SQL Server 2005 comes with a wide-ranging set of system data types that you can use for your application. The following list groups the system data types by their category:

Integer data types   If you need to store integer numbers such as 11 or –11, four system data types are designed for this purpose. The difference between them is the range of value and their length (the number of bytes required for storage).

tinyint   This has a range of values from 0 to 255 and needs a single byte for storage.

smallint   This can store a range of values from –32,768 to 32,767. It has 2 bytes in size.

int   This needs 4 bytes of storage and allows a range of values from –2,147,483,648 (-2^{31}) to 2,147,483,647 ($2^{31}-1$).

bigint   This is stored on 8 bytes and has a range of values from –9,223,372,036,854,775,808 (-2^{63}) to 9,223,372,036,854,775,807 ($2^{63}-1$).

Exact numeric   The exact numeric data types allow you to store decimal numbers such as 10.78954 or 1,232.55. They are not the only data types for storing decimal numbers but if you need to store values for scientific calculations or any number that requires precision, the exact numeric data types are the best choice. For ANSI compatibility reasons, SQL Server supports two exact numeric data types: decimal and numeric. If all data types have a range of values and a size, the exact numeric have two additional characteristics: precision and scale. Precision refers to the number of digits allowed to represent the decimal number. It also determines the size of the data type. The scale represents the number of digits after the decimal point.

decimal[(p[,s])]   This has a range of values from $-10^{38}+1$ to $10^{38}-1$. You can optionally specify a precision and a scale. The size of the decimal data type is determined by the specified precision. For p in (1,9) the size is 5 bytes, 9 bytes when p is in the (10,19) range, 13 bytes for p in (20,28), and 17 bytes if p is in (29,38).

In this chapter we will use the term *decimal numbers* to refer to floating-point numeric data.

numeric[(p[,s])]   This has the same characteristics as the decimal data type.

Approximate numeric   These are the second category of data types that can hold decimal numbers. The difference between exact and approximate numeric data types is that the latter type stores only an approximate value of the decimal number. You will see later in this topic an example that illustrates the difference between exact and approximate data types. There are two types in the approximate data types' category: float and real.

real The real data type requires 4 bytes for storage and can represent numbers in the following ranges: –3.40E + 38 to –1.18E – 38 and 1.18E – 38 to 3.40E + 38. The value 0 is also included in the possible values for this data type. It has a precision of 7 digits.

float[(n)] The float data type stores decimal numbers in the ranges 3.40E + 38 to –1.18E – 38 and 1.18E – 38 to 3.40E + 38. They can also store the value 0. The attribute n represents the number of bits used to store the mantissa of the float number in scientific notation and determines the precision and the size of the data type. When n is between 1 and 24 the precision of the data type is 7 digits and the size is 4 bytes. A value of n between 25 and 53 determines a size of 8 bytes and a precision of 15 digits for the data type.

You can find out more about the representation of floating-point numbers at the following article: "IEEE floating-point standard," http://en.wikipedia.org/wiki/IEEE_floating-point_standard.

To prove that float and real are approximate data types, we will use the next example. You will declare first two float variables and make a simple calculation:

```
DECLARE @F1 FLOAT(24),@F2 FLOAT(24);
SET @F1=1234567.5;
SET @F2=1234567.6;
SELECT
@F1 AS Nmb1,
@F2 AS Nmb2,
@F2-@F1 AS [Nmb2-Nmb1];
```

What do you think you will get as result? A 0.1 value? No, just look at the result:

```
-- Output
Nmb1       Nmb2       Nmb2-Nmb1
---------  ---------  ---------
1234567.5 1234567.6 0.125
```

The result is 0.125 instead of 0.1. The float data type has a 7 precision in this case and you are using 8 digits.

Now run the same example but change the type of the variables to decimal:

```
DECLARE @D1 DECIMAL(8,1),@D2 DECIMAL(8,1);
SET @D1=1234567.5;
SET @D2=1234567.6;
```

```
SELECT
@D1 AS Nmb1,
@D2 AS Nmb2,
@D2-@D1 AS [Nmb2-Nmb1];
```

This time you will get a better result—the right one:

```
== Output
Nmb1      Nmb2      Nmb2-Nmb1
--------- --------- ---------
1234567.5 1234567.6 0.1
```

As the float and real data types store inexact numbers, they are not recommended for key columns and they should be avoided in WHERE clauses. However they have the advantage of requiring less space and representing a wider range of values compared to exact numeric data types.

Monetary data types   If you work with currency values SQL Server 2005 offers you two specific choices: smallmoney and money data types. Both monetary data types are limited to four decimal points. If you need better accuracy for your calculations you can use decimal or numeric data types. The difference between the two data types is their size and implicitly the range of values.

> **smallmoney**   This is stored on 4 bytes and has a range of values from –214,748.3648 to 214,748.3647.

> **money**   The money data type needs 8 bytes of storage and has a range of values from –922,337,203,685,477.5808 to 922,337,203,685,477.5807. SQL Server stores only currency values (in money and smallmoney data types) not currency types. For example the next query returns 1000 and not 1000$:

```
DECLARE @m AS MONEY;
SET @m=$1000;
SELECT @m AS [Monetary value];
```

Date and time   data types stores, just like the name says, dates and times. One disadvantage of these data types is that they store both a date and a time together. Why we call this a disadvantage? For some situations you need to record just a date (like for example someone's birthday) and for other only a time. There are two date and time data types—smalldatetime and datetime. It may be interesting for you to know that they are stored internally as two integer values. The first integer value stored for smalldatetime data type represents the number of days since January 1, 1900 and the second one the number of minutes since midnight, while the first value stored for a datetime data type records the number of days between a date and January 1, 1753 and the second integer value stored represents the number of 1/300-second units after midnight. The two data types, smalldatetime and datetime, differ in size, range of values, and accuracy.

datetime   Compared to smalldatetime, a datetime value is twice the size (8 bytes), has an accuracy of 3.33 milliseconds, and gives you a range of values from January 1, 1753, to December 31, 9999.

smalldatetime   The storage required by a smalldatetime value is 4 bytes and it can store date and time values from January 1, 1900, to June 6, 2079, with an accuracy of 1 minute.

Character strings   There are actually two major types of character strings. One requires 1 byte to represent a range of characters and one needs 2 bytes for the same purpose. The first one is represented by American National Standards Institute (ANSI) character encoding and the second approach is the Unicode encoding. ANSI encoding is based on multiple character sets while the Unicode uses a single encoding scheme. Let's see the non-Unicode data types first.

char [(n)]   Stores non-Unicode character data. You can specify a length using a value from 1 to 8,000 for the n attribute. The storage size of the data type is n bytes. If you omit n, then for data definitions a value of 1 is assumed, and for CAST or for CONVERT functions a value of 30. The next examples illustrates this behavior:

```
DECLARE @V1 CHAR;
SET @V1='Short string';
SELECT @V1
-- Output:S


DECLARE @V2 CHAR(60);
SET @V2='This is a longer string' +
 ' having more than 30 characters';
SELECT CONVERT (CHAR, @V2);
-- Output: This is a longer string having
```

What is very important for you to remember is that CHAR is a fixed-length data type. That means that if you define a column as CHAR(60), each value stored needs 60 bytes for storage even if the value has less than 60 characters. Even one character value will consume 60 bytes of disk space.

varchar [(n|max)]   Provides a solution for storing variable-length character. The n attribute specifies the maximum length and it is in the 1 through 8,000 range. If you need more than 8,000 characters, you can use the max argument (new in SQL Server 2005) that allows a maximum length of 2^31-1 bytes. The main difference between variable- and fixed-length data types is the storage size required. Variable-length data types minimize the storage required for a data value, using a number of bytes equal to the length of the data value plus another 2 bytes overhead. If you have only a variable length column defined in a table, the overhead is 4 bytes. The storage savings using this data type can be huge.

text   Store variable-length non-Unicode data. It can store a maximum of 2^31-1 (2,147,483,647) characters. In SQL Server 2005, text data type is present for compatibility reasons. Microsoft recommends using the varchar(max) data type instead of text.

Unicode character strings   The Unicode counterparts of char, varchar, and text ANSI data types are nchar, nvarchar, and ntext. They use 2 bytes instead of one for storing a character. When you use Unicode expressions, you should prefix them with N (as in SET @Name= N'Kim') to avoid implicit conversion performance penalties.

  nchar [(n)]   Stores fixed-length Unicode character data. The attribute n indicates the maximum length and can have a value from 1 to 4,000. Each character stored requires two bytes so the storage required in n*2 bytes

  nvarchar [(n|max)]   Stores variable-length Unicode character data. The attribute n is in the range from 1 to 4,000 and indicates the maximum number of characters allowed and also the storage size required (n*2 + 2 bytes overhead). The keyword max allows a maximum storage of 2^31-1 bytes (roughly 1,073,741,823 characters).

  ntext   Stores variable-length Unicode character data just like the nvarchar(max) data type. As a matter of fact you should use nvarchar(max) instead of ntext because nvarchar(max) gives you more flexibility and functionality.

Binary data types   If you need to store binary data inside your database, you can use three data types: binary, varbinary, and image.

  binary [(n)]   For fixed-size binary data, you can use the binary data type. The n argument represents the size expressed in bytes and is in the range 1–8,000.

  varbinary [(n|max)]   For variable-length binary values, you can use the varbinary data type. It can store binary data between 1 and 8,000 bytes in size or if you use the max keyword the size of the data can be up to 2GB.

  image   The image data type can store the same type of data as varbinary(max) but has limited functionality. The Microsoft recommendation is to choose varbinary(max) over the image data type.

Other data types   Besides the data types we mentioned, there are another seven data types that we could not place in special category:

  bit   If you need to store just two values the bit data type is the right one. It can store only two values 0 and 1. When you have more bit columns in a table, the SQL Server groups them together to minimize the storage required. Thus, 8 columns of bit data type require a single byte of space and the same amount is needed by 1-, 2-, or 7-bit columns. For 9 bit type columns, there will be 2 bytes of storage and so on.

  cursor   The cursor data type is a reference to a cursor. The cursors as well as the XML data type have their own chapters in this book so we'll just mention them.

  sql_variant   A possible use of this data type is a situation when you cannot decide the data type for a column (parameter or returned value) or when you need multiple data types for a single column (parameter or returned value). It can store values for other data types of SQL Server 2005 with the exception of text, ntext, image, timestamp, and sql_variant, varchar(max), nvarchar(max), varbinary(max), xml, timestamp, and CLR user-defined types. For performance reasons, we recommend you to avoid this data type.

table   The table data type is somewhat similar to a real table, and you can use it to store results of function or as a local variable.

timestamp   This data type stores an 8-byte binary value that identifies the current version for a row.

uniqueidentifier   Also known as globally unique identifier (GUID), this data type stores a unique 16-byte binary value. If you use merge replication, SQL Server adds a GUID column to identify each row for each published table.

xml   New in SQL Server 2005, the XML data type can store XML documents.

Using Data Type Synonyms

Some of the data types of SQL Server 2005 have synonyms for SQL-92 compatibility reasons. Table 11.1 lists the SQL Server 2005 system data types and their synonyms.

TABLE 11.1   System Data Types and SQL-92 Synonyms

System Data Type	Synonym
varbinary	Binary varying
varchar	char varying
char	character
char(1)	character
char(n)	character(n)
varchar(n)	character varying(n)
decimal	Dec
float	Double precision
real	float[(n)] for $n = 1–7$
float	float[(n)] for $n = 8–15$
int	integer
nchar(n)	national character(n)
nchar(n)	national char(n)

TABLE 11.1   System Data Types and SQL-92 Synonyms *(continued)*

System Data Type	Synonym
nvarchar(n)	national character varying(*n*)
nvarchar(n)	national char varying(*n*)
ntext	national text
timestamp	rowversion

You can use synonyms instead of the base data types when you create objects. However, you should know that the object definition will store the base data type name.

For example, if you create the following table named Persons, SQL Server stores the definition of the table using the base data type names for the FirstName and LastName columns:

```
USE tempdb;
GO
CREATE TABLE Persons (
PersonID int PRIMARY KEY,
FirstName NATIONAL CHARACTER VARYING(32),
LastName NATIONAL CHARACTER VARYING(32)
);
GO
```

You can verify the result by running EXEC `sp_help N'Persons'` that the FirstName and LastName columns have the data type nvarchar(32). Don't be fooled by the value of Length column, which is 64, as you know the Unicode data types are use 2 bytes for each stored character so the actual length for the FirstName and LastName columns is 32.

Expanding the Existing Data Types

If necessary you can extend the existing data types using Microsoft .NET Framework or alias data types. The CLR user-defined types are beyond the scope of this chapter.

The alias data types are based on the system data types and can be used to maintain a consistent data type design strategy. To create an alias data type, you can use the CREATE TYPE statement. For example you can create a phone number alias data type and use it on all tables that need it:

```
USE tempdb;
GO
CREATE TYPE Phone
FROM VARCHAR(16) NOT NULL;
```

```
GO
CREATE TABLE Persons (
PersonID int PRIMARY KEY,
FirstName VARCHAR(32),
LastName VARCHAR(32),
PhoneNumber Phone
);
GO
```

You can see additional example of alias data types in the AdventureWorks database using the catalog view sys.types:

```
USE AdventureWorks;
GO
SELECT
[name]
FROM sys.types
WHERE is_user_defined = 1;
```

The output shows six user-defined data types:

```
-- Output
name
----------------
AccountNumber
Flag
Name
NameStyle
OrderNumber
Phone
```

To get more information about a specific type, you can use the DATALENGTH function to get the size of a data type or the sp_help stored procedure. For example, the Phone alias data type in the AdventureWorks database has the base type nvarchar(50), as you can see running this code:

```
EXEC sp_help N'Phone';
```

Using Data Types

To give you a simple example of how you should use data types, we suggest using a database named SalesDB that stores the sales data for a pharmaceutical company. The company has 10 locations and sells more than 2,000 products, each product having one category such as drugs, supplements, and medical equipment. The company has 20 categories of products and sales of more than 10,000 products per day.

The code that generated the current design of the SalesDB database follows:

```
CREATE TABLE Categories(
CategoryID INT PRIMARY KEY NOT NULL,
CategoryName CHAR(32));
GO
CREATE TABLE Locations(
LocationID INT PRIMARY KEY NOT NULL,
LocationName CHAR(32));
GO
CREATE TABLE Products(
ProductID INT PRIMARY KEY NOT NULL,
ProductName CHAR(32),
CategoryID INT
REFERENCES Categories(CategoryID)
);
GO
CREATE TABLE Customers(
CustomerID INT PRIMARY KEY,
CustomerName VARCHAR(64));
GO
CREATE TABLE Orders(
OrderID SMALLINT PRIMARY KEY,
TotalAmount DECIMAL(38,4),
CustomerID INT
 REFERENCES Customers(CustomerID)
);
CREATE TABLE OrderDetails(
OrderDetailID SMALLINT PRIMARY KEY,
OrderID SMALLINT
 REFERENCES Orders(OrderID),
ProductID INT
 REFERENCES Products(ProductID),
LocationID INT
 REFERENCES Locations(LocationID)
);
```

Is the database designed according to specifications? We would say that it is not. Here are several mistakes:

- Product names, people names, and category names should be variable-length data types not fixed length.

- The ProductID column from the Products table should be smaller—a smallint data type is enough. Using int would waste 4 bytes in Products table and, more important, in the Orders table.

- The CategoryID and LocationID columns also should be smaller. They should be tinyint.

- A special remark about the OrderID and OrderDetailID columns. They are too small. Considering the sales volume, they should be at least int—not smallint; otherwise if the company doesn't go broke, its current size doesn't allow you to record new orders after three days.

To put it simply, when you select a data type make sure that is not too large but also don't be too economical.

Optimizing Tables, Indexes, Extents, Pages, and Records

In Chapter 8, you saw that database objects are stored in pages and that eight physically contiguous pages make an extent. You also learned that that there are more types of pages, such as data pages that hold your data, index pages that hold index entries, text/image pages that contain large object data types, and several types of allocation pages that track data pages allocated to various objects. The next structure you should meet is the record (or the *row*).

At this point in the book, you should be familiar with the table and the index concepts. *Records* represent table and index rows stored physically on your disk by SQL Server. Besides table and index rows, records are also used for storing LOB values, allocation data, intermediate results for sort operation, and so on.

For this chapter, we focus on data and index records.

Data records   A row of a heap or from the leaf level of a clustered index is stored as a data record. Obviously, data records are stored on data pages. Some of the columns of the row may be stored separately but we will talk about it later.

Index records   Index records store the rows of nonclustered indexes and non-leaf level rows for clustered and nonclustered indexes. If the nonclustered index has an LOB data type included columns, those columns can be stored in different pages as text records and in the original page SQL Server leaves a pointer. Both data and index records have the same structure as you can see here:

Record Header	Fixed Length Data	NULL Bitmap	Variable Block	Variable Data	Versioning Tag

We can differentiate the following segments:

Record header   The record header take 4 bytes of storage. The first 2 bytes are for metadata indicating the record type. The other 2 bytes point forward in the record to the NULL bitmap.

Fixed-length data   The next portion of the row contains the values for the fixed-length columns (int, char, datetime). No matter the value stored for a fixed-length column, the same space is used. For example, if you store one character in a column defined as CHAR(10), the column still uses 10 bytes for storage. An exception to this rule makes the decimal data type when the vardecimal storage is enabled. More on this later.

NULL bitmap (or NULL block)   The NULL bitmap uses 2 bytes to count the columns of the record. Then, it uses a variable number of bytes to store the nullability of a column. Each column of the table needs a single bit so if the table has less than 9 columns, a single byte (8 bits) is necessary. If the column has between 9 and 16 columns, the null block requires 2 bytes for the null bitmap and so on.

Variable block   The variable block consists in 2 bytes for counting the variable-length columns and 2 bytes to indicate where the column value starts for each variable-length column. If your table has no variable-length columns, then the record does not contain a variable block.

Pop quiz: How can you improve the design of the next table if you know that the blood groups are 0, A, B, and AB?

```
CREATE TABLE BloodGroup(
PatientID INT NOT NULL,
BloodGroup VARCHAR(2));
```

The answer is to change the type of the BloodGroup column to CHAR(2) because in this particular case, using the VARCHAR(2) data type brings an overhead of 4 bytes.

Variable data   The variable data section stores the actual values for variable-length columns (if any).

Versioning tag   If you use row versioning, your rows (records) can have a 14 bytes versioning tag that contains a time stamp and a pointer to the Version Store.

Improving Performance through Database Design

You can improve the performance of your database following some simple design techniques such as normalization or keeping rows smaller. In this section, we explore several of the most used techniques.

Online Transaction Processing versus Online Analytical Processing

There are two main categories for most of the database applications:

- Online Transaction Processing (OLTP)
- Online Analytical Processing (OLAP) also know as Decision Support

OLTP Characteristics

Having many concurrent users perform small transactions characterizes OLTP database applications. For OLTP systems, you have to minimize I/O activity and use a design that facilitates concurrent activity. Usually an OLTP database is highly normalized to allow fast data modification and concurrent read and write operations. In general, historical and aggregate data in OLTP systems range from minimal to none. The index strategy is based on maintaining narrow indexes and keeping the number of indexes as low as possible to avoid the performance penalty for data modifications.

OLAP Characteristics

OLAP applications are usually based on a read-only, large volume of historical data accessed by a few users. Usually the users of OLAP systems do not modify the data so concurrency is not a problem. A large number of indexes support read queries, and the database structure is denormalized having pre-aggregated and summarized data.

Real-World Applications

In the real world you need both types of applications, and often you will meet them both in the same server instance. Ideally OLAP and OLTP are separated. When they are together, you have to design both for querying large volumes of data as well as for transactional performance.

The main tools you can use to achieve your performance objective are normalization and its counterpart, denormalization.

Understanding Normalization

Normalization is a process that consists of applying a set of rules. The goal of normalization is to eliminate redundancy and reduce potential anomalies that can occur during data modifications.

Table Orders (raw)

BookTitle	Publisher	Author1	Author2
70-442 Study Guide	Wiley	Marilyn White	Cristian Lefter
70-442 Study Guide	Wiley	Marilyn White	Cristian Lefter
...	...	...	...
70-442 Study Guide	Wiley	Marilyn White	Cristian Lefter

15000 rows

What is good about the table showed in the illustration? If you want to obtain all orders as well as the publishers' and the authors' names, then the Orders table is perfect as it is.

But if you want to delete the second row, what can you do? You cannot delete specifically the second row. Why? Nothing makes it unique compared to the other rows. You can delete or modify one row using, for example, the TOP operator but you cannot specify which one in this particular case. At least you cannot do it in a straightforward manner.

What if the book has a third author? What can you do? With this design you are pretty limited.

Another problem with the table Orders is that if you want to change the name of an author, for example, from Cristian Lefter to Cristian Andrei Lefter, you have to modify all 15,000 rows. You can imagine that updating so many rows for changing just a piece of information can have repercussions on your concurrency.

For contrast, the normalized version of the table is shown in the next image.

Orders

OrderID	BookID
1	1
2	1
...	...
15000	1

Books

BookID	BookTitle	PublisherID
1	70-442 Study Guide	1

Publishers

PublisherID	PublisherName
1	Wiley

Authors

AuthorID	AuthorName
1	Marilyn White
2	Cristian Lefter

Book Authors

BookID	AuthorID
1	1
1	2

This time if you want to modify the name of an author, a book, or a publisher, you modify a single row instead of 15,000. Add to that the fact that you have smaller tables that guarantee a better data modification performance and less disk storage. Also you can modify any row you want using columns, such as OrderID, PublisherID, BookID, or AuthorID. You can't tell from the picture but they are primary keys in their tables (Orders, Publishers, Books, and Authors) and foreign keys for other tables.

Another benefit is that you can have publishers that don't have any books ordered or published. Or you can have authors that are currently writing a book.

There is a downside for the new design: to obtain the complete data stored in a single table, you have to join five tables. How do we get five tables from the original one? We use normalization.

The process of normalization was first proposed by Edgar F. Codd, a British computer scientist working at that time at IBM. He defined originally three sets of rules also known as normal forms.

For a complete list of normal forms please refer to the "Database Normalization" article from Wikipedia at http://en.wikipedia.org/wiki/Database_normalization.

Though there are six normal forms, in practice only the first three are used.

First Normal Form

The first normal form requires that:

- Each table has a primary key (a set of attributes that identifies uniquely a record).
- Repeating groups should be eliminated.
- Each attribute contains a value, not a set of values.

Applying the first normal form to the original table, we add a primary key to the Orders table and replace the repeating group (Author1 and Author2 columns) with a single column Author. The combination OrderID, Author identifies uniquely a row.

Orders

OrderID	BookTitle	Publisher	Author
1	70-442 Study Guide	Wiley	Cristian Lefter
1	70-442 Study Guide	Wiley	Marilyn White
...	...	...	...
15000	70-442 Study Guide	Wiley	Cristian Lefter
15000	70-442 Study Guide	Wiley	Marilyn White

If you apply first normal form rules for a database, the database is said to be in first normal form.

Second Normal Form

The second normal form requires a database already in first normal form and comes with an additional rule: Data that is duplicated across multiple records should be moved to a separate table.

Applying this new rule to our single-table database, we move the BookTitle, Publisher, and Author columns to separate tables. The next illustration displays the result:

Orders

OrderID	BookID	PublisherID
1	1	1
2	1	1
...	...	...
15000	1	1

Books

BookID	BookTitle
1	70-442 Study Guide

Publishers

PublisherID	PublisherName
1	Wiley

Authors

AuthorID	AuthorName
1	Marilyn White
2	Cristian Lefter

Book Authors

BookID	AuthorID
1	1
1	2

Third Normal Form

Before applying the third normal form, the database should meet all the requirements of the second normal form. In addition, the third normal form comes with one more rule: Any field that is dependent on the primary key and also on another field should be moved to a separate table.

In our case, the PublisherID column depends on the BookID column so it should be in the Books table rather than in the Orders. Moving the PublisherID column is the last design operation. You've already seen the result.

Normalization Advantages

Normalized databases come with several packaged advantages such as:

- Narrower tables and implicitly narrower indexes. You will obtain:
    - More rows per page, hence less I/O activity (more rows per I/O operation).
    - Better cache utilization.
    - Easier index creation and maintenance (rebuild, recreate, reorganize).
    - Better and faster queries due to shorter index search operations.
- More clustered indexes per database (normalization generates more tables) but fewer indexes per table. The results are improved data modification performance and more flexibility for designing clustered and nonclustered indexes.
- Improved data integrity by reducing the probability of data modification anomalies. When the same piece of information exists in multiple places there is a potential for data modification problems and for inconsistency. Normalization eliminates redundancy and lowers the probability of data inconsistency.
- Less redundant data, which determines:
    - Better transactional performance.
    - Less storage.
    - Less time for maintenance operations such as backup and restore.
    - More compact databases and fewer NULLs.

Understanding Denormalization

If the normalization is the process of maintaining a specific piece of information in a single place, the denormalization is a step back. It adds redundancy by duplicating data.

You've seen an example of a denormalization technique in Chapter 10, when we combined three separate tables in a single table to reduce the number of joins required for a query.

The goal of denormalization is to enhance performance. It is very important to understand that denormalization assumes a prior normalized database. Keeping raw data does not qualify as denormalization. There are several techniques for denormalization such as adding redundant columns, collapsing tables, and so on. Let's take them in turns.

Adding Redundant Columns

To eliminate some of the most frequent table joins, you can add redundant columns to one or more tables.

Using the same example from the normalization topic, let's suppose that the most frequently run query in the database is the next query:

```
SELECT
  B.BookTitle,
```

```
 A.AuthorName,
 P.PublisherName
FROM Books B
JOIN Authors A
 ON A.AuthorID = B.AuthorID
JOIN Publishers P
 ON P.PublisherID = B.PublisherID
WHERE BookTitle LIKE @Pattern
```

To improve the performance of the query you can add the AuthorName column to the Books table and maintain it using a trigger. The resulting query would be faster through elimination of a join operation:

```
SELECT
 B.BookTitle,
 B.AuthorName,
 P.PublisherName
FROM Books B
JOIN Publishers P
 ON P.PublisherID = B.PublisherID
WHERE BookTitle LIKE @Pattern
```

The drawback of the solution is the presence of duplicate data (more disk space required) and maintaining the duplicated data.

Adding Derived Columns

Similar to adding redundant columns, you can add derived columns to reduce the number of joins or the time for calculating aggregate values.

For example, in the sample database Northwind that ships with SQL Server 2000, to get the total amount of money for each order, you have to use a join operation:

```
USE Northwind;
GO
SELECT
 O.OrderID,
 SUM(CONVERT(MONEY,(OD.UnitPrice*OD.Quantity*
(1-OD.Discount)/100))*100) AS TotalAmount
FROM Orders O
JOIN [Order Details] OD
 ON O.OrderID = OD.OrderID
GROUP BY O.OrderID
```

You could eliminate this join by adding a computed column to the Orders table.

Or, in the AdventureWorks database, an example of a derived column is the TotalDue column of the Sales.SalesOrderHeader table, which has the definition: TotalDue AS Subtotal + TaxAmt + Freight. In this case the TotalDue column is a computed column. You can store computed columns on disk using the PERSISTED keyword in the column's definition.

Disadvantages of this method are the same: required maintenance operations (through triggers, functions, and so on) and duplicate data.

Prejoined Tables

If you have queries with a lot of join operations, you can improve their performance by creating tables that contain prejoined data. For example, the next query can be improved from a performance point of view using prejoined tables technique:

```
SELECT
  T1.T1_COL,
  T2.T2_COL,
  T3.T3_COL,
  T4.T4_COL
FROM T1
JOIN T2
  ON T1.T1_ID = T2.T1_ID
JOIN T3
  ON T2.T2_ID = T3.T2_ID
JOIN T4
  ON T3.T3_ID = T4.T3_ID;
```

You can build a table T123 having the columns T3_ID, T1_COL, T2_COL, and T3_COL. To populate this table initially, use the next code:

```
INSERT INTO T123(
  T3_ID,T1_COL,T2_COL,T3_COL)
SELECT
  T3_ID,T1_COL,T2_COL,T3_COL
FROM T1
JOIN T2 ON T1.T1_ID = T2.T1_ID
JOIN T3 ON T2.T2_ID = T3.T2_ID;
```

To maintain the table, you can use DML triggers on all three tables. Then, the new form of the original query should be as follows:

```
SELECT
  T123.T1_COL,
  T123.T2_COL,
  T123.T3_COL,
  T4.T4_COL
```

```
FROM T123
JOIN T4
 ON T123.T3_ID = T4.T3_ID;
```

Duplicating Tables

If concurrent read-intensive and write operations block each other, you can minimize the problems using duplicate (or mirror) tables. This way one table can be used for data modifications and its mirror for read-intensive operations, reporting purposes, or aggregate queries. Also you can duplicate only a subset of the data from the original table.

Splitting Tables

There are two ways of splitting tables: horizontally and vertically. A vertical table split means creating two or more tables, each having a subset of the original table's columns. Take, for example, a table that stores books and was created using this code:

```
CREATE TABLE Books(
BookID INT PRIMARY KEY NOT NULL,
BookTitle VARCHAR(128),
ShortDescription VARCHAR(512),
CategoryID INT,
BookExcerpt VARCHAR(MAX),
BookDescription VARCHAR(MAX));
```

Two queries frequently run that use the Books table:

```
SELECT
BookTitle,
ShortDescription
FROM Books
WHERE CategoryID = @CategoryID;
```

```
SELECT
BookDescription,
BookExcerpt
FROM Books
WHERE BookID = @BookID;
```

The first query returns all books in the category specified by a parameter. The second one retrieves the details for a book.

To improve the performance of both queries, you can vertically split the original as follows:

```
CREATE TABLE Books(
BookID INT PRIMARY KEY NOT NULL,
```

```
BookTitle VARCHAR(128),
ShortDescription VARCHAR(512),
CategoryID INT);

CREATE TABLE BookDetails(
BookID INT PRIMARY KEY NOT NULL,
BookExcerpt VARCHAR(MAX),
BookDescription VARCHAR(MAX));
```

The horizontal partitioning involves two or more tables each having a subset of the original table's rows.

Partitioned tables and partitioned indexes are one of the methods of horizontal partitioning in SQL Server 2005. Horizontal partitioning can give you improved join and query performance and also improved management and backup operations. For example, you can horizontally partition a table Orders using the OrderDate column and month or year ranges.

Indexed Views

Maybe you never looked at indexed views as denormalization techniques though this is exactly what they are—duplicate data for improved query performance. You already know from the other chapters that indexes improve performance, but you have to pay a performance penalty for data modifications. There are more ways to denormalize data, but they're beyond the scope of the book.

 You can read more about denormalization techniques in an article by Craig S. Mullins, "Denormalization Guidelines," at `http://www.craigsmullins.com/ssu_1200.htm`.

Creating the Smallest Rows Possible

Optimal row width is the main goal in table design and especially for OLTP applications. The more rows you can store in a page, the more efficiency you get from each database operation on a table. The second benefit of small rows is better usage of cache. Also you can get efficient space usage as in the next example.

The following table named BlogComment records comments for blog entries.

 According to Wikipedia, a blog is a website where entries are made in journal style and displayed in a reverse chronological order. See `http://en.wikipedia.org/wiki/Blog`.

The table was created using this code:

```
CREATE TABLE BlogComments(
CommentID INT NOT NULL IDENTITY(1,1) PRIMARY KEY,
BlogEntryID INT NOT NULL,
CommentAuthor NCHAR(60) NOT NULL,
CommentText NCHAR(2000) NOT NULL,
Email VARCHAR(128) NULL,
AuthorURL VARCHAR(128));
```

What is wrong with this table? The first obvious mistake is using nchar data type instead of nvarchar for CommentAuthor and CommentText columns that probably would have values with varying sizes.

The second mistake, a little bit elusive, is the combination of choosing the nchar data type for the CommentText column and the size of the column 2000. A single row of this table can fit on a page and because of that almost half of the page space is wasted. Why? Because a page can store 8,060 bytes of data and a row of the BlogComment table is maximum 4,397 bytes in size. The formula used to calculate the maximum size of the row is: 4 bytes (the row header) + 4 bytes (the CommentID column) + 4 bytes (the BlogEntryID column) + 2*60 bytes (the CommentAuthor) + 2*2,000 (the CommentText) + 3 bytes (the null block) + 6 bytes (variable block) + 128 bytes (maximum size of the AuthorURL column) + 128 bytes (maximum size of the Email column).

A simple design remedy for this situation is to replace the NCHAR data type with NVAR-CHAR and to reduce the size of the CommentText column to 1,800 characters.

Using Variable-Length Columns Properly

The variable-length columns are most valuable when it comes to achieving the optimal row width. If they are used properly, they save disk space, cache and database maintenance time, and ultimately can increase the overall performance. The properties require two conditions—variable-length columns are not updated frequently and the values stored are variable in size. When frequently updated, the variable-length columns can generate page splits and create fragmentation. Also, when the values stored are fixed size, the variable-length columns bring unnecessary overhead.

Otherwise, the variable-length columns are very useful for many reasons from having large rows, making your tables and indexes more compact, to storing XML documents (when you want to preserve the formatting).

The vardecimal Storage Format

Decimal and numeric data types are stored as fixed-length data. Or, at least, they were stored this way until Service Pack 2 for SQL Server 2005 introduced the vardecimal storage format.

The vardecimal storage format allows the storage of decimal and numeric data types as variable-length data types. You already know from the data types topic that a decimal or numeric data type can use from 5 to 17 bytes of storage depending on its precision. A column declared as DECIMAL(38,2) will require 17 bytes of storage for each row, no matter if no value is specified or if you store the value 0.0.

Enabling the vardecimal storage format, you can save disk space for special situations where you can have multiple small-size values or NULLs stored in a column declared as a high-precision decimal. You can enable the storage format at the database level using the sp_db_vardecimal_storage_format stored procedure and then at the table level using the sp_tableoption stored procedure.

Here's an example (that requires you to have Service Pack 2 installed) of where this storage format can be useful. CompanyXYZ is a natural gas company from Russia. It sells natural gas both to individual consumers as well as to countries from the European Union. The following code represents the table that stored the bills for this company. We chose to create a new database instead of using tempdb or AdventureWorks. We set the recovery model of the database to SIMPLE for a little more speed and less log space:

```
USE master;
GO
CREATE DATABASE TestDB;
GO
ALTER DATABASE TestDB
SET RECOVERY SIMPLE;
GO
USE TestDB;
GO
CREATE TABLE Bills(
BillID INT PRIMARY KEY NOT NULL,
Amount DEC(38,4),
Overdue DEC(38,4),
CustomerID INT);
GO
```

The average individual customer pays around $50. We inserted some demo data to reflect that:

```
SET NOCOUNT ON;
GO
USE TestDB;
GO
DECLARE @I INT;
SET @I = 1;
WHILE @I<1001
  BEGIN
  INSERT INTO Bills (
  BillID,Amount,Overdue,CustomerID)
```

```
SELECT @I,50.25,0.0,@I;
SET @I=@I+1;
END;

INSERT INTO Bills (
 BillID,Amount,Overdue,CustomerID)
SELECT
 1001 as BillID,
 3975844935.242 AS Amount,
 30835933453.845 AS Overdue,
 1001 AS CustomerID;
```

The code inserts 1,000 rows with regular customers and one row representing an entire country. The current bill of the customer with the ID 1001 is \$3,975,844,935.242 and the debt \$30,835,933,453.845.

It makes sense to use a large decimal to store such numbers as the bill for customer 1001. But for the other 1,000 customers, this decision means wasted space.

The current space occupied by the table is returned using the sp_spaceused stored procedure:

```
EXEC sp_spaceused N'Bills';
```

You can see that the result reflects the number of rows and the total size of the table (the rows and the reserved columns):

```
-- Output
name   rows reserved data   index_size unused
-----  ---- -------- -----  ---------- -------
Bills  1001 72 KB    56 KB  16 KB      0 KB
```

The average record size can be obtained using the sys.dm_db_index_physical_stats dynamic management view:

```
SELECT
avg_record_size_in_bytes
FROM sys.dm_db_index_physical_stats(
 DB_ID(N'TestDB'),
 OBJECT_ID(N'Bills'),
 DEFAULT,
 DEFAULT,
 'DETAILED')
WHERE index_level = 0;
```

The result shows 49 bytes as the average size for the Bills table's rows:

```
-- Output
avg_record_size_in_bytes
------------------------
49
```

To decide if we should use or not the vardecimal storage format, we can use the sp_estimated_rowsize_reduction_for_vardecimal stored procedure that will tell you whether using the vardecimal storage format will result in less consumed space or not:

```
EXEC sp_estimated_rowsize_reduction_for_vardecimal N'Bills';
-- Output
avg_rowlen_fixed_format avg_rowlen_vardecimal_format row_count
----------------------- ---------------------------- ---------
49.00                   23.01                        1001
```

As you can see from the output, your average record size can be reduced from 49 to 23. That means that you will save more than half of the space occupied now by the Bills table.

To switch to the vardecimal storage format, you will enable it first at the database level and then at the table level:

```
USE master;
GO
EXEC sp_db_vardecimal_storage_format 'TestDB','ON';
GO
USE TestDB;
GO
EXEC sp_tableoption 'Bills', 'vardecimal storage format', 1 ;
GO
```

Now let's check again the space used:

```
EXEC sp_spaceused N'Bills';
```

The output should convince you that you do save space using this new storage format:

```
-- Output
name  rows reserved data  index_size unused
----- ---- -------- ----- ---------- -------
Bills 1001 48 KB    32 KB 16 KB      0 KB
```

The space used by the table is reduced from 72KB to 48KB—less than half if you are not taking into account the index pages and also the internal overhead (for rows and pages).

You can verify the average record size using the previous query:

```
SELECT
avg_record_size_in_bytes
FROM sys.dm_db_index_physical_stats(
 DB_ID(N'TestDB'),
 OBJECT_ID(N'Bills'),
 DEFAULT,
 DEFAULT,
 'DETAILED')
WHERE index_level = 0;
```

The output shows that the stored procedure that estimates the spaced saved didn't lie:

```
-- Output
avg_record_size_in_bytes
------------------------
23.012
```

You should be aware that in some cases using the vardecimal storage could result in more disk space required. Just think at the difference between a column declared as CHAR(17) and VARCHAR(17) (we choose 17 because 17 is the maximum length for decimal data type). If you store values that have variable sizes or no values at all, the VARCHAR(17) is the best choice. But if you store fixed-length strings, having 17 characters the VARCHAR(17) becomes a poor choice, adding up to 4 bytes of unnecessary overhead. The same holds true for the vardecimal storage but you should be aware of this new storage option.

Handling NULLs

We will not participate into the worldwide debate "should I use or not nulls." There are valid arguments for both using and not using NULLs. We recommend that you make your decision about using NULLs consistent in your application, in your database code, and in your database creation scripts.

Especially for database object creation scripts, we recommend you to be very specific about columns' nullability. Take, for example, the next two sample codes:

```
CREATE TABLE T1(I INT);
GO
CREATE TABLE T2(I INT NOT NULL);
GO
```

Though the code samples may appear to be equivalent, they are not. What can you say about the column I of the table T1? Does it allow NULL? Or it does not?

The answer is it depends. If the session setting ANSI_NULL_DFLT_ON is ON or if the database option ANSI_NULL_DEFAULT is ON, then the answer is yes. Otherwise the column I may not allow NULLs.

The best approach is to specify explicitly if a column allows nulls, which is just like the second statement. Some people recommend moving your nullable columns to a separate table. Whether you follow this recommendation is up to you.

Moving beyond the 8KB Row Size Limits

The only way to overcome the 8K row size barrier in SQL Server 2000 is to use the large object (LOB) data types. There are three LOB data types in SQL Server 2000—TEXT for storing large non-Unicode character data, NTEXT for storing Unicode text data, and IMAGE for binary data. All three can accommodate 2GB of data and still be supported by SQL Server 2005 for backward compatibility reasons.

 The *TEXT, NTEXT,* and *IMAGE* data types are deprecated and will be removed in future versions of SQL Server.

If you wonder how they can be larger than 8,000 bytes, the explanation is rather simple. They are stored usually off-row in a B-tree structure, maintaining in the data row a 16-byte pointer to root of the B-tree. You could store small- to medium-sized LOBs in-row using the 'text in row' table option. The TEXT, NTEXT, and IMAGE data types have a special type of allocation unit for managing the allocation of data pages.

What is wrong with SQL Server 2000 LOBs? They have a very limited Transact-SQL functionality and require special handling. Some examples of SQL Server 2000 LOB data types' limitations are as follows:

- You cannot use LOBs as parameters.
- Read and write operations require the use of text pointers.
- You can't compare or concatenate large objects.
- You can not use LOBs in your WHERE clause, except if you include them in a function, such as ISNULL, SUBSTRING, or PATINDEX, or if you use the IS NULL, IS NOT NULL, or LIKE expressions.

SQL Server 2005 gives you two new options for stretching the row size:

- Using the new large value data types: VARCHAR(MAX), NVARCHAR(MAX), and VARBINARY(MAX).
- The *row-overflow data* feature allows columns having the data type varchar, nvarchar, varbinary, or sql_variant to be stored off-row when the combined widths of the table's (or index's) columns is greater than 8,060 bytes.

Using the VARCHAR(MAX), NVARCHAR(MAX), and VARBINARY(MAX) Data Types

The MAX keyword applies to variable data types like varchar, nvarchar, and varbinary, expanding their maximum storage size to 2GB of data. You should know that the MAX specifier depends on SQL Server releases. In a future release, it could refer to a bigger value than the current 2GB.

The varchar(MAX), nvarchar(MAX), and varbinary(MAX) are similar to the legacy LOBs (text, ntext, and image) as they are also large objects. The main difference between new LOBs and legacy LOBs is functionality. New LOBs (or large value data types) give you anything you would expect from a regular data type:

- Data Manipulation Language (DML) support:
  - You can use new LOBs in joins or subqueries
  - You can also use them with the order by, group by, and distinct clauses
- Enhanced function support; the following functions allow large value data types as arguments:
  - COL_LENGTH
  - CHARINDEX
  - PATINDEX
  - LEN
  - DATALENGTH
  - SUBSTRING
- The ALTER TABLE statement allows a very simple migration from legacy to new LOBS.
- You can use large value data types in AFTER triggers (old LOBs being allowed only in INSTEAD OF triggers).
- You could define variables having large value data types.
- You can use large value data types in cursors.
- You can partially update a new LOB using chunked updates with the new .WRITE clause of the UPDATE statement.
- The OPENROWSET bulk rowset provider allows you to import large object data from data files.

The next examples illustrate several of the new features for the new large value data types.

We start with the migration from old LOBs. The procedure is very simple and consists of running an ALTER TABLE statement. What is remarkable about LOB migration is that it doesn't touch data. Only metadata is modified. Here's an example that creates a table having a text column and migrates the column to the new varchar(max) data type:

```
USE tempdb;
GO
CREATE TABLE BookStore(
```

```
BookID INT NOT NULL PRIMARY KEY,
BookExcerpt TEXT);
GO
INSERT INTO BookStore(BookID,BookExcerpt)
VALUES(1,REPLICATE(CAST('Text Is Not Available Yet' AS VARCHAR(MAX)),5000));
GO
```

We insert a single row in the table and, to generate a large value, we use the REPLICATE function to repeat the string argument 5,000 times.

To prove that no data changed, we use two catalog views to display the number of pages used by the table and their allocation unit type:

```
SELECT
OBJECT_NAME([object_id]) AS ObjName,
[rows] AS NmbOfRows,
type_desc AS AllocationUnitType,
total_pages AS NmbOfPages
FROM sys.partitions p
JOIN sys.allocation_units a
   ON p.partition_id = a.container_id
WHERE [object_id]=OBJECT_ID(N'BookStore');
```

As you can see from the output our table needs two pages of in-row data: one that holds the only row of the table and one allocation page. Also 25 pages store the LOB data.

```
-- Output
ObjName    NmbOfRows AllocationUnitType NmbOfPages
BookStore 1         IN_ROW_DATA        2
BookStore 1         LOB_DATA           25
```

As we already stated, the migration to the varchar(MAX) data type consists of a single ALTER TABLE statement:

```
ALTER TABLE BookStore
ALTER COLUMN BookExcerpt VARCHAR(MAX);
GO
```

If you run the previous code to check the allocation data, you should get the same two in-row data pages and 25 pages for LOB data.

Next, you will see how simple it is to read from a large value data type using the SUBSTRING function:

```
SELECT SUBSTRING(BookExcerpt,1,25)
FROM BookStore
WHERE BookID=1;
```

The output shows the first 25 characters stored in the BookExcerpt column:

```
-- Output
Text is Not Available Yet
```

For comparison, here's how you can do a read operation in SQL Server 2000 on a text column:

```
USE tempdb;
GO
CREATE TABLE OldStyleText(
ID INT NOT NULL PRIMARY KEY,
COL TEXT);
GO
INSERT INTO OldStyleText(ID,COL)
VALUES (1,'Stored Value');
GO
DECLARE @val varbinary(16)
SELECT @val = TEXTPTR(COL) FROM OldStyleText
WHERE ID = 1;

READTEXT OldStyleText.COL @val 0 6;
```

You have to use a text pointer and the READTEXT statement. The output shows the first 6 characters of the string stored in the COL text column:

```
-- Output
COL
Stored
```

The same result can be obtained in SQL Server 2005 using the next statement:

```
SELECT SUBSTRING(COL,1,6) FROM OldStyleText;
```

If you want to update only partially a large value text column the .WRITE clause of the UPDATE statement is a possible option. You have to supply a zero-based offset (that represents the start location) and the number of characters that will be replaced. The next code sample replaces the first 12 characters (' Text is Not ') of the BookExcerpt column with a new string:

```
UPDATE BookStore
SET BookExcerpt .WRITE (N'New Text is ',0,12)
WHERE BookID = 1;

SELECT SUBSTRING(BookExcerpt,1,21) FROM BookStore;
```

The output of the SELECT statement is:

```
-- Output
New Text is Available
```

The next code example is related to indexes. You cannot create indexes using text, ntext, or image columns. Let's prove that. First, you have to create a table and then you will try to create an index using a text data type column.

```
USE tempdb;
GO
CREATE TABLE BookCollection(
BookID INT NOT NULL PRIMARY KEY,
BookName VARCHAR(64),
BookExcerpt VARCHAR(MAX),
BookText TEXT);
GO
CREATE INDEX IDX_BookCollection_BookName
ON BookCollection(BookName, BookText);
GO
```

The output of the CREATE INDEX statement is an error message:

```
-- Output
Msg 1919, Level 16, State 1, Line 1
Column 'BookText' in table 'BookCollection' is of a type
that is invalid for use as a key column in an index.
```

You will get the same result if you try to include a text column in the leaf level of the index using an index with included columns:

```
CREATE INDEX IDX_BookCollection_BookName
ON BookCollection(BookName)
INCLUDE (BookText);
GO
```

The error message is a little different but you still get an error:

```
-- Output
Msg 1999, Level 16, State 1, Line 1
Column 'BookText' in table 'BookCollection' is of a type
that is invalid for use as included column in an index.
```

You cannot create indexes having as index keys large value data types, but you can include them in the leaf level of the index:

```
CREATE INDEX IDX_BookCollection_BookName
ON BookCollection(BookName)
INCLUDE (BookExcerpt);
GO
```

The previous statement will complete successfully because it uses a varchar(max) column instead of a text column. Including large value data types in the leaf level of an index allows better cover indexes.

The last example for this topic handles the loading of a large value data type using the OPEN-ROWSET bulk rowset provider. SQL Server 2005 allows you to load XML, varchar(max), nvarchar(max), or varbinary(max) columns or variables by using the BULK option of the OPENROWSET function. The partial syntax for this function is:

```
OPENROWSET
( {...
    }
  | BULK 'data_file' ,
      { FORMATFILE = 'format_file_path' [ <bulk_options> ]
      | SINGLE_BLOB | SINGLE_CLOB | SINGLE_NCLOB }
} )
```

You can read more about the OPENROWSET function in Books Online. For this topic, you should know that if you want to load a large value data type column or variable you have to specify the path to the data file and the content type using the SINGLE_BLOB, SINGLE_CLOB, or SINGLE_NCLOB options.

The SINGLE_BLOB option returns the content of a data file as one row with a single column having the type varbinary(max). Similarly, the SINGLE_CLOB options is used for reading the specified data file as ASCII and returns the content as a single row or single column of varchar(max) data type. The SINGLE_NCLOB considers the data file as Unicode encoded and returns the content as a single row having a single nvarchar(max) column. Here's a practical example that loads both a binary and a text document:

```
USE tempdb;
GO
CREATE TABLE LoadTable(
[FileID] INT IDENTITY(1,1) NOT NULL PRIMARY KEY,
[FileName] VARCHAR(128),
[FileType] NVARCHAR(60),
[Document] VARBINARY(MAX));
GO
```

```
-- Load a sample picture
INSERT INTO LoadTable([FileName], [FileType], [Document])
SELECT
'Soap Bubbles.bmp' AS [FileName],
'.bmp' AS [FileType],
BulkColumn
FROM OPENROWSET(BULK N'C:\WINDOWS\Soap Bubbles.bmp', SINGLE_BLOB) AS Document
GO

-- Load the Boot.ini file
INSERT INTO LoadTable([FileName], [FileType], [Document])
SELECT
'Soap Bubbles.bmp' AS [FileName],
'.ini' AS [FileType],
BulkColumn
FROM OPENROWSET(BULK N'C:\Boot.ini', SINGLE_BLOB) AS Document
GO
```

We load two files that exist initially on all Windows XP installations: a sample picture and the boot.ini file. The content of the picture cannot be displayed as an image in SQL Server Management Studio but we can see the content of the boot.ini file:

```
SELECT
CAST([Document] AS VARCHAR(MAX)) AS TextVersion
FROM LoadTable
WHERE FileID=2;
```

The output can be different on your machine but should look similar to the following:

```
--Output
TextVersion
--------------------------------------------------------------
[boot loader]
timeout=30
default=multi(0)disk(0)rdisk(0)partition(1)\WINDOWS
[operating systems]
multi(0)disk(0)rdisk(0)partition(1)\WINDOWS=
 "Microsoft Windows XP Professional" /noexecute=optin /fastdetect
```

Storing the Large Value Data Types

There are two options for storing columns having large value data types: in-row or off-row. Both options have advantages and disadvantages.

Storing the values for large value data type columns in-row may save additional I/O activity for retrieving the columns' values. On the other hand, that would make the table rows bigger, so store the large value data type columns in-row only if your queries retrieve them frequently. Obviously you can store LOBs in-row as long as they are small to medium in size or simply put smaller than 8,000 bytes for the new large value data types (and 7,000 bytes for ntext, text, and image).

To store legacy LOBs in-row, you could use the text in-row table option that can be set using the sp_tableoption stored procedure. For the new large value data types, you can use the same stored procedure with the large value types out of row option. The syntax for the sp_tableoption stored procedure follows:

```
sp_tableoption [ @TableNamePattern = ] 'table'
        , [ @OptionName = ] 'option_name'
        , [ @OptionValue = ] 'value'
```

The values for the text in-row option can be 0 or 'OFF' to store the LOB data type columns off row and 'ON' or an integer value between 24 and 7,000 to store the text, ntext, and image values in-row if their size is equal to or less than the specified integer value.

For the new large value data types you can use two values: 1 (or 'ON') for storing just a 16-byte pointer in the data row and the actual data in a B-tree structure in separate pages, and the value 0 (or 'OFF') for storing the values directly in the data row when they have a size smaller than 8,000 bytes and the value can fit in the record (the total size of the row is less than 8,060 bytes).

Here are some examples:

```
USE tempdb;
GO
CREATE TABLE MyTable(
ID INT NOT NULL PRIMARY KEY,
COL TEXT);
GO
EXEC sp_tableoption N'MyTable', 'text in row', '7000';
GO
INSERT INTO MyTable(ID,COL) VALUES (1,REPLICATE('0',5000));
GO
```

First, you've created a table and then enabled the in-row storage for text, ntext, and image data types. Then, you've inserted a row that contains a text value of 5,000 bytes. To verify that the value of the text column is stored inside the row, you can use the same query that displays the allocation units:

```
SELECT
OBJECT_NAME([object_id]) AS ObjName,
[rows] AS NmbOfRows,
type_desc AS AllocationUnitType,
total_pages AS NmbOfPages
```

```
FROM sys.partitions p
JOIN sys.allocation_units a
   ON p.partition_id = a.container_id
WHERE [object_id]=OBJECT_ID(N'MyTable');
```

In the output you can see that there are two in-row data pages (one that contains the row and one for the allocation unit) and zero pages of LOB data:

```
-- Output
ObjName NmbOfRows AllocationUnitType NmbOfPages
MyTable 1          IN_ROW_DATA        2
MyTable 1          LOB_DATA           0
```

It is important to know that when you enable the 'text in row' option, the existing LOB values are not affected unless they are updated. Only when an existing LOB value is modified will the database engine decide whether it can be stored in row or not. The behavior for disabling the 'text in row' option is different. All LOBs stored in-row are moved out of row in separate pages. The operation requires a table lock and can take a long time if you have a large table. To give you an example, the next code disables the 'text in row' option:

```
EXEC sp_tableoption N'MyTable', 'text in row', 'OFF';
GO
```

Using the same query, we can check that the text value is stored in a separate location:

```
SELECT
OBJECT_NAME([object_id]) AS ObjName,
[rows] AS NmbOfRows,
type_desc AS AllocationUnitType,
total_pages AS NmbOfPages
FROM sys.partitions p
JOIN sys.allocation_units a
   ON p.partition_id = a.container_id
WHERE [object_id]=OBJECT_ID(N'MyTable');
```

You have the same number of in-row data pages but also two new LOB data pages:

```
-- Output
ObjName NmbOfRows AllocationUnitType NmbOfPages
MyTable 1          IN_ROW_DATA        2
MyTable 1          LOB_DATA           2
```

The large value data types have a similar behavior:

```
USE tempdb;
GO
CREATE TABLE MyNewTable(
```

```
ID INT NOT NULL PRIMARY KEY,
COL VARCHAR(MAX));
GO
EXEC sp_tableoption N'MyNewTable', 'large value types out of row', 'ON';
GO
INSERT INTO MyNewTable(ID,COL)
VALUES (1,REPLICATE('0',5000));
```

Checking the page allocation, you would get a comparable result:

```
SELECT
OBJECT_NAME([object_id]) AS ObjName,
[rows] AS NmbOfRows,
type_desc AS AllocationUnitType,
total_pages AS NmbOfPages
FROM sys.partitions p
JOIN sys.allocation_units a
   ON p.partition_id = a.container_id
WHERE [object_id]=OBJECT_ID(N'MyNewTable');
```

Two pages for in-row data and two for LOB data:

```
-- Output
ObjName      NmbOfRows  AllocationUnitType  NmbOfPages
MyNewTable 1            IN_ROW_DATA         2
MyNewTable 1            LOB_DATA            2
```

When you disable the storage of large value data types out of row, you have to update the values if you want that the existing values to be stored in-row. So, you will disable the option, update the large value type column, and check the page allocation again:

```
EXEC sp_tableoption N'MyNewTable', 'large value types out of row', 'OFF';
GO
UPDATE MyNewTable
SET COL=COL
WHERE ID=1;
GO
SELECT
OBJECT_NAME([object_id]) AS ObjName,
[rows] AS NmbOfRows,
type_desc AS AllocationUnitType,
total_pages AS NmbOfPages
FROM sys.partitions p
JOIN sys.allocation_units a
```

```
ON p.partition_id = a.container_id
WHERE [object_id]=OBJECT_ID(N'MyNewTable');
```

As expected, you will reduce the number of LOB data pages to one from two, the one LOB data page being an allocation page:

```
-- Output
ObjName      NmbOfRows  AllocationUnitType  NmbOfPages
MyNewTable 1            IN_ROW_DATA         2
MyNewTable 1            LOB_DATA            1
```

Understanding the Row-Overflow Data

This new feature of SQL Server 2005 is another option for storing more than 8,060 bytes in a single row. It works with columns having the data type varchar, nvarchar, varbinary, sql_variant, or CLR user defined by moving one or more of these columns to a different page when the combined widths of the table (or index) columns is greater than 8,060 bytes. Each individual column is still limited to 8,000 bytes but their combined size can exceed the 8,060-byte limit. When a column is moved to a different page in the original row, a 24-byte pointer is maintained. You may find the row-overflow data under the name of SLOBs (small LOBs) or mini-LOBs.

The row-overflow data feature makes use of a new allocation unit named row-overflow data. To recap, SQL Server 2005 has three types of allocation units:

IN_ROW_DATA   Contains data for a heap or an index.

LOB_DATA   For large object (LOB) data types, such as xml, varbinary(max), or varchar(max).

ROW_OVERFLOW_DATA   For variable-length data stored in varchar, nvarchar, varbinary, sql_variant, or CLR user-defined columns for rows that exceed the 8,060-byte row size limit.

 For more information about the allocation units in SQL Server 2005, please refer to the "Managing Space Used by Objects" topic in Books Online.

In SQL Server 2000 you could create, theoretically, a row larger than 8,060 bytes when some of the columns that made the row were variable-length columns. If you try to create a row bigger than 8,060 bytes in SQL Server 2000, you will get an error:

```
-- On SQL Server 2000
USE tempdb;
GO
CREATE TABLE BigTable(
ID INT NOT NULL PRIMARY KEY,
COL1 CHAR(4000),
```

```
COl2 CHAR(4000),
COL3 CHAR(4000));
GO
```

The text of the error is:

```
Server: Msg 1701, Level 16, State 2, Line 1
Creation of table 'BigTable' failed because the row size would be
12025, including internal overhead. This exceeds the maximum
allowable table row size, 8060.
```

However, if you use variable-length columns, the statement works and a warning is displayed:

```
-- In SQL Server 2000
USE tempdb;
GO
CREATE TABLE BigTable(
ID INT NOT NULL PRIMARY KEY,
COL1 VARCHAR(4000),
COl2 VARCHAR(4000),
COL3 VARCHAR(4000));
GO
```

The warning is self-explanatory; any attempt to insert a row bigger than 8,060 will fail:

```
-- Output
Warning: The table 'BigTable' has been created but its maximum
row size (12031) exceeds the maximum number of bytes per row (8060).
 INSERT or UPDATE of a row in this table will fail if the resulting
row length exceeds 8060 bytes.
```

We challenged the warning on SQL Server 2000 box by running the next code that tries to insert a row of approximately 12,000 bytes:

```
INSERT INTO BigTable(ID,COL1,COL2,COL3)
VALUES (1,REPLICATE('A',4000),REPLICATE('B',4000),REPLICATE('C',4000));
```

Of course that the code failed, displaying the following error:

```
Server: Msg 511, Level 16, State 1, Line 1
Cannot create a row of size 12019 which is greater than the
allowable maximum of 8060.
The statement has been terminated.
```

Creating rows bigger than 8,060 will fail also in SQL Server 2005 if you use only fixed-length variables:

```
-- On SQL Server 2005
USE tempdb;
GO
CREATE TABLE BigTable(
ID INT NOT NULL PRIMARY KEY,
COL1 CHAR(4000),
CO12 CHAR(4000),
COL3 CHAR(4000));
GO
```

The output is somewhat different, but in essence it says the same thing: you are not allowed to create a row bigger than 8,060 bytes unless you use variable-length columns:

```
-- Output
Msg 1975, Level 16, State 1, Line 1
Index 'PK__BigTable__0F975522' row length exceeds the
maximum permissible length of '8060' bytes.
Msg 1750, Level 16, State 0, Line 1
Could not create constraint. See previous errors.
```

You can get a different result by using variable-length columns:

```
USE tempdb;
GO
CREATE TABLE BigTable(
ID INT NOT NULL PRIMARY KEY,
COL1 VARCHAR(4000),
CO12 VARCHAR(4000),
COL3 VARCHAR(4000));
GO
```

The command runs just fine and no warning is issued. You can test that you can have a bigger row using the previous INSERT statement:

```
INSERT INTO BigTable(ID,COL1,COL2,COL3)
VALUES (1,REPLICATE('A',4000),REPLICATE('B',4000),REPLICATE('C',4000));
```

To convince yourself of the row size, you can check the length for each column of the table:

```
SELECT
DATALENGTH(COL1) AS LEN_COL1,
DATALENGTH(COL2) AS LEN_COL2,
```

```
DATALENGTH(COL3) AS LEN_COL3
FROM BigTable
WHERE ID = 1;
```

Each of the varchar columns of the table is 4,000 bytes in size (the entire row having more than 12,000 bytes):

```
--Output
LEN_COL1 LEN_COL2 LEN_COL3
-------- -------- --------
4000     4000     4000
```

Let's check how the data is allocated:

```
SELECT
OBJECT_NAME([object_id]) AS ObjName,
[rows] AS NmbOfRows,
type_desc AS AllocationUnitType,
total_pages AS NmbOfPages
FROM sys.partitions p
JOIN sys.allocation_units a
   ON p.partition_id = a.container_id
WHERE [object_id]=OBJECT_ID(N'BigTable');
```

You have two in-row data pages (one for the allocation unit and one with the actual data) and two row-overflow pages (one for the allocation unit and one for the relocated column or columns):

```
-- Output
ObjName   NmbOfRows AllocationUnitType NmbOfPages
BigTable 1           IN_ROW_DATA        2
BigTable 1           ROW_OVERFLOW_DATA  2
```

If the total size of the columns changes, becoming smaller than 8,060 bytes, the row-overflow data can be moved back a row. Here's such a case:

```
UPDATE BigTable
SET
COL2=REPLICATE('B',1000),
COL3=REPLICATE('C',1000)
WHERE ID=1;

SELECT
OBJECT_NAME([object_id]) AS ObjName,
[rows] AS NmbOfRows,
```

```
type_desc AS AllocationUnitType,
total_pages AS NmbOfPages
FROM sys.partitions p
JOIN sys.allocation_units a
   ON p.partition_id = a.container_id
WHERE [object_id]=OBJECT_ID(N'BigTable');
```

Looking at the allocation units, you can see that you have just one row-overflow data page (the allocation page) and the same number of in-row data pages:

```
-- Output
ObjName   NmbOfRows AllocationUnitType NmbOfPages
BigTable 1            IN_ROW_DATA         2
BigTable 1            ROW_OVERFLOW_DATA   1
```

Row-overflow data columns can be included as nonkey columns for nonclustered indexes.

Summary

In this chapter, we focused on the optimization of the table, which is the basic structural unit for a database. You learned about the data types available in SQL Server 2005 and how and when to use them. Then, you learned that the performance of a database application is closely related to a proper row structure. Finally, you learned that performance can come from both normalization and its counterpart, denormalization.

Exam Essentials

Understand all the data types you can use.   You should know all the data types available in SQL Server 2005 and more importantly how to use them to achieve the best row structure possible.

Know how to customize the table's width.   OLTP and Decision Support (OLAP) applications are rarely independent. You will meet high transactional environments that also need performance from read and aggregate queries. The pure transactional application is a very rare bird so you should know to balance between highly normalized tables for transactional performance and adding redundant data (through denormalization) to support reads.

Be able to use variable-length data types.   Variable-length data types save disk space and increase the performance for your queries. Also, reduced size means reduced maintenance and recovery time. As every advantage comes with a hidden cost, if your data is modified with a very high frequency or its length is stable, you may want to use fixed-length data types instead.

Be able to use large value data types.   The MAX specifier made from varchar, nchar, and varbinary data types of true super-size structures allow you to stretch your row size to new limits. Furthermore, when your hunger for size is moderate, you can benefit from the row-overflow feature that allows you to have bigger rows without requiring the use of LOBs. You should know that in SQL Server 2005, rows can go beyond 8,060 bytes but you should use big rows only when you have to.

Review Questions

1. You have to design a database application for the Human Resources department of a publishing company. One table of this application, named Employees, stores the current and former employees of the company. You have to decide what data type to use for the EmployeeID column of the Employees table. The EmployeeID column is the primary key for the table and identifies each employee. To help your decision, you can use the following facts. (1) Currently 120 employees work in all locations of the company. (2) The forecasted number of employees for the next 5 years is 180. What should you do?

    A. Use uniqueidentifier as the data type for the EmployeeID column.

    B. Use int as the data type for the EmployeeID column

    C. Use smallint as the data type for the EmployeeID column

    D. Use float as the data type for the EmployeeID column.

2. You work for a company specialized in building interfaces between computers and industrial equipment. Each interface has between six and eight jumpers (switches) that configure the behavior of the interface. Each jumper has only two states: ON or OFF. To record all possible configurations of the jumpers for each interface type the following table was created:

```
CREATE TABLE InterfaceSettings(

SettingID INT NOT NULL PRIMARY KEY,

InterfaceID SMALLINT NOT NULL,

ConfigurationDescription VARCHAR(64),

Jumper01 INT NOT NULL,

Jumper02 INT NOT NULL,

Jumper03 INT NOT NULL,

Jumper04 INT NOT NULL,

Jumper05 INT NOT NULL,

Jumper06 INT NOT NULL,

Jumper07 INT NULL,

Jumper08 INT NULL);
```

    You want to minimize the storage for the InterfaceSettings table. What should you do? (Choose the best option.)

    A. Use the bit data type for all eight jumper columns.

    B. Use the tinyint data type for all eight jumper columns.

    C. Use the tinyint data type for the last two jumper columns.

    D. Use the smallint data type for all eight jumper columns.

3. You have to build a web application used for participants' registration for a conference event. The main table of the application was created using the following code:

```
CREATE TABLE EventParticipants(

EntryID INT IDENTITY(1,1) NOT NULL PRIMARY KEY,

FirstName CHAR(32) NOT NULL,

LastName CHAR(32) NOT NULL,

MiddleName CHAR(32) NULL,

Email CHAR(128) NOT NULL);
```

The conference planner expects no more than 500 registrations over the web for the conference. You want to redesign the table to minimize the storage required. Which of the following actions should you take? (Choose all that apply.)

   A. Change the data type for the EntryID column to tinyint.

   B. Change the data type for the EntryID column to smallint.

   C. Change the data type for the FirstName, the MiddleName, and the LastName columns to varchar(32).

   D. Change the data type for the Email column to nchar(128).

4. Which normal form is usually used for OLTP applications?

   A. First normal form

   B. Second normal form

   C. Third normal form

   D. Fifth normal form

5. Which of the following are normalization advantages? (Choose all that apply.)

   A. Better cache utilization

   B. Faster index operations

   C. More choices for clustered indexes

   D. Fewer indexes per table

6. Which of the following are denormalization techniques? (Choose all that apply.)

   A. Split tables.

   B. Add primary keys to each table.

   C. Use prejoined tables.

   D. Eliminate redundant data.

7. You have to optimize a database application used for selling car parts. Each car part has a serial number of exactly 50 characters that identifies uniquely the car part and contains several other sets of information, such as the factory that made the part, the manufacturing date, and the model of the car the part should be used for. The serial number is stored as CHAR(50) and is used as a primary key for the Parts table. It is also the clustered index key. A table named Orders has a foreign key to the SerialNumber column of the Parts table. You want to reduce the size for the indexes of the Parts table as well as the size of the Orders table. What should you do?

    A. Change the SerialNumber column's data type to NCHAR(50).

    B. Change the SerialNumber column's data type to VARCHAR(50).

    C. Change the SerialNumber column's data type to NVARCHAR(50).

    D. Use a surrogate primary key for the Parts table, such as an int column having the INDEN-TITY property. Use the new primary key column also as the clustered index key.

8. You need to select a column data type for storing XML documents. You want to preserve blank spaces and formatting. What should you do?

    A. Use a VARCHAR(MAX) data type column.

    B. Use a VARBINARY(MAX) data type column.

    C. Use an XML data type column.

    D. Use an IMAGE data type column.

9. You are developing a Human Resources application for a multinational company. What data type should you use for storing Employees' names?

    A. VARCHAR(128)

    B. NVARCHAR(128)

    C. CHAR(128)

    D. VARCHAR(MAX)

10. How many values could you store in a bit data type?

    A. 2

    B. 4

    C. 8

    D. 256

11. The Human Resources department of your company needs a web application that would allow interested candidates to review the job openings and to submit an application for a specific position. Another requirement of the application is to allow the candidates to submit a resume in Word or PDF format. What data type should you use for storing resumes?

    A. ntext

    B. text

    C. image

    D. varbinary(max)

12. You design a table named Books that contains computer-related books sold by an international publisher. The price for a book is expressed in USD and can have maximum two decimals. What data type should you use to store the price for a book?

    A. decimal(38,2)

    B. numeric(38,2)

    C. money

    D. smallmoney

13. You want to optimize the row length of a table named Employees by storing all varchar(max) columns of the table separately. Which of the following T-SQL code samples should you use?

    A. EXEC sp_tableoption 'Employees', 'large value types out of row', 'ON';

    B. EXEC sp_tableoption 'Employees', 'large value types out of row', 'OFF';

    C. EXEC sp_tableoption 'Employees', 'text in row', 'ON';

    D. EXEC sp_tableoption 'Employees', 'text in row', 'OFF';

14. You design a database application for a pharmaceutical company. The application is used to manage the products of the company. The products are stored in a table created using the following code:

```
CREATE TABLE Product(

ProductID SMALLINT NOT NULL PRIMARY KEY,

ProductCode CHAR(12) NOT NULL,

ProductName VARCHAR(30) NOT NULL,

ProductCategory TINYINT NOT NULL);
```

The product codes identify each product uniquely and for 99 percent of products it consists of 8 characters. The remaining 1 percent products represent retired drugs and have product codes of 6 and 7 characters. You want to optimize the physical structure of the Product table. What should you do?

    A. Check the average size for the ProductCode column using the following code:
    ```
    SELECT AVG(LEN(ProductCode))
    FROM Product;
    ```
    If the result is 8 then modify the data type for ProductCode column to VARCHAR(8).

    B. Verify the maximum size for the ProductCode column values using the next code:
    ```
    SELECT MAX(DATALENGTH(ProductCode))
    FROM Product;
    ```
    If the maximum is lower than or equal to 8, alter the Product table by changing the type of ProductCode column to VARCHAR(8).

C. Verify the maximum size for the values of the ProductCode column by running the next script:

```
SELECT MAX(LEN(ProductCode))
FROM Product;
```

If the resulting value is 8, modify the data type of the ProductCode column to be CHAR(8).

D. Verify whether the minimum size for the values of the ProductCode column is 6 and change the column data type to CHAR(6).

15. You work for a financial institution. As a part of your job you have to design a database application for recording daily operations. At the moment there are 20 categories of financial operations and the number may double in the next 10 years. A table named Category is designed to store the operations' types. The table has two columns: CategoryID and CategoryName. What data type should you use for the CategoryID column that identifies each category?

   A. `bit`
   B. `bigint`
   C. `tinyint`
   D. `float`

16. You work as a software developer for a bank. Your company decided to allow its customers to apply for loans using a web application. Among other details, the application should record the first and last name of the applicant, his or her date of birth, and the request date. Loans can be granted only to people born after 1910. Which of the following are proper design choices for the web application? (Choose all that apply.)

   A. Use a datetime data type to store the date of request.
   B. Use smalldatetime to store the date of birth.
   C. Use char data type to store the names of the applicants.
   D. Use varchar data type to store the names of the applicants.

17. What new feature of SQL Server 2005 allows you to have a row size greater than 8,060 bytes?

   A. The 'text in row' option
   B. The 'large value types out of row' option
   C. Row-overflow data
   D. The ntext data type

18. One of your company's customers is a car dealer. The customer needs a web application for selling car parts. You are responsible for designing the database scheme for the application. Each car part is identified by an alphanumeric code of 7 characters. How should you represent the car part identification code in the application's database?

   A. Use a char(7) data type.
   B. Use a varchar(7) data type.
   C. Use an int data type.
   D. Use a bigint data type.

19. You design a document management system that will handle primarily Microsoft Office files (Word, Excel) and PDF documents. The documents should be stored inside a SQL Server database and should be full-text indexed. What should you do?

A. Store the documents in a column having text data type.

B. Store the documents in a column having ntext data type.

C. Store the documents in a column having image data type.

D. Store the documents in a column having varbinary(max) data type.

20. Which denormalization technique consists of horizontal partitioning of a table?

A. Split tables

B. Duplicate table

C. Indexed views.

D. Prejoined tables

Answers to Review Questions

1. C. The best option for this scenario is to use an integer data type. Considering just the forecasted number of employees, you can use, theoretically, a tinyint column. However, a smallint column is a better choice because it leaves enough room to accommodate changes. You should take into account not just the current and forecasted numbers of employees but also the fact that some employees can leave the company.

    Using GUIDs is totally inappropriate as they will waste space and they are not required. Data types such as float and real are poor choices for primary key columns, not to mention that they are not required in this case. The int data type can be a good choice for this scenario, but it has a size of 4 bytes, which is two times more than the smallint data type.

2. A. The best storage savings you can get by using the bit data type for all eight jumper columns. Only one byte is used. The other options reduce the size of the initial table but not so drastically as the proposed solution.

3. B, C. A number of 500 participants to the event conference can be efficiently stored using a smallint column. A tinyint column is too small for that. The second measure you can take to improve the design of the table is to change the char columns to varchar columns as the names and email addresses of participants will vary in size.

    Using nchar instead of char for email addresses is not a solution and, on the contrary, using nchar data type will double the space occupied by email addresses.

4. C. OLTP applications are highly normalized for transactional performance. However, most of them do not go beyond the third normal form.

5. A, B, C, D. Eliminating redundant data as well as applying normalization rules has as its results among other things more rows per page, narrower tables and indexes, better cache utilization, faster index operations, more tables, and more choices for clustered indexes and less indexes per table.

6. A, C. Splitting tables or using prejoined tables are two denormalization techniques. Adding primary keys to each table or eliminating redundant data belong to the normalization process.

7. D. The question is intentionally misleading, suggesting a data type replacement for the Serial-Number column. However, a surrogate key is the best answer in this case. It will reduce the size for all other indexes of the Parts table and also the size of the Orders table that can refer a 4-byte column instead of a 50-byte column.

    Using NCHAR, VARCHAR or NVARCHAR data types can make the situation worse as they require more space than the original data type.

8. A. The best choice in this case is to use a VARCHAR(MAX) data type column. There is no need to store the XML document in a binary data type column such as VARBINARY or IMAGE. The XML data type does not preserve blank spaces or formatting.

9. B. Since a multinational company means employees from all over the world, you need a Unicode variable-length data type. The only possible answer in this case is to use the NVARCHAR(128) data type.

10. A. You can store only the values 0 and 1 in a bit data type column or variable. One may argue that you can also store NULL, but we do not count NULL as a value.

11. D. You will store binary files so the best option is the varbinary(max) data type. The text, ntext, and image data types are deprecated.

12. D. Unless the publisher sells a book with a price greater than $214,748 (we would love to see such a book), the smallmoney data type is a perfect fit. The money or decimal and numeric data types are not necessary in this scenario.

13. A. The 'large value types out of row' option determines the database engine's behavior in regards to storing values for varchar(max), nvarchar(max), varbinary(max), and xml columns in-row or off-row. The 'text in row' option refers to text, ntext, and image data types.

14. C. The best option is to determine whether the maximum size for the values of the ProductCode column is 8 and change the type of the column to CHAR(8). Using the VARCHAR(8) data type brings two additional bytes of overhead and you already know that 99 percent of the rows have exactly 8 characters for the value of the ProductCode column. Measuring the average size or the minimum size of the values for the ProductCode may lead to losing data. The average can be 8 if the table has, for example, 198 values of 8, one of 7, and one of 9.

15. C. The number of categories is an integer number and you can use tinyint, smallint, int, and bigint data types to identify each category. Considering the forecasted number of categories (40), the tinyint data type is the best choice. The bit data type can store only NULL and two values: 0 and 1. You need a minimum of 40 values. The float data type is not appropriate for this scenario.

16. B, D. A smalldatetime data type can accommodate values from January 1, 1900, to June 6, 2079. You should use the smalldatetime data type to store both the date of request and the date of birth for each applicant. If you use a datetime data type to record the request date, you are wasting 4 bytes unless your application will be used beyond 2079. Names of persons are variable length so you should use varchar or nvarchar data types to store them and not char data type.

17. C. You can work around the 8,060 row size limitation using large value data types such as text, ntext, image, varchar(max), varbinary(max), or xml. Also you can use row-overflow data, a new feature of SQL Server 2005 that allows a row greater in size than 8,060 by storing in a separate location data types such as varchar, nvarchar, varbinary, or sql_variant. When the combined widths of the columns for a table exceed the 8,060 limit, storing one or more columns in separate data pages make bigger rows a reality.

The 'text in row' and 'large value types out of row' options customize the behavior of the database engine allowing the in-row storage of large data type values.

The ntext data type can be a possible answer for solving the row size limitation but it is not a new feature. On the contrary, it is a deprecated data type.

18. A. Alphanumeric means both letters and numbers. So you cannot use INTEGER data types. In this scenario the data is fixed length so the CHAR option is better than the VARCHAR data type. Choosing VARCHAR instead of CHAR would add 2 to 4 bytes of unnecessary overhead for each car part stored.

19. D. You should select a binary storage format such as image or varbinary data type. As the image data type is deprecated you should use the varbinary(max) data type. The text and ntext data type are supported by SQL Server 2005 for backward compatibility and they can store non-Unicode and Unicode character data, respectively.

20. A. Both horizontal partitioning and vertical partitioning represent splitting the split tables denormalization technique.

Chapter 12

Case Studies

The 70-442 exam is built on performance-based case studies. You need to understand the essence of the organization in the study, the existing environment, the business requirements, and the technical requirements. You design solutions for some aspect of the database to meet these requirements.

The case studies incorporate all the objectives of the test. The questions are similar to those at the end of the individual chapters in this book; however, now you see them in the context of an overall plan to improve an organization's data access. The case studies test your knowledge of all the objectives in the exam.

The design exams are difficult, and exam 70-442, because of the scope of its programming concepts, is perhaps one of the most complex. You most likely have areas of the exam that are familiar to you and others in which you have had little or no experience. Even though total immersion and practical experience in SQL Server 2005 is certainly a help, we hope that our book has enabled you to recognize and understand the appropriate technologies to use even if you have not had a chance to experience them yet.

You have reached the heart of the matter.

If you need a little respite while working through the case studies, here is one last syllogism from Lewis Carroll's *Symbolic Logic* to help you clear your mind:

a. Showy talkers think too much of themselves.

b. No really informed people are bad company.

c. People who think too much of themselves are not good company.

You'll find the answer at the end of the case studies. The best of luck to you as you continue through the case studies and take the exam!

Case Study 1: Sequel Search

In an effort to provide assistance and resources for historians, a small group of history research scholars formed Sequel Search. The company currently has one office in Fort Worth, Texas, housing an internal Active Directory domain network with Microsoft Windows 2003 domain controllers. Currently, the only access users have to the local network is in the office.

Since the research capabilities of these scholars has become world recognized and many of the scholars travel extensively, the company wants them to have access to their research data through a web application. A web server will be purchased and configured for this purpose. It will be placed on a perimeter network between two separate firewalls, one to the Internet and the other to the internal network.

Existing Environment

In addition to the domain controllers, the internal Windows 2003 network consists of a member server running Microsoft Windows Server 2003 and Microsoft SQL Server 2005. In the office the clients access the network using their notebooks with Microsoft Windows XP SP2.

Currently a research database on the SQL Server stores reference articles and data, research works, general research guide catalogues, and research contacts.

A research project is assigned to a team according to area of expertise. Each project is assigned one master research scholar in charge of all aspects of the project. Since these scholars have several areas of expertise, a scholar may be assigned to several projects. The scholars use the research database for their background references. They connect to the database through a smart client application.

When scholars need to add new references or their own works to the research database, they use a database application written internally for them that transfers the text from a Microsoft Word document to the database.

Business Requirements

Research scholars want to search references or works that have been added to the research database using keywords. This requirement must be available through the web application also.

Documents stored in the research database need to be kept in their original format so that they can be easily accessed and printed if necessary.

Since multiple research scholars may work on a project, no scholar must overwrite another scholar's work. All team members contribute to the research and writing of the project and store their work for each project in the database. The master scholar does the final compilation and presentation.

Research data entered through the web application is stored as XML data type using the following defined type:

```
<refRoot>
     <refTitle>Title of Reference</ refTitle>
```

CASE STUDY

```
    <refAuthor>Author of Reference</ refAuthor>
    <refText>
        <intro>Introduction</intro>
        <subref Title= "Subref Title"> Subref Text </subref>
        <subref Title= "Subref Title"> Subref Text </subref>
    </refText>
</refRoot>
```

The XML data type column is named RefText and is in the CurrentProjects table. The CurrentProjects table has ProjectID, MasterID, TeamID, RefText, RefCategoryID, and RefDate.

Technical Requirements

The web server must be available for the research scholars 24/7.

Since much of the data contained in the research database is extremely rare, it is important that it is kept secure and is backed up regularly.

Review Questions

1. As the database developer for Sequel Search, you are creating a procedure for the web application to return all the authors of the reference data in the CurrentProjects table. You only want to have the data returned. You do not want to have any XML tags returned. Which of the following should you use?

    A. `SELECT RefText.query('\refRoot\refAuthor') FROM CurrentProjects`

    B. `SELECT RefText.nodes('\refRoot\refAuthor') FROM CurrentProjects`

    C. `SELECT RefText.value('\refRoot\refAuthor[1]','varchar') FROM CurrentProjects`

    D. `SELECT RefText.exist('\refRoot\@refAuthor','varchar') FROM CurrentProjects`

2. Since research scholars are adding, updating, and reading data concurrently on the same project, how should you handle concurrency requirements?

    A. Set the transaction isolation level to SERIALIZABLE.

    B. Set the transaction isolation level to READ_UNCOMMITTED.

    C. Set the transaction isolation level to REPEATABLE_READ.

    D. Set the transaction isolation level to READ_COMMITTED_SNAPSHOT.

3. The GuidesCat Table contains the documented listing of available research guide materials. Since it is used as a first step in the investigative study path for the research project, it is queried quite heavily and often retrieves a large result sets. However, its content does not often change. Since this is an extremely large table, you need to create an efficient index to minimize the locking in the table for the most frequently run query based on the CatID. Which of the following should you use?

    A. Use this:
    ```
    ALLOW_ROW_LOCKS = OFF
    ALLOW_PAGE_LOCKS = OFF
    ```

    B. Use this:
    ```
    ALLOW_ROW_LOCKS = ON
    ALLOW_PAGE_LOCKS = ON
    ```

    C. Use this:
    ```
    ALLOW_ROW_LOCKS = OFF
    ALLOW_PAGE_LOCKS = ON
    ```

    D. Use this:
    ```
    ALLOW_ROW_LOCKS = ON
    ALLOW_PAGE_LOCKS = OFF
    ```

4. Because the research database was originally designed for SQL Server 2000, you need to make certain all aspects of the database are compliant with SQL Server 2005 and versions forward. Several tables, especially those used for reference articles, contain columns using image data types. Which of the following should you use to replace the image data type?

   A. nvarchar(max)

   B. varbinary(max)

   C. varbinary

   D. nvarchar

5. The XP notebook clients the research scholars use need to have full functionality to your SQL Server 2005–built applications. Which of the following client libraries should they be using?

   A. OLE DB

   B. SQLCMD

   C. SQLNCLI

   D. ODBC

6. You have recently designed a database and application for a special project on Latin American relations. You have deployed the LatARel application to users in the Fort Worth office. Users report that some queries take a long time to process. You want to capture the queries and analyze the data with the minimum amount of impact on your current server. Which of the following should you do?

   A. Create a SQL Server Profiler replay trace and save the data to a file on the SQL server.

   B. Create a SQL Server Profiler replay trace and save the data to a file on another server.

   C. Create a SQL Server Profiler replay trace and save the data to a table in tempdb.

   D. Monitor the queries in System Monitor using SQL Server: Memory Manager counters.

7. You have recently designed and deployed a database and application for a special project on Latin American relations to the Fort Worth office. In resolving a problem with a specific query for the LatARel application, you want to determine if the query would perform more optimally if a different index were used. Which of the following SET options can you use to determine this?

   A. SET SHOWPLAN_TEXT ON

   B. SET STATISTICS XML ON

   C. SET SHOWPLAN_XML ON

   D. SET FORCEPLAN ON

8. What solution should be used to provide secure access between the web server on the perimeter network and the research database on the SQL Server in the internal network?

   A. Install IIS on the SQL Server 2005 server and access the data using XML queries.

   B. Create an HTTP endpoint and access the server data using ad hoc queries.

   C. Stop and restart the perimeter web server and access the server data using ad hoc queries.

   D. Create an HTTP endpoint and access the server data using stored procedures.

9. You have been asked to create a new feature for the web application that will list the subreferences for a given research reference that is stored in the database. Which of the following should you use?

    A. nodes() method

    B. OPENXML

    C. value() method

    D. query() method

10. You need to create indexes to improve the performance of queries for the CurrentProjects table. The most common queries return the title and author of reference material. Which indexes should you create? Choose all that apply.

    A. Create a clustered index on TeamID.

    B. Create a clustered index on RefText.

    C. Create a clustered index on ProjectID.

    D. Create a primary XML index on RefText.

Answers to Review Questions

1. C. The value method is used to return the value of an element or attribute without an XML tag. Although there may be only one refAuthor attribute in the XML instance, the syntax rule requires you to explicitly specify that the path expression returns a singleton. Therefore, you need to specify the additional [1] at the end of the path expression. The query, nodes, and exists methods are not correct because none of them return a scalar value.

2. D. Set the transaction isolation level to READ_COMMITTED_SNAPSHOT, which causes row versioning to be used. A consistent picture (copy) of the data in a transaction is handed off to tempdb at the beginning of the transaction. Users are able to read this data while the real data is being modified. There is no need for locks or hints or problems with dirty reads. You should not use the SERIALIZABLE isolation level since it is the most restrictive and will block all users reading data while others are updating. READ_UNCOMMITTED, the least restrictive, should also not be used because it can cause dirty reads that can overwrite data. Since other users may be inserting data while shared locks are held, you should not use the REPEATABLE_READ isolation level as you might get phantom data.

3. A. Set ALLOW_ROW_LOCKS = OFF and ALLOW_PAGE_LOCKS = OFF. When you access the table, a table lock will be used. There is less overhead if only one lock is used rather than several smaller locks. The queries will process more efficiently.

4. B. You should use varbinary(max) to replace the image data type. The image data type is deprecated and should no longer be used for any new development or works going forward. Nvarchar(max) is used to store large text data. You use the large-value data types to store up to 2^31-1 bytes of data.

5. C. SQL Native Client (SQLNCLI) was designed to provide a simplified method of gaining native data access to SQL Server using either OLE DB or ODBC. It is simplified in that it combines OLE DB and ODBC technologies into one library, and it provides a way to innovate and evolve new data access features used in SQL Server 2005. SQLCMD is the new command-line utility in SQL Server 2005.

6. A. Create a SQL Server Profiler replay trace and save the data to a file on the SQL server. If you save the file to another server, you will impact the network. Saving the data to tempdb does not ensure that the table will be available when you need it. Tempdb is flushed if SQL Server is restarted. System Monitor Memory Manager counters will not provide the analysis you need.

7. C. SET SHOWPLAN_XML ON is the only SET option that has the Missing Indexes element that contains information to help you determine what indexes would improve the performance of the specific query.

8. D. Create an HTTP endpoint and access the server data using stored procedures. To keep data secure, clients should not have direct access to the database server. You should use stored procedures or user-defined functions to access data. You should also use HTTP endpoints and XML web services and not install an IIS server on your SQL Server.

9. A. The nodes() method will give you the listing of the parsed nodes with their appropriate tag. You use XQuery to identify the named elements and the nodes() method to identify the subtree.

10. C and D. First, you should create a clustered index on ProjectID. Then, you can create a primary XML index on RefText. A clustered index must be created on the table prior to creating a primary XML index. The third index, which is not mentioned but should be created, is a property index on RefText. This is a secondary index of type property that can be used to index within the nodes of the XML column.

Case Study 2: H&S MedX

You are the database developer for H&S MedX, a research-driven pharmaceutical company. Through its two facilities in Gloucester Township, New Jersey, and White Settlement, Texas, it is discovering, developing, and delivering novel medicines and vaccines.

The New Jersey facility carries out the research and production. Sales are handled through the office in Texas. Both facilities house Phase I through Phase IV clinical trial studies.

Due to their recent successful medicines in the field of neurology, H&S is planning another research facility in Belgium.

Existing Environment

H&S has a single Windows Server 2003 Active Directory domain. New Jersey has two SQL Server 2005 Enterprise Edition servers: HSNJResearch hosts the research and clinical databases and HSNJProduction hosts the production database. Texas has three SQL Server 2005 servers. Two servers are enterprise edition: HSTXSales supports the sales database and HSTXResearch supports the clinical database. One server is standard edition: HSMedX hosts the internal employee database. All servers are Windows Server 2003 and all client computers are Windows XP SP2.

Business Requirements

H&S writes all its applications in house. The research laboratory application and each of the clinical trial phase applications are .NET applications. Clinical is considering making their application web based.

Phase I, II, and III clinical trials are monitored according to FDA regulations. Phase II and III trials are registered on the U.S. government website ClinicalTrials.gov, a service of the U.S. National Institutes of Health.

In Phase I trials, researchers test an experimental drug or treatment in a small group of people (20–80) for the first time to evaluate its safety, determine a safe dosage range, and identify side effects. Currently much of the study development and data for ClinTrial Phase I studies is paper driven and later entered into the system.

In Phase II and III trials, the experimental study drug or treatment is given to a larger group of people (100–300, 1,000–3,000) to monitor effectiveness, side effects, value, and safety.

Researchers often read through previous studies in the research database to gain knowledge in drug efficacy and safety. Usually they implement multiple queries at one time with not very large result sets. They need to be able to peruse the data in any order.

Technical Requirements

Since ClinTrial Phase I studies have a short delivery time, they need to develop procedures to handle their diverse tasks programmatically and still retain their flexibility.

All code and trial definitions must be within FDA compliance and have the approval of the regulatory division of the company.

The research facility in Belgium will be responsible for its own research projects. The same research application will be used company-wide.

Review Questions

1. Sales users are complaining that their sales applications and reports on HSTXSales are running slowly. One of the salespeople in the Texas facility is frequently implementing ad hoc queries on the sales database. You want him to be able to run the queries but limit those that may run for an extended time and negatively impact the performance of the server. Which of the following commands should you execute?

    A. `SET STATISTICS TIME ON`

    B. `SET QUERY_GOVERNOR_COST LIMIT 0`

    C. `sp_configure 'query governor cost limit', '8'`

    D. `SET QUERY_GOVERNOR_COST LIMIT 8`

2. You are developing stored procedures for the ClinTrials Phase I studies program. You need to create a stored procedure to make certain that participants in a new arthritis drug have not participated in a previous drug study just completing Phase III for etoricoxib. Since each study is stored separately in the ClinTrial database, what statement should you use to retrieve data from one table that is not in another?

    A. `LEFT JOIN`

    B. `INNER JOIN`

    C. `EXCEPT`

    D. `INTERSECT`

3. You are in charge of designing the research database implementation in Belgium. If each research facility is to handle it own projects and still wants to be able to have full access of all the projects in the research database, which of the following is the best scaleout solution for H&S?

    A. Peer-to-peer replication

    B. Snapshot replication

    C. Data-dependent routing

    D. Service-Oriented Data Architecture

4. To perform the study search for the researchers, the current research application uses a server-side static cursor with a separate connection for each query. With the advent of the new set of research projects to be started within the next fiscal quarter, you must modify the application so that it uses less network and server resources. Which of the following should you use?

    A. Dynamic server-side cursor

    B. Multiple active result sets (MARS)

    C. Fast-forward server-side cursor

    D. Keyset-driven server-side cursor

5. Users in the HR department have mentioned at times they cannot retrieve data from the database in a timely manner because it appears very busy. You need to identify the sessions that are creating the processes that are burdening the system. You want to collect the data in real time so that you can determine the connections causing the problems. Which of the following tools should you use?

    A. Task Manager

    B. Database Engine Tuning Advisor

    C. System Monitor

    D. Activity Monitor

6. You need to create a query for a ClinTrial Phase I study for HS0663. This is a double-blind study, meaning neither the participants nor the clinicians know what drug is being given, with 60Mg of the study drug given once daily versus 75Mg of diclofenac sodium, a comparable drug, given twice daily. The study proceeds for 4 weeks. The study monitors need to know the total amount of each drug given to all participants at the end of the study. Which of the following should you use to find the totals?

    A. ROLLUP and CUBE

    B. SUM and ROLLUP

    C. SUM

    D. CREATE AGGREGATE

7. The ClinTrial development team has written a .NET application to be used by ClinTrial Phase 1 programmers to build each unique trial application. Using this application, trial data can be initially entered into the system. To keep the initial data as clean as possible and to meet FDA standards, which of the following should you implement to validate data and report a custom error to the application whenever bad data is entered?

    A. Use a check constraint.

    B. Create an XML namespace that the data must conform with.

    C. Create an after trigger.

    D. Create another application to capture the data and test it before it is put into the database for the trial.

8. The sales manager wants each member of the sales department to be able to run a query for reporting purposes. Create a stored procedure that generates the query for the report that is run on the report server. You realize that the data for the stored procedure is only available to the manager and not the entire department. What should you do so that you can follow the manager's requirements?

    A. Give all the sales personnel the same permissions to the database as the manager so that they have access to the data for the stored procedure.

    B. Create the stored procedure using EXECUTE AS the sales manager within the procedure.

    C. Create the stored procedure using EXECUTE AS owner within the procedure.

    D. Create the stored procedure using EXECUTE AS caller within the procedure.

9. You are updating a procedure to use new features in error handling in SQL Server 2005. You have rewritten the following code using a TRY... CATCH block only to receive syntax errors in your code.

```
TRY

hsp_unvalidated_data

select * into phase1.H3000errors from dbo.errors

END TRY

GO

CATCH

SELECT ERROR_NUMBER() AS ErrorNumber;

END CATCH;
```

Which of the following correct the syntax errors? Choose all that apply.

A. Replace CATCH with BEGIN CATCH.

B. Replace TRY with BEGIN TRY.

C. Delete GO.

D. Replace END TRY with END.

E. Replace END CATCH with END.

10. In reviewing some of the queries for the sales application, you notice that some queries are not using valid search argument operators (SARGs) so that query results are limited. Which of the following are valid SARGs? Choose all that apply.

A. BETWEEN

B. =

C. <>

D. <=

Answers to Review Questions

1.   C. Execute sp_configure 'query governor cost limit', '8'. This statement will terminate the execution of queries within 8 seconds server-wide. Using the SET QUERY_GOVERNOR_COST LIMIT command will only set the cost limit for the particular connection. The SET STATISTICS TIME ON displays the number of milliseconds required to parse, compile, and execute the query.

2.   C. Use the EXCEPT statement. This statement will retrieve data that is not in the intersection or is common (INTERSECT) to both tables. Thus the retrieved data would be those new participants that were not in the etoricoxib study.

3.   A. Peer-to-peer replication propagates changes made to any copy of the data to all other copies. This is a new replication technology to SQL Server 2005. Snapshot replication does not propagate changes in both directions in its publication-subscription paradigm so both facilities would not have all research data. Data-dependent routing and Service-Oriented Data Architecture require significant changes in the research application.

4.   B. Use MARS and default result sets. Since the result sets generated by the researchers are reasonably small and all the queries are reads, this is an excellent opportunity to use MARS so that you can have multiple result sets open on a single connection. The other cursor choices will consume resources by using more connections and, as in the instance of the fast-forward cursor, may not provide the scrolling capabilities needed.

5.   D. Use Activity Monitor in SQL Server Management Studio. Using Activity Monitor you are able to collect information on running and blocked processes, locks, and user activity. None of the other tools give you information at the connection level.

6.   A. Once the study is unblinded, you are adding sums to find the total amount of each drug. The summation can be handled with ROLLUP and CUBE.

7.   C. Create an after trigger. Using an after trigger allows the bad data to be captured into a table for further investigation. It also allows a custom message to be reported. A check constraint will not report a message and it might be difficult to determine the criteria for out of range values—a trigger is better. The XML namespace does not meet the solution. Creating another application for testing is overkill and too much trouble. This app would need to be rewritten for each new trial.

8.   B. Use EXECUTE AS with the impersonation of the sales manager within the stored procedure itself. This will give the proper permissions to the procedure as it executes but not leave the user with elevated permissions after the execution of the stored procedure. None of the other EXECUTE AS options give the correct credentials. You should not give the entire sales personnel elevated privileges to the database.

9.   A, B, C. Both the TRY and CATCH blocks must start with BEGIN. Also there can be no code between the two blocks; therefore the GO must be deleted.

10.   A, B, D. BETWEEN, =, and <= are valid SARG operators. The is not equal to operator (<>) as well as any other negated operators are non-SARG operators and degrade query performance.

Case Study 3: Sequel Sails

You are the database developer for Sequel Sails, a marina and sailing school with two locations. The original marina is on the Delaware River in Cape Holly, New Jersey. Just recently Sequel Sails has expanded to be able to add coastal chartering and certifications to their offerings by purchasing a second marina, Jersey Boat Works, in Point Pleasant Beach.

Sequel Sails Sailing School (S4) provides certified instruction by USCG licensed captains for a variety of courses ranging from a basic learn-to-sail course to advanced coastal cruising course. The school is a member of the U.S. Sailing Association (USSA) and the American Sailing Association (ASA).

In addition to the course offerings, S4 provides special programs, workshops, gatherings, and events. They offer practice boat rentals and group sailing expeditions. They are offering many opportunities for New Jersey residents to comply with the recent safe boating laws by offering the NJ safe boating course.

Existing Environment

With the current addition of Jersey Boat Works, both facilities have been upgraded into one Windows Server 2003 Active Directory domain. The database servers used for warehouse, marina, and internal databases are SQL Server 2005 servers on Microsoft Windows Server 2003 member servers.

Business Requirements

Next year, Strictly Sail is coming to the Philadelphia Convention Center. Strictly Sail is the top acclaimed all-sail boat show in the United States. Since Sequel Sails is also an exhibitor, it expects a large boost in sales and course bookings from the show and wants to be able to handle the business.

Present customers have mentioned that they would like to have the inventory available online since quite often they need parts or like to shop after hours. An online marina sales component is to be added to the website.

Potential customers must be able to gain information and book offerings from the website. Currently reservations are handled by phone. When a customer makes an online reservation for a course, cruise offering, or boat rental, performance must be maintained and transactions must not be blocked. To give a more complete result set of cruise listings to potential customers, cruise offerings should be searchable within the text of the offering. When booking boat rental time, a customer can also request specific options of the rental at that time. However, the failure to choose an option should not prevent the booking from completing.

CASE STUDY

Technical Requirements

During the early spring to mid-summer bookings will be heavy and must be handled efficiently.

Inventory items and available seats for bookings that are available online need to be reported accurately and yet keep the website available.

All databases need to be recovered to a logical point in the event of failure. The action that is chosen should not consume resources such as filling the transaction log unnecessarily.

Review Questions

1. Several of the tables in the inventory database contain images of sailboats and boating supplies. Since image data will be removed in future versions of SQL Server, which of the following should you use to replace the image data type?

   A. varchar(max)

   B. varbinary(max)

   C. nvarchar(max)

   D. varbinary

2. Your user databases are in full recovery mode. To meet the requirements, you need to develop a strategy to ensure they are able to be recovered to a logical point in the event of a failure. Which of the following should you implement?

   A. Use the following statement at the beginning of all transactions:

   `BEGIN TRANSACTION WITH MARK`

   B. Use the following statement at the beginning of all transactions:

   `SET IMPLICIT TRANSACTION ON`

   C. Use the following statement at the beginning of all significant transactions:

   `BEGIN TRANSACTION WITH MARK`

   D. Use the following statement at the beginning of all significant transactions:

   `SET IMPLICIT TRANSACTION ON`

3. You are creating the application for lesson and boat rental reservations. You need to be certain that the customers see all accurate time slots available. You want to prevent dirty reads, non-repeatable reads, and phantom reads. Which of the following should you use?

   A. HOLDLOCK query hint

   B. NOLOCK query hint

   C. Set the transaction isolation level to REPEATABLE READ

   D. Set the transaction isolation level to READ UNCOMMITTED

4. You are designing the cruise table so that it will support full-text search for specific text in the cruise description listings. Which of the following should you use to create the cruise table?

   A. `CREATE TABLE CRUISE (CruiseID bigint PRIMARY KEY CLUSTERED, CruiseTitle nvarchar(50) NOT NULL, CruiseDesc image, ModifiedDate datetime NOT NULL)`

   B. `CREATE TABLE CRUISE (CruiseID bigint UNIQUE, CruiseTitle nvarchar(50) NOT NULL,CruiseDesc xml, ModifiedDate datetime NOT NULL)`

   C. `CREATE TABLE CRUISE (CruiseID bigint PRIMARY KEY CLUSTERED, CruiseTitle nvarchar(50) NOT NULL,CruiseDesc varbinary(max), FileExtension nvarchar(8) , ModifiedDate datetime NOT NULL)`

   D. `CREATE TABLE CRUISE (CruiseID bigint UNIQUE, CruiseTitle nvarchar(50) NOT NULL,CruiseDesc varchar(max), ModifiedDate datetime NOT NULL)`

5. The ownership of Jersey Boat Works has more than doubled the business. Users of the accounting application report that it is performing slowly when modifying customer records. You have isolated the stored procedure that updates the customer records. You want to view and analyze the query plan for the stored procedure without impacting resources or actually making any changes to the data in the database. Which of the following should you use when running the stored procedure in a batch?

   A. SET STATISTICS XML ON

   B. SET SHOWPLAN_XML ON

   C. SET STATISTICS PROFILE ON

   D. SET STATISTICS IO ON

6. You are designing the stored procedure ssp_BoatRental for customers to rent a sailboat. You need to follow the business requirements in the event that a customer does not choose any options for the booking. Which of the following should you use within the stored procedure?

   A. Use a TRY ...CATCH block and roll back the transaction if the customer does not choose an option.

   B. Use a CASE statement to handle the options with an @@ERROR. If there is an error, roll back the transaction.

   C. Use a WITH MARK option. Use the marked transaction to roll back the transaction.

   D. Use a SAVE TRANSACTION option. If an error occurs, roll back to the savepoint.

7. Some online orders, such as sails, need to be customized in that several parts will need to be configured. In designing the stored procedure for ordering sails, you need to take into account that one choice affects the next set of options offered and all options need to be filled out. Which of the following statements should you use?

   A. BEGIN DISTRIBUTED TRANSACTION

   B. BEGIN TRANSACTION

   C. NOLOCK

   D. SET TRANSACTION ISOLATION LEVEL READ UNCOMMITTED

8. You are designing an interface for the exhibit booth at Strictly Sail. You have an inventory of items that customers can purchase online and pick up at a later time, at the event. You want to improve data access by minimizing the number of connections to the database. Which of the following should you do?

   A. Use a System.Data.SqlClient.SqlDataReader object.

   B. Use multiple active result sets (MARS).

   C. Use server managed objects (SMO).

   D. Use a Common Language Runtime (CLR) aggregate.

9. Customers that purchase marina items online need to know the exact amounts that are in stock. Since this inventory must to be up to date, which of the following access strategies should you use?

   A. A Common Language Runtime (CLR) user-defined function

   B. A Common Language Runtime (CLR) stored procedure

   C. A System.Data.DataSet object

   D. A System.Data.SqlClient.SqlDataReader object

10. You are designing the web applications for Sequel Sails. You need to create objects to expose SQL Server as a web service. Which of the following should you use?

    A. TCP endpoint

    B. IIS virtual directory

    C. SSL Communications channel

    D. HTTP endpoint

Answers to Review Questions

1. B. Varbinary(max) should be used to store binary data type and image data type.

2. C. You should use the statement BEGIN TRANSACTION WITH MARK with significant transactions. The requirements state that the solution should not consume resources such as filling the transaction log unnecessarily. Transaction marks consume a lot of transaction log space so it is a recommendation that they be used only for significant transactions.

3. A. Use the HOLDLOCK query hint to further restrict the shared lock. Using the HOLDLOCK will ensure accuracy even though the query might run a little slower. You should not set the transaction isolation level to REPEATABLE READ since this might cause phantom reads. You should not set the transaction isolation level to READ UNCOMMITTED since this might also cause dirty reads, non-repeatable reads, and phantom reads.

4. C. Create the table using:

    ```
    CREATE TABLE CRUISE (CruiseID bigint

     PRIMARY KEY CLUSTERED, CruiseTitle

     nvarchar(50) NOT NULL,CruiseDesc

     varbinary(max), FileExtension

     nvarchar(8) , ModifiedDate datetime

     NOT NULL)
    ```

    A non-null unique index is required as the key column for full-text search; therefore the CruiseID column needs to be created as a primary key, not as unique. When you store the content of a document as a particular file type, you must also specify an additional column that stores the file type extension so that full-text search is able to apply the appropriate filter to read the document.

5. B. SET SHOWPLAN_XML ON returns the execution information for each statement without executing it. You will be able to analyze the stored procedure without modifying any data. All other choices execute the stored procedure and will modify the data in the database.

6. D. Use a SAVE TRANSACTION option. If an error occurs, roll back to the savepoint. Savepoints offer a mechanism to roll back portions of transactions. You create a savepoint using the SAVE TRANSACTION statement. You later execute a ROLLBACK TRANSACTION statement to roll back to the savepoint instead of rolling back to the start of the transaction.

    The TRY ...CATCH and CASE options are not correct because the entire transactions are rolled back. The WITH MARK option is not correct because this option is not used in a transaction; it is used in a RESTORE DATABASE statement.

7. A. Use BEGIN DISTRIBUTED TRANSACTION. You need to make certain that all the related transactions succeed, or the entire distributed transaction must be rolled back. None of the other options ensures this happening.

8. B. You should use multiple active result sets (MARS). MARS allows for applications to have multiple result sets open on a single connection. Using the System.Data.SqlClient .SqlDataReader object does not enable you to reuse the same connection. SMO and CLR are not correct because neither reduce the number of connections to the database.

9. D. You should use a System.Data.SqlClient.SqlDataReader object. The online marina items need to be queried in real time with each amount displayed prior to the customer's purchasing the item. The System.Data.SqlClient.SqlDataReader object uses a maintained streamed data connection to the data source, retrieving one row at a time. This type of data access works well for real time querying. Neither the System.Data.DataSet object nor any CLR implementation will ensure the real-time views desired.

10. D. You should use an HTTP endpoint. To expose SQL Server as a web service, you need to create an HTTP endpoint. The endpoint creates your communication link between SQL Server and the client application.

CASE STUDY

Case Study 4: Holly Culture

You are the database developer for Holly Culture, a symposium and culture center whose mission is to enable adults to continue to enrich their lives through the synergy of art, music, and cultural history. HC has found that these traditional values bring people together, allowing them to become more productive together. It is a work ethic that as been embraced by management teams throughout the United States and worldwide. Holly Culture has been acclaimed for their services to companies and communities.

In 2002, HC began as a team of four forward-thinking friends—a history professor, a professional musician, a famous artist, and an author in Blackwood, New Jersey. They interviewed and created a list of professionals in the fields HC was offering courses or symposiums. They designed courseware with open-ended pieces that would be tailored for each market or course, depending on the amount of granularity needed. They marketed to businesses, organizations, and communities. The response was overwhelming. It was a means of bringing arts to small communities of interested adults.

Existing Environment

HC has added three more locations to its company: Auburn, Washington, Fort Worth, Texas, and Virginia Beach, Virginia. There are full-time office staff and at least two training professionals at each location. Most of the training or symposiums, if not done by the traveling full-time professionals, are done by contracted professionals.

Symposium and training locations are usually held in corporate centers, hotel meeting rooms, or community locations. At times small groups can be accommodated at the office locations.

Holly Culture has a website explaining its mission, offerings, and contact information. The office facilities are configured as a Windows Server 2003 Active Directory domain. The database servers for all internal databases are SQL Server 2005 servers and are member servers in the domain.

Business Requirements

The courseware is stored on Microsoft Word documents for ease of modularity and redesigning. These documents are to be stored in the HollyCulture database in their original form so they can be used for parts when designing new or similar courses. Course writers want to search the document text for words, phrases, and synonyms.

Office personnel need to manage the database servers through an application. Company policy does not allow office personnel to use SQL Server Management Studio. SSMS can only be used by the IT department personnel.

Technical Requirements

All courses since 2002 are to be stored in the Courses table of the HollyCulture database. Since this table includes the Word documents of each of the courses or symposiums, it contains gigabytes of data. It is important that this table has good performance for searching, inserting, and updating.

Since customer profiles are updated regularly, it is important that resources used for the update be minimal. Updates should not block other transactions from reading the data.

Review Questions

1. Users report that the HC Customer Tracking application is running slowly. This application adds and deletes large numbers of rows to a few tables in the database quite often. Which of the following solutions will best correct this situation?

    A. Schedule indexes in the database to be periodically reorganized.

    B. Drop all the indexes and update statistics.

    C. Schedule indexes in the database to be periodically rebuilt.

    D. Drop all the nonclustered indexes and reorganize the clustered indexes.

2. Reports are run monthly at each of the locations. You create a report application that consists of a series of stored procedures that generate the desired reports run in a batch. If an error occurs while a stored procedure is running, you want to identify the procedure where the error occurred. You decide to run the procedures in the context of a TRY clause. Which of the following system functions should you use to retrieve the information you need?

    A. ERROR_PROCEDURE()

    B. ERROR_MESSAGE()

    C. ERROR_STATE()

    D. ERROR_SEVERITY()

3. You want to use a full-text search to query the course documents. You also need to make certain all business requirements are followed. Which of the following column structures should you to be able to hold and index the course documents in the Courses table?

    A. Create a CourseDocument column of type xml.

    B. Create a CourseDocument column of type nvarbinary(max) and FileExtension column of nvarchar(8).

    C. Create a CourseDocument column of type nvarchar(max) and FileExtension column of nvarchar(8).

    D. Create a CourseDocument column of type image.

4. You have rewritten some new queries for the HC Customer Tracking application. Users are reporting that the application is now performing more slowly than it had before you made the changes. You use System Monitor to retrieve some real-time data regarding Buffer Manager metrics and note that the page reads/sec and page writes/sec are quite high. Before purchasing new hardware, what should you do next to correct the problem?

    A. Use SQL Server Profiler to find the worst performing queries.

    B. Use SQL Server Profiler to find the duration of the worst performing queries.

    C. Use SQL Server Profiler to capture trace data while users are running the application. Use the Database Engine Tuning Advisor to recommend indexes.

    D. Use SQL Server Profiler to find the locking duration of the queries.

CASE STUDY

5. The Courses table is the largest table in the HollyCulture database and by far the most active. How can you make the Courses table more manageable while keeping the integrity of the database?

   A. Place the Courses table on its own disk drive.

   B. Place the Courses table in its own database on a separate disk.

   C. Reconfigure the database to have yearly Courses tables: courses2002 table, courses2003 table, and so on, each on its own disk

   D. Partition the Courses table by area of offerings and/or location horizontally across several filegroups, each on its own disk.

6. You have designed a special management tool for the office personnel to manage the database servers. You have used an application built on SQL management objects (SMO) using transaction processing. You need to make certain that the computers of the office staff using the management application can support SMO. Which of the following should you do?

   A. Install SQL Server Client Tools on computers of the management application users.

   B. Install SQL Server Native Client on computers of the management application users.

   C. Install SQL Server automation management objects (AMO) on computers of the management application users.

   D. Install a TSQL endpoint on each of the computers of the management application users

7. You are making some modifications to the transaction to modify a customer's profile. You need to make certain the requirements are also followed. Which of the following isolation levels should you use in the transaction?

   A. REPEATABLE READ

   B. SERIALIZABLE

   C. SNAPSHOT

   D. READ UNCOMMITTED

8. A sales focus stored procedure is a series of five parameterized queries. The parameter of one of the five queries is very unpredictable. When you check the performance of the stored procedure in SQL Server Profiler, you find that performance is good except when this one query's parameter is out of scope. What can you do to improve the performance of the stored procedure?

   A. Create a plan guide and use the RECOMPILE query hint for the unpredictable query.

   B. Use sp_recompile to recompile the stored procedure.

   C. Use sp_recompile to recompile the unpredictable query.

   D. Drop and recreate the stored procedure using WITH RECOMPILE.

9. You are reviewing some of the queries in the HC Customer Tracking application to make certain that they use valid search arguments for optimal performance. Of the following code snippets, which do not contain valid SARGs? Choose all that apply.

    A. `WHERE Customer.CustID > 1004`

    B. `WHERE Customer.CustID BETWEEN 1000 AND 3000`

    C. `WHERE Customer.CustID <> 2001`

    D. `WHERE Customer.CustID IN (2010, 2015, 2030)`

10. You are designing some code to retrieve course information for users of the website. You need to retrieve information on course name, course description, dates offered, location, and who to contact. What type of object should you create to retrieve this data?

    A. Table-valued user-defined function

    B. Stored procedure

    C. Extended stored procedure

    D. A Common Language Runtime (CLR) user-defined function

Answers to Review Questions

1.   C. Schedule indexes in the database to be periodically rebuilt. As rows are added or deleted from the tables, the tables and indexes are fragmented. Fragmentation impedes performance. The indexes need to be rebuilt. Reorganizing the indexes is not correct because it reorganizes only the leaf nodes. Since initially the application ran well, dropping the indexes is not correct.

2.   A. Use the ERROR_PROCEDURE() system function within the scope of the CATCH block of a TRY… CATCH construct. The ERROR_PROCEDURE() returns the name of the stored procedure in which the error occurred.

    ERROR_MESSAGE() returns the text of the message that would be returned to the application. ERROR_STATE() returns the state. ERROR_SEVERITY() returns the severity.

3.   B. Create a CourseDocument column of type nvarbinary(max) and FileExtension column of nvarchar(8). The Word document must be stored as nvarbinary(max) or image data type; however, image data type will be deprecated in future versions of SQL Server and should no longer be used for new work. A second column to read the data, the file extension column, must also exist for full-text search conditions to be met.

4.   C. Use SQL Server Profiler to capture trace data while users are running the application. Use the Database Engine Tuning Advisor (DTA) to recommend indexes. System Monitor Buffer Manager page reads/sec and page writes/sec can be minimized either by using a larger data cache, intelligent indexes, or more efficient queries. Thus, recommending indexes with the DTA would be a next step to correct the problem. None of the other options help correct the problem.

5.   D. Partition the Courses table by area of offering and/or location horizontally across several filegroups, each on its own disk. The table will still be visible to users and applications as a single table but will have less contention since it will reside on several separate disks. You need to implement the filegroups, create the partition function, create the partition scheme, and create the table on the partition scheme.

6.   B. Install SQL Server Native Client on computers of the management application users. SQL Server Native Client is required to connect to and manage a SQL Server using a SMO application. Normally, installing SQL Server Client Tools would also be correct; however, in this instance, users are not to use SSMS according to company policy and client tools gives them this capability.

7.   C. You should set the transaction isolation level to SNAPSHOT. The requirements state that updates should not block another transaction from reading the data. At the same time you want to make certain that the reads are protected from being dirty reads. Setting the transaction isolation level to SNAPSHOT gives you this capability.

8.   A. Create a plan guide and use the RECOMPILE query hint for the unpredictable query. The RECOMPILE query hint is much the same as the statement-level recompilation. Only that statement in the stored procedure is recompiled.

    You should not use sp_recompile to recompile the entire stored procedure. Sp_recompile does not recompile queries. It is also incorrect to use the WITH RECOMPILE since this would recompile the entire stored procedure each time it is executed.

CASE STUDY ANSWERS

9. C. WHERE Customer.CustID <> 2001 does not contain a valid SARG and would not perform optimally. All other options are valid SARGs.

10. B. Create a stored procedure to retrieve the data. The object you create needs to be exposed as a web method. This can be accomplished as a Transact-SQL stored procedure. Since the data is optimally retrieved using Transact-SQL, there is no need to create a CLR user-defined function. A table-valued user-defined function and an extended stored procedure cannot be exposed as web methods.

 And for the answer to the syllogism at the beginning of the chapter, showy talkers are not really well informed. (We hope you are! The best to you.)

Glossary

A

@@ERROR   Returns an error number if the previous statement encountered an error.

Activity data   *Data* generally relevant for a particular business activity and as such can be replicated or partitioned effectively.

Actual execution plan   A query plan that is generated by actually executing the query.

Ad hoc query   A batch that contains one SELECT, INSERT, UPDATE, or DELETE statement with no plan of reuse.

ADO   An API that wraps OLE DB and ODBC for use in languages such as Visual Basic.

ADO.NET   A data access architecture that provides the .NET programmer with access to relational data sources, XML, and application data.

AMO   Automation management objects. Features that are used for automating the management of your server.

Autocommit transaction   Default transaction mode for the SQL Server database engine in which each T-SQL statement committed or rolled back automatically.

Average page life expectancy   Should be greater than 300 seconds.

B

Binding to XML   The process of bringing in a value from a non-XML type column or a Transact-SQL variable inside XML.

Bit   Integer data type that can take a value of 1, 0, or NULL.

Blocked Process Report   Event that is triggered when the wait for a lock exceeds a threshold.

C

Caching   The process of using the pool of SQL Server memory to store both execution plans and data buffers.

Client cursor   A cursor that is implemented on the client such that the entire result set is first transferred to the client and the client application implements the cursor functionality from this cached result set.

Client libraries   A dynamic link library (DLL) on the client machine used to communicate with SQL Server over a particular network protocol.

CLR   Common Language Runtime. The engine that supplies .NET managed code execution.

Clustered index   A B-tree structure that stores the data rows of a table or view in an order dictated by the clustered index key.

Concurrency   The ability of multiple users to access data at the same time.

Concurrency effects   Effects of having concurrent users on the same data such as dirty reads, inconsistent analysis, and phantom reads.

Connection pooling   Enables an application to reuse a connection from a pool of connections rather than reestablishing one for each use.

Connection SET options   Options that are set at connection time that affect the query and its possible plan reuse.

Connection string   A list of keywords and associated values used to identify a particular connection attribute for an ADO or ADO.NET application.

CONTAINS predicate   One of four predicates used in full-text queries: *CONTAINS, CONTAINSTABLE, FREETEXT,* and *FREETEXTTABLE.* Used to search columns containing character-based data types for precise or fuzzy matches to words and phrases.

D

Data provider   Object used to connect to a specific data source by supplying necessary authentication information in a connection string.

Data-dependent routing (DDR)   Partitions the data among databases. An application or some middleware service routes queries to the correct database.

Database Engine Tuning Advisor   Utility that provides what-if analysis, partitioning recommendations, time-bound tuning and reports that give detailed information for each tuning recommendation.

DataReader   A read-only, forward-only stream of data that is returned by an ADO.NET query.

DataSet   The result of running a SELECT statement in .NET.

DateTime   Stored internally in SQL Server as an 8-byte integer and gives a range of values from January 1, 1753, to December 31, 9999, with an accuracy of 3.33 milliseconds.

Deadlock   Occurs when two or more tasks are each waiting for another to release a resource.

Decimal   Numeric data type having fixed precision and scale.

Default result set   Default mode that SQL Server uses to return a result set back to a client.

Default trace   A lightweight trace that logs changes in your server configuration as well as other events like Data Definition Language or Security events.

Distributed partitioned views   Table data that is partitioned among tables in several distributed databases, based on a partitioning key.

Distributed transaction   Transaction that spans two or more databases that can be located on the same or separate servers.

Dm_views/functions   See dynamic management view.

DMO   SQL Distributed Management Objects. A collection of objects that gives access to the administrative and development components of SQL Server 2000.

DSN   Data source name. A stored definition that records the ODBC driver to use for connections specifying the data source.

Dynamic cursor   A cursor that can reflect updates, deletes, and inserts to the underlying data while the cursor is open.

Dynamic management view   A SQL Server 2005 database object that exposes various internal memory structures, database engine components, and database components in a relational format.

E

Error function   Function that returns the error number for the error that triggered an ON ERROR routine.

Error handling   Process of creating code methods to handle exceptions.

Estimated execution plan   A query plan that is generated without executing the query.

Execution context   Execution context contains data specific to each user that executes a query such as parameter values.

Explicit transaction   Start and end of the transaction are explicitly defined using Transact-SQL statements (BEGIN TRANSACTION, COMMIT TRANSACTION, ROLLBACK TRANSACTION) or through API functions.

External fragmentation   Inefficient space usage for an index when the logical order of the index pages differ from the physical order.

F

Fast-forward cursor   A cursor that provides optimal performance by only supporting the NEXT argument.

Federation   A group of autonomous servers that cooperate to process a workload. Federated database servers are created using databases on each server and horizontally partitioning the data across the databases.

File DSN   Stores information for all users that have the same files stored on a local machine to connect to an indicated data provider.

Float   Approximate-number data type used with floating point, nonexact, numeric data.

FLWOR   Acronym for FOR, LET, WHERE, ORDER BY, and RETURN. Defines the XQuery iteration syntax.

FOR XML   Statement used to convert rowset data into XML data

Forward-only cursor   A cursor that can be read only in sequence from the first row to the last row.

FREETEXT predicate   One of four predicates used in full-text queries: *CONTAINS, CONTAINSTABLE, FREETEXT,* and *FREETEXTTABLE.* Used to search columns containing character-based data types for values that match the meaning and not the exact wording of the words in the search condition.

Full-text index   Special type of index used by the Microsoft Full-Text Engine service, allowing complex string searches in character as well as other data types.

H

Heap   A table without a clustered index defined.

HTTP endpoint   A registered service entry point for listening and receiving HTTP requests using the Windows Server 2003 operating system through the system HTTP listener process Http.sys.

I

Image   Variable-length binary data from 0 through $2^{31}-1$ bytes. Choose varbinary(max) over image data type for new development work since it is being deprecated.

Implicit transaction   When set on, SELECT, INSERT, DELETE, UPDATE, CREATE, and OPEN automatically begin a transaction. COMMIT or ROLLBACK needs to be specified to end a transaction.

Index on computed column   Used to improve the cardinality of your query and hence generate an improved query plan.

Index with included columns   Used to extend the functionality of nonclustered indexes by adding nonkey columns to the leaf level of the nonclustered index to cover a query.

Index rebuild   Drops the index and creates a new one.

Index reorganize   Defragments the leaf level of clustered and nonclustered indexes on tables and views by physically reordering the leaf-level pages to match the logical order (left to right) of the leaf nodes.

Integer data types   Used for storing integer numbers; includes int, bigint, smallint, and tinyint data types.

Interleave   The manner in which MARS executes multiple batches.

Internal fragmentation   Inefficient space usage for an index when the pages of the index are not full (or almost full).

Isolation level   The locking behavior for all SELECT statements for a particular session.

K

Keyset cursor   A cursor that shows updates made to its member rows by other users while the cursor is open, but does not show the effects of inserts or deletes.

L

Linked servers   Loosely coupled servers that give you the ability to query objects in remote databases as if they were local objects.

Locking   Mechanism to prevent multiple users or applications that access the same data at the same time from making simultaneous changes to the data.

Locking granularity   Acquiring locks on different types of resources.

Locking hints   Control the locking behavior of the query optimizer, giving you a more granular control than the isolation levels.

M

MARS   Multiple active result sets. A connection attribute that allows applications to have more than one pending request or more than one active default result set per connection.

MAX specifier   Allows a maximum storage of $2^{31} - 1$ bytes (roughly 1,073,741,823 characters).

Memory Grants Pending   Use the SQL Server: Memory Manager*Memory Grants Pending* performance counter. Must be less than one.

Money   Requires 8 bytes of storage and has a range of values from −922,337,203,685,477.5808 to 922,337,203,685,477.5807.

N

Native web services access   Provides the endpoint support for SODA from the client in the form of an HTTP listener.

Nonclustered Index   Similar to a clustered index, the difference being that in the leaf-level pages of a nonclustered index, each row of data contains a subset of the base table's columns (the columns that make the index key and included columns) and a pointer to the actual data row, not the actual data row itself.

Nontransparent scaleout   *Scaleout* technology that uses multiple servers running their own databases.

Normalization   Database process to eliminate redundancy and reduce potential anomalies that can occur during data modifications.

Ntext   Variable-length Unicode data with a maximum length of $2^{30} - 1$. Will be removed in a future version of Microsoft SQL Server so avoid using this data type in new development work; use nvarchar(max) instead.

Numeric   Fixed precision and scale numbers.

Nvarchar   Variable-length Unicode character data.

O

ODBC   Open Database Connectivity. A well-established industry standard for connecting to relational database systems.

OLE DB   Object Linking and Embedding Database. A set of COM interfaces that is higher-level replacement for, and successor to, ODBC, extending its feature set to support a wider variety of nonrelational databases.

Online index operations   Available in SQL Server 2005 Enterprise Edition. Allows creating, rebuilding, or dropping indexes online with minimal impact to the user.

OPENXML   Statement used to convert XML data into rowset data.

OPTIMIZE FOR   Query hint to optimize a query for a particular parameter.

P

Partition   Horizontal grouping of rows of data based on a specified column. The partitions can be put on one or more filegroups in the database.

Partition function   A database object that determines how data within a partitioned table will be split.

Partition scheme   A database object that maps the partitions of a partition function to a set of filegroups.

Partitioned table   A table that has been separated into a number of logical horizontal partitions (which are mapped to different physical files) through a partition scheme.

Peer-to-peer replication   Peer-to-peer replication, new in SQL Server 2005, propagates changes made to any copy of the data to all other copies.

Performance counters   Real-time monitoring metrics used to isolate problems.

Performance Monitor   Monitors the utilization of system resources and collects and views real-time performance data. Also used to configure performance logs and alerts.

Plan guide   A means to indirectly force the query optimizer to use a specific plan for a query.

Plan reuse   Strive for more than 90 percent reuse to conserve resources and not recompile every query statement.

Primary XML index   A persisted B-tree representation of an XML data type column.

Procedure cache   The part of SQL Server memory that is used to store query execution plans.

Q

Query governor   Used to prevent long-running queries by specifying an upper limit on the time within which a query can run.

Query notifications   Built on the Service Broker infrastructure introduced in SQL Server 2005, allows applications to be notified when data has changed.

Query plan   A read-only re-entrant data structure shared by multiple users.

R

RAISERROR   Generates an error message and initiates error processing for the session.

Read Committed Snapshot isolation   Based on row versioning instead of locking, provides statement-level read consistency.

Real   Four-byte approximate-number data type for use with floating point numeric data.

Reference data   Relatively stable data like airline schedules or parts catalog references. Since this type of data seldom changes, scaleout is easily implemented.

Resource data   High availability data, such as account data, inventory, customer list, and invoices.

RMO   Replication management objects. Managed code assembly that encapsulates replication functionalities for SQL Server.

Row-overflow data   Feature that allows columns having the data type varchar, nvarchar, varbinary, or sql_variant to be stored off-row when the combined widths of the table's (or index's) columns is greater than 8,060 bytes.

Row versioning   Maintaining different versions of modified data.

Row versioning–based isolation level   Copies the data before modification to tempdb. Reduces the number of locks acquired by a transaction by eliminating the use of shared locks on read operations.

Row-based operations   The act of retrieving data one row at a time.

S

Savepoints   Allows partial rollback for a transaction.

Scalable shared databases   A scaleout solution where processing power is scaled out but only a single disk image of the data is used.

Scaleout   Expanding the data to multiple servers.

Scaleup   Increasing a server's resources such as memory, CPU speed, and disk subsystems to handle larger amounts of data.

Search argument (SARG)   Using the following operators to filter the result set of a query: =, >, <, >=, <=, BETWEEN, and LIKE.

Secondary XML index   Defined after a primary XML index. Can be of type PATH, VALUE, or PROPERTY.

Server cursor   A cursor built and implemented on the server such that only the rows fetched by an application are sent to the client.

Service Broker   Provides a reliable, secure, asynchronous, and scalable messaging infrastructure for applications and scaleout solutions.

Service interaction data   Used to communicate between services. It is a basis for Service-Oriented Data Architecture in SQL Server 2005.

Service-Oriented Data Architecture (SODA)   Builds service-centric applications making SQL Server a full-service provider for loosely coupled distributed applications.

SET SHOWPLAN_ALL   Similar to SET SHOWPLAN_TEXT, includes additional information.

SET SHOWPLAN_TEXT   When set to ON, the queries that follow are not executed and their execution plan is returned as text.

SET SHOWPLAN_XML   When set to ON, a well-formed XML document of a query plan is returned without the query executed.

SET STATISTICS IO   When set to ON, queries executed and information displayed about the disk activity are generated.

SET STATISTICS PROFILE   The execution counterpart for the SET SHOWPLAN_ALL option. Queries are executed, then the query plans and execution information is returned.

SET STATISTICS TIME   When set to ON, queries are executed and additional information, including the number of milliseconds required for parsing, compiling, and executing each statement for every query executed is returned.

SET STATISTICS XML   Similar to the SET SHOWPLAN_XML but with queries executed and then the XML form of the query plan returned. Also contains execution information.

Set-based operations   Method of processing data such that the server's resources and memory utilization have all been optimized to use result set algorithms to provide the best performance possible.

Severity levels   Values between 0 and 25 indicate the importance of the problem and also some of the consequences of an error.

Showplan   Different formats (text, graphical, and XML) of the query plan.

Signal wait   A high value greater than 25 percent could mean possible CPU problems.

SmallDateTime   Stored internally as 2-byte integer data type that gives a range of values from January 1, 1900, through June 6, 2079, with an accuracy of 1 minute.

SmallMoney   Four-byte data type that represents monetary or currency value with values from –214,748.3648 to 214,748.3647.

SMO   SQL Server management objects. A collection of objects that are designed for programming all aspects of managing Microsoft SQL Server.

Snapshot isolation   Provides transaction-level consistency (instead of statement level) for read operations using the last version of each row that had been committed at the time the transaction.

SNI   SQL Server Network Interface. The protocol layer replacing the Net-Libraries for SQL Server 2000 and Microsoft Data Access Components (MDAC) that encapsulates the TDS packet inside a standard communication protocol to enable SQL Server database engine to communicate with an application.

SOAP   Simple Object Access Protocol. A protocol used to exchange XML-based messages over the network, normally using HTTP.

Sp_executesql   System stored procedure that executes a Transact-SQL statement or batch that can be reused or one that has been built dynamically.

SQL injection   A security vulnerability occurring at the database application level that allows unintended T-SQL code to be executed against a SQL Server instance.

SQL Server Lock Manager   Internal part of the SQL Server database engine that manages locks.

SQL Server Profiler   A SQL Server 2005 utility used to capture network traffic/trace activity between client applications and a SQL Server instance.

Sql:column()   Function used to insert row data values into the XML.

Sql:variable()   Function used to expose a variable that contains a relational value inside an XML.

SQLCLR   Provides the logic host for a Service-Oriented Data Architecture scaleout solution.

SQLNCLI   SQL Native Client. Client library for SQL Server 2005 that combines OLE DB and ODBC technologies into one library. Provides new data access features without changing the current Microsoft Data Access Components (MDAC).

SQLXML   Initial versions enable XML support for SQL Server 2000, bridging the gap between XML and relational data. The updated version, SQLXML 4.0, includes the new features in SQL Server 2005.

State   An integer between 1 and 127 used to identify the situation in which an error occurred for errors that occur in multiple situations.

Statement-level recompile   In SQL Server 2005, only the statement inside the batch causes recompilation.

Static cursor   A cursor that shows the result set exactly as it was at the time the cursor was opened.

sys.dm_db_index_operational_stats   Returns current low-level I/O, locking, latching, and access method activity for each partition of a table or index in the database.

sys.dm_db_index_physical_stats   Returns size and fragmentation information for the data and indexes of the specified table or view.

sys.dm_db_index_usage_stats   Returns counts of different types of index operations and the time each type of operation was last performed.

sys.dm_exec_query_stats   Identifies queries that generate the most I/O activity.

sys.dm_os_wait_stats   Determines if you have an I/O bound system by specifying wait time, count, and wait type.

sys.messages   System view that contains a row for each message id or language id of the error messages in the system, for system-defined and user-defined messages.

System DSN   Stores information for all users and services on a local machine to connect to an indicated data provider.

System Monitor   Windows operating system utility used to monitor performance object counters.

T

TDS endpoint   Tabular data stream endpoint. The SQL Server object that represents the communication point between SQL Server and a client.

Text   Variable-length non-Unicode data in the code page of the server and with a maximum length of $2^{31}-1$. Will be removed in a future version of Microsoft SQL Server so avoid using this data type in new development work; use varchar(max) instead.

Transaction   A unit of interaction processing with the database system that must be either entirely completed or aborted.

Transparent scaleout   Loosely coupling many networked database computers, each with the same database, such that the user sees one virtual server.

TRY...CATCH   Transact-SQL construct to process error handling.

U

Unique index   An index whose index key has no duplicate values.

USE PLAN   Query hint specifying the execution plan the query optimizer uses.

User DSN   Stores information for a particular user on a local machine to connect to an indicated data provider.

User input validation   Validates input through two approaches: disallowing certain characters or certain strings of characters or allowing only required characters.

User-defined messages   Error messages created by the user for specific error handling.

V

Varbinary   Variable-length binary data.

Varchar   Variable-length, non-Unicode character data.

W

W3C   The World Wide Web Consortium. The main international standards organization for the World Wide Web.

Wait type   Occurs when trying to synchronize the parallelism operator.

X

XACT_ABORT   When ON, if a Transact-SQL statement raises a runtime error, the entire transaction is terminated and rolled back.

XACT_STATE   Function that reports the user transaction state of a current running request.

XML DML   XML Data Modification Language. A Microsoft extension to the XQuery language to provide Data Modification Language against the XML data type.

XML namespace   Method for qualifying element and attribute names used in XML documents by associating them with namespace identified by URI reference.

XML Schema   Method for validating XML by associating it with a schema name.

XML showplan   Gives the most comprehensive type of query plan information. New in SQL Server 2005.

XQuery   Query language of XML.

XQuery expression   Contains a prolog, namespace, and a body, which define the result of the query.

XQuery method   Extracts the sections of an XML instance from an XML data type, column, or parameter.

XQuery syntax   Rules valid in XQuery, such as XQuery is case sensitive; XQuery elements, attributes, and variables must be valid XML names.

Index

Note to the Reader: Throughout this index **boldfaced** page numbers indicate primary discussions of a topic. *Italicized* page numbers indicate illustrations.

Q

R

Wiley Publishing, Inc.
End-User License Agreement

The Absolute Best MCITP Developer: SQL Server Book/CD Package on the Market!

Get Ready for the new MCITP Developer: Designing and Optimizing Data Access by Using Microsoft SQL Server 2005 (70-442) exam with the most comprehensive and challenging sample tests anywhere!

The Sybex Test Engine features:

- All the review questions, as covered in each chapter of the book.

- Challenging questions representative of those you'll find on the real exam.

- Bonus Case Study Questions, found only on the CD.

- An Assessment Test to narrow your focus to certain objective groups.

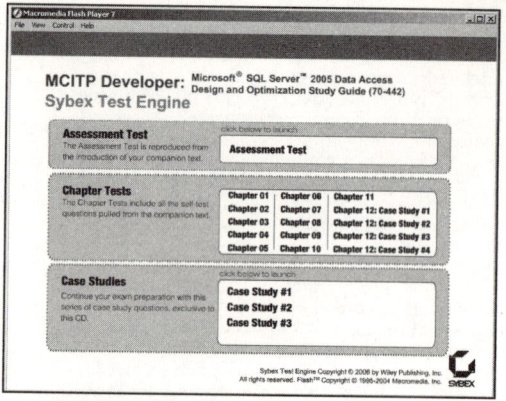

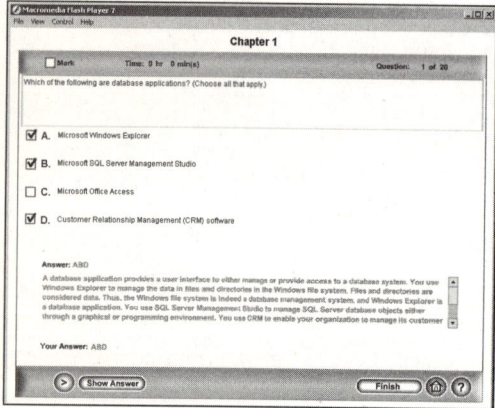

Search through the complete book in PDF!

- Access the entire *MCITP Developer: Microsoft SQL Server 2005 Data Access Design and Optimization Study Guide*, complete with figures and tables, in electronic format.

- Search the *MCITP Developer: Microsoft SQL Server 2005 Data Access Design and Optimization Study Guide* chapters to find information on any topic in seconds.

Use the Electronic Flashcards for PCs or Palm devices to jog your memory and prep last-minute for the exam!

- Reinforce your understanding of key concepts with these hardcore flashcard-style questions.

- Download the Flashcards to your Palm device and go on the road. Now you can study for the *MCITP Developer: Designing and Optimizing Data Access by Using Microsoft SQL Server 2005* exam any time, anywhere.

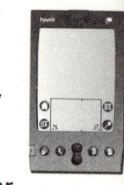